The Constitution and the Economy

The Constitution and the Economy

Objective Theory and Critical Commentary

by Michael Conant

University of Oklahoma Press : Norman and London

By Michael Conant

Antitrust in the Motion Picture Industry (Berkeley, 1960)
Railroad Mergers and Abandonments (Berkeley, 1964)
The Constitution and Capitalism (Saint Paul, 1974)
The Constitution and the Economy (Norman, 1991)

Library of Congress Cataloging-in-Publication Data

Conant, Michael.
　The constitution and the economy : objective theory and critical
commentary / by Michael Conant.
　　p.　cm.
　Includes bibliographical references and index.
　ISBN 0-8061-2363-X (alk. paper)
　　1. United States—Constitutional law—Economic liberties.
2. Industrial laws and legislation—United States. 3. Trade
regulation—United States. 4. Interstate commerce—United States.
I. Title.
KF1600.C54　1991
343.73'07—dc20
[347.3037]　　　　　　　　　　　　　　　　　　91-13536
　　　　　　　　　　　　　　　　　　　　　　　　CIP

The paper in this book meets the guidelines for permanence and durability of the
Committee on Production Guidelines for Book Longevity of the Council on
Library Resources, Inc. ⊗

Contents

Preface

THIS CRITICAL COMMENTARY on the Constitution of the United States and its interpretation in Supreme Court opinions is aimed at readers who are familiar with elementary economics. Judges, lawyers, and law students will find that economics proposes solutions to difficult constitutional issues that earlier treatises merely describe. The economic approach offers new frameworks of reasoning for constitutional cases that can be the starting point for more intensive research on novel issues in litigation. A second group of readers who should find this commentary of interest includes institutional economists, political scientists, and historians. While this commentary is only partially a study of history based on original sources, a digest of research on original meanings of constitutional language and an economic critique of two hundred years of leading cases should assist social scientists in understanding why some Court decisions favored special-interest groups to the detriment of the public. The emphasis on separated powers and the primacy of the legislative function in a democracy offers a framework for further critical studies of the scope of judicial discretion in constitutional decision making.

The concern here is with those clauses of the Constitution that directly affect the economy and with those constitutional limitations that have been construed by the Supreme Court to have significant effect on the economy. The hypothesis is that the structure and functioning of government, like that of firms, is subject to efficiency criteria. Within the constraints of constitutional structure and language, such as separated powers and checks and balances, the framers of the Constitution were trying to create an efficient government. They expected those who would carry on the functions of the three departments of government to attempt to minimize the costs of executing their tasks and not to waste economic resources. It is thus appropriate to investigate the economics of separated powers and the economics of federalism. Furthermore, the framers used efficiency criteria to determine the scope of the powers delegated to Congress such as those over commerce and taxation.

A second focus of this study is the constitutional limitations. The contract clause, for example, which is directly concerned with preventing state interference with the enforcement of executory contracts is subject to economic analysis. But the more general limitations are also subject to economic inquiry. For example, the question of whether corporations should be treated as persons under the due process clauses is easily answered affirmatively. If corporations were denied the full and fair procedure that constitutes due process of law, there would be no corporations; absent large-scale equity financing there could have been no industrial revolution. All of the clauses in section 1 of the Fourteenth Amendment are treated to economic analysis in this study. The conclusion is that the due process clause, which was used so widely by the Supreme Court to invalidate economic regulation before 1937, should not have been used at all. On the other hand, the privileges-or-immunities clause and the equal protection clause, which were little used by the Supreme Court for economic regulation, should have been used much more widely as a bar to governmental grants of monopoly.

The hypothesis of this study differs radically from those of studies of the economics of the common law. While the courts have worked out many common-law rules that are efficient guides to behavior, they are less apt to apply efficiency guidelines to interpreting the Constitution, and have frequently allowed special interests to prevail over public welfare. Rules of documentary interpretation that would have sharply limited judicial discretion have not been pleaded and argued in key constitutional cases, and as a result, they have been ignored and forgotten by the courts. Great dissenters, such as Justice Holmes, were unable to assemble Supreme Court majorities for adherence to original meanings of constitutional language. Instead, the Supreme Court majority has at times succumbed to ideologies of the era, such as laissez-faire and states' rights. As a result, much of this study is negatively critical of Supreme Court opinions.

This study concurs with two main sections of the massive study of William W. Crosskey, *Politics and the Constitution in the History of the United States* (1953): his analyses of the commerce clause and of the Fourteenth Amendment. Crosskey demonstrates the plenary character of the commerce clause with overwhelming evidence of eighteenth-century usage. Crosskey's analysis is reinforced by the conclusion herein that the Congress was to have the final say on the scope and breadth of the language in the enumerated powers in Article I. This study also supports Crosskey's analysis of the Fourteenth Amendment, that the privileges-or-immunities clause incorporates the Bill of Rights as against the states, by assembling evidence on the historical use of that language starting with the Charter of Virginia.

But this study sometimes veers notably from Crosskey. The analysis in chapter 7 rejects Crosskey's conclusions on the federal common law, showing instead that the commercial law for interstate transactions, as a branch of private international law, was correctly a national case law but was distinct from the local common law. In chapter 9, Crosskey's view of the contract clause is rejected, but his analyses of the imports-and-exports clause and the ex post facto clause are accepted.

This study adopts the objective theory of documentary interpretation that is summarized by Oliver Wendell Holmes, The Theory of Legal Interpretation, 12 Harv. L. Rev. 417 (1899). This theory holds that written language can be interpreted only in terms of the meaning to reasonably educated readers of the time it was written. Holmes's theory rejects the possibility of finding the subjective intent of a single writer or the various subjective intents of the group of writers of a collective document. Collective intent does not exist. The conclusion is that statements of individual framers of a constitutional clause are useful only if they confirm the generally accepted meaning to readers of those times of the language that was ratified. This method does not confine interpretation to the text alone. All objective evidence of the circumstances and context in which the language was adopted can contribute to its meaning.

In order to contain the study within a reasonable length, the facts of the key cases are summarized with emphasis on economic implications. Persons who wish more detailed discussions of opinions are referred to comprehensive legal handbooks such as J. E. Nowak, R. P. Rotunda, and J. N. Young, Constitutional Law (2d ed. 1983).

I wish to acknowledge the assistance of many persons in the preparation of this study. Professors William Fletcher, Dow Votaw, and Douglas Laycock reviewed the manuscript and offered critical advice. I alone am responsible for errors that remain. Professor Edwin Epstein encouraged the writing and also assisted in advising on the publication. I am indebted to the Bureau of Economic and Business Research of the University of California for financial assistance. Research assistance was ably provided by Teri Prezant, John Henderson, and David Abramovitz. Margo Sercarz typed the many versions of the manuscript with great skill and patience. I also acknowledge the permissions to use previously published materials granted by the *Emory Law Journal,* the *Journal Maritime Law and Commerce,* and the West Publishing Company. I am especially indebted to my wife, Helene M. Conant, for her patience. Special recognition must be paid to my closest chow-chow friend who stayed by my side through years of work, AKC Champion Ho-Yam of Kensington.

MICHAEL CONANT

Berkeley, California

The Constitution and the Economy

Economic Analysis and the Law

THIS STUDY UTILIZES basic economic analysis to comment critically on the original meanings and the interpretations of those clauses of the Constitution that have particular bearing on the economy. Many of the conclusions are markedly different from those of the Supreme Court and earlier commentators. The view presented here is that the commerce clause and the equal protection clause, if they had been construed consistently with their comprehensive original meanings, would have given much greater protection against state laws that impaired free markets. On the other hand, the Constitution vested most of the final determination of economic policy for the nation in Congress. To the extent that special interests could buy congressional favor for their anticompetitive activities, free markets could be impaired within the constitutional constraints as interpreted by the Court. Many of the cases discussed here are criticized for their failure to recognize the incorporation of the British antimonopoly tradition in the Ninth Amendment or their failure to recognize equal protection of the laws as incorporated into the Fifth Amendment.

Three leading cases that are explained in detail in later chapters illustrate the markedly different conclusions one reaches from the critical view of normative economics. The first, *Swift* v. *Tyson*,[1] was a correct application of the law merchant to an interstate bill of exchange and should never have been overruled.[2] Efficient negotiation of transactions in international and interstate trade required a uniform commercial law upon which merchants could rely. The law merchant applied by Justice Story for the unanimous Court in *Swift* was then considered part of maritime law and not a precedent for later common-law decisions.

The *Carolene Products*[3] case is an example of a decision that, from an economic viewpoint, was wrong. Free markets require equal legislative treatment of rivals. Prohibition of shipment of one nonfat milk product and not others should have been held to violate equal protection of the laws as incorporated in the due process clause.[4] The famous footnote 4 of *Carolene* is also arguably wrong.[5] The very-low-income persons who bought filled milk were a discrete minority who were exploited by the monopoly power of the dairy interests in causing the prohibition to be enacted. Is there a rational basis to argue that freedom of expression is more important to very-low-income persons than freedom from monopoly in the food supply?

Another key example, on a broader level of economic and social analysis, demonstrates that *Plessy* v. *Ferguson*,[6] the lead opinion validating statutory racial segregation, was wrong. The legal concept approved in that case of racially "separate but equal" facilities was judicial fantasy. From time immemorial, the primary function of caste systems has been to impose and perpetuate ethnic inequality, and jim crowism could not be an exception.[7] The result of *Plessy* v. *Ferguson* was to limit materially and delay the economic development of the South by highly unequal education that left the majority of Afro-Americans semiliterate and unskilled.

This introduction summarizes for the noneconomist the basic economic concepts used in the critical analysis of the Constitution and its interpretations by the courts. Some readers may find this chapter too brief. They are urged to read the first few chapters of a basic text on law and economics or to study the articles cited in the notes to this chapter.[8] It is most important to observe that the economic approach to law is only partial. It cannot solve all of the problems of public choice related to the economy, let alone the other multiple social problems of a society.[9]

Economic policy can best be understood by dividing the issues into three main categories: (1) microeconomics—resource allocation in the productive processes; (2) macroeconomics—national-income analysis and monetary policy; and (3) distribution of income. Although governmental policies in any of these three areas can have effects in the other areas, rigorous analysis must begin by determining effects in the primary area. Thus, attempts to use microeconomic solutions for macroeconomic problems are foredoomed to failure. For example, the macroeconomic problem of the economic depression of the 1930s resulted in Congress's adopting microeconomic policies approving price fixing in the National Industrial Recovery Act and the Agricultural Adjustment Act. As economists predicted, the monopoly pricing aggravated the national-income problem.

Economic analysis is of least use in regard to policy issues concerned primarily with the distribution of income. The ultimate distribution of income is the result of redistribution of income pursuant to legislative policy.[10] The major policy issues are philosophical rather than economic. Redistribution of income through taxation and spending can have negative effects on the economy, if taxation reaches a level that impairs incentives to produce goods and services. But the basic issues of whether to adopt a marginal increase in taxes for public schools, subsidized health care for the poor, or welfare payments for dependent children are philosophical.

This leaves microeconomic and macroeconomic issues as the main concern of normative economics. In this study, only chapter 8 on the monetary and fiscal powers is concerned primarily with macroeconomics. The remainder of the chapters address the microeconomics of constitutional language, structure, history, and judicial interpretation.

The primary standard of microeconomic policy is efficiency. Knight defines efficiency as the ratio between useful output and total input in any production process.[11] Useful output has meaning only because it has value in the marketplace. Modern welfare economics defines efficiency in terms of Pareto superiority.[12] Taking the distribution of wealth and income as given for purposes of this microeconomic analysis, an efficient allocation of resources is one in which value is maximized. A Pareto-superior transaction is one that makes at least one person better off and no person worse off. Each person is assumed to be the best judge of his own welfare. If a person enters a transaction that leaves him better off and no one worse off, that transaction is presumed to increase total value.

If there is no situation where a Pareto-superior shift can be made, then the state of affairs is Pareto-optimal. This approach to maximizing value has the advantage that it does not require interpersonal comparisons of utility. It has the disadvantage that it is generally not useful as a guide for the adoption of regulatory statutes. Most statutes are designed to make some set of persons better off, but there are usually some others upon whom the impact is negative.

A less-restrictive definition of efficiency is that of Kaldor-Hicks, which most economists have adopted. Kaldor-Hicks efficiency exists if in moving to a potentially Pareto-superior state, the parties could compensate anyone who is made worse off. If the compensation is actually paid, the transaction becomes Pareto superior. But in large numbers of situations, measurement of harm to third parties and the transaction costs of negotiating payment make it infeasible to compensate third parties. Thus a move toward freer trade, such as a reduction in the protected price for sugar, is Kaldor-Hicks efficient because it lowers the sugar price for all consumers closer to the cost of efficient sugar-cane producers. This is true even if there is no compensation to the formerly protected, higher-cost–sugar-beet growers who had to shift to a less profitable crop and scrap some specialized farm machinery.

There are two general classes of cases for not compensating losers even if the amount of loss is subject to reasonable estimation. Where the regulatory statute is designed to correct a market failure, there is no reason to compensate losers. If antitrust laws are enforced against a cartel, the public gains and those who had restrained trade lose. If deregulation occurs in a regulated industry such as airline transport that had blocked entry of new firms, negative effects will accrue, but only to the income of former monopolists. Thus, those who have profited by restraint of trade need not be compensated for loss.

There is also no logical reason for compensation if the transaction costs of administering compensation would be greater than the losses of those disadvantaged. Transaction costs include search costs. The problem is especially severe where there is involuntary exchange. If political activists cause an ordinance to be passed allowing loudspeakers in a public park, they and those who like political speeches gain. Those who can no longer enjoy a quiet park are an indeterminate number and the correct compensation for any one of them is not subject to reasonable estimation.

Productive efficiency within firms and among firms exists when any given level of output is produced with the least cost combination of inputs.[13] Presuming inputs can be obtained in effectively competitive markets, efficiency is obtained by minimizing long-run average costs. If such a condition is met, there is no possible shift in resource use within firms or between firms that would create greater output. If competitive prices prevail, there is incentive in all firms to achieve productive efficiency. Thus, competitive markets are said to have, through the bidding of buyers and sellers in input and output markets, an automatic allocation of resources that is efficient. This automaticity is sometimes labeled an "invisible hand."

Minimizing long-run average costs has the effect of determining the optimal sizes of plants and firms in relation to the sizes of markets in which they operate.[14] Before 1940, for example, because of relatively low labor costs and the fact that a significant proportion of the working class and the unemployed had no automobiles, the optimal size and location of an urban grocery store was small and within walking distance of most of its customers. When the postwar economic expansion brought rising labor costs, economies of large-scale purchasing, and a great majority of customers with autos, the optimal retail food store was very large and accompanied by a parking lot. When a larger size of plant or firm results in lower average costs of production, we say that the plant or firm is benefiting from economies of scale. The corollary is diseconomies of scale, in which average costs rise because costs of coordination exceed any economies resulting from larger size. This same terminology can be applied to the costs of government. The very large bureaucracy of the United States government and the lack of coordination in control of expenditures has caused many persons to decry its diseconomies of large scale.

Statutory controls of the economy are justifiable in economic theory if they are designed to remedy market failures and thereby increase efficiency. If statutes are passed to interfere with markets and create market inefficiencies for the benefit of special-interest groups, they are to be condemned under the standards of normative microeconomics. There are four main classes of market failure: monopoly, externalities, public goods, and informational asymmetry.

Monopoly may occur in many ways. A single firm may control the output of a product or the supply of an input of production. Where the number of firms in a market is few, they may combine to form a monopoly in a product market or an input market. Since monopoly raises prices above competitive levels by curtailing supplies, it makes for inefficiencies. The antitrust laws are designed to replace monopoly with competition, where this is possible. In some instances, economies of scale in relation to the size of market are such that a monopoly is the least-cost firm. Examples include structural monopolies such as water, electric, and local-telephone utilities. Statutory regulation to control monopoly pricing by such firms has received judicial approval at least since *Munn* v. *Illinois*.[15] Another class of monopolies that is promoted by federal statutes enacted pursuant to a specific power in Article I, section 8 of the Constitution includes patents and copyrights. Patents and copyrights grant monopolies for a limited time period in order to promote invention and creative written works.

The second class of market failures are externalities. While free exchange in a market is voluntary and increases value to the parties, some transactions or production processes have effects on third parties that are involuntary and sometimes harmful. A negative or harmful externality imposes costs on third parties without their consent. The most common example of this is pollution of streams or air by a production process. The action of a factory can impose involuntary costs on those downstream or within the air pollution area. The costs imposed on any particular third party may be small in any single year, but may have large cumulative effects. The damage is hard to prove and litigation costs for an action in the tort of nuisance may be very high. The lack of a feasible remedy can be thought of as either a market failure or a judicial failure. The solution is statutory regulation that forces the firm to pay the total social cost of its production by forcing it to expend funds to reduce the level of pollution. While total elimination of pollution in an industrial nation might bring most factory production to a halt, there is some optimal level of pollution consistent with continued benefits of most productive processes.[16]

The third class of items making for market failure are public goods. A public good has two primary characteristics. First is the fact of nonrivalous consumption: consumption of the good or service by one person leaves it equally available to others. Second, the cost of excluding nonpayers from a public good or service is so high that no private enterprise will supply the good. Paving city streets is a key example. If one householder on a block were to pay for paving the street, all other householders on the block could use it for free. Hence the term "free ride." The cost of administering toll gates is so great that no private enterpriser could undertake the paving profitably. Consequently, only government, which has the power of taxation, is able to create public goods successfully. Other common examples of public goods are the police and national defense. Protection available to one citizen protects all others from the same harm. If payment were voluntary, it would not be possible to exclude those who would refuse to pay from those receiving the benefits of the service.

The fourth class of market failure is asymmetric information. Sellers very often know much more about the quality of goods than do buyers, and buyers may not even have enough knowledge to ask the right questions in the ordinary bargain in the market. This fact rebuts the presumption of the law of contract that sane adults are equal bargainers. If sellers know significantly more about a good or service, there is material informational asymmetry in the market. In some cases this asymmetry is corrected by market forces as sellers offer express warranties of quality in order to meet the competition of rivals. In other cases, the market fails to evoke express warranties to offset informational asymmetries, and statutory intervention is necessary to correct the market failure. The Uniform Commercial Code, following the earlier model in the Uniform Sales Act, imposes implied warranties of quality and fitness for purpose upon sellers of goods. Similar statutes to induce more nearly optimal exchange are found in state statutes requiring termite inspection paid for by sellers of houses. In a key case under the commerce clause, an 1838 statute remedied asymmetry of information between owners of ships and passengers on inland waters by requiring licensing and safety inspection of ships.[17]

One important emphasis in this study is that litigation costs are analogous to transaction costs. If legal principles and rules are clearly and precisely defined by the Supreme Court when they are first construed on appeal, litigation and its costs will be minimized, the bar will have meaningful standards for advising clients, and trial courts will have clear bases for granting demurrers to frivolous actions. In contrast, if legal principles or rules have a high degree of uncertainty because they lack definable standards, the number of legal actions filed and the costs of litigation will be much greater. There are many examples of this uncertainty phenomenon in constitutional law. One outstanding example in the economic sector, as treated in detail in chapter 11, was the judicial creation of substantive due process. After a five-man majority joined in an erroneous opinion in *Lochner* v. *New York*,[18] trial courts, relying on this opinion, heard hundreds of cases concerning the reasonableness of statutes regulating the economy. The period from 1905 to 1937 came to be known as the *Lochner* era. The impossibility of defining standards of reasonableness in what was essentially a legislative issue led to other five-man erroneous decisions in the Supreme Court such as *Adkins* v. *Childrens Hospital.*[19] This in turn promoted additional litigation challenging the many statutes enacted to remedy asserted market failures in an expanding industrial economy.

CHAPTER 1

Constitutional Structure and Functions

A NATIONAL CONSTITUTION is primarily a political document whose main function is to create a structure of government and a set of limitations on government to protect individual rights.[1] From an economic viewpoint, citizens with freedom to create a republican form of government establish a constitution to allocate resources to acquire that protection of life, liberty, and property necessary for long-term peaceful existence. Absent government, persons might spend most of their time defending themselves, their families, and their meager assets. Establishing a government with a monopoly on physical force is the most efficient means of obtaining a general peaceful environment so that most citizens can produce goods and services other than defense. Government is thus a machine with a set of processes that allow collective action in a free society.[2]

As a control on human aggression, government clearly benefits from economies of scale. The larger the geographic area under common governmental control, the less likely it is that a tribe or nation will have to engage in war with neighboring tribes or nations. The urge to extend the realm of peace through law and the finding of the means to do it are clearly as old and as enduring as the urge to fight.[3] In 1437, for example, the Florentines went to war with Lucca.[4] The modern unification of Italy under a single government leads many to forget the centuries of wars between the city states.[5] The potential for violent conflict between the thirteen former English colonies was greatly reduced by replacing the Articles of Confederation with a national Constitution that created a single free trade area and allocated military force to the national government.[6]

From an economic viewpoint, the constitutional principles of government can be seen as a set of given goals or constraints. The economic issue is how to allocate human and other resources in order to achieve these goals with efficiency, at minimum cost. In this context, the primary cost must be defined in terms of social conflict, the breaking down of political institutions. Consequently, efficient government is first that which fosters long-term social stability. Such a system concentrates social-policy differences in institutions that function well in resolving them peacefully, usually legislatures. Although legislative processes may be inefficient in procedures, their responsiveness to the electorate makes them the most efficient social institutions for resolving social conflict.

Evidence of inefficiency of key operative institutions of government in resolving social conflict are revolution and civil war. The *Dred Scott*[7] case is an outstanding example. The judiciary attempted to usurp the resolution of the major political conflict of the time, the issue of whether slavery should be expanded into the western territories. The issue had been tentatively settled by the Congress in the Missouri Compromise,[8] which the Court in *Dred Scott* held unconstitutional.[9] The majority decision was a significant factor in destabilizing social relations on an issue that had been partially settled. The Court could have avoided the constitutional issue and ruled on the narrower one of whether the voluntary return of Scott to Missouri precluded a challenge to his status.[10] Instead the majority adopted a view that aggravated the controversy that led eventually to civil war.

The Constitution of the United States is held to be basic and superior law because it is derived from the people themselves through the process of ratification. This is immediately apparent from the Preamble, which begins, "We the people of the United States, in order to form a more perfect union, . . ."[11] Chief Justice Marshall pointed out that the Constitutional Convention created a mere proposal to be submitted to the conventions of delegates in each of the states for ratification. He concluded "The government of the Union . . . is emphatically, and truly, a government of the people. In form and in substance, it emanates from them. Its powers are granted by them, and are to be exercised directly on them, and for their benefit."[12]

The key clauses of a constitution are the general principles of government. They differ from the narrow rules of liability found in most of the common law and statutes, both in their magnitude of generality and their function of creating a structure for public law. Nevertheless, it is error to presume that most constitutional principles were wholly designed in the Convention of 1787. Like the common law and most rules enacted into statutes,[13] the origin of many constitutional principles is evolutionary. The vesting of all legislative powers in the Congress, for example, derives from the British parliamentary supremacy over the king, incorporated in the Bill of Rights of 1689.[14] This was the result of centuries of conflict to establish effective representative government.[15] As to civil rights, the British Habeas Corpus Act of 1679[16] was the result of a long fight against arbitrary imprisonment.[17] Even though the act was not operative in the colonies, every former colonist in America claimed the benefit of this principle as a common-law right, whether incorporated in a written constitution or not.

In economic terms, votes needed to get law enacted can be viewed as costs. The Constitution of the United States differs from statuary law in its higher costs of enactment and amendment.[18] The general principles creating a representative government and a set of civil rights are not to be easily withdrawn, even by a majority of the populace. The majority could be affected by some hysteria of the time, fostered by fanatic leaders. The costs of amendment must be high in order to prevent amendment in response to such hysteria. But lesser changes can be enacted by legislative adjustment to social change. The general principles that make up the main clauses of the Constitution need not change their language to adapt to a changing society. The broad national power to regulate commerce, for example, does not need amendment to encompass all the new methods of commerce and any negative externalities such methods might create.[19]

Representative government is much less costly than pure democracy, in which political issues are always submitted to the entire electorate. The information costs of explaining all political issues to every citizen, especially those with little education, would be so large that the society would reject pure democracy. Representatives, on the other hand, develop special skills in policy formation and are thus the least-cost method of government that is responsible to the citizens. As to election of representatives, there are at least three arguments supporting universal suffrage.[20] Denial of the franchise to any groups gives opportunity to those in power to redistribute income from disenfranchised persons to themselves. Such redistribution has social costs and the effect on the disenfranchised is to provoke protest and even rebellion. Second, general elections are the least-cost way for policymakers to learn majority preferences. Thirdly, the larger the electorate, the more difficult it is for groups of voters to form coalitions to do harm to specific minorities.

Economics of Federalism

A workable division of legislative power between the national and state governments was essential to long-term survival of the union.[21] Madison noted that states' rights were protected in part by the fact that the national government was one of limited powers. He stated that "its jurisdiction extends to certain enumerated objects only, and leaves to the several States a residuary and inviolable sovereignty over all other objects."[22] He later compared the numbers of powers. "The powers delegated by the proposed Constitution to the federal government are few and defined. Those which are to remain in the State governments are numerous and indefinite."[23]

Although the national government is one of enumerated powers, some of these are the basic essentials of government. Powers of taxation, spending, war, and regulation of private commerce are stated as general principles, not narrow legal rules. They are meaningful only if broadly construed. In order to ensure broad construction, the draftsmen inserted the "sweeping" clause, giving Congress the power "to make all laws which shall be necessary and proper for carrying into execution the foregoing powers, and all other powers vested by this Constitution in the government of the United States, or in any department or office thereof."[24] As Madison said, "Without the substance of this power, the whole Constitution would be a dead letter."[25] In their arguments against ratification, the opponents of the Constitution, repeatedly charged that the clause amounted to an unlimited grant of power to Congress.[26] As to the effect on the breadth of the enumerated powers, they correctly interpreted the meaning of the language. So long as a regulatory statute could be subsumed under an enumerated power and did not violate a constitutional limitation, it was valid.

The primary economic issues of federalism concern economies and diseconomies of scale. Certain of the national powers in Article I, Section 8 are exclusive, because the character of the activities is national in scope, and they are more efficiently executed on a national level. Example of such powers are the powers to declare war, to coin money, to establish post offices, to establish uniform laws of bankruptcy, and to regulate commerce between the states.[27] The exclusive national bankruptcy power, for example, was adopted because some state laws prior to union had created havens for dishonest debtors. Those states "created an ignoble array of legislative schemes for the defeat of creditors and the invasion of contractual obligations."[28] The national power to regulate the interstate segment of commerce among the several states is exclusive because conflicting state regulations of any single transaction between parties in different states could greatly impede commerce.

Some governmental powers are shared by the nation and the states in the sense that they may possibly be exercised by either one but not both at the same time. Delegates to the Convention of 1787 quickly realized that efficient government could not function if national and state laws on the same subject conflicted, and in response, they proposed a congressional veto of state laws.[29] The eventual solution was to transfer this resolution to the judiciary by adoption of the supremacy clause.[30] A prominent example of shared power has been the regulation of local commerce that affects more states than one. In almost all cases, the Supreme Court has given broad application to federal preemption under the supremacy clause.[31] In one narrow area where the Court deviated from this principle, there has been costly promotion of much litigation. In *Parker* v. *Brown*,[32] the Court expressly noted conflict between the Sherman Antitrust Act and a state statute giving regulatory approval of cartel pricing of raisins. Yet it upheld the state policy, partly on grounds that there also existed a congressional policy to aid distressed agriculture.

The state-action defense to the antitrust laws developed thereafter without thorough consideration by the Court of the scope of the supremacy clause.

Concurrent powers, those which may be exercised by the nation and the states at the same time, are best illustrated by taxation and spending. In the fiscal area, the competitive concept of federalism that prevailed for about one hundred years from the 1830s to the 1930s has given way to a dominant concept of cooperative federalism. A prime example is national grants in aid to the states for numerous welfare purposes.[33] Although the states have been unable or unwilling to tax themselves for all these local activities, the federal government has become a major source of finance. The chief objection to cooperative federalism is that it fosters continuing enlargement of national power and expanded national bureaucracy. The superior taxing power and borrowing power of the national government means that the Congress is the dominant force and the state legislatures are submissive to directions from Washington.

Diseconomies of scale are a significant result of national subsidy and control of local government functions.[34] Public school education, for example, has largely been under the control of local school districts. Local interests insist on continued local control because they fear bureaucratic centralized management of schools. But local financing, especially in the poorer states, has been difficult. Persons voting in local elections to increase school taxes internalize the costs and may underinvest in education in terms of its long-run benefits.[35] But because they do not internalize the costs of national grants in aid, they may therefore give political support for such aid. The creation of the U.S. Department of Education superimposed an additional layer of governmental administration, whose cost must be added to the total social cost of public education.[36]

As to shared or concurrent powers, according to the Tiebout hypothesis, absent economies of scale, local government will be a more efficient provider of services than the national government.[37] Public choice is greatly enhanced when services are provided locally because municipalities and even states have much less monopoly power as providers than does the national government. If persons dislike the mix of taxes and services in one town or state, they may move to another so long as they can earn a living there. This citizen mobility should cause localities and states to compete with one another for productive citizens by responding to consumer demand with a desirable mix of services. Only imperfect information and imperfect mobility should limit the practical effect of the Tiebout hypothesis.

One of the key economic effects of federalism is interstate externalities. The issue is the incentive each state has to improve its income position by imposing costs on residents of other states.[38] States export costs by taxation or regulation, the incidence of which is borne by those in other states.[39] They import benefits by attracting investors through tax benefits and other public services. The Supreme Court has power under the commerce clause and the equal protection clause to prevent such interstate discrimination. It has exercised this power to invalidate taxes on nonresident consumers and tariffs on state imports. But it has sometimes failed to invalidate state statutes whose effect is an export of taxation. In *Commonwealth Edison Co. v. Montana*,[40] for example, the Court failed to see that a state's 30 percent severance tax on coal would have its main impact on out-of-state consumers. The Court's failure to meet the issue of the incidence of the taxation distorts resource allocation from true comparative advantage and in effect upholds interstate taxation.

Economics of Separated Powers

The separation of governmental powers into legislative, executive and judicial, together with a set of checks and balances, has the political objective of preventing monopolization of the coercive power of the state.[41] Separated powers promote rival interests in the branches and avoid the collusion that could lead to totalitarian control.[42] The costs of collusion increase with the increase in the number of people necessary to make it effective. A majority of the legislature may succumb to the hysteria of an era and pass totalitarian legislation, but if the executive avows that such laws are unconstitutional and refuses to execute them, tyranny may be forestalled. Even if the executive should carry out such laws, the judiciary may refuse to use its sanctions for noncompliance and may under the *habeas corpus* principle order the release of those who have been detained. As Justice Brandeis observed, the doctrine of separated powers was adopted "not to promote efficiency but to preclude the exercise of arbitrary power. The purpose was, not to avoid friction, but, by means of the inevitable friction incident to the distribution of the governmental powers among three departments, to save the people from autocracy."[43]

Separated powers are effective only if the officers of the three departments are independent of one another.[44] The first essential of independence is that persons holding office in one department do not owe their tenure to the will or preferences of persons in another of the branches.[45] Thus under the U.S. Constitution, the president and members of Congress are continued in office or not at the will of the electorate at general elections,[46] and the federal judges hold office during good behavior, and their compensation may not be reduced.[47] The second essential of independence is that officials in one department may not concurrently hold office in either of the other two departments[48] and may not usurp or encroach upon the powers which the Constitution clearly assigns to another department.[49]

While checks and balances of governmental powers are said to impair government efficiency, another argument hypothesizes that separated powers are merely an example of the division of labor. Locke observed that while a legislature may be in session for only a short time each year, the execution of laws requires continuous activity throughout the year.[50] Furthermore, the representative character of a legislature makes it too large and too slow to carry out the executive function.[51] Many of the founding fathers commented on this phenomenon.[52] Justice Wilson contrasted legislative and executive methods as follows:

> In planning, forming, and arranging laws, deliberation is always becoming, and always useful. But in the active scenes of government, there are emergencies, in which the man, as in other cases, the woman, who deliberates, is lost. Secrecy may be equally necessary as despatch. But, can either secrecy or despatch be expected, when, to every enterprise and to every step in the progress of every enterprise, mutual communication, mutual consultation, and mutual agreement among men, perhaps of discordant views, of discordant tempers and of discordant interests, are indispensably necessary? How much time will be consumed! and when it is consumed; how little business will be done! . . . If, on the other hand, the executive power of government is placed in the hands of one person, who is to direct all the subordinate officers of the department, is there not reason to expect, in his plans and conduct, promptitude, activity, firmness, consistency, and energy?[53]

Hamilton emphasized that, unlike the contesting legislature, efficiency in the executive required that it be vested in a single person. "It is essential to the protection of the community against foreign attacks; it is not less essential to the steady administration of laws, to the protection of property against those irregular and high-handed combinations which sometimes interrupt the ordinary course of justice, to the security of liberty against enterprises and assaults of ambition, of faction, and of anarchy."[54] He concluded, "Decision, activity, secrecy, and despatch will generally characterize the proceedings of one man in a much more eminent degree than the proceedings of any greater number; and in proportion as the number is increased, these qualities will be diminished."[55]

An efficient judiciary is one with maximum independence from the other two branches.[56] Strict separation is necessary for pursuit of the ideal of deliberative objectivity, especially in the enforcement of constitutional limitations against the legislature and executive. The effectiveness of the judicial bar to arbitrary and oppressive government can be guaranteed only by a judiciary that is free from executive or legislative control.[57] In the classic statement of Lord Coke: "No man may be a judge in his own cause."[58] Neither the legislature that has exercised the sovereign lawmaking power in enacting a statute nor the executive officers charged with enforcing a statute may sit in judgment of a defendant charged with violating the statute. For both the legislature and executive, in their efforts to govern, have a vested and therefore biased interest in unlimited statutory enforcement.[59] They cannot be impartial judges of the constitutional limitations on their own acts.[60] Only an independent judiciary can perform this function.

The doctrine of the separation of powers is a general constitutional principle and was not conceived as rigid.[61] It has exceptions. Although the legislature is granted exclusive lawmaking power,[62] efficient government makes it necessary for secondary legislative power to be delegated to executive agencies.[63] The legislative power is general and prospective.[64] Although the primary legislative function of setting general rules is assigned to the legislature, there are many instances where it would be highly inefficient and perhaps impossible for the legislature to set all the detailed secondary rules. As a prime example, consider rate regulation. In order to remedy the market failure of monopoly, the legislature has adopted statutes regulating maximum rates or prices.[65] But the legislature would be making an inefficient allocation of its time if it spent thousands of hours setting individual rates for a railroad or an electric utility. In fact, the legislature may lack the technical skill to set such rates. Instead, the legislature is basically a duty-assigning body that delegates to a specialized administrative agency the power to do such acts as are necessary to achieve the results required by the statute.[66]

Legislative bodies have high transaction costs. The cost to a legislator of acting when the public is sharply divided on the need for and scope of proposed legislation may be the loss of a seat. The legislature can avoid some of these costs by passing a very general statute and leaving the executive to fill in the substance. The degree of generality in statutes may become very great as factions in a legislature compromise by adopting indefinite, general language.[67] There are other instances where complexity makes detailed legislation impossible, for example when the legislature lacks the skill to construct a multifaceted statutory remedy. In such cases, the legislature must leave the detailed rules to the executive.[68] Furthermore, dynamic changes may make it essential that some detailed rules be under constant change. It can be argued that the necessary-and-proper clause of the Constitution gives Congress explicit authority to delegate secondary legislative functions.[69]

The primary negative criticism of the delegation of legislative powers is that the elected representatives shirk their responsibilities and, by general language, shift most of the legislative function to nonelected appointees in the executive branch. But the Supreme Court has invalidated statutes on the ground that the primary legislative power is nondelegable only in a few extreme cases. Two cases arose under the National Industrial Recovery Act of 1933,[70] where the president approved codes of "fair competition" designed by representatives of labor and management.[71] Under vague standards, the statute largely delegated legislative power to private persons to engage in monopoly pricing, thereby aggravating market failure. In the *Schechter* case, Chief Justice Hughes, writing for a unanimous Court, held the statute void, stating, "The Congress is not permitted to abdicate or to transfer to others the essential legislative functions with which it is thus vested. . . . Congress cannot delegate legislative powers to the President to exercise an unfettered discretion to make whatever laws he thinks may be needed or advisable for the rehabilitation and expansion of trade or industry."[72]

This bar to the delegation of primary legislative functions has not survived. Vague and indeterminate legislative standards have been upheld, although the background of the doctrine of nondelegation has in a few instances caused narrow construction of delegated power.[73] Justice Rehnquist, in dissent, has urged broader application of the nondelegation doctrine.[74] In fact, the Supreme Court approval of almost unlimited delegation of primary legislative power has encouraged Congress to ignore its duties to create definable, limited standards of regulation, even though in many fields, the drafting of more precise standards would not have a high cost. Substantive regulations in many fields, with the exception of price controls, require only that the congressional staff assemble sufficient data from interested parties so that the issues can be detailed to the elected Congress. If coalitions cannot be formed to achieve the majority needed to adopt rigorous regulatory language, the principle of separated powers dictates that regulation should not become law. Politicians facing a demand for legislative remedies do not want to face the cost of taking clearly identifiable stands on the controversial political and economic issues of the day. The issue is whether, under representative government, they have the power to pass vague laws that enable executive employees to make general public policies for the nation.[75]

In order to offset the great legislative power delegated to administrative agencies, Congress in recent years has often adopted a method to recover control, the legislative veto. Congress enacts legislation with an express condition that the executive may enact regulations if one or both houses of Congress do not veto them. Under the statute, proposed regulations are submitted to Congress. Under some statutes, one or both houses of Congress may by resolution veto them. Under other statutes, the regulations gain the force of law only after one or both houses approves them.

The transaction costs in Congress of reviewing for approval or disapproval many separate regulations adopted over time to effectuate a single statute should be much greater than the costs of negotiating a single detailed and precise statute at the outset. The majority of legislators prefer, however, to defer considering the detailed application of some legislation, probably to avoid the political costs of enactment.

While the legislative veto had been upheld in the lower courts,[76] it had been attacked by the commentators.[77] Until 1983 the Supreme Court had avoided the issue.[78] Then, in *Immigration and Naturalization Service* v. *Chadha*,[79] the Court, in very general language, held the congressional veto unconstitutional. Under the statute, the suspension of deportation of an alien by the executive had to be reported to Congress. In this case, the House of Representatives passed a resolution vetoing the decision of the attorney general to suspend the deportation of Chadha. Under the statute, the resolution was not treated as "legislation," and it was not sent to the Senate or the president. The Court held that the resolution was legislation and the failure to submit it to the president violated the presentment clause.[80] It also violated the bicameral requirement and the separation of governmental powers.[81] The case points out the relatively high costs in congressional time of reviewing individual deportations as opposed to the public benefits from allocating legislative time to statutes having broad effects on the public welfare.

While *Chadha* concerned congressional review of one deportation and thus seemed a replication of a long executive proceeding, the invalidation of the legislative veto has been followed in other areas. In two summary affirmances, the Court disapproved the veto. The first applied to the regulation of natural gas pricing by the Federal Energy Regulatory Commission.[82] The second applied to rulemaking by the Federal Trade Commission.[83]

Constitutional Limitations

The second main function of the national Constitution is to guarantee the civil rights of persons within the United States by express limitations on the powers of national and state governments. The idea of protecting individual liberties in the Anglo-American legal system has a long history that goes back at least to Magna Charta.[84] Given the totalitarian dictatorships in most of the world, both in the past and in the present, the idea of representative government that effectively limits the powers of those delegated the authority to govern is the most fundamental concept of human liberty. Protection of individuals from oppression by agents of government must be considered the primary function of government in a free society and the allocation of governing power merely subservient to it. In fact, the separation of powers in government, with a set of checks and balances, was designed to protect individuals from arbitrary and unjust treatment by governmental officials.

The enforcement of constitutional limitations by judicial review is treated in chapter 3. Chapters 9 through 12 are devoted to the economic implications of express constitutional limitations. Chapter 9 is devoted to the contract clause. Chapters 10 through 12 are devoted to the three clauses of section 1 of the Fourteenth Amendment: privileges or immunities, due process, and equal protection. There are also express limitations on the taxing power and on barriers to international trade. The Supreme Court has held in addition that there are also implied constitutional limitations. As noted in chapter 5, the plenary power in Congress to regulate commerce among the several states carries the implication that the states may not regulate parts of that commerce. Transactions between parties in different states may not be regulated by the conflicting statutes of the two states because such state regulation would bring interstate commerce to a halt.

Some express constitutional limitations, such as those enforcing procedural protections for the accused in criminal cases, present only two-sided controversies between citizens and government. Others are more complex. Substantive constitutional limitations may be invoked in controversies between private factions in which one special interest gets legislation enacted that is detrimental to other persons. This is especially true of the equal protection clause. Economic-interest groups have subsidized legislators and thereby bought special legislation for their control of the supply of some goods or services in the market.[85] Such statutes bar the entry of rivals into the market and result in the market failure of monopoly. Supply of the resource or product is reduced and prices are increased to all users. Challenges to such legislation usually originate not with the state but rather with other suppliers that are barred from the market. The economic history of the Constitution is full of examples. *Gibbons v. Ogden*[86] concerned a long-term state grant of monopoly to one steamboat operator. The *Slaughter-House Cases*[87] concerned a state grant of monopoly to a small group of New Orleans butchers. Numerous other examples under the equal protection clause are reviewed in chapter 12. In these cases, judicial intervention to curtail legislative grants of monopoly is clearly appropriate.

In fact, one of the earliest precedents in English constitutional law for enforcing constitutional limitations concerned a Crown grant of monopoly. In *Dr. Bonham's Case*,[88] letters patent from King Henry VIII to the Royal College of Physicians in London granted the College the power to impose fines on persons practicing medicine in London who had not been admitted to practice by the college. The college further claimed the right to govern the professional conduct of all physicians in London and implement its rules, if necessary, by fines and imprisonment. The letters patent in this case had been confirmed by statute.[89] This statute was in derogation of the common-law precedents against Crown grants of monopoly in the ordinary trades or professions.

Dr. Thomas Bonham, a medical graduate of Cambridge University, was cited by the college for practicing medicine in London without their certificate. He was fined, and when he persisted, he was imprisoned for seven days. Bonham brought a tort action for false imprisonment against the leading members of the Royal College of Physicians. Chief Justice Coke held for Bonham and asserted five arguments to support his view. The one that is important here was that since the college was to receive one-half of all fines, the members were both parties to the cause of action and judges therein.[90] The lack of fundamental fairness in procedure was a denial of the due process of the law. In dictum, Coke asserted that "when an Act of Parliament is against common right and reason, or repugnant, or impossible to be performed, the common law will control it and adjudge such Act to be void."[91] Thus one of the earliest pronouncements on judicial enforcement of constitutional limitations was this application of Coke's strong views against governmental grants of monopoly power.[92]

There is space here for only one illustrative example of how the courts have in many areas given decreased enforcement of constitutional limitations when applied to economic activity. The relation of the First Amendment to commercial expression, especially advertising, shows the judicial failure to comprehend the significance of information systems to the efficient functioning of markets. Hayek long ago pointed out the importance of prices in free markets as signals for decision making in resource allocation.[93]

The economic theory of perfect competition presumes perfect and costless information in all parties to transactions and to those who consider transactions and reject them.[94] This theoretical ideal of efficient markets, those that maximize welfare under any given distribution of assets and income, is the objective of the free-market system. In the real world, access to information is imperfect and search for information has costs.[95] Thus, imperfect information makes for imperfect competition. Fully rational economic decisions are impossible because of the presence of uncertainty about factual aspects of the subject matter of transactions.[96] In this sense, the subject matter includes not only the price and quality characteristics of one seller or buyer but also the same facts about the offers of all rival sellers or buyers. Uncertainty about current facts in a market thus makes for disutility on the part of those lacking information. If the flow of factual information about goods and services can be improved, efficiency of markets will be improved.

A key impediment to effective competition is asymmetric information of sellers and buyers. For most goods and services, sellers are specialists in the item, and buyers are not. Buyers who must act in ignorance of significant facts about the item or its market are unlikely to make purchase decisions that maximize utility. Furthermore, buyer ignorance increases the risk that false advertising will provoke transactions and not be detected. From the viewpoint of economics, any activity that makes for more symmetrical access to information increases competition. Thus informative advertising reduces ignorance on the part of buyers concerning the price and quality of goods and services and thereby contributes to the efficiency of markets. Statutes that bar informational advertising from the mails, such as that for contraception, impede efficiency.[97]

Supreme Court opinions on abridging freedom of speech and of the press are notable for their lack of rigor, and they often ignore the most fundamental distinction in the topic: the dichotomy between protection of the *content* of speech and publications on the one hand and the necessary regulation of time, place, and manner of speaking and distributing publications on the other.[98] It is clear that the underlying purpose of these sections of the First Amendment was to protect *content* of expressions.[99] Leading commentators have pointed out that most expressions are subject to regulation of time, place, and manner.[100] The Congress of the United States has rules prohibiting speech when the speaker has granted the floor to another member.[101] Courts have large sets of rules regulating what may be spoken and admitted as evidence and the order in which persons may speak.[102]

The failure of the Supreme Court to begin analysis of each case concerning freedom of expression by determining whether it concerns content has caused confusion in the Court's discussion of its own earlier opinions and left lower courts without clear guidelines for decision making. This has caused especially severe problems in the field of commercial expression. The leading early cases holding that commercial speech and publication were not protected by the First Amendment concerned only time, place, or manner. *Valentine* v. *Chrestensen*,[103] upheld a New York City ordinance prohibiting distribution of commercial advertising materials in the streets. Chrestensen had printed and distributed in the streets handbills advertising tours of a former U.S. Navy submarine that he exhibited for profit. There was no assertion that the First Amendment would not protect the content, true statements concerning legal events. The problem was with Chrestensen's distribution of the handbills on the street, rather than by mail or at gatherings on private property. The Court had previously upheld the constitutional right peacefully to distribute handbills with political content on public ways.[104] But in *Chrestensen,* Justice Roberts noted that while the state may regulate distribution of political matter on the streets, they may not unduly burden or proscribe it. He then concluded, "We are equally clear that the Constitution imposes no such restraint on government as respects purely commercial advertising."[105] The inference from this statement that commercial expression had no constitutional protection was misinterpreted as applying to content and was subject to attack. In 1959 Justice Douglas asserted that the *Chrestensen* "ruling was casual, almost offhand. And it has not survived reflection."[106]

The Court adopted its reasoning in *Chrestensen* in another case concerning time, place, and manner of commercial expression. In *Breard* v.

Alexandria,[107] the Court upheld an ordinance prohibiting door-to-door selling as applied to persons selling magazine subscriptions. The commercial aspect was emphasized because eight years earlier the Court had voided an ordinance that prohibited door-to-door distribution of printed matter as applied to free publications of Jehovah's Witnesses.[108] The Court recently invalidated an ordinance that limited door-to-door solicitation for political canvassing to the hours 9A.M. to 5P.M.[109] The distinction between political and commercial solicitation had no logical basis. Both disturb the solitude of the thinking householder and should be subject to statutory prohibition. There seems to be a denial of equal protection of the laws to commercial solicitors.

Later courts, not observing that *Chrestensen* was concerned only with time, place, and manner, felt they had to distinguish cases concerning content of publication from *Chrestensen.* In *New York Times* v. *Sullivan,*[110] the Court reversed a judgment for defamation as applied to a paid advertisement containing political criticism. The Court found it necessary to conclude that a paid advertisement soliciting funds for a civil rights group was not a "commercial" advertisement in the sense in which "commercial" was used in *Chrestensen.*[111] Given the political content of the advertisement, the profit motive of the newspaper was not relevant.

The second fundamental issue relating to commercial expression is whether the original meaning of the First Amendment applies to it at all. Although the context of the adoption of the amendment was to protect political expression, the unqualified language is not limited to political issues. Even Meikeljohn, whose early writing centered on the political function of free expression, conceded that the First Amendment protected expression in the form of literature, philosophy, education, and science.[112] The protection must extend to both informative expression of facts and opinions. In practice, the borderline between political or scientific expression and commercial expression is not easy to determine. In *Bigelow* v. *Virginia,*[113] for example, the Court upheld the right to advertise when the advertisement contained factual material of clear public interest. *Bigelow* held invalid a Virginia statute barring publication to encourage or prompt the procuring of an abortion as to advertisements in a Virginia newspaper by a New York City abortion referral service. Persons not in need of an abortion could learn of the difference in law between New York and Virginia.[114]

Those who would limit the protection of the First Amendment to political expression would protect prices of prescription drugs in a consumer's journal that advocated new statutes deregulating the pharmaceutical industry, an industry where existing special-interest statutes promote monopoly pricing.[115] But if this publication is protected by freedom of the press as political, can there be a logical reason not to protect dissemination of the raw data, price advertisements by druggists for prescription drugs? This was the issue in *Virginia State Board of Pharmacy* v. *Virginia Citizens Consumer Council, Inc.*[116] The plaintiffs attacked a Virginia statute that prohibited the advertising of prices for prescription drugs, claiming that lack of effective competition increased prices. The Court first held that the First Amendment right to expression could be asserted by the recipients of the information.[117] Next the Court set aside the purported ruling of the *Chrestensen* case that there was no protection for commercial speech, and recognized that *Chrestensen* concerned only the manner of distributing the advertising.[118] It held that speech that does no more than propose a commercial transaction was entitled to First Amendment protection.[119] If one of the objectives of free expression is individual self-fulfillment, relief from high drug prices through dissemination of price information furthers that objective.[120] The society has a strong interest in the free flow of commercial information, and there is little point in forcing sellers to frame their advertisements as political comments in order to free them from legislative suppression. Furthermore, "no line between publicly 'interesting' or 'important' commercial advertising and the opposite kind could ever be drawn."[121]

The breadth of the constitutional protection for advertising is illustrated by the cases concerning advertising by attorneys.[122] The law on the topic was reviewed in *Zauderer* v. *Office of Disciplinary Counsel.*[123] The Court invalidated rules that forbade soliciting clients through advertisements containing information or advice regarding specific legal problems.[124] But in *Zauderer*, discipline of an attorney for misleading advertising was upheld when his ads failed to reveal that clients would be liable for litigation costs even if their lawsuits were unsuccessful.[125] The one case barring a class of truthful expression by attorneys was *Ohralik* v. *Ohio State Bar Association*,[126] where the Court upheld a ban on direct, in-person solicitation of clients because of the likelihood of overreaching and undue influence. Here again, the Court failed to note that this was a regulation of time, place, and manner of speech and not of content. The Court did note that physically approaching a potential client was conduct, not expression, and that the regulation was primarily one of conduct.[127]

The failure of the Court to make a clear preliminary distinction between free expression cases that concern not content, but rather time, place, and manner of expression, has continued to cause confusion. *Pacific Gas & Elec.* v. *P.U.C. of California*[128] is a recent example concerning place. The utilities commission ordered the utility to enclose a newsletter of a public-interest group in its billing envelopes. The content of the newsletter was political and clearly protected by the First Amendment, but the Court held the utility commission order to be an impermissible burden on the utility. The issue here was solely one of place and manner, for the Court had earlier upheld the right of a utility to include political matter with its bills.[129] But the commission wished to give access only to those who disagreed with the utility, and its order might provoke the utility to stop expressing its views, thus reducing the free flow of information and ideas.[130] The place, namely the envelope, forced the utility to associate with speech of other private parties with which it disagreed. This was an unreasonable regulation, quite different from the surgeon general's warning that the government requires on cigarette packages. The latter does not abridge free expression because it requires the truthful factual findings on health be distributed in order to make the assertions of the seller not misleading.[131]

The issues of freedom of expression in regulated industries are complex. In an industry where a regulatory commission controls prices or rates and costs, every expenditure is conduct subject to regulation. When the expenditure is for the purpose of publishing information or opinions, conduct and expression are joint acts. In *First National Bank of Boston v. Bellotti,*[132] the Court invalidated a state statute that prohibited banks and other regulated industries from expenditures to influence voters on taxation of income, property, or transactions. Such political expression was at the heart of the concern of the First Amendment,[133] and the content will be protected even when published by a corporation.[134] Three of the four dissenters felt that regulating expenditures on issues that did not directly concern the corporation, such as personal income taxation, was well within the regulation of conduct necessary to protect shareholders.[135]

The issue of whether the protection of the content of expressions extended to commercial advertising by a firm with regulated costs was presented in *Central Hudson Gas* v. *Public Service Commission of N.Y.*[136] The state commission extended a policy begun during the oil shortage of 1973 to prohibit promotional advertising by electrical utilities. The 1973 ban did not apply to institutional and informational advertising and was adopted as part of a national policy to conserve energy. The Supreme Court held the ban to violate the First Amendment. It easily could have distinguished *Virginia Pharmacy Board* because the industry here was one of regulated cost structure and the ban was only on noninformational advertising. While noting the state grant of monopoly, the Court failed to discuss the issue of regulating conduct (costs) that was related to expression in regulated industries. The Court did reiterate its distinction between commercial speech, which is subject to regulation for deception, and other types of speech, adopting a four-part analysis.[137] First, commercial speech is protected only if it concerns lawful activity and is not misleading. Second, there must be a substantial governmental interest in regulation. Third, the regulation must directly advance the governmental interest. Fourth, regulation must not be more extensive than is necessary to serve that interest.

Here it was clear that the expressions related to lawful conduct and were not deceptive. The Court found that monopoly in the service area did not reduce the value of commercial advertising, but it appears to have forgotten that informational advertising had not been banned by the commission.[138] The state interests were energy conservation and inequities caused by failure to base the utilities' rate on marginal cost.[139] The former was found to be advanced by the commission order; the latter was not. As to the fourth test, the commission order was found to be more extensive than necessary to promote conservation.[140]

Justice Rehnquist, the sole dissenter, recognized that the case primarily concerned economic regulation and that the issues of free expression were subordinate.[141] He failed, however, to explain the distinction between regulating conduct that has secondary effects on expression and direct suppression of speech or press. In this case, economic policy strongly supported curtailing conduct, namely advertising expenditures, and an emphasis on this aspect should have justified the regulation.

The issue of commercial advertising in regulated industries was again litigated in *Posadas De Puerto Rico Assoc.* v. *Tourism Co.*[142] Casino gambling as a regulated industry differs greatly from the electric utilities in *Central Hudson* since casino costs structures are not subject to regulation. By a 5-to-4 decision the Court upheld the facial constitutionality of a Puerto Rico statute that prohibited advertising of licensed casinos to the public in Puerto Rico but permitted such advertising outside Puerto Rico. The Court's application of the four-step test of commercial speech in *Central Hudson* illustrates the arbitrary character of the second test, the substantiality of the asserted governmental interest.[143] The legislature's interest in protecting the health, safety, and welfare of its citizens can be found in any statute regulating expression. Here the effects from casino gambling harmful to Puerto Ricans are not harmful to tourists. Justice Brennan, in dissent, points out that the legislative legalization of casino gambling is a determination that it will not have "serious harmful effects" on Puerto Ricans.[144] The Court also found that the third and fourth tests of *Central Hudson* were satisfied. The restrictions prevented the increase in demand that would result from local advertising, and they were not more extensive then necessary.

The Court made the additional argument that since the legislature could have prohibited casino gambling, it could also take the lesser step of reducing demand through restricting advertising.[145] This again confuses regulation of conduct with regulation of expression. Control of gambling is control of conduct, exercised by many legislatures, while control of expression is a distinct activity protected by the First Amendment.[146] This is just one more example of the fallacious reasoning based on the view that "abridge" in the First Amendment applies differently to truthful commercial expression and to other truthful expression.

Justice Stevens's dissent emphasized the issue of unequal treatment under the First Amendment.[147] If there were a constitutional right to advertise this legal activity, could the state validly deny the information to one specific group of citizens? The discriminatory ban on advertising was a system of prior restraint with standards that were hopelessly vague and unpredictable.

Conclusion

The economics of information explains why maximizing factual information to actors in a market increases the likelihood of maximizing utility, the measure of total welfare. The First Amendment, in barring abridgment of freedom of speech and of the press, was designed to protect dissemination of truthful facts and opinions on all the controversial issues in the society. In effectively competitive markets, the bids of sellers and buyers are the information signals that enable the economy to function efficiently. The underlying facts of the market contest are analogous to the facts asserted by politicians in their arenas. Governmental restriction on the dissemination of truthful facts in either arena invades the core protection of the First Amendment.

In early cases, the Supreme Court mistakenly relegated factual advertising to second-class protection in cases concerning time, place, and manner of expression. Even though the Court later recognized that these early cases did not concern content, it continues to assert that commercial speech is entitled to less protection than other varieties of speech. There is no logical basis for this when applied to truthful speech. On the other hand, false or misleading advertising, like libel, is not a class of communication subject to constitutional protection. As to truthful advertising, it is time for the Court to recognize that it is part of that general class of expression that government may not abridge.

CHAPTER 2

An Objective Theory of Interpretation

CONSTITUTIONAL THEORY MATTERS, not just to scholars, but to the entire community.[1] The constitutional theory or theories adopted by justices on the Supreme Court of the United States fix their approach to decision making. The substantive methodology the justices adopt determines the scope of judicial discretion in real cases. This scope can, in turn, determine decisions.

This chapter begins with an explanation of the necessary rejection of *stare decisis* in constitutional cases in the Supreme Court. This is followed by a demonstration that the search for the intent of the framers, a popular slogan of some political conservatives, is an impossibility. The conclusion is not, however, that judicial discretion in the highest court is unlimited. Instead, the chapter presents an objective theory of interpretation that is tied to original meanings of constitutional language, but to the meanings to readers at the time of adoption, not to the unknown intent of writers. The theory urged here emphasizes text, rules of documentary interpretation, and evidence of total context that points to search for social purposes. The methodology presented by Justice Story in 1833 is shown to be just as relevant and applicable today as it was then.

The primary constitutional principles underlying a rational and rigorous theory of constitutional interpretation are the separation of governmental powers and the reservation of the amending power to the people in Article 5. The Supreme Court is an appointed elite, and under the present system of judicial review its majority of five can hold any statute unconstitutional.[2] But the Constitution does not provide for maximum governance by the judiciary. When interpreting the principles incorporated in the more general constitutional clauses, the Court must determine the scope and breadth of judicial discretion in the Court in the frame of its own countermajoritarian character.

All legislative and judicial officers take the same oath to support the Constitution.[3] The legislature as initiator of law must be given the presumption of acting in good faith to write laws. The judiciary must frame its interpretation in this light. When invalidating a statute as unconstitutional, the Court must exercise its discretion with clear recognition of the presumption of constitutionality.[4]

The first principle of interpretation is the rejection of a strong or binding version of *stare decisis* as it applies to the Supreme Court when interpreting the Constitution. This rejection is unique to constitutional interpretation in the highest appeals court. The strong version of *stare decisis* applies to all statutory interpretation,[5] including that in the Supreme Court, and it applies to constitutional interpretation in lower courts.[6]

The rejection of binding precedent in interpretation of the Constitution by the highest court arises directly from the superior status of constitutions. A constitution is supreme law because it is derived from the people themselves through their ratification of proposals adopted at a constitutional convention.[7] No constitutional decisions of the Supreme Court, or of any other court, are submitted to the people for ratification.

A workable system of constitutional interpretation requires the Supreme Court to give dominant status only to that which the people have ratified, not to what a majority of justices may have said about a particular constitutional clause in some earlier decision concerning a specific and narrow-fact situation. As Justice Frankfurter said in *Graves* v. *New York,* "The ultimate touchstone of constitutionality is the Constitution itself and not what we have said about it."[8] An erroneous constitutional interpretation by the Supreme Court cannot become a binding precedent on that Court in later, similar cases. If *stare decisis* were applied to constitutional interpretation by the Supreme Court, judicial error could amend the Constitution. If, for example, the erroneous decision in *Hammer* v. *Dagenhart*[9] were binding precedent, the necessary federal regulation of national economic problems would be impossible. As Senator Garrett Davis said in 1866, when the *Dred Scott*[10] decision was argued to be controlling law, "this is not a Government of precedents; it was never intended to be; and there cannot be any more dangerous principle established in our government than that precedents shall make Constitutional law."[11] Justice Douglas, in language similar to Justice Daniel has concluded: "A judge looking at a constitutional decision may have compulsions to revere past history and accept what was once written. But he remembers above all else that it is the Constitution which he swore to support and defend, not the gloss which his predecessors may have put on it."[12]

A second reason for the highest court to reject *stare decisis* in constitutional cases is that the people do not stand ready to amend the broad language of the Constitution just because the majority of electors think one case was wrongly decided. Amendment was designed to be a costly, time-consuming process.[13] And broad, general language is difficult to amend while still retaining most of the same meaning in the clause. For this reason, the highest court has adopted an efficient method to correct what it considers errors in its earlier constitutional interpretations: it exercises its power to overrule them in subsequent similar cases. And the methodology of overruling is the exact opposite of *stare decisis*. The contrast between correcting errors in statutory interpretation and in constitutional interpretation was stated by Justice Brandeis: "*Stare decisis* is usually the wise policy, because in most matters it is more important that the applicable rule of law be settled than that it be settled right. . . . This is commonly true even where the error is a matter of serious concern, provided correction can be had by legislation. But in cases involving the Federal Constitution, where correction through legislative action is practically impossible, this Court has often overruled its earlier decisions. The Court bows to the lessons of experience and the force of better reasoning, recognizing that the process of trial and error, so fruitful in the physical sciences, is appropriate also in the judicial function."[14]

In effect, a constitutional decision is law only if it is correct. Chief Justice Taney noted this in observing that the majority of the Supreme Court had refused to follow his earlier interpretations: "After such opinions, judicially delivered, I had supposed that question to be settled, so far as any question upon the construction of the Constitution ought to be regarded as closely by the decision of this court. I do not, however, object to the revision of it, and am quite willing that it be regarded hereafter as the law of this court, that its opinion upon the construction of the Constitution is always open to discussion when it is supposed to have been founded in error, and that its judicial authority should hereafter depend altogether on the force of the reasoning by which it is supported."[15]

The best authority for the rule that the Supreme Court has the power and the duty to reject *stare decisis* and overrule its earlier constitutional decisions which it considers erroneous is the fact that it has done so in over 170 cases.[16] The exact figure cannot be stated because some overrulings are not explicit, and legal historians disagree on the real effect of some implied overrulings. *Erie R.R. Co* v. *Tompkins*,[17] for example, expressly overruled only *Swift* v. *Tyson*,[18] but it impliedly overruled a large group of Supreme Court cases that had erroneously created federal common law in many areas. The true significance of these figures can be realized only if one knows how high courts try to avoid admitting their own clear errors.[19] If two cases have many identical facts but the later court can find one material fact which is different, that court will likely distinguish the two cases and avoid the issue of direct conflict in law. Consequently, each overruling in the highest court comes only after a clear admission that the cases cannot be distinguished. They are essentially identical in reference to the constitutional issue before the court. Rejecting *stare decisis* as not apposite, the highest court is bound to point out its error and correct it.

Rejection of Intent of Framers

The modern definition of "intent" is, in its true subjective sense, the thoughts that were in the minds of the persons who spoke or drafted or approved a document. Search for intent in this sense is an impossibility. No one knows the thoughts of each person at the Constitutional Convention and at the ratifying conventions that turned the proposed document into law.[20] Some commentators assert that statements by leaders at the convention imply the intent of a silent majority on any given topic.[21] This speculation has no basis in fact. The framers probably had varying and conflicting intents. The Convention of 1787 was deliberately closed to all outsiders and no official report made on the speeches in order to bar the influence of statements of leaders on the interpretation of the final document. This was later emphasized by Madison: "As a guide in expounding and applying the provisions of the Constitution, the debates and incidental decisions of the Convention can have no authoritative character."[22] Since no official record of proceedings of the framers was made, none could be sent to the ratifying conventions. Those who voted for ratification voted for the language in the text, not the unknown subjective thoughts of 55 framers. The predominance of the text also applies to the amendments. As Justice Gray noted, "Doubtless the intention of the Congress which framed and of the states which adopted [the Fourteenth] Amendment of the Constitution must be sought in the words of the Amendment; and the debates in Congress are not admissible as evidence to control the meaning of those words.[23]

The background for those who drafted and ratified the Constitution in 1787 were the common-law rules of documentary interpretation.[24] Although the idea of intent had some ambiguity at that time, it was not used in the subjective sense because lawyers knew that searching for the thoughts of writers of documents was impossible. The emphasis was on the language itself and evidence of generally accepted meanings. Thus John Powell wrote in 1790 that contract was not concerned with "internal sentiments" but only with the "external expressions" of the parties.[25] The "intent" of the maker was to be found in the meaning of the document in common understanding of English. This view of common-law contract has been restated for modern times by Judge Learned Hand: "A contract has, strictly speaking, nothing to do with the personal, or individual intent of the parties. A contract is an obligation attached by the mere force of law to certain acts of the parties, usually words, which ordinarily accompany and represent a known intent. If, however, it were proved by twenty bishops that either party, when he used the words, intended something else than the usual meaning which the law imposes upon them, he would still be held, unless there were some mutual mistake, or something else of the sort."[26]

The eighteenth-century courts recognized that it was also impossible to find subjective intent in interpreting statutes.[27] Absent total expressed consensus on the meaning of the words, there is no such thing as collective intent. Committee reports and legislative record may show the intent of a few legislators, but even some of those may have been misstating their views. One or more may have been totally against a statute and still have signed a report in favor of it because the language had been so weakened in committee that its effect would be minimal. The economics of regulation hypothesizes that, regardless of their subjective evaluation, many legislators' votes can be purchased with money or the promise of future power.[28] Congressmen may feel totally opposed to tobacco growers and their cancerous product or to milk cartels that exploit the consumers, but for a large gift, they may vote in favor of subsidies to the special interests.[29]

But perhaps the most important reason that it is impossible to find intent of legislators in statutory language is that most legislators have no intent. The majority are not sponsors of the particular bill and have time to give it only superficial thought. They take the advice of party leaders in voting or trade votes on bills sponsored by others for votes on bills they sponsor. A modern statement of the interpretive issue was made by Justice Jackson: "For us to undertake to reconstruct an enactment from legislative history is merely to involve the Court in political controversies which are quite proper in the enactment of a bill but should have no place in its interpretation."[30]

The delegates to the Constitutional Convention and the ratifying conventions acted in the framework of the existing rules to interpret common law and statutes.[31] None of these rules provided for the impossible search for subjective intent.[32] The emphasis was on the intrinsic meaning of the language and the extant methods of statutory construction. Those who attended the ratifying conventions were mere agents of the people as a whole. The intentions of the majority of people were to ratify the stated language of the Constitution, not what was in the many differing minds of their agents, nor the conflicting views voiced by the minority who spoke at the ratifying conventions. The expectations of the legal community and others familiar with the legislative process was that the broad constitutional clauses would receive interpretation according to currently effective rules of documentary construction. Supreme Court interpretation would give lower courts and the people a more detailed understanding of the intrinsic meaning of constitutional language as of the date of adoption.

Objective Interpretation

To most scholars, the constitutional language itself and methods for finding its most general meaning at the time of adoption are the first and dominant elements of a theory of interpretation.[33] The integrity of the constitutional text must be the starting point.[34] The Committee of Detail at the Constitutional Convention of 1787 worked long and laboriously to refine an internally consistent document that would be subject to the extant rules of interpretation.[35] As to the prime importance of the language itself, Chief Justice Hughes quoted Chief Justice Taney: "In expounding the Constitution of the United States, every word must have its due force, and appropriate meaning; for it is evident from the whole instrument, that no word was unnecessarily used, or needlessly added. The many discussions which have taken place upon the construction of the Constitution, have proved the correctness of this proposition; and shown the high talent, the caution, and the foresight of the illustrious men who framed it. Every word appears to have been weighed with the utmost deliberation, and its force and effect to have been fully understood."[36]

A few words and phrases in the Constitution have narrow, specific meanings determinable by the text alone. They can be employed without resort to extrinsic evidence of meaning. The age requirements for congressmen and the president are examples.[37] But the important contested clauses of the Constitution contain general principles to allocate governing power and to delineate the civil rights of persons.[38] Such general clauses require interpretation. Some such phrases use common words of the English language of the time, such as "commerce among the several states."[39] Others are technical legal terms, such as "privilege of the Writ of Habeas Corpus."[40] In either case, scope and breadth of the language is subject to debate. How one uses extrinsic evidence to determine meaning is often helped by rules of documentary interpretation. The leading authorities on eighteenth-century interpretation of documents were Rutherforth and Bacon.[41] Their work was a prime source for Mr. Justice Story's long chapter on rules of interpretation in his *Commentaries*.[42] The following discussion is based on those rules.

Justice Story cited three Supreme Court decisions that hold that interpretation must be contemporary with the document.[43] In effect, he reiterated the rule that the changing meanings of words over time cannot be allowed to amend the Constitution. He explained the scope of this rule as follows: "Contemporary construction is properly resorted to, to illustrate, and confirm the text, to explain a doubtful phrase, or to expound an obscure clause; and in proportion to the uniformity and universality of that construction, and the known ability and talents of those, by whom it was given, is the credit, to which it is entitled. It can never abrogate the text; it can never fritter away its obvious sense; it can never narrow down its true limitations; it can never enlarge its natural boundaries."[44]

Commentators today who assert that eighteenth-century interpretation makes us slaves of a bygone age do not understand that the language incorporates into the stated principles a broad general scope of national powers and civil rights. It will be shown that "commerce among the several states" vested a plenary power in Congress to regulate every transaction in the United States.[45] Likewise, it will be shown that "due process of law" meant required or appropriate procedure, not the actual procedure of 1791, but whatever procedure the current judges consider required for full and fair hearing in criminal and civil actions.[46] The broad principles in the Constitution are couched in words of general classification. The actual facts or events falling in any class in 1789 or 1791 have no affect on and put no limit on those that fall in the same class today. Selling microchip computers is a valid example of commerce, and *Miranda*[47] warnings are a valid example of modern rules necessary to enforce the privilege against self-incrimination.

The only principled method of construing a written constitution is an objective theory of documentary interpretation. Such a theory is based on the meaning of language to reasonably educated readers of the time, not the unknown intents of the writers. Objective interpretation has been best described by Justice Holmes: "What happens is this. Even the whole document is found to have a certain play in the joints when its words are translated into things by parol evidence, as they have to be. It does not disclose one meaning conclusively according to the laws of language. Thereupon we ask, not what this man meant, but what those words would mean in the mouth of a normal speaker of English, using them in the circumstances in which they were used, and it is to the end of answering this last question that we let in evidence as to what the circumstances were. . . . We do not inquire what the legislature meant; we ask only what the statute means."[48]

Justice Story used the word "intention," but following the usual method of the times, he clearly indicated that he is really concerned with objective meaning. Quoting Blackstone, he wrote, "That the intention of a law is to be gathered from the words, the context, the subject-matter, the effects and consequences, or the reason and spirit of the law."[49] Story applied this as follows:

> In construing the constitution of the United States, we are, in the first instance, to consider, what are its nature and objects, its scope and design, as apparent from the structure of the instrument, viewed as a whole, and also viewed in its component parts. Where its words are plain, clear, and determinate, they require no interpretation; and it should, therefore, be admitted, if at all, with great caution, and only from necessity, either to escape some absurd consequence, or to

guard against some fatal evil. Where the words admit of two senses, each of which is conformable to common usage, that sense is to be adopted, which, without departing from the literal import of the words, best harmonizes with the nature and objects, the scope and design of the instrument. ... In examining the constitution, the antecedent situation of the country, and its institutions, the existence and operations of the state governments, the powers and operations of the confederation, in short all the circumstances, which had a tendency to produce, or to obstruct its formation and ratification, deserve a careful attention. Much, also, may be gathered from the contemporary history, and contemporary interpretation, to aid us in just conclusions.[50]

Story thus emphasized that law has purposes, and for the general, ambiguous clauses of the Constitution, one may have to search the institutional context for purpose in order to determine the scope of the language.[51] As to the technical legal language in the Constitution, as Sir Henry Maine reminded us, "The Constitution of the United States is a modified version of the British Constitution; but the British Constitution which served as its original was that which was in existence between 1760 and 1787."[52] The due process clause, for example, has meaning only in terms of its developmental history going back to Magna Charta.[53] The privilege of the writ of habeas corpus has meaning only in light of the British Habeas Corpus Act of 1679.[54] The meaning of these technical legal terms in the late eighteenth century was known to the lawyers at the convention and to those in the general public who urged ratification. Hence, one can argue that there were known meanings of both ordinary English and technical legal terms. If the scope of these meanings were in contest at the time, current interpretation should center on the relative suitability of the various eighteenth-century meanings.

Justice Story viewed broad construction as directed by the Constitution itself. "(1) It is to be construed as a *frame* or *fundamental law* of government, established by the PEOPLE of the United States, according to their own free pleasure and sovereign will."[55] He urged reasonable interpretation. "By a reasonable interpretation, we mean, that in case the words are susceptible of two different senses, the one strict, the other more enlarged, that should be adopted which is most consonant with the apparent objects and intent of the constitution; that which will give it efficacy and force as a *government*, rather than that which will impair its operations."[56] He followed this with a series of more specific rules of construction, all of which have as much applicability today as they had when written.[57] Like all canons of construction, however, they are more difficult to apply than they are to state. The point is that controversies over the meaning of language in the text should center on these canons and the reasonableness of their application in any particular situation.

The writings of Story, Holmes, and Hand present forcible arguments that the original meaning of language is to be found under objective standards: the meaning of language to reasonably educated readers of the time of adoption. This view of constitutional construction emphasizes historical linguistics supplemented by contemporaneous rules of documentary interpretation. Such rules assist in exploring extrinsic evidence needed in order to resolve ambiguities of general language. A judge is not a slave to these rules of interpretation, but rather adopts those that his or her sound reason indicates will be helpful.

A prime example, treated fully later, is the equal protection clause of the Fourteenth Amendment.[58] Scattered evidence of possible intent of some framers from speeches at the 39th Congress indicates that the equal protection clause was designed to assure that former slaves received equality of treatment by the state with that afforded white citizens.[59] But because construction can never abrogate the text, the very comprehensive, general language of the clause is not controlled by evidence of a limited purpose to protect African-Americans.[60] The clause applies to all classifications of persons and firms who are discriminatorily treated differently from others who are in like circumstances.

One of the most neglected aspects of the theory of constitutional interpretation is that the language incorporates the ideals of the community.[61] In fact, constitutional language is often general so that it can incorporate the conflicting ideals of the community. The compromises of contesting blocs of delegates at a constitutional convention or of a legislature adopting an amendment are reached by rising to higher levels of generalization in the final language. The framers do not want to constitutionalize their current, imperfect behavior. They are people with a mission to design a better government and a better set of civil rights, ideal citizen-government relationships.[62]

Again, the equal protection clause of the Fourteenth Amendment is a prime example. The radical Republicans were determined to wipe out all aspects of slavery and to prevent inferior treatment of former slaves.[63] They deplored the remnants of state-sponsored racial segregation in the North and were determined to excise it. The radicals convinced the majority to adopt the most general language for the amendment, ideal behavior that incorporated absolutely equal state treatment for all persons in like circumstances. As will be shown in chapter 12, state segregation statutes of the 1880s and 1890s were a deliberate attempt to evade the clear meaning of the clause with the fiction that separate could be equal.[64] The dissent of Justice Harlan in *Plessy* v. *Ferguson*[65] emphasizes that in racial matters the ideal character of the clause mandates a colorblind Constitution.

Purpose in Modern Interpretation

The original meaning of constitutional language, as supplemented by rules of documentary interpretation of the time if they are helpful in a particular case, may still leave substantial ambiguities. In such instances, it may be useful to search for the purpose of a clause. Purpose is not a subjective concept. It is concerned with the social issues, problems, or conflicts that caused the adoption of the particular clause. As Llewellyn said of statutes, language "must be read in the light of some assumed purpose."[66] Judge Wright argued that in the interpretation of the broad language of constitutional limitations, analysis of purpose is primary: "A judge or scholar should begin by expounding his view of the theory and purpose behind the constitutional provision in question. . . . The proper approach for the judiciary, then, is to state 'principled goals' and general rules with a comprehensiveness and degree of clarity sufficient to establish at least a very strong presumption against a range of government actions violative of the articulated purpose."[67]

The search for purpose at the time of adoption requires the use of extrinsic materials, and for this task the research of modern historians can be helpful. This was explained by Judge McCurn when he met the rare case requiring him to interpret the allocation of power in our first Constitution: "Although interpreting the Articles of Confederation is more difficult than contemporary statutory construction because of the passage of time, the approach is the same. To determine the Articles' meaning the court must examine the Articles' language, the legislative history, the interpretations that the period's statesmen and historical experts have given the Articles, how the Articles were applied, the period's general history, and relevant secondary sources."[68]

Since key constitutional clauses incorporate very broad principles for structuring government and delegating powers, it may not be easy to pinpoint the history of the social problems that were to be resolved by any particular clause. Nonetheless, some fundamental background facts are significant. The Articles of Confederation had not created an effective government. The Constitution was written to create a national government with comprehensive power to enforce a single national economy and with a power to tax and spend for the general welfare. The purposes of the congressional powers can be explained by social facts and structural needs alone. But the purposes of the procedural constitutional limitations in the Bill of Rights are grounded in substantial legal history.[69] There is not always one purpose that will be found for any given clause. Hence, dissenting opinions will not disappear when and if all justices follow objective interpretation. Controversy should center, however, on the original meaning of the text and its purpose.[70]

The first canon of interpretation is that evidence of purpose may never be used to contradict or curtail broad constitutional language. As Chief Justice Marshall noted: "[A]lthough the spirit of an instrument, especially of a constitution, is to be respected not less than its letter, yet the spirit is to be collected chiefly from its words."[71] This is clearly illustrated in the economic clauses of the Constitution. The linguistic history of the commerce clause presented in chapter 5 shows that the meaning of the clause was not ambiguous, and thus a search for purpose would be inappropriate. The words "nations" and "states" in the commerce clause unambiguously refer to groups of people with a common government. Consequently, commerce "among the several States" means commerce among the several groups of people who formed the United States. This means all their transactions. The fact that the primary purpose of the commerce clause was to terminate state barriers to interstate trade could not diminish the plenary affirmative power to regulate commerce delegated to Congress by the language.[72] Another example is the dictum of Justice Miller in the *Slaughter-House Cases*[73] about the purpose of the Fourteenth Amendment. He noted that the primary purpose of the amendment was to end discrimination and injustice against the ex-slaves. But his dictum erroneously suggested that the purpose would curtail the broad language of the equal protection clause.[74] Later Supreme Courts, as shown in chapter 12, have correctly applied the broad equal protection clause to persons and firms throughout the society.

When drafting the Constitution, the framers were aware that they could not anticipate the many future controversies that would arise concerning the meaning and purpose of any given clause. They tried to incorporate the ideals of representative government for the long-term future. As John Ely has noted, they wanted to create open channels for political change.[75] This is illustrated in *United States* v. *Classic*,[76] where the court determined that Article I, Section 2 included the right to choose representatives in primary elections. Justice Stone noted: "To decide it we turn to the words of the Constitution read in their historical setting as revealing the purpose of the framers, and in search for admissible meanings of its words which, in the circumstances of their application, will effectuate those purposes."[77] He explained the latitude to be given language that is to endure for the ages:

> We may assume that the framers of the Constitution in adopting that section, did not have specifically in mind the selection and elimination of candidates for congress by the direct primary any more than they contemplated the application of the commerce clause to interstate telephone, telegraph and wireless communication which are concededly within it. But in determining whether a provision of the Constitution applies to a new subject matter, it is of little significance that it is one with which the framers were not familiar. For in setting up an enduring framework of government they undertook to carry out for

the indefinite future and in all the vicissitudes of the changing affairs of men, those fundamental purposes which the instrument itself discloses. Hence we read its words, not as we read legislative codes which are subject to continuous revision with the changing course of events, but as the revelation of the great purposes which were intended to be achieved by the Constitution as a continuing instrument of government.[78]

Where the meaning of constitutional language has been contested and viewed as unclear, legal-linguistic research in confirming original meanings can be supplemented by the results of studies that search for the social purposes of clauses. In chapter 10, the linguistic history of the terms, "privileges" and "immunities," from the Charter of Virginia in 1606 to 1868 demonstrates that they were together a synonym for constitutional limitations. This history supports the conclusion that the privileges-or-immunities clause of the Fourteenth Amendment incorporates the Bill of Rights as effective against the states. The recent comprehensive study of Michael Curtis on the purposes of this clause reinforces this conclusion.[79] This conclusion confirms the dissenting opinion of Justice Black in *Adamson* v. *California*[80] and rebuts those who would search for subjective intents of framers.

Presumptions in Constitutional Method

Some of the most difficult cases appealed to the Supreme Court present head-on conflicts between two or more constitutional clauses. In such cases, neither the text nor the historical meaning of language assist a solution, and the Court must create solutions on the basis of the total structure of constitutional law. Many such cases fall into one or the other of two large groups. The first group concerns conflicts between national or state legislative power and one or more of the constitutional limitations. The second group concerns conflicts between national legislative powers and state legislative powers. The argument presented here is that these conflicts of constitutional clauses in the most difficult cases on appeal cannot result in a consistent pattern of decisions if decided on an *ad hoc* basis. Therefore, the Court must approach constitutional conflicts in terms of the total structure of the Constitution. Out of this structure, the Court should be able to derive principles that create a set of rebuttable presumptions on the relationships between national legislative powers, state legislative powers, and constitutional limitations. These presumptions of the priority of one group of constitutional clauses over another are abstract structural principles. Like scientists' theories, the principles do not by themselves solve cases. They merely create a framework of relationships that point toward a solution unless some sound, reasoned policies rebut the presumptions.

Chapter 3 argues departmental finality for the national legislative powers. If they are litigated, the rule of *McCulloch* v. *Maryland*[81] requires
broad construction. The Court has held that broad construction is also
to be given to the express constitutional limitations. Justice Brewer explained:

> We are not here confronted with a question of the extent of the
> powers of Congress but one of the limitations imposed by the Consti-
> tution on its action, and it seems to us clear that the same rule and
> spirit of construction must also be recognized. If powers granted are
> to be taken as broadly granted and as carrying with them authority
> to pass those acts which may be reasonably necessary to carry them
> into full execution; in other words, if the Constitution in its grant of
> powers is to be so construed that Congress shall be able to carry into
> full effect the powers granted, it is equally imperative that where
> prohibition or limitation is placed upon the power of Congress that
> prohibition or limitation should be enforced in its spirit and to its
> entirety. It would be a strange rule of construction that language
> granting powers is to be liberally construed and that language or
> restriction is to be narrowly and technically construed.[82]

Since both national powers and limitations are to be given broad construction, no insight to priorities between them can be gained from looking
at their breadth. Nonetheless, the structure of constitutional law creates
a decisional presumption in favor of constitutional limitations. Denial of
the civil rights of Englishmen against government led to the American
Revolution. The primary basis for a written constitution and for adoption
of the Bill of Rights was enforcement of these rights against the new
government. Unlike legislative acts, which are primarily general substantive regulations to limit human behavior, constitutional limitations are
particular substantive and procedural prohibitions on the action of government against oppression of individual citizens. Thus, generality and
constraint on freedom are the key characteristics of legislative acts, and
particularity and constraint on government are the key characteristics of
constitutional limitations. Thus, considering the fundamental objective of
protecting human freedom that pervaded the writing of the Constitution,
presumptive priority must go to the constitutional limitations.

Presuming the priority of constitutional limitations over national legislative powers would have pointed the direction of solution in many past
Supreme Court cases. Though not explicitly stated, the principle was
applied in *Ex Parte Milligan*[83] in 1866. In this case, the judicial conflict
was between the war powers of Article I, Section 8, and the rights to due
process of law and jury trial under the Fifth and Sixth Amendments. The
Court ordered the release of Milligan, a civilian who had been tried and
sentenced to death in Indiana by a military commission even though the
civil courts were open there. The Court held that the military commission

was without jurisdiction as long as civil legal process was unobstructed. The same principle was followed, although belatedly, in 1944, in *Ex Parte Endo*,[84] where detention without trial in a relocation camp of a U.S. citizen of Japanese ancestry whose loyalty was conceded was held unconstitutional. But the presumptive priority of constitutional limitations was not followed in 1944 in *Korematsu v. United States*.[85] In a 6-to-3 decision, the Supreme Court upheld forcible evacuation of American citizens of Japanese ancestry from the western United States even though the civil courts were fully operative and there had been no declaration of martial law. The judicial contest was between the war powers and (1) the prohibition of bills of attainder in Article I, Section 9, (2) the right to due process of law in the Fifth Amendment, which incorporates a concept of equal protection, and (3) the right to a jury trial before punishment in the Sixth Amendment. Citizens who the government later conceded were loyal were banished from the states where they had homes, employment, and businesses. Banishment of citizens has been considered penal in nature in the Anglo-American and European legal systems for hundreds of years.[86] Had the courts in this case commenced their consideration with a presumption in favor of constitutional limitations, it is unlikely the decision would have upheld the evacuation.

The necessary priority of constitutional limitations is demonstrated in chapter 4, which elucidates the chief substantive protection for property in the Bill of Rights, the eminent domain clause. This final clause of the Fifth Amendment creates an immunity that is a necessary component of any social system whose economic development depends on private saving and investment. For this reason, Chief Justice Marshall was clearly wrong in his dictum that "The power to tax involves the power to destroy."[87] Many later cases have recognized that the taxing power is subject to the limitation on eminent domain.[88] And Justice Holmes stated this succinctly when he said, "The power to tax is not the power to destroy while this Court sits."[89] Similarly, because of the constraint on eminent domain, rate regulation under the commerce power must have an ultimate limit,[90] as must national bankruptcy power.[91] Because of such limitations, a court may not deprive a mortgagee of substantial property rights solely in the interest of a mortgagor. The purpose of bankruptcy law, however, is to forgive debts. Hence, it would seem that a presumption toward protecting the lender's property could in many instances be rebutted.

As to state legislation conflicting with national constitutional limitations, the failure of the Court to confirm a strong presumption in favor of the latter has often led to confusion. The flag-salute cases are a prime example. Here the conflict is between state police power and the First Amendment as incorporated into the Fourteenth. In *Minersville School Dist. v. Gobitis*,[92] a small, isolated, powerless minority proved that saluting the flag conflicted with their serious, deeply felt religious beliefs.[93]

Justice Frankfurter, for the majority, noted that "a grave responsibility confronts this Court whenever in the course of litigation it must reconcile the conflicting claims of liberty and authority."[94] He then upheld the local requirement that all children must salute the flag. His view that a small and powerless minority group might protect itself through the electoral process was a legal fiction. He held that "except where the transgression of constitutional liberty is too plain for argument, personal freedom is best maintained—as long as the remedial channels of the democratic process remains open and unobstructed—where it is ingrained in a people's habits and not enforced against popular policy by the coercion of adjudicated law."[95]

In spite of the patriotic fervor of wartime, *Gobitis* was overruled in *West Virginia State Bd. of Educ.* v. *Barnette.*[96] True patriotism is not created by flag salutes. Exempting a tiny religious minority from engaging in a symbolic act in no way causes material harm to the state. Justice Jackson, for the Court, stated the controlling rule: "The very purpose of a Bill of Rights was to withdraw certain subjects from the vicissitudes of political controversy, to place them beyond the reach of majorities and officials and to establish them as legal principles to be applied by the courts."[97] He concluded that "the test of legislation which collides with the Fourteenth Amendment, because it also collides with the principles of the First, is much more definite than the test when only the Fourteenth is involved."[98] His example of legislation involving only the Fourteenth was public-utility regulation and the "rational basis" test under the due process clause. In contrast, free speech, press, assembly, and worship "are susceptible of restriction only to prevent grave and immediate danger to interests which the state may lawfully protect."[99]

The modern cases are merely examples of a continuing failure of the Court to articulate a clear presumption of constitutional limitations over state legislation. Chapter 9 presents the one outstanding early example bearing on the security of transactions under capitalism: the prohibition of Article I, Section 10 that no state shall pass any law impairing the obligation of contracts. Starting in 1827 with *Ogden* v. *Saunders,*[100] the Court majority gave the contracts clause a narrow interpretation and held it to prohibit only retrospective state insolvency laws. In the leading mortgage-relief case of this century, *Home Building and Loan Association* v. *Blaisdell*[101] in 1934, a 5-to-4 decision again gave the contracts clause a narrow interpretation. Again there was no mention of the supremacy clause of Article VI as setting the mandatory framework in favor of national powers and limitations over state laws. The leading recent case holding the state police power superior to the contracts clause was *City of El Paso* v. *Simmons,*[102] which held constitutional a Texas statute that materially altered the contracts rights of prior purchasers of public lands. In dissent, Justice Black argued that the Court did not have the power to set its own balance between a state law and the national constitutional limitation whose language was admittedly violated. He argued in vain for the supremacy of the constitutional limitations.

When one turns to the relationships between national legislative powers and state legislative powers, there are more than presumptions in favor of the federal law. Article VI, Clause 2, states an explicit mandate in favor of the national constitution and laws. Justice Holmes noted its crucial importance: "I do not think the United States would come to an end if we lost our power to declare an Act of Congress void. I do think the Union would be imperiled if we could not make that declaration as to the laws of the several States. For one in my place sees how often a local policy prevails with those who are not trained to national views and how often action is taken that embodies what the Commerce Clause was meant to end."[103]

The supremacy clause of Article VI was the cement the framers chose to hold the nation together when state and national policies conflicted. They predicted that national supremacy would usually make for national unity while state supremacy would make for disintegration and possibly civil war. As the industrial revolution brought specialization in manufacture and national channels of marketing, most commerce affected more states than one. The mandate in the Court to protect the national commerce power and to prohibit interstate barriers to trade created a legal environment that fostered economic growth. Judicial enforcement of the constitutional prohibition on state autarchy may well have prevented the kind of trade barriers that fostered many of the wars in Europe.

The supremacy clause is an express rejection of the theory of dual federalism, that the national and state governments are equal sovereigns. Chief Justice Marshall declared both in *McCulloch* v. *Maryland*[104] and in *Gibbons* v. *Ogden*[105] that Article VI established the principle of national supremacy in the law. Nonetheless, for a hundred years a number of Supreme Court majorities chose to ignore Article VI and assert that the Tenth Amendment withdrew some matters of internal police from the reach of power expressly granted to Congress. This viewpoint was asserted shortly after Marshall's death in *New York* v. *Miln*,[106] which has since been overruled. The conception of a "complete, unqualified, and exclusive" police power residing in the states and limiting the power of the national government was also asserted ten years later by Chief Justice Taney in the *License* cases.[107]

The doctrine of independent power in the Tenth Amendment was first used to hold a federal statute unconstitutional in 1871 in *Collector* v. *Day*,[108] which was also later repudiated. As noted in chapter 5, in 1918 the Tenth Amendment was also asserted as one basis for the 5-to-4 decision nullifying the Federal Child Labor Law in *Hammer* v. *Dagen-*

hart.[109] The complete repudiation of this interpretation in the later cases has restored the mandate of national supremacy.[110] But, in spite of this relegation of the Tenth Amendment to its original and proper place in constitutional structure, the Supreme Court has failed to revive the supremacy clause of Article VI to its status as the prime analytical tool for every case where federal and state legislative powers conflict.

The inconsistency of the court in applying the supremacy clause is exemplified by the state-action defense to the federal antitrust laws under the doctrine of *Parker* v. *Brown*.[111] This doctrine created an exception to the general principle of the supremacy clause: that state legislation that conflicts with national law or would frustrate the scheme of a national statute must fall.[112] In spite of the quasi-constitutional status of the national antitrust laws,[113] the Court in *Parker* upheld the validity of the California Agricultural Prorate Act,[114] a state-established price-fixing program as applied to raisin growers. Justice Stone devoted the bulk of his opinion to the indisputable rule that state officers acting in a governmental regulatory capacity were immune from injunction under section 4 of the Sherman Act.[115] His other basis of decision was state sovereignty,[116] and there he ignored the paramount position of the supremacy clause in issues of federalism.

As to the substance of the state act, the Court stated, "We may assume for present purposes that the California prorate program would violate the Sherman Act if it were organized and made effective solely by virtue of a contract, combination or conspiracy of private persons, individual or corporate."[117] If the Court had used preemption analysis, the opinion would have drawn to a quick conclusion. The California statute establishing cartel pricing was in actual conflict with the Sherman Act. Injunction against state officials to enforce the supremacy clause was the appropriate remedy.[118]

While the Court admitted that a state cannot give immunity to "those who violate the Sherman Act by authorizing them to violate it,"[119] it held that command and supervision by the state creates an antitrust exemption. However, the Sherman Act contained no express exemption for persons and firms violating its provisions under state compulsion and supervision, and its language does not imply one.[120] Sections 1 and 2 of the Sherman Act begin with the unambiguous word "every."[121] Section 1 has been interpreted consistently with the word "every" to hold all horizontal combinations to fix prices and other private cartels illegal per se.[122] No reasonable user of English would interpret the statutory language to imply an antitrust exemption for violators of the Sherman Act because their cartel was state imposed and administered. And the Supreme Court had no power to create one on the basis of mere legislative omission. Furthermore, the presumptions of our legal system are just the opposite. The supremacy clause controls the relationship between federal and state law, not unexpressed statutory intent. National statutes generally do not have supplementary clauses prohibiting conflicting state statutes because they are unnecessary. The Constitution obviates this task.

In *Parker,* there was no discussion by the Court of the language and scope of the supremacy clause. The state-action defense was approved with full knowledge that the state law was inconsistent with, and contrary to, the mandate of competition in the Sherman Act.[123] The Court noted that there were similar federal statutes protecting agricultural prices in derogation of the Sherman Act. But this was not relevant. Congress may create such exemptions to the antitrust laws as required by political expediency. The states have no power to create exemptions for federal statutes. That is the essence of the supremacy clause.

Judicial Review of Legislation:
Scope and Limits

JUDICIAL REVIEW IS the final determination by the courts in a litigated case of the constitutionality of state and national executive or legislative actions.[1] It is thus not a power in the courts that exists generally to review acts of state or national officers or legislatures, but is restricted to cases of which the particular court has jurisdiction. This Court resorts to judicial review only when a case puts the question of constitutionality in issue and the Court must determine constitutionality as part of its obligation to dispose of the case according to law. This chapter centers on judicial review of the national legislative powers.

A typical focus for the economist might be which aspects of judicial review are efficient methods of facilitating effective representative government and also protecting civil rights of persons.[2] From the viewpoint of efficiency, judicial review of the scope and breadth of delegated legislative powers is very different from judicial review to enforce constitutional limitations. A statute that imposes taxes or regulates commerce is of a different class from a bill of attainder or a law regulating the content of newspapers. The first class is concerned with powers delegated by the people solely to the legislature; the second class is concerned with limitations on the invasion of civil rights of individuals by officials in any department of government. Since the legislature and the executive have strong biases toward political objectives, only the independent judiciary has an incentive toward impartiality. Thus judicial review may be the only efficient method of enforcing constitutional limitations. But judicial review of the scope of delegated legislative powers is not efficient, primarily because of the different functions of the two branches.

The legislature is a democratic institution designed to absorb political pressures and to resolve the major social conflicts of the society. Legislative finality on the scope and meaning of the constitutional language in the delegated powers is the only efficient method to resolve social conflict. The appointed elite of the judiciary are not a democratic institution and were not created to resolve major legislative issues. The Supreme Court has little ability to respond to political attack by a majority or significant minority of citizens because it is not structured as a political institution.

This distinction is demonstrated in the literature attacking judicial review as being undemocratic.[3] The Anglo-American constitutional system has a tradition going back to Magna Charta for judicial enforcement of constitutional limitations against the executive. This judicial enforcement of constitutional limitations was expanded in the U.S. Bill of Rights to be effective against the legislature.[4] But judicial protection of individual rights from legislative oppression was seldom termed undemocratic until the due process clause was, without foundation in the constitutional text, converted from a protection of individual procedural rights into a general enforcement of freedom of contract.[5] The main area for the modern charge of undemocratic judicial review is judicial review of the scope and breadth of legislative powers, a process for which there was in 1789 no Anglo-American tradition. The framers of the Constitution adopted as their starting point the English constitutional tradition of legislative supremacy.[6] Judicial review of legislation other than that challenged as invading civil rights must be found in facts or arguments that rebut the English tradition.

In the national government, judicial review of legislative powers was and is attacked as undemocratic because it gives the appointed judiciary a veto over the elected Congress for all statutes of enough social importance to be litigated.[7] The public has expressed great dissatisfaction with judicial review of substantive legislation of Congress since early in this century. Justice Frankfurter, before his appointment to the Court, wrote to President Roosevelt in 1937 as follows:

> Dissatisfaction with a few isolated judicial decisions would never have given rise to deep and widespread disquietude concerning the relation of the Supreme Court to the national welfare. *With accumulating disregard of its own settled canons of constitutional construction,* the Supreme Court for about a quarter of a century has distorted the power of judicial review into a revision of legislative policy, thereby usurping powers belonging to the Congress and to the legislatures of the several states, always by a divided court and always over the protest of its most distinguished members. With increasing frequency a majority of the Court have not hesitated to exercise a negative power on any legislation, state or federal, which does not conform to their own economic notions.[8]

Forty years earlier, Justice Holmes spoke of similar extraconstitutional decisions as unconscious expressions of extreme laissez-faire judicial bias: "When socialism first began to be talked about, the comfortable classes of the community were a good deal frightened. I suspect this fear has influenced judicial action both here and in England, yet it is certain that it is not a conscious factor in the decisions to which I refer. I think that something similar has led people who no longer hope to control the legislatures to look to the courts as expounders of the Constitutions, and that in some courts new principles have been discovered outside the bodies of those instruments, which may be generalized into the acceptance of the economic doctrines which prevailed about fifty years ago."[9]

Thus Holmes charged that a conservative Supreme Court majority had imposed its laissez-faire biases on the nation.[10] Beginning in the 1870s and extending to 1937, the Supreme Court had constricted the scope of the commerce clause to a fraction of its original plenary meaning.[11] Starting about 1890, the Supreme Court adopted, without constitutional basis, the concept of substantive due process.[12] The Court used its commerce limitations and due process creation to hold unconstitutional large numbers of statutes designed to remedy market failures, especially in the field of labor relations.[13] Since these statutes had represented the majority will for regulated expansion of industrial society, the Court's misinterpretations became a great countermajoritarian force.

The primary historical conclusion of this chapter is that the judiciary was never delegated power to review the constitutionality of substantive acts of Congress enacted pursuant to Article I, except those challenged as violating specific constitutional limitations. It will be shown that the decision on judicial review of Chief Justice Marshall in *Marbury* v. *Madison*[14] was precedent only for the construction of Article III, the subject matter of that case. His statements on the general nature of judicial review, which have been adopted as binding law to this day, were unnecessary to the *Marbury* decision.[15] His simplistic view of a self-applying constitution with no uncertainties about the meaning of language and a self-evident function of judicial review assumed as a premise the conclusion he intended to reach. Leading modern scholars have objected to Marshall's generalizations,[16] claiming that they should not have been binding on lower courts as the law on judicial review of the general legislative powers since *Marbury* did not concern Article I.

Under the American system of separated powers, judicial review of legislation can be justified as constitutional only on three bases: textual, historical, or structural.[17] Before explaining these bases, it is important to note that the issue is one of jurisdiction: In what classes of cases does the constitutional text, history, or structure require or permit the courts to exercise judicial review? It is essential to distinguish this issue from the issue of what methodology the Court may utilize after taking jurisdiction. The scope of constitutional doctrines and the issue of conflict between constitutional clauses in a particular situation are in the area of methodology of decision making and are not our concern here.

The textual basis of judicial review is also historical. It is concerned with the connotation of language on the date of adoption. The changing meaning of words in the English language over time is not supposed to amend the Constitution.[18] If maritime law, for example, included the law merchant in 1789, the law merchant should be included today.[19]

"Connotation," however, does not mean "denotation." Many constitutional clauses enact broad principles. It will be shown that in 1789 "commerce" included all transactions. Using the same connotation today, "commerce" includes the sale of computers—even though computers were unknown in 1789. Furthermore, the common use of language at the time of adoption cannot be determined in the abstract. Evidence of context is needed to give language meaning. To the extent that language in the Constitution was borrowed from English charters and statutes, the meaning of those writings in the late eighteenth century may be significant aids in determining constitutional meanings.

Absent a textual basis, there may still be historical bases of judicial review. As noted, the Constitution of the United States was not created in a historical vacuum. Judicial review of executive actions in England had been established only after a long, hard-fought battle, eventually leading to the statute known as the English Bill of Rights of 1689. The most significant aspect of this history is that it pertained to constitutional limitations on the executive. But any historical argument for judicial review of legislation that invades civil rights must be found not in the English tradition, but in the peculiar history and structure of the U.S. Constitution.

Some aspects of judicial review may be grounded in a structural base even though this base is not specified in the text or derived from English constitutional history.[20] The issue is what areas of judicial review are necessarily implied by constitutional structure. The separation of governmental powers is the most important example of an area implied by constitutional structure. One key issue is whether this separation creates three coequal departments, each of which has final say on the constitutionality of actions delegated to it. Such a system of review is known as departmental review or the tripartite theory of review. On another level, the separation of powers between the national and state governments is the prime structural element in determining the constitutionality of national laws enacted though unmentioned in Article I and thus openly usurping residual powers of the states.

Review of State Laws: Umpiring the Federal System

While most contests between the nation and the states are settled politically on the floors of Congress, a few of them lead to litigation and must be decided by the courts. There is a textual basis for judicial review of state laws challenged in litigation as conflicting with national laws or the Constitution.[21] The provision for judicial review to enforce the supremacy of national law over state law is in Article VI, Clause 2: "This Constitution, and the Laws of the United States which shall be made in Pursuance thereof; and all Treaties made, or which shall be made, under the Authority of the United States, shall be the supreme Law of the Land; and the Judges of every State shall be bound thereby, any Thing in the Constitution or Laws of any State to the Contrary notwithstanding."[22] State judges are expressly bound by this national law, "anything in the Constitution or Laws of any State to the Contrary notwithstanding." This final phrase was necessary because in addition to their oath pursuant to Article VI, Clause 3[23] to support the national constitution, state judges take oaths to support state constitutions and laws. Judges of the United States courts are different. They take only the oath to support the national Constitution and laws. Hence, the general supremacy language of Article VI, Clause 2 is sufficient to bind federal judges to give primacy to the national law over state law in any litigation where such an issue is tested.

The initial proposal in the Constitutional Convention was for a congressional negative of unconstitutional state laws. The sixth resolution of Randolph of Virginia at the opening of the convention moved that the national legislature have power "to negative all laws passed by the several States, contravening in the opinion of the National Legislature the articles of the Union."[24] One objective of this resolution was to give Congress the opportunity to negative acts of state legislatures before the date that they became effective. Since the original resolution dealt only with constitutionality and not conflict between national and state law, Pinkney later moved that Congress have "authority to negative all [state] laws which they should judge to be improper."[25] This indeterminate language was debated and the proposal was defeated.[26] Continuous review by the Congress of state laws as they were passed was not an efficient form of control. Most state laws would conform to the national Constitution, and review of these would not be an efficient use of the time of congressmen.

Having rejected the congressional negative, the framers began drafting a supremacy clause directed at the judiciary. The original version of the supremacy clause provided only for the priority of national laws and treaties over state laws and did not specify constitutions.[27] Luther Martin, the draftsman, said it contemplated the supremacy of state constitutions over national statutes and treaties.[28] The Committee of Detail remedied this by adding "the constitutions of the states" to the final "notwithstanding" clause.[29] Subsequently, the convention adopted without further debate the final version that preceded "Laws of the United States" with "This Constitution."[30] It was thus clear that the entire convention saw the necessity of resolving conflict between state laws and the Constitution and the need for national supremacy.

A federal system requires a final umpire to resolve conflicts between state and national laws and constitutions. The final umpire of the federal system is the Supreme Court of the United States. Local biases of state supreme courts cannot be allowed to stand as law if the mandate of the supremacy clause is to prevail.

The supremacy clause plus the comprehensive appellate jurisdiction vested in the Supreme Court in Article III, Section 2 confirm the national judicial review of state court judgments on national law.[31] The judicial power extends to all cases arising under the Constitution, laws, and treaties of the United States. For cases other than in the Supreme Court's original jurisdiction, the Court has general appellate jurisdiction. The language does not limit these cases to those arising in national courts. Consequently, issues arising under the national constitution and laws that have been litigated in the state courts are subject to the appellate jurisdiction of the Supreme Court. Section 25 of the Judiciary Act of 1789[32] was designed to implement this appellate jurisdiction of the Supreme Court over state courts. Section 25 enacted that a final judgment in the highest court of a state might be reexamined and reversed or affirmed in the Supreme Court if the judgment held a statute or treaty of the United States unconstitutional, or if it upheld a statute or an authority exercised under a state against a charge that it violated the federal constitution, statutes, or treaties.

The constitutionality of this section was tested and upheld by the Supreme Court in *Martin* v. *Hunter's Lessee*.[33] The case concerned thousands of acres of rich timber and tobacco lands in Virginia which had belonged to Lord Fairfax. The State of Virginia, under claim of having confiscated the estates in 1777 during the Revolution, granted title to a part of the land in 1789 to David Hunter. Hunter brought an action in the state court to eject Martin, who held title under the will of Lord Fairfax. Martin argued in defense that the Treaty of Peace and Jay's Treaty of 1795 confirmed the titles of British subjects to land in America. The trial court and the Virginia Court of Appeals held against Martin and upheld Hunter's claim to title from the state. The Supreme Court of the United States, having granted review on a writ of error pursuant to Section 25 of the Judiciary Act, reversed this decision in 1813 and upheld the superior status of federal treaties.[34] The Virginia Court of Appeals refused to comply with the mandate of the Supreme Court, its view being that the Supreme Court had no appellate jurisdiction over state courts, and so Section 25 was unconstitutional. This refusal was brought before the Supreme Court in 1815.

Since Chief Justice Marshall had disqualified himself because of financial interest in the Fairfax estates, Justice Story gave the opinion of the Court. In holding Section 25 to be constitutional, Story rejected the Virginia contention of state sovereignty. He began by noting that the Constitution of the United States was created by the people themselves. The powers in the federal government could be broader than that vested by the several peoples in their state governments. To the extent that these powers conflicted, Article VI clearly indicated that the people of the United States wished to limit state sovereignty.

The Constitution could be implemented to create a national government only if the enumerated powers were construed broadly. Justice Story held that since Article III extends the judicial power to all cases arising under the Constitution, laws, or treaties of the United States, there must be power in Congress to give the courts appellate jurisdiction over these matters. The language of Article III does not limit these cases to those originating in federal courts. Consequently, the fact that a federal issue arises in the state courts rather than the lower federal courts is no ground to limit this appellate jurisdiction. In fact, the underlying issue is one of equal protection of the laws. Uniform interpretation of the national Constitution, laws, and treaties could be enforced only if judgments of all courts where such issues arose were subject to appeal to the single Supreme Court of the United States. The constitutional language demonstrated that the framers clearly recognized that the unity of the nation depended on the supremacy of the national constitution and laws over any state legislation that conflicted with them.

Legal scholars have disputed the meaning of the word "pursuance" in the supremacy clause. Crosskey, quoting Dr. Johnson's 1755 *Dictionary*, says the term most commonly meant "done in consequence or prosecution of anything."[35] Bickel concurred, stating that "pursuance of the Constitution" meant "that the statutes must carry the outer indicia of validity lent them by enactment in accordance with the constitutional forms."[36] From this view of pursuance, and in light of the necessary-and-proper clause,[37] any act of Congress that could possibly carry out one of the enumerated powers and is duly enacted should preempt conflicting state law.

National Laws Violating Constitutional Limitations

Historical analysis confirms the existence of the one area of judicial review that until recently has received the least comment as a separate class. That area is federal statutes that are challenged as being in violation of the constitutional limitations. The function of constitutional limitations is exactly the opposite of the substantive clauses that delegate governing power. The function is to prohibit government officials in any department from depriving any person of specified privileges or immunities. In fact, the first Supreme Court ruling on constitutionality of national legislation concerned the limitation on direct taxation.[38]

The national constitutional limitations begin with Article 1, Section 9, which protects the privilege of the writ of habeas corpus and prohibits bills of attainder and *ex post facto* laws. The remainder of the national constitutional limitations are found primarily in Amendments I to X, XIII to XV, XIX, and XXIV. While most of the constitutional limitations are procedural, some of them are substantive. Amendments I to IV, XIII, XV, XIX and XXI are primarily substantive.

The judicial function of enforcing constitutional limitations in all three departments of government is not spelled out expressly in the Constitution. Nonetheless, its historical development from Magna Charta to the time of the Constitutional Convention confirms that it was the legal context in which the Constitution and especially the Bill of Rights were written. The idea of civil rights developed in England as protection of the individual against the Crown and is known there as the "rule of law."[39] Dicey noted that as a part of the English Constitution, the rule of law includes under one expression at least three distinct, though kindred, conceptions: "We mean in the first place, that no man is punishable or can be lawfully made to suffer in body or goods except for a distinct breach of law established in the ordinary legal manner before the ordinary courts of the land."[40] The second is that not only is no person above the law, but every person, regardless of rank, is subject to the ordinary law and the jurisdiction of the ordinary courts.[41] The third is that the general principles of the Constitution are the result of judicial decisions determining the rights of private persons in particular cases brought before the courts.[42]

Thus one sees the whole idea of civil rights of persons developing either out of court decisions or the great charters, culminating in the English Bill of Rights of 1689. All of these rights are enforceable against the Crown in the ordinary courts. As Dicey pointed out, these rules of law are supplemented by the conventions of the Constitution, a body of constitutional and political ethics.[43] Under these conventions, the Parliament, though supreme, would never pass legislation to invade those civil rights that have become part of the English Constitution.

The civil rights of English citizens and the tradition of judicial enforcement of those rights was brought to the American colonies by the settlers. Most of the colonial charters actually recited the colonist rights to the "liberties of Englishmen."[44] As the struggle developed against oppressive legislation passed by Parliament, the colonists started looking to the courts to enjoin what they considered violations of their constitutional rights. The most famous was the Writs of Assistance case of 1761.[45] These general warrants enabled royal officers to search any house or ship, force entry, and seize goods at will. James Otis, relying on the opinion of Lord Coke in *Bonham's Case*,[46] challenged the validity of the writs under the English Constitution.[47] Although Otis was unsuccessful, his argument has been characterized as the firing of the opening gun in the American Revolution.[48]

The colonists continued to demand these rights against the Crown before the Revolution and against their state governments during and after the Revolution. For example, the privileges and immunities of citizens in Article IV of the Articles of Confederation were primarily those of the English Constitution. This fact is clearly seen in the first committee draft of July 12, 1776, in which Clause VI read: "The Inhabitants of each Colony shall henceforth always have the same Rights, Liberties, Privileges, Immunities and Advantages, in the other Colonies, which the said Inhabitants now have, in all Cases whatever, except in those provided for by the next following Article."[49] Since this language was written before most states had adopted constitutions, the phrase "which the said inhabitants now have" had to refer to the English constitutional limitations. In other words, the Declaration of Independence discarded those parts of the English Constitution that imposed a framework of government, but not the constitutional privileges and immunities of Englishmen that the colonists had for so long argued were theirs.

The original U.S. Constitution did contain some constitutional limitations, such as Article I, Sections 9 and 10, but it did not contain a bill of rights. When the issue of a proposed declaration of civil rights was raised near the end of the Constitution Convention, it was voted down. The debates indicate that the delegates felt that the civil rights of Englishmen against government, which they argued were theirs, did not need enumeration.[50] When the subsequent demand for an express bill of rights became so great that it was a condition of ratification, Madison promised to introduce the proposals for amendment in the first Congress.[51] The adoption of the Bill of Rights did more than codify existing civil rights. Enumeration of some of them in absolute form, such as the first amendment, made them more comprehensive than they were in the English Constitution.[52]

A key function of codifying and ratifying the U.S. Bill of Rights was to rebut the English presumption of legislative supremacy, and thus to impose constitutional limitations on both the executive and the legislative branches. Madison, in proposing the national Bill of Rights, noted the great differences between the English and U.S. constitutions. He observed that "it may not be thought necessary to provide limits for the legislative power in that country, yet a different opinion prevails in the United States. The people of many States have thought it necessary to raise barriers against power in all forms and departments of Government. . . . It therefore must be levelled against the legislative, for it is the most powerful, and most likely to be abused, because it is under the least control."[53]

The broad jurisdictional clause of Article III, Section 2 of the Constitution, extending the judicial power "to all cases, in Law and Equity, arising under this Constitution," was specifically designed to protect the constitutional limitations. Such cases might arise in the absence of any act of Congress. If, for example, a U.S. marshall incarcerates a citizen without trial, legal action is based directly on rights defined in the Constitution. It is clear that this same tradition of civil liberties extends to acts of Congress that attempt to impose any similar infringement of civil rights. As Madison declared when introducing the Bill of Rights to the First Congress: "If they are incorporated into the Constitution, independent tribunals of justice will consider themselves in a peculiar manner the guardians of those rights; they will be an impenetrable bulwark against every assumption of power in the Legislature or Executive; they will be naturally led to resist every encroachment upon rights expressly stipulated for in the Constitution by the declaration of rights."[54] Jefferson, who was a leading opponent of general judicial review, expressly supported judicial enforcement of the Bill of Rights.[55] James Wilson, Samuel Adams, John Hancock, Patrick Henry, Richard Henry Lee, and others also stated this view.[56]

Comprehensive judicial review of the acts of Congress, while not provided in the substantive sense, is effective procedurally under the Bill of Rights. Under the Fifth Amendment, the general procedural limitation is that one may not be deprived of life, liberty, or property without due process of law.[57] This rule applies to all three branches of government. All national procedural statutes are subject to judicial review on the challenge that they violate due process by failing to provide full and fair hearing pursuant to established law. Any substantive act of Congress also can be challenged on the limited procedural ground that the constitutional or statutory requirements for enacting a statute have not been fully met.[58]

In concluding that judicial review of national laws challenged as violating constitutional limitations is clearly founded in the history and structure of the Constitution, one can conclude likewise that the paramount function of judicial review is to guard against governmental infringement of individual liberties secured by the Constitution.[59] In light of this emphasis, it is useful to reconsider *Marbury* v. *Madison*.[60] After asserting the general power of judicial review in the Supreme Court, Chief Justice Marshall presented illustrations, all of which are constitutional limitations. They are (1) "no tax or duty shall be laid on articles exported from any state," (2) no bill of attainder or ex post facto law shall be passed," and (3) "no person shall be convicted of treason unless on the testimony of two witnesses of the same overt act, or on confession in open court."[61] One can only hypothesize that Marshall might have adopted a rationale that was less than a general power of judicial review if counsel had argued a more limited power of judicial self-defense plus securing constitutional limitations.

One final issue emerges about this limited or partial judicial review. Most of the state precedents before 1789 allegedly supporting a general power of judicial review, even if they survive the charge of being spurious,[62] are cases concerning constitutional limitations.[63] They are as follows: *Case of Josiah Philips*[64] (bill of attainder), *Holmes* v. *Walton*[65] (right to jury of twelve persons), *Commonwealth* v. *Caton*[66] (legislative pardon; separation of powers), *Rutgers* v. *Waddington*[67] (state statute violated national treaty of peace), *Symsbury Case*[68] (legislature was highest judicial tribunal; hence, no judicial review), *Trevett* v. *Weeden*[69] (denial of jury trial in criminal case), *Bayard* v. *Singleton*[70] (denial of jury trial in common law action to recover real property). None of these cases support a *general* power of judicial review in the highest appeals court of a state. *Rutgers* v. *Waddington*[71] was the only civil action upholding judicial review, and this case was not concerned with a traditional constitutional limitation. In this case, a state statute was held to violate a national treaty, thus merely supporting the supremacy of national law over state law. At most, these state cases illustrate limited judicial review of alleged violations of constitutional limitations.

National Laws Regulating the Judicial Function

Judicial review of congressional acts regulating the judicial function, while not expressly stated in the text of the Constitution, is clearly implied by the text and also is founded on the structure and historical background of the Constitution. The first basis is textual. As noted, the Bill of Rights provides for judicial review of all national procedural laws under the due process clause of the Fifth Amendment.[72] Amendments V through VIII are procedural and are clearly directed at the judiciary for enforcement. The due process clause, requiring full hearing and fair procedure according to established law, requires the judiciary to rule on whether statutes setting judicial procedures violate that standard.

The second basis of judicial review of statutes regulating the judiciary is structural and is based on the separation of powers. Under Article III, the entire judicial power is vested in the "Supreme Court and in such inferior Courts as the Congress may from time to time ordain and establish."[73] Statutes regulating this function, including statutes on federal jurisdiction, must conform to Article III. The final determination of this conformity must rest with the Supreme Court, the authoritative head of the judicial branch. As Elbridge Gerry said of the judiciary at the Constitutional Convention, "They will have a sufficient check agst. encroachment on their own department by their exposition of the laws, which involved a power of deciding on their Constitutionality."[74] This is an application of the theory of departmental review, that each of the three branches is coequal and has final say on the scope of constitutional powers vested in it. This application of judicial review is known as "judicial self-defense."[75]

Under the above rule, the Supreme Court in *Marbury* v. *Madison*[76] correctly assumed jurisdiction to pass on the constitutionality of Section 13 of the Judiciary Act of 1789.[77] The power of the Congress to add to the original jurisdiction of the Supreme Court was clearly an issue under Article III, Section 2. Leading constitutional historians have severely criticized the decision in *Marbury*.[78] Since the criticism of the merits of the decision has no bearing on the more general issue of judicial review, it will not receive comment here.

The primary issue of *Marbury* was not the scope of judicial review, but whether the executive could defy the law. Most of the opinion is devoted to the latter topic.[79] Here it is important to note that Marshall's generalizations on the Court's power of judicial review were *obiter dicta* and erroneous.[80] The correct principle of judicial review of *Marbury* is the narrower one stated above, that under departmental review the Court has final say on the meaning of Article III. Marshall's general statements that, under a written constitution, the judiciary must determine all constitutional controversies appealed to it are not consistent with his earlier language in the opinion. He noted that under the separation of governmental powers, the political acts of the president and executive officers acting for him are not subject to judicial review.[81] Just as the Court refuses to hear clearly political controversies, it could and should refuse to hear constitutional challenges to substantive acts of Congress—except for claims of violation of civil rights.

Marshall adopted the generalizations of Hamilton in *Federalist* 78.[82] But Hamilton's political generalizations were not law, and in this case they were clearly misleading.[83] One can hypothesize why Hamilton made these statements. The key public fear about the Constitution was that it put too much power in the legislature.[84] Hamilton, whose antidemocratic proposals had been rejected at the Constitutional Convention,[85] was writing a political tract to urge ratification. He decided to assuage public fear by declaring the existence of a general judicial control over possible legislative excesses. Hence, he presented judicial review of all acts of Congress that are litigated as a necessary result of a written constitution. While asserting this general judicial supremacy, he also asserted disingenuously in the very same paper that the judiciary will always be the *least dangerous* department of government.[86] Many judges and scholars who should know better put great weight on all of the *Federalist*. But careful discrimination is required.[87] While many, perhaps most, *Federalist* papers are useful analyses, some of them are exaggerations, and a few are totally misleading.[88]

Choper has pointed out that congressional regulation of judicial authority has from the earliest days been a matter for judicial review.[89] Under the separation of powers, the Congress may not impose nonjudicial functions on the courts or subject judicial determinations to executive revision. This is illustrated by *Hayburn's Case*,[90] the first case of judicial self-defense holding a federal statute unconstitutional. Three different circuit courts, on which five of the six Supreme Court justices sat, held that they could not perform the executive function of ruling on the validity and amount of veterans' pension claims. On the other hand, the Court has approved statutes creating legislative courts as long as their decisions are reviewable in a U.S. court of appeals.[91] Recently, however, the Court held a congressional grant of general jurisdiction to legislative courts under the bankruptcy act to be unconstitutional.[92]

National Substantive Laws Enacted Pursuant to Article I

Neither the constitutional text, nor its history, nor its structure provides support for judicial review of congressional statutes enacted pursuant to the delegated powers of Article I. On the contrary, the history and structure of the Constitution point to legislative finality on the scope and breadth of such statutes as long as they do not also contain violations of the express constitutional limitations. Most authorities assert that there is no textual basis for judicial review of national substantive laws. Such judicial review is not explicitly mentioned in the Constitution and cannot be reasonably inferred from Article III, which is merely jurisdictional.[93] That the framers excluded it while expressly providing for judicial review of state legislation in Article VI is a strong indication that no general power of judicial review of national laws was to be inferred from the document.

Legal historians point out that there was no settled public opinion at the time on whether general judicial review was implied.[94] Although Hamilton wrote of judicial review in the broadest terms, both Madison and Jefferson opposed a general power of judicial review of acts of Congress. Madison, who clearly supported judicial review to enforce the Bill of Rights, voiced strong objection at the convention to general judicial review. The original proposal of the Committee of Detail on the jurisdiction of the Supreme Court was first for "cases arising under laws passed by the Legislature of the United States."[95] On August 27, 1787, Dr. Johnson moved to insert the words "this Constitution and the" before the word "laws."[96] Madison reports his reaction: "Mr Madison doubted whether it was not going too far to extend the jurisdiction of the Court generally to cases arising Under the Constitution, & whether it ought not to be limited to cases of a Judiciary nature. The right of expounding the Constitution in cases not of this nature ought not to be given to that Department. The motion of Docr. Johnson was agreed to nem:con: it being generally supposed that the jurisdiction given was constructively limited to cases of a Judiciary nature."[97] "Cases of a judiciary nature" is nowhere defined. Madison could have meant arising under the judicial function, judicial self-defense. He could also have meant to include enforcing the Bill of Rights and other constitutional limitations, as was the historical judicial function of the British courts. He surely was voicing opposition to general judicial review of legislation, a practice unknown in British or American legal history. On possible judicial refusal to enforce legislative acts, Madison wrote in 1788, "This makes the Judiciary Department paramount in Fact to the Legislature, which was never intended and can never be proper."[98] In the first Congress, discussing the question of granting to the president the power of removal, Madison stated: "I beg to know upon what principle it can be contended that any one department draws from the Constitution greater power than another, in marking out the limits of the powers of the several departments. The Constitution is the charter of the people in the government; it specifies certain great powers as absolutely granted, and marks out the departments to exercise them. If the constitutional boundary of either be brought into question, I do not see that any one of these independent departments has more right than another to declare their sentiments on that point."[99]

Jefferson, who also supported judicial review to enforce the Bill of Rights, strongly opposed the generalizations of Chief Justice Marshall in *Marbury* v. *Madison* concerning judicial review. He wrote: "That instrument [the Constitution] meant that its co-ordinate branches should be checks on each other. But the opinion which gives the Judges the right to decide what laws are constitutional, and what not, not only for themselves in their own sphere of action, but for the Legislative and Executive also in their spheres, would make the Judiciary a despotic branch."[100]

The inference from constitutional structure of legislative finality on legislative powers is supported by the comments of James Wilson at the Constitutional Convention. In supporting the view that the judiciary should share with the executive in the veto power, he recognized that the Supreme Court could hold unconstitutional statutes regulating the judiciary, but implied that the Court could not invalidate statutes enacted pursuant to Article I: "It had been said that the Judges, as expositors of the Laws would have an opportunity of defending *their* constitutional rights. There was weight to this observation; but this power of the Judges did not go far enough. Laws may be unjust, may be unwise, may be dangerous, may be destructive; and yet not be so unconstitutional as to justify the Judges in refusing to give them effect."[101]

The framers did not include language providing for general judicial review of substantive Acts of Congress because that would have been inconsistent with the historical context of English legislative supremacy and with the basic separation of governmental powers. "The Constitution of the United States is a modified version of the British Constitution, but the British Constitution that served as its original was that which was in existence between 1760 and 1787."[102] The British Constitution in existence during the years of the federal Constitutional Convention was dominated by the English Bill of Rights of 1689, which established parliamentary supremacy.[103] This fact was the basic framework of government in Blackstone's *Commentaries,* the leading lawbook in the colonies.[104] The idea of legislative supremacy, as borrowed from the writings of John

Locke, had great influence in the American colonies.[105] Although the framers of the Constitution were concerned with limiting possible abuses of legislative supremacy, they did not adopt as a remedy judicial supremacy over all those acts of Congress that are litigated. The historical presumption in favor of legislative supremacy was rebutted for statutes violating constitutional limitations and judicial self-defense, but not for substantive acts of Congress.

The basic structural characteristic of the Constitution is the separation of governmental powers.[106] In this context, those sections of the Constitution vesting substantive governing power in one department of government are not expressly subject to a general veto by another department. Such a veto would make the separation of powers a hollow gesture. Yet, a general veto power in the judiciary for all acts of Congress that are litigated was the rationalization that Chief Justice Marshall adopted in *Marbury* v. *Madison*.[107] The more reasonable inference from separated powers is that each coequal department should make its own final determination on the breadth of the affirmative governing powers vested in it by the people. As has been noted, this is labeled "departmental review."[108] Bickel has concluded that the requirement of Article VI, Clause 3 for officials of all three departments of government to take oaths to support the Constitution means that each department is to construe with finality the performance of its own peculiar functions.[109] A leading constitutional historian has pointed to the application of departmental review in the executive,[110] and it is easily illustrated in the legislative branch. Article I, and especially Section 8 of that article, for example, delegates broad legislative powers to the Congress. The members of Congress, following their oaths of office to support the Constitution, are rightly presumed to conform to their oaths. Since both constitutions and statutes must be expounded in written language that contains some level of uncertainty of meaning, Congressmen are just as qualified as justices to assess the scope of both and determine the constitutionality of powers vested in them. As Justice Holmes admonishes, "it must be remembered that legislatures are ultimate guardians of the liberties and welfare of the people in quite as great a degree as the courts."[111]

Given the overwhelming power of the judiciary when it assumes the prerogative of final review of substantive powers of the legislature, it is not surprising that persons of such diverse views as President Jackson and President Lincoln should make statements in opposition. In his veto message of July 10, 1832, Jackson supported coequal departmental review: "The Congress, the Executive, and the Court must each for itself be guided by its own opinion of the Constitution. Each public officer who takes an oath to support the Constitution swears that he will support it as he understands it, and not as it is understood by others. . . . The opinion of the judges has no more authority over Congress than the opinion of

Congress has over the judges, and on that point the president is independent of both. The authority of the Supreme Court must not, therefore, be permitted to control the Congress or the Executive when acting in their legislative capacities, but to have only such influence as the force of their reasoning may deserve."[112]

President Lincoln, in his first inaugural address, sought to limit the impact of the *Dred Scott* case.[113] Though he conceded that the nation must accept the decision as it applied to the particular parties, he challenged its finality for the other branches of government: "[I]f the policy of the Government upon vital questions affecting the whole people is to be irrevocably fixed by decisions of the Supreme Court, the instant they are made in ordinary litigation between parties in personal actions, the people will have ceased to be their own rulers, having to that extent practically resigned their Government into the hands of that eminent tribunal."[114]

The idea of a general veto power in the Supreme Court over all substantive laws enacted by Congress that are litigated is further repudiated by another structural element, the character of representative government created in the Constitution. The Congress is a representative body, responsible to the people at every general election. If the majority of voters should conclude that a national statute exceeds the delegated powers of Congress, it may within the next two years vote out of office those congressmen who supported such enactment. The judiciary, in contrast, is an appointed elite with lifetime tenure. If the Supreme Court should hold a national law unconstitutional that the overwhelming majority of citizens views as clearly within a delegated power of Congress, there is no remedy short of impeachment. One must conclude that the theory of electively responsible government would rank legislative finality of substantive legislative powers over review by an appointed judiciary. A rejection of any general veto power in the appointed judiciary is further reinforced by the fact that the Constitutional Convention voted down a proposed Council of Revision with veto power over Congress that was to contain "a convenient number" of the national judiciary.[115]

The conclusion that judicial review of the constitutionality of national substantive statutes was not adopted in the Constitution has effect not only in the Supreme Court, but in all lower courts, both national and state. This conclusion means that Section 25 of the Judiciary Act of 1789,[116] allowing appeal to the Supreme Court for specified classes of state and national constitutional issues decided in state courts, should have been divided by the Court into two groups. As to national laws, judicial review of the issues should have applied only to procedural statutes and those substantive statutes challenged as violating constitutional limitations. Since the state courts, like the national, has no power to rule on the constitutionality of all other national substantive laws, appeals from unwarranted assumption of jurisdiction in such cases should have resulted in summary orders of dismissal of the actions.

Recent scholarship points to the conclusion that Chief Justice Marshall did not consider his generalizations about judicial review in *Marbury* to apply to legislative acts of Congress under its delegated powers in Article I.[117] The idea of legislative finality for decisions concerning the scope and breadth of delegated powers is reasonably inferred from Marshall's opinion in *McCulloch* v. *Maryland*.[118] One key issue was the constitutionality of the Congressional act creating the second Bank of the United States. The particular question was whether the creation of a nationally chartered banking corporation was valid in the absence of an express power in the Constitution. In upholding the constitutionality of the second Bank, Chief Justice Marshall made a structural analysis based on the concept of implied powers.[119] Even before his discussion of the "necessary-and-proper clause," he found that workable government could function only if Congress could choose the most efficient means to execute its express powers.[120] Marshall gave the following primarily structural explanation of the existence of broad, implied legislative power:

> A constitution, to contain an accurate detail of all the subdivisions of which its great powers will admit, and of all the means by which they may be carried into execution, would partake of the prolixity of a legal code, and could scarcely be embraced by the human mind. It would probably never be understood by the public. Its nature, therefore, requires, that only its great outlines should be marked, its important objects designated, and the minor ingredients which composed those objects be deduced from the nature of the objects themselves. That this idea was entertained by the framers of the American Constitution, is not only to be inferred from the nature of the instrument, but from the language. Why else were some of the limitations, found in the ninth section of the first article, introduced? It is also, in some degree, warranted by their having omitted to use any restrictive term which might prevent its receiving a fair and just interpretation. In considering this question, then, we must never forget, that it is a constitution we are expounding.[121]

Like Hamilton in *Federalist* 33, Marshall minimized the significance of the necessary-and-proper clause.[122] In answering the argument that the word "necessary" precluded implementing the fiscal powers by incorporating a national bank, Marshall stated:

> The subject is the execution of those great powers on which the welfare of a nation essentially depends. It must have been the intention of those who gave these powers, to insure, as far as human prudence could insure, their beneficial execution. This could not be done by confining the choice of means to such narrow limits as not

to leave it in the power of Congress to adopt any which might be appropriate, and which were conducive to the end. This provision is made in a constitution intended to endure for ages to come, and, consequently, to be adapted to the various crises of human affairs.[123]

* * *

We admit, as all must admit, that the powers of the government are limited, and that its limits are not to be transcended. But we think the sound construction of the Constitution must allow to the national legislature that discretion, with respect to the means by which the powers it confers are to be carried into execution, which will enable that body to perform the high duties assigned to it, in the manner most beneficial to the people. Let the end be legitimate, let it be within the scope of the Constitution, and all means which are appropriate, which are plainly adapted to that end, which are not prohibited, but consist with the letter and spirit of the Constitution are constitutional.[124]

The implication of *McCulloch* is that the final word on implementation of express powers in the legislature is left to the legislature. This is only a short step from saying that the scope and breadth of legislative powers are to be determined with finality by Congress. Marshall did not go so far as to assert the departmental theory of judicial review. If he had done so, it would have been consistent with the holding of *Marbury,* which concerned judicial self-defense, but not with his *obiter dicta* in that case on the general character of judicial review.

What of the highly unlikely situation that Congress should enact a statute that is openly and obviously not pursuant to any of the powers enumerated in the Constitution? Examples would be a national wills act or a national statute defining negligence for local vehicular torts.[125] Such a national statute could be in direct conflict with existing state statutes and common-law rules on these topics. Where such a statute is beyond reasonable doubt outside the subject matter of any enumerated power, the Supreme Court would hold it ineffective under the supremacy clause and would uphold conflicting state law under the Tenth Amendment.[126] This principle must be strictly construed.[127] Holding a national statute ineffective under the supremacy clause technically does not make it void.[128] If the decision that held it ineffective is later overruled by the Court, the statute again becomes legally effective.[129]

Criticism of Judicial Review

Most of the critics of judicial review have failed to distinguish its application to constitutional limitations from its application to delegated powers. As a result, they tend to make sweeping statements for or against its continuance. Professor Commager, after reviewing the Court's misuse of judicial review between 1870 and 1937, suggested that the only way to end such abuse of power was to terminate judicial review.[130] He felt that legislative supremacy, even with extremist statutes enacted in time of national crisis, would be less detrimental to society than the abuses by the Court majority under judicial review. His view is that judicial review leads inevitably to judicial legislation and that, consequently, judicial review destroys the true separation of governmental powers. The school of legal realists, concerned with the social and economic background of judges and their effects on decision making, deal very harshly with the whole notion of judicial objectivity.[131] They feel that bias is unavoidable. Commager preferred the biases of the majority of the elected Congress to the biases of the appointed elite on the Supreme Court. He felt that the Congress was basically conservative and would seldom deliberately attempt to evade the clear language of the Constitutional limitations. Consequently, he was prepared to place his trust in a majority of Congress to respect civil liberties as opposed to placing his trust in a majority of the Supreme Court.

The proponents of judicial review marshal many defenses against the charge of its undemocratic character.[132] They argue that the misuse of judicial review by some Supreme Court majorities through abuse of judicial discretion should be remedied by techniques to prevent recurrence of abuses, not by the total termination of this vital judicial check on possible legislative tyranny. They further argue that abuses of judicial discretion before 1937 have taught present and future justices a lesson, so that future excesses are much less likely. The essential effect of terminating all judicial review, they argue, would be the termination of all constitutional limitations. But the Constitution specifically designed limitations to prevent a duly elected majority of the legislature from oppressing minorities. The judiciary are given life tenure so that they will act fearlessly to enforce constitutional limitations against the public's unbridled passions of the moment that may result in the passage of oppressive legislation.

Justice Cardozo spoke of judicial review as a vital background factor affecting legislatures in their consideration of proposed laws:

> The utility of an external power restraining the legislative judgment is not to be measured by counting the occasions of its exercise. The great ideals of liberty and equality are preserved against the assaults of opportunism, the expediency of the passing hour, the erosion of small encroachments, the scorn and derision of those who have no patience with general principles, by enshrining them in constitutions, and consecrating to the task of their protection a body of defenders. By conscious or subconscious influence, the presence of this restraining power, aloof in the background, but none the less always in reserve, tends to stabilize and rationalize the legislative judgment, to infuse it with the glow of principle, to hold the standard aloft and

visible for those who must run the race and keep the faith. . . . The restraining power of the judiciary does not manifest its chief worth in the few cases in which the legislature has gone beyond the lines that mark the limits of discretion. Rather shall we find its chief worth in making vocal and audible the ideals that might otherwise be silenced, in giving them continuity of life and of expression, in guiding and directing choice within the limits where choice ranges. This function should preserve to the courts the power that now belongs to them, if only the power is exercised with insight into social values, and with suppleness of adaptation to changing social needs.[133]

There is a counterargument that judicial review cannot save a nation bent on destroying its freedoms, and that the judiciary should not be assigned the impossible duty of ultimate savior. Judge Learned Hand has argued for limits on judicial review in the Supreme Court even in cases concerning constitutional limitation:

And so to sum up, I believe that for by far the greater part of their work it is a condition upon the success of our system that the judges should be independent; and I do not believe that their independence should be impaired because of their constitutional function. But the price of this immunity, I insist, is that they should not have the last word in those basic conflicts of "right and wrong—between whose endless jar justice resides." You may ask what then will become of the fundamental principles of equity and fair play which our constitutions enshrine; and whether I seriously believe that unsupported they will serve merely as counsels of moderation. I do not think that anyone can say what will be left of those principles; I do not know whether they will serve only as counsels; but this much I think I do know—that a society so riven that the spirit of moderation is gone, no court *can* save; that a society where that spirit flourishes, no court *need* save; that in a society which evades its responsibility by thrusting upon courts the nurture of that spirit, that spirit in the end will perish.[134]

History has shown that when the tide of opinion favors suppression of political minorities, the Supreme Court majority will many times find a way of upholding oppressive statutes.[135] If the Court does resist the oppression and orders protection for a minority, its order may be ignored. Such was the case when the Supreme Court held unconstitutional certain Georgia statutes depriving the Cherokee Indians of their lands.[136] It is thus clear that the willing cooperation of all three departments of government is the prime prerequisite for effective judicial review to enforce constitutional limitations.

The general judicial review of congressional legislation that prevails today was founded on the *obiter dicta* of Chief Justice Marshall in *Marbury* v. *Madison*.[137] Scholars have pointed to the holding of *Marbury* as a case of judicial self-defense that does not support Marshall's generalizations, but the courts have not recognized this elementary fact. There seems small likelihood that the Supreme Court will soon recognize legislative finality for federal statutes not challenged under constitutional limitations. The development of general judicial review after the Civil War and up to the present time makes it an established institution.[138]

There is no present movement to restore national legislative finality through constitutional amendment.[139] Since 1937 the court has recognized very broad powers in Congress under the taxation and commerce clauses.[140] This removes any urgency to restore federal legislative finality. Should a swing of the judicial pendulum result in the return to the narrow interpretations like those in the decades just before 1937, however, a movement for constitutional amendment could arise.

CHAPTER 4

Economic Origins and Protections for Property

SINCE 1913 the academic world has argued over the importance of economic factors in the origin of the Constitution. Since the early issues centered on different types of property, they form an introduction to a general treatment of property rights in the Constitution. This chapter reviews the historical meaning of property in relation to changing definitions in the twentieth century. The economics of property law is used to explain the interactive character of components of the traditional common law and constitutional protections. This chapter uses this total background to ground a critique of the "new property" with a comment on the social costs of such litigation.

Economic Origins of the Constitution

The modern controversy over the economic origins of the Constitution begins with Charles Beard, *An Economic Interpretation of the Constitution of the United States.*[1] Though Beard admits in his introduction that his study is fragmentary and not based on exhaustive historical research, his book nevertheless had a very great influence on historians of the Constitution.[2] Later, more extensive studies, however, have rejected most of Beard's conclusions.[3]

Beard's method of historical interpretation is economic determinism. His hypothesis is that economic elements are the chief factors in the development of political institutions.[4] It was one thing to note that economic factors had been ignored in most earlier historical studies, but Beard's assertion that they were the primary factors was a significant leap. Applying economic determinism is especially difficult in studying a document whose primary task was to create a set of political institutions, and especially one that did not delegate voting qualification to the national government. To assert economic determinism, one must imply that the few clauses relating to commerce, taxation, money and bankruptcy somehow were the primary factors in the Constitution.

The economic determinism of Beard, while based on classes of property owners, is not Marxian. It could not be so because Marx wrote after the

English industrial revolution about industrial society and the significance of the working class. In writing of a preindustrial society in which manufactures were of minor significance, Beard could not find a class conflict between those owning capital (including land) and those without. Consequently, he hypothesizes a conflict between owners of two kinds of property.[5] One class comprised the owners of real property, most of whom were small landowners that Beard presumed were largely debtors. The other class comprised owners of personal property, which Beard asserts were divided into four subgroups: owners of money, public securities, manufacturing and shipping facilities, and titles to western lands held for speculation. He leaves the fourth of these subgroups out of his conclusions.[6]

Beard's thesis is that the owners of personal property instigated and controlled the Constitutional Convention,[7] creating a Constitution primarily for their economic benefit. He argues that the new nation was highly undemocratic and that the Constitution was adopted primarily by representatives of the owners of personal properties. More recent studies have refuted this argument,[8] noting that even though most states restricted voting for representatives to the ratifying conventions to male property owners, most of these owners were small holders of real property. The fact that over three-quarters of this restricted electorate did not bother to vote for representatives to the ratifying conventions is probably evidence that most saw no reason to oppose the ratification.

Furthermore, the evidence does not support Beard's thesis that the primary holdings of the delegates to the Constitutional Convention were personal property. Only six delegates had personal property in excess of their real property.[9] The delegates were not a solid economic group. One-fourth of them had previously voted in state legislatures for state issues of paper money and state bankruptcy laws for relief of debtors.[10] Although the final Constitution barred such laws,[11] the evidence demonstrates that there was not a solid block of delegates urging clauses to protect creditors.

In the ratification conventions, personal property interests were not in control. The majority of delegates were small farmers, but there is no evidence that a majority of them were debtors. Both holders of real property and merchants supported ratification by a large majority.[12] Even the majority of known debtors favored ratification. The expected long-run monetary stability from national control seems to have been more important than short-run relief from debt accompanied by continuous monetary instability. The evidence further demonstrates that holders of national securities did not vote as a bloc in favor of ratification, as one might have expected.[13]

Thus, the critics have shown that Beard's main thesis of conflict between real property and personal property interests was just wrong. He collected inadequate evidence and misinterpreted the evidence that he had. Among his primary misinterpretations was his assertion that Madison in *Federalist* 10 supported his view.[14] But Madison was not an economic determinist. Just as John Locke recognized an unequal distribution of property was necessary for saving because saving would be done by the "industrious and rational,"[15] so Madison expounded on the same issue:

> The diversity in the faculties of men, from which the rights of property originate, is not less an insuperable obstacle to a uniformity of interests. The protection of these faculties is the first object of government. From the protection of different and unequal faculties of acquiring property, the possession of different degrees and kinds of property immediately results; and from the influence of these on the sentiments and views of the respective proprietors, ensues a division of the society into different interests and parties.

> * * *

> [T]he most common and durable source of factions has been the various and unequal distribution of property. Those who hold and those who are without property have ever formed distinct interests in society. Those who are creditors, and those who are debtors, fall under a like discrimination. A landed interest, a manufacturing interest, a mercantile interest, a moneyed interest, with many lesser interests, grow up of necessity in civilized nations, and divide them into different classes, actuated by different sentiments and views. The regulation of these various and interfering interests forms the principal task of modern legislation, and involves the spirit of party and faction in the necessary and ordinary operations of the government.[16]

Madison wrote of many divisions in society, economic, political, and religious. The division he considered most fundamental was between the free states and the slave states, a division not on class lines.[17] Majority rule with broad legislative power in the Congress over commerce and finance was the first protection of the citizenry from oppression. A constitutional system of checks and balances was the first step to protect minorities from oppression by the majority. But the offsetting interests of many factions, aired in the legislature of a republic, was the best safeguard against breakdown of the society through factional conflict.[18]

But although conflict between various property interests was not the foundation of the Constitution, its primary objective was the protection of life, liberty and property.[19] The subsequent sections on the law and economics of property rights demonstrate why the founders of the nation considered it essential for a constitution to protect the institution of property.

Definition of Property

Property is the legal right to possess, use, and dispose of things.[20] Things may be tangible, such as land, goods, and money, or they may be intangible, such as patents, copyrights, franchises, and charters.[21] Intangible assets induce investment in tangible things and, since they are often grants of monopoly, they are a substantial asset in the valuation of an activity or enterprise. The key characteristics of property rights are ownership and use of external things, not one's own person. In order to distinguish property rights from other legal rights created by the common law and legislatures, our legal system classifies property rights as being *in rem*.[22] They delineate status relationships to external things, enforceable by the owner against all other persons.

In defining property rights, the concept of ownership is crucial. Legal scholars have analyzed the elements of ownership in great detail.[23] Becker has extended the basic concepts of possession, use, and disposition into thirteen elements.[24] The right to use includes the right to manage, the right to income, the right to consume, and the right to modify. Of these, the right to income is of primary significance to the economist. We define the value of a capital good as the discounted present value of an expected stream of income calculated after depreciation. Thus, a vested right in a stream of income, such as an annuity, is considered property.[25] The creation of property rights by grant from government has long been recognized in the form of patents,[26] copyrights,[27] and franchises.[28]

As background to the later critical review of the "new property," it is useful to note with Justice Bradley that "property interest" and "ownership" are words of precise legal signification.[29] Justice Roberts has pointed out that it is not useful to use "property" in the vulgar and untechnical sense of the physical thing. The term is "employed in a more accurate sense to denote the group of rights inhering in the citizen's relation to the physical thing, as the right to possess, use, and dispose of it."[30] He explained its application to condemnation: "When the sovereign exercises the power of eminent domain it substitutes itself in relation to the physical thing in question in place of him who formerly bore the relation to that thing, which we denominate ownership. In other words, it deals with what lawyers term the individual's "interest" in the thing in question. That interest may comprise the group of rights for which the shorthand term is 'a fee simple' or it may be the interest known as an 'estate or tenancy for years,' as in the present instance. The constitutional provision is addressed to every sort of interest the citizen may possess."[31]

Rigor in defining "property" is essential to the evaluation of public policies such as use of land. A person entitled to possession of property may not use it to cause harm to others. Disposal of waste onto adjoining properties or the public way is remediable in tort and subject to regulation by the state. Such physical invasion of the property of others is the easiest case to justify social control on the use of property.[32] Where the effects of wrongful use, such as air pollution, are widely dispersed, there may be market failure in the form of high transaction costs for hundreds or thousands of remedies for minor harm to others. Such market failure justifies intervention by the state in the use of its police power to curtail the harm.

The content of the bundle of property rights is a crucial issue in cases asserting condemnation through regulation. Noise pollution near airports and its social regulation is an example. Regulation of billboards along scenic highways is another. Legal theorists who urge the expansion of state regulatory power over property center on aspects of disposition and use. Reduction of elements of these aspects without compensation on the basis of judicial views of fairness can undermine the security aspect of property rights.[33] Efficient use of resources requires the enforcement of reasonable expectations of owners about the legal protections for the different elements of their property rights.

The Economics of Property Rights

The economic basis of property rights in things was recognized by Locke.[34] Writing of a period when population was so small that land was a free good and capital goods were of little significance, Locke asserts that resources in a state of nature, untouched by human beings, do not have value, and argues that it is the addition of human labor to resources that gives them value.[35] Goods found in the commons become property by the use of labor to appropriate them. Thus, even in the most primitive society, property is a necessary incident of social organization. Locke's example is the Indian who hunts a deer for his family knowing that he lives in a tribe that will recognize and protect his ownership in the possession of a good on which he expends his labor.[36] On the other hand, no one will take time to produce goods if others may appropriate the output. Even agriculture will not exist if the crop may be taken from the farmer by someone with greater physical force.[37]

In modern terms, property rights are essential to the accumulation of "capital"—a quantity of funds invested in capital goods, those which produce other goods or a long-run stream of services.[38] In this context, land that has been occupied and improved is a capital good. No person or association of persons will abstain from consumption and save part of income for investment in capital goods if the society will not create and protect property rights in those goods. All of the advantages of specialization in production derive from combining labor and capital. And since capital accumulation will occur only if there are property rights, economic growth is dependent on the prior existence of such rights and a long-term expectation of their continuance.

To understand the interaction of human liberty and property, one must realize that property other than consumption goods represents someone's savings. As Justice Stewart wrote: "The dichotomy between personal liberties and property rights is a false one. Property does not have rights. The right to enjoy property without unlawful deprivation no less than the right to speak or the right to travel is in truth a 'personal' right, whether the 'property' in question be a welfare check, a home or a savings account. In fact, a fundamental interdependence exists between the personal right to liberty and the personal right to property. Neither could have meaning without the other. That rights in property are basic civil rights has long been recognized."[39] The same social institutions that protect the person from harm must also protect his savings as represented by his property. Liberty has little meaning if all one's assets may be taken by force. Those aggressive, totalitarian individuals that would take one's liberty and enslave him are the same ones who would use force to take his property. If savings in the form of property are not protected by law, savings will not exist and the economy will not function. No production or exchange can exist without property protections for the means of production and the output.

The necessary existence of property rights for all scarce resources either in the state, individuals, or some association of individuals is illustrated by the tragedy of the commons.[40] If the allocation of use of property rights in a scarce asset is not allocated to persons or to government, there is an incentive to use the asset to exhaustion and no incentive to maintain it. If specific grazing lands may be used in common by all owners of animals, each owner will have the incentive to put more animals on the land, and no owner of animals will have an incentive to preserve the land. This indicates one of the necessary requisites of the law of property, universality. Assets must be owned by some person, agency, or government if they are to be maintained.

The issue of whether most of the capital goods in a society will be private property or state property is the central contest between capitalism and socialism. At the time of the framing of the Constitution, transactions were preindustrial, centering in land and in products of agriculture, fishing, and mining. These transactions developed into a system of private property. For over two centuries before 1787, rules of private property in England and on the continent had been changing in order to facilitate the expanding commercial capitalism.[41] Since the growing internal and international trade of Europe was created by private-enterprise merchants, state ownership of enterprises was not within the contemplation of the framers of the constitution.

The basis for the preference for private property in most capital goods is economic efficiency.[42] For public goods, however, such as national defense and city streets, economies of scale and free-rider problems make public ownership necessary. The efficiency functions of private property are the creation of incentives to produce goods and services and to internalize the costs of such production. The three criteria for efficient use of property are universality, exclusivity, and transferability.[43] All property must be owned by some person or agency in order to prevent its waste. Ownership must be sufficiently exclusive so that others may not impair its use in production. Property must be transferable from less productive uses to more productive uses by voluntary exchange.

Private property forces owners to internalize costs. Private property in assets will be used in productive processes only if they earn sufficient return to maintain them and a market return on investment. Because there are market failures and because productive processes impose costs on third parties who cannot feasibly recover from the producer, government regulation may be necessary to force firms to internalize these external costs.[44]

Protection of Private Property

For seven centuries before Blackstone, the common-law courts had been developing the law of property.[45] Since land was the most valuable asset, the law of real property was the most important concern of the royal courts. The presumption of Blackstone and of the American colonists was the existence of a legal system that protected private property, both in land and in movables. Blackstone states, "There is nothing which so generally strikes the imagination, and engages the affection of mankind, as the right of property; or the sole and despotic dominion which one man claims and exercises over the external things of the world, in total exclusion of the right of any other individual in the universe."[46] At the Constitutional Convention, leading delegates spoke of the protection of property rights as the main or primary object of government.[47] Justice Patterson, who had been a delegate to the convention, declared, "The preservation of property is a primary object of the social compact."[48] Justice Story, for the Court in *Wilkinson* v. *Leland*, explained the significance of property rights to human security:

> That government can scarcely be deemed to be free, where the rights of property are left solely dependent upon the will of a legislative body, without any restraint. The fundamental maxims of a free government seem to require, that the rights of personal liberty and private property should be sacred. At least, no court of justice in the country would be warranted in assuming that the power to violate and disregard them—a power so repugnant to the common principles of justice and civil liberty—lurked under any general grant of legislative authority, or ought to be implied from any general expressions of the will of the people. The people ought not to be presumed to part with rights so vital to their security and well-being without very strong and direct expressions of such an intention.[49]

While the founders of the nation could not have fully understood the necessity of property law for a functioning economy, they considered property rights to be fundamental. As John Adams wrote, "Property must be secured or liberty cannot exist."[50] In a lecture at Harvard, Justice Story observed that property represented someone's savings. After restating his previous judicial pronouncement that the sacred rights of property must be guarded, he queried: "What is personal liberty, if it does not draw after it the right to enjoy the fruits of our own industry? What is political liberty, if it imparts only perpetual poverty to us and all our posterity? What is the privilege of a vote, if the majority of the hour may sweep away the earnings of our whole lives?"[51]

The American legal system protects private property by enforcing the common law and through several constitutional protections. The American colonists overthrew British rule, but they consistently maintained that they retained the rights of Englishmen against government.[52] These included the inheritance of the common law.[53] John Adams asserted that "the liberty, the unalienable and indefeasible rights of man, the honor and dignity of human nature . . . and the universal happiness of individuals, were never so skillfully and successfully consulted as in that most excellent monument of human art, the Common Law of England."[54] The law of property protected rights relating to ownership of things. The law of torts, through the legal action of trespass, provided a remedy for wrongful entry onto land and wrongful damage to real or personal property.

The original Constitution does not expressly mention property rights, but the separated governmental powers with its system of checks and balances was designed to prevent governmental oppression against personal liberty or property,[55] and there were express restrictions designed to prevent state governments from diminishing property rights. The prohibition on state creation of paper money, for example, was designed to prevent debtors from using inflation to reduce materially the true value of their obligations.[56] The prohibition against state impairment of the obligation of contract was to prevent state bankruptcy laws that would also relieve debtors of their liabilities.[57]

All of the civil rights of Englishmen against government were presumed to be effective against the government of the United States.[58] Those who opposed a Bill of Rights in the main body of the Constitution emphasized this point.[59] Consequently, the two protections for property that were incorporated into the Fifth Amendment were long-established rights of Englishmen.

The due process clause of the Fifth Amendment originated in Chapter 39 of the Magna Charta.[60] The clause provides that no person shall be "deprived of life, liberty or property without due process of law."[61] This is a procedural protection, since "process" in 1791 was a synonym for procedure.[62] One's property can be seized by government as a fine in a criminal case or as damages for a successful plaintiff in a civil action, but the Fifth Amendment guarantees that this will be done according to the appropriate procedures of established law of the nation.

Similarly, the eminent domain clause of the Fifth Amendment is historically founded on Chapter 28 of Magna Charta.[63] The amendment provides "nor shall private property be taken for public use without just compensation." Since 1897, this substantive immunity has been held effective against the states by Section 1 of the Fourteenth Amendment.[64] Kent points out that eminent domain is an inherent sovereign power that in modern times gives to the legislature the control of private property for public use. He notes that the national Constitution and most early state constitutions have imposed a "great and valuable check" upon the exercise of this legislative power:

> A provision for compensation is a necessary attendant on the due and constitutional exercise of the power of the lawgiver to deprive an individual of his property without his consent; and this principle in American jurisprudence is founded on natural equity and is laid down by jurists as an acknowledged principle of universal law.
>
> It undoubtedly must rest, as a general rule, in the wisdom of the legislature, to determine when public uses require assumption of private property; but if they should take it for a purpose not of a public nature, as if the legislature should take property of A give it to B, or if they should vacate a grant of property, or of a franchise, under the pretext of some public use or service, such cases would be gross abuses of their discretion, and fraudulent attacks on private right, and the law would be clearly unconstitutional and void.[65]

Justice Story, citing Blackstone's *Commentaries*, notes the importance of the right to compensation in takings: "Indeed, in a free government almost all other rights would become utterly worthless if the government possessed an uncontrollable power over the private fortune of every citizen. One of the fundamental objects of every good government must be the administration of justice; and how vain it would be to speak of such an administration, when all property is subject to the will or caprice of the legislature and the rulers."[66]

There is no definition of "property" in the Constitution. Under the federal system, the law of property is left to the states, so the definition of property is presumptively left to the states.[67] Congress, however, could by statute designate additional items as property.

The Supreme Court has lacked rigor in distinguishing the procedural protections of the due process clause from the substantive protection of the eminent domain clause. One notable example of misapplication is *Fleming* v. *Nestor*,[68] a 5-to-4 decision. In *Fleming*, the Supreme Court reversed a finding of a district court that a person who, together with his employer, had paid into the Old Age and Survivors Insurance Trust Fund[69] (Social Security) from 1936 to 1955 had an accrued property right. The Court upheld a section of the Social Security Act[70] that terminated old-age insurance payments to aliens who were deported for having been members of the Communist party during their U.S. residence. Nestor had been a member of the Communist party from 1933 to 1939. Communist party membership was a legal act at the time, but only fifteen years later, in 1954, Congress passed the statute providing for deportation of former Communists. The statute applied to all aliens, even those with permanent residence and families in the United States like Nestor, who had been in the United States for forty-three years. The financial consequence of the deportation was upheld in *Fleming* even though banishment had been considered penal under the Anglo-American legal system for hundreds of years.[71]

The district court had held the statute that terminated old-age insurance benefits to be unconstitutional under the due process clause of the Fifth Amendment, finding that the statute deprived Nestor of an accrued property right.[72] The Supreme Court majority reversed this ruling. It did note that "the interest of a covered employee under the Act is of sufficient substance to fall within the protection from arbitrary governmental action afforded by the Due Process Clause."[73] Since there was no issue of deprivation of life or liberty in the insurance termination, logically the only issue was deprivation of property. But the Court held just the opposite: "It is apparent that the non-contractual interest of an employee covered by the Act cannot be soundly analogized to that of a holder of an annuity, whose right to benefits is bottomed on his contractual premium payments."[74] The Court concluded: "To engraft upon the Social Security System a concept of 'accrued property rights' would deprive it of the flexibility and boldness in adjustment to ever-changing conditions which it demands."[75] The Court found that the classification was not patently arbitrary or lacking in rational justification.[76]

Even if one concedes that the statute was a product of rational congressional behavior and thus no violation of the due process clause, the Court still failed to treat the primary constitutional issue, which was one of compensation under the eminent domain clause. Justice Harlan's confused assertion that there was a right to a due-process hearing on deprivation of property but that there was no property demonstrates that he was lost in the wrong clause. The decision failed to penetrate the true meaning of "property" and failed to review the precedents on the status of paid-up insurance as a property interest.[77] If the Court had found Nestor to have a right similar to an insurance contract, instead of similar to a gift, then it would have seen that a contract for money or property, fully performed on one side, creates a vested right in the party who has performed.[78] Such a vested contract right, when taken by government, has been held by the Court to be property under the eminent domain clause.[79]

Eminent Domain

A review of the law and economics of eminent domain will illustrate how the judiciary has whittled away at the key substantive civil right relating to property. The recent commentators have written extensive reviews of the topic.[80] This survey will develop some economic tests for eminent domain and criticize the major recent cases in terms of these tests.

The economic argument for the governmental power of eminent domain is the control of monopoly. The pertinent economic model is bilateral monopoly.[81] A common example is the acquisition of a right-of-way, for a highway by the state or for a rail line by a regulated carrier. Once a plan for the most efficient line between places has been announced, each landowner in the projected right-of-way has an incentive to hold out for a monopoly price. This price could be greatly in excess of the cost of acquiring similar land or building nearby but not in the right-of-way. In the absence of the power of eminent domain, the cost of the property and the transaction costs of negotiating its purchase would be based on the monopoly price and could be very much higher. Some owners in the projected way may have a very high subjective value for property, perhaps because it has been possessed by their families for many generations. But under the more objective standards of fair market value under eminent domain, they will be entitled only to reasonable replacement cost.

The economic model of bilateral monopoly does not have a determinant solution for price in the open market.[82] Bargaining can result either in a monopoly gain for the seller or a monopsony gain for the buyer. Public agents make offers to owners of land in a designated area for public acquisition at their estimate of market value. The owner of a small parcel may not want to undertake the transaction cost of employing legal counsel and it may, in fact, be difficult to employ such counsel. The fee for such counsel is often one-third the increase in price over the initial offer, a sum that may not cover the cost of extended negotiation. An empirical study of condemnations for the urban-renewal program of Chicago concluded that eminent domain did not ensure that fair market value was paid in the assembly of sets of contiguous properties.[83] Owners of low-valued parcels systematically received less than fair market value; owners of high-valued parcels received more than market value. The amount of legal services devoted to each acquisition by the state agency cannot vary significantly with the size of the parcel, so the result is to spend a higher percentage of the parcel value on those that are low valued.

A first issue is the distinction between the taxation of income from property and the condemnation of property. Thomas Cooley observed that the distinction is one of degree. "Everything that may be done under the name of taxation is not necessarily a tax; and it may happen that an oppressive burden imposed by government, when it comes to be carefully scrutinized, will prove, instead of a tax, to be an unlawful confiscation of property, unwarranted by a principle of constitutional government."[84] While the taxation of income is necessary to finance government, immunity from uncompensated forfeiture of the capital that produces the income is a necessary component of a social system whose economic growth depends on private savings and investment. For this reason, Chief Justice Marshall was clearly wrong in his dictum that "the power to tax involves the power to destroy."[85] And, indeed, many later cases have recognized that the taxing power is subject to the limitation of eminent domain.[86] Justice Holmes stated this succinctly when he said, "the power to tax is not the power to destroy while this Court sits."[87] Similarly, federal price and rate regulation under the commerce power have an ultimate limit in the constraint on eminent domain.[88] And the Court has held the national bankruptcy power to be limited by the eminent domain protection.[89] A court may not deprive a mortgagee of substantial property rights solely in the interest of a mortgagor.

Justice Holmes noted the similar relation between the state police power and eminent domain:

> Government hardly could go on if to some extent values incident to property could not be diminished without paying for every such change in the general law. As long recognized some values are enjoyed under an implied limitation and must yield to the police power. But obviously the implied limitation must have its limits or the contract and due process clauses are gone. One fact for consideration in determining such limits is the extent of the diminution. When it reaches a certain magnitude, in most if not in all cases there must be an exercise of eminent domain and compensation to sustain the act. So the question depends upon the particular facts. The greatest weight is given to the judgment of the legislature but it always is open to interested parties to contend that the legislature has gone beyond its constitutional power.[90]

The police powers relate to the "safety, health, morals, and general welfare of the public."[91] The necessarily imprecise definition creates great ambiguity. This aggravates the problem of setting the borderline between valid statutory application of the police power and regulation that is of such magnitude that it constitutes a taking of property. A key example is the power of the states to regulate public-utility rates and other prices charged by sellers in order to curtail monopolistic exploitation of consumers.[92] Under the police power, the state may reduce the value of property by compelling the reduction of output prices whose effect is to lower earnings from a monopoly level to a competitive level.[93] If, however, state regulations set prices in an industry so low that it is impossible to attract capital, there would be an issue of inverse condemnation.

Historically, any statute or ruling that directs a permanent physical invasion of another's property is an unconstitutional "taking" under the eminent domain clause. The right of the owner to exclusive possession is the first element of property. This rule was recently reconfirmed in *Loretto* v. *Teleprompter Manhattan CATV Corp.,*[94] in which the Court invalidated a New York statute that compelled a landlord to permit a cable-television company to install cable facilities on the roof of his apartment building in order to serve the tenants. The law barred payment in excess of that set by a state commission, and the commission had set a one-time fee of $1 as reasonable. The Court ruled that the owner was entitled to just compensation for the use of her property.

The right to exclusive possession of property has also been held to allow an owner the power to bar temporary occupation of any of its property. In *Lloyd Corp* v. *Tanner,*[95] the Court held that the private owner of a shopping center was not compelled by the free speech and petition clauses of the First Amendment to provide access to persons wishing to distribute political handbills on its property. The owner of a shopping center, like the owner of an office building, is a real-estate enterpriser trying to provide the optimal setting for commercial transactions and related activity. The public are invited onto the property to negotiate and to engage in transactions and for no other purpose. Neither the sidewalks of the shopping center nor the halls of the office building are part of the public way. The Court concluded that it "would be an unwarranted infringement of property rights to require them to yield to the exercise of First Amendment rights."[96]

But the *Lloyd* rule was not followed in *Pruneyard Shopping Center* v. *Robbins,*[97] where persons collecting signatures for a political petition were excluded by the owners of a shopping center. The key difference from *Lloyd* was a ruling by the California Supreme Court that the California Constitution's general protection of liberty of speech and press and right to petition government gave plaintiffs the right to solicit signatures, even in a privately owned shopping center. This judicial expansion of the state constitution was held to be a valid exercise of the state's police power, adopting reasonable restrictions on the use of private property. Justice Rehnquist, for the Court, ruled that the requirement that owners permit plaintiffs "to exercise state-protected rights of free expression and petition on shopping-center property clearly does not amount to an unconstitutional infringement of [owner's] property rights under the Taking Clause."[98] The fact that the plaintiffs were orderly and limited their activity to the common areas of the shopping center provoked Rehnquist to assert that "the fact that they may have 'physically invaded' [the owners'] property cannot be viewed as determinative."[99] This is clearly inconsistent with the precedents that any use of the state police power to condone physical invasion of another's property is a partial taking under eminent domain. The opinion lacks an analytical explanation of the meaning of exclusive possession in the law of property, and it also fails to recognize the supremacy clause as a framework that assures the supremacy of national constitutional limitations over state police power.

Inverse Condemnation

Inverse condemnation occurs when a court finds that though no condemnation action has been filed, governmental regulation has materially impaired one or more elements of a person's property rights—a *de facto* taking.[100] Under the language of the Fifth Amendment, such partial taking should be remedied by compensation to the owner of the rights. Unlike a general property tax, which has a uniform effect on income from all property, inverse condemnation affects particular persons or classes of owners and materially reduces the value of their capital investment. The basic economic approach is that the owner of property earning a competitive return in the market should be compensated if any material aspect of the property is taken by the state.

A classic case of inverse condemnation is *Pumpelly* v. *Green Bay Co.*[101] The defendant canal company had erected a dam pursuant to legislative authorization, and the waters backed up by the dam flooded the plaintiff's property. The plaintiff's action was under the eminent domain clause of the Wisconsin Constitution, which was almost identical to the eminent domain clause of the Fifth Amendment. The court held that there must be compensation when there is almost complete destruction of the value of the land. Justice Miller, for the Court, stated:

> It would be a very curious and unsatisfactory result, if in construing a provision of constitutional law, always understood to have been adopted for protection and security to the rights of the individual as against the government, and which has received the commendation of jurists, statesmen and commentators as placing the just principles of the common law on that subject beyond the power of ordinary legislation to change or control them, it shall be held that if the government refrains from the absolute conversion of real property to the uses of the public it can destroy its value entirely, can inflict irreparable and permanent injury to any extent; can, in effect, subject it to total destruction without making any compensation, because, in the narrowest sense of that word, it is not taken for the public use. Such a construction would pervert the constitutional provision into a restriction upon the rights of the citizen, as those rights stood at the common law, instead of the government, and make it an authority

for invasion of private right under the pretext of the public good, which had no warrant in the laws or practices of our ancestors.[102]

Pennsylvania Coal Co. v. Mahon[103] supplied a key precedent supporting the application of inverse condemnation as a remedy for a material diminution of property value by a regulatory statute. The coal company sold surface rights over its mining operations under express terms allowing further removal of coal with a waiver by grantees of all claims for damages for subsidence. The state subsequently enacted a statute that forbade mining that caused subsidence. The Supreme Court held in this case that the statute operated as an unconstitutional taking that would materially diminish the value of the property rights. On the necessary judicial protection under eminent domain, Justice Holmes, for the Court, stated: "When this seemingly absolute protection is found to be qualified by the police power, the natural tendency of human nature is to extend the qualification more and more until at last private property disappears. But that cannot be accomplished in this way under the Constitution of the United States. The general rule at least is that while property may be regulated to a certain extent, if regulation goes too far it will be recognized as a taking."[104]

In most cases, arguments based on police power have been upheld in denying compensation for the regulatory taking of material property rights. Even where investment was made in reasonable reliance on valid laws, in most cases no compensation is awarded when a changed law destroys the values of the investment. In *Mugler* v. *Kansas*,[105] for example, the defendant had built and operated a brewery at a time when this was legal. When brewing was made illegal, a state action was brought to shut up and abate the brewery. The Supreme Court upheld this action under the police power, noting the broad power of the state to abate a public nuisance in protecting public health. The Court rejected application of the compensation rule in *Pumpelly* to the brewing equipment, which was vastly reduced in value.[106] In its decision, the Court failed to separate the police power of the legislature to prohibit manufacture of alcoholic beverages from the issue of compensation for the brewing machinery and the cost of refitting the building for other uses.

Some of the leading denials of remedies for economic loss in inverse condemnation cases have occurred in judicial approvals of zoning ordinances. *Euclid* v. *Ambler Realty*[107] is a leading case upholding modern urban zoning laws whose effect is substantially to decrease property values. The plaintiff owned sixty-eight acres between a principal highway, Euclid Avenue, and the Nickel Plate Railroad. This was viewed as an area of expanding industrial development until the city ordinance reduced the zoning of a significant portion of it to single-family dwellings. The trial court held the rezoning an unconstitutional taking of part of plaintiff's property value and enjoined enforcement of the ordinance.[108] The Supreme Court reversed, giving the police power broad construction and drawing analogies to the tort law of nuisance. The zoning was upheld even though "the exclusion is in general terms of all industrial establishments, and it may thereby happen that not only offensive or dangerous industries will be excluded, but those which are neither offensive nor dangerous will share the same fate. . . . It cannot be said that the ordinance in this respect 'passes the bounds of reason and assumes the character of a merely arbitrary fiat.' "[109] Thus the inherent police power was held to override the express constitutional right to compensation because the zoning "bears a rational relation to the health and safety of the community."[110]

While the Court has invalidated a zoning ordinance found to have no substantial relation to public health, safety, morals, or general welfare,[111] most recent cases follow *Euclid* and uphold zoning laws that materially reduce the market value of land. In *Goldblatt* v. *Town of Hempstead*,[112] the town had expanded to surround a quarry. The town adopted a series of ordinances to limit the operation of the quarry. An amendment in 1958 that prohibited excavation below the water line had the effect of stopping the use of the quarry. In spite of the material reduction in land values by prohibiting the most beneficial use of the property, the Court upheld the ordinance. The court's holding that the partial taking was permitted when "not unduly oppressive on individuals" violates the economic purpose of eminent domain.[113] Since there was an admitted partial taking of property, compensation should have been paid.

This case is quite different from coming-to-nuisance litigation. When a brickyard was in a rural area outside of town, its noise and other impositions on nearby empty property disturbed no one.[114] But after the area was incorporated into the city and housing was built close to the brickyard, the city enacted an ordinance making it a misdemeanor to operate a brickyard in that area. Even though the value of the property was reduced by over 80 percent, there was a valid exercise of the state police power to remedy a nuisance and no taking of property by the state.

In *Agins* v. *City of Tiburon*,[115] the Court unanimously upheld a downzoning that greatly decreased the value of land. Agins owned five acres of land with a view of San Francisco Bay. Under the law prevailing when he acquired this land, it could have been subdivided for a large number of homes. The city passed an "open space" zoning ordinance that reduced the number of homes that could be built on the land to five. Shortly after, Agins filed a claim against the city for largely destroying the developmental value of his land. The city brought eminent domain proceedings to acquire the property, but later abandoned the action. The reasonable inference is that the city could accomplish most of its open space objectives through zoning rather than paying for land. The California Supreme Court upheld the city ordinance first on the ground that asserted deprivation of substantially all use of land may be challenged only through declaratory relief or mandamus to invalidate the ordinance.[116] Plaintiff may not "sue in inverse condemnation and thereby transmute an excessive use of police power into a lawful taking for which compensation in eminent domain must be paid."[117] Second, it held that the "trial court was justified in finding that the ordinance did not unconstitutionally interfere with plaintiff's entire use of the land or impermissibly decrease its value."[118] In affirming the judgment, Justice Powell, for the U.S. Supreme Court, held that the ordinances "neither prevent the best use of appellant's land, . . . nor extinguish a fundamental attribute of ownership."[119] In spite of the major decrease in values, he held that no taking of Agins's property had occurred.

Landmark designation of buildings is similar to downzoning. In *Penn Central Transp. Co. v. City of New York,*[120] Grand Central Station was designated under the New York Landmarks Preservation Law. Penn Central's lessee was denied permission to build a fifty-three-story office tower over the terminal. The record was clear that the proposed office building was in full compliance with all New York zoning laws and height limitations. Nonetheless, the Supreme Court affirmed the New York Court of Appeals ruling that there had been no "taking" in violation of the eminent domain protection. The opinion noted that "this Court, quite simply, has been unable to develop any 'set formula' for determining when 'justice and fairness' require that economic injuries caused by public action be compensated by government, rather than remain disproportionately concentrated on a few persons."[121] Here the majority held there was no taking as long as Penn Central could earn a reasonable return on its original investment.[122] Such reasoning displays fallacious economics. The original cost is only a historical incident. When we look at market value of property in the context of uniform zoning laws we can identify infinite factors that have had impact on the owner as risk taker since original investment. If, for example, when property is condemned, its market value is half the original cost to the owner, the measure of compensation is not the original cost.

As a partial mitigation, Penn Central was issued transferable development rights that could be used on at least eight parcels in the vicinity of the terminal. To the extent that these rights were usable on property nearby that owned by Penn Central, they were redundant—unless those properties were previously downzoned under another exceptional law. In any case, the rights had an uncertain and contingent market value and were not a substitute for cash compensation.[123]

For a long time the Supreme Court avoided meeting the issue of a constitutional right to just compensation for temporary taking of property rights by operation of a regulatory statute. In a number of cases the Court refused to review the substance of the issues because it found factual disputes yet to be resolved by the state courts.[124] But the issue was finally decided in *First English Evan. Luth. Ch.* v. *Los Angeles Cty.*[125] The church had built a retreat center for handicapped children on land it owned in a canyon in the Angeles National Forest. Following a forest fire upstream, a flood destroyed the buildings of the retreat center. Los Angeles County then adopted an interim ordinance prohibiting reconstruction of buildings in the area. The church filed an action for inverse condemnation against the county, seeking damages in compensation. The trial court dismissed the allegation on the basis of the rule in *Agins* v. *Tiburon,*[126] that a landowner may not maintain an inverse condemnation suit in state courts based on a "regulatory" taking. Under *Agins,* the owner must first bring an action for declaratory judgment or mandamus and prove the taking. If, thereafter, the government decides to continue the regulation in effect, compensation will be required. The California Court of Appeal affirmed.

The Supreme Court reversed. Chief Justice Rehnquist, for the court, noted that a landowner is entitled to bring an action for inverse condemnation because of the "self-executing character of the provision with respect to compensation."[127] Since the government may abandon its intrusion or discontinue regulations, the question is whether government must pay compensation for the period of time during which regulations deny a landowner all use of his land. The cases concerning temporary appropriation of property during World War II awarded monetary relief to the owners.[128] This applied even to a temporary taking of a leasehold.[129] Later invalidation of the law authorizing the use of private property, though converting the taking into a "temporary" one, is not a sufficient remedy to meet the demands of the just compensation clause.[130] The action for inverse condemnation for temporary denial of all use does not force the government to exercise eminent domain. But "where the government's activities have already worked a taking of all use of property, no subsequent action by the government can relieve it of the duty to provide compensation for the period during which the taking was effective."[131]

The cases reviewed here demonstrate inconsistency and lack of principled application of the general values incorporated in the eminent domain clause. The Court has reiterated a sound fundamental principle: "It is axiomatic that the Fifth Amendment's just compensation provision is 'designed to bar Government from forcing some people alone to bear public burdens which, in all fairness and justice, should be borne by the public as a whole.' "[132] Yet the Court has failed to apply the principle.

Miller v. *Schoene*[133] stands as a classic illustration of this failure. In the state of Virginia, through no fault of the owners, a rust fungus developed in ornamental red cedar trees. The cedar rust attacked nearby apple trees, owned by others, causing severe damage. At the behest of apple growers, the state enacted a statute that authorized the state entomologist, upon petition from ten freeholders in the area, to investigate, and if necessary, cut down affected cedar trees without compensation to the owners. The plaintiffs whose trees were cut were left with the cut timber as partial compensation. They sued the state for the difference in value between the live trees and the cut timber.

It was clear that the value of the apple orchards greatly exceeded the value of the ornamental cedars that were destroyed. One can assume that the statute was enacted because no private bargaining of owners of apple trees to compensate owners of cedar trees could be effected as a solution. The transaction costs and the free-rider problem would make this theoretical solution impracticable.[134] The consequent ideal statutory solution, given no fault by any parties, would have been a tax on apple growers to compensate owners of cedars. The Supreme Court upheld the denial of compensation, thus inflicting a public burden on the owners of cedars. While the police power could be rightfully used to prohibit the planting of new cedars, public destruction of property rights in existing cedars violated the express language of the constitutional limitation, and compensation should have been paid.

The New Property: A Critique

The expanded concept of property under the due process clauses of the Fifth and Fourteenth Amendments has been labeled the "new property." Based on the writings of Charles Reich, the public policy is to expand the procedural protections for persons receiving benefits from government.[135] Since the courts could not possibly undertake this expansion under the traditionally accepted definitions of property, they have labeled certain government benefits as "entitlements," and they have treated entitlements as a synonym for property.

The key holding that the right to government largesse is a property right is *Goldberg* v. *Kelly*.[136] The issue here was whether New York could terminate Aid to Families with Dependent Children (AFDC) without affording the recipient an evidentiary hearing prior to termination. The New York Social Welfare Law provided only for a posttermination hearing. The district court held that only a pretermination hearing would satisfy the requirements of the due process clause of the Fourteenth Amendment. Since there was no deprivation of life or liberty, the first issue was whether a statutory right to governmental benefits constitutes property. Instead of contesting this issue and litigating the scope and breadth of the property concept, the state conceded the point and merely argued that the posttermination hearing satisfied due process. In affirming, the Supreme Court relegated the property issue to a footnote, stating: "It may be realistic today to regard welfare entitlements as more like 'property' than a 'gratuity.' "[137] The cited authority was the two articles of Reich.[138]

Justice Black, in dissent, argued that requiring constitutional due process in this context was without precedent.[139] The Court "in effect says that failure of the government to pay a promised charitable installment to an individual deprives that individual of *his own property,* in violation of the Due Process Clause of the Fourteenth Amendment. It somewhat strains credulity to say that the government's promise of charity to an individual is property belonging to that individual when the government denies that the individual is honestly entitled to receive such a payment."[140]

In *Board of Regents* v. *Roth,*[141] a five-person majority gave greater recognition to the need to define property. The Court held that a nontenured college teacher who was discharged with full notice but no statement of reasons had no due process right to a hearing. To have a property interest, a person "must have more than a unilateral expectation of it. He must instead have a legitimate claim of entitlement to it."[142] The Court further stated: "Property interests, of course, are not created by the Constitution. Rather they are created and their dimensions are defined by existing rules or understandings that stem from an independent source such as state law—rules of understanding that secure certain benefits and that support claims of entitlement to those benefits."[143] Following this principled declaration, the Court then rationalized *Goldberg* v. *Kelly*[144] as an entitlement grounded in statute. It is clear that the Court majority refused to accept the logic of Justice Black's dissent in *Goldberg,* demonstrating that statutes creating state benefits had never before been classed as a type of ownership.

The companion case of *Perry* v. *Sindermann*[145] held that a nontenured college teacher with ten years service was, under the due process clause, entitled to a hearing before discharge for two reasons: (1) he alleged that he was terminated solely because he exercised a First Amendment right to criticize the college administration, and (2) he alleged that the college had a *de facto* tenure program under which he qualified.[146] This asserted contract right to tenure was labeled by the Supreme Court as a "property" interest. Citing *Roth,* the Court held, "A person's interest in a benefit is a "property" interest for due process purposes if there are such rules or mutually explicit understandings that support his claim of entitlement to the benefit and that he may invoke at a hearing."[147] The Court confused the right to litigate a contract claim, during which trial one would receive the full process of the law, with a property deprivation by government, a violation of the due process clause.

Arnett v. *Kennedy*[148] was another case where some justices viewed a government employment contract to be property. When a nonprobationary federal employee was discharged, he alleged that the hearings provided in the federal statute were inadequate and denied him due process of law. Though the Supreme Court held the statutory hearings adequate, Justice

Powell stated that the employee had "a legitimate claim of entitlement which constituted a 'property' interest under the Fifth Amendment."[149]

In *Goss* v. *Lopez*,[150] a ten-day suspension from high school for misconduct was held to violate the due process clause because the student was not granted a hearing. "[T]he state is constrained to recognize a student's legitimate entitlement to a public education as a property interest which is protected by the Due Process Clause and which may not be taken away for misconduct without adherence to the minimum procedures required by the Clause."[151] While many courts had recognized total expulsion from public school to be penal in nature and therefore a deprivation of liberty,[152] earlier decisions had not recognized day-to-day school discipline to be of that character.

The jurisprudential effect of this group of cases is to class any conditioned benefit from government as a type of property. Thus, any statutory rights could be classed as property rights though they have none of the traditional characteristics of property.[153] Such creations are unconnected with constitutional language or constitutional history.[154] They are philosophical ventures of Supreme Court majorities adopted in contest with the sharply conflicting philosophies of Court minorities. Since there is no constitutional principle that applies, the majority must tie the cases to law by holding that any legal right may be labeled a property right. The closest analog to this methodology is the creation of substantive due process in a case like *Lochner* v. *New York*.[155]

Underlying the whole issue of welfare rights is the basic separation of governmental powers. Redistribution of national income is a legislative function, not a judicial one. The taxing and spending powers of the national government are vested in the Congress, and the legislature is the center of public choice.[156] The social cost of affording every person receiving governmental largesse a constitutional right to litigate the process of distributing such benefits is very great.

CHAPTER 5

The Commerce Clause

THE COMMERCE CLAUSE IS a prime example of a delegated legislative power whose final interpretation should have been in the Congress under departmental review. Article I, Section 8, Clause 3 states: "The Congress shall have power . . . to regulate commerce with foreign nations, and among the several states, and with the Indian tribes."[1] The economic test is the effectiveness of this language in creating efficient nationwide markets unimpeded by state barriers to trade and governed by uniform congressional regulation to remedy market failures. In 1789 most transactions were local and without effect on national commerce, though a substantial amount moved between states going to and from ocean ports. Over two hundred years, however, economic development, especially in transportation and communications, has given most transactions some national impact. Consequently, most state regulation of commerce has national impact, and if restrictive, will reduce efficiency in the national market.

The evidence presented in this chapter shows that the original meaning of the commerce clause delegated to Congress a plenary power to regulate all private transactions in the nation. In order to prevent state barriers to trade and conflicting state regulations of transactions between states, the national power over interstate and foreign commerce had to be exclusive. The national power over intrastate trade was to be shared with the states, and any conflicts were to be resolved by the supremacy clause. The extent to which this power would be used was left to the political arena, the Congress. Citizens expected their elected representatives—not the appointed, life-tenured, Supreme Court majority—to determine when national regulations would be the most effective.

The commerce clause must be assessed in relation to the prohibitions on state tax of exports and imports in Article 1, Section 10, Clause 2.[2] Legal historians argue that the language and background of this clause demonstrate that it was designed to enforce a national free-trade area by barring all duties on interstate or foreign trade.[3] The Supreme Court, however, has construed this clause to apply only to foreign imports.[4] Consequently, the commerce clause stands alone as a prohibition on customs duties between states.[5]

Mercantilist Background

Before the American Revolution, the colonies were part of the internal free-trade area of the British empire.[6] But on the international level, the political-economic outlook was still one of mercantilism. The strength of the nation was believed to be tied to maximizing exports and minimizing imports. The accumulation of precious metals was thought necessary for the needed increased supply of money that would enable the increased number of transactions characteristic of economic growth. The political economy of the period from 1600 to 1800 centered in a spirit of nationalism that led to interminable conflicts of the European powers.[7] A nominal peace was only a state of undeclared hostility. It is easier to understand the economic nationalism of the mercantile system in the context of these conditions.

The spirit of mercantilism was still dominant when the Revolution made each of the thirteen colonies a sovereign nation. Although Adam Smith's *Wealth of Nations*[8] had been published in 1776, its arguments on the benefits of free trade had not become politically significant by 1787. Thus, leading historians have labeled the economic issues of the Constitutional Convention a "debate among mercantilists."[9] An influential leading document in this tradition is Alexander Hamilton's *Report on Manufactures*,[10] of which Tench Coxe was a probable coauthor. The report recommended barriers to international trade, such as duties high enough to prohibit import of foreign articles that were rivals of domestic ones, prohibitions on the export of materials of manufacture, bounties, premiums, statutory encouragement of new inventions, and laws facilitating transportation.

It is not surprising that merchant groups in most states sought legislative barriers to trade when the colonies became independent. And since the Articles of Confederation did not contain a national commerce power, a likely outcome of prevailing ideology was mercantilist enactments in the separate states. Justice Jackson noted the result:

> When victory relieved the Colonies from the pressure for solidarity that war had exerted, a drift toward anarchy and commercial warfare between states began. "* * * each state would legislate according to its estimate of its own interests, the importance of its own products, and the local advantages or disadvantages of its position in a political or commercial view." This came "to threaten at once the peace and safety of the Union." Story, The Constitution, §§ 259, 260. . . . The sole purpose for which Virginia initiated the movement which ultimately produced the Constitution was "to take into consideration the trade of the United States; to examine the relative situations and trade of the said states; to consider how far a uniform system in their

commercial regulation may be necessary to their common interest and their permanent harmony" and for that purpose the General Assembly of Virginia in January of 1786 names commissioners and proposed their meeting with those from other states.[11]

Representatives of only five states met at Annapolis in September 1786,[12] but they concluded that they alone could not remedy the problem. Consequently, they recommended that a convention be called to review and to revise the Articles of Confederation. Pursuant to this resolution, the Continental Congress requested all of the states to send delegates to Philadelphia in May 1787.[13]

The Virginia delegation was led by Washington, Madison, and Randolph. Since Virginia was largely responsible for calling the convention, its delegates had prepared a series of resolutions that became the basis for initial discussions. These were read by Randolph at the opening of the Convention of 1787.[14] Part of the sixth resolution stated that the national legislature should be empowered "to legislate in all cases to which the separate states are incompetent, or in which the harmony of the United States may be interrupted by the exercise of individual legislation."[15] This resolution was passed by the convention.[16]

There was very little discussion of the domestic commerce power in the Constitutional Convention. Paterson of New Jersey presented a plan that included a power in Congress "to pass acts for the regulation of trade and commerce as well with foreign nations as with each other.[17] The Committee of Detail reported on August 6 with proposed language that was much broader. It gave the legislature power "to regulate commerce with foreign nations, and among the several states."[18] The terms "with the Indian tribes" was added later.

Historians assert that the purpose of the broad power to regulate domestic commerce must be found in all of the prior problems it was designed to remedy. Keeping in mind the canon of construction that the Constitution must be read as an integrated whole, one leading historian of federal jurisdiction wrote in 1934:

> The history and proceedings of the Convention and of the ratifying conventions in the states indicate that the purpose of the commerce clause was to give the Federal Government as much control over commercial transactions as was and would in the future be essential to the general welfare of the union, and there is no suggestion that this power was to be limited to control over movement. The framers of the Constitution would have been exceedingly surprised if they had thought that by the language employed to accomplish that purpose— "commerce among the several states"—they had so restricted the national power as to create a union incapable of dealing with a commercial condition even more serious than the one that had

brought them together. They were acutely conscious that they were preparing an instrument for the ages, not a document adapted only for the exigencies of the time.[19]

Original Meaning

The word "commerce" in 1789, like today, had many meanings. The issue is which meaning applied to a national constitution adopted, in part, to enable the legislature to remedy the many problems of trade and of state regulation of trade that then existed. The narrowest dictionary definition of "commerce" as trade in goods was used in 1789 in the context of marketing merchandise. But the lawyers who drafted the commerce clause as fundamental law for the nation could not have had such a narrow conception. The context of their dealing with commerce was in commercial litigation. The commercial law, also known as the "law merchant," comprehended all transactions for money and in barter.[20] The English and American law reports in the second half of the eighteenth century contained many commercial cases concerning transactions for shipping and insurance services[21] and transactions in legal rights such as bills of exchange and promissory notes.[22]

Legal historians present massive evidence that the idea of general commerce included all gainful activity.[23] This would mean all transactions in agriculture, manufacturing, transportation, and finance, among others. Among the many treatises illustrating this point is Anderson's four-volume history of commerce.[24] A significant part of this study concerns service transactions in the shipping trade. Tench Coxe, noted economist and delegate to the Annapolis convention, wrote, "The commerce of America, including our exports, imports, shipping, manufactures, and fisheries, may properly be considered as forming one interest."[25] Hamilton wrote in the *Federalist* of American marine transport services as "an ACTIVE COMMERCE in our own bottoms."[26]

Chief Justice Marshall noted in *Gibbons* v. *Ogden* that in the eighteenth century the verb "to regulate" was a synonym for the verb "to govern."[27] Regulation included both promotion through subsidy and limitation, including total prohibition.

In the eighteenth century, the preposition "among" also had more than one meaning. In a few contexts, it was used as a synonym for "between." In "treaties among nations" and "hostilities among nations," "among" was substituted for "between" in the context of nations as governments.[28] But in most other contexts, "between" and "among" were not synonyms. At the Constitutional Convention, the Committee of Stile would surely have adopted the words "between states" if they had meant from one territory into another.[29] "Among" would not have been used in an interterritorial sense when territories were contiguous because it would not have been idiomatic English. The enacted language was not the narrower "commerce between the several states" or its synonym, "interstate commerce."

The most common use of "among" in the eighteenth century was "intermingled with" or "in the midst of."[30] Such a use made idiomatic sense when applied to groups of persons, but not when applied to contiguous territories. Chief Justice Marshall noted in *Gibbons* that "among" in the commerce clause meant "intermingled with."[31] The commerce clause seems easier to understand when one uses the definition "in the midst of."

The final step is determining which of the three main uses of the word "state" in the eighteenth century made idiomatic sense with the word "among."[32] As just noted, the territorial sense of state does not fit. This is in contrast to Article IV, where "state" preceded by the preposition "in" could be interpreted in a territorial sense. Second, "state" in the sense of government does not make sense in the commerce clause. The thrust of Article I, Section 8 is not the governance of intergovernmental relations but of the citizens as a whole.

The idiomatic use of "state" in the eighteenth century, like the word "nation" in the same clause, must be determined here in the context of the word "commerce." The third and most common use of "state" in the eighteenth century was as a synonym for "nation," a group of people with a common government.[33] Article I, Section 2, for example, provides that "representatives and direct taxes shall be apportioned *among the several states . . .* according to *their respective numbers.*"[34] It is this collective use of the noun "state" that makes idiomatic sense with "among." This is reinforced by the evidence that the phrase "several states" was a collective term used to refer to the states as a unified group.[35] Commerce in the midst of the several groups of peoples forming the United States meant all of the commerce in which they engaged, which, in modern usage, would include both interstate and intrastate. The conclusion is that by ratifying this clause, the people vested in Congress a plenary power to regulate all commercial transactions of the people of the United States. Thus, it is not surprising that Tench Coxe spoke of one of the measures of the Convention of 1787 as "the establishment of a national legislature with complete powers over commerce and navigation."[36]

Congress's view of its plenary power over commerce is confirmed by the first Congress's passage of the Coasting Act of September 1, 1789.[37] The Congressmen, many of whom were leaders at the Constitutional Convention, adopted a statute licensing vessels "destined from district to district, or to the bank or whale fisheries." This would include both interstate and intrastate travel on the coasts and navigable rivers of the United States. It is notable that this early statute, enacted pursuant to the commerce clause, licensed persons engaging in transactions for the sale of transport services. The first Congress, like the later Supreme Court in

Gibbons v. *Ogden,* viewed commerce as not limited to transactions in goods.

The effect of the Coasting Act was to require a national license even if a shipowner was going to operate only between ports in one state. Thus, there was general acceptance at the time of this regulation that Congress had the power to regulate intrastate commerce. The constitutionality of the statute was not challenged.

Early Cases

The early cases indicate the broad scope of the language, "regulate commerce among the several states." In *United States* v. *William,*[38] which upheld the constitutionality of the Embargo Act of 1807, the issue concerned the scope of the power to regulate foreign commerce. In holding that the power to regulate included the power to prohibit entirely, Judge Davis wrote that "the power to regulate commerce is not to be confined to the adoption of measures, exclusively beneficial to commerce itself, or tending to its advancement; but, in our national system, as in all modern sovereignties, it is also to be considered as an instrument for other purposes of general policy and interest."[39] Noting that the congressional power over foreign commerce was exclusive, Judge Davis went on to speak of those objects that require national regulation: "Commerce is one of those objects. The care, protection, management and control, of this great national concern, is, in my opinion, vested by the Constitution, in the Congress of the United States, and this power is sovereign, relative to commercial intercourse qualified by the limitations and restrictions expressed in that instrument."[40]

In 1820 Chief Justice Marshall, on circuit, had to face the issue of whether shipping service or navigation was part of commerce. In *Wilson* v. *United States,*[41] the issues were whether statutory duties on imports and tonnage applied to foreign privateers and whether a statutory prohibition on bringing a "negro, mulatto or any person of colour" into ports where states barred their entry applied to "coloured" seamen. In holding that under the commerce clause, ships as well as their cargoes may be regulated, Marshall noted that such laws had never been questioned. He stated: "From the adoption of the Constitution, till this time, the universal sense of America has been, that the word 'commerce,' as used in that instrument, is to be considered a generic term, comprehending navigation."[42]

In the 1823 case of *Elkinson* v. *Deliesseline,*[43] Justice Johnson, on circuit, held that the power of Congress to regulate foreign commerce and the interstate part of commerce among the several states was exclusive. An 1822 statute of South Carolina provided that free Negro seamen brought into that state from any other state or foreign port should be seized and jailed until the ship departed the state. If the captain of the ship failed to pay the expenses of such detention, the free seamen were to be declared slaves and sold. Although the action for writ of habeas corpus concerned a British subject, a free Negro seamen in foreign trade, Justice Johnson held the entire South Carolina statute to violate the commerce clause. He rejected the state's argument that it had concurrent regulatory power over interstate and foreign commerce. Johnson, a noted Jeffersonian, wrote: "The right of the general government to regulate commerce with the sister states and foreign nations is a paramount and exclusive right; and this conclusion we arrive at, whether we examine it with reference to the words of the Constitution, or the nature of the grant. That this has been the received and universal construction from the first day of the organization of the general government is unquestionable; and the right admits not of a question any more than the fact. In the Constitution of the United States, the most wonderful instrument ever drawn by the hand of man, there is a comprehension and precision that is unparalleled."[44]

Steamboat Monopoly

The series of cases that arose over the New York state steamboat monopoly provided major additions to the interpretation of the commerce clause. The original grant in 1798 by the New York legislature to Livingston and Fulton was an exclusive right to navigate the waters of the state with steam-propelled vessels.[45] This grant probably came under an exception to the British constitutional tradition against governmental grants of monopoly in the ordinary trades.[46] The exception was designed to promote invention and innovation of a new technique, which thus was not in the ordinary trades. But under the precedents, exceptions to the antimonopoly tradition were to be limited in time. Only short-term monopolies were held to benefit the public by fostering innovation. Thus, when the monopoly of Livingston and Fulton was renewed and extended in 1808 for another thirty years, it was no longer short term, and its validity under English constitutional principles became questionable.

New York enforced the steamboat monopoly both against local vessels and those in interstate commerce. This resulted in retaliatory statutes by New Jersey, Connecticut, and Ohio.[47] If the New York and New Jersey grants of monopoly to rival steamboat companies on the Hudson River had been enforced, steamboat travel between those two states would have had to cease. The greatest public outcry, however, was from New York customers of the monopoly. This provoked New York firms to enter the steamboat business on the Hudson River without securing a license from the monopolists.

The intrastate enforceability of the steamboat monopoly was tested in the New York courts in 1811 in *Livingston* v. *Van Ingen*.[48] The action was for injunction to restrain Van Ingen and associates from operating a steamboat on the Hudson River between New York and Albany. The defendants had failed to obtain a license under the Federal Coasting Act of 1793,[49] even though that statute applied to navigable rivers. Consequently, they did not allege conflict with a national statute. Chancellor Lansing avoided ruling on the commerce clause, denying the injunction on the ground that it violated the natural right of all citizens to free navigation of the waters of the state.[50] The Court of Errors reversed Chancellor Lansing, ruling that since all persons were free to navigate the waters of New York by every power other than steam, no fundamental principle of government was violated. Furthermore, Chief Justice James Kent ruled that the state monopoly had not violated commerce clause in its dormant state. Kent held a broad view of state power over intrastate commerce: "All the internal commerce of the state by land and water remains entirely, and I may say, exclusively, within the scope of its original sovereignty."[51] In 1825, in another intrastate steamboat case subsequent to *Gibbons,* Kent's view of the exclusive state power over intrastate commerce was overruled by the New York court.[52]

The Supreme Court held the application of the New York steamboat monopoly to interstate commerce invalid in *Gibbons* v. *Ogden*.[53] Ogden had an assignment from Livingston and Fulton to operate steamboats from New York to New Jersey. Gibbons was licensed to engage in the coasting trade under the Federal Coasting Act of 1793 and entered the shipping trade in competition with Ogden. Ogden secured an injunction against Gibbons in the New York courts for violation of his monopoly. Chancellor Kent, sitting as trial judge, treated the decision in the *Van Ingen* case as controlling.[54] He held that a federal coasting license, being a mere permission to operate, did not override the New York statute. This was affirmed in the highest court of New York,[55] and appeal was taken to the Supreme Court of the United States.

The Supreme Court reversed the New York decision and held the state monopoly to violate the commerce clause.

The first issue was whether commerce included the sale of transport services, navigation. Given the long-standing acceptance of statutes regulating navigation, the Embargo Act and the Coasting acts, together with lower federal court decisions upholding their constitutionality, it is surprising that this issue was seriously argued. Chief Justice Marshall held navigation to be an integral part of commerce, following his earlier opinion in *Wilson* v. *United States*.[56] "Commerce, undoubtedly, is traffic, but it is something more,—it is intercourse. It describes the commercial intercourse between nations and parts of nations, in all its branches, and is regulated by prescribing rules for carrying on that intercourse."[57] He concluded: "All America understands, and has uniformly understood, the word 'commerce' to comprehend navigation. It was so understood, and must have been so understood when the constitution was framed."[58]

The second issue was the meaning of "regulate commerce among the several states." Marshall noted that "among" meant "intermingled with" and that "to regulate" meant "to govern."[59] But he defined the phrase "among the several states" somewhat differently from what modern historians say it meant in 1789. This was because he failed to recognize that the most common meaning of "state" had changed by 1824. Marshall used "state" to mean a territory, not a group of people with a common government.

Marshall defined "commerce among the several states" as "commerce which concerns more states than one."[60] In modern terms, this is interstate commerce plus that part of intrastate commerce that affects other states. While the facts of the case concerned commerce between states, Marshall's opinion centered on defining the breadth of the phrase. He excluded from national power only that commerce that was completely internal to one state and that did not affect other states. In Marshall's language: "Commerce among the states cannot stop at the external boundary-line of each state, but may be introduced into the interior. . . . The genius and character of the whole government seems to be, that its action is to be applied to all the external concerns of the nation, and to those internal concerns which affect the states generally; but not to those which are completely within a particular state, which do not affect other states, and with which it is not necessary to interfere for the purpose of executing some of the general powers of the government."[61]

Marshall could have confined his opinion to those facts demonstrating the New York attempt to regulate commerce between states (interstate) and ruled that regulation of this sector of commerce among the several states was delegated exclusively to the national government.[62] Had he done this, his negative implication would have been that the New York decision in the *Van Ingen* case was valid law because it applied to ports within one state. But Marshall did not want to do this. The Coasting Act of 1793 expressly applied to transport between custom districts and between ports within one district.[63] Marshall needed the fact of this statute to state a rule broad enough to imply that the decision in the *Van Ingen* case was wrong. Hence, he said, "the sole question is, can a state regulate commerce with foreign nations and among the states, while Congress is regulating it?"[64] He could answer the question with a rule that applied to interstate and intrastate transport on the coasts and the navigable rivers that ran to the coasts.

In conclusion, Marshall held that the commerce clause and the supremacy clause combined vested in the national government the power to preempt regulation of commerce among the several states.[65] The Coasting Act, under which Gibbons was licensed, was treated as a significant national regulation of commerce. It was held to preempt the New York grant of monopoly to Ogden's assignors to navigate the coastal waters of New York.

Justice Johnson, concurring, had a broader view of "commerce among the several states" than did the chief justice.[66] Following his opinion in *Elkinson* v. *Deliesseline*,[67] Johnson in effect stated that the Constitution delegated to Congress a plenary power to regulate commerce. He further viewed the power in Congress to be exclusive. "It can reside but in one potentate; and hence, the grant of this power carries with it the whole subject, leaving nothing for the state to act upon."[68] Under this view, the Federal Coasting Act was not relevant. The national commerce power had ousted the state commerce power. Johnson noted, however, that state health and safety laws applied to goods arriving by ship would not be regulations of commerce and thus would not conflict with an exclusive power in Congress to regulate commerce.[69] Likewise, he viewed the state laws supplying or fostering ferries and turnpikes not to be regulations of commerce.[70]

The application of the national commerce power to intrastate commerce was confirmed by the highest appeals court of New York in holding the steamboat monopoly invalid even in local operation. *North River Steamboat Co.* v. *Livingston*[71] applied the national preemptive rule of *Gibbons* to navigation between ports within New York. The chancellor had originally denied an injunction against operation of a steamboat competing with the monopoly between New York City and Troy even though he viewed the commerce power as limited to interstate commerce.[72] His reason was that under the facts of this case, the boat had stopped en route in Jersey City and thus was for a short time in interstate commerce. By petition and affidavits, the plaintiff asserted that the stops in New Jersey were not bona fide. The chancellor then issued an injunction against direct trips from New York to Troy, but denied an injunction for trips when there was a stop in another state.[73]

Upon appeal, the Court of Errors reversed the order for injunction against intrastate voyages and affirmed the denial of injunction against interstate voyages. The court held that the rule of *Gibbons* v. *Ogden* necessarily applied to intrastate commerce. If ships arriving from other states could make numerous stops in the state of New York under the rule of *Gibbons,* enforcing the monopoly only against local carriers with no interstate stops in their routes would foster the unequal treatment in commerce that the commerce clause was designed to prevent.

There were more fundamental reasons for applying the Coasting Act to intrastate voyages. The court held that the constitutional language vested a plenary power in Congress to regulate all commerce. Chief Justice Savage noted the original meaning of the language: "It was the thought that commerce among the States meant among the people of the states;

that this commerce was internal as related to the Government of the U.S. and its citizens, and as contradistinguished from foreign commerce. It was at that time supposed that the Constitution intended to guaranty to the citizens of the Whole U.S. an equality of commercial rights and privileges."[74]

Pursuant to this broad commerce power in the Coasting Act of 1793,[75] Congress adopted a direct application to intrastate commerce. The act was to apply to ships operating between different districts in different states, between different districts in the same state, and between different places in the same district, on the seacoast or on a navigable river. Given the competition of carriers from many states for this trade, even intrastate trips involved commerce that concerned more states than one. Such trade would not come under Chief Justice Marshall's narrow exception in *Gibbons* for purely internal commerce that did not affect other states.

Limiting State Regulation

In *Brown* v. *Maryland*,[76] the Supreme Court reaffirmed the Constitution as the protector of free markets. Maryland had passed a license tax of $50 on importers or wholesalers before they could sell at wholesale goods brought into the state. The statute was held unconstitutional on two grounds. Even though it was a license tax on importers, it was levied on foreign imports while they were still in their original packages. Thus, it violated Article 1, Section 10, the prohibition on state duties on imports and exports.[77] It also violated the commerce clause because it regulated foreign and interstate commerce. As to the commerce power, Chief Justice Marshall wrote: "The power is coextensive with the subject on which it acts, and cannot be stopped at the external boundary of a state, but must enter its interior. . . . Congress has a right, not only to authorize importation, but to authorize the importer to sell."[78]

The next test of the scope of the commerce clause was in 1829 in *Wilson* v. *Black Bird Creek Marsh Company*.[79] This case explained the operation of the shared national and state powers over intrastate commerce. Chief Justice Marshall sustained a Delaware statute that authorized landowners to build a dam that blocked navigation on a small, navigable tidal creek that ran into the Delaware River. The defendant's sloop broke and injured the dam. Although the defendant was licensed under the Federal Coasting Act, this fact was not relevant because no transport between ports on the coast or navigable rivers was involved. Thus, the "dormant" commerce clause would not override this type of state regulation of local intrastate commerce. But Marshall's dictum noted that Congress could have passed a valid statute concerning small, navigable creeks and the national statute would have preempted that of Delaware.[80] In this case, the Court used cost-benefit analysis. The clear economic benefits from draining marshes greatly outweighed the smaller losses of those forced to terminate navigation. In modern legal terminology, the state burden imposed on commerce among the several states was not undue.

In the first commerce case of the Taney era, a sharply divided Supreme Court had to define the borderline between the police power of the states and the national commerce power. In *New York* v. *Miln*,[81] a New York statute of 1824 required the master of each ship arriving from another country or another state to file a report to the mayor of New York of a set of facts on each passenger debarking. The second section of the statute allowed the mayor to require each master to give a bond of $300 for each foreign passenger to protect the city from the cost of maintenance of those who were destitute. The action was to recover a statutory penalty of $75 per person for one hundred passengers for whom the master filed no report. Justice Barbour, writing for five of the seven justices, held that the statute was not a regulation of commerce in violation of the commerce clause, but a valid exercise of the state's police power.[82] He further stated that even if the statute were considered a commercial regulation, it did not violate the commerce clause because Congress had not acted on the topic.[83] In fact, Congress had recognized the state police power in a 1799 law requiring customs officers to aid in the enforcement of state quarantine and health laws.[84]

Justice Story dissented in the *Miln* case. Though admitting that states have the power to pass health, quarantine, and poor laws, he denied that they have the power to "trench upon the authority of Congress in its power to regulate commerce."[85] The statute required bond in dollars and regulated masters of ships before they landed, and Story found this to be either a regulation of foreign commerce or of commerce with other states, depending on the origin of the ship. Story, citing *Gibbons*, was of the view that the power to regulate foreign and interstate commerce was delegated exclusively to the national government.

Story was subsequently vindicated. In *Henderson* v. *New York*,[86] the requirement of bond for persons arriving from foreign ports was held unconstitutional. In *Edwards* v. *California*,[87] a state barrier to the entry of immigrants was held to violate the commerce clause. *New York* v. *Miln* was overruled.

In the *License Cases* of 1847,[88] the Supreme Court again had to fix a borderline between the local police power of the states and the dormant national commerce power. With six justices delivering separate opinions, the Court upheld statutes of three states regulating and taxing the intrastate sale of alcoholic liquors. In the New Hampshire case, the approved tax was levied on alcoholic beverages from other states still in their original packages, apparently rejecting the general rule of *Brown* v. *Maryland*.[89] Since the regulations and taxes were on goods that had become part of intrastate commerce, and there was no conflicting federal statute, the decision was not inconsistent with earlier cases. Chief Justice Taney's statement on the concurrent national and state power over commerce are not a reversal of earlier law if read, as they should be, to apply to intrastate commerce.[90]

In the *Passenger Cases*[91] of 1849, with eight justices writing separate opinions, the Court held unconstitutional state statutes imposing a tax per passenger on operators of ships bringing immigrants to their ports. This was an attempt at direct taxation of foreign commerce and thus violated the commerce clause.

Before 1850 the Supreme Court had created a consistent pattern of cases and an efficient division of powers: exclusive national power over foreign and interstate (between states) commerce, and a shared national and state power over intrastate commerce. But the many opinions in the *License* and *Passenger* cases left the legal community unsure of this law. The *obiter dictum* of Cooley v. *Board of Wardens*[92] was an attempt to state a general rule. The law of the *Cooley* case was affected by an act of Congress of 1789[93] providing that ship pilots in the bays and harbors of the United States be regulated by existing state law and state law enacted in the future until Congress should provide otherwise. A Pennsylvania statute required pilots on all vessels entering and leaving the state's ports, even though they would be in interstate or foreign commerce. Any master refusing a pilot still had to pay one-half the pilotage fee. As Chief Justice Marshall noted in *Gibbons v. Ogden,*[94] the 1789 act was a congressional adoption of state law passed before 1789 because under the Constitution, Congress may not delegate the exclusive portion of its commerce power to the states. Since the Pennsylvania law was passed in 1803, another rule was needed. The Court held that for state pilot statutes passed after 1789, the act of Congress was a designation that the commerce power was not exclusive on this topic. Justice Curtis, in upholding the constitutionality of the Pennsylvania statute, undertook to categorize the statutes. He wrote: "Whatever subjects of this power are in their nature national, or admit of only one uniform system, or plan of regulation, may justly be said to be of such a nature as to require exclusive legislation by Congress."[95] This broad statement of principle is too general to be useful guidance to counsel in any particular controversy. Although some commentators hailed it as reconciling the law, the rule of the case in allowing state regulation of interstate and foreign commerce was inconsistent with prior law. Justices McLean and Wayne dissented.

Transportation Cases

It was only in the area of transportation that the Supreme Court continued a broad construction of the commerce power as applicable to intrastate commerce. Even though the Court adopted the limiting phrase "interstate commerce" as a synonym for "commerce among the several states," local activities affecting interstate transportation were held subject to federal regulation. A key decision was the *Daniel Ball*.[96] Congress had exercised its plenary power to regulate commerce in a statute designed to remedy the market failure of asymmetric information about safety between owners of and passengers on steamboats. An act of 1838 required licenses and safety inspection of all ships on inland navigable waters. In spite of the fact that the *Daniel Ball* operated entirely in Michigan, the Supreme Court held her subject to the statute because part of the merchandise transported by her originated in or was destined to other states.

This broad construction of the commerce power was applied to railroads after the passage of the Interstate Commerce Act of 1887.[97] The principle that commerce among the several states extended to local acts directly affecting the movement of goods between states was explicitly embodied in the *Minnesota Rate Cases*[98] and the *Shreveport Case*.[99] Local rates could be regulated by Congress because of their competitive relation to interstate rates[100] and their general effect upon railroad revenues.[101] Local trains were subject to federal safety appliance legislation because of the danger to interstate traffic on the same lines if they went unregulated.[102] Maximum hours were validly prescribed for employees engaged in local work connected with the movement of interstate trains.[103]

The Supreme Court also upheld federal statutes prohibiting the transportation between states of some types of goods and persons, though it felt compelled to rationalize such prohibitions on the basis of harmful effects or moral pestilence of the subject matter.[104] Most of the affected statutes were criminal statutes. Among them were the Lottery Act,[105] and Pure Food and Drug Act,[106] the Mann Act,[107] the Adamson Act,[108] the Bill of Lading Act,[109] the Motor Vehicle Theft Act,[110] and the Animal Industry Act.[111] The Court also upheld federal regulation of local stockyards and grain exchanges whose business affected transactions throughout the country.[112] The Court emphasized that the stockyards were but one step in a stream of commerce, since both the cattle shipped in and the meat shipped out were transported between states.

Reduction of the Commerce Power

Starting in 1869 and accelerating toward the turn of the century, the Supreme Court majority made a series of decisions that reduced the national commerce power to substantially less than its original meaning. Like the prior transition of the word "state" from a group of people to a territory, none of the reinterpretations noted here was founded on eighteenth-century meanings. Allowing changes in common usage of words to amend the Constitution is more than just a violation of canons of documentary construction. It violates Article 5, which reserves the amending power to the people. The decisions during this period did not fit the structural and commercial realities of an integrated industrial economy. It is not surprising that starting in 1937 most of these cases were overruled, expressly or impliedly, though again without reference to the original meaning of the commerce clause.

Two ideologies were prominent in American society after the Civil War, whose existence were inconsistent with continuance of the early broad construction of the national commerce power. First, the ideology of laissez-faire, recognized no exceptions in terms of market failures and thus viewed the American industrial revolution of the time as best nurtured without legal controls.[113] The second, the ideology of states' rights, was one element of the effort to heal the social wounds of the Civil War. Both became instruments in the arsenal of the business attorneys to attack national regulation. One would expect that these ideologies would have underlain arguments in the Congress, since the legislative branch of government is where conflicting viewpoints are to be aired and resolved. But, if commercial regulation passed Congress over the opposition of the business community, it was because the majority of citizens in the largely agricultural nation supported such regulation. In contrast, under a government of separated powers it was not expected that the appointed elite that formed the Supreme Court majority would be so overcome with the ideologies of the times that they would remold constitutional language in order to veto Congress. Unfortunately, during this era they were so overwhelmed, and the countermajoritarian use of the judicial power to veto the legislative power became widespread.

The reduction of the commerce power began in 1869 with a limit of the term "commerce" in *Paul* v. *Virginia*.[114] The Court upheld a Virginia statute requiring bonds of foreign insurance corporations up to $50,000. This effectively barred their entry and promoted local monopolies. One basis for the decision was Justice Field's assertion that insurance contracts "are not articles of commerce in any proper meaning of the word. ... Such contracts are not inter-state transactions, though the parties may be domiciled in different states."[115] The decision was contrary to the explanation of Marshall in *Gibbons* v. *Ogden*[116] that all transactions (intercourse), including those for services, were part of commerce.

In 1870 the Court rejected Congress's attempt to assert its plenary power over commerce to regulate the quality of goods in transactions. A federal statute made it a misdemeanor to sell illuminating oils that were flammable at less than 110 degrees. The economic rationale of this regulation is the asymmetric information of sellers and buyers. The regulation was most efficient at the national level. But in *United States* v. *Dewitt*[117] the statute was held unconstitutional as applied to intrastate commerce. Ignoring the view of Marshall in *Gibbons* that commerce among the several states had to extend into the interior of the states, Chief Justice

Chase said the commerce clause implied "a virtual denial of any power to interfere with the internal trade and business of the separate states."[118]

A key shift in interpretation of the word "among" occurred in the *Case of the State Freight Tax*,[119] in which the Court correctly invalidated a state tonnage tax as applied to interstate cargo. The importance to the commerce clause is that this case contained the Court's first authoritative limitation on the word "among." The Court used "between" as a synonym for "among" in this context, and as a result of the Court's adoption of "between," commerce among the several states was to be limited to interstate commerce.

This total exclusion of intrastate commerce from the congressional power was reiterated in 1879 in the *Trademark Cases*.[120] In the Trademark Act of 1870, Congress had exercised what they considered their plenary power to regulate commerce by enacting a general statute for registration and enforcement of trademarks. This was another regulation founded in the economics of information, and it too was most efficient at the national level. Identifying the origin of articles and protection against "passing off" enables consumers to know the producer and attach quality valuations.[121] Following the *Freight Tax* ruling, Justice Miller invalidated the statute. He wrote: "Commerce among the several States means commerce between the individual citizen of different states."[122] All application of the Trademark Act was held unconstitutional because separation of the interstate application from the intrastate application was not possible.

Another major shift in language that further reduced the meaning of "commerce" arose from later courts' misunderstanding of *Kidd* v. *Pearson*.[123] An Iowa statute of 1884 prohibited the manufacture of intoxicating liquors except for medicinal or similar purposes. The law was held constitutional against a distiller whose total output was to be shipped to other states. Justice Lamar stated: "No distinction is more popular to the common mind, or more clearly expressed in economic literature, than that between manufactures and commerce. Manufacture is transformation—the fashioning of raw materials into a change of form for use."[124] Lamar distinguished the physical manufacture of goods from their sale, which is part of commerce. He held, in effect, that state control of the physical manufacture of a dangerous substance was within the police power of the state. Later courts incorrectly cited *Kidd* v. *Pearson* as holding that sale of goods by manufacturers was not commerce.

The effect of this set of cases was that "among" and "commerce" were completely redefined. "Commerce among the several states" was reduced to mean transport between states. This was a fraction of Chief Justice Marshall's "commerce which concerns more states than one." The effect of the shifts in language was to limit the commerce power to interstate movements and those few local activities found to be part of the "stream of interstate commerce" or to have a direct effect on interstate commerce.

Some of the earliest applications of the new, narrow interpretation of the commerce clause were to frustrate the initial fifteen years of the Sherman Antitrust Act[125] except as applied to interstate railroads. The act was designed to remedy the market failure of monopoly. The jurisdiction clause of the Sherman Act, "commerce among the several states," was borrowed directly from the commerce clause. Section 1 applied to agreements in restraint of trade. In *United States* v. *E. C. Knight Co.,*[126] a suit to enjoin agreements to combine almost all the sugar refiners in the United States into one company was dismissed even though the complaint centered on restraint of trade in sales. Although most of the sugar was eventually shipped to other states, the local manufacture of sugar was held not to be commerce. This was an erroneous extension of the rule of *Kidd* v. *Pearson.*[127] In *Knight,* sales transactions by sugar refiners were exempt from antitrust because they were found to have only "indirect" effects on interstate commerce.[128] The same narrow interpretation was applied in dismissing antitrust actions against local stockyards.[129]

It was not until 1905 in *Swift & Co.* v. *United States*[130] that the *Knight* case was distinguished and antitrust revived. A price-fixing combination of local meat packers in one state was held illegal. Since they made purchase and sales agreements with firms in other states, Justice Holmes held that they were "in a current of commerce among the states." In later cases this was called a "stream" of commerce. In *Standard Oil Co.* v. *United States*[131] in 1911, the narrow jurisdictional concept of the *Knight* case was finally overruled.

The laissez-faire bias of the Court majority had its greatest impact in invalidating congressional acts designed to protect employees. The view of the public and the majority of Congress that there were market failures in labor relations requiring legislative action was repeatedly vetoed by five or six members of the Court. Surprisingly, some of these vetoes even occurred in the interstate railroad industry. One railroad case concerned workmen's compensation for injury. The economic basis for statutes requiring such compensation is to force firms to internalize the costs of an externality that arises from the production process.[132] In the first *Employers' Liability Cases,*[133] a 5-to-4 decision invalidated a federal statute making interstate carriers liable for negligent injuries of any employee because it included shop workers who were not in interstate commerce. Congress retreated and passed a similar statute applying only to interstate employees,[134] and this statute was held constitutional.[135] In *Adair* v. *United States,*[136] the Court, with three dissents, invalidated a federal act that forbade interstate carriers from requiring employees not to join unions or from discharging those who did join unions. The Court found no direct connection between membership in a union and the carrying on of interstate commerce.

The leading case invalidating federal labor legislation concerned national uniformity in prohibiting child labor. The economic rationale for regulation was not only the market's failure to protect the health of children. In an industrial economy, where income levels are high enough so that child labor is not necessary for survival, laws prohibiting child labor force parents to keep children in school. The economic effect is to prevent underinvestment in education so that children will acquire the knowledge and skills needed for this highest possible lifetime productivity and income.[137] But in *Hammer* v. *Dagenhart*,[138] a 5-to-4 decision, the Federal Child Labor Act of 1916 was held unconstitutional. The act was drafted in terms of interstate transport because the Court's decisions had reduced the commerce clause to that. It prohibited the shipment in interstate commerce of manufactured articles from factories in which children under fourteen years old were employed in production. Citing the Tenth Amendment, Justice Day held that the regulation of labor transactions of manufacturers was reserved to the states. Commerce begins by "actual delivery to a common carrier for transportation."[139] The Court held that the congressional power to prohibit interstate commerce was limited to articles in themselves harmful or deleterious, such as lottery tickets, impure food and drugs, and prostitutes. Justice Holmes dissented, noting that the constitutional power to regulate interstate commerce was delegated to Congress without qualification: "The Judicial cannot prescribe to the Legislative Departments of the Government limitations upon the exercise of its acknowledged powers."[140]

The Court also frustrated an attempt to control child labor through taxation. In *Bailey* v. *Drexel Furniture Co.*,[141] the Child Labor Tax Law of 1919 was held unconstitutional. This statute had assessed a 10 percent tax on profits of firms employing children under fourteen years of age. This too was ruled an indirect method of governing local manufacture. The unreal distinction between transactions of manufacturers and commerce in these cases inhibited Congress from passing effective labor legislation for another fifteen years.

The economic depression of the 1930s brought new public demands for federal remedies. The resulting National Industrial Recovery Act of 1933[142] provided for industrial codes of self-regulation of output, prices, wages, and hours of work. Economists who were critical of the statute knew that these particular controls were foredoomed attempts at microeconomic solutions for macroeconomic problems of deflation and unemployment. Since the statutes created exceptions to the Sherman Act and promoted monopoly pricing, they would accentuate the depression rather than effect a partial remedy. The legal issues, however, were the administrative standards and the scope of the federal commerce power.

In 1935 in *Panama Refining Co.* v. *Ryan*,[143] output controls in the oil industry were held to be an unconstitutional delegation of legislative power because the indefinite standards in the statute put no controls on the administration. In *Schechter Poultry Corp.* v. *United States*,[144] which concerned the sale of chickens in New York, the Court unanimously struck down the main sections of the statute on the same ground. As a second ground, the Court held the particular application in the poultry code in New York was outside the power of Congress under the commerce clause. It found the effects on interstate commerce to be indirect and that, under the Tenth Amendment, control of such matters was reserved to the states.

Three weeks before the *Schechter* decision, the Court in a 5-to-4 decision, had invalidated the Railroad Retirement Act of 1934.[145] The act had established compulsory retirement and pension systems for railroad employees. The majority held that the statute had purely social ends and no direct relation to interstate commerce. As a result, Congress had to take a new statutory approach to railroad retirement.[146]

Following the *Schechter* case, the Congress attempted a few selective controls of particular industries. The Bituminous Coal Conservation Act of 1935 provided, *inter alia,* for minimum wages and maximum hours for miners whose coal output would subsequently be shipped in interstate commerce. In *Carter* v. *Carter Coal Co.*,[147] by a 5-to-4 decision, the Court held this statute unconstitutional on the ground that mining preceded commerce and here had only an indirect effect upon interstate commerce. This part of the act was also deemed invalid on the ground of unlimited delegation of legislative power.

Restoration of the Commerce Power

The Supreme Court's frustration of the congressional attempts to regulate business and labor relations in a time of economic crisis led President Roosevelt in 1937 to call for legislation of "reorganize the judicial branch."[148] Roosevelt's so-called court-packing plan was to increase the size of federal courts by allowing new additional appointments whenever an incumbent judge reached voluntary retirement age and refused to retire. At that time, six of the nine members of the Supreme Court were past the voluntary retirement age. Coincidentally with this proposal, which was ultimately rejected, the Supreme Court majority shifted, and the restrictive interpretations of the commerce clause and other constitutional constraints on the regulation of business came to an end.

The Supreme Court initiated its return to a broad construction of the commerce clause in 1937 with *N.L.R.B.* v. *Jones & Laughlin Steel Corp.*,[149] a 5-to-4 decision. The National Labor Relations Act of 1935 prohibited unfair labor practices affecting commerce among the several states.[150] Its economic objective was to reduce the transaction costs of negotiating long-term relational contracts between employers and workers.[151] Specifically, it protected the freedom of employees to choose their own representatives and bargain collectively. Chief Justice Hughes, for the majority, upheld the constitutionality of the act and its application to one factory in Pennsylvania. The Court held that congressional authority was not limited by the stream-of-commerce cases. It also explicitly rejected the reasoning of the *Schechter* and *Carter* cases, based on indirect effects upon interstate commerce. The Court stated: "We have often said that interstate commerce itself is a practical conception. It is equally true that interferences with that commerce must be appraised by a judgment that does not ignore actual experience."[152] The conclusion was that the stoppage of the company's manufacturing operations by industrial strife would have a most serious effect upon interstate commerce. In the next two years, the Court reaffirmed the application of the Labor Relations Act to intrastate producers.[153]

In *United States* v. *Darby*[154] in 1941, a unanimous Supreme Court upheld the constitutionality of the Fair Labor Standards Act of 1938.[155] The act prohibited interstate shipment of manufactures where the producer violated the prescribed minimum wages of maximum hours.[156] Darby cut lumber at his Georgia sawmill and sold to customers in other states. He paid less than the legal minimum wage. In the *Darby* case, the government, for the first time in the century, made a major argument based on the meaning of "commerce among the several states" adopted by Chief Justice Marshall in *Gibbons* v. *Ogden*.[157] Unfortunately, though the word "interstate" is not found in *Gibbons,* the Court continued to employ this limiting language. "The power of Congress over interstate commerce is 'complete in itself, may be exercised to its utmost extent, and acknowledges no limitations other than are prescribed in the Constitution.' "[158] In *Darby,* the rule of *Hammer* v. *Dagenhart,*[159] that the power to prohibit articles from commerce was limited to items in themselves harmful or deleterious, was expressly rejected and that case expressly overruled. Justice Stone concluded by noting the relation to the commerce clause of the necessary-and-proper clause and of the Tenth Amendment. As to the former, Congress "may choose the means reasonably adapted to the attainment of the permitted end, even though they involve control of intrastate activities."[160] As to the latter, the Tenth Amendment "states but a truism that all is retained which has not been surrendered."[161] The Fair Labor Standards Act was subsequently held applicable to employees in various occupations in intrastate commerce.[162]

Agriculture cases approving monopoly pricing through regulations demonstrated the most comprehensive federal governance of purely local commerce. The fact that price elasticity of demand for farm output is very low means that farm income can be materially raised by controlling supply.[163] This was achieved through acreage controls and marketing orders limiting domestic sales. In *United States* v. *Rock Royal Cooperative, Inc.,*[164] the Court upheld milk-marketing orders under the Agricultural Adjustment Act of 1935. In *Wickard* v. *Filburn*,[165] the Court upheld wheat-marketing quotas under the Agricultural Adjustment Act of 1938. The decision sustained the allocation of quotas even to crops that were fed to livestock on the same farm. Justice Jackson concluded that "even if appellee's activity be local and though it may not be regarded as commerce, it may still whatever its nature, be reached by Congress if it exerts a substantial economic effect on interstate commerce, and this irrespective of whether such effect is what might at some earlier time have been defined as 'direct' or 'indirect.' "[166]

Restoration of the broad application of federal power to regulate local commerce was also seen in litigation under the antitrust laws. In *United States* v. *South-Eastern Underwriters Ass'n.*[167] in 1944, the Court overruled a 1868 decision and held insurance contracts, each of which is made in a single state, to be a part of commerce. To hold that insurance was not commerce would give the words of the Constitution "a meaning more narrow than one which they had in common parlance of the times in which the Constitution was written."[168] Justice Black referred to Chief Justice Marshall's statement that commerce is among the several states when it "concerns more states than one," or when it will "affect the people of more states than one."[169] In *Mandeville Island Farms Co.* v. *American Crystal Sugar Co.,*[170] in 1948, the Sherman Act was held applicable to an agreement among processors in a single state to fix prices paid farmers in the same state for their sugar beets, on the ground that these fixed input prices would inevitably affect the processors' output price in interstate commerce. Justice Rutledge, speaking of the line between federal and state power over commerce, states, "The essence of the affectation doctrine was that the exact location of this line made no difference, if the forbidden effects flowed across it to the injury of interstate commerce or to the hindrance or defeat of congressional policy regarding it."[171] In the *Women's Sportswear Case*[172] of 1949, the Sherman Act was applied to price-fixing combinations of manufacturers in a single city who dealt only with local jobbers who in turn shipped the goods in commerce. Justice Jackson remarked, "If it is interstate commerce that feels the pinch, it does not matter how local the operation which applies the squeeze."[173]

Recent litigation affirming the broad scope of the commerce clause has been under the Civil Rights Act of 1964.[174] The act guaranteed equal enjoyment of the goods, services, and accommodations of business establishments serving the public without discrimination on the ground of race, color, religion, or national origin. In *Heart of Atlanta Motel, Inc.* v. *United States*,[175] the Court upheld constitutionality of the act in reference to hotels and motels. The statutory language was limited to enterprises having a direct and substantial relation to the interstate flow of goods and people. "The power of Congress to promote interstate commerce also includes the power to regulate the local incidents thereof, including local activities in both the States of origin and destination, which might have a substantial and harmful effect upon that commerce."[176] In *Katzenbach v. McClung*,[177] the Court also upheld the section of the 1964 act pertaining to restaurants. The decision was based on the fact that in one year the restaurant purchased $69,683 of meat from a local supplier who had procured it from outside the state.

The modern interpretation of the commerce clause has in effect returned the clause to its original meaning, a plenary power to regulate American commerce. Thus, Justice Stevens asserted: "Today, there should be universal agreement on the proposition that Congress has ample power to regulate the terms and conditions of employment throughout the economy."[178] Citing *Gibbons* v. *Ogden*,[179] he further stated: "Neither the Tenth Amendment, nor any other provision of the Constitution, affords any support for . . . judicially constructed limitation on the scope of the federal power granted to Congress by the Commerce Clause."[180] The Court may continue to use the limiting phrase "interstate commerce," but it now finds that commerce is affected by all local transactions.

Dormant Commerce Power as a Bar to State Regulation

The dormant commerce power protects interstate and foreign commerce from state regulation when Congress has not enacted regulatory statutes on a topic nor expressly adopted state regulation as effecting national policy. "For a hundred years it has been accepted constitutional doctrine that the commerce clause, without aid of congressional legislation, thus affords some protection from state legislation inimical to the national commerce, and that in such cases, when the Congress has not acted, this Court, and not the state legislature, is under the commerce clause the final arbiter of the competing demands of state and national interests."[181] From an economic viewpoint, the only efficient regulator of carriers or goods moving between states or of transactions between parties in different states is the national government. Conflicting state regulations of such movements or transactions create costs that have to be characterized as economic waste. To raise the key public policy issues, we review the leading cases here.[182]

The Supreme Court has rendered a series of inconsistent decisions on state regulation of commerce over the last fifty years because it has failed to adhere to first principles as found in the structure of the Constitution. The primary principle that the Court has correctly announced and then ignored is that the national power over interstate commerce is exclusive.[183] This should bar all state laws that attempt directly to regulate interstate commerce and those local regulations that discriminate against or materially burden interstate commerce. The classic case is *Wabash, St. Louis &*

Pacific Ry. Co. v. Illinois,[184] in which the Court invalidated a state statute that regulated railroad rates on the in-state portion of interstate shipments even though Congress had not at that time acted to regulate rates.

The leading modern case invalidating a state attempt directly to regulate commerce moving between states is *Southern Pacific v. Arizona.*[185] The state statute limited all passenger trains to fourteen cars and all freight trains to seventy cars during operation within the state. In Arizona, approximately 93 percent of the freight traffic and 95 percent of the passenger traffic was interstate. This statute required Southern Pacific to haul over 30 percent more trains in Arizona than would otherwise have been necessary. The increased cost to the two railroads in Arizona of breaking up and remaking interstate trains was about $1 million per year. Instead of summarily holding the state law an illegal regulation of interstate commerce, the Court made an extensive review of the facts in order to find a serious burden on interstate commerce.[186] It thus treated the alleged safety law when applied to interstate trains as if it were merely a state regulation of local commerce that affected other states.

State regulation of interstate trains in terms of full-crew laws received the opposite treatment. It was validated by the Court in *Brotherhood of Locomotive Firemen & Enginemen v. Chicago R.I. & P.R. Co.*[187] Under an Arkansas statute, railroads operating a line of more than fifty miles and freight trains of more than twenty-five cars were required to have crews of at least six persons. The mileage exemption freed all of Arkansas's seventeen intrastate carriers from the coverage of the statutes, but the Court found this not discriminatory, partly because "the smaller railroads would be less able to bear the cost."[188] Most transport economists characterize full-crew laws as legislative enactment of featherbedding, mandating inefficiency by forcing railroads to hire more labor than needed for safe operations.[189] The district court here had agreed with the economists. It had found that the full-crew requirements had "no substantial effect on safety of operations," placed "substantial financial burdens" upon the carriers, and caused "some delays" and interference with the continuity of railroad operations.[190] The Supreme Court reversed, holding that "the District Court indulged in a legislative judgment wholly beyond its limited authority to review state legislation under the Commerce Clause."[191]

The Court also failed to enforce the exclusive national regulatory power over interstate commerce in ruling on state statutes regulating interstate motor carriers. Like the railroad cases, these decisions were inconsistent. In *South Carolina Highway Dept. v. Barnwell Bros.,*[192] the state statute prohibited on its highways any trucks over ninety inches wide or heavier than ten tons. The statute applied to all trucks, so it did not discriminate against interstate commerce. The Court sustained the state regulation of interstate trucks, asserting that it was for Congress to decide when "local interests should be required to yield to the national authority and interest."[193] Furthermore, it adopted a rational-basis test. When Congress has not acted, the judicial function stops with the inquiry "whether the means of regulation chosen are reasonably adapted to the end sought."[194] "[C]ourts are not any the more entitled, because interstate commerce is affected, to substitute their own for the legislative judgment."[195] *Barnwell* seems inconsistent with *Southern Pacific*.

Later decisions, however, have not been so tolerant of state regulation of national commerce. In *Bibb* v. *Navajo Freight Lines, Inc.*,[196] the Court invalidated an Illinois statute, as applied to an interstate trucker, requiring all trucks operating on Illinois highways to be equipped with contour rear-fender mudguards. The Illinois law had the effect of prohibiting an equally safe mudguard that was legal in forty-five other states. Instead of treating this law as an interference with the exclusive national power over interstate commerce, the Court excused its ruling. "This is one of those cases—few in number—where local safety measures that are nondiscriminatory place an unconstitutional burden on interstate commerce."[197]

In *Raymond Motor Transport, Inc.* v. *Rice*,[198] the Court invalidated a Wisconsin statute that prohibited trucks of over fifty-five feet in length on the state highways. The plaintiffs, operating under Interstate Commerce Commission certificates, were interstate carriers between Illinois and Minnesota over interstate highways in Wisconsin. They were denied permission to operate sixty-five-foot double trailers. In spite of the state's direct regulation of commerce between the states, Justice Powell wrote "that the inquiry necessarily involves a sensitive consideration of the weight and nature of the state regulatory concern in light of the extent of the burden imposed on the course of interstate commerce."[199] Here the state had "failed to make even a colorable showing that its regulations contribute to highway safety."[200]

In *Kassel* v. *Consolidated Freightways Corp.*,[201] the Court invalidated an Iowa law prohibiting sixty-five-foot double-trailer trucks on its highways. The plaintiff was an interstate carrier crossing Iowa on interstate highways. Although Iowa produced substantial evidence to support its safety rationale, the Court found this outweighed by the evidence of burden on interstate commerce.[202] The law added about $12.6 million per year to the costs of trucking companies.[203] Here again, a balancing of interests replaced a general rule that would summarily protect interstate commerce from local control.

Other direct regulations of interstate commerce include state statutes creating barriers or limitations on the movement of goods between states. Such protectionist legislation has been in a few cases summarily invalidated by the courts as an invasion of the exclusive national power over interstate commerce. As Justice Frankfurter wrote: "The very purpose of the Commerce Clause was to create an area of free trade among the several States."[204] In *Baldwin* v. *G.A.F. Seelig, Inc.*,[205] the Court struck down the application of the New York law setting minimum prices paid farmers for milk to producers in other states. The New York law, designed to increase milk prices to all New York consumers, had been sustained as applied to New York producers.[206] The aspect invalidated in *Baldwin* prohibited New York milk dealers from selling milk in that state that had been acquired from out-of-state producers at below the regulated price. Justice Cardozo explained: "Such a power, if exerted, will set a barrier to traffic between one state and another as effective as if customs duties, equal to the price differential, had been laid upon the thing transported."[207]

H.P. Hood & Sons v. *Du Mond*[208] was a milk case whose facts were converse to *Baldwin* since the regulation in question barred the export of milk from New York. By a 5-to-4 decision, the Court held the denial of a license to a Massachusetts milk distributor to operate a third receiving station in New York as in violation of the commerce clause. The bulk of the milk was to be shipped for sale in the Boston market, thus reducing the supply to towns near the plant. The asserted statutory objective of preventing "destructive competition" was found to discriminate against interstate commerce. As to the underlying principle, Justice Jackson noted: "The desire of the Forefathers to federalize regulation of foreign and interstate commerce stands in sharp contrast to their jealous preservation of power over their internal affairs. No other federal power was so universally assumed to be necessary, no other state power was so readily relinquished."[209]

In *Dean Milk Co.* v. *Madison*,[210] a Madison, Wisconsin, ordinance requiring all milk sold in the city to be pasteurized and bottled within five miles of the center of town was held an unlawful discrimination against interstate commerce. Dean Milk Company's plants were in Illinois, sixty-five and eighty-five miles away. The Court concluded that this barrier to trade was unlawful even in the exercise of the city's unquestioned power to protect health and safety of its citizens, if reasonable nondiscriminatory alternatives, adequate to conserve legitimate local interests, were available.[211] The Court found that such alternatives were available, since Madison could impose the cost of inspecting distant milk plants on the processor, or alternatively, could rely on inspection by local officials in other areas, whose standards of inspection were graded by the U.S. Public Health Service. "To permit Madison to adopt a regulation not essential for the protection of local health interests and placing a discriminatory burden on interstate commerce would invite a multiplication of preferential trade areas destructive of the very purpose of the Commerce Clause."[212]

In cases where state statutes or regulations have operated directly to restrict interstate commerce, the Court has often mislabeled them controls on "local public interests." In *Pike* v. *Bruce Church, Inc.*,[213] for example, the Court affirmed the invalidation of an Arizona statute prohibiting the export of uncrated cantaloupes. The grower had efficient packing facilities in California, thirty-one miles from his Arizona ranch. Building a packing facility in Arizona would have required an additional investment of $200,000. Justice Stewart stated the test: "Where the statute regulates even-handedly to effectuate a legitimate local public interest, and its effects on interstate commerce are only incidental, it will be upheld unless the burden imposed on such commerce is clearly excessive in relation to the putative local benefits."[214] As to this case, he concluded: "[T]he Court has viewed with particular suspicion state statutes requiring business operations to be performed in the home state that could more efficiently be performed elsewhere. Even where the state is pursuing a clearly legitimate local interest, this particular burden on commerce has been declared to be virtually *per se* illegal."[215]

Similar failures to recognize the exclusive national power over interstate commerce have caused the Court to treat barriers to trade between states as requiring a balancing act. The Court mistakenly believes that it must make a "delicate adjustment of the conflicting state and federal claims."[216] In *Great A & P Tea Co.* v. *Cottrel*,[217] the Court invalidated a Mississippi reciprocity statute that barred the importation of milk products from other states unless those states signed agreements to admit Mississippi milk products. Adopting the balancing test from *Pike,* Justice Brennan for the Court stated the key finding: "Mississippi's contention that the reciprocity clause serves its vital interests in maintaining the State's health standards borders on the frivolous."[218] He concluded: "Mississippi is not privileged under the Commerce Clause to force its own judgments as to an adequate level of milk sanitation on Louisiana at the pain of an absolute ban on the interstate flow of commerce in milk. However available such methods in an international system of trade between wholly sovereign nation states, they may not constitutionally be employed by the States that constitute the common market created by the Framers of the Constitution."[219] In *Hunt* v. *Washington State Apple Advertising Com'n*[220] the Court affirmed an injunction against a North Carolina statute that in effect prohibited the display of Washington State apple grades on the closed crates shipped into the state. The statute, designed to regulate interstate commerce, was invalidated only because it burdened and discriminated against interstate commerce, and the state failed to justify it in terms of local benefits.[221]

In *Edgar* v. *MITE Corp.*,[222] the Court finally restated the principle that it should have applied in most of the earlier cases: state law that directly regulates interstate commerce is unconstitutional. In voiding the Illinois Business Takeover Law that directly regulated interstate transactions in securities, the Court said: "It is therefore apparent that the Illinois statute is a direct restraint on interstate commerce and that it has a sweeping extraterritorial effect."[223] The Court also found the law unconstitutional under the test of *Pike* because it presented a burden on interstate commerce not offset by the local interests it served. The latter test seems superfluous even though the economic analysis borrowed by the Court is correct.[224]

In a few of the modern cases, the Court has actually approved the direct regulation of interstate commerce by the states. In *Huron Portland Cement Co. v. Detroit*,[225] the Court sustained the application of the Detroit Smoke Abatement Code to ships docked at Detroit, even though the ships were regularly engaged in commerce between states. The fact that the ordinance was nondiscriminatory and the record showed no conflicting regulations of other cities was held to justify local control of interstate carriers.[226] In *Exxon Corp. v. Governor of Maryland*,[227] the Court sustained a Maryland statute providing that no producer or refiner of petroleum products could operate any retail service station within the state. Exxon, which sold mostly in bulk to wholesalers and independent retailers, was forced to divest its thirty-six company-owned stations. These stations were clearly part of the interstate operations of an integrated firm, designed to test innovative marketing concepts or products.[228] Justice Blackmun, in dissent, pointed out that the legislation was protectionist discrimination against what might be the most efficient method of interstate marketing for gasoline. "The Commerce Clause forbids discrimination against interstate commerce, which repeatedly has been held to mean that states and localities may not discriminate against the transactions of out-of-state actors in interstate markets."[229]

In the minority of dormant commerce clause cases where the state regulation is directed at local business activities that have only incidental effects on other states, the Court has correctly upheld the state law. The leading case is *California v. Thompson*.[230] All travel agents in the state were required to pay a license fee of $1 and post a bond of $1,000. The statute was upheld as applied to agents booking interstate tours on interstate highways. The license requirement was designed to prevent fraudulent and unconscionable conduct and did not materially affect the flow of commerce.

The continuing failure of the Supreme Court to distinguish between state regulation of interstate commerce and state regulation of local commerce that affects other states has been the prime source of confusion in applying the dormant commerce clause. Even as strong a supporter of the national commerce power as Justice Black seems mistaken in his dissents to the invalidation of state regulation of interstate commerce.[231] Failing to recognize the exclusive national power over interstate commerce, he argued that the doctrine of the *Cooley* case went too far in limiting state power over commerce. Although Black would strike down state laws discriminating against interstate commerce, his view was that in estimating a mere burden on interstate commerce, the courts had no definite judicial standards. Consequently, they were not performing a truly judicial function, but rather the legislative function of passing on the wisdom of state statutes. He felt it was the duty of Congress to exercise the legislative function of prohibiting any particular nondiscriminatory state regulations of commerce that the Congress thought would be detrimental. He thus interpreted the absence of such statutes as implied congressional approval of state regulation of commerce, both local and interstate. He failed to understand that Congress cannot, by inaction or other means, delegate its exclusive power to regulate commerce between states.

CHAPTER 6

National Commerce Power and State Transactions

THE EXTENT TO WHICH the national commerce power is to apply to transactions of states and their municipalities raises particular issues of federalism and intergovernmental immunities. The plenary power in Congress to regulate commerce among the several states was adopted in a historical context of regulating transactions between private persons or firms.[1] A corollary is that the structure of federalism creates a presumption against national regulation of transactions of the states and their agencies. But the presumption should be rebuttable when states act like proprietors. This chapter will show that state proprietary transactions are so like private transactions that nondiscriminatory regulation of these transactions in order to remedy market failures fits logically and functionally into efficient national markets. In contrast, state purchase of goods and services to be used in executing internal governmental functions does not require national regulation, and states may lose efficiency as a result of such regulation.

Since the monopoly power of the national government to tax and to regulate markets far exceeds the power of any state, there is a great potential for national law to supersede state law entirely. In their efforts to gain or maintain monopoly profits, nationally organized business associations, farmers' groups, and trade unions may find it more feasible and less costly to "buy" legislation from the Congress than from fifty state legislatures.[2] The issue here is the extent of state immunities when federal statutes are extended to control state transactions. The extreme case would be a federal statute regulating the wages that states may pay their governors, cabinet members, legislators, and judges.

This chapter centers on the national commerce power and possible state immunities as illustrated by *Garcia* v. *San Antonio Metro. Transit Auth.*,[3] which overruled *National League of Cities* v. *Usery*.[4] Both of these cases concerned wage transactions between state agencies and their employees.

State transactions like those treated here must be distinguished from state regulation of private commerce. Conflicting national and state regulation of private commerce raises issues under the supremacy clause.[5]

Such issues were recently illustrated in *Federal Energy Regulatory Com'n* v. *Mississippi*,[6] in which the Court held that the national government may set mandatory regulatory standards for electric utilities and that if states choose to regulate such utilities, their regulations must follow the national standards.[7] The issue here was one of national preemption. It was not like national regulation of state transactions in the market, which raises issues of the structure of federalism but not the particular federalism issue raised in preemption.

Structural issues such as federalism and separated powers are not treated explicitly in the Constitution. When such issues are litigated, the Supreme Court often tries to reframe them as issues of individual rights governed by express constitutional limitations.[8] The federal structure created by the U.S. Constitution, with enumerated national powers and residual powers in the states, is emphasized by the Tenth Amendment.[9] It is not useful to regard this structure as state sovereignty acting as a restraint on federal power.[10] Rather, there is merely a division of powers between two coordinate governments. The presumption arising from federalism is that the national and state governments are distinct entities, and that each will administer its own governmental offices. If, for example, Congress enacted a statute requiring all potential state and municipal employees to take and pass U.S. civil service examinations as a precondition to state employment, most commentators would label it unconstitutional.

There has not been much litigation over congressional invasion of the internal administration of state governments because Congress, being composed of representatives of the states, has generally refrained from such incurrences.[11] Chief Justice Chase noted that "the Constitution, in all its provisions, looks to an indestructible union, composed of indestructible states."[12] As Madison observed, "The Federal and State governments are in fact but different agents and trustees of the people, constituted with different powers, and designed for different purposes."[13]

The one pertinent example of federal invasion of state internal administration was *Coyle* v. *Smith*.[14] The national statute admitting Oklahoma as a state had an express condition that the capital remain fixed for a stated period and that no state funds be appropriated for building a capital. This statute was held unconstitutional on the ground that it invalidated "essentially and peculiarly state powers."[15] The structure of state government, as long as it meets the requirement of a republican form of government, is peculiarly a state issue.[16] Thus, the size of state legislative bodies, and the number and terms of office of state executives are presumed to be independent of congressional control. The further issue, raised in *Garcia* and *National League of Cities*, is whether internal employment policies of the states are subject to federal control.

A key issue, contested in *Garcia*, is whether the judiciary has a part in enforcing federalism by declaring federal statutes that invade the residual powers of the states to be unconstitutional. As noted, historically, the answer to this issue of judicial review is affirmative.[17] Judicial review was a key basis of persuading the public to support ratification.[18] Chapter 2 argued, however, that the final determination of the scope and breadth of the enumerated powers in Article I was vested in Congress. Here the limit of that power is tested. When congressional acts under the tax or commerce power are asserted directly against the states as governments, the issue is one of federalism subject to judicial review. The scope of the commerce power when applied to transactions of private persons and firms should be determined finally by Congress. But attempts of Congress to extend the commerce power to state transactions puts in contest issues of the federal structure of government, ultimately a judicial issue.

National regulation of state transactions presents a potential conflict between an enumerated power of Article I and the residual power of the states under federalism to administer their own governments. The fact that one constitutional clause is stated expressly and the other is implicit in constitutional structure should not determine any given case.[19] The Supreme Court must resolve the potential conflict by setting the border-lines between the two. Since the commerce clause was adopted in the context of regulating private transactions, one might expect the commerce power to extend only to state transactions that are like private ones, proprietary transactions. On the other hand, state transactions for the administration of government should be immune from national regulation to enforce the principle of federalism. The distinction between governmental and proprietary transactions is the basis of the following critical analysis.

State Proprietary Transactions

The distinction between governmental and proprietary transactions has been controversial.[20] When the function of a state agency centers on commercial or proprietary transactions, both this function and the input transactions of the agency, such as employment relations, are subject to national regulation. Although the Supreme Court prefers to classify activities negatively, identifying those that are not traditional governmental functions, it extends a positive classification to proprietary functions. An activity is "proprietary" when the function centers on buying or selling goods or services. While state agencies often operate at a loss, which means that purchasers receive a partial subsidy, the goods or services they offer do not fall in the economic class "public goods." The goods or services they offer can be supplied by private firms, and each consumer can purchase the amount of service he desires without conferring benefits on others.

The leading precedent on national regulation of state proprietary services was *United States* v. *California*,[21] which held a railroad operated by California in commerce among the several states subject to national safety statutes. Although the activity was clearly proprietary, Justice Stone wrote, "[W]e think it unimportant to say whether the state conducts its railroad in its 'sovereign' or in its 'private' capacity."[22] Instead, he emphasized that the plenary power in Congress to regulate commerce applied to all the activities of an intrastate carrier operating in interstate commerce, even if owned by a state.

Proprietary activities of states were held subject to national taxation in *New York* v. *United States*.[23] There, a nondiscriminatory federal tax on sellers of bottled mineral waters was applied to New York, and its immunity was denied. Justice Frankfurter, for the Court, held that denying state immunity because an activity was proprietary was too narrow a characterization. He held that states were subject to all nondiscriminatory federal taxes except those that would tax states as states.[24] He exempted functions that were uniquely governmental like the statehouse and the states' tax income. In *Garcia*, Justice Blackmun wrote that the *New York* case abandoned the distinction between governmental and proprietary functions,[25] but this seems to overstate the case. Frankfurter cited state proprietary cases as one class of those subject to nondiscriminatory federal taxes.[26]

The leading recent case concerning state proprietary transactions is *United Transp. Union* v. *Long Island R. Co.*[27] The railroad, primarily a commuter carrier that also carried freight from Long Island to New York, was owned by an agency of New York. The Supreme Court held that the railroad was subject to the federal Railway Labor Act that permitted collective bargaining instead of New York law that prohibited strikes by public employees.[28] The railroad, founded in 1834 and acquired by the Metropolitan Transportation Authority in 1966, was subsidized by the state, but operated as a separate and distinct public corporation.[29] The state maintained that the national regulation impaired the ability of the state to carry out a constitutionally preserved sovereign function and was thus a violation of the Tenth Amendment. A unanimous Supreme Court held that operation of railroads in interstate commerce was not a traditional governmental function.[30] National regulation of a state-owned railroad would in no way hamper the state government's ability to fulfill its role in the Union nor endanger its "separate and independent existence."[31] National regulation of railway labor relations had been in effect since 1888, and a uniform regulatory scheme was held necessary to the operation of the national rail system.

As background to *Garcia*, it is notable that three courts of appeal have treated public transit as a proprietary function.[32] Relying on the *Long Island* opinion, the courts held that local transit authorities are subject to national regulation under the Fair Labor Standards Act. In *Kramer* v. *New Castle Area Transit Authority*,[33] the Court emphasized the finding that local mass transit is not a traditional governmental function. Rather, mass transit has historically been owned and operated by private companies, and the recent socialization of most local transit does not alter "historical reality." In *Alewine* v. *City Council of Augusta, Ga.*,[34] the Court cited the reasoning of the *Kramer* case.[35] Noting that both the commuter railroad in the *Long Island* case and local buses in Augusta carried commuters for payment, it held that selling transport service is not a traditional governmental function. In *Dove* v. *Chattanooga Area Regional Transportation Authority*,[36] the Court also cited and followed *Kramer*.[37] Quoting the *Long Island* case, the Court noted that "there is no justification for a rule which would allow the States, by acquiring functions previously performed by the private sector, to erode federal authority in areas traditionally subject to federal statutory regulations."[38]

The concept of proprietary functions has been elaborated in two recent cases concerning the commerce clause.[39] In essence, the Supreme Court has held that state proprietary activities cannot be challenged under the commerce clause as a burden on commerce among the several states. This view is, of course, consistent with the view that proprietary activities are subject to national regulation and can be curbed or totally banned by Congress.

Hughes v. *Alexandria Scrap Corp.*[40] is the modern authority that state proprietary activity may not be challenged as a burden on interstate commerce. The main problem with the case is that the state action in question was in fact not proprietary. A Maryland state subsidy for delivering abandoned automobiles to a licensed processor discriminated against out-of-state processors.[41] Justice Powell, missing a key distinction of economics,[42] treated the subsidy as a state purchase.[43] Having erroneously held Maryland the equivalent to a private participant in the market, the Court held that Maryland as "purchaser" could have offered the subsidies only to domestic processors.[44] The derelict autos were found to have remained in the state, not because of trade barriers, but in response to market forces. "Nothing in the purposes animating the Commerce Clause prohibits a State, in the absence of congressional action, from participating in the market and exercising the right to favor its own citizens over others."[45]

While the facts of the *Alexandria Scrap* case did not concern proprietary state action, the principle announced was clearly correct. This is illustrated by *Reeves* v. *Stake*.[46] South Dakota had engaged in the proprietary activity of operating a cement plant for over fifty years. The plant had been built to assure users in South Dakota of a supply of cement in times of shortages. In 1978, a time of construction boom, the state cement commission reaffirmed its policy of supplying all local customers first. Reeves, a

Wyoming customer of the plant, was informed that the South Dakota state cement plant could not continue to fill Reeves's orders, and Reeves sued for an injunction, which the district court granted. After two appeals,[47] the Supreme Court upheld the South Dakota policies on the basis of *Alexandria Scrap*.[48] The state as market participant could not be found to burden commerce in violation of the commerce clause. As Professor Tribe has noted,[49] the dormant commerce clause was a limitation only on the regulatory and taxing actions taken by states in their sovereign capacity. The court noted, however, that state proprietary activities may be, and often are, subjected to the same national regulation that is imposed on private market participants.[50] The South Dakota plant, together with all other cement plants in the United States, could be subjected to a congressional allocation statute. But absent such a statute, each producer was free to choose its own customers.

State Governmental Transactions

In terms of economic efficiency, the services of states and municipalities can best adjust to market conditions through local control. Given different levels of economic development in different areas and some immobility of labor, both per capita income and market wage levels may vary from state to state.[51] States with lower incomes as a source of taxation may also have lower wages for unskilled and semiskilled labor.[52] Nevertheless, powerful national unions have been able to convince a majority of both houses of Congress to extend the Fair Labor Standards Act to all government employees.[53]

The minimum-wage requirements of the law have particular application to unskilled and part-time workers such as high school students, but they have not been the major source of litigation. Instead, the main challenge to national regulation has been in connection with overtime requirements, as applied to workers with wages far above the minimum, including workers like policemen, firemen, and bus drivers, with necessarily extended work-time patterns.

Governmental transactions concern the supply of public goods, those which it is not economically feasible for a citizen to provide for himself because of economies of scale and the "free-rider" problem.[54] The latter problem concerns uncompensated benefits conferred on others. If one citizen, in fear of criminals, hired private police to protect a sector of the city where he lived, other citizens would benefit though they would not pay.

In most cases, public goods can be feasibly provided only by government, the one agency able to finance them by compulsory taxation. The consumption of public goods is "nonrival" which means that consumption by one person does not reduce the benefits received by others. The same benefits are available to all without mutual interference.[55] Taxpayers, for example, vote collectively to purchase primary education for all children in the community. There is private gain to the children and their parents. But taxpayers are also purchasing the externalities, the benefits to the general public from a literate society. The public good is a citizenry that is able to read instructions necessary to hold semiskilled jobs, and a citizenry able to read sufficiently to understand the issues of a democratic society and vote intelligently. No taxpayer could buy these public benefits by himself, and the public benefits are shared by all, so that it would be inefficient to try to exclude anyone from the benefits even if this were feasible.

Maryland v. *Wirtz*[56] was the first case to test the extension of the Fair Labor Standards Act to state and municipal employees. A 1966 amendment to the act applied to state hospitals, institutions, and schools.[57] In upholding the statute, Justice Harlan discussed the great breadth of the commerce clause without recognizing that it was adopted in the context of private transactions, not state transactions. He then asserted that "it is clear that the Federal Government, when acting within a delegated power, may override countervailing state interests whether these be described as 'governmental' or 'proprietary' in character."[58] Relying on the proprietary case of *United States* v. *California*,[59] Harlan stated that the Court "will not carve up the commerce power to protect enterprises indistinguishable in their effect on commerce from private business, simply because those enterprises happen to be run by the States for the benefit of their citizens."[60] Justices Douglas and Stewart dissented. Douglas asserted that "what is done here is . . . such a serious invasion of state sovereignty protected by the Tenth Amendment that is it in my view not consistent with our constitutional federalism."[61] Douglas agreed with the dissenting judge in the district court that Congress was forcing the state either to increase taxes or curtail services. Recognizing that the Court must draw the line between the commerce power and the residual powers of the states, he concluded: "In this case the State as a sovereign power is being seriously tampered with, potentially crippled."[62]

National League of Cities v. *Usery*[63] overruled *Wirtz*. For the first time the Court held that the state as employer was in some activities immune from national commerce regulation. The 5-to-4 decision has received voluminous comment.[64] In the 1974 amendments to the Fair Labor Standards Act,[65] Congress extended the wages and hours provisions to all employees of states and agencies created by states except for executive, administrative, and professional personnel. Actions by a number of states and municipalities challenged the application of the amendments to "traditional" governmental functions such as fire protection, police protection, sanitation, public health, and parks and recreation. The Court invalidated the application of the amendments to traditional governmental functions. Justice Rehnquist's opinion for the majority indicated that the decision rested not on the scope of the commerce clause, but on the character of federalism.[66] Although Congress clearly had a plenary power under the commerce clause to regulate local wages and hours of employment in private endeavor that affected other states, regulating those of state governmental employees raised issues of intergovernmental immunity.

Justice Rehnquist held that when the output functions of the state employees were traditional governmental ones, the input function of determining wages was an "undoubted attribute of state sovereignty."[67] He reviewed a number of examples where increased labor cost would materially affect governmental policies. The national policies "may substantially restructure traditional ways in which the local governments have arranged their affairs."[68] The conclusion was that the wages and hours provisions would "impermissibly interfere with the integral governmental functions"[69] of the states and their subdivisions. They would "significantly alter or displace the States' abilities to structure employer-employee relationships in such areas as fire prevention, police protection, sanitation, public health, and parks and recreation."[70] These were typical examples of public goods.

Although *National League of Cities* was obviously based on the structure of constitutional federalism, the opinion was not articulate on this primary issue. The opinion did note the states' contention that their residual powers are an affirmative limitation on delegated national powers, but it offered no full explanation of intergovernmental immunities.[71] Instead, Rehnquist introduced the issue in terms of the Tenth Amendment as an express declaration of "the constitutional policy that the Congress may not exercise power in a fashion that impairs the States' integrity or their ability to function effectively in a federal system."[72] This whole approach seems wrong, or at least unnecessary, since the entire federal structure was in the original Constitution.[73] To discredit the argument that the Tenth Amendment created distinct policy, the dissenting justices in *National League of Cities* correctly quoted Justice Stone's statement.[74] But this did not meet the underlying issue of the scope of implied intergovernmental immunities in the federal system.

Rehnquist cited dicta from two earlier decisions that had upheld national regulation of state transactions. In *Wirtz*, the Court had noted that it had "ample power to prevent . . . the utter destruction of the State as a sovereign political entity."[75] In *Fry* v. *United States*,[76] the Court recognized that federalism is expressly declared in the Tenth Amendment: "The Amendment expressly declares the constitutional policy that Congress may not exercise power in a fashion that impairs the States' integrity or their ability to function effectively in a federal system."[77]

Rehnquist's use of the ambiguous term "traditional" may have misled him.[78] Some proprietary functions, such as subways in New York, have a "tradition" of government operation. But the true issue for the purposes of federalism ought to be whether the function is necessarily governmental—whether it is a public good. In overruling *Wirtz*, the Court recognized that the public hospitals, institutions, and schools of that case were different from the fire and police departments affected by *National League of Cities*.[79] Nevertheless, both classes were nonproprietary governmental services, essential to the public as a whole. The free hospitals and institutions for the destitute or insane in the *Wirtz* example benefited those unable to purchase these services in the market; but they also gave external benefits to all other citizens, who were protected, *inter alia,* from contagious diseases and injury or theft by insane persons.

Although the legal criteria for state immunity set by *National League of Cities* were not precise, it seems clear that its application only to "states as states" meant the internal government of states and not state regulation subject to the supremacy clause. But later court decisions have demonstrated confusion on this primary distinction.

Hodel v. Virginia Surface Mining & Reclamation Ass'n[80] arose under the Surface Mining Control and Reclamation Act of 1977 (SMCRA), a federal statute designed to guarantee that surface mining will be completed with least possible disturbance to the earth's surface.[81] The statute allowed the states to submit reclamation plans for approval by the secretary of interior, but the secretary was directed to prepare a federal program for those failing to submit programs.[82] The lower courts[83] failed to recognize that the federal statute was a regulation of private behavior, and erroneously relying on *National League of Cities,* they held key sections of the statute to violate the Tenth Amendment.

In the *Virginia Surface Mining* case a unanimous Supreme Court reversed the district courts' holding of sections of SMCRA unconstitutional. Justice Marshall should have distinguished *National League of Cities* as inapplicable to statutes regulating private industry. But instead, he attempted to clarify the vague tests of *National League of Cities* by extracting from the opinion a three-step test for determining whether a federal statute enacted pursuant to the commerce clause violates the constitutional structure of federalism.[84]

Regulation of "states as states" seems to indicate regulation of state governmental institutions rather than of individuals and corporations. But in the *Virginia Surface Mining* case, the congressional objective was to regulate private mining companies. "Indisputable attributes of state sovereignty" seems to concern policymaking for or administration of internal functions of operating a state government, for example, power to locate the state capitol or to set wages for those employed to carry out governmental functions.[85] "Directly impair the States' ability to structure integral operations in areas of traditional functions" is more complex.

The Court speaks of it as congressional displacement of state decisions that "may substantially restructure traditional ways in which the local governments have arranged their affairs."[86] The effects on state managerial decisions must be more than material. They must significantly change state operating procedures.

The final statements by the Court on the preemptive power of Congress under the supremacy clause should have impressed upon all lower courts and critics that *National League of Cities* did not apply to state regulation of private economic activity.[87]

Federal Energy Regulatory Commission v. *Mississippi*[88] reiterated the ruling of the *Virginia Surface Mining* case. Here the Court, faced with issues of federal conditional preemption of state regulation of private economic activity, upheld the constitutionality of the federal Public Utility Regulatory Policies Act of 1978 (PURPA).[89] The act concerned regulatory policies for gas and electrical utilities, requiring state public-utility commissions to "consider" the adoption and implementation of specific "rate design" and regulatory standards.[90] It prescribed procedures for considering proposed standards. One section encouraged cogeneration by requiring the Federal Energy Regulatory Commission to promulgate rules in consultation with state agencies.[91]

The district court held that PURPA (1) exceeded the power of Congress under the commerce clause, and (2) under *National League of Cities*, violated federalism by trenching on state sovereignty.[92] The Supreme Court reversed the trial court on the commerce clause issue unanimously, and reversed the lower court on the federalism issue by a vote of 5 to 4. As to the latter, Justice Blackmun, for the Court, noted that "the commerce power permits Congress to preempt the States entirely in the regulation of private utilities."[93] PURPA gave the states a choice of adopting federal standards or abandoning regulation of the field altogether, even though Congress had not yet adopted alternative regulation. The Court noted that this was only one step beyond *Virginia Surface Mining*. Since PURPA did not regulate the "states as states" but was concerned with utility regulation, the act did not impair the states' abilities "to structure integral operations in areas of traditional functions."[94]

The surprising aspect of the federalism part of *FERC* was the four dissents. Justice O'Connor, in the principal dissent, was primarily concerned that the federal scheme required the states to use their regulatory machinery in a fashion dictated by the national government. But she failed to see that the key explanatory point of *Virginia Surface Mining:* that *National League of Cities* applies only to state transactions and not to state regulation of private economic activity.[95] She erroneously viewed PURPA as analogous to the statutory provisions in *National League of Cities*. But the conditional preemption of regulation in *FERC* was based on the supremacy clause, while *National League of Cities* concerned intergovernmental immunity.

One recent case that seems inconsistent with *National League of Cities* approved national regulation of state transactions with an employee performing a police function. In *Equal Employment Opportunity Commission* v. *Wyoming*,[96] the issue of age discrimination was treated under the commerce clause rather than the Fourteenth Amendment.[97] The Age Discrimination in Employment Act of 1967,[98] prohibiting discrimination on the basis of age for employees between the ages of forty and seventy, was extended in 1974 to include employees of state and local governments.[99] When a supervisor for the Wyoming Game and Fish Department was involuntarily retired at age fifty-five, the supervisor filed a complaint with the Equal Employment Opportunity Commission (EEOC), which ultimately brought an action against the state. The district court dismissed the suit on the basis of the rule in *National League of Cities*,[100] but the Supreme Court reversed in a 5-to-4 decision.

In applying the tests derived from the *National League of Cities*, the final one was found wanting. The first requirement, that the national statute must regulate "states as states," was plainly met.[101] The second, that the national statute must address an undoubted attribute of state sovereignty, was not clear. But, even assuming the second test to be met, the third was not met. The Age Discrimination in Employment Act did not "directly impair" the State's ability to "structure integral operations in areas of traditional governmental functions."[102] Thus, the Court concluded that the degree of federal intrusion in the *Wyoming* case was "sufficiently less serious than it was in *National League of Cities* so as to make unnecessary . . . to override Congress's express choice to extend its regulatory authority to the States."[103]

The small impact of the Age Discrimination Act on Wyoming was shown by the fact that the state could continue its mandatory retirement age if the state could demonstrate that age was a *bona fide* occupational qualification for a job as a game warden.[104] Furthermore, unlike in *National League of Cities*, in *Wyoming* there was no potential impact of the mandate of the Age Discrimination Act on the "State's ability to structure operations and set priorities over a wide range of decisions."[105] The large potential financial impact of national regulation in the former case was absent in the *Wyoming* case. The final distinction was that in *Wyoming*, there was no impairment of the state's ability to use its employment relationship with its citizens as a tool for pursuing social and economic policies beyond their immediate managerial goals.[106]

Having found application of the Age Discrimination Act to state employees to be a valid exercise of Congress's powers under the commerce clause, the Court held that it need not decide whether the statute could be upheld as an exercise of Congress's powers under Section 5 of the Fourteenth Amendment.[107] Critics of the opinion often find this to be an evasion of an essential issue.

The Age Discrimination Act had material impact on those able to avoid compulsory retirement and on those not promoted because the lack of retirements meant that there were no new openings. The problem is whether constitutional issues of federalism should turn on the relative size of admittedly material impacts of statutes. If the majority opinion as based on the commerce clause is basically unsound, then it is crucial whether the statute can be based on Section 5 of the Fourteenth Amendment. Since the statute is an amendment to the Civil Rights Act[108] and is concerned with equality of treatment for the aged, its primary purpose would seem to be to enforce the equal protection clause. Any functional analysis would treat the statute as one enforcing equal protection.[109]

Chief Justice Burger, for the four dissenters, also analyzed the case in terms of the three tests of National League of Cities as delineated in the Virginia Surface Mining case. As to the first, he concurred with the majority opinion that the legislation was aimed at regulating states as states.[110] As to the second, he found that the Age Discrimination Act addressed matters that were "attributes of state sovereignty."[111] Mandatory retirement laws to assure physical preparedness for game wardens were viewed as an attribute of sovereignty because National League of Cities identified parks and recreation services as traditional state activities. And, the chief justice also found that Wyoming met the third test. He felt that the federal intrusion would materially impair the ability of the state to structure integral operations. He emphasized the evidence that employment costs and disability costs could potentially increase materially.[112] He also concluded there would be noneconomic hardships if the state could not hire those physically best able to do the job and had to impede promotion opportunities as upper-level, supervisory personnel refused to retire.

The majority and dissenters both adopted without question the three-step approach to National League of Cities that was outlined in Hodel v. Virginia Surface Mining and Reclamation Ass'n.[113] Since the latter case was one of preemptive regulation, its statements on National League of Cities were dictum. One would have expected the dissenters to reject the idea that general principles of federalism can turn on detailed factual issues of financial impact of a federal regulation. But the dissent could have easily rested on the key distinction that the state employee in the Wyoming case was performing a police function, an admitted governmental regulatory activity. And if one adopts this analysis, the majority opinion in the Wyoming case is inconsistent with National League of Cities.

Lower-Court Confusion

The lower federal courts also showed great uncertainty in applying *National League of Cities*. Many opinions centered on the word magic of "traditional governmental functions" rather than on the impact on federalism. Justice Blackmun in *Garcia* cited five cases that granted state immunity under this concept.[114] It is clear in these cases that the lower courts did not understand the primary distinction between state transactions and state regulation of private business. Two of the five cases concerned municipal grants of monopoly to private firms and the possible exemption from antitrust preemption under the supremacy clause.[115] One concerned conflicting federal and state judicial powers and not federal regulation of states.[116] Two cases granted immunity from the Fair Labor Standards Act for employment activities found to be integral government functions.[117]

Justice Blackmun in *Garcia* also cited eight cases denying state immunity under *National League of Cities*.[118] Three of these cases concerned conflicts between national and state regulation and should have been governed by the supremacy clause,[119] since issues of federalism were not present. Three other cases concerned state transactions that were not uniquely governmental.[120] Two other cases concerned application of the Fair Labor Standards Act to state welfare workers.[121] Such activity was held not to be a traditional or integral function of a state, and immunity was denied.

Some of the lower-court decisions can be reconciled if one applies the primary distinction between state regulation and state transactions. The air-transport cases exemplify the issue. In *Hughes Air Corp* v. *Public Utilities Com'n*,[122] state regulation of air transport was ruled to be preempted by federal regulation. This was a simple application of the supremacy clause, and *National League of Cities*, cited in denying immunity, should have not been mentioned. In contrast, *Amersbach* v. *City of Cleveland*,[123] which concerned employment transactions, application of the Fair Labor Standards Act to employees of a municipal airport, correctly posed the issue of federalism. Although some critics disagree, it is within reason to find this function uniquely governmental and grant state immunity.

The San Antonio Cases

The San Antonio cases, litigated in *Garcia* v. *San Antonio Metro Transit Auth.*[124] concerned mandatory overtime pay under the Fair Labor Standards Act (FLSA) as applied to local transit. The economic issue is the necessity of overtime in industries with two demand-peak loads that do not occur in one eight-hour period.[126] Labor unions have negotiated that workers cannot be employed on a split shift where some (with less seniority) are off the payroll for four hours in midday. Given this constraint, the most efficient payroll employs some drivers more than eight hours on certain days with compensatory time off on other days.[127] The FLSA amendments required overtime pay at time-and-one-half rates, paid in cash. The budget effects on local transit, operating at a loss and surviving on taxpayer subsidies, was significant. In fact the wage levels previously established far above the minimum wage, had resulted from collective bargaining that took account of the often-extended workday. The bargaining result in most cities was high standard wages with compensatory time off for work beyond the eight-hour day. This equilibrium compensation was upset by the imposition of mandatory overtime pay by the FLSA.[128] Established union contracts and great union power made it impossible ever to lower basic wages to offset the new, high overtime pay.

Garcia brought the issue of overtime pay under FLSA for public mass-transit workers to the Supreme Court. The legal background to this case was the rule of National League of Cities that exempted from FLSA only traditional governmental functions. San Antonio had been served from early in the century by privately owned companies. Only in 1959 was the tradition of private ownership replaced by a public authority.[129] Nonetheless, four months after National League of Cities was handed down, the San Antonio Transit System notified employees that it was relieved of overtime pay obligations under FLSA.[130]

In 1979 the Wages and Hours Administration of the Department of Labor issued an opinion that San Antonio Metropolitan Transit Authority's (SAMTA) operations were not constitutionally immune from FLSA under National League of Cities.[131] SAMTA then filed this action for declaratory judgment against the secretary of labor, and Garcia and other employees brought suit against SAMTA for overtime pay. The district court ruled twice, once before and once after the Long Island R. Co. decision, that public mass-transit was an immune traditional governmental function.[132]

In reversing the district court in a 5-to-4 decision, the Supreme Court did not take the easy course of holding transactions of local transit districts a proprietary function outside the scope of National League of Cities immunity.[133] Rather, the majority overruled National League of Cities, holding that "traditional governmental functions" were not a workable standard.[134] The Court noted the apparently conflicting opinions of lower federal courts in trying to apply the standard.[135] It noted cases in the area of state-tax immunity and the difficulty of concepts such as "essential," "usual," "traditional," or "strictly" governmental functions.[136] But it was in the tax field that the Court came to reject the distinction between governmental and proprietary functions. It found that a nonhistorical standard is also likely to be unworkable, noting the rejection of the concept "uniquely" governmental functions in the field of government tort liability.[137]

Justice Blackmun, for the majority, held that none of the distinctions in governmental functions could be "faithful to the role of federalism in a democratic society."[138] He concluded that classifying governmental functions as "traditional," "integral" or "necessary" "inevitably invites an unelected federal judiciary to make decisions about which state policies it favors and which it dislikes."[139] He therefore rejected any such rule of state immunity as "unsound in principle and unworkable in practice." The Court did not deny that the federal structure of government imposes limitations on the commerce clause as applied to the states. But the conclusion was: "We doubt the courts ultimately can identify principled constitutional limitations over the State merely by relying on *a priori* definitions of state sovereignty."[140]

The Court found that the portion of sovereignty remaining in the states was protected by the states' position in the national political process.[141] It noted the local interests of congressmen and the equal representation in the Senate. It also noted that the federal political process was demonstrably effective in protecting the states, as illustrated by the large revenue sharing by the national government with the states.[142] As to the specific application of FLSA to local transit, the Court found nothing destructive of state sovereignty or violative of any constitutional provision.[143] The Congress provided substantial fiscal aid to local mass transit because it required conformity in minimum wages and overtime pay.

Justice Powell for the four dissenters, criticized the majority for overruling *National League of Cities*.[144] Justice Blackmun, who had concurred in that case, and other justices in the majority had joined in subsequent decisions that applied the tests of *National League of Cities*. In *Garcia*, they could have reversed the district court by applying the proprietary classification of *Long Island R. Co.*, but instead they chose to overrule their own reaffirmed views of the tests of federalism.

As to the commerce clause, Powell, like the majority, failed to recognize that its original function was the regulation of private transactions, creating a presumption against national regulations of state transactions. As to the borderline between the commerce power and the residual powers of the states, Powell emphasized the necessity of weighing the respective interests of the states and the federal government.[145] Noting that Blackmun had concurred in *National League of Cities* in urging a balancing approach, Powell submitted that such an approach was needed to weigh the state and national powers.

Powell asserted that the majority had failed to explain how the electoral process guarantees the Congress will not impinge the residual powers of the states.[146] The majority noted the ability of the states to obtain grants in aid from the national government. But this is evidence that the states are only one of the many interest groups to which Congress must respond. The negative inference could be that national taxing has increased so greatly that the states' taxing power has diminished. The people are able to control state taxation, but they are demonstrably unable to stop the growth of national taxing and spending. In any case, this does not show that the political processes are sufficient to enforce constitutional limitations like the Tenth Amendment.

Powell perceived the origins and avowed purposes of the framers in designing a federal system of government. He concluded:

> The framers believed that the separate sphere of sovereignty reserved to the States would ensure that the States would serve as an effective "counterpoise" to the power of the federal government. The States would serve this essential role because they would attract and retain the loyalty of their citizens. The roots of such loyalty, the Founders thought, were found in the objects peculiar to state government. For example, Hamilton argued that the States "regulat[e] all those personal interests and familiar concerns to which the sensibility of individuals is more immediately awake. . . ." Thus, he maintained that the people would perceive the States as "the immediate and most visible guardian of life and property," a fact which "contributes more than any other circumstance to impressing upon the minds of the people affection, esteem and reverence towards the government."[147]

Powell noted that subsequent Supreme Court opinions have observed the narrow area of immunity carved out by *National League of Cities*.[148] He noted that that case was limited to fire and police protection, sanitation, and public health—activities remote from usual commercial relations.[149] He concluded by pointing out that the facts of *Garcia* concerned only city-owned transit. Overruling *National League of Cities* was not necessary for the *Garcia* decision. The majority, in asserting otherwise, gave the national commerce power over the states a seemingly unlimited scope.

The commentators are in total disagreement on the soundness of *Garcia*. Some support it, drawing parallels between *National League of Cities* and the *Lochner* era.[150] They do this in spite of a clear recognition that the rule of *National League of Cities* applied only to state transactions, not to those of private persons and firms. The *Lochner* analogies are often combined with an argument that federalism is merely derived from constitutional structure, an approach that goes very far in cutting the justices loose from the constraints of constitutional language.[151] This whole framework of critique is supported by the errors of Justices Powell and O'Connor in pointing as a primary cause "the recent expansion of the commerce powers."[152] This statement is contrary to the theory of interpretation outlined in chapter 1, that neither the Congress nor the judiciary is vested with the constitutional power to expand any clause. Either legislative power of a given scope and breadth was delegated in the Constitution or the amendments or it does not exist. As noted in chapter 5, the Congress was delegated in Article I the plenary power to regulate all private commerce in the United States. After 1937 the Supreme Court merely restored that power; it could not validly expand it.

Other commentators have been negatively critical of *Garcia* as wrongfully curtailing the federal structure of government.[153] Of the two structural elements implicit in the Constitution, separated powers has received strong judicial support, and federalism has not.[154] To citizens this may seem surprising, because federalism is the only structural element restated in the Tenth Amendment, which means that it is an element of the Bill of Rights. Protecting federalism is thus an express constitutional limitation. Commentators support Justice Powell in citing statements of both leading framers and historians to support this view of the original understanding.[155] Federalism was one aspect of the checks and balances designed to prevent tyranny. Constitutional amendments since 1789, especially the Seventeenth, have not diminished the residual powers of the states, even if they have removed some safeguards to protecting those powers.[156]

But the most important issue, on which the Court split and the commentators disagree, is whether the political processes perform such a safeguard to internal state government that judicial enforcement of federalism is unneeded. The issue is whether state governments, as distinct from the peoples of the states, are represented in the political process so that their internal administration will not be overrun by the Congress.

The Supreme Court has historically developed principles to determine the borderline between the powers of the national government and the states.[157] It has had to do so because the assertion that there exist operative political safeguards to protect state governments is just untrue: representatives elected in the states do not represent the states as governments. Chief Justice Marshall noted long ago that the measures adopted in Congress are those of people in the states, not the measures of the state governments.[158] The people are divided into factions or interest groups, which assert pressure on members of Congress to pass legislation favorable to them.[159] An economic theory of governmental regulation suggests that interest groups with money to support elections will be the most powerful influence in a legislature.[160] In modern times, political action committees, which represent business and labor union interests with large bankrolls, have more political power in Congress than do state governments.

The expected financial impact on cities of *Garcia* was so severe that immediate appeal was made to Congress for relief from the duty to pay employees in cash for overtime work. Mayor Koch of New York presented estimates of the National League of Cities that the total cost of compliance by all municipalities would exceed $2 billion per year.[161] Since citizens would not vote for such substantial increases, enforcing the overtime provisions of the Fair Labor Standards Act could lead to significant decreases in services of police, fire, and transit workers. In response, Congress modified the law so that overtime could be paid by compensatory time off at a rate of one-and-one-half hours for each overtime hour worked.[162] Thus the impact of *Garcia* could reduce services, but the municipalities would not have to pay overtime in cash.

CHAPTER 7

The Commerce Clause and the Law Merchant

THE PURPOSE OF the commerce clause has been seen as promoting an efficient national market unimpeded by state barriers to trade and governed by uniform congressional regulation to remedy market failures. But regulation by Congress was not the only legal control on commerce. The law merchant, a body of international commercial law, was also applied to commerce to resolve controversies over interstate and international private transactions. This body of judgemade, customary law became part of the national law of the United States through its adoption by the federal courts in deciding commercial cases.

International and interstate commercial controversies were brought into the federal courts by both the admiralty and the diversity jurisdictions under Article III.[1] The commerce clause vested the power to make the substantive law in these areas in Congress.[2] But, absent congressional action, the federal courts still had to decide mercantile cases. In doing so, they utilized the only available law on the topic, the principles and rules of the law merchant. The constitutional foundation for this federal decisional law of private transactions is the mandate of the commerce clause for uniform law in commerce among the several states. While not recognized by the early courts, the theory of the supremacy clause[3] of Article VI mandates national preemption of this part of private commercial law. The supremacy clause requires in litigation of interstate and international transactions that all national and state courts follow independently determined decisions of the Supreme Court of the United States.

Efficiencies deriving from the mandate for uniform national regulation of commerce merged with international efficiencies of the law merchant. The latter resulted from its customary origins. The basis of mercantile law was the customary behavior of merchants, acting under private incentive to minimize costs as part of maximizing profits. In mercantile cases counsel had to prove that contested customs had been in use for sufficient time that they had become accepted methods of trade before the courts would adopt such customs as legal rules. In England the adoption was by court decisions. In France and other major trading countries on the continent, the adoption was by statute. Consequently, the early federal courts in the United States used both English decisions and continental codes in deciding mercantile litigation.

The most noted case in the American law merchant was *Swift* v. *Tyson*.[4] Recent studies have restored the reputation of the opinion of Justice Story in *Swift* as a principled application of private international law.[5] Detailed analysis of opinions before *Swift* shows that the decision on the interstate commercial issues in that case was based on settled rules of the law merchant. Analysis of statutory language and early cases shows that Section 34 of the Judiciary Act of 1789[6] applied only to legal actions at common law. At the time of adoption of the Judiciary Act and in 1842, the commercial law or law merchant was not part of the common law in the narrow sense of that term. The law merchant had become part of the common-law system, but it was an independent branch, as were equity and maritime law. The widest sense of the rule of *Swift* as precedent should have been the refusal to apply Section 34 of the Judiciary Act to the law merchant.[7]

A review of cases shows that after the Civil War, the Supreme Court misinterpreted the Judiciary Act and the *Swift* opinion to create a federal common law. It mistakenly held many areas of local common law, such as property and torts, to be of a general nature, and ruled that the federal courts were not bound by the Judiciary Act to follow state precedents on these topics. This led to forum shopping. Parties would change their state of residence in order to obtain federal diversity jurisdiction and application of the federal common law to their controversy. Great objections to the expanding federal common law were voiced by dissenting justices, legal scholars, and the bar. Finally, in *Erie* v. *Tomkins*,[8] the Supreme Court overruled itself and terminated the federal common law. Unfortunately, in overruling the federal common law the Court also overruled *Swift*. This was because it failed to understand that *Swift* was not a common-law case or precedent. Thus, the Court not only corrected their predecessors' past error of creating a general federal common law; they also incorrectly eliminated the national customary commercial law for interstate and international transactions.

The Law of Nations

Historians have demonstrated that one cannot truly understand the rule of *Swift* v. *Tyson* until one understands the distinct character of private international law in 1789 when the Constitution and the Judiciary Act became law.[9] Admiralty, maritime and commercial law and the conflict of laws were a highly integrated body of law. No sharp distinctions or borderlines existed between these branches of the law of nations. Lawyers had described conflict-of-laws principles as a branch of commercial law since the doctrines first arose in international commercial transactions.[10]

The commercial law or law merchant was an integral part of maritime law. International contracts for the sale of goods and a bills of exchange drawn on foreign merchants or financiers for payment were closely tied to maritime contracts to ship the goods by sea and to insure them.[11] In 1821 Justice Story spoke of maritime and commercial law interchangeably, noting their high degree of uniformity throughout the commercial world:

> As to commercial law. From mutual comity, from the natural tendency of maritime usages to assimilation, and from mutual convenience, if not necessity, it may reasonably be expected, that the maritime law will gradually approximate to a high degree of uniformity throughout the commercial world. This is, indeed, in every view exceedingly desirable. Europe is already, by a silent but steady course, fast approaching to that state, in which the same commercial principles will constitute a part of the public law of all its sovereignties. The unwritten commercial law of England at this moment differs in no very important particulars from the positive codes of France and Holland. Spain, Portugal, and the Italian States, the Hanseatic Confederacy, and the Powers of the North, have adopted a considerable part of the same system.[12]

The customary origin of the commercial law was a key aspect of its character.[13] It meant that courts did not, as in some areas of the common law, create descriptive categories of legal wrongs and remedies. Rather, the merchants created the patterns of customary behavior that were most efficient in marketing goods and facilitating payment, and the courts adopted rules to enforce these customs. The historical origins of this customary law precede the recognition of the law merchant by the common-law courts. The merchant courts from the fourteenth to the sixteenth centuries in the port cities and at the fairs were created by merchants for the purpose of applying established and known business practices as the standards for settling controversies.[14]

The earliest mercantile cases reported in the common-law courts also cite the proof "declared upon the customs of merchants" as the applicable law.[15] A typical declaration began "whereas by the custom of London between merchants trafficking from London into the parts beyond the seas."[16] Once a general custom had been defined and proved in a number of cases, the courts would take judicial notice of it.[17]

The customary character of commercial law was emphasized continuously by the courts into the latter part of the nineteenth century. It was best described by Chief Justice Cockburn:

> It is true that the law merchant is sometimes spoken of as a fixed body of law, forming part of the common law, and as it were coeval with it. But as a matter of legal history, this view is altogether

incorrect. The law merchant thus spoken of with reference to bills of exchange and other negotiable securities, though forming part of the general body of the lex mercatoria, is of comparatively recent origin. It is neither more nor less than the usages of merchants and traders in the different departments of trade, ratified by the decisions of Courts of law, which upon such usages being proved before them, have adopted them as settled law with a view to the interests of trade and the public convenience, the Court proceeding herein on the well-known principle of law that, with reference to transactions in the different departments of trade, Courts of law, in giving effect to the contracts and dealings of the parties, will assume that the latter have dealt with one another on the footing of any custom or usage prevailing generally in the particular department.[18]

Contract and commercial law are based on a single primary principle: enforcement of the reasonable expectations of parties to transactions. The objective theory of contract requires courts to enforce reasonable expectations in promisees induced by the promises of promisors.[19] In contract and commercial law, however, there is a second set of expectations in parties. This set of expectations concerns the legal framework of transactions. Agreements are made with the expectation that the established customary behavior of merchants that has been recognized as law by the courts will be applied to any controversy that arises. Risk allocation for the hundreds of market contingencies that have not been provided for in the agreement will be allocated by the courts according to customary rules. The expectation is that standing customary law is in a sense part of transactions, ready to resolve ambiguities and fill gaps in agreements of merchants.

Throughout the history of mercantile law, its customary rules of behavior have always been subject to exception by express agreement of parties to a transaction. In *The Reeside*[20] Justice Story on circuit explained the function of custom in the judicial decision process for mercantile controversies. The action was a libel under maritime law for damage to goods being shipped from New York to Boston. Story explained the priority of express promises in transactions and the use of custom as a device to construe the incomplete or ambiguous terms of an agreement that led to litigation.[21]

The dynamic character of the law merchant is its most useful trait. As more efficient methods of shipping, communication, and transacting business were developed, new customary behavior was incorporated into the law. "When a general usage has been judicially ascertained and established, it becomes part of the law merchant, which Courts of justice are bound to know and recognize."[22] The dynamics of the law merchant was aptly described by Justice Bigham, in holding corporate bearer bonds to be negotiable.[23]

The law merchant was brought to England from the continent, and like modern contract law, many of its rules originated in the civil law.[24] It is not surprising that a special court established in London in 1601 to hear insurance cases, comprised the following personnel: the recorder, *two doctors of civil law,* two common lawyers, and eight "grave and discreet" merchants.[25]

Before 1600, mercantile cases were heard in the merchant courts.[26] Between 1600 and 1755, mercantile cases were heard in common-law and equity courts, but few of the merchant customs had been litigated sufficiently to be accepted as established legal rules.[27] Most customs still had to be proved at trial in the same manner that one proved foreign law.[28] Lord Mansfield is credited with making the great advance toward integration of merchant customs into law. His opinions incorporated the rules of the law merchant into the common-law system during his tenure as Chief Justice of Kings Bench from 1756 to 1788.[29]

Although the rules of mercantile law became part of the common-law system, no one spoke of them as common-law rules. There was ambiguity, however. The common-law system was sometimes called the general Common Law. Consequently, some courts stated that the "custom of merchants is part of the Common Law."[30] Nevertheless, lawyers and scholars who specialized in commercial law always spoke of it as distinct from the common law in the narrow sense of that term. Professor Bigelow has explained that this distinction continued through the nineteenth century: "The mischief of them lies in the mistaken notion implied, that the law merchant is a sort of poor relation of the common law, or rather it is a dependent of the common law, subject to it wherever its own language is not plain. Such instances, in other words, overlook the fact that the law merchant is an independent, parallel system of law, like equity or admiralty. The Law Merchant is not even a modification of the common law: it occupies a field over which the common law does not and never did extend."[31]

In order to understand the American law merchant and *Swift* v. *Tyson,* one must understand that the term "commercial law" was used by Justice Story in *Swift* as a synonym for law merchant or mercantile law. These terms were clearly synonyms at the time of the enactment of the Judiciary Act of 1789. In a leading case on bills of lading in 1787, Justice Buller spoke of the "established course among merchants" as the source of commercial law.[32] Justice James Wilson in lectures of 1790–91 cited Mansfield in *Luke* v. *Lyde,*[33] the case later used by Story as authority for *Swift,* and spoke of the law of merchants as that of the commercial world.[34] And Blackstone had written that "the affairs of commerce are regulated by a law of their own, called the law merchant or *lex mercatoria,* which all nations agree in and take notice of. And in particular it is held to be part of the law of England, which decides the causes of merchants by the general rules which obtain in all commercial countries."[35]

The titles of leading treatises on commercial law both before and after *Swift* indicate the synonymy of commercial law and the law merchant. One of the earliest is George Caines, *An Enquiry into the Law Merchant of the United States;* or *Lex Mercatoria Americana, on Several Heads of Commercial Importance* (1802). The title of a textbook on commercial law by Professor Theophilus Parsons of Harvard was *Elements of Mercantile Law* (1856).

The law merchant was not just the commercial law of the federal courts for interstate and international transactions. It was also the law adopted in state courts, when no state statute existed, to decide controversies arising in intrastate commercial transactions.[36] In 1805 Chief Justice James Kent of New York, in deciding a maritime case, said: "The *law merchant* is, however, the general law of commercial nations; and, where our own positive institutions and decisions are silent, it is to be expounded by having recourse to the usages of other nations. This has been the maxim from the time of *Rhodian* law to this day."[37] Justice Gibson of Pennsylvania, in an action on a promissory note, stated that "equity and the commercial law perfectly agree, that being founded on principles of reason as well as convenience."[38] Justice Redfield of the Vermont Supreme Court, in an action on a bill of exchange, explained the evolutionary process of the law merchant in which a growing body of reliable evidence of customary behavior developed into legal precedents.[39]

The Judiciary Act and Actions at Common Law

Section 34 of the Judiciary Act of 1789, also known as the Rules of Decision Act, read as follows: "The laws of the several states, except where the constitution, treaties or statutes of the United States shall otherwise require or provide, shall be regarded as rules of decision in trials at common law in the courts of the United States in cases where they apply."[40] Section 34 was to apply to the substantive issues; the Process Act, passed five days later, governed procedure in the federal courts.[41]

Historians have presented overwhelming evidence that in 1789 the word "laws" in the phrase "laws of the several states" included both state statutory law and settled rules of state decisional law in the reports of the highest state appeals courts.[42] Even though there were no operative state supreme courts in 1789 except Virginia's and no published reports of settled state common-law rules, the Congress used general language that anticipated the creation of such specialized appeals courts and the issuance of authoritative opinions on purely local controversies. The opinions of the Supreme Court that antedated *Swift* demonstrate that the Court understood this usual contemporary meaning and was employing it.[43]

It was a misreading of both Section 34 and *Swift* that caused later courts and scholars to hold that the word "laws" included only state statutes. Justice Field, dissenting in *Baltimore & Ohio R. Co. v. Baugh*[44] to the Supreme Court's later unwarranted creation of a federal common law of torts, noted that only in exceptional cases was "laws" in 1789 restricted to statutes, i.e., where it was so declared or clearly indicated by context.[45] Neither of these exceptions applied to Section 34. Field illustrated the continuing usual comprehensive meaning of "laws" by the illustration of the Fourteenth Amendment phrase "equal protection of the laws,"[46] which does not apply only to statutes. If state judges in common-law decisions created one definition of negligence for white persons and a different one for African-Americans, there would be a clear violation of the equal protection clause of the Fourteenth Amendment.

The phrase "except where the Constitution, treaties or statutes of the United States shall otherwise require or provide" assists the understanding of the other terms that create the exemption of the law merchant. The Constitution vests the governing power over interstate and international commerce exclusively in the national government.[47] The power in the national judiciary in maritime and diversity cases to establish a uniform commercial law for interstate transactions by incorporating the international law merchant into a body of national case law is constitutionally based on the commerce power and on the power to utilize established conflict-of-laws rules.[48] The first issue is one of federalism. The extraterritorial commercial transactions that were the subject matter of the law merchant, as they arose in diversity cases, raised legal issues beyond the exclusive legislative authority of any single state. The application by federal courts of the traditional judicial practices of the law of nations would in no way invade that part of law reserved to the states by the structure of the Constitution and restated in the Tenth Amendment.[49] As to intrastate transactions, absent preemptive congressional enactments, the states were free to deviate by statute or judicial decision from the general commercial law in any manner they chose.

The objective of uniform regulation of interstate transactions underlying the commerce clause also has a negative implication. Even if Congress fails to regulate transactions or shipments between states, the states have no power to regulate that sector of commerce.[50] The states have power only to regulate local commerce; they share power with the national Congress to regulate intrastate commerce that affects other states. But state regulation of intrastate commerce that affects other states is valid only if it does not conflict with national regulation and does not burden commerce among the several states.[51] In light of these allocations of regulatory power, the state legislatures cannot regulate extraterritorial commercial transactions. That which state legislatures cannot do without invading the national commerce power, the state judiciaries are also barred from doing. *Ipso facto,* the Supreme Court of the United States may not delegate to the state judiciaries the power to make binding law for interstate transactions litigated in the federal courts.

In the absence of congressional legislation on the topic, the constitutional separation of powers between the legislative and judicial branches also was no barrier to the adoption by the Supreme Court of the law merchant as a national case law for interstate transactions. The controlling framework of analysis of the Constitution of the United States is that it is a modified and expanded version of the English Constitution extant in the 1780s.[52] Adoption of the law merchant into the English legal system in order to settle private international disputes followed the English tradition of judgemade law.[53] Since commercial law originated in customary behavior rather than in sovereign command, codification of it was not the British approach. The courts were the governmental agency best able to adopt and modify mercantile rules from case to case as the business community developed new, more efficient methods of marketing and financing. Following the English tradition, the federal courts applied mercantile rules derived from English precedents or from the civil codes of France and other European nations.[54]

The phrase "in trials at common law" referred to the judicial hearing of legal actions at common law. Chief Justice Marshall on circuit stated in 1807 that he had always conceived "the technical term 'trials at common law' " of Section 34 to apply "to suits at common law as contradistinguished from those which come before the court sitting as a court of equity or admiralty."[55] Marshall's view is corroborated by the Process Act of 1789,[56] passed five days after the Judiciary Act, which provides different procedures for actions at common law from those in equity, admiralty, and maritime jurisdiction. The latter group are according to "the course of the civil law." At the time, some states did not have equity branches in their legal systems. Rawle has explained Congress's intentional omission of "equity" in Section 34: "[a] construction that would adopt the state practice in all its extent would at once extinguish in such states the exercise of equitable jurisdiction."[57] As Justice McLean later explained: "The rules of the High Court of Chancery of England have been adopted by the courts of the United States. . . . In exercising this jurisdiction, the courts of the Union are not limited by the chancery system adopted by any state, and they exercise their functions in a state where no court of chancery has been established."[58] Thus the negative implication of Section 34 was that conflict-of-laws rules in diversity cases should apply only to the common law in its narrower sense. By definition, this excluded the law merchant. Since common law excluded maritime law, and the general commercial law at that time was considered part of maritime law, the reasonable conclusion is that Section 34 was not applicable to commercial law.

The final clause of Section 34, "in cases where they apply," reinforces the above analysis of the status of commercial law. The primary reason to add this clause must have been to enable the Supreme Court to decide the breadth of application of the statute according to the principles of federalism. Although the traditional common law was reserved to the states and would have been even without passage of Section 34, the federal judiciary was required to adopt decisional rules for those areas of the customary law that were truly national. The chief component of this national customary law was the law of nations, of which the commercial law was a major part.

This was the key distinction that Justice Story made in *Swift* v. *Tyson*.[59] The distinction made was between state statute law and settled state case law of a strictly local character on the one hand, and customary or case law of an extraterritorial character on the other hand.[60] The latter body of law was to be governed by the law of nations, so *Swift* held that the Judiciary Act did not apply in this area. Since there could be only one law of nations to govern interstate and international transactions, no state statutory or case law purporting to govern controversies in the law of nations could control decisions in extraterritorial disputes decided in the federal courts.

Section 34 was a conflict-of-laws directive to the federal courts. The Supreme Court and leading commentators asserted that Section 34 merely codified for legal actions at common law the standing conflict-of-laws rules.[61] Although there were few American law reports at the time of the enactment of Section 34 and even fewer decisions on conflicts of law, there was a body of law in European nations that dealt with conflicts.[62] It was argued that for the common law, Section 34 was merely precautionary. It reaffirmed that national courts were not free under their general jurisdiction in diversity-of-citizenship cases to create a federal common law. Such a creation would have meant a dual common law, so that federal decisions on matters where there was settled local state law could differ from state precedents. In fact, this is exactly what happened in the latter part of the nineteenth century and the first third of the twentieth century when the Supreme Court, misreading *Swift*, created a federal common law.[63]

Legal historians have demonstrated that before the Civil War, the federal courts adhered to the distinction outlined above, applying Section 34 to actions at common law and following settled state rules of decision, but refusing to apply state law to the commercial law and other branches of the law of nations.[64] In *Swift*, Justice Story noted that Section 34 clearly applied to *in rem* and other strictly local common-law actions. He described these as "right and titles to things having a permanent locality, such as the rights and titles to real estate and other matters immovable and intraterritorial in their nature and character."[65] The classic Supreme Court precedent holding federal courts bound by settled decisions of state's highest appeals courts on title to property is *Jackson ex dem. St. John* v. *Chew*[66] and Justice Story had earlier asserted that general principle in *United States* v. *Crosby.*[67]

Section 34 also required federal courts to follow settled state common law generally. In *Wheaton* v. *Peters,*[68] an action concerning the applicability of state common-law rules of copyright, Justice McLean for the Supreme Court made general observations: "It is clear, there can be no common law of the United States. The federal government is composed of twenty-four sovereign and independent states; each of which may have its local usages, customs and common law. There is no principle which pervades the Union and has the authority of law that is not embodied in the Constitution or laws of the Union. The common law could be made a part of our federal system, only by legislative adoption. When, therefore, a common-law right is asserted, we must look to the state in which the controversy originated."[69] It is significant that Justice Story joined in this opinion. Eight years later, he wrote the unanimous opinion in *Swift* v. *Tyson,*[70] affirming federal judicial adoption of the international customary commercial law for interstate transactions. Unfortunately, in writing the *Swift* opinion, Story failed to mention *Wheaton, Chew,* or *Crosby* when he distinguished local common law from the general commercial law.

A classic case applying Section 34 to statutes is *Green* v. *Neal's Lessee.*[71] The Supreme Court of the United States had construed a Tennessee statute of limitations relating to land claims. Some months later, the Tennessee Supreme Court gave a contrary interpretation. In *Green,* the U.S. Supreme Court explained why it would conform to the Tennessee precedents rather than its own in order not to create two rules of property on the same issue within a state.[72] An important underlying factor was the general-conflicts rule of *lex loci rei sitae* in real property cases.

But this view was not followed where the Supreme Court could reverse itself only by denying the reasonable expectations of parties to contract. In *Rowan* v. *Runnels,*[73] the Court refused to abandon its own first interpretation of the Mississippi constitutional clause prohibiting trade in slaves that it had made in *Groves* v. *Slaughter.*[74] Although the action was on a promissory note, the issue was not one of commercial law but of the common-law contract rule on legality of object. Since transactions totaling over $3 million had been entered in reliance on the decision in *Groves,* a subsequent contrary state precedent was rejected by the Supreme Court. In *Rowan,* the Court followed *Groves.* Writing for the Court, Chief Justice Taney refused to impair the obligations of contracts in litigation outside the field of bankruptcy. Taney admitted, however, that future contracts would be governed by state-court decisions.[75]

A special problem arose when there was no settled state law on a common-law issue. If there were no unequivocal state precedents from its highest appeals court or if precedents were in conflict in the state whose law was to be applied, Section 34 could not operate, and the Supreme Court had to apply general principles of common law found in the English law reports and those of other states. Chief Justice Marshall explained that even in a property case, it was impossible to apply *lex loci rei sitae* when the case was of first impression and there were no precedents.[76]

The Commercial Law and *Swift* v. *Tyson*

The federal courts early took the view that interstate and international commercial transactions were not bound by state common-law precedents. Unfortunately, the judges and justices did not seem to realize that this view was mandated by the commerce clause of the Constitution. The largest group of law-merchant cases in the United States before 1840 were in the area of marine insurance.[77] The federal courts and the state courts knowingly exercised independent judgment as they shared in adopting and clarifying a body of national customary law. In a case of double insurance in 1800 Judge Peters stated that the United States "should have a national, uniform and generally received law-merchant."[78] In 1806 Justice Paterson reviewed the status of a settled marine insurance rule and noted: "It has grown up into a clear, known and certain rule for the regulation of commercial negotiations, and is incorporated into the law merchant of the land."[79] In all the marine insurance cases in the period to 1820, the federal courts agreed that they were applying the general commercial law.[80] In no case, even in the few instances where state courts had decided the issue differently, was it even argued that federal courts were bound by Section 34 of the Judiciary Act to follow local law.

Justice Story was thoroughly familiar with the body of decisions on marine insurance in the lower federal courts that relied on general principles of the law merchant for decision.[81] Between 1836 and 1838, he wrote three opinions on circuit that treated the issue. Not local law but law-merchant rules governed marine insurance.[82] Story's clearest statement of the standing law was in *Williams* v. *Suffolk Ins. Co.*: "The doctrine being founded, not upon local law, but upon the general principles of commercial law, would be obligatory upon this court, even if the decisions of the state court of Massachusetts were to the contrary; for upon commercial questions of a general nature, the courts of the United States possess the same general authority, which belongs to the state tribunals, and are not bound by the local decisions. They are at liberty to consult their own opinions, guided, indeed, by the greatest deference for the acknowledged learning and ability of the state tribunals, but still exercising their own judgment, as to the reasons, on which those decisions are founded."[83] This was the generally accepted understanding of the commercial law found in the then-available treatises on the common-law system.[84]

In *Findlay's Executors* v. *Bank of the United States,*[85] Justice McLean on circuit resolved a conflict between Ohio and federal precedents in a case of suretyship, another branch of the law merchant. He noted that "[t]his great head of equity is derived from the civil law, and is founded upon immutable principles of justice and benevolence."[86] Since the Ohio precedent and the conflicting federal precedent both purported to stand on principles of general commercial law, McLean had to use independent judgment on the issue of which was correct. He adopted a principle from an opinion in the Supreme Court of the United States and noted that Chancellor Kent had adopted that view in a New York case.[87]

Many of the most notable opinions on the application of the general commercial law concerned bills of exchange. In *Buckner* v. *Finley,*[88] the Supreme Court made an unqualified holding that bills of exchange drawn in one state on persons living in another state were foreign bills for the purpose of applying the rules of protest. Justice Washington pointed out that almost all reported state cases took the same view.[89] He did not note the constitutional foundation: interstate and international bills of exchange, being extraterritorial to any single state, were part of the national commerce, whose regulation was delegated exclusively to the national government by the commerce power of Article 1. One of the functions of the "dormant" commerce clause was to prevent attempted enforcement of the conflicting statutes of two different states on any single interstate transaction.

One of the earliest expositions of the law applicable to international transactions was that of Justice Story on circuit 1812 in *Van Reimsdyk* v. *Kane.*[90] The case was in equity and presented issues under the international conflict of laws. At that time, however, conflicts rules and commercial law were still considered one integrated branch of the law of nations,[91] so the principles applied here would also apply to the law merchant. The defendants, citizens of Rhode Island, through an agent in Java, had drawn a bill of exchange on a mercantile house in Amsterdam payable to the plaintiff, a Dutch resident of Java. The bill of exchange had been presented to the drawee and protested for nonpayment. The defendant-drawers pleaded in defense that all their debts had been discharged in a proceeding under the Rhode Island insolvency statute of 1756. Without deciding whether this statute, having the effect of a general bankruptcy law, violated the constitutional prohibition on state law impairing the obligation of contracts, Story admitted its existence and exercise. The question was whether the Rhode Island insolvency statute was a bar to this legal action on an international bill of exchange, "whether the courts of the United States are bound to enforce against foreigners or citizens of other states, rightfully suing therein, the full effect of a bar of this nature."[92] In rejecting this defense, Story held that under international conflict-of-laws rules, a valid contract made in another country could not be nullified by the insolvency law of the place where the suit was brought. Even though this action was brought in equity, Story also explained why a suit of this nature would not be subject to enforcement under Section 34 of the Judiciary Act:

> There must then be some limitation to the operation of this clause, and I apprehend such a limitation must arise whenever the subject matter of the suit is extraterritorial. In controversies between citizens of a state, as to rights derived under that state, and in controversies respecting territorial interests, in which, by the law of nations, the lex rei sitae governs, there can be little doubt, that the regulations of the statute must apply. But in controversies affecting citizens of other states, and in no degree arising from local regulations, as for instance, foreign contracts of a commercial nature, I think that it can hardly be maintained, that the laws of a state, to which they have no reference, however narrow, injudicious and inconvenient they may be, are to be the exclusive guides for judicial decision. Such a construction would defeat nearly all the objects for which the constitution has provided a national court.[93]

A leading precedent on the interpretation of interstate bills of exchange is *Coolidge* v. *Payson*,[94] in which Chief Justice Marshall affirmed a circuit court opinion of Justice Story.[95] He held that a written promise of a drawee to a drawer to accept a bill of exchange that is about to be drawn, which is communicated to a third party and induces him to take the bill, is equivalent to an actual acceptance. One fact of the case, though not in contest, was to regard a preexisting debt as valuable consideration for transfer of a bill of exchange. This was to be the primary issue in *Swift* v. *Tyson*. The method of interpretation was to adopt English law-merchant cases as evidence of the law and make no reference to local state law on the topic. In the circuit court, counsel for the losing defendant had cited a Massachusetts precedent.[96] The possible application of Section 34 of the Judiciary Act was not raised in the case.

In *Townsley* v. *Sumrall*,[97] Justice Story decided a case on interstate bills of exchange on the basis of law-merchant principles and without citation of authority on the key issues. One of the holdings was that a pre-existing debt was a valuable consideration for a bill of exchange, the issue later contested in *Swift*. Here again, the possible application of Section 34 of the Judiciary Act was not raised.

In 1841, in *Riley* v. *Anderson*,[98] Justice McLean on circuit decided the same issue that was to be litigated a year later in *Swift*. An antecedent debt was held sufficient consideration upon the endorsement of a promissory note to cut off defenses that would been good between the original parties to the instrument. Although the notes for the interstate transaction were made in Ohio, McLean refused to adopt the contrary Ohio rule. He cited *Coolidge* and *Townsley* and the English mercantile cases.

Swift v. *Tyson*,[99] concerning an interstate bill of exchange, required Justice Story again to construe Section 34 of the Judiciary Act of 1789. As has been noted, a significant group of circuit-court opinions had held that statute did not apply to the law merchant. The specific circuit-court ruling of *Riley* v. *Anderson*[100] one year before had decided the same issue on negotiable paper as *Swift* without referring to the statute. But *Swift* was the first Supreme Court opinion expressly ruling that the commercial law was general in nature and not subject to Section 34, which meant that federal courts were to use independent judgment in applying commercial law to interstate and international transactions.

A bill of exchange was drawn in New York on the defendant Tyson in Maine, who accepted it; the payee was one Norton who endorsed it to the plaintiff, Swift. The bill was dishonored at maturity. This was a case of acceptance procured by fraud, the bill subsequently being taken by plaintiff in "payment" of a prior debt due from his endorser. Justice Story held that, assuming the unsettled New York law to the contrary, a pre-existing indebtedness by the endorser of a bill of exchange was consideration that would cut off defenses that were good between the original parties to the instrument.[101] The Supreme Court had twice before reached this decision on this issue by following the general rule of the law merchant.[102] Thus *Swift,* certified to the Supreme Court on a narrow issue of negotiable-instruments law, is an easily understandable case in its context, the commercial law. After 1860, some judges and justices found the decision puzzling because they mistakenly thought it referred to the common law.

In the key paragraph of the opinion, Story began with an *obiter dictum* that was an excursion into abstract jurisprudence. Referring to decisions of "local tribunals," he wrote: "In the *ordinary* use of language it will hardly be contended that the decisions of courts constitute laws. They are, at most, only evidence of what the laws are, and are not of themselves laws. The laws of a State are *more usually* understood to mean the rules and enactments promulgated by legislative authority thereof, or long established local customs having the force of law."[103] The words "ordinary" and "more usually" in the dictum are important qualifying terms. Local customs do have the force of law when there is a settled opinion by the highest appeals court in the jurisdiction. But in 1842, there were still relatively few settled common-law rules in the reports of the highest court of any single state. State trial courts often had to apply common-law, equity, and mercantile principles and rules by using English law reports and those of other states as evidence of the law. In any case, this excursion into jurisprudence was unnecessary. *Swift* did not rest on the definition of "laws" because, as Justice Story noted, the Supreme Court would not be bound by state statutes or decisional law when deciding issues that were extraterritorial to a state.

Story then explained why Section 34 of the Judiciary Act did not apply to the federal courts as they heard diversity cases under the general commercial law. He wrote:

> It never has been supposed by us, that the section did apply, or was designed to apply, to questions of a more general nature, not at all dependent upon local statutes or local usages of a fixed and permanent operation, as, for example, to the construction of ordinary contracts or other written instruments, and especially to questions of general commercial law, where the State tribunals are called upon to perform the like functions as ourselves, that is, to ascertain upon general reasoning and legal analogies, what is the true exposition of the contract or instrument, or what is the just rule furnished by the principles of commercial law to govern the case. And we have not now the slightest difficulty in holding, that this section, upon its true intendment and construction, is strictly limited to local statutes and local usages of the character before stated, and does not extend to contracts and other instruments of a commercial nature, the true interpretation and effect whereof are to be sought, not in the decision of the local tribunals, but in the general principles and doctrines of commercial jurisprudence. Undoubtedly, the decisions of the local tribunal upon such subjects are entitled to, and will receive, the most deliberate attention and respect of this court; but they cannot furnish positive rules, or conclusive authority, by which our own judgments are to be bound up and governed. The law respecting negotiable instruments may be truly declared in the language of Cicero, adopted by Lord Mansfield in Luke v. Lyde, 2 Burr. R. 883, 887, to be in a great measure, not the law of a single country only, but of the commercial world. Non erit alia lex Romae, alia Athenis, alia nunc, alia posthac, sed et apud omnes gentes, et omni tempore, una eademque lex obtinebit.[104]

Justice Story itemized only two of the questions of a "more general nature" not subject to Section 34. These were the rules of documentary construction and the general commercial law.[105] Only the latter was at issue in *Swift*. Section 34 did not apply to the law merchant because all mercantile principles were totally independent of state statutes and state common law. Story cited the opinion of Lord Mansfield in the shipping case of *Luke* v. *Lyde*[106] to illustrate that the law of negotiable instruments, like all of the law merchant, was "not the law of a single country only, but of the commercial world."[107]

There is nothing puzzling about the *Swift* decision, even though the *obiter dictum* on the meaning of the word "laws" in the opinion is ambiguous. Chief Justice Taney and other Jacksonian justices must have joined in the opinion of Justice Story, because it was a reasonable declaration of standing law.[108] It was clear to competent lawyers of the time that the commercial law meant the law merchant. The Taney court were not using law as an instrument of change to promote expansion of the national judicial function. They were deciding a narrow commercial issue, not approving the foundation of a federal common law. The illegitimate extension of *Swift* to create a federal common law was to come later in the century, when the true meaning of "commercial" law was forgotten.

Swift v. *Tyson* was the culmination of a series of cases on negotiable instrum ents that had established the distinct position of the law merchant in the common-law system. It should be noted, however, that there were some aspects of the commercial law that, under conflict-of-law rules, were decided according to the place of contract. In the law of bills of exchange, three of these items were days of grace, rates of interest, and rights to damages, all of which were determined on the basis of *lex loci*.[109]

In the same year as *Swift*, Justice Story wrote an opinion that combined elements of the law of nations that he had mentioned in *Swift*, the canons of documentary construction and the commercial law. *Carpenter* v. *Providence Washington Insurance Co.*[110] concerned the construction of an interstate contract for fire insurance. Story adopted the same rationale as in *Swift* to reject state-law precedents and to apply general principles of commercial law.[111]

Thirteen years after *Swift*, the Taney Court again confirmed the *Swift* rule on national mercantile law. In *Watson* v. *Tarpley*,[112] the Court denied the application of a Mississippi statute on bills of exchange to an interstate transaction. The statute denied legal action on a bill of exchange until after the date of its maturity. Under the law merchant, action could be brought at any time after protest and notice founded upon the refusal to pay. Justice Daniel for the Court stated that the state statute was "a violation of the general commercial law, which a state [had] no power to impose, and which the courts of the United States [were] bound to disregard."[113] In effect, in 1855 the Court gave the same interpretation to Section 34 of the Judiciary Act as Justice Story had given on circuit in *Van Reimsdyk* v. *Kane*[114] in 1812. States rules of decision, whether statutes or decisional, did not apply to extraterritorial commercial transactions.

The Supremacy Clause

The Supremacy Clause of Article VI, Clause 2 reads as follows: "This Constitution, and the Laws of the United States which shall be made in Pursuance thereof; and all Treaties made, or which shall be made, under the Authority of the United States, shall be the supreme Law of the Land; and the Judges in every State shall be bound thereby, any Thing in the Constitution or Laws of any State to the Contrary notwithstanding."[115]

The first issue in determining the expected impact of this language in the establishment of uniform commercial law for the United States is the meaning of "laws" in the phrases "Laws of the United States" and "Laws of any state."

As was noted in the discussion of "laws" in the Judiciary Act of 1789, the usual meaning of "laws" then included both statutory and decisional law.[116] Only if additional language or the context so demonstrated was the term limited to statutes.[117] As to "laws of the United States" in the broad context of a constitutional article mandating national supremacy, there is no textual or contextual basis for less than the broadest interpretation. It is clear that the framers were concerned with national supremacy for international issues since they included in the supremacy clause "all Treaties made, or which shall be made under the Authority of the United States."[118]

The law of nations would be the key substantive customary law that the national judiciary would adopt and make a part of the laws of the United States. There is substantial evidence that in Article III, "laws of the United States" included the "law of nations."[119] The context of Article VI seems comparable. Both the jurisdiction of federal courts and the supremacy of national law are necessary elements of a uniform legal system on which all parties to international transactions can rely. In contrast, if state courts were allowed to impose their various statutes and case law on issues of private international law that arise in state litigation, uniformity of the law of nations would be lost and forum shopping would be encouraged.

The phrase "law of any state" in the supremacy clause must be compared with the language "laws of the several states" in Section 34 of the Judiciary Act. As has been noted, the latter included both state statute law and state common law. The context of the supremacy clause indicates the same broad definition of "laws." Judges in every state are bound to recognize that national law preempts conflicting state law, both statutory and decisional. Recent cases illustrate the national preemption of conflicting state common law.[120]

The future tense of the verbs in the supremacy clause circumscribes the scope of the clause. "Laws of the United States" applies only to laws of Congress to be enacted in consequence of its powers under this second Constitution and to those rules of the law of nations to be adopted by the national courts. As to the latter, the Supreme Court was, of course, not bound to the precedents or statutes of any nation.[121] On the other hand, to the great extent that English precedents and continental statutes coincided on issues of the law of nations, counsel could advise American shipowners and shippers of goods in interstate and international trade on the high probability of rules that would be adopted in the national courts. This prediction is supported by the preconstitutional efforts of state supreme courts to conform to the law merchant in litigation of international transactions in hope that courts of other nations would give recognition to their judgments.[122]

The future tense of the supremacy clause was additional evidence of the existence of federalism. The common law of England and British amendatory statutes existing at the time of ratification were not within the class of national laws described in the supremacy clause. While many state constitutions and statutes expressly adopted the common law of England and even British amendatory statutes to the extent that they fit in the American setting,[123] the national constitution did not. The negative implication of the language of the supremacy clause is that "laws of the United States" in Article VI did not include the standing English or state common law. On the other hand, the exclusive power in the national government to regulate foreign relations and foreign commerce meant that only the national government could act to make the law merchant a part of American law.

Since the law merchant and admiralty are both branches of the law of nations, the operation of national preemption in admiralty cases indicates the way the law merchant should have been treated. Under Article III, Section 2 of the Constitution, the judicial power of the United States extends to "all cases of admiralty and maritime jurisdiction."[124] The Supreme Court interpreted this clause, together with Section 9 of the Judiciary Act of 1789,[125] to give the national courts a much broader jurisdiction than the British courts of admiralty had in 1789.[126] The language of the clause is merely jurisdictional. By itself, it provides no key to the substantive law to be applied in admiralty and maritime cases.[127]

It is clear that Section 34 of the Judiciary Act could not apply to maritime cases based on events occurring on the high seas. If substantive maritime law was to have any uniformity, Section 34 also could not apply to events occurring in the territorial waters of a state.[128] In fact, it is clear that the substantive law to be applied in maritime cases was and is the maritime branch of the law of nations.[129] This has been consistently applied in maritime cases. In the recent *Moragne*[130] case, the Court utilized the traditional civil law methodology of admiralty in recognizing a customary remedy for wrongful death due to unseaworthiness,[131] and deriving public policy from a set of statutes treating the same problem but not directly applicable in the case. The Court also reemphasized the need for uniformity in private international law, the theme of *Southern Pacific* v. *Jensen*.[132]

The preemption of conflicting state law by national maritime law is clearly established.[133] The supremacy of national maritime law as the only means to uniformity is illustrated by recent decisions. "While states may sometimes supplement federal maritime policies, a state may not deprive a person of any substantial admiralty rights as defined in controlling acts of Congress or by interpretative decisions of this Court."[134] "A state law, even though it does not contravene an established principle of admiralty law will, nevertheless, not be applied where its adoption would impair the uniformity and simplicity which is a basic principle of the federal admiralty law."[135] In the *Wilburn Boat*[136] case, concerning a marine-insurance contract, the Supreme Court stated: "Congress has not taken over the regulation of marine insurance contracts and has not dealt with the effect of marine insurance warranties at all; hence there is no possible question here of conflict between state and any federal statute. But this does not answer the questions presented, since in the absence of controlling Acts of Congress this Court has fashioned a large part of the existing rules that govern admiralty. And States can no more override such judicial rules validly fashioned than they can override Acts of Congress."[137]

Maritime legal actions may begin in state courts[138] or in the national courts. In either case, the national customary maritime law preempts state substantive statutes and common-law rules in all aspects of the litigation.[139] It makes no difference whether the maritime case originates under admiralty jurisdiction or under diversity of citizenship.[140] The substantive maritime law is preemptive.

The preemption of Supreme Court commercial decisions could have the breadth of maritime cases only if commercial law were considered a part of maritime law for plenary federal jurisdiction. Although the meaning of "maritime" included "commercial" in 1789, it has not since then been so construed by the courts. The national commercial law before 1938 was a mandate only in transaction litigated in the federal courts. Unlike maritime cases, commercial cases are subject to federal jurisdiction only when there is diversity of citizenship. All others are entirely local and are governed by state statutes and state-court decisions.

In spite of their autonomy under the principle of federalism, early state courts usually recognized the Supreme Court of the United States as the final authority on the customary commercial law. Absent local statutes to the contrary, state courts recognized that the law merchant was the law of the commercial world and that a uniform national law would promote trade and economic growth. Justice Wilson referred to Mansfield and noted this in his 1790–91 lectures:

> One branch of that law, which, since the extension of commerce, and the frequent and liberal intercourse between different nations, has become of peculiar importance, is called the law of merchants. This system of law has been admitted to decide controversies concerning bills of exchange, policies of insurance, and other mercantile transactions, both where citizens of different states, and where citizens of the same state only, have been interested in the event. This system has, of late years, been greatly elucidated, and reduced to rational and solid principles, by a series of adjudications, for which

the commercial world is much indebted to a celebrated judge, long famed for his comprehensive talents and luminous learning in general jurisprudence.[141]

The view of the bar on the stature of Supreme Court commercial decisions can be seen from the comments of the justices and the official reporters. In *Coolidge* v. *Payson*,[142] Chief Justice Marshall decided an issue concerning bills of exchange and stated: "It is of much importance to merchants that this question should be at rest."[143] The implication was that this decision would determine the issue for all courts. Reporter Wheaton noted that Marshall's opinion would be "considered as settling the law of the country on this subject."[144]

As to *Buckner* v. *Finley*,[145] holding interstate bills of exchange to be foreign bills, reporter Peters noted the question was now "settled."[146] The truth of his comment is verified by the fact that the New York courts, the only ones previously stating a contrary view, thereafter followed *Buckner*.[147] In *Riley and Amrings* v. *Anderson*,[148] Justice McLean made the point that he was not bound to follow Ohio decisions on the negotiability of promissory notes, but also asserted that "on all questions of a general and commercial character, the rule established by the federal courts should be followed by the local tribunal."[149]

The effect of *Swift* on state-court decisions illustrates the attitude of judicial deference in that era. In *Carlisle* v. *Wishart*,[150] the Ohio Supreme Court adopted the rule of *Swift* and overruled its own prior contrary precedent. Justice Wood state: "It is believed that the law, as thus settled by the highest judicial tribunal in the country, will become the uniform rule of *all*, as it now is of *most* of the states. And, in a country like ours, where so much communication and interchange exists between the different members of the confederacy, to preserve uniformity in the great principles of commercial law, is of much interest to the mercantile world."[151] The appeals court of many states recognized *Swift* as the correct authority and applied its rule to intrastate transactions.[152] The New York Court of Appeals, however, refused to adopt the *Swift* rule on the issue.[153]

Over time, however, uniformity in state law did not prevail. In local commercial transactions, the statute and case law of the various states developed many differences.[154] Even though settled rules for federal courts did come from appeals to the Supreme Court, such rules were rejected by many state supreme courts. With state court rejection of uniform commercial law, the federal courts in this century also deviated from the *Swift* doctrine. In determining the negotiability of bills of exchange, for example, federal courts stopped applying the national law and instead applied conflict-of-law rules to adopt the law of one state.[155] The failure of Congress to enact national private commercial law left parties to interstate transactions in great uncertainty about which state's law would apply if controversies arose.

With the decision in *Erie* v. *Tompkins*,[156] the last vestiges of national commercial law disappeared. After *Erie*, the federal courts could no longer apply national rules to interpret the Negotiable Instruments Law and other uniform codes; all commercial cases in diversity actions were thereafter treated like common-law contracts. But the Supreme Court went even further. It wiped out the international conflict-of-laws rules. In *Klaxon Co.* v. *Stentor Electric Mfg. Co.*,[157] the Court followed *Erie* and interpreted the Judiciary Act to require federal courts to follow state-court decisions on the conflict of laws. *Erie* not only corrected the previous erroneous creation of a federal common law. It also led to elimination of the customary law of nations in commercial cases and in the conflicts of laws.

The application of *Erie* to the commercial law has in most cases not raised extreme problems of diverse rules because the Uniform Commercial Code is considered the federal law of commerce.[158] But in international bills of exchange controversies, the issues are more complex. In determining whether a party is a holder in due course, a federal court may choose to apply not the Uniform Commercial Code but alternate choice-of-law Rules.[159] In marine-insurance cases, in the absence of federal statue or settled federal decisional law, the courts will apply state law.[160] In any case, there is no longer any reference to a general commercial law of the international community.

Conclusion

Much of the misunderstanding of *Swift* and confusion in its later interpretation seems to have arisen from ambiguity in language. The fact that before 1850 "commercial law" was a synonym of and limited to "the law merchant" had been forgotten. The fact that "common law" in 1789 was almost always used in a narrow sense that excluded equity, admiralty, and law merchant had also been forgotten. The national decisional law in the various branches of the law of nations was never labeled "federal common law" until long after *Swift*. Ambiguity could be avoided if it again were labeled "national customary law."

Great justices and leading scholars have misunderstood *Swift*. Justice Holmes correctly dissented to the existence and application of federal common law,[161] but he did not understand that *Swift* was not a common-law case.[162] Justice Brandeis in *Erie* v. *Tompkins*[163] correctly stated that "[t]here is no federal general common law."[164] He did not see the distinction, however, between common-law torts and their conflicts rules based on place of wrong, the subject of *Erie,* and disputes over interstate commercial transactions that by definition are extraterritorial to any single state.[165] He mistakenly overruled *Swift* because he too did not realize that this law-merchant case was not a precedent for common-law decisions.[166]

Section 34 of the Judiciary Act of 1789, as amended to substitute "civil actions" for "trials at common law," is still the national law.[167] It is not applied to admiralty,[168] but is applied to the interstate commercial law.[169] The conclusion of this study is that the latter application is wrong. The Supreme Court's holding that state decisional law should regulate inter-state and international commercial transactions—even though the Consti-tution delegates this area of law exclusively to the national government—is clearly wrong. For interstate transactions, the federal courts should apply the Uniform Commercial Code as the national law merchant, not peculiar state statutes that deviate from that code, even if they are the law of the place of contract. The federal courts should make their own interpretations of the Uniform Commercial Code using the principles of the civil law.[170] Under the commerce clause, they are not bound to follow state decisions when adopting a national law merchant to apply to transac-tions in commerce among the several states.

A more difficult issue arises when, in the absence of congressional legislation, interstate transactions are litigated in the state courts. If the national decisional law is recognized as the only constitutionally valid law for such transactions, it is clear that state courts should be bound to follow federal court precedents in such cases. The Supreme Court should acknowledge that the national customary commercial law is part of the "laws of the United States" under Article III[171] and under the Judiciary Act.[172] Then decisions of state supreme courts that apply this law to interstate transactions would be subject to review in the Supreme Court upon petition for *certiorari*.

It is notable that recognition of a national customary commercial law would not encourage for mercantile cases the forum shopping that was characteristic of the federal common law before *Erie*. If the commercial case is interstate, national and state courts would apply the national decisional law. On the other hand, if a commercial case concerned transac-tions that were entirely intrastate, the courts would apply local state statutory and decisional law. The choice of law is not based on the procedural issue of whether there is diversity of citizenship. Rather, it is based on the character of the transactions.

CHAPTER 8

Monetary and Fiscal Powers

Macroeconomic Background

MONEY IS SUPPLIED by government because the transaction costs of arranging the "double coincidence" of barter are very high. In fact, money is a necessary medium for the development of market economies.[1] Money serves as a measure of value, as a medium of exchange, and as a short-term means of retaining a quantity of purchasing power. Part of modern monetary theory centers on the optimal quantity of money in an economy.[2] Government should control the supply of money so as to minimize its effects on production and consumption decisions. Since inflation and deflation can have negative effects on efficiency, the long-run goal is stability in an index of the general level of prices.[3] One hypothesis of this chapter is that the framers of the Constitution adopted language to vest exclusive monetary powers in the national government because they valued monetary stability. The rational inference is that money issued by states or banks under state control is an unconstitutional invasion of the national monetary power.

Prominent New England writers in the seventeenth century recognized the need for paper money as the medium of exchange in a growing economy.[4] The limited quantity of specie brought from England or received in international trade was subject to constant drain to pay for manufactures imported into the colonies. Absent significant paper money, commodities used as money and foreign coins were bid up in price far above their value in the world market. In order to prevent deflation and the negative expectations for prices that deflation would create, conservative leaders proposed banks of credit that would issue notes for circulation. Early in the eighteenth century, all of the colonies undertook to relieve the critical shortage of a medium of exchange by issuing paper money of some kind.[5] There were no central banks in the colonies comparable to the Bank of England to issue bank notes on the basis of a partial reserve of specie. Consequently, the states undertook to issue bills of credit in anticipation of taxes.[6] Other bills were issued and loaned to merchants on the security of real property. Some classes of notes were interest bearing, and others were not. Some were declared legal tender, and others were legally enforceable only to pay taxes. The colonial bills of credit were issued in such great quantities that they depreciated to a fraction of their original value in relation to British coins. This so disrupted business relations that in 1751 Parliament passed an act prohibiting any of the New England colonies from emitting bills of credit and from making them legal tender.[7] In 1764 Parliament passed similar legislation for the other plantations and required that outstanding bills of credit should be gradually retired.

The background to the constitutional clauses on money was the issue of paper money by the states and the Continental Congress after the Declaration of Independence. The long-term opposition to British taxes created a mind-set in the former colonies that made it impossible to finance the revolutionary war through taxation. Before the Continental Congress ever met, the states had set a pattern; many of them began to emit bills of credit to finance the war.[8] Soon thereafter, all of the states followed this policy. Congress, lacking the power to levy taxes, began by issuing $6 million in paper money before the end of 1775 and requested the states to redeem their respective quotas of these bills by imposing taxes.[9] The states refused. By the end of 1779, Congress had issued $241.5 million in bills of credit and the states had emitted over $200 million.[10] Early in 1781, a paper dollar was traded at less than two cents in specie, and within the year it became practically worthless. The effect of state laws making congressional and state bills of credit legal tender was to cause people to refuse to sell their lands or goods. Merchants closed their stores, and many were mobbed, fined, and imprisoned.[11] Thus the economic stagnation and social disruption that could derive from unstable money was within the actual experience of the delegates to the Constitutional Convention.

The other source of paper money before the Constitutional Convention convened was bank notes. The Bank of North America was chartered by the Continental Congress on December 31, 1781.[12] Since it was doubtful that Congress had power under the Articles of Confederation to grant any charters, some states issued supplementary charters. Massachusetts and New York granted charters of incorporation that gave the firm a banking monopoly in the two states for the duration of the war.[13] Pennsylvania granted the bank a charter identical to that granted by Congress, which was operative long after the founding of the United States. In 1784 banks of issue were founded in New York and Boston, and soon thereafter banks were founded in other cities.[14] Each of the banks operated independently and issued bank notes purportedly convertible to specie. Since many of these banks had grants of monopoly in their areas and centered on financing government and commerce, they were opposed by agrarian interests, which urged greater increases in the supply of money.

Paper Money

The constitutional powers in Congress to control the supply of money are derived mainly from the power to borrow and the power to coin money. These clauses of Article I, Section 8 reads as follows: "The Congress Shall have power . . . (2) To borrow money on the credit of the United States. . . . (5) To coin money, regulate the value thereof, and of foreign coin.[15] As a corollary to this federal power, the states are prohibited from exercising power over money in Article I, Section 10: "No state shall . . . coin money, emit bills of credit, make anything but gold and silver coin a tender in payment of debts."[16]

The Committee of Detail had submitted the original wording of Section 8, Clause 2 as "to borrow money, and emit bills on the credit of the United States."[17] Gouverneur Morris of Pennsylvania moved to strike the phrase "and emit bills" asserting: "If the United States had such credit such bills would be unnecessary; if they had not, unjust and useless."[18] The motion carried. At that time, "bill of credit" meant paper money issued by a government and not currently redeemable in coin. The effect of striking the phrase was debatable, as shown by the comments of the delegates. It was agreed that the issue of public notes redeemable in coin would not be affected by the omission. There was concern that in times of emergency, bills of credit would have to be issued, a they had been by the Continental Congress to finance the Revolution.

It was an open question whether the borrowing power together with the necessary-and-proper clause still enabled the Congress to emit bills of credit.[19] In fact, Congress in 1812 resorted to the issue of treasury notes in small denominations that were not payable on demand, and these circulated as money.[20] Although they were not made legal tender, they were receivable for public dues and payable to public creditors.

As has been noted, the emission of bills of credit by the states and their statutes making this paper legal tender were prime causes of economic instability after independence.[21] Madison explained the constitutional prohibition:

> The extension of the prohibition to bills of credit must give pleasure to every citizen, in proportion to his love of justice and his knowledge of the true springs of public prosperity. The loss which America has sustained since the peace, from the pestilent effects of paper money on the necessary confidence between man and man, on the necessary confidence in the public councils, on the industry and morals of the people, and on the character of republican government, constitutes

an enormous debt against the States chargeable with this unadvised measure, which must long remain unsatisfied; or rather an accumulation of guilt, which can be expiated no otherwise than by a voluntary sacrifice on the altar of justice, of the power which has been the instrument of it.[22]

Story pointed out that the prohibitions on state bills of credit and on the enactment of legal tender laws are distinct and independent of each other: "Both are forbidden. To sustain the one because it is not also the other; to say that bills of credit may be emitted, if they are not made a tender in payment of debts, is, in effect, to expunge that distinct, independent prohibition, and to read the clause as if it had been entirely omitted. No principle of interpretation can justify such a course."[23]

The scope of the prohibition on state bills of credit was tested in *Craig* v. *Missouri*,[24] a suit on a promissory note that had been issued for state certificates that circulated as money. In 1830, the Supreme Court, by a 4-to-3 decision, invalidated the state statute providing for the issuance of loan certificates by the state bearing 2 percent interest. The loan certificates were issued in denominations of from $.50 to $10.00. Although the statute did not declare them legal tender, the certificates were receivable in discharge of taxes and debts to the state and local governments, salaries of state officers, and for salt sold by lessees of the public saltworks. Chief Justice Marshall first defined the terms: "To 'emit bills of credit' conveys to the mind the idea of issuing paper intended to circulate through the community for its ordinary purposes, as money, which paper is redeemable at a future day."[25] The law directed the auditor and treasurer to redeem annually one-tenth of the bills from circulation. The fact that the issue was labeled "certificates" was not determinative. "We think the certificates emitted under authority of this act are entirely bills of credit as if they had been so denominated in the act itself."[26] The functional analysis of Marshall explained why the prohibition applied whether state bills of credit were made legal tender or not. The object was to terminate unstable paper money emitted by the states and accepted by the people regardless of its lack of legal tender.

The effectiveness of *Craig* in barring paper money issued by states was eliminated seven years later in *Briscoe* v. *Bank of Kentucky*,[27] in which the Court upheld the constitutionality of a state statute creating a banking corporation owned and controlled by the state and authorized to issue bank notes. The bank was clearly the agent of the state. The key distinction of Justice McLean turned on a technicality. The corporation was a distinct legal entity, whose funds stood behind its obligations. The bank could be sued without its consent and its assets were subject to execution to satisfy its debts. Justice McLean held that since the bank notes were not issued on the credit of the state government or redeemable by it, they were not state bills of credit.[28]

The lone dissent of Justice Story followed the functional analysis of Chief Justice Marshall in *Craig*. Story noted that at the earlier hearing of the case before the death of the Chief Justice, Marshall agreed with him that the statute was unconstitutional.[29] Bills of credit "mean negotiable paper, intended to pass as currency, or as money, by delivery or endorsement."[30] In this sense, bank notes are bills of credit. The nature and object of negotiable paper are not changed, whether it is issued by a corporation or by a state. Story noted "that the bank corporation is here the sole and exclusive instrument of the State, managing its exclusive funds, for its exclusive benefit, and under its exclusive management."[31] The bank existed for the sole benefit of the state. "The whole funds possessed by it, whether they were capital stock, or debts, or securities, or real estate, or bank notes, belonged in fact to the State."[32] As equitable owner, the state might repeal the bank charter and take over the assets. And if the state assumed the status of legal owner, it would have to perform the bank's contracts so that its takeover would not be an unconstitutional impairment of contract. This would raise issues of enforcement in light of the Eleventh Amendment.

In his treatise, Justice Story cited Daniel Webster for a further textual argument against the state power to charter banks to issue notes that circulate as money. The states are prohibited from coining money. Do they have the power to "coin that which becomes the actual and almost universal substitute for money?"[33] In contrast to the states, Congress was given the power to create the Bank of the United States with authority to issue bank notes. This power was founded in part on the exclusive national power to coin money. It might have been difficult to justify the bank on the basis of taxing and commerce powers alone.

Both the national power to coin money and to authorize its substitute, bank notes, can be argued to be exclusive if the goal is to delegate monetary power solely in Congress. In fact, at the time, national control of the supply of money through coinage and through issuing national bank notes was highly ineffective because the majority of paper money was state bank notes. As Story noted, "It would be a startling proposition in any other part of the world, that the prerogative of coining money, held by government, was liable to be defeated, counteracted, or impeded by another prerogative, held in other hands, of authorizing a paper circulation."[34]

Story's viewpoint is reinforced by the express power in the national government to determine the value of money.[35] This power could be narrowly interpreted to mean only the value of coins. But if legal-tender statues make paper money convertible into coins, the power to determine the value should also extend to paper such as bank notes. Although the quantity theory of money was not known in the era before the Civil War, the fear of great increases in the supply of bank notes was real. The power to control the supply in order to regulate the value should have enabled Congress to prohibit the issuance of bank notes by state-chartered banks.

From 1800 to 1860, and especially after the charter of the second Bank of the United States expired in 1836, state-bank notes were a major part of the money supply in the United States.[36] The consequence was monetary instability, alternate cycles of inflation and economic collapse.[37] Unsound banking meant suspension of specie payments in times of economic crisis. Inconvertible state bank notes sold at discounts of 50 percent to 60 percent.[38] Such an unstable monetary system was not adequate when the nation went to war. In 1861 the first federal statute was passed authorizing the issue of notes by the Treasury Department.[39] This was followed by a number of other statutes, some of which also contained sections imposing small taxes on the notes of national and state banks.

In 1866 Congress imposed a tax of 10 percent on the notes of state banks. The obvious purpose was to tax them out of circulation.[40] The constitutionality of the statue was upheld in 1869 in *Veazie Bank* v. *Fenno*.[41] The tax was held not to be a direct tax under Article I, Section 2, Clause 3 and Article I, Section 9, Clause 4: "[I]n the practical construction of the Constitution by Congress, direct taxes have been limited to taxes on land and appurtenances, and taxes on polls, or capitation taxes."[42] Hence, this tax on currency did not have to be apportioned among the states according to the census. More important, it was held that a tax designed to destroy the power of banks to issue notes was clearly within the powers of Congress. The Court was without power to hold this tax rate excessive when it was used to supplement the congressional power to coin money and control the value thereof. "Having thus, in the exercise of undisputed constitutional powers, undertaken to provide a currency for the whole country, it cannot be questioned that Congress may, constitutionally, secure the benefit of it to the people by appropriate legislation."[43] The same rule was applied in 1880 in upholding a similar 10 percent tax as applied to national bank notes.[44]

The issues of United States notes by the treasury after 1861 led to three major cases testing their unconstitutionality, the legal-tender cases.[45] As background to the issues in those cases, one must recall that there was a contest at the Constitutional Convention about whether to give Congress an express power to emit bills of credit.[46] In the legal-tender cases, the Supreme Court noted without citation that it was established law that under its fiscal powers and the necessary-and-proper clause, the Congress could emit bills of credit. The only issue was whether the notes could be made legal tender for private debts.

In *Hepburn* v. *Griswold*,[47] a 4-to-3 decision in 1870, the Court held unconstitutional the 1862 statutes making United States notes legal tender for private debts contracted before passage of the statute. Chief Justice Chase first ruled that making bills of credit legal tender was not a necessary and proper means of executing the express power in Congress to coin money.[48] Although issuance of bills of credit was necessary to execute the war powers, making them legal tender in payment of pre-existing debt was not. The legal-tender statute was also held to violate the due process clause of the Fifth Amendment. "We are obliged to conclude that an Act making mere promises to pay dollars a legal tender in payment of debts previously contracted, is not a means appropriate, plainly adapted, really calculated to carry into effect any express power of Congress; that such an Act is inconsistent with the spirit of the Constitution; and that it is prohibited by the Constitution."[49]

Following the *Hepburn* decision, President Grant filled two vacancies on the Court with Justices Bradley and Strong, men known to support the constitutionality of United States notes.[50] Subsequently, in 1871, by a 5-to-4 decision, in *Knox* v. *Lee*[51] and *Parker* v. *Davis,* the Court upheld all the constitutional aspects of the legal-tender acts. The statutes were held necessary and proper to execute the fiscal and war powers in time of emergency. Justice Strong, for the Court, noted the effect of such statutes on contracts made before enactment: "Every contract for the payment of money simply is necessarily subject to the constitutional power of the government over the currency, whatever that power may be, and the obligation of the parties is, therefore, assumed with reference to that power."[52] He further noted that the federal government is not explicitly barred from impairing the obligation of contracts, and that this statute, whose effect was to lower the value of currency, did not violate the eminent domain protection. He concluded by expressly overruling *Hepburn* v. *Griswold,* and commented on the method of constitutional interpretation: "[I]t is no unprecedented thing in courts of last resort, both in this country and in England, to overrule decisions previously made. We agree this should not be done inconsiderately, but in case of such far-reaching consequences as the present, thoroughly convinced as we are that Congress has not transgressed its powers, we regard it as our duty so to decide, and to affirm both these judgments."[53]

It was not until 1884 in *Juilliard* v. *Greenman,*[54] that the Supreme Court upheld the legal tender of treasury notes without reliance in part on the war powers. In that case, it upheld the constitutionality of an act of 1878 providing for reissue of United States notes. Speaking for an 8-to-1 majority, Justice Gray concluded that enumerated fiscal powers and the necessary-and-proper clause were sufficient grounds to uphold the statute.[55]

None of the statutes in the legal tender cases required acceptance of treasury notes when bonds or contracts were expressly payable only in gold or coin.[56] It was only in 1933 that a joint resolution of Congress abrogated gold-payment clauses in government bonds and private contracts.[57] In *Perry* v. *United States,*[58] a 5-to-4 decision in 1935, the abrogation of the gold clause in a government bond was successfully challenged as violating the borrowing clause of the Constitution, but the creditor was denied a remedy in the absence of proof of actual damages. In 1935 Congress prevented further legal actions relating to its debts payable in gold by withdrawing its consent to be sued in such cases.[59] In *Norman* v. *B. & O. R. Co.*[60] also a 5-to-4 decision in 1935, the Court upheld the abrogation of gold clauses in private contracts as a valid application of the coinage clause. The law was effective even though the contracts were executed before the legislation was passed. The affirmative regulatory power of Congress was held to enable it to impair the obligation of private contracts without violation of the eminent domain and due process clauses of the Fifth Amendment. These latter clauses were held limited to direct appropriation.

National Banks to Control the Supply of Money

When the nation began its existence in 1789, the only national currency was coins.[61] Given the constitutional prohibition on state bills of credit, the only paper money was the bank notes of three banks, chartered in Philadelphia, New York, and Boston. The national government had to use state banks for deposit of treasury funds and as fiscal agents to transfer funds. The state banks controlled the supply of money through their issuance of bank notes.

At the Constitutional Convention, the issue of whether the national government should have the power to create private corporations, such as a national bank, was left open. Madison suggested that Article I, Section 8 should include the power "to grant charters of incorporation where the interest of the U.S. might require & the legislative provisions of the individual States may be incompetent."[62] Rufus King of Massachusetts thought that the power was unnecessary. "The States will be prejudiced and divided into parties by it."[63] He mentioned Philadelphia and New York as not wanting competing banks and other places as fearing a general power of incorporation as the power to create mercantile monopolies. James Wilson of Pennsylvania disagreed. The issue was not brought to a vote.

On December 14, 1790, the secretary of the treasury, Alexander Hamilton, transmitted to the House of Representatives his proposal for a national bank.[64] Its first function would be to operate as a commercial bank with partial reserves of gold and silver, and, through loans, augment the productive capital of the country. Hamilton explained the functions of a bank as a financial intermediary and as a creator of funds for economic expansion so that interest rates would remain low. Following the pattern of the Bank of England, the bank would also assist public finance with loans to the national government. It would facilitate the payment of taxes by loans and discounts for persons in business who did not have liquid capital when taxes were due, and by adding to the quantity of paper money acceptable for payment of taxes. Furthermore, the establishment of a national bank with many branches would lower the transaction costs of collecting and transporting coins paid as national taxes.

The bill to charter the Bank of the United States provided for a capital stock of $10 million of which one-fifth was to be subscribed by the government. The bill was first heard in the Senate. In those early days, the debates and proceedings of the Senate were not open to the public. The record shows only a resolution without recorded dissent: "That this bill do pass; that the title it be, 'An act to incorporate the subscribers to the Bank of the United States.' "[65] In the House of Representatives, four members spoke against the constitutionality of the bank bill. James Madison led the opposition. He observed that the monetary and fiscal powers of Article I, Section 8 gave Congress no express power to create a bank. He dismissed the necessary-and-proper clause as "in fact merely declaratory of what would have resulted by unavoidable implication, as the appropriate, and, as it were, technical means of executing those powers."[66] He concluded: "If implications, thus remote and thus multiplied, can be linked together, a chain may be formed that will reach every object of legislation, every object within the whole Congress of political economy."[67] But the majority of speakers supported the bill, and the final vote was 39 in favor and 20 against.[68] Of those voting against, fifteen were from Virginia, the Carolinas, and Georgia.[69] It is reasonable to infer that most opponents of the bill were motivated not by the constitutional issue, but by the agrarian fear of the financial power of a national bank.

When the bill was transmitted to President Washington, he referred it to the secretary of state, Thomas Jefferson, and to the attorney general, Edmund Randolph, for their opinions. Both of them replied with reports indicating that they considered the bank bill unconstitutional.[70] When their written opinions reached Secretary Hamilton, he wrote a long memorandum in defense of the bill.[71] He repeated the efficiency argument of his original proposal. The president signed the bill, which granted a charter for twenty years.

The Bank of the United States came to perform a central banking function that its sponsors had not anticipated. The state banks were not regulated by state governments, and their managers had various attitudes concerning the reserves that should be held in currency to meet demands. The Bank of the United States, by promptly returning bank notes and checks to the issuing or drawee state banks, pressured them to keep adequate reserves. In spite of the bank's fine record of performance, two groups of Jeffersonians opposed renewal of its charter in 1811.[72] The first group were those agrarians who opposed its original creation. The second were those who had established local banks and wished to end the competition of the Bank of the United States and to stop its prompt return of their bank notes and checks drawn on them. Much of the public argument of these partisans attacked the constitutionality of the bank. Of the thirty-nine speeches in Congress on the issue of renewal, thirty-five centered on constitutionality.[73] The renewal was blocked when a vote in the House to postpone indefinitely the consideration of the renewal bill carried by 65 to 64.[74]

Upon demise of the first Bank of the United States, many new banks were chartered by the states. This was just before the War of 1812, which disrupted trade and greatly reduced the demand for loans. Absent the regulatory effect of the Bank of the United States in returning notes and checks for payment, the state banks could lower specie reserves. In 1814, when the British attacked Washington, there were runs on banks for payment in specie.[75] Except in New England, banks throughout the country had to suspend payment because their reserves were exhausted. State-bank notes were discounted in varying percentages depending on the likelihood of resumption of specie payments. The problem of bank regulation, that could have an efficient solution only on the national level, was left to the states. The necessary movement of treasury business to the state banks also reduced efficiency of transfers of federal funds and left the treasury with no source of short-term loans.

Beginning in 1814, there were proposals in Congress to charter a new national bank.[76] The issue of constitutionality, which was given so much insincere prominence in 1811, was hardly mentioned. President Madison indicated that the issue should be waived "as being precluded, in my judgment, by repeated recognitions, under varied circumstances, of the validity of such an institution, in the acts of the legislative, executive, and judicial branches of the Government, accompanied by indications, in different modes, of a concurrence of the general will of the nation."[77] The national government clearly needed a fiscal agent and a national bank was the only efficient solution. The bill to charter the second Bank of the United States for a period of twenty years was approved in the Senate by a vote of 22 to 12 and in the House by a vote of 91 to 67.[78] It was signed by President Madison on April 10, 1816.[79] Like the first bank, the government controlled only a minority interest. Only 20 percent of the shares were owned by the government and twenty of the twenty-five directors were elected by the shareholders. The judgment of history is that the bank achieved notable success in providing a note issue of high quality and in serving as fiscal agent of the government.[80]

The opponents of the Bank did not give up. Local banking interests had powerful influence in their state legislatures. Maryland, Tennessee, Georgia, North Carolina, Kentucky, and Ohio passed taxes on the bank sufficient to force it from their states.[81] This raised the constitutional issue of whether states could by taxes annihilate a nationally chartered bank.

McCulloch v. *Maryland,*[82] in 1819, brought to the Supreme Court the issues of whether the Congress had constitutional power to charter the second Bank of the United States and whether a state could tax the notes of the federal instrumentality. The state legislature had imposed an annual tax of $15,000 on all banks established "without authority from the state." The Maryland branch of the Bank of the United States was the only bank in the state that fit the description. McCulloch, the local cashier of the bank, refused to pay the tax, claiming federal incorporation as his defense. As noted earlier, in upholding the constitutionality of the bank, Chief Justice Marshall emphasized the scope of the incidental powers in Congress under Article 1, Section 8.[83] In its application here, he pointed to the bank's function of financing government and as a transfer agent of federal funds: "Although, among the enumerated powers of government, we do not find the word 'bank' or 'incorporation,' we find the great powers to lay and collect taxes; to borrow money; to regulate commerce, to declare and conduct a war; and to raise and support armies and navies. The sword and the purse, all the external relations, and no inconsiderable portion of the industry of the nation, are entrusted to its government.[84]

After an extended explication of the character of incidental powers to a constitution that enunciated the general governing principles of a nation, he applied his conclusions to this case:

> That a corporation must be considered as a means not less usual, not of higher dignity, not more requiring a particular specification than other means, has been sufficiently proved. . . .
>
> If a corporation may be employed indiscriminately with other means to carry into execution the powers of the government, no particular reason can be assigned for excluding the use of a bank, if required for its fiscal operations. To use one, must be within the discretion of Congress, if it be an appropriate mode of executing the powers of government. That it is a convenient, a useful and essential instrument in the prosecution of its fiscal operations, is not now a subject of controversy. All those who have been concerned in the administration of our finances, have concurred in representing its importance and necessity.[85]

The chief justice went on to hold the Maryland tax on the bank to be unconstitutional. This aspect of the case is treated in the next section of this chapter.

The state of Ohio had passed a severe tax of $50,000 on each bank not chartered by the state. When the decision in *McCulloch* v. *Maryland* was handed down, Ohio chose to ignore it. Osborn, the Ohio state auditor, after demanding and being refused payment of the tax, seized the assets of the local branch of the Bank of the United States. The bank then sued the state officials and the case reached the Supreme Court in 1824 as *Osborn* v. *The Bank of the United States.*[86] The primary holding was that, even though under the Eleventh Amendment there was no federal jurisdiction in such actions against a state, the federal court could hear this action against state officials. When enforcing an unconstitutional state statute, state officials were not truly acting for the state and were personally responsible for their wrongs. In the decision, the Supreme Court reviewed and reaffirmed its decision in *McCulloch* v. *Maryland* on the constitutionality of the bank. The Court specifically upheld the power of the bank to engage in all banking operations for ordinary persons as necessary for its existence so that it could also carry on the fiscal duties for the federal government.[87]

Public acceptance of the rule in the *McCulloch* and *Osborn* cases was so general that the 1864 federal statute for the chartering of national banks was not even challenged.[88] In *Farmers' and Mechanics Natl. Bank* v. *Dearing*,[89] the Supreme Court struck down state regulation of such banks. Justice Swayne, for the Court, explained the scope of congressional power.[90] The Federal Reserve Act of 1913 created a set of regional reserve banks and the Federal Reserve Board to execute national monetary policy.[91] The act gave national banks a new power to act as trustee of stocks and bonds. This delegation was held constitutional in *First Natl. Bank of Bay City* v. *Fellows*.[92] The competitive rationale of upholding even this power was stated by Chief Justice White.[93]

Taxation: Scope and Immunities

The fiscal powers of taxation and spending have objectives and effects that alter resource allocation, distribution of income, and stabilization of the economy. Taxing the income of persons and firms in order to supply public goods diverts a large proportion of national income to spending based on political values derived from legislative compromises rather than on private utility valuations in the market.[94] This diversion of resources and transfer payments designed to assist particular groups of citizens result in income redistribution.[95] Monetary and fiscal policies combine and interact in the implementation of national income-stabilization policies. As noted in the section below on the spending power, national and state governments exercising concurrent powers of taxation create special issues of federal grants in aid. The superior taxing powers of the national government and its use of the borrowing power for huge deficit financing have led some economists to recommend constitutional amendments to limit the taxing power.[96]

The federal tax power is delegated to Congress in broad language in Article I: "The Congress shall have Power to lay and collect Taxes, Duties, Imposts and Excises, to pay the Debts and provide for the common Defence and general Welfare of the United States; but all Duties, Imposts and Excises shall be uniform throughout the United States."[97] This national power is constrained by the provision that "No Tax or Duty shall be laid on Articles exported from any State."[98]

The original meaning of "uniform throughout the United States" was geographical uniformity.[99] Such uniformity does not require Congress to devise taxes that fall equally or proportionately on each state. Rather a "tax is uniform when it operates with the same force and effect in every place where the subject of it is found."[100] Justice Story explained the purpose of the clause: "It was to cut off all undue preferences of one state over another in the regulation of subjects affecting their common interests. Unless duties, imposts, and excises were uniform, the grossest and most oppressive inequalities, vitally affecting the pursuits and employments of the people of different states, might exist. The agriculture commerce, or manufactures of one state might be built up on the ruins of another; and a combination of a few states in Congress might secure a monopoly of certain branches of trade and business to themselves, to the injury, if not the destruction, of their less favored neighbors."[101]

The limited scope of the requirement of uniformity is illustrated by two modern decisions. In *Fernandez* v. *Weiner*,[102] the Supreme Court upheld an amendment to the Internal Revenue Act that included in the gross estate of the decedent all community property including life insurance proceeds on the decedent's life. The effect was uniform in all states having community property, and its inapplicability to other states did not violate the uniformity requirement. The Court also held that the Tenth Amendment had placed no restriction upon the power delegated to the national government to lay an excise tax *qua* tax.

Even geographical uniformity has functional exceptions. In *United States* v. *Ptasynski*,[103] the Court upheld the Alaskan oil exemption in the Crude Oil Windfall Profit Tax Act against a charge of violation of the uniformity clause. In fact, less than 20 percent of Alaskan production was exempt. This came from an area where climatic and geographical conditions make the average cost of drilling as much as fifteen times that elsewhere in the United States. The Court commented on the origins of the clause: "There was concern that the National Government would use its power over commerce to the disadvantage of particular States. The Uniformity Clause was proposed as one of several measures designed to limit the exercise of that power."[104]

The Supreme Court has emphasized the broad scope of the tax power by characterizing it as "exhaustive" and holding that it "embraces every conceivable power of taxation."[105] But under the thesis of this study, there should be legislative finality on the scope and breadth of the national taxing power within the constraints of the express constitutional limitations. The Court has never recognized this power. Instead, it has created and dismantled a series of intergovernmental tax immunities that lacked a principled understanding of state exemptions.

In a federal system where the national government and the states have concurrent powers of taxation, there is great potential for one to harm the other through oppressive taxation. In a recent regulatory case the court has said that protection for the states lies only in the political process,[106] but this contention is highly debatable. In terms of judicial enforcement of federalism, a reasoned principle would state that neither the national government nor the state governments may impose taxes on the other that would materially impair the function of governing.

As stated in the rule of *McCulloch* v. *Maryland*, the tax immunity of the national government is most secure. *McCulloch* held the state tax on the bank notes of the second Bank of the United States unconstitutional. The case could have been decided on the narrow issue of discriminatory taxation. Chief Justice Marshall chose a much broader approach. Reasoning on the basis of the national supremacy clause of Article VI, he offered the following deductions: "1st. That a power to create implies a power to preserve. 2d. That a power to destroy, if wielded by a different hand, is hostile to, and incompatible with these powers to create and to preserve. 3d. That where this repugnancy exists, that authority which is supreme must control, not yield to that over which it is supreme."[108] Marshall further asserted that the state power of taxation is measured by the extent of the sovereignty of the people of a single state. This, he stated, places beyond state reach all those powers that the people of the United States have conferred on their government and all those means for executing federal governmental powers. For this reason the Maryland tax on the notes of the Bank of the United States was unconstitutional.

In *Osborn* v. *Bank of the United States*,[109] the Court reiterated the rule of *McCulloch* that a state may not tax an instrumentality of the national government. It rejected the argument that the exemption should have been expressly stated in the legislation of creating the bank. Chief Justice Marshall observed: "It is no unusual thing for an act of Congress to imply, without expressing, this very exemption from state control, which is said to be so objectionable in this instance."[110] Marshall also rejected the argument that a bank of which the government owned only 20 percent was not a public institution. A contractor acting as fiscal agent of the government was entitled to immunity because this was necessary for the execution of the government's agency functions.[111]

The tax immunity of the national government and its agencies is now unquestioned. But serious difficulties arose on whether that immunity should be extended to recipients of income from the government or the suppliers of goods and services to the government. The income from United States bonds, for example, is not subject to a state tax on securities.[112] If, however, the income has been received and is held as an asset, it is subject to the general state property tax.[113] The one principle that seems clear is that, under the necessary-and-proper clause, Congress may confer immunity from state taxation. It may protect governmental functions from state taxation even if those functions are not exercised by federal officers. In *First Agricultural Nat. Bank* v. *State Tax Com'n.*,[114] for example, the application of a Massachusetts sales-and-use tax to a nationally chartered bank was held not permitted by federal statute.

A number of cases that had extended the national governmental immunity to its public officials and to companies hired by public agencies have been overruled. In *Graves* v. *N.Y. ex rel. O'Keefe*,[115] the Court overruled its earlier decisions and held that the salary of a federal officer was not immune from state income taxation. The earlier courts had erroneously held that salaries that had been paid to federal or state officials were still in the hands of a governmental instrumentality. Another earlier decision was overruled to hold that royalties received from patents or copyrights are subject to a nondiscriminating state income tax.[116]

National governmental tax immunity under the supremacy clause and the rule of *McCulloch* has also been tested in this century in cases concerning extension of the immunity to suppliers of goods and services to the government. From an economic viewpoint, if the tax becomes part of the cost function of the supplier, its incidence will be on the government as final purchaser. Applying Article VI, Clause 2, the Court followed the economics rule and held state laws imposing excise taxes on the sale of gasoline void as assessed on sales to federal agencies.[117] The immunity was not extended, however, to gasoline purchased by a government contractor who used the gasoline to operate his machinery in the construction of levees.[118]

It is debatable whether a gross-receipts tax on a government supplier will become part of his costs or operate more like a net income tax, whose incidence is upon the taxpayer. In *Alward* v. *Johnson*,[119] the Court sustained a state gross-receipts tax levied in lieu of a property tax upon the operator of an automobile-stage line. About two-thirds of his gross receipts were derived from carriage of the U.S. mails. In *James* v. *Dravo Contracting Co.*,[120] by a 5-to-4 decision, the Court sustained a state occupation tax on an independent contractor measured by his gross receipts under a contract to construct locks and dams for the national government. The Court noted its effort "in this difficult field to apply the practical criterion" it had used in earlier cases.[121] It found no direct burden on the government. But the Court broke new ground when it stated: "[I]f it be assumed that the gross receipts tax may increase the cost to the government, that fact would not invalidate the tax."[122] The Court analogized state property tax on contractor's equipment to the gross-receipts tax. It is notable that the solicitor general of the United States supported the contention of the state that the tax was valid.[123]

In *Alabama* v. *King & Boozer*,[124] the Court went even further in upholding state taxes with an ultimate incidence on the national government.

The Court sustained a state sales tax charged on lumber sold by King and Boozer to contractors building an army camp on cost-plus-fixed-fee basis. It was acknowledged that the economic incidence was on the government, but immunity was denied because the legal incidence was on the contractor.[125] The Court refused to invoke the supremacy clause because Congress had failed to pass express legislation immunizing such transactions from state taxation.[126]

The Supreme Court held the opposite view in *Kern-Limerick, Inc.* v. *Scurlock*.[127] Here again a state sales tax was assessed on a contractor purchasing goods to be used in construction for the government. In this case, however, the contractor was appointed an agent of the navy to buy the goods in the name of the navy. "We find that the purchaser under this contract was the United States. Thus King & Boozer is not controlling for, though the Government also bore the economic burden of the state tax in that case, the legal incidence of the tax was held to fall on the independent contractor and not upon the United States."[128]

Two recent cases have reiterated the rule of *King & Boozer*. In *United States* v. *New Mexico*,[129] a special bank account in which U.S. treasury funds were deposited was available to contractors managing a national atomic laboratory. New Mexico sales taxes were assessed on goods and services sold to the contractors and paid from the account. In sustaining the tax, the Court ruled that "immunity may not be conferred simply because the tax has an effect on the United States, or even because the Federal Government shoulders the entire economic burden of the levy."[130] The Court concluded that "tax immunity is appropriate only in one circumstance: when the levy falls on the United States itself, or on an agency or instrumentality so closely connected to the Government that the two cannot realistically be viewed as separate entities."[131] A similar ruling was made in *Washington* v. *United States*,[132] a 5-to-4 decision. Justice Blackmun, for the dissenters, noted the issue: "The Court by its ruling in this case continued its recent tendency to be sympathetic with States in their urgent quest for new taxes. In my view, however, the Court now oversteps the important and significant boundary that separates appropriate state taxation, having only an incidental effect on federal operations, from inappropriate state taxation that is imposed directly or indirectly upon the United States and is therefore invalid under the Supremacy Clause, Art. VI, cl. 2, of the United States Constitution."[133]

In the field of property taxes, national immunity from state taxation is narrowly defined. In *United States* v. *Detroit*,[134] the Court upheld application of a Michigan statute that provided that when tax-exempt property was leased, loaned, or used by a private person for business for profit, taxes would be assessed as though the operator owned the property. The tax was assessed on the lessee of a federally owned industrial plant.

Potential state immunity from federal taxation faces the opposite side of the supremacy clause from national immunity. Federal taxation carries the armor of the supremacy clause when conflict arises with state law. As a general principle, Congress may not assess a tax on state governments that would impair their sovereignty. But Congress has seldom enacted laws to tax directly the incomes or properties of the states or municipalities. The Court held in 1873 that the federal income tax could not be imposed on a municipality for income from investments in securities of private corporations.[135] But it is clear that recipients of income from the states are not immune from federal taxation. In *Helvering* v. *Gebhart*,[136] the Court held that the salaries of state officers are not immune from federal income taxation. Similarly, in *Helvering* v. *Mountain Producers Corp.*,[137] the Court overruled its earlier views and held the profits of private oil companies from oil produced on land leased from a state where subject to federal taxation. Earlier the Court had sustained federal taxation of income derived by independent engineering contractors from the performance of state functions[138] and duties on the importation of scientific apparatus by a state university.[139]

The most recent ruling on state immunity concerns the power of the national government to assess federal income tax on the interest paid to owners of municipal bonds. In *Pollock* v. *Farmers' Loan & Trust Co.*,[140] the Court had held that income from municipal bonds "could not be taxed because of want of power to tax the source."[141] In *South Carolina* v. *Baker*,[142] the Court validated the 1982 act in which Congress removed from federal income-tax exemption the interest on publicly offered long-term bonds issued by state and local governments unless those bonds were issued in registered form. By a 7-to-1 decision, the Court first rejected an argument based on the Tenth Amendment and related constitutional principles of federalism.[143] It noted that under the rule of *Garcia*[144] states must find their protection from congressional regulation through the national political process. As to the second argument, based on intergovernmental immunity, the Court expressly overruled this aspect of the *Pollack*.[145] Instead of relying on the supremacy clause, the Court adopted the questionable doctrine derived from cases such as those concerning state taxes on suppliers to the national government. "States can never tax the United States directly, but can tax any private parties with whom it does business, even though the financial burden falls on the United States, as long as the tax does not discriminate against the United States or those with whom it deals."[146] The Court's analysis treated both the national and the state aspects of intergovernmental immunity as equal, although the supremacy clause makes them unequal.

State immunity from federal taxation does not extend to nongovernmental or proprietary activities. The leading case on federal taxation of such state activities is *New York* v. *United States*.[147] The state operated the Saratoga Springs recreation facility at a loss, but recovered part of its expenses by selling mineral water taken from the property. The federal government imposed a tax of two cents per gallon on the sale of mineral waters. The Supreme Court, in a 6-to-2 decision, upheld the imposition of this tax on New York. Two of the justices felt it was constitutional as long as it was nondiscriminating. Chief Justice Stone and three others, while rejecting the distinction between governmental and proprietary functions, stated a general rule. The Court held that "the limitation on the taxing power of each, so far as it affects the other, must receive a practical construction which permits both to function with the minimum of interferences each with the other; and that limitation cannot be so varied or extended as seriously to impair either the taxing power of the government imposing the tax . . . or the appropriate exercise of the functions of the government affected by it."[148]

Taxation as Regulation

Special constitutional issues arise when the primary purpose of a taxation statute is not to secure revenue but to regulate other activity.[149] It is established that regulatory or destructive taxation may properly be used as a means to execute the delegated powers of Congress. As was noted above, in 1869 *Veazie Bank* v. *Fenno*[150] held that a destructive 10 percent tax on state-bank notes, which earned no revenue, was constitutional because it was enacted to effect the delegated currency powers.

A much broader rationale was needed to sustain the 1902 statute in which Congress imposed a prohibitive tax of ten cents per pound on oleomargarine colored to look like butter.[151] This statute, designed to protect the creamery interests from competition, was professedly a public-health measure and not subsumed under any of the other delegated regulatory powers. In 1904, in *McCray* v. *United States*,[152] the oleomargarine statute was held constitutional because, on its face, the law purported to be for the purpose of taxation. Justice White presented what has come to be known as the doctrine of objective constitutionality.[153]

This application of objective constitutionality is arguably wrong. In *McCray*, there is a conflict between the delegated power to tax and the fundamental constitutional limitation, equal protection of the law. It is demonstrated in chapter 12 that equal protection is a necessary component of a fair legal system, even though it is not explicitly stated in the Bill of Rights.[154] It is necessarily implied by chapters 39 and 40 of the Magna Charta and should be inferred from the due process clause of the Fifth Amendment.[155] The different treatment of yellow margarine from white and from butter when they all are in like circumstances as competitors in the market for healthful spreads is a denial of equal protection. Under the general principle that constitutional limitations override delegated powers, the statute should have been invalidated.

Many regulatory taxes have been upheld by the Supreme Court, either on the theory of delegated power of the *Veazie* case or on the theory of objective constitutionality of the *McCray* case.[156] Under the necessary-and-proper clause, Congress may regulate some aspects of local business within a state in order more effectively to tax it. The broad construction of the taxing power has even been applied to the preservation of inefficient business through high protective tariff barriers. In *Hampton & Co.* v. *United States*,[157] Chief Justice Taft stated: "Whatever we may think of the wisdom of a protection policy, we can not hold it unconstitutional. So long as the motive of Congress and the effect of its legislative action are to secure revenue for the benefit of the general government, the existence of other motives in the selection of the subject of taxes cannot invalidate Congressional action."[158]

The laissez-faire bias of those justices who voted to constrict the commerce power in this century until 1937 also led them to vote against the use of the tax power as an indirect means of regulating commerce. In a few cases they assembled a majority. In the *Child Labor Tax*[159] case of 1922, Congress had passed a statute imposing a tax of 10 percent on the income of firms that had employed workers under fourteen years of age in mills and factories or those under sixteen years of age in mines and quarries. This was a patent attempt to regulate indirectly a practice that the Court had barred from federal commerce regulation in the case that is now known as one of the Court's great errors, *Hammer* v. *Dagenhart*.[160] In Child Labor Tax the Court rejected the objective constitutionality of the *McCray* case and struck down the statute. Furthermore, the Court held that Congress had violated the Tenth Amendment by invading the reserved powers of the states. "The so-called tax is a penalty to coerce people of a state to act as Congress wishes them to act in respect of a matter completely the business of the state government under the Federal Constitution."[161]

In 1922 the Court also invalidated the Future Trading Act, which levied a tax of twenty cents per bushel on grain in futures contracts except when made through a member of the Board of Trade designated by the secretary of agriculture.[162] The Court found this to be a penalty and an attempt to regulate local commerce. In the *Constantine* case of 1935, the Court struck down a special federal excise tax of $1,000 on liquor manufacturers and dealers operating in states where such business was illegal.[163] The statute was held to be a penalty rather than a tax, and to have no constitutional basis following repeal of the Eighteenth Amendment. In the *Butler* case of 1936, the Court held the Agricultural Adjustment Act of 1933 to be unconstitutional on the ground that the proceeds of a tax on processors of agricultural commodities were to be used to regulate local agriculture, a matter reserved to the states under the Tenth Amendment.[164]

The Supreme Court's sharp reversal of interpretation of the commerce clause in 1937 marked a renewed recognition of the extremely broad original character of national constitutional power.[165] This renaissance of federal regulatory power was also expressed in the tax decisions. Although the *Child Labor Tax* case and the *Butler* case were never overruled because later statutes did not concern precisely the same subject matter, the legal significance of those cases was essentially destroyed. The Court has unequivocally asserted that the power to tax is not restricted by the Tenth Amendment.[166]

The first two tax cases in the new era upheld the constitutionality of the Social Security Act of 1935. In *Steward Machine Co.* v. *Davis,* [167] by a 5-to-4 decision, the Court sustained the unemployment compensation sections of the act. The statute imposed a tax on employers, but they could receive a credit of up to 90 percent of the tax if they made contributions to a state unemployment-compensation fund approved by the Social Security Board. One obvious purpose of the statute was to force the states to set up approved unemployment-compensation plans. In spite of the penal nature of the tax if a state chose not to conform, the statute was upheld. In *Helvering* v. *Davis*[168] with two dissents, the Court sustained the old-age pension sections of the act.

In *United States* v. *Sanchez*[169] in 1950, the Supreme Court sustained the tax on marijuana and rejected the argument that the tax was penal, in effect returning to the doctrine of objective constitutionality of the *McCray* case. Justice Clark wrote: "Nor does a tax statute necessarily fall because it touches on activities which Congress might not otherwise regulate."[170] This comment may not be applicable here since, under the commerce power, Congress has plenary power to prohibit all transactions in marijuana.

The broad scope of the tax power was continued in *United States* v. *Kahriger,*[171] which sustained a statute that assessed a tax of 10 percent on the amount of all wagers and required registration of persons in the trade. The Court distinguished the *Constantine* case on the basis that this tax applied not only in states where wagers were illegal, but also in states where wagers were legal. Justice Reed distinguished pure penalty cases from those having some revenue objective.[172] One must conclude that the laissez-faire majority of the court that struck down those few statutes between 1922 and 1936 had narrowed the tax power to conform to the enumerated powers in a manner inconsistent with its true meaning. The doctrine of objective constitutionality upholds the original meaning of the tax power by giving legislative finality to its scope and breadth, though subject to the express constitutional limitations.

Taxation: Apportionment

Two sections of Article I require that direct taxes be apportioned: "Representatives and direct Taxes shall be apportioned among the several States which may be included within this Union, according to their respective Numbers;" "No Capitation, or other direct, Tax shall be laid, unless in proportion to the Census or Enumeration herein before directed to be taken."[174]

It is clear that in 1787 "capitation tax" meant poll tax. There was no clear meaning in the language for the phrase "direct tax," so one must resort to the special meaning given that phrase by the members of the convention who took part in the drafting of it.[175] All the evidence supports the conclusion that it referred to taxes on land.[176] The clause was a result of one of the compromises at the convention, in which the representatives of the South wished to prevent federal taxation on land by area or taxation on slaves by number.

Hylton v. *United States*[177] in 1796 was the first case to test the meaning of "direct tax." Congress had levied a specific tax on all carriages, for personal use, for hire, or for conveyance of passengers. The tax met the requirement of Article I, Section 8 for geographical uniformity of all duties, impost or excise, but it was attacked as a direct tax not apportioned according to the census. The Court, which sustained the tax, contained three members of the Constitutional Convention, two of whom, Wilson and Patterson, participated in the writing of the direct-tax clause. The Court took the logical position that the direct-tax clause was an exception to the general taxing power of Congress. As a practical matter, the court felt no tax should be excepted that could not be conveniently apportioned. The tax on carriages was found to be assessed on their use, and was therefore an excise.

The statements of the framers and of the *Hylton* case, that direct taxes pertained only to poll and land taxes, was not challenged until after the Civil War. Rejecting such challenges, the Supreme Court sustained as excises or duties a tax on the receipts of insurance companies from premiums and assessments,[178] a tax on the notes (paper money) issued by state banks,[179] and an inheritance tax as applied to real estate.[180] Finally, in 1881 the Civil War general income tax was held not to be a direct tax in *Springer* v. *United States*.[181] In this case, a unanimous Supreme Court reiterated that direct taxes were only capitation and land taxes.[182]

The preceding cases are background to the challenge of the income tax, which was incorporated in the Wilson-Gorman Tariff Act of 1894.[183] In *Pollock* v. *Farmers' Loan & Trust Co.*,[184] by a 5-to-4 decision, this tax on income from real and personal property was held to be a direct tax that had not been apportioned among the states and was therefore unconstitutional. The decision demonstrated a confusion of a tax on income with a tax on the source of income. Justice Fuller, for the Court, noted, however, that the decision did not apply to income taxes on "business, privileges or employments."[185] Subsequently, in *Flint* v. *Stone Tracy Co.*,[186] the Court sustained a corporate income tax enacted under the Corporate Excise Tax Act of 1909.[187] It was not possible to apportion such a tax among the states according to the census. It was treated as an excise tax even though part of a firm's income might come from real or personal property.

Like the *Dred Scott* case,[188] the *Pollock* case has been characterized by Chief Justice Hughes[189] as one of the Court's great self-inflicted wounds. Not only were the majority of citizens aroused by the *Pollock* decision, but many leading lawyers felt it was clearly erroneous. *Pollock* was handed down by the same court that had almost wiped out the effectiveness of the Sherman Act by its erroneous construction of the commerce clause in the *Knight*[190] case. In *Pollock,* the Court strained the meaning of constitutional language and overruled the *Hylton*[191] case of a hundred years earlier. The Court majority found a way to impede the adoption of the progressive income tax. From an economic point of view, taxes on wealth are in a different class from taxes on income. While income taxes are progressive, most local property taxes have been regressive.[192] Although the property tax can be viewed as a tax on capital income, its burden is not necessarily uniform.[193] Large areas of land, for example, can be held vacant for speculative purposes and have no current income, and yet be subject to land taxes. Farmers pay land taxes even in years when drought or insects destroy their crops.

One can only conclude that the majority in *Pollack* were determined to find a way to impede the adoption of a national income tax. The result, as in the *Dred Scott* case, was to provoke the Congress and the people to amend the Constitution. The Sixteenth Amendment reads as follows: "The Congress shall have power to lay and collect taxes on incomes, from whatever source derived, without apportionment among the several states, and without regard to any census or enumeration."[194] It was not until 1913 that the Sixteenth Amendment became law. Thus the *Pollock* decision barred effective federal income taxation for over fifteen years. Ironically, in the first test of a federal income tax after the passage of the amendment, the Court seemed to feel the amendment was not essential. "The Sixteenth Amendment conferred no new power of taxation but simply prohibited the previous complete and plenary power of income taxation possessed by the Congress from the beginning from being taken out of the category of indirect taxation to which it inherently belonged."[195]

Spending Power and the General Welfare

The economic relations between the taxing and spending powers vary according to the public-spending objectives.[196] Some public goods, such as national defense and local police, are social goods that must be consumed in equal amounts by all persons in the community.[197] Because no person can be excluded from the benefits and most persons will not engage in voluntary payments, the market will not supply such goods. Other public goods, such as highways, are not consumed in equal amounts by all persons. But the transaction costs of charging each user on a per-mile basis and the cost of excluding nonpayers makes it infeasible to apply unit pricing to users. Nonetheless, highways are not a social-welfare activity of the state, so the general application of user charges in the form of license and fuel taxes is appropriate.

Still other types of public spending are not for true public goods and would be provided by the private market if public institutions were not available. Primary and secondary schools are an example. This is not to say that public subsidy to parents for education of a large segment of lower-income children cannot be economically justified. Education should be subsidized in order to prevent underinvestment in education in terms of its long-run benefits to the lifetime income of the students and to productivity of the economy.[198] In addition, education produces citizens capable of participating effectively as voters in a democratic society.

Yet another large category of public spending is pure transfer payments to individuals who are unable to care for themselves. Even this type of expenditure can be justified on an economic basis in terms of persons with higher incomes having a demand for charity. The issue is the extent to which charitable decisions should be made by legislatures or by individuals.

The constitutional power in Congress to spend is an express element of the tax clause. It is stated as the power "to pay the debts and provide for the common Defense and general Welfare of the United States." Some authorities argue that this clause of Article I, Section 8 by itself vests in the Congress a general power to spend for the general welfare.[199] The scope of this power, however, is reinforced by the fact that it reiterates part of the purposive statement in the Preamble: "to promote the general Welfare." The effect of the Preamble under the rules of documentary interpretation of the time was to assure to the government that the Constitution was creating powers fully adequate, on a national scale, to all the objects for which governments commonly were formed.[200] Consequently, it is clear that the original meaning of the language was that the Congress was granted a general power to tax and spend for all activities that would promote the general welfare.[201] The courts have universally followed this broad construction of the spending power.

Since its first session Congress has appropriated money for projects ranging from roads and canals to disaster relief. It was not until 1936, however, that the Supreme Court construed the general-welfare clause. In *United States* v. *Butler*,[202] in spite of holding that the particular tax invaded the reserved powers to the states, Justice Roberts presented a broad dictum supporting the spending power under the general-welfare clause. After noting that Madison had argued that the general-welfare clause was limited by the other enumerated powers while Hamilton and Story had argued it was not, Roberts concluded: "Study of all these leads us to conclude that the reading advocated by Justice Story is the correct one. While, therefore, the power to tax is not unlimited, its confines are set in the clause which confers it, and not in those of § 8 which bestow and define the legislative powers of the Congress. It results that the power of Congress to authorize expenditure of public moneys for public purposes is not limited by the direct grants of legislative power found in the Constitution."[203]

In *Steward Machine Co.* v. *Davis*,[204] the Court held unemployment relief was a legitimate object of federal expenditure under the general-welfare clause and that the credit allowed for state taxes bore a reasonable relation "to the fiscal need subserved by the tax in its normal operation."[205] State unemployment-compensation payments would relieve the burden of direct relief borne by the United States treasury. In the companion case of *Helvering* v. *Davis*,[206] Justice Cardozo further elaborated on the scope of the power: "The line must still be drawn between one welfare and another, between particular and general. Where this shall be placed cannot be known through a formula in advance of the event. There is a middle ground or certainly a penumbra in which discretion is at large. The discretion, however is not confided to the courts. The discretion belongs to Congress, unless the choice is clearly wrong, a display of arbitrary power, not an exercise of judgment."[207]

After these landmark decisions, there has been no case in which the courts have curtailed the national spending power. There have been some cases where the power was questioned and the government prevailed. *United States* v. *Gerlach Live Stock Co.*,[208] in 1950 confirmed that the general-welfare clause could be the basis of federal expenditures without resort to rationalization under other constitutional clauses. Justice Jackson wrote: "Thus the power of Congress to promote the general welfare through large-scale projects for reclamation, irrigation, or other internal improvement, is now as clear and ample as its power to accomplish the same results indirectly through resort to strained interpretation of the power over navigation."[209]

The issue of which government has primary control of public spending in a federal system is determined by which government has the greater power to tax. The increased dominance of the national government over the last fifty years has led to a continuous expansion of federal grants in aid to the states.[210] Aid to Families with Dependent Children and grants by Federal Aid to Public Education are two prominent examples. But the cost of national administration of local spending functions raised efficiency issues.[211] The total cost of national, state, and local officials is augmented by the reduced efficiency resulting from greatly extended spans

of control. Politicians create new federal agenc
tions, but they do not seem to consider potential disc

In *King* v. *Smith*,[212] among others, the Court upheld the ⊦
Congress to impose conditions on grants in aid to states. In *South L*.
v. *Doyle*,[213] the Court reconfirmed the power of Congress to con
local activities through conditions on the spending power. The statute
authorized the secretary of transportation to withhold a percentage of
federal highway funds from states where it was lawful for persons under
twenty-one years to purchase or possess alcoholic beverages. Although
the main arguments centered on denial of exemption under the Twenty-
First Amendment, the rest concerned the spending power of Congress.
Chief Justice Rehnquist restated the rule of *Helvering* v. *Davis* that although the spending must be in pursuit of the general welfare, the courts
should defer substantially to the judgment of Congress on the issue.[214]
Here, the differing drinking ages in the states created an incentive for
underage persons to drive to a nearby state with a lower statutory drinking
age in order to imbibe. A national solution was needed to remedy a
problem of interstate transportation for the purpose of transactions in
alcoholic beverages.

CHAPTER 9

The Contract Clause and Efficient Markets

THE CONTRACT CLAUSE of Article I, Section 10 mandates that no state shall pass any "Law impairing the obligation of contracts."[1] Since the historical record indicates that the main state laws that had impaired contract were bankruptcy or insolvency relief laws, this clause must be read as at least partially a reinforcement of the national bankruptcy power. Article I, Section 8 vests in Congress the power to establish "uniform Laws on the subject of Bankruptcies throughout the United States."[2] The negative implication of the comprehensive national power is that the states were to have no bankruptcy power. If the prohibition on the states in Section 10 had been worded in terms of bankruptcy laws, it would have been redundant. The broad language adopted in the contract clause indicates the importance of contract in the preindustrial era and the need to protect both private and state transactions from legislative impairment.

The Economics of Contract Law

Contracts are promises enforceable at law. Usually there is an agreement, a set of voluntary promises to exchange things of value in the future.[3] The economics of contract law is concerned with efficient exchange, promoting value-maximizing exchanges and minimizing transaction costs.[4] These costs include all those incurred in negotiating or enforcing agreements.

The objective theory of contract is an efficiency principle. Contract is based on the promissory expressions of the parties and reasonable reliances of promisees.[5] Enforcing the reasonable expectations of promisees enables them to prepare to perform and to make third-party contracts in reliance on the original one. Any rule that disappoints reasonable expectations of promisees increases transaction costs materially.

Efficient exchange can be viewed in terms of three primary functions: (1) increasing security of transactions; (2) allocating and transferring risks and uncertainties; and (3) providing standard rules for contingencies not contemplated by the agreement.

Contract law first promotes value-maximizing exchanges by enforcing promises in order to achieve greater security of transactions. Markets function well only if promisees in transactions have a high level of confidence that promisors will keep their promises. Breached agreements can impose substantial costs on promises. Contract law creates incentives to contract through incentives to perform promises by enforcing remedies against those who breach agreements.

The development of large-scale trade in England during the period of commercial capitalism (for at least three hundred years before the industrial revolution) created the need for legal enforcement of promises to perform transactions in the future. Transactions in the products of agriculture and mines became so large and complex that they could not be based on immediate and present exchange of goods for money. Reliable promises to perform in the future were needed so that production and transport could be planned by traders in wheat, wool, wine, coal, iron, and other commodities.[6] Furthermore, large-scale trade meant dealing with strangers as opposed to the person in one's own village. One has less confidence that informal social controls, such as reputation in the community and basic shared notions of morality, will cause strangers living hundreds of miles away to keep their promises. In order to promote economic growth through specialization in production and exchange, nationwide legal rules were needed to assure that most people would keep their commercial promises.

Second, contract law allocates and enables transfer of market risks and uncertainties. "Risks" are unknown future events that can be statistically estimated in the aggregate and are therefore insurable. "Uncertainties" are unknown future events that cannot be statistically estimated and thus are not insurable. Entering transactions in free markets necessarily involves undertaking risks and uncertainties. An enterpriser who acquires inventory or delivery trucks has the risk that they will be destroyed by fire or theft. One can minimize the cost of this risk by transferring it to an insurance company through a contract of insurance. When contract does not provide expressly for transfer of insurable risks, rules of law allocate the risks to promisors. A seller who promises to deliver goods to a buyer assumes the risk of loss of the goods until they are delivered. If the seller bargains to transfer the risk of loss before delivery, he must accept a lower price because the buyer must purchase additional insurance.

Uncertainties are also allocated by legal rules to parties who make promises. The most important market uncertainties are the future prices of goods and services. An enterpriser undertakes market uncertainties because all the factors that may cause shifts in demand functions or supply functions cannot be predicted. Under the obligation of contract, an enterpriser reasonably expects profits if he predicted well, and losses if he predicted poorly. His reasonable expectations include a legal environment in which all contract duties will be enforced, with the only exception being the national bankruptcy laws. He will not undertake the market uncertainties inherent in transactions for future performance if the state may excuse the duties of the party with whom he is dealing.

Third, contract law minimizes transactions costs by providing for uncontemplated contingencies. Hundreds of uncertain circumstances may surround a complex contract. It is very costly to negotiate terms and draft a contract that provides for every conceivable contingency, and it is impossible to provide for contingencies not perceived. For large numbers of minor contingencies that are viewed as unlikely to happen or that are not likely to affect costs much, it is not worth the expense to negotiate in advance how to allocate costs if the events do occur. Parties to contract rely on the standard allocation rules developed over time by the common-law courts. Their reasonable expectation is that these standard rules will not be changed by the legislature to have retroactive effect on pending contracts.

Modern economic analysis offers an explanation of why it is important to have constitutional protection for contract relations. The economic theory of "rent-seeking" behavior explains why political factions try to use legislative power to transfer wealth from others to themselves.[7] The theory applies to many items in addition to the economic rent of land. The modern industrial economy is characterized by many highly specialized productive assets with long lives. Many have a much higher value in their best use than in their second-best use, which may be salvage value. The difference in value between the best use and the second-best use is a "quasi-rent."[8] A legislature may appropriate a large part of this quasi-rent either through taxation or regulation, reducing the return to the owner, without causing the owner to shift the asset out of its best use.

Madison, in discussing the contract clause and related clauses, noted that they were designed to limit the many legislative interferences "in cases affecting personal rights" that "become jobs in the hands of enterprising and influential speculators, and snares to the more industrious and less informed part of the community."[9] State legislation to tax or to regulate prices that would redistribute economic rents from the enterprising to those in power or to voters who would support those in power were to be constitutionally curtailed. From this viewpoint, the constitutional limitations were to be given broad construction to eliminate the excesses now categorized as rent seeking. As the cases will demonstrate, this objective failed: the Supreme Court held the state police power broad enough to outweigh the contract clause in large numbers of instances.

The attempts to redistribute income and wealth by taxing or regulating economic rents are not costless to society. Those favoring and those opposing such legislation will spend large amounts of money to influence state legislators.[10] Thus, the economic rents in any given area of enterprise can be largely dissipated in efforts to purchase or repel legislative favor.

Origins and Meanings

In the era of the confederation, two main policies of state governments tended to reduce security of transactions and thereby impede trade. The first was the policy of issuing paper money in quantities that created hyperinflation, together with statutes declaring such money to be legal tender. This was remedied in Article I, Section 10 by prohibiting state emission of bills of credit or making anything but gold and silver coin a tender in payment of debts.[11] The second policy reducing security of transactions was state laws to relieve debtors. In 1787 the impetus for uniform laws on bankruptcies and prohibition of state laws impairing the obligation of contracts was from creditors. As Chief Justice Hughes has written:

> The widespread distress following the revolutionary period and the plight of debtors had called forth in the States an ignoble array of legislative schemes for the defeat of creditors and the invasion of contractual obligations. Legislative interferences had been so numerous and extreme that the confidence essential to prosperous trade had been undermined and the utter destruction of credit was threatened. "The sober people of America" were convinced that some "thorough reform" was needed which would "inspire a general prudence and industry, and give a regular course to the business of society." The Federalist, No. 44. It was necessary to interpose the restraining power of a central authority in order to secure the foundations even of "private faith."[12]

The differing state laws for relief of debtors fostered the removal of persons and property to those states where debtors' relief was greatest. Some of the statutes giving relief to debtors were "stay laws," which postponed the payment of private debts beyond the time stipulated in the contract; installment laws, which provided that debts could be paid in monthly installments rather than the time stipulated in the contract; and commodity payment laws, which permitted payment in specified commodities rather than in the contract money.[13] Most important, the general insolvency laws of the states varied greatly, depending on the relative influence of creditors and debtors in state legislatures. Some of the clauses of these statutes provided for the discharge of debtors' contracts without full performance, and thus came under the general definition of bankruptcy laws. To this extent, such statutes would also seem to fit the definition of impairing the obligation of contracts.[14]

The available notes of the Constitutional Convention of 1787 reveal little about the contract clause. They do reveal that it was discussed in the same context as prohibiting state bills of credit, limiting debtor relief.[15] Madison asserted that a general negative was necessary. Otherwise "[e]vasions might and would be devised by the ingenuity of the Legislatures."[16] The Committee of Stile reported a clause that no state shall pass laws "altering or impairing the obligations of contracts."[17] Subsequently, without explanation, the word "altering" was dropped.[18] The clause, like much of the Constitution, was drafted as a general principle, the appropriate form for fundamental law. The historical origins of creditor protection do not control its scope; the controlling factor is the language of the text in terms of English usage of the times.

Although later Supreme Courts found the contract clause to be ambiguous and encrusted a body of ignoble case law onto it, the literal meaning in 1787 should have been clear to an educated user of the English language. Furthermore, the meaning of the language of the contract clause has not changed in meaning since the eighteenth century. Chief Justice Marshall defined the obligation of contract as "the laws which binds the parties to perform their agreement."[19] Thus, the obligation is the legal duty of a promisor to perform in all of the terms of a valid contract. A corollary to the duty is the legal right in the promisee to receive the full performance. The term "impairing" was defined by Marshall as that which renders contracts "invalid, or releases or extinguishes them."[20] Chief Justice Hughes pointed out that impairment would also include those "laws which without destroying contracts derogate from substantial contract rights."[21] Clearly, the prime objective was to ensure security of transactions in the area of private contracts.

Given the accepted definition of "contract," the courts should have limited application of the clause to statutes impairing executory contracts, those in which some duty was still to be performed. The clause should not have applied to executed contracts because no obligation of contract would be in existence. By definition, an executed contract is one in which the rights and duties have been discharged. Rights created by an executed charter or franchise, for example, are not contract rights, but property rights. These were protected from congressional invasion, but not from state attack, by the eminent domain clause of the Fifth Amendment.[22] Since 1897, the Supreme Court has held that the due process clause of the Fourteenth Amendment incorporates the takings clause as enforceable against the states.[23]

Chief Justice Marshall also noted the distinction between the state power to pass laws regulating the making of contracts, which the Constitution does not restrain as long as the state regulation does not discriminate against or burden commerce among the several states, and state laws impairing the obligation of contracts. "The obligation must exist before it can be impaired; and a prohibition to impair it, when made, does not imply an inability to prescribe those circumstances which shall create its obligation."[24] Thus, state laws requiring that certain contracts be in writing or have a seal merely regulate the creation of contract duties or obligations; they do not impair existing obligations. And laws regulating remedies, such as statutes of limitations, as long as their operation is not *ex post facto*, would also be legal constraints on the making and enforcing of contracts. They, too, would not impair the obligation. Statutes delineating or revising remedies for breach of contract would not impair the obligation as long as they did not materially reduce the value of the obligation.[25]

State laws regulating intrastate commerce in areas not preempted by national law cannot impair contract as long as the laws are prospective only. Such laws are prohibitions on future contracting and delineate which classes of agreements have illegal objects. Thus, a usury law prohibits certain interest charges, and a zoning law prohibits certain structures. Subsequent to the passage of the laws, agreements for interest above the legal limit or agreements to build structures barred by zoning laws are void; they can never become contracts. There can be no impairment of contract if an illegal object prevents an agreement from becoming a contract.[26] This rule is clearly consistent with the objective theory of enforcing reasonable expectations of promisees. As long as the regulatory statute is not retroactive, the public is forewarned. No person should reasonably expect performance of an agreement that has an illegal object.

A key aspect of the original meaning of the contract clause is that the language is unqualified. The later Supreme Court ruling, over Chief Justice Marshall's dissent, that the clause had application only to retrospective statutes, was an error.[27] Language designed to ensure the security of transactions against state invasion and to reserve the bankruptcy power to the national government should be applicable to all state laws impairing contract, whether the contracts are made before or after passage of the state law. A state insolvency law, excusing debtors from part of their debts, violates the clear language of the contract clause both when applied to contracts made before enactment of the statute and to contracts made after enactment of the statute. In either case, there is state excuse from the obligation of executory contract.

In part, the contract clause came to be treated as a type of *ex post facto* law because the *ex post facto* clause was misconstrued to apply only to the criminal law.[28] Justice Chase, in *Calder* v. *Bull*[29] failed to recognize that "*ex post facto*" was merely a synonym for "retrospective." Because most of the examples in the precedents were criminal cases, he held the clause to be enforceable only against criminal statutes. This left no express constitutional protection against retrospective civil statutes of the states. The fundamental inequity of imposing retroactive liabilities is that one cannot make current economic decisions to adjust to law that will be enacted in the future. Later Supreme Court justices who failed to see the essential error of *Calder* embarked on a search for other constitutional clauses to protect individuals against the injustice of retrospective civil laws. The use of the contract clause to invalidate retroactive state insolvency laws carried the false impression that it was merely an *ex post facto* law, and therefore inapplicable to prospective laws impairing contract. In fact, the ex post facto clause should have invalidated all retrospective state laws impairing contract, thereby reinforcing part of the effect of the contract clause. The main function of the contract clause, by itself, should have been to invalidate prospective state laws impairing the obligation of executory contracts.

State Grants and Corporate Charters

The earliest cases under the contract clause concerned not private contracts, but, rather, state legislative acts that were analogized to contracts. The decisions in these cases formed the basis for what commentators have labeled the "doctrine of vested rights." The doctrine has been described as a notification by the courts that they would disallow any legislative act that they found to bear unduly harshly upon existing property rights.[30] Although the contract clause was the express constitutional basis for the doctrine of vested rights, it was also argued that property rights were of transcendental origin and were protected by natural law.[31] Chief Justice Marshall, who had pointed to the positive language of a written constitution as one key foundation of judicial review,[32] shifted to reliance on natural law when he found it useful.[33]

Fletcher v. *Peck*[34] is the early example of applying the contract clause to protect property rights even though no obligation of executory contract was extant. As a result of bribery and corruption, the Georgia legislature passed a statute in 1795 directing the governor to convey land that is now most of Alabama and Mississippi to certain land companies for about 1.5 cents per acre.[35] The companies then resold millions of acres to speculators and prospective settlers. The public reaction to this sale of the Yazoo lands was so great that in the Georgia legislative elections of 1795, a new anti-Yazoo majority was swept into office. On February 13, 1796, the new legislators repealed the act that had authorized the sale, declaring it a "usurped act" that was "null and void." This was affirmed in the Georgia Constitution of May 30, 1798.[36]

Since the statute repealing the grant was legal notice relating to an *in rem* transaction, all persons anywhere who had acquired parcels of the land after enactment of the statute could be charged with notice of defective title. Peck acquired title to the litigated lands in 1800 and conveyed them to Fletcher in 1803 with covenants of good title. Fletcher sued in federal court for breach of the covenant of title. He asserted that either the original sale had been unlawful and ineffective, or the sale had been lawfully rescinded by statute in 1796. Chief Justice Marshall, for the Court, failed to treat the issue of legal notice of defective titles. Instead, he accepted Peck's defense of good-faith purchaser and held for the defendant on both counts.[37]

As to the first statute, granting the sale of Yazoo lands, the Court held that it could not be attacked collaterally. "It would be indecent, in the extreme, upon a private contract, between two individuals, to enter into an inquiry respecting the corruption of sovereign power of a State."[38] There was no express clause in the Georgia constitution prohibiting the sale. It would be difficult to determine how much legislative corruption was necessary to vitiate a sale.

As to the second statute, annulling the grant, Marshall held it invalid. "It is, then, the unanimous opinion of the court, that, in this case, the estate having passed into the hands of a purchaser for a valuable consideration, without notice, the State of Georgia was restrained, either by general principles, which are common to our free institutions, or by the particular provisions of the constitution of the United States, from passing a law whereby the estate of the plaintiff in the premises so purchased could be constitutionally and legally impaired and rendered null and void."[39]

The first general principle asserted by Marshall was the separation of governmental powers.[40] He argued that the Georgia legislature, as a party to the transaction, should not have had final determination of its invalidity. Rather, the issue of a voidable contract should have been submitted to judicial determination. Marshall asserted that this aspect has a natural-law basis.[41]

Marshall's application of separated powers to the annulling statute seems wrong on the basis of two alternate arguments. First, legislative annulment may have been the only available remedy for this massive fraud and corruption of governmental officials. Judicial invalidation of the prior statute might have been impossible because a statute that is facially valid and was enacted following constitutional procedures is usually held by courts to be unimpeachable. Second, the function of the annulling statute was remedial, to make an open admission that the prior statute authorizing the giveaway sale lacked a valid governmental purpose and therefore violated legislative due process.[42] This would be a rationale for the legislative annulment or for a judicial determination that the annulling statute was valid.

The second general principle asserted by Marshall was the rule of the common law of property protecting good-faith purchasers for value. The economic purpose of this rule is to promote the transfer assets to their most productive use. Without this rule, uncertainties in potential buyers concerning defects in the chain of title to assets would greatly impede the working of markets. But it is not efficient to protect those who commit

fraud or those potential purchasers who should have notice of wrongdo-
ing. As noted, Marshall should not have upheld the defense of good-faith
purchase in the defendant. He failed to discuss the statute as notice, nor
did he distinguish purchasers before the repeal statute as the only ones
who might have purchased in good faith.

The additional basis of the decision was the particular provision of the
Constitution's contract clause. Marshall began this section of his opinion
by stretching the clause, in clear violation of its literal meaning, to apply
to executed contracts. He ignored accepted law that an executed contract
may create continuing property rights, but that the contract obligations
are discharged. Rather, he asserted that an executed contract contains
obligations binding on the parties. "A grant, in its own nature, amounts
to an extinguishment of the right of the grantor, and implies a contract
not to reassert that right."[43] Clearly, he was stretching the contract clause
to operate as a prohibition on the taking of property by the state. "It
would be strange if a contract to convey was secured by the constitution,
while an absolute conveyance remained unprotected."[44]

In fact, the language of the contract clause demonstrates that it was
designed only to protect executory contracts. Marshall apparently did not
realize that he needed an eminent domain clause in order to protect vested
rights in property. The Georgia constitution of 1789 did not contain an
express eminent domain clause.[45] Nonetheless, Marshall could have found
such a right to be an inherent element of the Georgia Constitution, because
it was one of the constitutional rights of Englishmen that Americans had
insisted prevailed against state and national governments even before the
adoption of the express bill of rights.[46] As Chancellor Kent wrote: "A
provision for compensation is a necessary attendant on the due and
constitutional exercise of the power of the lawgiver to deprive an individual of his property without his consent; and this principle in American
constitutional jurisprudence is founded on natural equity, and is laid
down by jurists as an acknowledged principle of universal law."[47]

Having asserted that an executed grant was still a contract, Marshall
met the issue of whether state transactions were subject to the contract
clause. The language of the contract clause has no exceptions. The history
of adoption shows no basis to infer that state transactions were to be
exempted. The people "having manifested a determination to shield themselves and their property from the effects of those sudden and strong
passions to which men are exposed."[48] Article I, Section 10 "contains
what may be deemed a bill of rights for the people of each State."[49] The
structure of Article I, Section 10, with its prohibitions on *ex post facto*
laws and bills of attainder, clearly limited state action in all its aspects.[50]
There was thus no reasonable basis to infer an exception for state contracts.

The contract protection, as applied to land grants, was extended to an immunity from taxation in *New Jersey* v. *Wilson*.[51] In 1758, the colonial government of New Jersey, in the name of the king of England, had created a tribal reservation for the Delaware Indians in exchange for the agreement of the Indians to release all claims to the southern portion of the province. The consideration to the Indians was perpetual immunity from taxation, but the land could not be conveyed. In 1801, upon petition of the Indians, the New Jersey legislature permitted the land to be sold. The sale was executed in 1803, and in 1804 the legislature repealed the 1758 tax exemption. Upon suit by the purchasers, the New Jersey courts upheld the repeal of the tax exemption.[52] The Supreme Court, in a unanimous opinion, reversed, holding that the state had impaired the obligation of contract.

The findings of the lower courts seem more consistent with the theory of efficient contracts.[53] The continuing contract duty to exempt the Indian lands from taxation was personal in nature and in part international in character. The Indians as a "nation" could contract for tax exemption as a part of the state's recognition of their distinct, independent, political community.[54] In these circumstances, no reasonable purchaser of Indian lands should expect the same exemption. He should expect the exemption to be extinguished with the restraint on alienation, even if not expressly stated. He should expect equal treatment with all other citizens in property taxation.[55]

In *Wilson*, however, Marshall adopted the rule of *Fletcher* that the contract clause applied to state transactions. By asserting that the exemption was attached to the land, he assumed as a premise the key conclusion he wanted to reach.[56] He also put great weight on what appears to be an inadvertence: the legislature had not demanded release of the tax exemption as a condition to consent to resale.

Marshall failed to mention the key policy issue. Taxation is an indispensable sovereign power. May one legislature grant an exception to ordinary voting citizens, as distinct from an Indian nation receiving a bargained consideration, and bind all future legislatures to this exemption? Marshall's dictum in *Fletcher* had been that, as to general legislation, one legislature cannot abridge the powers of the next.[57] But the Court has held that a state may in a bank charter agree to tax a bank by a given method and be bound under the contract clause not to revoke this promise.[58] As to *Wilson*, Wright has concluded, "Marshall was so desirous of placing limitations on state legislatures to the end of protecting the vested rights of property that he did not even pause to consider the handicap to state financial powers that this principle might produce.[59]

Trustees of Dartmouth College v. *Woodward*[60] established the principle that a corporate charter was a contract constitutionally protected from impairment by the state. The college was established by royal charter in 1769 with twelve trustees who were empowered to govern the college and appoint their successors. In 1816 the New Hampshire legislature passed statutes increasing the trustees to twenty-one and authorizing the governor to appoint the nine new members. A statute subjected key decisions of the trustees to a new Board of Overseers controlled by the governor. The state courts upheld the statutory changes,[61] but the Supreme Court reversed on the basis of the contract clause.

From an economic viewpoint, the key questions were whether there was contract and whether contract reliances were defeated. Early in his opinion, Chief Justice Marshall begged the question by asserting: "It can require no argument to prove that the circumstances of this case constitute a contract."[62] Justice Story, in his concurring opinion, elaborated on this view by adopting the fallacious reasoning of *Fletcher* v. *Peck.*[63] "A grant in its own nature amounts to an extinguishment of the right of the grantor, and implies a contract not to reassert that right."[64] In spite of these bold assertions, most authorities agree that a corporate charter lacks both promise and bargained consideration.[65] The charter here, like most charters, did not contain promissory language. Nor did the trustees promise the Crown to perform specific acts on exchange. These facts, of course, illustrate that there was also a failure of consideration.[66] Although the founder performed acts in reliance to the charter and donors gave money to the college, none of this was in a bargain with the Crown.[67]

A charter or franchise, once granted, may be viewed as property. In fact, the theory of this case seems to be a taking of property without just compensation. But the protections for vested property rights are not found in the contract clause. In fact, any charter issued by the Crown was subject to legislative amendment because of the general principle of legislative supremacy in English constitutional law.[68] The conclusion of the New Hampshire court had been that the state legislature had merely exercised this power.[69] No reasonable reliances in the law of property had been defeated because a holder of a Crown charter must expect possible legislative amendment.

The doctrine of the Dartmouth College case was mitigated in *Charles River Bridge* v. *Warren Bridge.*[70] This case presented the principle of strict construction of public grants.[71] The Charles River Bridge Company had been granted a state franchise to operate a toll bridge, with no mention of whether its privilege was exclusive. Later, the Warren Bridge Company was granted a franchise to build a nearby bridge on the condition that after the costs were recovered from tolls, the bridge would be turned over to the state as a free bridge. The Supreme Court, in an opinion by Chief Justice Taney, held that because the first franchise contained no express provision for exclusive operation, no such provision was implied. The state had not undertaken an obligation to exclude rival bridges, so there was no impairment of contract. The decision followed the accepted principles of documentary interpretation and the common-law principle against implied grants of monopoly.[72] In conclusion, Chief Justice Taney wrote: "It is well settled by the decisions of this court, that a State law may be retrospective in its character, and may devest vested rights; and yet not violate the constitution of the United States unless it also impairs the obligation of a contract."[73]

The effect of the doctrine of vested rights adopted in the *Dartmouth College* case was to give security to the growth of American business corporations. However, under the logic of that case, the state may reserve in a corporate charter the right to amend, alter, or repeal it. Such reservation becomes part of the contract between the state and the incorporators, the obligation of which is not impaired by the exercise of the right. Later decisions recognized that the state may reserve the amending power, and it is a general practice for states to do so.[74] It must be noted, however, that the power of the state to amend or repeal a corporate charter does not allow the state to invade property or contract rights that accrue while the corporation is in existence. The eminent domain and contract clause protections apply to all such corporate legal rights.

Even if a state fails to reserve the power to amend or repeal a corporate charter, a corporation is subject to the police power of the state. The prohibition on impairing the obligation of contract will in some cases be held inferior to the power of the state to tax and to regulate business for the general welfare. In *Providence Bank* v. *Billings*,[75] Chief Justice Marshall held that, in the absence of express stipulation or reasonable implication to the contrary in its charter, the state bank was subject to the taxing power of the state. In *Beer Company* v. *Massachusetts*,[76] Justice Bradley, for a unanimous Court, held that a state law forbidding the sale of malt liquor was not an unconstitutional impairment of the charter of a beer company. The leading case concerning the police power was *Stone* v. *Mississippi*,[77] in 1880. In 1867, the state legislature had granted a twenty-five year charter to a company to conduct a lottery. The state constitution of 1868 outlawed lotteries, and in 1870 an enforcing act was passed canceling all the lottery privileges granted in the charter. A unanimous Court upheld the rescinding statute. Chief Justice Waite concluded: "No legislature can bargain away the public health or the public morals. The people themselves cannot do it, much less their servants."[78]

State Insolvency and Foreclosure Laws

Because a key purpose of the contract clause was to bar state laws relieving debtors of their contract duties, one might have expected the states to refrain from passing insolvency laws. But the absence of national bankruptcy laws for most of the first seventy-eight years of the United States led some states to try to relieve the many hopeless debtors resulting from periodic economic crises.[79] The validity of such state insolvency laws reached the Supreme Court in *Sturges* v. *Crowninshield*.[80] The debtor, Crowninshield, had been discharged from debt under a New York state insolvency law that had been enacted after the issuance of the notes upon which the suit was based. The plaintiff sued in federal court on the basis of diversity of citizenship and asserted the invalidity of the New York statute. Chief Justice Marshall, for the Supreme Court, held the statute in this instance to violate the contract clause.

From an economic standpoint, all retroactive laws affecting commerce reduce the security of transactions. Credit is extended and loans are made in light of existing bankruptcy laws. If merchants must take the risk that later, much more liberal bankruptcy laws will be retroactive, they will not enter into riskier transactions.

The underlying reaction of most persons is that retroactive laws other than remedial statutes are fundamentally unfair. The essence of fair law is that one can plan ahead to conform to the law. Retroactive laws imposing costs or other burdens on persons make it impossible to conform to the law. Chief Justice Marshall, at the end of his opinion in *Sturges*, notes that statutes of limitations and usury laws operating retroactively are unconstitutional impairments of contract.[81] But such laws operating only prospectively are valid public constraints on the making of contract because they define remedies or legality of object for future contracts.

Although the facts of *Sturges* concerned retroactive application of a state insolvency law, Marshall announced an opinion in general terms that applied to all state insolvency laws. The first issue was whether the delegation to Congress of the power to establish "uniform laws on the subject of bankruptcies, throughout the United States"[82] preempted all state insolvency laws. The answer was negative. "Insolvency laws operate at the instance of an imprisoned debtor."[83] Remedial laws that terminate imprisonment for debt without changing contract obligations do not violate the contract clause.[84]

As to the relation between national and state debtor-relief laws, Marshall asserted "that until the power to pass uniform laws on the subject of bankruptcies be exercised by Congress, the states are not forbidden to pass a bankruptcy law, provided it contain no principle which violate the 10th section of the first article of the Constitution of the United States."[85] In judging whether the New York insolvency law violated the contract clause in this instance, he observed that the promissory notes bound the debtor to pay money on a fixed date. This was the obligation. "Any law which releases a part of this obligation, must in the literal sense of the word, impair it."[86] The fact that the Constitution did not expressly bar state insolvency laws was not controlling. Laws impairing the obligation of contract include insolvency laws that release debtors' duties, because they violate the general principle found in the constitutional language. "The spirit of the law is to be collected chiefly from its words. It would be dangerous in the extreme, to infer from extrinsic circumstances, that a cure for which the words of an instrument expressly provide, shall be exempted from the operation."[87] In this case, the New York law was invalid because it relieved the debtor of part of his contract duties.

The generality of the rule in *Sturges* was confirmed in the companion case of *McMillan* v. *McNeill*,[88] concerning a contract made in South Carolina in 1811. When defendant McMillan moved to Louisiana, he was released from the contract under an insolvency statute that had been enacted in 1808. Marshall found the case not distinguishable in principle from *Sturges* and held the Louisiana statute to violate the contract clause. "That the circumstances of the state law, under which the debt was attempted to be discharged, having been passed before the debt was contracted, made no difference in the application of the principle."[89] In spite of this general language, the rule of the case was narrow. A state insolvency law, though enacted before the litigated contract was entered, could not discharge a contract made in another state.

It was 1821 before the Court had to meet the issue of the validity of state laws for relief of insolvent debtors on subsequent contracts entered by citizens of the same state. In *Ogden* v. *Saunders*,[90] the Court upheld such state bankruptcy laws by a vote of 4 to 3. This is the only constitutional case during Chief Justice Marshall's thirty-four years on the Supreme Court in which he dissented. The majority were concerned to sustain some kind of debtor relief from economic crises in the context of a Congress that could not assemble a majority to pass a national bankruptcy law. The majority of Washington, Johnson, Thompson, and Trimble wrote seriatim opinions that were very similar. They held that the *Sturges* decision had to be limited to its facts, and that the contract clause is a prohibition on retrospective state insolvency statutes.[91] They rejected Marshall's general statement in the *Sturges* case that the only state insolvency laws that were constitutional were those that modified the remedy but did not discharge the obligation. They held that state insolvency laws were a condition under which subsequent contracts were made.[92]

Justice Washington, who had been Marshall's closest ally in most decisions, broke with him here.[93] His legal rationale is more than strained. He stated that he had always considered the national bankruptcy power exclusive.[94] He felt bound, however, to follow the dictum of *Sturges* that he understood to limit the contract clause. He thus voted to uphold a state law that he felt was invalid. This adherence to precedent in the Supreme Court was clearly inconsistent with the principle that only the Constitution is fundamental law because the Constitution, not previous Supreme Court decisions, was ratified by the people.

Justice Johnson's reasoning was even more strained. He asserted that the national bankruptcy power was not exclusive in spite of the clause's objective of geographical uniformity. Absent national law, nonuniform state bankruptcy laws could relieve debtors. In spite of the plain language of the contract clause and its historical origins, Johnson viewed it as totally inapplicable. The state insolvency laws limited remedies in order to prevent creditors from continuing to pursue hopelessly insolvent debtors.[95] Laws controlling remedies were separate and distinct from the obligation. States must have the power to set the conditions for contracting, such as by passing statutes of frauds and limitations and usury statutes.[96] Limitations on remedies were of the same class. The preexisting insolvency statute could not impair contract because all parties had previous notice that the statute limited the contract.[97] Johnson went even further and disavowed his part in the "unanimous" vote in *Sturges*, holding that retroactive insolvency laws were valid in order to do justice to the hopeless debtor.[98] This seems inconsistent with his further view that the *ex post facto* clause applied to civil matters.[99]

Chief Justice Marshall, for the minority, conceded a general power in the state to regulate local contracts and "to prohibit such as may be deemed mischievous."[100] He was not, however, trying to create a general liberty of contract, as the later Court did by creating substantive due process.[101] Bankruptcy and insolvency laws excusing debt were of a special class. Their whole purpose was to allow defeat of executory contracts that were once obligatory.[102] Labeling them "remedial" in no way lessened the fact that they impaired the obligation of contract: this principle had been established by prior decision.[103] One underlying purpose of the contract clause was to reinforce the exclusive national bankruptcy power. There was no principled ground to distinguish retroactive insolvency laws of *Sturges* from the prospective insolvency laws of *Ogden*. In fact, the state insolvency statutes impairing contracts during the period of the confederation, which the contract clause was to cure, usually had both retroactive and prospective application.[104]

The majority decision is contrary to the unqualified language of the contract clause. The Committee on Stile wrote the contract clause to do more than just repeat as to contracts the more general *ex post facto* clause, which precedes it. But as Justice Johnson pointed out, the earlier Supreme Court had erroneously limited the *ex post facto* clause to criminal cases.[105] And that error in the interpretation of one clause fostered error in interpretation of the second. The effect was to leave the nation with many diverse state bankruptcy laws. The costs to lenders and other creditors of acquiring information on all of these changing laws was much greater than it would have been than under a national bankruptcy law.

During the rest of the nineteenth century, state bankruptcy laws operated to relieve debtors in contracts made after the passage of particular statutes. After 1898, however, the general national Bankruptcy Act preempted the field and excluded state insolvency laws.[106]

Statutes regulating mortgages and the conditions for foreclosure of mortgages, though concerned with debt, are not bankruptcy laws. Land mortgages condition the title and rights to possession of properties as a security device for a loan of money. They do not depend on the general solvency or insolvency of the debtor. For an insolvent debtor, however, a bankruptcy proceeding may result in a statutory stay of foreclosure proceedings.[107] State laws regulating the conditions for foreclosure of mortgages invoke the possibility only of violation of the contract clause. Many of the cases dealing with such statutes center on the principle stated by Chief Justice Marshall in *Sturges* that the remedy may be modified so long as the obligation of contract is not impaired.

Bronson v. *Kinzie*[108] in 1843 was the leading nineteenth-century case on mortgage-relief legislation. At issue was the validity of two Illinois statutes enacted in 1841 to alleviate some of the effects of the panic of 1837. Both statutes were to have retrospective application. The mortgage, made before the laws were enacted, had given the mortgagee an unrestricted power of sale upon the mortgagor's default. The first statute allowed the mortgagor a year to redeem the foreclosed property by repaying the purchase price plus 10 percent interest. The second statute provided that no foreclosure sale could be made unless two-thirds of the appraised value of the property was bid.

Chief Justice Taney, for the Court, held that the prior Illinois statute formed a part of the mortgage, even though there was no express stipulation to that effect.[109] The reasonable reliance on parties to contract are not only on the other's promises but also on the law setting conditions to contract. The first new statute, extending the right of redemption, injected terms not present in the mortgage and thus impaired this obligation.[110] The second new statute, requiring a sale price of at least two-thirds of appraised "value" merely affected the remedy.

Similar statutory provisions in three other states were also held unconstitutional.[111] One other type of legislation for debtors was also held invalid. Two statutes, based on newly adopted state constitutional provisions, exempting homesteads from execution to satisfy contract debts were ruled unconstitutional when applied retrospectively.[112]

The rule of *Bronson*, giving strong protection to the reasonable expectations of mortgagees, remained in effect for ninety years. The economic depression of the 1930s brought its end. In *Home Building and Loan Association* v. *Blaisdell*,[113] in 1934, a 5-to-4 decision of the Supreme Court upheld the constitutionality of the retrospective Minnesota Mortgage Moratorium Law of 1933. The statute provided that during the emergency created by the depression, the period of redemption from foreclosure sales could be extended by a state court, but not beyond May 1, 1935. A condition of the extension was that the mortgagor be ordered to pay a reasonable rental value toward payment of taxes, insurance, interest, and principal as fixed by a court.

The economic theory of the statute was that the price of real property in the depth of the economic depression was a short-run phenomenon reflecting downward price expectations of that phase of the business cycle. The presumption of the legislature in 1933 in passing this two-year statute was that land prices were below the "real values" that would prevail under stable prices. Chief Justice Hughes noted that emergency does not create power, but "emergency may furnish the occasion for the exercise of power."[114] The issue, however, was whether relief from obligation during economic crisis was vested exclusively in the bankruptcy power of the national government. Hughes construed the contract clause narrowly and allowed the state to act. He recognized that this statute went beyond mere modification of the remedy and changed essential terms of the mortgage contract. In justification, he wrote: "Not only are existing laws read into contracts in order to fix obligations as between the parties, but the reservation of essential attributes of sovereign power is also read into contracts as a postulate of the legal order. The policy of protecting contracts against impairment presupposes the maintenance of a government by virtue of which contractual relations are worth while,—a government which retains adequate authority to secure the peace and good order of society. This principle of harmonizing the constitutional prohibition with the necessary residuum of state power has had progressive recognition in the decisions of this Court."[115]

Justice Sutherland, for the dissenters, correctly wrote that this case was in direct conflict with the meaning of the contract clause. He presented an exhaustive analysis of the historical context in which the language of the contract clause was adopted, showing that the economic crisis of the preconstitutional period was just as severe as the crisis of the 1930s. He concluded: "If it be possible by resort to the testimony of history to put any question of constitutional intent beyond the domain of uncertainty, the foregoing leaves no reasonable ground upon which to base a denial that the clause of the Constitution now under consideration was meant to foreclose state action impairing the obligation of contracts *primarily and especially* in respect of such action aimed at giving relief to debtors *in time of emergency.*[116]

A short time after the *Blaisdell* decision, the Supreme Court decided *W. B. Worthen Company* v. *Thomas,*[117] holding unconstitutional a 1933 Arkansas law that provided that all benefit payments received in life, sickness, and accident insurance policies were exempt from legal process for indebtedness existing at the time the act was passed. Chief Justice Hughes distinguished the *Blaisdell* case by pointing to the unlimited exemption here: "In the existent case, the relief sought to be afforded is neither temporary nor conditional. In placing insurance moneys beyond the reach of existing creditors, the act contains no limitation as to time, amount, circumstances or need."[118] On the other hand, the Court later upheld legislation for relief of mortgages that extended payment over ten years, holding that creditor interests were protected.[119]

One must conclude that the Supreme Court has assumed the power materially to diminish the scope of the contract clause as applied to private contracts. They may be impaired by state statute whenever the Court majority feel that the reasons are imperative and the conditions of the statute limited.

Recent Cases

The subordination of the contract clause to the police power of the states continued into the 1960s. A leading case was *City of El Paso* v. *Simmons*[120] in 1965. From early in the century, a Texas statute allowed certain public agencies to sell lands to purchasers with small down payments. In case of forfeiture for nonpayment, the buyer or his assignee could reinstate their rights at any future time by paying up the delinquent interest if no rights of third parties had intervened. In 1941 Texas amended the law to limit the reinstatement right to five years. This was admittedly more than just a modification of remedy. But the fact that reinstatement was not the central undertaking and that there was a policy to remove clouds from titles caused the majority of the court to hold this a reasonable invasion of contract rights.

Justice White, for the majority, held it unnecessary to chart the dividing line between remedy and obligation. "For it is not every modification of a contractual promise that impairs the obligation of contract under federal law."[121] Relying on *Blaisdell,* he concluded that "we think the objects of the Texas statute make abundantly clear that it impairs no protected right under the contract clause."[122] Unexpected and unforeseen events meant that unlimited reinstatement conferred considerable advantages on purchasers, and costly and difficult burdens on the state. "Laws which restrict a party to those gains reasonably to be expected from the contract are not subject to attack under the contract clause, notwithstanding that they technically alter an obligation of a contract."[123]

Justice Black dissented to the Court's balancing away the plain guarantee of the contract clause.[124] Noting that the clause was in the same section as that prohibiting bills of attainder and *ex post facto* laws, he wrote: "All three of these provisions reflect the strong belief of the Framers of the Constitution that men should not have to act at their peril, fearing always that the State might change its mind and alter the legal consequences of their past so as to take away their lives, their liberty or their property."[125] He pointed out that the state could clear titles by condemning the land and paying compensation. Only this method would conform to the eminent domain clause of the Fifth Amendment as incorporated into the Fourteenth.

It appeared that the contract clause had lost its force. But there was a partial revival in 1977. In *United States Trust Company* v. *New Jersey*,[126] by a vote of 4 to 3, the Court invalidated a state statute that materially modified the state's contractual obligations. A statutory covenant in 1962 between New York and New Jersey, upon acquisition of the bankrupt Hudson and Manhattan Railroad by the Port Authority of New York and New Jersey, provided that none of the authority's future income would be used to subsidize deficits of mass-transit facilities taken over later. The object was to secure financing by giving bondholders a guarantee that revenues and reserves pledged as security for the current bonds would not be used to subsidize other mass transit. In 1974, however, both states passed statutes whose effect was a retroactive repeal of the 1962 covenant. The trustee for the bondholders brought suit, alleging violation of the contract clause. The state courts upheld the repeal, but the Supreme Court reversed.

The facts showed a clear, material impairment of the obligation of contract. The statutes modified a transaction between a public agency and lenders and thus contained no aspect of conflict with general legislative powers of the state. "Such a promise is purely financial and thus not necessarily a compromise of the state's reserved powers."[127] Instead of a summary reversal, however, the Court adopted the balancing technique of *El Paso* and stated that "an impairment may be constitutional if it is reasonable and necessary to serve an important public purpose."[128] Fostering mass transportation, energy conservation, and environmental protection were the general goals of the statute. Encouraging users of private automobiles to shift to public transportation was the specific goal. But the evidence showed that these goals could be achieved by alternative public policies, so repeal of the 1962 covenant was not necessary. Thus the Court found a balance in favor of the contract clause in a situation where applying the plain language of the clause would have invalidated the repeal statute on its very facts.

In 1978 the Supreme Court applied the contract clause to facts that contained no impairment of promissory obligations. In *Allied Structural Steel Company* v. *Spannus*,[129] the Court, reviewing state regulation of private contracts, revived the contract clause. In April 1974, Minnesota had enacted a pension law requiring firms that terminated their pension plans or closed a Minnesota office to fund their previously voluntary plans for all employees who had worked at least ten years. The statute was retroactive. Allied Structural Steel had adopted a pension plan in 1963 to which it was the sole contributor, and Allied retained the right to amend the plan or terminate it at any time and for any reason. Allied closed its Minnesota office and in July 1974, it discharged eleven of its thirty Minnesota employees. Upon suit by Allied, the district court upheld the act, but the Supreme Court reversed.

Justice Stewart, for a majority of five, attacked the retroactive character of the statute in increasing the pension liabilities of firms. Allied had planned a pension system without the funding requirement. "It relied heavily, and reasonably, on the legitimate contractual expectation in calculating its annual contributions to the pension fund."[130] In fact, the regulatory statute merely added duties to those created by contract. In spite of the fact that no party's contract duties were diminished, the Court labeled Allied's increased duties as a substantial impairment of a contractual relationship.[131] Justice Brennan, for the three dissenters, reviewed the history of the contract clause and concluded: "[T]he clause was thus intended by the Framers to be applicable only to laws which altered the obligations of contracts by effectively relieving one party of the obligation to perform a contract duty."[132] In this case, the Court ignored the first rule of documentary interpretation, which emphasizes the primacy of constitutional or statutory language.

The fundamental problem in *Allied Structural Steel* was that it involved a regulatory statute that was retroactive. The basic unfairness of imposing retroactive liabilities arises because one cannot make economic decisions to adjust to law that will be enacted only in the future. In *Calder* v. *Bull*,[133] the Court, failing to recognize that *ex post facto* was merely a synonym for "retrospective," was led to limit the *ex post facto* protection to criminal statutes. The legacy of *Calder* has been oppressive retroactive civil legislation. Other constitutional clauses were ruled unavailable as substitute remedies. Tax statutes, applicable to income received in years before the legislation was enacted, have been unsuccessfully attacked under the due process clause.[134] Medical benefits for mine workers who left employment long before passage of the statute requiring the benefits have also been upheld against a due process challenge.[135] Until *Calder* is overruled, civil legislation violating citizens' expectations about regulatory liabilities will continue.

In 1983 the Court ruled on the validity of prospective state price regulation that negates operation of escalator clauses in previously existing long-term supply contracts. In *Energy Reserve Group Incorporated* v. *Kansas Power & Light Company*,[136] the supplier of natural gas (ERG) agreed in 1975 to supply gas to the utility (KPL) for the lifetime of a certain gas field. The price clauses permitted ERG to increase the price if a governmental regulatory agency permitted higher prices. In 1978 the Congress extended federal regulation to the price of gas in intrastate commerce. The federal maximum price was substantially above the existing contract price between ERG and KPL, thus triggering the escalator clause. The Kansas legislature, pursuant to power delegated by the federal act, enacted a statute setting ceiling prices for gas delivered pursuant to contracts executed before April

1977. The ceiling stopped ERG from raising the price to KPL under the escalator clause. The Supreme Court unanimously affirmed the Kansas court in upholding the state statute.

Citing *Blaisdell*, the Court held that the judicial duty was to balance "the language of the contract clause against the state's intent in exercising its police power."[137] The first test was whether there was a substantial impairment of a contractual relationship. The court emphasized that this was an industry that historically was subject to price regulation by entering private contracts.[138] Here, there was not substantial impairment because the reasonable expectation of all parties dealing in gas should be that regulating statutes will be amended and apply to all future deliveries and payments. "In short, ERG's reasonable expectations have not been impaired by the Kansas Act."[139] The Court stated, in dictum, that if there had been substantial impairment, it was offset by the legitimate interest of the state under its police power to correct a market imbalance.

Exxon Corporation v. *Eagerton*[140] again brought to the Court a conflict between the state's taxing power and the contract clause. An Alabama statute increased the severance tax on oil and gas from Alabama wells. The issue relating to the contract clause was a statutory prohibition on producers from passing on the tax increase to their purchasers. Pre-existing contracts required purchasers to reimburse producers for severance taxes paid. The Supreme Court held that the pass-through prohibition of the state act, as applied to intrastate sales, did not violate the contract clause. Here, as in *Energy Reserves*, the Court emphasized that one may not obtain immunity from state regulation by making private contractual arrangements.[141] The statute regulating the incidence of taxation was a generally applicable rule of conduct to advance a broad societal interest.[142] The objective was to shield consumers from the burden of tax increase. A state's power to tax and determine the incidence of its tax cannot be controlled by private contract.

Recent cases have partially revived the contract clause, but have not restored it to its original meaning. On the contrary, the majority in *El Paso* ruled that a state may impair its obligations when the judiciary finds it reasonable. The plurality in *United States Trust* merely applied this rule in balancing the factors and finding there was not reasonable impairment. In its confusion, the Court applied the contract clause in *Allied Structural Steel* when there was no evidence of impairment of obligation: the contract clause was used as civil *ex post facto* clause. In *Energy Reserves Group*, a statute regulating prices was allowed to impair long-term supplier contracts. And in *Exxon Corporation*, a tax statute stipulating the incidence was allowed to impair standing contracts.

Although the Court has held that the states may not contract away their general legislative powers, the plain language of the contract clause has clearly been violated by the interpretation that state police power can override the contract clause in other situations. The balance technique of *Blaisdell* and *El Paso* was a Court creation without constitutional foundation. Furthermore, the rule of *Ogden* v. *Saunders,* limiting the clause to retroactive application clearly violates its social purpose. For laws whose primary purpose is to impair contract, such as insolvency laws, the contract clause is unlimited. It was designed to prohibit both retroactive and prospective insolvency laws.

CHAPTER 10

Privileges and Immunities: The Ninth Amendment and the Antimonopoly Tradition

THE FOURTEENTH AMENDMENT PROVIDES in part: "No state shall make or enforce any law which shall abridge the privileges or immunities of citizens of the United States."[1] This clause has been interpreted by the Supreme Court to have almost no effect.[2] The view of this study, based on a historical review of the English and American origins of the phrase, is that "privileges or immunities" was a synonym for constitutional limitations. The conclusion is that the proscription against abridgement of privileges and immunities means that the states shall not make laws that abridge the constitutional limitations of citizens of the United States. The language must mean that all types and classes of civil rights of citizens protected by the Constitution against invasion by the national government are also protected from invasion by the state governments.

The language of the clause was probably deemed an efficient way to secure against state infringement a minimum set of civil rights to all citizens. Some state constitutions might have fewer civil rights clauses than the national constitution, but no citizen was to have fewer civil rights than the national standard. Absent this clause, the objective of protecting civil rights of former slaves would not be satisfied by the equal protection clause alone if any state had few express constitutional limitations and also rejected those derived from the British Constitution, the rights of Englishmen. Furthermore, extant state constitutional limitations could be repealed in the future by amendment of state constitutions. A clear example is the privilege of the writ of habeas corpus, which is effective against the national government in Article I, Section 9.[3] If this privilege was not in a state constitution in 1868 or was there but was subsequently repealed by amendment, the privileges-or-immunities clause would still assure every citizen the privilege of the writ when incarcerated by state officers.

This chapter treats a neglected issue, the significance in the United States of the British common law and constitutional tradition barring governmental grants of monopoly in the ordinary trades. The thesis is that this constitutional limitation was retained for the American people by the Ninth Amendment, which made the limitation an original immunity of citizens of the United States. Through the privileges-or-immunities clause of the Fourteenth Amendment, the limitation became operative against state action. The conclusion is that the majority decision in the *Slaughter-House Cases*,[4] upholding a state grant of monopoly in butchering, was erroneous. Of the four dissenters, the opinion of Justice Field, emphasizing the privileges-or-immunities clause, at least pointed to the correct law based on the Anglo-American antimonopoly tradition. But the failure to raise and argue the Ninth Amendment in that case was fatal to the decision because this was the only way to make the antimonopoly tradition an immunity of citizens of the United States.

Privileges and Immunities: Historical Meanings

The word "privileges," when used in the context of the relationship of a citizen to government, as found in the interstate privileges-and-immunities clause of Article IV, Section 2 of the Constitution, was a synonym for the words "liberties" or "franchises."[5] "Privileges" represented a class of activities in which citizens were free to engage: affirmative or active liberties that government had no legal right to restrain. The word "immunity," when used in the context of the relationship of citizens to government, meant "exemption."[6] It designated negative or passive liberties, the citizens' freedom from the legal power of government to act on some topic. An "immunity" was an exemption from possible future legal liability, such as the immunity from unreasonable searches and seizures.

Privileges and immunities, or synonymous terms, had their origins in U.S. law in the Charter of Virginia of 1606 which read as follows: "Alsoe wee doe, for us, our heires and successors, declare by theise presentes that all and everie the parsons being our subjects which shall dwell and inhabit within everie or anie of the said severall Colonies and plantacions and everie of theire children which shall happen to be borne within the limitts and precincts of the said severall Colonies and plantacions shall have and enjoy all liberties, franchises and immunities within anie of our other dominions to all intents and purposes as if they had been abiding and borne within this our realme of Englande or anie other of our saide dominions."[7]

The phrase "liberties, franchises and immunities of free denizens or natural borne subjects" appears also in the Charter of New England of 1620,[8] in the Charter of Maine of 1639,[9] and in the Charter of Georgia of 1732.[10] The phrase "liberties and immunities of free and natural born subjects" is in the Charter of Massachusetts Bay of 1629,[11] in the Charter of Connecticut of 1662,[12] and in the Charter of Rhode Island and Providence Plantations of 1663.[13] The Charter of Maryland of 1632 used "privileges, franchises and immunities,"[14] and the Charter of Carolina of 1663 used "liberties, franchises and privileges."[15]

The significance of the language of privileges and immunities is that it

referred to the civil rights of Englishmen against their government—
constitutional limitations. The colonial charters did not use the word
"rights" because a colonist was not entitled to every interpersonal right
created by English law for citizens of England. Because much of the
detailed municipal law in England might be unsuitable in the colonies,
the colonists were granted power in their charters to make their own
laws—as long as these were consistent with the charters and with the part
of English law that in its language was expressly made applicable to the
colonies.[16]

The privileges and immunities of Englishmen were reaffirmed in the
declarations of civil rights made by the colonists pursuant to their limited
lawmaking power. For example, the Massachusetts Body of Liberties of
1641 had a preamble that began: "The free fruition of such liberties
Immunities and privileges as humanitie, Civilitie and Christianitie call
for."[17] In 1664 Richard Nicolls, governor of New York, wrote to assure
the people of Long Island that they would have "equall (if not greater
freedomes & Immunityes) than any of his Majesties Colonyes in New
England."[18] In 1682 William Penn proclaimed a Frame of Government
of Pennsylvania in which he confirmed "these liberties, franchises and
properties, to be held, enjoyed and kept by the freemen, planters, and
inhabitants of the said province of *Pennsilvania* for ever."[19] Penn's Pennsylvania Charter of Privileges of 1701 confirmed the enjoyment of certain
stated "Liberties, Franchises and Privileges," such as liberty of conscience
and the rights to witnesses and counsel in criminal cases.[20]

In the eighteenth century, as the conflicts with England increased,
new resolutions were made, again using the language of privileges and
immunities. In 1765 the Massachusetts legislature resolved that "no Man
can justly take the Property of another without his Consent" and that
"this inherent Right, together with all other, essential Rights, Liberties,
Privileges and Immunities of the People of Great Britain, have been fully
confirmed to them by Magna Carta."[21] Similar language was in the Resolutions of the House of Burgesses of Virginia against the Stamp Act[22] and
the Resolutions of the Stamp Act Congress,[23] both in 1765. In 1774 the
colonists were still asserting loyalty to the Crown, but they were becoming
more insistent in their demands for their civil rights as English subjects.
In Virginia, the Fairfax County Resolutions asserted this claim in terms
of privileges, immunities, and advantages.[24] A series of intolerable acts by
the English government led to the calling of the First Continental Congress. On October 14, 1774, the Congress issued its Declaration and
Resolves and asserted the civil rights of Englishmen, this time in terms of
rights, liberties, and immunities.[25]

Thus, 170 years of legal-linguistic history establishes that the words
"privileges" and "immunities" had established meanings when they were
included in Article IV of the Articles of Confederation.[26] They were a

summary phrase to connote all constitutional rights of citizens against government, the constitutional limitations on the legitimate power of government to invade those rights.[27]

The evidence indicates that the privileges and immunities of citizens in Article IV of the Articles of Confederation were primarily those of the English Constitution. This is clearly seen from the first committee draft of July 12, 1775, in which the language in Article VI was: "The inhabitants of each Colony shall henceforth always have the same Rights, Liberties, Privileges, Immunities and Advantages in the other Colonies, which the said Inhabitants now have, in all Cases whatever, except in those provided for by the next following Article."[28] This was before most states had adopted constitutions, so that the phrase "which the said Inhabitants now have" had to refer to the English constitutional limitations. In other words, the Declaration of Independence discarded those parts of the English Constitution that imposed a framework of government, while retaining the constitutional privileges and immunities of Englishmen that the colonists had argued so long were theirs.

The final version of November 11, 1777, dropped the words "rights," "liberties," and "advantages," and the language became "privileges and immunities."[29] Each of the states, as a sovereign nation, thus agreed to give visitors from other states the benefit of constitutional limitations. Each did not, however, want to give visitors the benefit of rights and advantages created by ordinary statutes. Citizens of a state taxed themselves to provide many benefits, such as fishing and hunting grounds, and these benefits were meant not for visitors but for the local citizens who had paid for them.

The Articles of Confederation were superseded by the Constitution in 1789. The interstate privileges-and-immunities clause of Article IV, Section 2 of the Constitution is clearly a modified form of the clause in the Articles of Confederation. The constitutional clause states: "The Citizens of each State shall be entitled to all Privileges and Immunities of Citizens in the Several States."[30] In the articles, the beneficiaries of comity had been the "free inhabitants" of each state, which included all free residents regardless of race.[31] In the Constitution, this was changed to "citizens." Both Chief Justice Taney and Justice Curtis later presented the view that in the late eighteenth century the words "free inhabitants," "citizens," and "the people" were synonymous.[32] They were the men and women who, as the Preamble indicates, ordained and established the Constitution.[33]

Hence, it is unlikely that this change in wording made a difference.[34] The free residents of one state, whether they had met the technical requirements of state citizenship or not, were, under English constitutional tradition, entitled to the benefit of the constitutional limitations where domiciled.[35] No common-law lawyer would expect resident aliens to lose the benefits of such limitations when visiting another state. A resident alien, living in one state, would reasonably have expected, for example, the privilege of trial by jury in criminal cases and immunity from attainder in any other state he entered.

Given its derivation from Article IV of the Articles of Confederation, the interstate privileges-and-immunities clause of the Constitution must also refer to the English constitutional limitations plus the additions to them and expansions of them found in the state constitutions. In 1789, and for some time thereafter, some states did not have bills of rights, and others had only partial enumeration of the established constitutional rights inherited from England. Given the essential similarity of the state constitutional limitations in the early days of the union and the view that the national Bill of Rights was also mostly an enumeration of previous English civil rights, it is not surprising that some persons spoke of all of them collectively. Thus the Republicans at the time of the Civil War argued that Article IV, Section 2 was more than interstate.[36] It could connote all constitutional rights of Americans, including those found in state and federal constitutions. They argued that "in the several states" meant in the United States and was not equivalent to "of the several states." The majority interpretation, generally accepted today, restricts the privileges-and-immunities clause to its interstate character. Citizens of one state, visiting a second, are entitled to all the privileges and immunities found in the law of the second.[37]

The courts and commentators have largely failed to realize that privileges and immunities meant constitutional limitations. Instead of referring to the prerevolutionary origins of the constitutional language, they have relied on the dictum of Justice Washington, on circuit, in *Corfield* v. *Coryell*,[38] and have misinterpreted him. He wrote: "We feel no hesitation in confining these expressions to those privileges and immunities which are, in their nature, fundamental; which belong, of right, to the citizens of all free governments; and which have, at all times, been enjoyed by the citizens of the several states which compose this Union, from the time of their becoming free, independent, and sovereign."[39]

Because of the phrase "which belong of right, to the citizens of all free governments," some courts and commentators have labeled this a natural-law approach.[40] This is probably wrong. The free governments to which Justice Washington referred were England and the nations and states with English constitutional heritage. Analysis of the whole paragraph shows that Justice Washington was using the word "fundamental" not in its natural-law sense but in its positive-law sense, as a synonym for "constitutional." The latter was by far the most common use of "fundamental" at the time.[41] Washington said that these are the privileges and immunities that Americans have had since declaring independence and recites a list of some of the specific ones. All of these examples are positive constitutional limitations derived from our English legal heritage.[42]

Justice Washington's insight in *Corfield,* that "privileges and immunities" meant "constitutional limitations," was misunderstood by later courts because he used the label "fundamental." This history has been reviewed by others and does not deserve further treatment here.[43] Two recent Supreme Court opinions illustrate the state of the law on interstate privileges and immunities. In *Baldwin* v. *Montana Fish & Game Commission,*[44] a state statute with substantially higher hunting licensing fees for nonresidents to hunt elk was held not to deny privileges and immunities under Article IV, Section 2. Justice Blackmun summarized the view of Justice Field in *Paul* v. *Virginia*[45] that the objective of the clause was to relieve nonresidents from "disabilities of alienage in other states." He also noted that the clause has been interpreted not to enforce natural law but to prevent states from discriminating against citizens of other states in favor of their own. The test of violation of the clause is whether the discrimination is of such significance that it would frustrate the purposes of the formation of the union. Elk hunting "is not basic to the maintenance or well-being of the Union."[46] The Court failed to realize that the true distinction is between privileges and immunities, which are constitutional, as opposed to those rights that are created by ordinary statutes.

In *Baldwin,* Justice Blackmun raised an issue pertinent to this study, noting that earlier cases have held that the interstate privileges-and-immunities clause prevents a state from "imposing unreasonable burdens on citizens of other States in their pursuit of common callings within the State."[47] One would expect such an issue to be argued under the commerce clause rather than the privileges-and-immunities Clause.[48] Nonetheless, the earlier cases he cited give at least collateral support for the view that grants of monopoly in the ordinary callings and trades are unconstitutional.

In *Supreme Court of New Hampshire* v. *Piper,*[49] the practice of law was held to be a "privilege" under Article IV, Section 2. A rule of the New Hampshire Supreme Court limited admission to the bar to state residents. Kathryn Piper lived in Vermont, about 400 yards from the New Hampshire border, and she had passed the New Hampshire bar examination. Upon denial of admission, she brought this action. The practice of law was held a privilege "bearing on the vitality of the nation as a single entity."[50] The justifications offered by the state court were held not to be substantial reasons for difference in treatment.[51] Furthermore, the discrimination did not bear a close and substantial relationship to the state's objectives.

The treatment of Piper was radically different from that of Myra Bradwell in 1873, when the practice of law was held not to be a "privilege" under the Fourteenth Amendment.[52] The problem is that both cases concern equal protection of the laws, and not privileges and immunities. The practice of law is not a civil right of all persons and therefore should not be ruled a "privilege" under the Constitution. Both Piper and Bradwell were denied equal protection of the laws: they met all the requirements for admission to the bar, but were still denied admission. Neither residence nor gender has a rational relationship to being a qualified attorney.

The Privileges-or-Immunities Clause

The privileges-or-immunities clause of the Fourteenth Amendment adopts the phrase "privileges [or] immunities of citizens" from Article IV, Section 2.[53] That part of the language of the two sections are *in pari materia* and must have the same meaning. It has been shown that 260 years of American legal-linguistic history between the Charter of Virginia and the drafting of the Fourteenth Amendment gave a clear meaning to "privileges" and "immunities" in a constitutional context. Since the terms together meant constitutional limitations, the Fourteenth Amendment refers to the national constitutional limitations. These privileges and immunities of citizens of the United States are found in the original Constitution, in the Bill of Rights, and in English constitutional protections of 1791 preserved by the Ninth Amendment. Under this theory, the states are prohibited by the Fourteenth Amendment from making or enforcing any laws that would abridge the classes of civil rights against government delineated in those three sources of constitutional limitations.

The meaning of the privileges-or-immunities clause is further confirmed by the fact that Section 1 of the Fourteenth Amendment was designed to overrule the doctrine of *Scott* v. *Sandford*.[54] It was standing constitutional law under that case that a person of African descent, even if a citizen of one of the states, could not be a citizen of the United States and therefore had no protections under the national Constitution. Chief Justice Taney wrote: "[T]he question is simply this: can a negro, whose ancestors were imported into this country, and sold as slaves, become a member of the political community formed and brought into existence by the Constitution of the United States, and as such become entitled to all the Rights, and privileges, and immunities, guaranteed by that instrument to the citizen?"[55] His answer was negative. The primary decision of this case was that persons of African descent were not entitled to the privilege of suing in courts of the United States under the interstate diverse-citizenship jurisdiction.[56] Taney further stated that such persons, even if citizens of a state, would not be entitled to civil rights guaranteed to "the citizens of each state" in Article IV, Section 2. They were not entitled "to the privileges and immunities of citizens in the other states."[57]

In overruling *Dred Scott*, the Fourteenth Amendment enjoined the states from abridging all "the privileges or immunities of citizens of the United States." These were not just those of citizens of a state, such as suing in national courts on the basis of diversity of citizenship. They also included items in the original constitution, such as the privilege of the writ of habeas corpus and all of the privileges and immunities guaranteed in Amendments I to VIII. The effect of the comprehensive language of the privileges-or-immunities clause should have been to overrule the decision in *Barron* v. *Baltimore*.[58] The most efficient way to assure minimum civil rights to former slaves and even to poor whites, who also were without political power, was to make the Bill of Rights effective against states. Otherwise, such fundamental privileges and immunities as those guaranteed by the First Amendment could be massively abridged by white elites controlling governments in some of the states.

This interpretation vindicates the dissenting views of the first Justice Harlan in some early cases.[59] It also confirms the view of Justice Black, stated in his dissenting opinion in *Adamson* v. *California*,[60] that the Fourteenth Amendment incorporated, *inter alia,* the Bill of Rights as effective against the state governments. The Court majority in *Adamson,* and consistently thereafter, rejected Black's view on general incorporation of the Bill of Rights, but, via the due process clause, subsequently engaged in selective incorporation on a case-by-case basis, to accomplish much the same result.[61] The Court later expressly overruled the generalizations against incorporation of the Bill of Rights that had been expounded in the early case of *Maxwell* v. *Dow,*[62] and in effect repudiated another early case denying incorporation, *O'Neil* v. *Vermont.*[63] It also overruled the specific holdings of *Adamson* v. *California,*[64] and of the leading early case, *Twining* v. *New Jersey,*[65] which had relied on *Maxwell* to deny incorporation of the Bill of Rights. But the Court steadfastly has refused to adopt the rule of total incorporation.

The refusal of the Court to adopt the privileges-or-immunities clause of the Fourteenth Amendment as one vehicle to incorporate the Bill of Rights against the states has created an irrationality in the law. Amendments I to IV are substantive. During the 1920s and 1930s the Court used the doctrine of substantive due process to incorporate the First Amendment into the Fourteenth as effective against state governments.[66] In economic-regulation cases, the Court subsequently repudiated the doctrine of substantive due process as an unwarranted judicial fabrication, a usurpation of the amending power by the judiciary.[67] Since the due process clause correctly refers only to procedural protections, the use of due process to incorporate the First Amendment remains an illogical anomaly in our law.

The leading case on the meaning of the privileges-or-immunities clause is the *Slaughter-House Cases,*[68] but the issue of incorporation of the Bill of Rights by the privileges-or-immunities clause was mentioned by the majority in the case only in dictum. As Professor Ely suggests, however, a close reading of the various opinions in that case points to the possibility that all nine justices took the position that the language of the clause directed incorporation.[69] The majority opinion held that state grants of monopoly in the ordinary trades were solely an issue of state constitutional law. As to the Fourteenth Amendment, the majority stated: "[L]est it should be said that no such privileges and immunities are to be found if those we have been considering are excluded, we venture to suggest some which owe their existence to the Federal government, its National character, its Constitution, or its laws. . . . The right to peaceably assemble and petition for redress of grievances, the privilege of the writ of habeas corpus, are rights of the citizen guaranteed by the Federal Constitution."[70] This was a clear recognition by the majority that the privileges-or-immunities clause incorporated the First Amendment.

Only one of the dissenting justices found it necessary to treat incorporation expressly. Justice Bradley summarized a number of the specific privileges and immunities in the Bill of Rights and then stated, "These, and still others, are specified in the original Constitution or in the early Amendments of it, as among the privileges and immunities of citizens of the United States, or, what is still stronger for the force of the argument, the rights of all persons whether citizens or not."[71]

Additional support for the incorporation theory as the reasonable meaning of the language of the privileges-or-immunities clause at the time of adoption is found in the circuit court opinion in the first case decided under the clause. *United States* v. *Hall*[72] was a criminal prosecution of Ku Klux Klan members for violation of the Voting Rights Enforcement Act of 1870. The indictment, which was held valid, charged defendants with unlawfully preventing one Hays from exercise of freedom of speech and peaceable assembly in violation of the Constitution. Judge Woods quoted some of the language of *Corfield* v. *Coryell*[73] and then observed that the Fourteenth Amendment makes the first eight amendments enforceable against the states.[74]

The Ninth Amendment

A thesis of this study is that one of the unenumerated rights preserved for the people by the Ninth Amendment was the prohibition of grants of domestic monopolies in the ordinary trades. The historical background of this amendment will only be summarized here, because others have treated the history in detail.[75]

When the issue of a proposed declaration of civil rights was raised near the end of the Constitutional Convention, it was voted down. The debates indicate that the delegates felt that the civil rights of Englishmen against government, which they argued were theirs, did not need enumeration.[76]

When the subsequent demand for an express bill of rights became so great that it was a condition of ratification, Madison promised to introduce the proposals for amendment in the first Congress.[77]

Once the adoption of a bill of rights was agreed upon, a clause relating to unenumerated civil rights was urged for two reasons. The first was to indicate that the express restraints did not imply that Congress had been delegated power to act on the listed topics. The second was to indicate that there was no implication that unenumerated civil rights were forfeited to the national government. Madison's original proposal read as follows: "The exceptions here or elsewhere in the Constitution, made in favor of particular rights, shall not be so construed as to diminish the just importance of other rights retained by the people, or as to enlarge the powers delegated by the Constitution; but either as actual limitations of such powers, or as inserted merely for greater caution."[78] The language used here and Madison's proposal that it be inserted in Article I, Section 9 of the Constitution indicate that the constraints were on the national government only, and not on the states.[79]

After revision by the select committee, of which Madison was a member, the portion indicating that no additional powers in Congress were implied by the enumeration was dropped. The final version that was enacted read: "The enumeration in the Constitution, of certain rights, shall not be construed to deny or disparage others retained by the people.[80] The language states a rule of construction for those government agencies that will interpret the Constitution. It notes that certain of the civil rights of citizens against government have been enumerated in the Constitution and Bill of Rights and implies that other rights existent at the time were not. The objective was to preserve the latter. "This clause was manifestly introduced to prevent any perverse or ingenious misapplication of the well-known maxim, that an affirmation in particular implies a negation of all others."[81]

The first premise in a search for unenumerated rights is to recall that constitutional language must be interpreted as of date of adoption.[82] This is reinforced here by the key verb in the Ninth Amendment, "retained," which meant "to keep hold or possession of that which one already had." Consequently, unenumerated civil rights can be found in the substantive standing constitutional law of England and the American states in 1791.[83]

None of the meager literature on the Ninth Amendment has approached its content in these terms. Irvin Kent has attempted the most comprehensive survey of unenumerated rights under four categories: (1) personal freedoms, (2) family relationships, (3) economics, and (4) participation in organized society.[84] The majority of rights he lists are really enumerated rights or derived from them, such as the right to engage in political activity or to vote or to seek office.[85] Others are those created by courts more recently and fail to meet the criterion of existence in 1791. Kent lists one right that relates to immunity from monopoly, the right to earn a livelihood.

Ely has argued that the literal meaning of the Ninth Amendment, as a reference to standing, unenumerated constitutional rights, is conclusively shown by its subsequent adoption in twenty-six state bills of rights.[86] That the clause was not in the few partial bills of rights adopted by states before the national convention indicates that Americans in those times must have thought it unnecessary. They automatically considered all the privileges and immunities of Englishmen as their birthrights, part of their heritage.[87] After the Congress thought it wise to preserve these same unenumerated rights expressly in the Ninth Amendment, most of the later state conventions in the nineteenth century, in drafting their more comprehensive bills of rights, considered it wise to adopt a similar clause.

One key example of an unenumerated substantive civil right is the right to possess, use, and dispose of property according to the common-law rules, subject to such statutory regulation as the legislature enacts for the public welfare. This right can be traced in part to chapters 28, 30, and 31 of the Magna Charta and the English Bill of Rights of 1689.[88] Protection of some aspects of the property right is found in two sections of the Fifth Amendment.[89] The due process clause assures full and fair procedure when one is deprived of property by a rule of law. The takings clause assures just compensation when property is taken for public use by the national government. For 150 years, American courts have continued to cite as authority the statement of Justice Bushrod Washington that one of the fundamental or constitutional privileges and immunities of our heritage, comprehended under Article IV, Section 2 of the Constitution, is the right "to take, hold and dispose of property, either real or personal."[90] One can conclude that there was not a general protection for property in the Bill of Rights because it was such an agreed principle of Anglo-American constitutional law that restating it was unnecessary.

The antimonopoly tradition of the English Constitution, as restated in the original constitutions of two states and in the recommendations of five states to the first Congress for inclusion in the Bill of Rights, was a significant element of American constitutional heritage. This tradition was augmented in 1776 by publication of Adam Smith's *An Inquiry into the Nature and Causes of the Wealth of Nations*. His was a powerful statement for the supreme value of individual liberty and free trade as an element of that liberty. Holdsworth recounts the substantial influence of the *Wealth of Nations* on political and legal institutions.[91] Thus, the arguments against mercantilism, which had promoted monopoly in international trade, reinforced the policy against domestic monopolies that had been confirmed in the law a century before. Like the right to property, the rule against governmental grants of monopolies in the ordinary trades was taken for granted. It was so completely accepted as part of the constitutional foundation of England and America that enumeration was unnecessary.

The Ninth Amendment has had little hearing in the courts and has never been more than a partial basis for a Supreme Court decision.[92] The most prominent Supreme Court case in which the Ninth Amendment was introduced as a partial basis of decision was *Griswold* v. *Connecticut*.[93] Though he did not elaborate on the Ninth Amendment, Justice Douglas, writing for the majority in *Griswold*, listed the Ninth Amendment as one of six constitutional clauses that had penumbras combining to create a civil right of privacy. And Justice Goldberg, in his concurring opinion, relied heavily upon the Ninth Amendment.[94] From the viewpoint presented here, *Griswold* was a poor fact setting in which to raise the Ninth Amendment. In effect, both Douglas and Goldberg sought to create a new constitutional right of privacy out of personal value judgments against the state statute limiting birth control. There was, however, no class of English constitutional immunities against government in 1791 relating to privacy in the general sense under which a statute preventing birth control could be subsumed.[95] The justices therefore had no real support for a Ninth Amendment argument, and it is unfortunate that *Griswold* stands as the foremost reference to the meaning of the amendment.[96]

Antimonopoly Tradition in England

The tradition against governmental grants of domestic monopolies in England seems to have begun with chapter 41 of the Magna Charta.[97] This chapter was designed to protect one small sector of competition, that of foreign merchants. Because these merchants had not been protected by the common law of the land, King John had extracted large tolls from them, impeding the introduction to England of types of goods not previously known there or not amenable to efficient production there. Chapter 41 guaranteed them safe conduct, liberty to buy and sell, and confirmation of the ancient rates of "customs."[98]

The right of the English sovereign to grant monopolies to inventors and to persons introducing new goods from abroad as a reward for benefit given to the community had always been recognized as part of the common-law prerogative.[99] In theory, a monopoly could not be granted by the Crown without some consideration moving to the public, since monopolies were considered to be in derogation of the common right to freedom of trade. In practice, however, the sovereigns of England from the fourteenth to the sixteenth centuries granted all types of monopolies, some as royal favors and some to finance the Crown treasury. Royal grants of monopolies to merchants were common. Consequently, Parliament enacted statutes in the fourteenth century designed to curtail these grants.[100]

During this era, the superiority of Parliament was not established. Kings granted monopolies in spite of statutory prohibitions. The response of Parliament was to re-enact statutes asserting the liberty of English merchants to buy and sell goods without governmental restraint.[101] Cunningham quotes Sandys's paper on *Instructions towchinge the Bill for Free Trade* on the broad scope of the 1497 statute.[102] In the sixteenth century, patents of monopoly were issued primarily to promote the introduction into England of the advanced knowledge of industrial arts on the continent. In the latter part of the century, however, Queen Elizabeth granted many patents of monopoly on commodities in general use, including alum, salt, soap, and playing cards. Universal discontent led to an address from the House of Commons to the queen in 1597 and a declaratory bill in Parliament to restore common-law freedom of trade.[103] The queen responded by conceding that the courts could determine the legality of patents of monopoly. This was followed by a proclamation revoking some of the patents, and the bill in Commons was withdrawn.

The common-law rule that monopolies were void unless they were for the common good is cited in two leading cases. In *Davenant v. Hurdis,*[104] the Company of Merchant Tailors had been empowered in its charter from the Crown, which had been confirmed by Parliament, to make ordinances to govern the corporation. One ordinance required each member to send at least one-half of the cloth sent out to be dressed to another member of the corporation. The penalty for violation was ten shillings for each cloth. The ordinance was held void as a monopoly in violation of the common law.

The second leading case was *Darcy v. Allin,*[105] best known as the *Case of Monopolies*. In 1598 the queen had granted Darcy a patent for the manufacture and transport of playing cards for twenty-one years. Darcy brought an action against Allin, who began manufacture of cards in competition. Darcy's grant was held void as a monopoly against the common law and in violation of earlier statutes protecting free trade. The case is famous as the most comprehensive statement of the common law of monopolies at the beginning of the seventeenth century. The exaggerations of Lord Coke that Crown grants of monopolies had been forbidden by law since Magna Charta became part of the accepted law.[106] The significance of this case in Anglo-American constitutional law has not been overlooked. Professor Thayer of Harvard Law School included a full report in his *Cases on Constitutional Law*.[107]

The *Case of Monopolies* was reinforced in 1614 by the Kings Bench decision in *Cloth Workers of Ipswich*.[108] This was an action for a penalty by the Corporation of Tailors of Ipswich charging that defendant had practiced the trade of tailor without serving an apprenticeship of seven years. The royal charter granting the monopoly was held unenforceable on the ground that it took away the common-law right of any man to work at a lawful trade. The rule was reiterated in the *Dubin Corporation Case*,[109] an action *in quo warranto* holding a Crown grant of monopoly to a guild of merchants within one city to be void. These cases are evidence that control of trades by the guilds, dating back at least to the thirteenth century, was in decline.

In spite of the decision in the *Case of Monopolies*, King James continued to exercise his royal prerogative to issue patents of monopoly. The number became so great that the House of Commons filed petitions of protest with King James in 1606 and 1610. The second protest provoked a declaration of the king, or *Book of Bounty*, that monopolies were against the laws of the realm.[110] Finally, on July 10, 1621, King James issued a proclamation revoking certain monopolies.[111] The culmination of these protests was the proceeding in the House of Commons against Sir Giles Mompesson for abuse of monopolies.[112] He was expelled from the House.

Another petition of grievance of the House of Commons against monopolies in 1623 led to a second legal milestone of constitutional status in England, the Statute of Monopolies.[113] The first section of the statute declared all royal grants of domestic monopolies to be void. The second section provided that the validity of letters patent should be determined by the courts according to the common law. The third section disabled all persons and corporations from exercising monopolies. The fourth section gave any party aggrieved by action of a monopoly a right to recover treble damages and double costs. Other sections provided exemptions of fourteen years for new manufactures.

Section 9 of the Statute of Monopolies exempted municipalities and existing corporations or companies of craftsmen or merchants. This is easily understandable in the mercantilist setting of the times. It was 150 years before the free-market philosophy of Adam Smith. Nevertheless, the decisions in the *Davenant, Ipswich*, and *Dublin Corporation* cases indicate that monopoly power in corporations was limited. In the seventeenth century, persons outside the corporations could enter the same trade in competition if they could find customers who were not concerned by the lack of a guild stamp of quality.

Despite the rule of *Darcy* v. *Allin* and the Statute of Monopolies, King Charles continued to assert his prerogative to grant monopolies to corporations for the sale of many manufactures.[114] The Company of Playing-Card Makers, for example, received a patent in 1615 and was awarded another in 1637.[115] In 1631, as a technique of taxation, an office was erected for the sealing of playing cards, which further entrenched the monopoly.[116] This resurgence of monopolies again provoked many protests from the House of Commons. In response, the king issued proclamations in 1639 and 1640 canceling most patents of monopoly.[117] This marked the decline of the monopoly system. In 1641 the Parliament abolished the Court of Star Chamber, where many patents of monopoly had been enforced.[118] During the commonwealth patents were not granted, and after the restoration Charles II agreed to submit patent applications to the Royal Society for examination to determine invention. The Bill of Rights of 1689[119] abolished the royal prerogative and established parliamentary supremacy. The House of Commons, having fought the battle against monopolies and won, has never since issued a patent for a domestic monopoly except for invention.[120]

Under the conventions of the English Constitution, the *Case of Monopolies* and the Statute of Monopolies were established fundamental law in 1791 when the Ninth Amendment preserved unenumerated civil rights.[121] The fact that legislative supremacy in England made it possible for Parliament to reverse its long-standing view and start granting domestic monopolies has no bearing on legislative power in the United States. A key function of the United States Bill of Rights was to impose constitutional limitations on both the executive and the legislative branches. Madison, in proposing the national Bill of Rights, noted the great differences between the English and United States constitutions. He observed that "it may not be thought necessary to provide limits for the legislative power in that country, yet a different opinion prevails in the United States. . . . The people of many States have thought it necessary to raise barriers against power in all forms and departments of Government."[122]

Antimonopoly Tradition in America

The *Case of Monopolies* and the Statute of Monopolies enunciated one of the claimed liberties or immunities of Englishmen, and the American colonists could claim the same benefits by virtue of the colonial charters.[123] Pursuant to the authority granted in their charters, the colonists enacted local law consistent with the charters. The first mention of monopolies was in the Massachusetts Body of Liberties of 1641.[124] Item 9 therein states: "No monopolies shall be granted or allowed amongst us, but of such new Inventions that are profitable to the Countrie, and that for a short time."[125] The Body of Liberties was adopted at the same time when the greatest victories were won in England against Crown grants of monopolies to domestic companies. It was adopted by the General Court of Massachusetts only after consideration by the magistrates and elders in each town and publication for the citizens. As one historian has commented, "a more careful process of legislation is perhaps nowhere recorded."[126]

William Penn, in *The Excellent Privilege of Liberty & Property Being the Birth-Right of the Free-Born Subjects of England*,[127] also examined monopolies. In the section of this pamphlet that is a commentary on the Magna Charta, largely from Lord Coke, Penn wrote of chapter 29 (chapter 39 in the revised version) and described some practices that were against the law of the land. After summarizing the facts of *Davenant* v. *Hurdis*[128] and *Darcy* v. *Allin*,[129] he concluded: "Generally all Monopolies are against the great charter because they are against the Liberty and Freedom of the Subject, and against the Law of the Land."[130]

No other mention of monopolies has been found in the American constitutional documents of the seventeenth century. Sir Edwin Sandys, who played a leading role in obtaining the revised royal charters of Virginia of 1609 and 1612,[131] was one of the outspoken opponents of the grants of monopolies to companies in England. Since Sandys prepared the first draft of the charter of 1609 and did not specifically mention monopolies, historians can only hypothesize that the general protection for free trade in the charter was sufficient to preclude grants of monopoly.[132]

The issue of constitutional immunity against monopolies did not arise in the eighteenth century until the American Revolution. This can be understood only in light of the fact that the colonists claimed all the constitutional protections of Englishmen,[133] which included the benefit of the Statute of Monopolies and its antecedent common law. When the first state constitutions were enacted, starting with Virginia in 1776, the conventions were more concerned with the structure of their new governments than with civil rights. Only seven states enacted bills of rights, though four more included some civil rights within their constitutions.[134] These states codified only part of the existing English constitutional limitations. Connecticut and Rhode Island did not adopt constitutions and continued state government under their colonial charters. In this context of partial codification, it is not surprising that only two states included specific constitutional provisions against monopolies. The Maryland Constitution of November 3, 1776, contained the following clause: "XXXIX. That monopolies are odious, contrary to the spirit of free government, and the principles of commerce; and ought not to be suffered."[135] The similar clause of the Constitution of North Carolina of December 14, 1776, stated "XXIII. That perpetuities and monopolies are contrary to the genius of a free State, and ought not to be allowed."[136] One reasonably can conclude that these two constitutional clauses merely codify one element of the standing constitutional law of all Americans, derived from their heritage as English citizens.

Upon adoption of the proposed national constitution by the Convention of 1787, the dominant issue in the ratification controversies was whether an express bill of rights should be appended.[137] In his first letter to Madison commenting on the proposed constitution, Jefferson wrote: "I will now add what I do not like. First the omission of a bill of rights providing clearly and without the aid of sophisms for freedom of religion, freedom of the press, protection against standing armies, *restriction against monopolies*, the eternal and unremitting force of the habeas corpus laws, and trials by jury. . . . Let me add that a bill of rights is what the people are entitled to against every government on earth, general or particular, and what no just government should refuse, or rest on inference."[138] In so writing, Jefferson seemed to attach as much importance to the English constitutional immunity from grants of monopoly as he did to those privileges and immunities that eventually appeared in the First Amendment.

Five of the states that ratified the Constitution and urged adoption of an express Bill of Rights recommended a prohibition on monopolies. The proposal of the Massachusetts Convention of February 6, 1788, was "[t]hat Congress erect no Company of Merchants with exclusive advantages of commerce."[139] New Hampshire and North Carolina adopted the same language on June 21, 1788, and August 1, 1788, respectively.[140] The New York recommendation of July 26, 1788 was "[t]hat the Congress do not grant Monopolies or erect any Company with exclusive Advantages of Commerce."[141] The belated ratification of Rhode Island on May 29, 1790, contained the same recommendation as New York.[142] Although the Rhode Island proposal came too late to have had an effect on Congress in its decisions on which rights should be enumerated in the Bill of Rights, the proposal indicates one more state that found this issue significant. This must be compared with the fact that only four states considered it necessary for express statement in the Bill of Rights of provisions for due process of law, speedy and public trial, and the rights to assembly and petition.[143]

The surprising fact was that neither Virginia nor Maryland recommended a prohibition of monopolies. George Mason of Virginia, major author of the Virginia Declaration of Rights of 1776, refused to sign the Constitution in 1787, primarily because it failed to contain a bill of rights.[144] One of his stated objections was that "Congress may grant monopolies in trade and commerce."[145] There is no explanation why Mason did not persuade the Virginia Convention to include a ban on monopolies among its twenty recommendations for a bill of rights. Maryland had adopted a prohibition on monopoly in its state constitution,[146] and one can only surmise that the Maryland convention in this preindustrial era did not consider monopoly a national issue.

The express prohibition of monopolies was not among the amendments offered in Congress by Madison nor among those reported by the Select Committee of the House of Representatives. Proposals on the floor of the House and the Senate to add prohibitions on monopolies were defeated.[147] Since Madison had to assuage the Federalists, who controlled both Houses and thought a bill of rights was unnecessary, he eschewed controversial topics that might engender substantial opposition in ratification.

There is no expressed explanation why the due process clause was expressly included in the Bill of Rights and the ban on monopolies was not. Both received the recommendation of four states before action by the Congress. It is clear, however, that those civil rights that were not expressly included in the Bill of Rights were to be preserved. This was the sole purpose of the Ninth Amendment.

Slaughter-House Cases

The *Slaughter-House Cases*[148] was provoked by the grant from the legislature of Louisiana in 1869 to one corporation of a monopoly over the slaughtering of animals for food in New Orleans. The grant deprived over a thousand trained butchers of a living, and there was a general feeling of outrage in the community.[149] The result was several hundred suits for injunctions. Five of the actions, either attacking or attempting to enforce the monopoly, were heard on writ of error to the Supreme Court of the United States.[150] After the monopoly had been upheld in the Louisiana Supreme Court, and before the appeal was heard in the Supreme Court of the United States, an action to enjoin enforcement of the Louisiana judgments was heard in the United States Circuit Court for Louisiana.[151] Justice Bradley, on circuit, was of the view that the state grant of monopoly violated the Civil Rights Act[152] and the privileges-or-immunities clause of the Fourteenth Amendment. As to the latter, he declined to submit a general definition, stating: "But so far as relates to the question in hand, we may safely say it is one of the privileges of every American citizen to adopt and follow such lawful industrial pursuit—not injurious to the community—as he may see fit, without unreasonable regulation or molestation, and without being restricted by any of those unjust, oppressive, and odious monopolies or exclusive privileges which have been condemned by all free governments."[153]

He noted exceptions to the antimonopoly rule for inventions, for structural monopolies such as railroads, canals, and turnpikes, and for regulating sale of intoxicating drinks and drugs. In this case, however, he found the pretense of a health regulation false. He stated: "But this pretense is too bald for a moment's consideration. It certainly does confer on the defendant corporation a monopoly of a very odious character. If it be not fairly and fully within the definition of a monopoly given in the great case of monopolies (11 Coke, 85), it is difficult to conceive of a case which would be within it.[154] Justice Bradley denied the injunction, however, reasoning that Section 3 of the Judiciary Act of 1793[155] prohibited federal courts from enjoining proceedings in state courts.

When the cases from the Louisiana Supreme Court reached the Supreme Court of the United States, they were affirmed by a vote of 5 to 4.[156] Writing for the majority, Justice Miller asserted that the appellant's argument rested wholly on the assumption that the privileges and immunities guaranteed by Article IV, Section 2, and the Fourteenth Amendment were the same,[157] and consequently rejected that assumption. Justice Miller's assertion, however, was erroneous. Retired Justice Campbell, for the appellants, had merely used ambiguous language. He should have argued more precisely that both classes of privileges and immunities had the same foundation in English constitutional law. Every lawyer and most educated citizens knew that although the state and national bills of rights had many clauses in common, they also had some constitutional limitations that differed. However, Justice Miller went further and, in effect, asserted, also erroneously, that the two sets of privileges and immunities did not overlap, that only state constitutions and the interstate privileges-and-immunities clause protected the many civil rights derived from our English heritage that Justice Washington had labeled "fundamental."[158] The national privileges and immunities, he reasoned, were only those enumerated in the national Constitution or implied by it, such as the right to travel to the seat of government. He ignored the Ninth Amendment.

Justice Miller viewed the appellant's argument to be that the Fourteenth Amendment made the Supreme Court of the United States the final arbiter on all civil rights, state and national. Part of the effect would have been to make the Court the final reviewer of state legislation under state constitutions. Having given this extreme, and arguably wrong, interpretation to the appellants' arguments, Justice Miller of course rejected them as inconsistent with the structure and spirit of the constitutional division of powers between national and state governments. He concluded that the right to pursue a common calling free from grants of monopoly to others was solely an issue of state privileges and immunities under state constitutional law. Not being enumerated in the Constitution or Bill of Rights, it posed no federal issue under the Fourteenth Amendment, he argued. The Louisiana courts, with their French legal tradition, had the final say when a grant of monopoly was constitutional.[159]

Professor Lusky, in a penetrating critique of Justice Miller's opinion, calls it an anomaly and considers it based on shabby reasoning.[160] He argues that it also is intellectually dishonest,[161] noting that Justice Miller deliberately misquoted Article IV, Section 2 to end with "of the several states,"[162] and trimmed a quotation from *Corfield* v. *Coryell* to hide the fact that it harmed rather than helped his argument.[163] Furthermore, Professor Lusky argues that Justice Miller denied that Congress had ever undertaken to define any of the privileges or immunities of citizens of the United States, even though the Civil Rights Act of 1866 had an extensive, though incomplete, enumeration.[164] Given Lusky's critique and many prior ones,[165] it is surprising that Justice Miller's opinion is still part of our standing constitutional law. Yet the Supreme Court has held to the opinion that the privileges-or-immunities clause is without significant effect.[166]

Justice Field, for the four dissenters in the *Slaughter-House Cases,* viewed the privileges and immunities of citizens of the United States to be much broader. Although he incorrectly held the privileges and immunities protected by the Fourteenth Amendment to be the same as those protected by the comity clause of Article IV, he correctly viewed the civil rights derived from our English heritage and labeled by Justice Washington as "fundamental" as not only the foundation of state privileges and immunities but also the foundation of national privileges and immunities.[167] In effect, he held both privileges-and-immunities clauses to be types of equal protection clauses. Unfortunately, however, and unlike the majority opinion, Field found it unnecessary even to mention the issue of whether the privileges-or-immunities clause incorporated the Bill of Rights. If he *had* adopted the incorporation principle, his opinion would have more closely paralleled the viewpoint of this study, and would have been a stronger argument against the Louisiana statute.

Justice Field showed that the substantive privilege or immunity in question in the *Slaughter-House Cases,* immunity from government grants of domestic monopolies in the ordinary trades, was part of our English constitutional heritage. He stated: "All such grants relating to any known trade have been held by all the judges of England, whenever they have come up for consideration, to be void at common law as destroying the freedom of trade, discouraging labor and industry, restraining persons from getting an honest livelihood, and putting it in the power of grantees to enhance the price of commodities."[168] Field cited the *Case of Monopolies,*[169] *Davenant* v. *Hurdis,*[170] and the Statute of Monopolies[171] as authorities. He then cited the Declaration and Resolves of the First Continental Congress as preserving these "indubitable rights and liberties" for Americans.[172] He further noted state cases applying the rule against monopolies and concluded by tying the immunity to "the right of free labor, one of the most sacred and imprescriptible rights of man."[173]

The one major legal argument that appellants failed to raise, and that could and should have enabled them to win, was the applicability of the Ninth Amendment to the states. The political and legal context of the adoption of the Ninth Amendment demonstrates that the national government was, like the state governments, based on the English constitutional tradition, and Justice Field was therefore right to assert that the antimonopoly tradition of English constitutional law was part of our national law. If only the Ninth Amendment had been pleaded in the *Slaughter-House Cases* and the history of its origins argued, Justice Field possibly could have persuaded at least one more justice that the rule against monopolies was part of the Bill of Rights. The incorporation of the Bill of Rights by the privileges-or-immunities clause as effective against state governments already had been at least noted by the majority, and, consequently, grants of domestic monopolies for ordinary goods or services, whether by the national or the state governments, could have been held unconstitutional.[174]

Ignored until recently, the unenforced Ninth Amendment has left citizens of the United States without the full benefit of their unenumerated substantive civil rights. One result is that Congress has been free to pass regulatory statutes whose effect is equivalent to outright grants of domestic monopolies for ordinary goods and services.[175] In addition, the misconstrued Fourteenth Amendment has left citizens of the United States without remedies against infringement by state governments of unenumerated national civil rights. State statutes granting monopolies in the ordinary trades flourish in many jurisdictions.[176] Overruling the *Slaughter-House Cases* would revive the privileges-or-immunities clause and enable challenge of modern state regulatory statutes granting monopoly power.

CHAPTER 11

Due Process and the Substance of Law

THE AMENDMENTS TO THE CONSTITUTION CONTAIN two due process clauses. The Fifth Amendment states in part: "No Person shall be . . . deprived of life, liberty, or property, without due process of law." In spite of its unqualified language and its origin in the fundamental rights of Englishmen, the Fifth Amendment has been interpreted by the Supreme Court as a limit only on the national government.[1] The Fourteenth Amendment, Section 1 puts the same limitation on the states: "nor shall any state deprive any person of life, liberty, or property without due process of law." "Due process" is a technical term of the law that was in the Fifth Amendment when the Fourteenth was adopted. Under the basic rules of documentary interpretation, the latter clause must make good as against the states every constraint that the former effected against the national government.[2]

Chapter 10 established that the original meaning of the language in the privileges-or-immunities clause of the Fourteenth Amendment required incorporation of the Bill of Rights against the states. Incorporation of the Fifth Amendment entitled all citizens of the United States to the benefit of that due process clause against the states. But if the courts were to interpret the word "citizens" in the privileges-or-immunities clause in its literal, narrow sense, state governments might still be free to deprive aliens residing within their territories of due process of law. The due process clause of the Fourteenth Amendment remedied this. It prohibited the states from depriving any *person*, including aliens[3] and corporations,[4] of the full and fair procedure that constitutes due process of law.

Efficient interpretation of the due process clauses begins with the rule of documentary interpretation that technical words are to be given their technical meaning unless this is repelled by the context.[5] This rule must be taken in light of another rule of construction, that words are not construed in isolation: they have meaning only as part of a clause and a section of a document. In order to resolve any ambiguity, we must resort "to the context, and shape the particular meaning so as to make it fit that of the connecting words and agree with the subject matter."[6] These rules dictate that the due process clauses be interpreted as integrated wholes in light of their technical sense in the law of the time.

It is shown here that the original meaning of "due process" was "required procedure." In construing the due process clauses, the first and foremost interpretive rule of the courts should have been to limit the clauses to the original meaning: procedural protections. This conclusion is reinforced by the requirement to interpret the clauses as integrated wholes. The clauses do not protect "liberty" or "property" in isolation. In a proper judicial proceeding, one's liberty or one's property may be taken as a punishment or remedy as long as there is compliance with all the required procedures of law. The judicial creation of substantive due process had no foundation in the Constitution. Substantive due process was a set of judicial usurpations of legislative powers.[7] This action was inefficient because it imposed judges' personal views of reasonable regulation on the law. The due process rulings precluded definition and consequently fostered litigation. The hundreds of cases between 1890 and 1937 seeking judicial remedies under that theory represent a great economic waste by courts, lawyers, and litigants.

Original Meaning: Required Procedure

The accepted understanding of the phrase "due process of law" in 1791 was much broader than its earlier English meaning. Its alleged origins in the "law of the land" in chapter 39 of the Magna Charta[8] and its statutory adoption as due process in chapter 3 of 28 Edw. III in 1335 do not explain later usage. Coke's definition in terms of criminal procedure at common law was but a fraction of its later meaning.[9] It is clear that in 1791, due process was not limited to criminal law, nor to common law. It applied to all legal procedures, both civil and criminal, and to procedural statutes as well as common-law procedure.

In 1791, "process" was a synonym for "procedure." The foremost element of legal classification was and is the distinction between adjective law and substantive law. A typical example of process as the usual way of referring to judicial procedure was the first federal statute regulating procedures in lower federal courts. This statute was called the Act to Regulate Processes in the Courts of the United States.[10] The bill that led to the enactment was the Senate Process Bill.[11] The leading law dictionary of the time defined "process" as "proceedings in legal actions from the beginning to the end."[12] The usual way of comparing procedures was to speak of different "modes of process."[13] It is thus clear that in 1791 the word "process" was the most common way of denoting procedure.

Historians have established that in 1791 "due process of law" meant required or appropriate procedure in the broadest sense.[14] The constitutional context indicates that the constraint is imposed on all three departments of government. In a criminal prosecution, a convicted defendant may be deprived of his life, liberty, or property. In a civil lawsuit, a losing defendant may be deprived of property. But in either case, there is a required judicial procedure. Daniel Webster explained it as "a law which hears before it condemns; which proceeds upon inquiry and renders judgment only after trial."[15] Following legislative due process requires the Congress and state assemblies to follow all their respective constitutional and statutory procedures for enacting laws. And under due process, executive officers must administer laws in ways that give citizens such full and fair hearings as are appropriate to the particular administrative functions.

An explanatory definition of "due process" or "required procedure of law" has three elements. The first two were explained by Justice Curtis in the leading case of *Murray's Lessee* v. *Hoboken Land and Improvement Company* in 1855:

> The Constitution contains no description of those processes which it was intended to allow or forbid. It does not even declare what principles are to be applied to ascertain whether it be due process. It is manifest that it was not left to the legislative power to enact any process which might be devised. The article is a restraint on the legislative as well as on the executive and judicial powers of the government, and cannot be so construed as to leave Congress free to make any process "due process of law," by its mere will. To what principles, then, are we to resort to ascertain whether this process enacted by Congress, is due process? To this the answer must be twofold. We must examine the Constitution itself, to see whether this process be in conflict with any of its provisions. If not found to be so, we must look to those settled usages and modes of proceeding existing in the common and statute law of England, before the emigration of our ancestors, and which are shown not to have been unsuited to their civil and political condition by having been acted on by them after the settlement of this country.[16]

The first category enumerated by Justice Curtis included the various specific "process" or procedural guarantees of the Fifth, Sixth, Seventh, and Eighth amendments and those in the original Constitution. His second category noted the constitutional incorporation of the then-existing procedural guarantees under the common and statute law of England. This second group of limitations is directly supported by the language of the Ninth Amendment: "The enumeration in the Constitution of certain rights shall not be construed to deny or disparage others retained by the people." Justice Harlan confirmed that due process included this second category of guarantees, "which had long been deemed fundamental in Anglo-Saxon institutions." He went on to quote Justice Story: "It was under the consciousness of the full possession of the rights, liberties and immunities of British subjects that the colonists in almost all the early legislation of their respective assemblies insisted upon a declaratory Act, acknowledging and confirming them."[17]

It was not necessary for Justice Curtis to go further, because the "process" in the *Hoboken* case conformed to the Constitution and had been followed as common law in England. But there must be a third category of due process. The framers of the Fifth Amendment clearly contemplated that Congress would pass new procedural statutes. And Congress, in framing the Fourteenth Amendment, contemplated that the state legislatures would pass new procedural statutes. Furthermore, executive officers of both the nation and the states could be expected to invent novel procedures for the new administrative agencies created by Congress and the state legislatures. Even if they conformed to the specific process guarantees of Amendments V to VIII, any of the innovative procedures of later legislatures or administrators might have an essential unfairness or inequity to the persons governed. Hence, in addition to the two elements of due process explained by Justice Curtis, there had to be a third, general limitation on all procedures of all departments of government: they must also be *fair* and *equitable* under the general value standards of American society.

This third aspect of due process of law is not subject to more precise definition than "total fairness" in procedure, including notice, hearing, and decision making.[18] It has been summarized by Justice Cardozo as those procedures that embody "some principle of justice so rooted in the traditions and conscience of our people as to be ranked as fundamental."[19] Although reflecting traditional notions of fair play and substantial justice, the concept of total fairness is not static. As Justice Frankfurter has written: "It is thus not a stagnant formulation of what has been achieved in the past but a standard for judgment in the progressive evolution of the institutions of a free society."[20]

The due process limitation is one of those few areas of constitutional law in which the original language provides for a growing concept. As the community's notion of fair play evolves, the scope of the due process limitation can be expected to expand. The Supreme Court may impose new procedural requirements to be added to those established in earlier eras.

One key implication of *Murray's Lessee* has received little recognition by the Supreme Court. Because due process is a phrase of comprehensive connotation that includes the particular process guarantees of the original Constitution and the Bill of Rights, the due process clause of the Fourteenth Amendment must incorporate Amendments V through VIII. This creates a partial redundancy, since the privileges-or-immunities clause also incorporated the entire Bill of Rights for citizens of the United States. It was the failure to understand and answer the incorporation implications of *Murray's Lessee* that led the majority in *Hurtado* v. *California*[21] and other procedural cases to deny incorporation.[22] It was only in the 1960s that most of the erroneous denials of incorporation were overruled.[23]

The procedural character of the due process clauses was emphasized by Justice Miller in *Davidson* v. *New Orleans*.[24] An assessment on real estate in New Orleans for draining the swamps of the city was upheld against a charge that it violated the due process clause of the Fourteenth Amendment. If "those laws provide for a mode of confirming or contesting the charge thus imposed, in ordinary courts of justice, with such notice to the person, or such proceeding in regard to the property as is appropriate to the nature of the case, the judgment in such proceedings cannot be said to deprive the owner of his property without due process of law, however obnoxious it may be to other objections."[25] The statute contested here clearly provided the required procedures of law. In contrast, as Miller pointed out, a statute confiscating property without hearing on the issue of compensation would violate due process. "It seems to us that a statute which declared in terms, and without more, that the full and exclusive title of a described piece of land, which is now in A, shall be and is hereby vested in B, would, if effectual, deprive A of his property without due process of law, within the meaning of the constitutional provision."[26] In this sense, the taking of property by the state cannot be solely statutory. Owners are entitled to a judicial due process in which eminent domain is inextricably entwined.

Miller noted that although there had been little litigation under the due process clause of the Fifth Amendment, the docket in his day was crowded with cases under the due process clause of the Fourteenth. "There is here abundant evidence that there exists some strange misconception of the scope of this provision as found in the XIVth Amendment."[27] Petitioners were requesting review of the merits of legislation, and a reversal on the basis of the Court's view of the substance of the law. The pressure on the Court to adopt substantive due process was growing.

Creation of Substantive Limitations

"Substantive due process" is the label for holding unconstitutional those regulatory statutes that the Court finds to be unreasonable interferences with liberty or property. The approach was created by lawyers, especially Thomas M. Cooley, who convinced courts to ignore and eliminate from consideration the phrase "due process of law" from the end of the two constitutional clauses.[28] In this group of cases, the clause came to be read as "No person shall be deprived of life, liberty or property" whenever a court could be convinced that a statute was unreasonable. The Supreme Court majority adopted a constitutional ideology for economic individualism that was based on a premise of inherent antagonism between the people and the government. Although Cooley rejected a theory of natural rights, he viewed human rights against government as incorporated in an organically growing Constitution. He asserted that pre-existing common-law rights of freedom of contract and unfettered property were preserved in the Constitution by virtue of implied limitations. The sanctity of these vested rights, though not present in specific clauses, was found from reading the constitutional limitations as a unified whole. Judicial review was a necessary instrument to enforce the implied limitations on the substance of relations between the individual and the state. Cooley viewed the judicial expansion of constitutional meanings as a direct response to the expression of popular will, which was superior to the will of elected legislators.

Freedom of contract was elevated to a constitutional principle. Business lawyers had created the idea as part of the laissez-faire philosophy of the business community. They convinced the majority of the justices to use it in holding unconstitutional federal and state statutes that attempted to regulate prices, wages, and other business practices. Thus, many times the courts frustrated the will of the people for regulated economic development in order to remedy asserted market failures. Arrogating unto them-selves the status of a superlegislature, the courts held the regulatory statutes unreasonable and therefore unconstitutional. This conversion of a procedural protection into a substantive one not only violated canons of documentary interpretation; it had no basis in the Constitution.

The attempts to convert liberty and property into distinct constitutional standards began in state courts before the Civil War.[29] Graham records the extrajudicial rise of substantive due process in the antislavery move-ment and in the litigation of the rights of free Negroes.[30] The leading case in which a court clearly adopted the doctrine was the 1856 decision of *Wynehamer* v. *The People*[31] in the New York Court of Appeals. That court held unconstitutional a state prohibition act that barred the sale of liquor except for medicinal purposes and forbade storing all other existing liquor in any place other than a dwelling house. This criminal statute declared that liquors kept in any other place were a nuisance, and it provided for summary destruction. Such change of property rights was found unreasonable and was therefore held to violate the state due process guarantee, although such uncompensated forfeiture was not unusual in prohibition statutes. Analogous modern laws provide for summary de-struction of other dangerous drugs.

The *Dred Scott* case[32] was the first opinion under the Fifth Amendment to distort "due process of law" into "due substance of law." As a second aspect of that case, the Supreme Court held the Missouri Compromise of 1820 unconstitutional. The Missouri Compromise prohibited slavery in certain territories west of the Mississippi. Dred Scott had been taken into Illinois and into the western territory by his master. He sued after he was taken to the slave state, Missouri. In holding the federal law invalid, Chief

Justice Taney wrote: "An act of Congress which deprives a citizen of the United States of his liberty or property merely because he came himself or brought his property into a particular territory of the United States and who had committed no offense against the laws could hardly be dignified with the name of due process of law."[33] In Taney's view, the owners of slaves had a vested right in their property that was absolute. The total prohibitions of slavery in the Illinois Constitution and in the federal statute for the western territory were not effective for a slave brought temporarily into those territories.

Justice Bradley initiated substantive due process under the Fourteenth Amendment in his dissenting opinion in the *Slaughter-House Cases*[34] of 1873. Under the pretense of enacting sanitary regulations, the legislature of Louisiana had granted a corporation of seventeen citizens a monopoly on the slaughter of meat in New Orleans. As noted in chapter 10, the majority of the Supreme Court held this grant not to violate any of the three clauses of Section 1 of the Fourteenth Amendment. The dissent of Justice Field stressed the privileges-or-immunities clause, but Justice Bradley emphasized that the due process clause afforded substantive protection to liberty and property. He asserted: "This right to choose one's calling is an essential part of that liberty which it is the object of government to protect; and a calling, when chosen, is a man's property and right."[35] He concluded: "In my view, a law which prohibits a large class of citizens from adopting a lawful employment, or from following a lawful employment previously adopted, does deprive them of liberty as well as property without due process of law."[36]

State regulation of carrier rates and other prices was adopted largely at the political demand of agricultural interests as a remedy for the market failure of monopoly. History shows, however, that in the railroad industry the carriers supported rate regulation as a technique to reinforce price-fixing cartels.[37] State regulation of rates or prices was first upheld by the Supreme Court in *Munn* v. *Illinois*[38] in 1876, with two justices dissenting. Chief Justice Waite, for the majority, held the state regulation of charges by grain elevators was not a deprivation of property without due process of law. He held it a legislative question whether a business was "affected with a public interest" and likewise a legislative question of what rates were reasonable. "For protection against abuses by legislatures, the people must resort to the polls, not to the courts."[39] Justice Field, in dissent, urged adoption of substantive due process. He viewed governmental regulation to control and limit monopoly pricing by unincorporated firms as subversive to the rights of property and liberty. This was clearly inconsistent with Field's strong views against governmental grants of monopoly in his dissent in the *Slaughter-House Cases*.

The effectiveness of *Munn* v. *Illinois* was short-lived. As more states passed statutes regulating intrastate rates, the reasonableness of the rates was repeatedly challenged under the due process clause. In the *Railroad Commission Cases,* Chief Justice Waite admitted that railroad rates can not be set so low that it "amounts to a taking or private property for public use without just compensation, or without due process of law."[40] By 1890 in *Chicago, Milwaukee & St. Paul Ry.* v. *Minnesota,*[41] essentially the entire court was won over to the substantive due process idea that the reasonableness of rates was a judicial question. This view was confirmed in 1898 in *Smyth* v. *Ames,*[42] in which the Court invalidated a Nebraska regulation of railroad rates. The distinction between confiscatory and unreasonable rates disappeared. "What the company is entitled to ask is a fair return upon the value of that which it employs for public convenience." The Supreme Court became a superlegislature to review the reasonableness of rates in all regulated industries.

State regulation of three other industries contributed to the development of substantive due process. In *Mugler* v. *Kansas*[43] the Supreme Court upheld a state statute prohibiting the manufacture and sale of intoxicating liquors. The statute was a measure to protect public health, safety, and morals. Justice Harlan, for the Court, did not limit due process to procedure. He warned: "It does not at all follow that every statute enacted ostensibly for the promotion of these ends is to be accepted as a legitimate exertion of the police power of the State."[44] He further stated that the courts "are at liberty—indeed, are under a solemn duty—to look at the substance of things, whenever they enter upon the inquiry whether the Legislature has transcended the limits of its authority."[45]

In *Powell* v. *Pennsylvania,*[46] the Court approved a state statute prohibiting the manufacture and sale of oleomargarine against challenges under the due process and equal protection clauses. Justice Harlan, for the Court, stated: "If all that can be said of this legislation is that it is unwise, or unnecessarily oppressive to those manufacturing or selling wholesome oleomargarine, as an article of food, their appeal must be to the legislature, or to the ballot-box, not to the judiciary."[47] But he cautioned that the courts would have to hold a statute unconstitutional "if the State Legislature, under the pretense of guarding the public health, the public morals, or the public safety, should invade the rights of life, liberty, or property, or other rights, secured by the supreme law of the land."[48] Justice Field dissented in an opinion urging the adoption of substantive due process. In fact, the sole purpose of the legislation in this case was to promote monopoly power in one of the ordinary trades, the dairy industry. This clearly violated the Anglo-American constitutional tradition against governmental grants of monopoly in the ordinary trades.[49] The failure of the Court in the *Slaughter-House Cases*[50] to recognize this historic immunity under the privileges-or-immunities clause or the equal protection clause of the Fourteenth Amendment left the Court with no valid tool to invalidate legislation promoting monopoly.

Allgeyer v. *Louisiana*[51] stands as the founding case in which the Supreme Court expressly confirmed substantive due process as constitutional law. A Louisiana statute created a deliberate barrier to interstate commerce by making it a misdemeanor for its citizens to contract for insurance with companies outside the state that had not complied with state law requiring them to have an agent within the state. Justice Peckham, for the Court, held the state statute unconstitutional. He ignored the fact that there was a violation of the commerce clause. Instead, he isolated the word "liberty" in the due process clause and wrote liberty of contract into the Fourteenth Amendment. "The liberty mentioned in that amendment means, not only the right of the citizen to be free from the mere physical restraint of his person, as by incarceration, but the term is deemed to embrace the right of the citizen to be free in the enjoyment of all of his faculties; to be free to use them in all lawful ways; to live and work where he will; to earn his livelihood by any lawful calling; to pursue any livelihood or avocation, and for that purpose to enter into all contracts which may be proper, necessary, and essential to his carrying out to a successful conclusion the purposes above mentioned."[52] Justice Peckham adopted this view in spite of the fact that one of the leading lawyers in the country had six years earlier written a comprehensive article establishing that the word "liberty" in the due process clauses was concerned only with freedom of movement of the individual, an immunity from imprisonment.[53]

Labor Relations Cases

Labor relations was a prime field for substantive due process litigation. The laissez-faire bias of the court majority offered employers a good likelihood of successful attack on statutes limiting hours of work or setting minimum wages.[54] In many states, organized-labor interests had convinced the legislatures to pass laws remedying asserted market failures in this field. Limiting hours of work was urged as a health and safety measure that would reduce the short-run supply of labor (total hours worked) but materially protect the health of workers and in the long run increase the total supply of healthy laborers. Such an analysis may have overlooked the facts of the real world. At the turn of the century, immigrant workers, unschooled in the English language, worked at a market wage that was very low. They may have needed seventy hours of work in order to purchase what they considered the necessities of life. Likewise, modern studies have shown the main effect of minimum wage laws is to cause unemployment. The policy issues of whether to adopt these types of regulations were clearly legislative, not judicial.

A majority of the Supreme Court transformed these policy issues into judicial ones because they viewed "liberty" in the due process clauses to incorporate the idea of freedom of contract. Many times the justices disagreed on whether a particular statute regulating wages or hours was an unreasonable interference with freedom of contract. Because there were no standards for reasonableness, no one could predict whether a majority of the court would approve of any particular labor relations statute.

In *Holden* v. *Hardy*,[55] the Court upheld a Utah health-and-safety statute setting a maximum eight-hour day for workers in dangerous occupations at smelters and underground mines. Justice Brown commented generally on the constitutionality of statutes regulating labor relations: "The question in each case is whether the legislature has adopted the statute in the exercise of a reasonable discretion, or whether its action be a mere excuse for an unjust discrimination or oppression, or spoliation of a particular class."[56]

Lochner v. *New York*,[57] a 5-to-4 decision, was the leading early labor case. The majority held unconstitutional a New York law limiting hours of work in bakeries to ten per day and sixty per week. Justice Peckham, for the majority, wrote: "In every case that comes before this court, therefore, where legislation of this character is concerned, and where the protection of the Federal Constitution is sought, the question necessarily arises: Is this a fair, reasonable, and appropriate exercise of the police power of the state, or is it an unreasonable, unnecessary, and arbitrary interference with the right of the individual to his personal liberty, or to enter into those contracts in relation to labor which may seem to him appropriate or necessary for the support of himself and his family?"[58] The majority found that the limit of the police power had been reached. They held that there was no reasonable foundation for holding this statute to be necessary and appropriate as a health law.

Three of the dissenters felt the New York law was a reasonable remedy for diseases resulting from long hours of work. But this case is most famous for the separate dissent of Justice Holmes and his fundamental attack on substantive due process:

> This case is decided upon an economic theory which a large part of the country does not entertain. If it were a question whether I agreed with that theory, I should desire to study it further and long before making up my mind. But I do not conceive that to be my duty, because I strongly believe that my agreement or disagreement has nothing to do with the right of a majority to embody their opinions in law. . . . The fourteenth amendment does not enact Mr. Herbert Spencer's *Social Statistics*. . . . [A] Constitution is not intended to embody a particular economic theory, whether of paternalism and the organic relation of the citizen to the state or of *laissez faire*. It is made for people of fundamentally differing views, and the accident of our finding certain opinions natural and familiar, or novel, and

even shocking, ought not to conclude our judgment upon the question whether statutes embodying them conflict with the Constitution of the United States.[59]

Unfortunately, Justice Holmes failed to add an explanation that his opinion was based on the original meaning of "due process," that "process" was a synonym for "procedure." This definition precluded substantive review.[60] If Holmes had emphasized the conservative nature of his originalist interpretation, he might have been able to persuade one or more of the majority justices to join him in judicial restraint, and thus formed a different majority. Substantive due process would have been less influential, and the *Lochner* decision might not have ushered in what has been labeled the "*Lochner* era."

The *Lochner* majority view on reasonableness was not followed by the Court in 1908 in *Muller* v. *Oregon*,[61] in which the Court sustained a law limiting hours of work for women to ten per day and sixty per week. Louis D. Brandeis, counsel for Oregon, realized the Court had assumed the role of a superlegislature. Consequently, he filed a brief of over one hundred pages that was essentially like a presentation of facts to a legislative committee.[62] Brandeis's brief reviewed scientific opinion to the effect that long hours of work were especially dangerous to women because of their physical structure and their maternal functions. The Brandeis brief, in part, convinced even Justice Brewer, the Court's standard bearer for laissez-faire, that state regulation was appropriate. The Court later upheld similar statutes in other states. By 1917, in *Bunting* v. *Oregon*,[63] the Court also sustained a state law limiting hours of work for both men and women. Because this was a general statute, not limited to dangerous occupations like *Holden,* it was presumed by most commentators to have overruled *Lochner, sub silentio.*[64]

Minimum-wage laws were given the opposite treatment by the Supreme Court. In 1923, in *Adkins* v. *Childrens Hospital,*[65] a minimum-wage law for women in the District of Columbia was held violative of the due process clause of the Fifth Amendment. Evidence supported the view that such statutes cause unemployment. The five-justice majority who rendered this decision declined, in light of the Nineteenth Amendment, to treat wages of females differently from that of males. They viewed all wage regulation as violative of due process because it was an unreasonable infringement of freedom of contract. Justice Holmes dissented, reiterating his view that such issues are legislative: "[P]retty much all law consists of forbidding men to do some things that they want to do, and contract is no more exempt from law than other acts. . . . The criterion of constitutionality is not whether we believe the law to be for the public good."[66] The majority view, however, was followed in cases of attempted state regulation of women's wages.[67] The last of these cases was in 1936 in *Morehead* v. *New York ex rel. Tipaldo,*[68] a 5-to-4 decision that voided the New York minimum-wage law for women. The restricted appeal in this case concerned only whether the facts were distinguishable from *Adkins*. No review of the constitutional issue was requested in the Supreme Court, but Justice Stone, in dissent, felt the constitutional issue could not be avoided.

The Supreme Court also used substantive due process to invalidate federal and state labor legislation that had been designed to protect workers' rights to join labor unions. In *Adair* v. *United States*,[69] the Court held unconstitutional a federal act of 1898 that made it a crime for a railroad to dismiss an employee for being a member of a labor union. Justice Harlan, for the Court, again asserted the constitutional status of liberty of contract. He held that it was "not within the functions of government . . . to compel any person, in the course of his business and against his will, to accept or retain the personal services of another, or to compel any person, against his will, to perform personal services for another."[70] Justice Holmes, dissenting, urged: "I confess that I think that the right to make contracts at will that has been derived from the word 'liberty' in the Amendments has been stretched to the extreme by the decisions; . . . It cannot be doubted that to prevent strikes, and, so far as possible, to foster its scheme of arbitration, might be deemed by Congress an important point of policy, and I think it impossible to say that Congress might not reasonably think that the provision in question would help a good deal to carry its policy along."[71] In *Coppage* v. *Kansas*,[72] a 6-to-3 decision, a state statute forbidding labor contracts in which the workers agreed not to join unions was held to violate the due process clause of the Fourteenth Amendment. Justice Holmes again dissented: "Whether in the long run it is wise for the workingmen to enact legislation of this sort is not my concern, but I am strongly of opinion that there is nothing in the Constitution of the United States to prevent it."[73]

Regulation of Business Practices and Prices

To implement its laissez-faire philosophy, the Supreme Court majority used substantive due process to void many more state statutes regulating business practices. In *Adams* v. *Tanner*,[74] by a 5-to-4 vote, the Supreme Court in 1917 voided a Washington state statute that effectively decreed the end of private employment agencies for profit by prohibiting the collection of fees from clients for whom the agencies had found employment. The majority felt that complete prohibition of a type of private business exceeded the bounds of reasonable regulation. In *Burns Baking Co.* v. *Bryan*,[75] by a 7-to-2 decision, the Court invalidated a Nebraska statute designed to prevent deception by requiring that loaves of bread must weigh one-half pound, one pound or multiples thereof. And in *Weaver* v. *Palmer*,[76] a 6-to-3 decision, a Pennsylvania statute designed to protect health and prevent fraud by forbidding the use of shoddy in bedding was held to violate the due process clause.

The regulation of prices in various industries by state legislatures, which attempted to follow the method in *Munn* v. *Illinois,*[77] were many times held by the Supreme Court to be an unreasonable invasion of "property" under the due process clause.[78] The Court took the dictum from the *Munn* case that warehouses were "affected with a public interest," and used this concept to reverse its ruling that it was a legislative question to determine which industries needed regulation. From 1923 to 1932, the Court majority voided price regulation in five major decisions by interposing its view that these industries were not "affected with a public interest."[79] In the *Tyson* case, Justice Holmes in dissent made one of his classic attacks on substantive due process. His view was "that the notion that a business is clothed with a public interest and has been devoted to the public use is little more than a fiction intended to beautify what is disagreeable to the sufferers. The truth seems to me to be that, subject to compensation when compensation is due, the legislature may forbid or restrict any business when it has a sufficient force of public opinion behind it."[80]

In at least one of these cases, however, the decision can be justified on other grounds. In *New State Ice Co.* v. *Liebmann,*[81] a 6-to-2 decision, the Court held violative of due process an Oklahoma statute requiring a state certificate of convenience and necessity to enter the ice business. As to due process, Justice Brandeis was correct in his dissent when he concluded: "The notion of a distinct category of business 'affected with a public interest' employing property 'devoted to a public use,' rests upon historical error."[82] But the facts of the case show an objective to create local monopolies in ice manufacture by barring entry of new firms.[83] The facts are most closely analogous to the *Slaughter-House Cases*[84] in that the statute was designed to bar entry into an ordinary trade. As Justice Sutherland wrote: "We are not able to see anything peculiar in the business here in question which distinguishes it from ordinary manufacture and production."[85] If tested under the privileges-or-immunities clause, as noted in chapter 10, or the equal protection clause, the statute should have been invalidated. *New State Ice Co.* presented an ideal opportunity to overrule the *Slaughter-House* decision.

This survey of the rise of substantive due process has reviewed only the leading cases. From 1890 to 1937, there were over 150 cases before the Supreme Court on the validity of economic regulations under the due process clause.[86] In the majority of the cases the Court upheld state regulatory statutes, but the other cases were significant enough to impede substantially the economic controls that were justified by market failures. If the majority of the Court had adhered to the rejection of substantive due process that was clearly enunciated in *Davidson* v. *New Orleans,*[87] most of the later cases would never have reached the Supreme Court.

Repudiation of Substantive Limitations of Economic Regulation

The vindication of Justice Holmes's constitutional method began in 1934. *Nebbia* v. *New York*[88] initiated the decline that led to the ultimate demise of substantive due process as a standard to judge economic regulation. In *Nebbia* the Court finally discarded the concept of "business affected with a public interest." The 5-to-4 decision upheld the constitutionality of a New York law delegating to the Milk Control Board the authority to set minimum retail prices for milk. The opinion was written by Justice Roberts, who, with Chief Justice Hughes, switched from the majority in the *New State Ice*[89] case, which had interposed the economic due process barrier, to the majority in this case, which rejected economic due process. He noted that "neither property rights nor contract rights are absolute; for government cannot exist if the citizen may at will use his property to the detriment of his fellows, or exercise his freedom of contract to work them harm."[90] He interpreted *Munn* v. *Illinois* as holding that "affected with a public interest" is the equivalent of "subject to the exercise of the police power."[91] Consequently he concluded: "It is clear that there is no closed class or category of businesses affected with a public interest. . . . The phrase 'affected with a public interest' can, in the nature of things, mean no more than an industry, for adequate reason, is subject to control for the public good."[92]

From an economics viewpoint, the statute in *Nebbia* was predestined to fail in its objective of raising farm incomes.[93] It was a microeconomic policy reaction to the macroeconomic problem of a large drop in aggregate demand. Legislated minimum retail prices could result only in lower total sales, the amount of decrease depending on the elasticity of demand. By eliminating price competition in milk retailing, the statute guaranteed the markup of distributors at the expense of consumers.

Seven years later, in *Olsen* v. *Nebraska*,[94] a unanimous Court adopted the approach of the *Nebbia* case. A Nebraska statute licensing employment agencies and setting maximum prices for their services was held constitutional under a due process challenge. In *Olsen*, the Court expressly overruled the *Ribnik* case, which had voided regulation of employment agencies. Justice Douglas concluded: "We are not concerned, however, with the wisdom, need, or appropriateness of the legislation. Differences of opinion on that score suggest a choice which should be left where . . . it was left by the Constitution—to the States and to Congress."[95]

The view based on substantive due process that the judiciary must determine the reasonableness of rates charged by regulated industries was finally rejected in 1944 in *Federal Power Commission* v. *Hope Natural Gas Co.*[96] The "fair return on fair value" fallacy of *Smyth* v. *Ames*[97] was repudiated. Justice Douglas wrote: "The fixing of prices, like other applications of the police power, may reduce the value of the property which is being regulated. But the fact that the value is reduced does not mean that the regulation is invalid. . . . It does, however, indicate that "fair value" is the end process of rate-making not the starting point as the Circuit Court of Appeals held. The heart of the matter is that rates cannot be made to depend upon 'fair value' when the value of the going enterprise depends on earnings under whatever rates may be anticipated."[98] The effect of discontinuing the due process clause as a constraint on rate making was that the Court returned to the view that the eminent domain clause was the one ultimate constitutional limitation on regulation, i.e., "nor shall private property be taken for public use without just compensation." "Rates which enable the company to operate successfully, to maintain its financial integrity, to attract capital, and to compensate it for the risks assumed certainly cannot be condemned as invalid, even though they might produce only a meager return on the so-called 'fair value' rate base."[99]

As to minimum-wage legislation, the great reversal restoring constitutionality came in 1937 following President Roosevelt's proposed court-packing plan. In *West Coast Hotel Co.* v. *Parrish,*[100] the Court upheld the constitutionality of the Washington State minimum-wage law for women and minors. In doing so, it expressly overruled the *Adkins*[101] decision of 1923 and in effect overruled the *Morehead*[102] decision of 1936. In fact, the 5-to-4 decision in *West Coast Hotel Co.* v. *Parrish* came about without a change in court personnel from the *Morehead* case. Like in the *Nebbia*[103] case, Justice Roberts again made a quick switch from supporting due process as a barrier to economic regulation to denying it. This was the same Roberts who was later to complain that too many overrulings tend "to bring adjudications of this tribunal into the same class as a restricted railroad ticket, good for this day and train only."[104]

Chief Justice Hughes, writing for the majority in *West Coast Hotel Co.*, directed the decline, but not the final demise, of substantive due process. He quoted from the dissents of Chief Justice Taft and Justice Holmes in the *Adkins* case as authoritative interpretations of the due process clause. He concluded: "The Constitution does not speak of freedom of contract. It speaks of liberty and prohibits the deprivation of liberty without due process of law. In prohibiting that deprivation the Constitution does not recognize an absolute and uncontrollable liberty. Liberty in each of its phases has its history and connotation. But the liberty safeguarded is liberty in a social organization which requires the protection of law against the evils which menace the health, safety, morals and welfare of the people."[105]

Thirty years of decisions subsequent to *West Coast Hotel Co.*, upholding all state and national regulatory statutes challenged as violating substantive due process, signaled the demise of this barrier to economic regulation. Only four leading decisions can be reviewed here. *Lincoln*

Federal Labor Union v. *Northwestern Iron & Metal Co.*[106] in 1949, was the first notable case in the field of labor relations. A labor union challenged a state statute that provided that no person should be denied an opportunity to obtain or retain employment because he is or is not a member of a labor union. It also forbade employers from entering agreements with unions to exclude persons from employment because they were or were not members of a union. In response to a due process challenge, the Court unanimously upheld the constitutionality of this "right to work" statute. Justice Black wrote of the Court's trend in these cases. "This Court beginning at least as early as 1934, when the *Nebbia* case was decided, has steadily rejected the due process philosophy enunciated in the *Adair-Coppage* line of cases. In doing so it has consciously returned closer and closer to the earlier constitutional principle that states have power to legislate against what are found to be injurious practices in their internal commercial and business affairs, so long as their laws do not run afoul of some specific federal constitutional prohibition, or of some valid federal law."[107]

In *Day-Brite Lighting* v. *Missouri*,[108] the Court upheld the constitutionality of a Missouri statute, first enacted in 1897, that provided that an employee could absent himself for four hours on election days without penalty. Any employer who deducted wages for the absence was guilty of a misdemeanor. In rejecting the due process challenge, Justice Douglas wrote: "Our recent decisions make plain that we do not sit as a superlegislature to weigh the wisdom of legislation nor to decide whether the policy which it expresses offends the public welfare."[109]

In two cases, the objective of the statute in question was suppression of competition. In *Williamson* v. *Lee Optical of Okla.*[110] in 1955, the Court upheld a state statute that made it unlawful for any person not a licensed optometrist or ophthalmologist to fit glasses, duplicate lenses, or replace lenses into frames except on prescription from one of the two types of professionals. The effect was to forbid a mere optician from doing mechanical tasks he was clearly qualified to do without a prescription from one of the professionals. The statute was clearly designed to reduce market efficiency, but Justice Douglas, for the Court, said: "The Oklahoma law may exact a needless, wasteful requirement in many cases. But it is for the legislature, not the courts, to balance the advantages and disadvantages of the new requirement."[111] As noted in chapter 12, the state grant of monopoly should have been enjoined as a denial of equal protection of the laws.

Ferguson v. *Skrupa*[112] in 1963, marked the final demise of substantive due process as a barrier to economic regulation. The Kansas statute made it a misdemeanor for any person to engage in debt adjusting except licensed Kansas lawyers. It thus prohibited nonlawyer credit advisors and debt adjustors, regardless of their training and skills. The statute should have been invalidated as a violation of the equal protection clause. In rejecting the due process challenge, Justice Black stated:

> The doctrine that prevailed in Lochner, Coppage, Adkins, Burns, and like cases—that due process authorizes courts to hold laws unconstitutional when they believe the legislature has acted un-wisely—has long since been discarded. We have returned to the original constitutional proposition that courts do not substitute their social and economic beliefs for the judgment of legislative bodies, who are elected to pass laws. . . . Nor are we able or willing to draw lines by calling a law "prohibitory" or "regulatory." Whether the legislature takes for its textbook Adam Smith, Herbert Spencer, Lord Keynes, or some other is no concern of ours. The Kansas debt ad-justing statute may be wise or unwise. But relief, if any be needed, lies not with us but with the body constituted to pass laws for the State of Kansas.[113]

While substantive due process is certainly dead as a constraint on economic regulation by the national or state governments, the concept is not extinct. As will be noted, substantive due process has been revived by the Supreme Court in spite of the overwhelming judicial demonstration that it has no constitutional foundation.

Noneconomic Substantive Due Process: "Liberty" as a Substitute for the First Amendment

The failure of the Supreme Court to recognize that the privileges-or-immunities clause of the Fourteenth Amendment incorporated the Bill of Rights against state action left the states free to violate the substantive immunities of the First Amendment.[114] In the 1920s, the Court majority turned to the term "liberty" in the Fourteenth Amendment to develop a substantive due process substitute for rights in the First Amendment. In *Meyer v. Nebraska,*[115] the Court invalidated a state statute that prohibited the teaching of foreign languages in public or private elementary schools. Meyer had been convicted of teaching German in a private grade school. Justice McReynolds, for the Court, reversed, holding there was a violation of liberty under the Fourteenth Amendment. Today's courts would term this an issue of freedom of speech under the First Amendment as incorporated into the Fourteenth.

In *Pierce v. Society of Sisters,*[116] the Court invalidated an Oregon state constitutional amendment that required all children except the handi-capped to attend public school between the ages of eight and sixteen. Upon challenge by a Catholic school and a private military academy, the Court held that there was a violation of liberty in that the amendment unreasonably interfered with the liberty of parents to direct the upbringing and education of children.[117] Federal courts today would surely treat this as an attempt to prohibit the free exercise of religion[118] and to abridge the freedom of speech.

In *Gitlow* v. *New York*,[119] the Supreme Court upheld a conviction under the New York criminal anarchy statute. Gitlow was found to have advocated and published a manifesto containing the doctrine that organized government should be overthrown by force and violence. In dicta, the Court stated: "[W]e may and do assume that freedom of speech and of the press—which are protected by the 1st Amendment from abridgement by Congress—are among the fundamental personal rights and 'liberties' protected by the due process clause of the 14th Amendment from impairment by the states."[120] Unfortunately, the dissenting Justice Holmes, who had so fiercely objected to the concept of substantive due process in *Lochner,* here used the word "liberty" in the Fourteenth Amendment to incorporate the First Amendment.[121] Seemingly without reflection, Holmes joined the majority in asserting that a procedural constitutional clause incorporated substantive rights. Modern cases treat the First Amendment as incorporated generally by the Fourteenth without emphasizing terms such as "liberty."[122]

The express incorporation of the First Amendment in the due process clause of the Fourteenth Amendment came in 1931. *Stromberg* v. *California*[123] invalidated a state law as violating the guarantee of free speech in the First Amendment as applied to the states by the Fourteenth. In *Near* v. *Minnesota,*[124] the Court applied the same due process rule to freedom of the press. In *Hamilton* v. *Regents,*[125] the Court rejected the claims of religious conscientious objectors to mandatory military training at state universities. It centered its reasoning on "liberty" in the due process clause as including protections of religion rather than on the First Amendment as an incorporated national immunity. Subsequently, the First Amendment rights of assembly[126] and of petition[127] were incorporated in the due process clause of the Fourteenth Amendment.

Resurrection of Substantive Due Process

Starting in 1965 the Supreme Court revived substantive due process under the Fourteenth Amendment to create constitutional human rights that could not be derived from the express constitutional limitations. Most of these concerned sexual, marital, and family relationships.[128] Unlike economic regulation, there would seem to be a fundamental issue of federalism here. None of the enumerated powers of the national government concerned sexual, marital, or family relations. If the national government assumed powers in these areas, presumably the courts would hold such statutes invalid on the grounds of federalism. Since there were no national powers in these areas, it was reasonable to expect no national constitutional limitations in these areas. Since the law relating to personal relations is reserved to the states, one should expect civil rights against the states for these activities to be stipulated in state constitutions.

In spite of this federalism background, in 1965 the Supreme Court began to create a constitutional right of privacy against state government. *Griswold* v. *Connecticut*[129] was a contrived case to test a disused state statute that made it a crime to use artificial birth control.[130] The defendants were a director of Planned Parenthood and a Yale professor of medicine. The defendants were convicted of abetting violation of the statute. In reversing the conviction and finding an invasion of a constitutional right of privacy, Justice Douglas, for the majority, had great trouble in finding a basis for the decision in constitutional language. He first repudiated a return to substantive due process under *Lochner* v. *New York*,[131] asserting, "We do not sit as a super-legislature to determine the wisdom, need of laws."[132] He then seemed to contradict himself by citing as partial authority for creating a right of privacy the two substantive due process cases, *Pierre* v. *Society of Sisters*[133] and *Meyer* v. *Nebraska.*[134] To make sure the reader believed this confusion, he stated: "And so we reaffirm the principle of the Pierce and the Meyer cases."[135] He then asserted that there are "penumbras formed by emanations" from the First, Third, Fourth, Fifth and Ninth Amendments that result in a general guarantee of privacy.[136] Justices Harlan and White wrote concurring opinions, specifically relying on the concept of liberty in the Fourteenth Amendment. Justice Black, joined by Justice Stewart, dissented and criticized substantive due process in the same language he had used in the majority opinion of the *Ferguson* case two years earlier.[137] After 1965 some lower courts used *Griswold* as precedent to apply a right of privacy to a number of other circumstances.[138]

The Supreme Court opinions on privacy have not been consistent. In an electronic surveillance case under the Fourth Amendment, the majority dicta seemed to limit the right of privacy against government to specific constitutional limitations. "But the protection of a person's *general* right to privacy—his right to be let alone by other people—is like the protection of his property and of his life, left largely to the law of the individual states."[139] This restricted view was short-lived.

The express revival of substantive due process occurred in *Roe* v. *Wade,*[140] in which the Supreme Court invalidated a Texas law making it a crime to secure an abortion. Justice Blackmun, for the court, concluded that a right of privacy, founded in the Fourteenth Amendment's concept of personal liberty, includes the abortion decision. Among others, he cited *Griswold, Meyer,* and *Pierce* as authorities for the general right of privacy.[141] Having found the right to abortion to be fundamental, meaning constitutional, the Court found some state regulation permissible. There was a compelling state interest to regulate maternal health after the first trimester. At some point in time, the health of the mother and that of a potential human life overrides the right to privacy.

Justice White, joined by Justice Rehnquist, dissented. He stated:

> I find nothing in the language or history of the Constitution to support the Court's judgment. The Court simply fashions and announces a new constitutional right for pregnant mothers and, with scarcely any reason or authority for its action, invests that right with sufficient substance to override most existing state abortion statutes. The up-shot is that the people and the legislatures of the 50 states are constitu-tionally disentitled to weigh the relative importance of the continued existence and development of the fetus, on the one hand, against a spectrum of possible impacts on the mother, on the other hand. As an exercise of raw judicial power, the Court perhaps has authority to do what it does today; but in my view its judgment is an improvi-dent and extravagant exercise of the power of judicial review that the Constitution extends to this Court.[142]

The constitutional right to abortion was reaffirmed by the Court in 1976[143] and in 1983.[144] The general constitutional right of privacy, derived from substantive due process, was reconfirmed by the Supreme Court in two opinions in 1977. In *Moore* v. *City of East Cleveland*, the Supreme Court in a 5-to-4 decision reversed the conviction of a homeowner who had violated a city ordinance limiting occupancy of dwelling units to a single family.[145] *Carey* v. *Population Services International*[146] invalidated a New York law that granted a monopoly to pharmacists to sell nonmedi-cal contraceptive devices to persons over the age of sixteen and prohibited the sale to any child under sixteen. The existence and viability of substan-tive due process was even affirmed in 1986 when the Supreme Court refused to extend the right of privacy to the practice of sodomy. In *Bowers* v. *Hardwick*,[147] the Court held that sodomy failed the tests of being such a fundamental liberty that is "implicit in the concept of ordered liberty"; nor could it be characterized as a liberty "deeply rooted in this Nation's history and tradition."[148]

The constitutional right of privacy under substantive due process and its major applications, such as *Roe* v. *Wade*, have become important and divisive political issues in American society.[149] The *Roe* decision must be viewed in historical context. It represents a major judicial addition to the gains achieved in a hundred-year campaign for the rights of women in American society. Even before *Roe*, liberal abortion statutes had been en-acted in a majority of northern and western states. This was achieved with the political support of the majority of women, and as an evolutionary development, it cannot be significantly reversed. Nonetheless, the judicial foundation for the "political" decision of the Supreme Court in *Roe* is the quicksand of substantive due process. If the *Roe* decision were overruled, the political decision on the legality of abortion would be returned, at least temporarily, to the state legislatures. If women's groups supporting the right to abortion could not prevail in some state legislatures because their representatives feared offending key religious groups, they would have to initiate campaigns for constitutional amendment on the state or national level or both. This would return the political decision to the people. Recognition that the Bill of Rights is incomplete and that additions by amendment are the prescribed means for fundamental change would relieve the judiciary of some of the pressures to be the prime agency of constitutional development.

The philosophy of *Griswold, Roe* and their progeny is that the due process clauses and the Ninth Amendment vest essentially unlimited authority in the Supreme Court to create new substantive civil rights.[150] In effect this would empower the Court to use natural law as its standard in determining the constitutionality of statutes. As Justice Holmes pointed out, however, the standard of natural law is both egocentric and ethnocentric.[151] The modern commentaries supporting this view are cited by Ely.[152] A natural-law interpretation of due process or the Ninth Amendment would in effect empower the justices to impose their personal value judgments on the law. Arguments for such a power seem mistaken. Vesting the Supreme Court with the unlimited power to veto legislation has already made the judicial department a very powerful branch of government. Denying any duty to follow constitutional language expands this power. The framers, on the other hand, were concerned only that they had created insufficient checks on the legislature, that only the Congress had the possibility of becoming too powerful. They considered the judiciary the least dangerous branch.[153]

Leading historians and legal scholars have concluded that the founding fathers rejected natural law as a judicial decision tool.[154] Conclusive statements voicing this view have been made by Chafee,[155] Rossiter,[156] and Cover.[157] Only a few of the early constitutional opinions relied on natural law, and some of these used natural law only to reinforce express constitutional limitations.[158] In *Calder* v. *Bull*[159] in 1798, Justice Iredell objected to Justice Chase using the so-called principles of natural law as one of the bases of his decision on the validity of retrospective legislation. Justice Iredell explained as follows:

> [I]t has been the policy of all the *American* states, which have, individually, framed their state constitutions since the revolution, and of the people of the *United States,* when they framed the Federal Constitution, to define with precision the objects of the legislative power, and to restrain its exercise within marked and settled boundaries. If any act of Congress, or of the Legislature of a state, violates those constitutional provisions, it is unquestionably void; though, I admit, that as the authority to declare it void is of a delicate and awful nature, the Court will never resort to that authority, but in a clear and urgent case. If, on the other hand, the Legislature of the

Union, or the Legislature of any member of the Union, shall pass a law, within the general scope of their constitutional power, the Court cannot pronounce it to be void, merely because it is, in their judgment, contrary to the principles of natural justice. The ideas of natural justice are regulated by no fixed standard: the ablest and the purest men have differed upon the subject; and all that the Court could properly say, in such an event, would be, that the Legislature (possessed of an equal right of opinion) and passed an act which, in the opinion of the judges, was inconsistent with the abstract principles of natural justice.[160]

In spite of the warning by Justice Iredell and others that natural law is a matter of personal value judgments that should not be substituted for the express language of the constitutional limitations, some justices set sail knowingly into this sea of doubt. As noted, majorities on the Court have used a natural-law outlook to impose their own views on which economic regulations have a reasonable relation to public health, safety, morals, or welfare, thereby creating substantive due process. Justice Holmes's dissents in those cases were demonstrations of his humility and pleas to his associates to end their usurpations of the amending power. Dissenting in 1930 in *Baldwin* v. *Missouri,*[161] he wrote: "As the decisions now stand, I see hardly any limit but the sky to the invalidating of those rights if they happen to strike a majority of this Court as for any reason undesirable. I cannot believe that the [Fourteenth] amendment was intended to give us carte blanche to embody our economic or moral beliefs in its prohibitions. . . . Of course the words "due process of law," if taken in their literal meaning, have no application to this case."[162]

After 1936 the Supreme Court majority adopted what was essentially a natural-law measure of which of the procedural protections of the Bill of Rights would be enforceable against the states. The selective incorporation was based on the finding that a clause protected a "fundamental" aspect of liberty. Justice Black, in the footsteps of Justices Iredell and Holmes, objected to the majority's departure from historical analysis of constitutional language in interpretation of the scope of the Bill of Rights and their substitution of vague, natural-law concepts. Dissenting in *Adamson* v. *California,*[163] a 5-to-4 decision in 1947 denying incorporation of the privilege against self-incrimination, which was later overruled, Justice Black wrote: "To pass upon the constitutionality of statutes by looking to the particular standards enumerated in the Bill of Rights and other parts of the Constitution is one thing; to invalidate statutes because of application of 'natural law' deemed to be above and undefined by the Constitution is another. 'In the one instance, courts proceeding within clearly marked constitutional boundaries seek to execute policies written into the Constitution; in the other, they roam at will in the limitless area of their own beliefs as to reasonableness and actually select policies, a responsibility which the Constitution entrusts to the legislative representatives of the people.' "[164]

The common conclusion of Justices Iredell, Holmes, and Black was that the value judgments expressed in the language of the Constitution are the primary rules and principles that bind the Court in constitutional cases. Judicial humility and respect for separated governmental powers requires that these rules and principles shall not be supplemented by or supplanted by any justice's views of natural law. As Professor Wechsler has asserted: "The main constituent of the judicial process is precisely that it must be genuinely principled, resting with respect to every step that is involved in reaching judgment on analysis and reasons quite transcending the immediate result that is achieved."[165] But these must be principles founded in constitutional language and rules of interpretation, not in the personal value systems of the justices.

In spite of the natural-law character of substantive due process with its unprincipled assumption of governing power by the judiciary, a small group of scholars urge the revival of substantive due process to void economic regulation.[166] In effect, they advocate rehabilitating the rule of Lochner.[167] Advocates of substantive due process point out that new economic liberties and new political liberties are likely to be created and expanded by the Courts in tandem. But Justice Scalia, in an extrajudicial speech, warned against a return to such broad governance by the judiciary.[168] For if we object to the Court acting in the absence of express constitutional limitations as a superlegislature to reverse legislative choices, we must oppose judicial creation of new liberties.

Furthermore, there is no reason to believe that the courts will limit their constitutionalizing of economic rights to those that an economist would approve as maximizing some recognized social goal. Even where a true market failure is perceived, the costs of regulation may or may not exceed the social loss of the uncontrolled practice. There is no reason to believe that judges will have adequate evidence before them and the perception needed to do economic cost-benefit analysis. The history of court behavior in the earlier period of substantive due process does not encourage its resumption.

There is a world of difference between advocating broad application of the eminent domain clause, the contract clause, the privileges-or-immunities clause, and the equal protection clause to protect economic liberties and to advocating substantive due process. This study has shown that the modern Court has diluted or avoided express constitutional limitations when economic interests have sought protections for free markets. Denying protection to economic interests under the express constitutional limitations in the name of judicial restraint is just as wrong as the judicial activism of the Lochner era with its use of substantive due process.

CHAPTER 12

Equal Protection of Persons and Firms in the Market

THE FINAL CLAUSE OF Section 1 of the Fourteenth Amendment provides "that no state shall deny to any persons within its jurisdiction the equal protection of the laws."[1] Following generally accepted rules of documentary interpretation, the clause must be viewed as a complement to the earlier clauses in Section 1 and also as having a specific function of its own.[2]

The privileges-or-immunities clause was designed to make all national constitutional limitations protecting citizens effective against the states. The due process clause mandated full and fair procedure to any person whose life, liberty, or property was to be taken by a state. The equal protection clause complemented the earlier ones by providing a specific substantive protection for all persons within a state in order to bar oppressive state legislation that would not have contravened the earlier prohibitions. Equal protection does not refer to fundamental civil liberties that are protected by the privileges or immunities clause. Rather, it primarily concerns statutes that classify persons in order to regulate human behavior in some substantive way.[3] The most prominent examples of application of the clause have been to the classification of children by race involved in the state regulation of public schools.

From an economic viewpoint, equal protection of the laws sets efficiency criteria for governmental regulation: no state may deny any person equal access to any market. The word "person" would have to include firms, since efficiency requires that persons form firms, such as corporations,[4] in order to engage in many activities. Equal access to every market in which a person or firm can compete effectively is essential to the maximization of the number of value-increasing exchanges. Any statute or administrative rule that denies persons who are qualified by skill from entering a market reduces economic efficiency. If the numbers that are excluded from a market are significant, the state has promoted monopoly.

The realities of the decisional law are in sharp contrast with this viewpoint. Justice Brandeis, who was not known as a promoter of monopoly, noted in 1935: "[T]he grant of a monopoly, if otherwise an appropriate exercise of the police power, is not void as denying equal protection of the law."[5]

The legal standard for violation of equal protection in the area of economic and business regulation has been the rational-basis test:[6] To define a class subject to legislation all that is required is that the distinctions drawn have some relevance to the purpose for which the classification is made.[7] But it is always possible to define the legislative purpose of a statute in such a way that the statutory classification is rationally related to it.[8] And furthermore, if the legislative record shows multiple purposes of a statute, the classification need be related to only one of them. Thus the Court need not openly recognize that some statutes are designed for the monopolistic exploitation of consumers. It can find some other aspect of public health, safety, or welfare to be the statutory objective.

The thesis of this chapter is that the equal protection clause should reinforce the privileges-or-immunities clause as a bar to state grants of monopoly power to private persons and firms. The Anglo-American anti-monopoly tradition, as retained against the national government by the Ninth Amendment and enforceable against the states through the privileges-or-immunities clause, should have barred state grants of monopoly in the ordinary trades.[9] The equal protection clause should have supplemented this by barring all unequal state regulation of persons and firms that were found to be in like circumstances.

In a system of representative government where most legislation is sponsored by special-interest groups, attempts to purchase grants of monopoly power from legislators are pervasive.[10] Although the Fourteenth Amendment was adopted primarily to protect the civil rights of former slaves,[11] the comprehensive language of the equal protection clause has clear application to the economy. Whether state statutes foreclose tobacco farming to Afro-Americans or instead to persons not raising tobacco at the time of the passage of the restrictive statute, all excluded farmers are denied equal treatment under the law. The equal protection clause has been applied by the courts to some economic activities,[12] but the thesis here is that it should have had a much broader application. The possible correct utilization of the equal protection clause has been discouraged by the erroneous creation and use of substantive due process in the field of economic regulation.

Original Meanings

Unlike the privileges-or-immunities clause and the due process clause, both of which had hundreds of years of legal-linguistic history, the equal protection clause brought new language to the Constitution.[13] The word "equal" is found in natural-law contexts in the Declaration of Independence and in the "free and equal" clauses of some state constitutions.[14] These clauses were the basis in a few states for the judicial termination of slavery where it was a dying institution opposed by the majority of citizens.[15] The clauses did not function as controlling law on other topics.

The word "protection" is derived from the Latin term meaning "to cover or to save from harm." Equal protection means equal coverage for all persons.[16] The shield of the law is to be the same for any individual or firm found by the courts to come within the definition of "person."[17] The close connection between the idea of equality and its protection by government was stated by Senator Timothy Howe, abolitionist from Wisconsin: "I have thought that it belonged to republican institutions to carry out, to execute the doctrines of the Declaration of Independence, to make men equal. That they are not equal in social estimation, that they are not equal in mental culture, that they are not equal in physical stature, I know very well; but I have thought the weaker they were the more the government was bound to foster and protect them. If government be designed for the protection of the weak, certainly the weaker men are the more they need its protection."[18]

In this context, the word "laws" must mean both the common law and statutes. The hearings in the 39th Congress demonstrate that one primary purpose of the equal protection clause was to invalidate the Black Codes that had been adopted by many of the southern states.[19] Another primary purpose was to assure equality in the right to contract and to hold property, key elements of the common law.[20] Even the objective of overruling the doctrine of *Scott* v. *Sandford*[21] vindicated a common-law principle, that persons of African descent could be free and equal citizens of the nation. This was the principle that Lord Mansfield had enunciated in 1772 in *Somerset's Case*,[22] when he held that a slave brought into England became a free person.

The phrase "equal protection of the laws" must mean that persons in like circumstances are to receive the same treatment.[23] There is no issue of inequality if persons are not in like circumstances. Barbers and lawyers do not expect to take the same state licensing examination to enter their professions. Equal protection thus requires classification in order to determine if persons are in like circumstances in relation to a constitutionally valid statutory objective. Legislative classification defines the class to which the law applies. Most statutes are not general legislation applying to all persons in the state, but rather are special laws regulating a particular group. "Indeed, the greater part of all legislation is special, either in the extent to which it operates, or the objects sought to be attained by it."[24]

The idea of equality before the law in the Anglo-American legal system has its beginnings in chapter 40 of the Magna Charta, which states: "To no one will we sell, to no one will we refuse or delay, right or justice."[25] As one key aspect of the English concept, "Rule of Law" means "equality before the law, or the equal subjection of all classes to the ordinary law of the land administered by the ordinary law courts."[26] The protection was incorporated in the Massachusetts Body of Liberties of 1641 as follows: "Every person within this Jurisdiction, whether Inhabitant or forreiner shall enjoy the same justice and law, that is generall for the plantation, which we constitute and execute one towards another without partialities or delay."[27] The religion clause of the Massachusetts Constitution of 1780 declared that "every denomination of Christians, demeaning themselves peaceably, and as good subjects of the common wealth, shall be equally under the protection of the law."[28]

The absence of express equal protection clauses in most state constitutions at that time can probably be attributed to the existence of slavery. After ratification of the Fourteenth Amendment, the dicta on equality became more general. As Chief Justice Waite observed: "The equality of the rights of citizens is a principle of republicanism. Every republican government is in duty bound to protect all its citizens in the enjoyment of this principle, if within its power. That duty was originally assumed by the States; and it still remains there. The only obligation resting upon the United States is to see that the States do not deny the right. This the Amendment guaranties, but no more. The power of the National Government is limited to the enforcement of this guaranty."[29]

Since the equal protection clause was adopted primarily to protect the legal rights of former slaves, the foremost group of cases under the clause have concerned racial segregation. These cases illustrate the difficult issues of interpretation when a constitutional clause incorporates the ideals of revolutionary change in a society. The language of the clause, drafted by the radical Republicans on the Committee of Fifteen on Reconstruction, was couched in the broadest possible terms in order to express the committee's ideal of a legal system where all persons were absolutely equal.[30] Although the language did not treat social or political equality,[31] its mandate for legal equality was unequivocal.

The inclusive character of the language in the equal protection clause must be emphasized because a few recent scholars have erroneously suggested that the alleged intent of some of the framers controls and narrowly limits its meaning.[32] Their argument is that evidence of the intent of some members of the 39th Congress, though highly controversial and not within the knowledge of the ratifiers, can be used to cut the meaning of the language to a fraction of its facial definition to ordinary readers of those times.[33] By asserting that the comprehensive language of the Fourteenth Amendment was designed solely to constitutionalize the narrower language of the Civil Rights Act of 1866,[34] they conclude that wholly different language is equivalent. This attempt to curtail the meaning of the language of the clause by interpretation violates a basic rule of documentary construction.[35]

Section 1 of the Civil Rights Act of 1866 provided former slaves with the same right to contract, to sue, and to hold property as whites and for "the full and equal benefit of all laws and proceedings for the security of person and property, as is enjoyed by white citizens."[36] This language is narrower in scope than "the equal protection of the laws" in the Fourteenth Amendment. As noted, the latter applies to all laws, both common law and statutes. There is no doubt that one primary function of the Fourteenth Amendment was to supply a constitutional foundation for the Civil Rights Act. Congressman John A. Bingham of Ohio, the radical Republican who was later the primary author of Section 1 of the Fourteenth Amendment, opposed the Civil Rights Act because he thought that Congress was without power to pass such a bill.[37] He felt this defect could be cured only by constitutional amendment. But the equality of civil rights that were provided in the 1866 act did not include equality under statutes dispersing public benefits. State statutes providing public education for whites only would not violate the 1866 act. The language of the equal protection clause of the Fourteenth Amendment was broader and would apply to all state statutes, including those dispensing state benefits, and to all regulations of the marketplace that might be administered to the detriment of nonwhites.

For efficient judicial review of cases arising under the equal protection clause, the courts should have adopted a two-step process of analysis. The first issue is whether there is a constitutionally valid objective. "The sovereign may not draw distinctions between individuals based solely on differences that are irrelevant to a legitimate governmental objective."[38] This would apply both to trial judges in common-law actions and to legislatures. If a trial judge in common-law litigation should indicate by language or rulings that he will grant motions to exclude all members of a certain race, religion, or ethic group from serving on juries, his objective is constitutionally invalid.[39] Similarly, a state statute limiting jury service to whites is also invalid.[40] In these examples, the objective of the judge or the statute is discrimination on the basis of race or some other arbitrary characteristic. The unequal treatment makes the actions unconstitutional, whether or not prohibited by federal statute.[41] The Supreme Court has consistently held that the judiciary has the power to enforce the Fourteenth Amendment whether or not Congress has passed an enforcement statute pursuant to Section 5.[42]

The second step to test conformity to the equal protection clause is necessary only if there has been a finding of a constitutionally valid objective of the common-law rulings or statute in question. If such finding has been made, the second test is whether the classification that has been adopted assigns all persons who are in like circumstances or "similarly situated" to the same class.

In applying this two-step analysis to the case of school segregation by race, for example, the first finding should be whether the objective of the statutes was arbitrary separation on the basis of race. If so, an immediate conclusion of unconstitutionality should follow. But if the court should find that the statutory objective was to subsidize elementary and secondary education and regulate quality in the operation of schools, then the second test would have to be applied: the determination if all persons similarly situated were treated equally. The persons similarly situated for purpose of education are all children. Separating any one or group of them on the basis of noneducational criteria would be arbitrary and therefore unequal. Legislative segregation on the basis of race, religion, height, weight, country of ancestor's origin, or any other noneducational criterion is a badge of differentiation that indicates inequality.

Equality of Persons: Racial Segregation

The economic theory of racial discrimination postulates that there exists a dominating ethnic group in a society and that many of the members of that group have a taste not to associate with members of other ethic groups.[43] To the extent that members of the dominant group refuse to engage in value-increasing exchanges within other groups, incomes of both groups are reduced. Before World War I in the United States, African-Americans were largely barred from skilled trades and factory work and were relegated by a caste system to the lowest income levels.[44] In a caste society, transactions between dominant and dominated members are not discouraged so long as minority members remain in the areas and tasks assigned by the system to their group. Contractual relations between whites and African-Americans after the Civil War were necessary for the functioning of the economy in the South. Whites entered sharecropping agreements with African-Americans in rural areas and hired them as unskilled labor in urban areas.[45] Large numbers of African-American women worked as domestic laborers in white homes.

A key factor maintaining the lower caste status of African-Americans after the Civil War was separate and unequal education.[46] Before passage of the Fourteenth Amendment, there were few public schools in the South, and most states provided public schools only for whites. Other states required African-Americans to pay separate taxes for their own schools. The percentage of African-American children in school rose from 1.9 in 1860 to 9.9 in 1870 and to 33.8 in 1880, but it dropped to 31.1 in 1900.[47] Even though some courts held that dual systems of taxes violated equal protection,[48] county administrators allocated general tax funds on an unequal per capita basis, largely in favor of white schools.[49] Thus, the assumption in the South that African-Americans were being educated at the expense of whites was false.

Racial segregation and economic deprivation were interrelated phe-

nomena. In those southern states with large African-American popula-
tions, the underinvestment in public education left the economy with a
large segment of semiliterate persons, ill-prepared to hold jobs in an
industrializing economy.[50] Part of the lag in economic development in the
South must be attributed to this limited investment in African-American
public education.

If the courts had followed the original meaning of the equal protection
clause, statutes requiring racial separation would have been invalidated
upon the enactment of the Fourteenth Amendment. Such laws are today
immediately suspect because their objective is discriminatory—treating
some persons as second-class citizens.[51] But the invidious character of
statutory racial classification had been recognized by the Court as early
as the *Strauder* case of 1879, where Justice Strong observed: "The words
of the Amendment, it is true, are prohibitory, but they contain a necessary
implication of a positive immunity, or right, most valuable to the colored
race—the right to exemption from unfriendly legislation against them
distinctively as colored,—exemption from legal discriminations, implying
inferiority in civil society, lessening the security of their enjoyment of the
rights which others enjoy, and discriminations which are steps toward
reducing them to the condition of a subject race."[52]

A few racial segregation laws have an antebellum origin.[53] Although
the rural South had the ultimate caste system in slavery, a few major
cities had large numbers of free African-Americans. Segregation laws and
ordinances were enacted in these cities to define and defend the caste
system for free African-Americans. The Civil War brought an end to
slavery and an end to statutory racial segregation in public places for a
long period of time. It was more than ten years after the federal troops
left the South in 1877 that the first state segregation statute for public
places was passed.[54] The capitulation to racism allowed extremist views
to take control of social relations through legislation. The essence of white
supremacy was to relegate and maintain African-Americans in a lower
caste, and this was the function of segregation laws.[55]

The national case law on racial segregation after the Civil War begins
with an act of the Louisiana reconstruction legislature to prohibit discrimination. In *Hall* v. *DeCuir*,[56] the Supreme Court held such a law invalid
as violating the commerce clause. A Louisiana statute of 1869 forbade
racial segregation in public conveyances. An African-American intrastate
passenger on an interstate steamboat on the Mississippi was denied passage in a cabin reserved for white passengers. Since different states along
the route could have different rules on racial mixing, the state law was
held an unconstitutional burden on commerce. "If the public good requires such legislation, it must come from Congress and not from the
States."[57] The decision is questionable. The Louisiana statute was enforc-

ing a particular state constitutional clause for public conveyances analogous to the more general equal protection clause of the Fourteenth Amendment for all laws. The court at that time only hypothesized segregation
statutes in adjacent states. It is those hypothetical segregation statutes
that would have violated equal protection and burdened commerce among
the several states, not the Louisiana statute enforcing equal protection in
public conveyances.

In *Louisville, New Orleans, and Texas Ry. Co.* v. *Mississippi*,[58] the
court upheld a Mississippi statute of 1888 requiring railroads to provide
separate accommodations for the "white and colored races." The statute
applied only to intrastate commerce, and the litigation tested only the
carrier's duty to provide facilities, not the segregation of passengers.
Nonetheless, Justice Harlan dissented.[59] The defendant was an interstate
carrier, and the objective of the statute was to segregate all passengers,
including interstate travelers. Harlan viewed the facts to be within the
rule of *Hall* v. *DeCuir*.

A possible explanation of the discrepant cases is that between the two
trials the Supreme Court assumed the power to cut the scope of the
commerce clause to a fraction of its earlier meaning.[60] Following the
restoration of the commerce clause to its broad original meaning, state
segregation statutes for transport of persons were held to burden commerce. In *Morgan* v. *Virginia*,[61] a state segregation statute applying both
to intrastate and interstate buses was held to burden commerce among
the several states. "It seems clear to us that seating arrangements for the
different races in interstate motor travel require a single, uniform rule to
promote and protect national travel."[62]

The *Civil Rights Cases*[63] represent another narrow interpretation of the
Constitution that was later corrected. The Civil Rights Act of 1875[64]
provided for full and equal accommodation in inns, public conveyances,
theaters, and other places of public amusement. Since the carriers and
inns were regulated by common-law duties of access to all, and theaters
were subject to many state regulations, the statute was viewed by Senator
Sumner and its other sponsors as a supplemental control for regulated
industries.[65] The Supreme Court, with Justice Harlan dissenting, invalidated the statute as not concerned with state action.[66] This narrow interpretation of Section 5 of the Fourteenth Amendment was made without
regard to the commerce clause, in spite of the fact that the act was
primarily a regulation of facilities for travelers on the nation's highways.[67]
This ignoring of the commerce clause may also be explained by the fact
that by 1883 the Supreme Court had assumed the power to reduce the
clause to a fraction of its original meaning. Ninety years later, Congress,
exercising its plenary power over commerce in Article 1, Section 8, enacted
similar legislation, barring discrimination in places of public accommoda-

tion. This part of the Civil Rights Act of 1964,[68] being an exercise of the commerce power restored to its original meaning, was held constitutional.[69]

The most significant and socially damaging case on racial segregation under the equal protection clause in the nineteenth century was *Plessy* v. *Ferguson*,[70] in which the Supreme Court upheld a Louisiana statute of 1890 that mandated racial separation of railroad passengers.[71] Plessy, who was seven-eighths white, was charged with violating the law by trying to sit in a coach reserved for whites. In denying Plessy a writ of prohibition, the Court approved the doctrine of separate-but-equal facilities. Since the majority of citizens were unsure of the breadth of the equal protection clause in that era, this decision was instrumental in curtailing its scope.

The *Plessy* decision fostered the ideology of racial separation and statutes enforcing racial segregation for almost sixty years. The decision was more than just a travesty of justice. It was part of the common understanding of Americans in 1890 that racial segregation was a badge of inferior status. This truth is confirmed by historians and sociologists who in this century have made scientific studies of the origins of "jim crow."[72] Charles Black has characterized the acceptance of the separate-but-equal doctrine as the point where "the curves of callousness and stupidity intersect at their respective maxima."[73] Robert Harris has labeled *Plessy* "a compound of bad logic, bad history, bad sociology, and bad constitutional law."[74]

The majority in *Plessy* made an assumption of fact that was clearly against the manifest weight of the available evidence. Justice Brown first admitted that "the object of the amendment was undoubtedly to enforce the absolute equality of the two races before the law."[75] But he erroneously concluded: "We consider the underlying fallacy of the plaintiff's argument to consist in the assumption that the enforced separation of the two races stamps the colored race with a badge of inferiority. If this be so, it is not by reason of anything found in the act, but solely because the colored race chooses to put that construction upon it."[76] But from time immemorial, the primary function of caste systems has been to impose and perpetuate inequality.

Justice Harlan, the lone dissenter in *Plessy*, observed that racial segregation of former slaves was a badge of second-class citizenship and therefore a denial of equal protection. "There is no caste here. Our constitution is color-blind, and neither knows nor tolerates classes among citizens. In respect of civil rights, all citizens are equal before the law."[77] He concluded: "In my opinion, the judgment this day rendered will, in time, prove to be quite as pernicious as the decision made by this tribunal in the *Dred Scott* case."[78] As many commentators predicted, Justice Harlan has been vindicated on the meaning of equal protection.[79] The modern

Court has unqualifiedly asserted that: "The Equal Protection Clause was intended to work nothing less than the abolition of all caste-based and invidious class-based legislation."[80]

In fact, the common-law and statutory background of *Plessy* included the duty of public carriers to serve all persons willing to pay the stipulated fares.[81] Justice Harlan, in dissent, cited numerous cases upholding the public character and public duties of carriers.[82] The equal protection clause prohibited states from evading the obligation to treat all persons alike in the regulation of carriers. In *Railroad Co. v. Brown*,[83] twenty-three years before *Plessy*, the Court had recognized the congressional declaration that segregation in transportation was negative discrimination, not equality. The charter to the railroad included a clause that "no person shall be excluded from any car on account of color."[84] The carrier provided separate-but-equal cars for white and colored. Mrs. Brown, a "colored" woman, attempted to sit in the "white" car and was ejected. A judgment for Mrs. Brown against the railroad was affirmed by a unanimous Supreme Court. The inequality was explained: "Congress, in the belief that this discrimination was unjust, acted. It told this company, in substance, that it could extend its road in the District as desired, but that this discrimination must cease, and the colored and white race, in the use of the cars, be placed on an equality."[85]

Segregation in Public Education

The doctrine of *Plessy* confirmed the constitutionality of a caste society. Applied to education, it validated existing segregation of public schools[86] and discouraged legal attacks on segregation because all trial courts would be bound to follow the precedent of *Plessy*. An African-American community, one generation out of slavery and largely illiterate, was at the mercy of the white supremacists who had instigated the passage of segregation statutes. The result was not a society that was separate and equal. Like other caste systems, it was a society that was separate and unequal.[87] The most pronounced aspect was highly inferior schools for African-Americans and in many areas the absence of public high schools for them.[88]

The school segregation cases began in 1850, long before the Fourteenth Amendment, with a key Massachusetts decision that was overruled by legislative action. *Roberts v. City of Boston*[89] challenged regulations of the Boston School Committee assigning "colored" children to two of the 161 primary schools in Boston. The plaintiff, a five-year-old "colored" girl, attempted to enter the school nearest her home, a distance of 900 feet, and was denied admission.[90] The segregated school was 2,100 feet from her home. The qualification of instructors in white and "colored" schools was equal, and the physical deficiencies of the "colored" school appear not to have been put in issue. Chief Justice Shaw, for the Supreme Judicial Court, upheld the Boston School Committee. The clause of the Massachusetts Declaration of Rights, "All men are born free and equal,"[91] was a natural-law proclamation, not operative law. "The province of a declaration of rights and constitution of government, after directing its form, is to declare great principles and fundamental truths, to influence and direct the judgment and conscience of legislators in making laws, rather than to limit and control them, by directing what precise laws they shall make."[92] Charles Sumner, for the plaintiff, had argued that discrimination on the basis of race was a perpetuation of caste, and necessarily a violation of equality.[93] The court upheld the discretion of the School Committee and held that separate schools did not violate any constitutional rights. But the *Roberts* decision was law for only five years. Citizens organized and convinced the legislature that separate schools were in their nature unequal. In 1855 the Massachusetts legislature enacted a statute prohibiting the separation of children in schools on the basis of race, color, or religious opinion.[94] Given the factual basis of the legislative rejection of the *Roberts* decision, the opinion should never have stood as a precedent for separate-but-equal schools.

After the Civil War, radical Republicans began what was to be an unsuccessful campaign to end racial segregation in the public schools. The new constitutions of 1868, drafted by the conventions controlled by the radicals in Louisiana and South Carolina, expressly prohibited racial segregation in public schools.[95] In 1870, the radicals in Congress were successful in incorporating bars against racial segregation in state schools as a condition subsequent in the acts to readmit Mississippi, Texas, and Virginia to the Union.[96] These conditions were subsequently evaded.

The controversies over school segregation in the Congress demonstrate that most members recognized that the power to order racially mixed schools was within the power of Congress under Section 5 of the Fourteenth Amendment.[97] But the attempts of the radical Republicans to get such laws passed failed. Even some Southern Republicans opposed such bills. Thus, though there was a recognition that the Fourteenth Amendment could apply to schools, it was politically impossible to pass national statutes mandating mixed schools. This left open the issue of whether the courts could hold segregated schools in any state or district to violate the equal protection clause in the absence of Congressional legislation. In fact, the grant to Congress could not be exclusive if the equal protection clause was to be meaningful. If the Congress was divided in blocs and there was an impasse on antisegregation legislation, only the judiciary could block flagrant violation of equality of the races.

For fifty years after *Plessy*, the African-American community, with few lawyers and few friends among skilled white lawyers who would donate time to an impoverished group, did not begin a direct attack on school segregation. Instead, most actions centered on showing the inequality of schools for African-Americans. In *Cumming* v. *Board of Education*,[98] a high school for African-Americans was closed to convert it to a larger primary school for African-Americans. The plaintiffs petitioned the court to enjoin tax expenditures for the white high schools until a school was provided for African-Americans. The Supreme Court upheld a denial of this remedy, whose effect would have been to leave both races without high schools. In *Berea College* v. *Kentucky*,[99] the Court upheld a state statute that prohibited private institutions from teaching white and non-white students in the same place and at the same time. Following this expansion of the doctrine of *Plessy*, laws were passed throughout the South requiring racial segregation in public places, including privately operated facilities such as theaters and pool halls.[100]

As to education, the segregation principle was restated in *Gong Lum* v. *Rice*,[101] in which the Court upheld the denial of admission of a Chinese-American to a white school in Mississippi. Absent evidence thereon, the Court assumed that a school with equal facilities was provided in the county for the "colored races."[102] The Court held that assignment of a Chinese citizen of the United States to such school was not a denial of equal protection of the laws, citing *Plessy* as authoritative law.

The first successful attacks on racial segregation in education came after 1930. These attacks applied to law schools and graduate schools, where it was not economically feasible to supply segregated institutions.[103] It was only after World War II that a frontal attack was mounted against racial segregation in public schools, an attack on the idea that separate schools could be equal. In the four cases that were on appeal together in *Brown* v. *Board of Education*,[104] attorneys for the plaintiffs seeking admission to white schools presented the testimony of many expert witnesses on the demeaning character of enforced segregation of minority children.[105] Although three of the trial courts ruled that they were bound to follow *Plessy*, one of these, the Topeka court, made a finding of fact accepting the social-science evidence on the detrimental effect of segregation on the African-American children.[106] In the Delaware case, the district court found the inequalities of education of such magnitude that they ordered immediate admission of the African-American children to the white schools.[107] The chancellor found that segregation itself results in an inferior education for African-American children, but he did not rest his decision on that ground.[108]

The Supreme Court in *Brown* held for the plaintiff children in all the cases. It accepted the finding of fact in the Topeka case as correct.[109] Segregation by law was a badge of inferiority: "We conclude that in the field of public education the doctrine of 'separate but equal' has no place. Separate educational facilities are inherently unequal."[110] Although the Court did not expressly overrule *Plessy*, *Plessy*'s rule was held inapplicable to public education in the 1950s.[111] Critics of the Court's reliance on social-science data must have failed to read the transcripts of the trial courts, where such evidence was overwhelmingly in favor of the plaintiffs' cases.[112]

The Court in *Brown* heard argument on whether the original understanding of the equal protection clause was to invalidate segregated schools. After review of the sources, the Court concluded: "At best, they are inconclusive."[113] Bickel has demonstrated that history cannot answer the question of whether a particular set of acts occurring today do or do not violate broad general constitutional principles such as the equal protection clause of the Fourteenth Amendment: "It is thus quite apparent that to seek in historical materials relevant to the framing of the Constitution, or in the language of the Constitution itself, specific answers to specific present problems is to ask the wrong questions. With adequate scholarship, the answer that must emerge in the vast majority of cases is no answer."[114] Most often today's problems did not even exist when the applicable constitutional clause became law. Those that did exist, such as racial segregation in public schools in the northern states, were subject to diverse and conflicting views among the ratifiers. Most of the hundreds of representatives at the ratifying conventions did not speak on this narrow topic. But even if they had spoken and said that separate-but-equal public facilities for the races satisfied the equal protection clause at that time, this would not control courts today. A finding of fact at a trial in 1951 that racial separation is a badge of inferior status would require a holding of unconstitutionality regardless of the views of ratifiers in 1867 and 1868.

In the companion case to *Brown*, *Bolling v. Sharpe*,[115] the Court held that the segregation of public schools in the District of Columbia violated the due process clause of the Fifth Amendment. Since "due process" means "required procedure" and there is no equal protection clause in the Fifth Amendment, the reasoning of *Bolling* is much more difficult than *Brown*. The Court resorted to substantive due process: "Classifications based solely upon race must be scrutinized with particular care, since they are contrary to our traditions and hence constitutionally suspect."[116] The Court concluded: "Segregation in public education is not reasonably related to any proper governmental objective, and thus it imposes on Negro children of the District of Columbia a burden that constitutes an arbitrary deprivation of their liberty in violation of the Due Process Clause."[117] A more direct approach would have established a national civil right to equal protection from the English right to equal justice as founded in chapter 40 of the Magna Charta and preserved by the Ninth Amendment.[118] In this framework, the proclamation of equality in the Declaration of Independence can be viewed both as a statement of natural law and of positive law.

Equality of Firms in the Market

An efficient economy requires that business firms receive equal protection of the law. The efficiencies resulting from division of labor in large-scale factory production can occur only if underlying risk capital can be secured from large numbers of small investors. These stockholders have no part in day-to-day management, so ownership is separated from control.[119] Under such circumstances, stockholders will invest only if they are guaranteed limited liability. Nicholas Murry Butler remarked in 1911 on the legal technique of limited liability: "I weigh my words, when I say that in my judgment the limited liability corporation is the greatest single discovery of modern times, ... Even steam and electricity are far less important than the limited liability corporation, and they would be reduced to comparative impotence without it."[120]

In light of the economic realities, it is not surprising that Chief Justice Waite announced for the Court in *Santa Clara County* v. *Southern Pacific R. Co.*[121] that "[t]he court does not wish to hear argument on the question whether the provision in the Fourteenth Amendment to the Constitution, which forbids a state to deny to any person within its jurisdiction the equal protection of the laws, applies to these corporations. We are all of opinion that it does."[122] Although a corporation is not a "citizen" within the meaning of the privileges-or-immunities clause,[123] it is a "person" within the meanings of the due process and equal protection clauses. The Court has reaffirmed the right of corporations to equal protection of the laws many times, though its application to specific controversies has been uneven.[124]

The Supreme Court's treatment of the equal protection clause in the marketplace begins with its refusal to apply the principle in the 5-to-4 decision in the *Slaughter-House Cases*.[125] In that decision, Justice Miller, for the majority, held that the pervading purpose of the amendments was to protect the newly emancipated Afro-Americans and that no strong case of other state oppression had been made.[126] From an economics viewpoint, the Court's refusal to apply the equal protection clause to stop a state grant of monopoly for twenty-five years in an ordinary trade, like its refusal to apply the privileges-or-immunities clause, was patently wrong. All butchers were in like circumstances for the enactment of any health or safety statute, and the creation of a monopoly was not necessary for any police regulation of the trade. Furthermore, the grant of monopoly was not only an injury to all other butchers, it was an injury to the public as consumers, forcing them to pay monopoly prices for butchering services and for meat. The equal protection clause, by enforcing the Anglo-American constitutional precedents against governmental grants of monopoly in the ordinary trades, should have been a second, additional basis for invalidating the statute granting the monopoly.

In 1879 the state of Louisiana adopted a new Constitution, which read in part: "The monopoly features in the charter of any corporation now existing in the State, save such as may be contained in the charters of railroad companies, are hereby abolished."[127] In *Butchers Union Co.* v. *Crescent City Co.,*[128] the Supreme Court held that the grant of monopoly that had been validated in the *Slaughter-House Cases* was legally terminated. Justice Miller, for the majority, emphasized the contract clause. After holding that the grant was a contract, he adopted the rule of *Stone* v. *Mississippi*[129] that the state may not contract to surrender its police power to regulate industry. Justices Bradley and Field wrote concurring opinions. Adopting their dissenting views in the *Slaughter-House Cases* that the original grant of monopoly was void, they restated their opinions that the grant violated the privileges-or-immunities clause.[130] Justice Bradley also noted a violation of the equal protection clause: "If it is not a denial of equal protection of the laws to grant to one set of men, the privilege of following an ordinary calling in a large community, and to deny it to all others, it is difficult to understand what would come within the constitutional prohibition."[131]

One of the earliest cases under the equal protection clause concerned both racial and monopoly issues. In *Yick Wo* v. *Hopkins,*[132] a San Francisco ordinance made it unlawful to operate a laundry in a wooden building without a permit from the board of supervisors. Yick Wo proved that his wooden laundry had equipment that was not a fire hazard, but he was refused a permit. In fact, two hundred other Chinese laundry operators were denied permits while only one of eighty non-Chinese laundry operators with wooden buildings was denied a permit. Though the ordinance was neutral on its face, it was obviously administered to grant a monopoly to non-Chinese. Justice Matthews, for the Court, reversed the convictions for operating laundries without permits. "The fact of this discrimination is admitted. No reason for it is shown, and the conclusion cannot be resisted, that no reason for it exists except hostility to the race and nationality to which the petitioners belong, and which in the eye of the law is not justified."[133]

Statutory monopoly in the labor market was invalidated under the equal protection clause in *Truax* v. *Raich.*[134] An Arizona statute required firms employing five or more workers to reserve 80 percent of its positions for United States citizens. In an action by a resident alien, the Supreme Court affirmed a holding that a person could not be denied opportunity for employment. Justice Hughes noted that "[i]t requires no argument to show that the right to work for a living in the common occupations of the community is of the very essence of the personal freedom and opportunity that it was the purpose of the Amendment to secure."[135] He concluded: "If this could be refused solely on the ground of race or nationality, the prohibition of the denial to any person of the equal protection of the laws would be a barren form of words."[136]

Absent a classification based on race or alienage, the equal protection clause has not been utilized significantly to protect the right to compete in markets. A key early example was *Powell* v. *Pennsylvania*,[137] in which a state law prohibiting the manufacture and sale of oleomargarine was upheld. The Court devoted the bulk of the opinion to a denial of relief under substantive due process. It then disposed of the equal protection claim in one unreasoned sentence by noting that the statute applied to all makers of margarine.[138] The avowed purpose of the statute was the protection of public health, but the trial court had denied admission in evidence of all offers of proof of the healthfulness of the margarine.[139] In fact, the purpose of the statute was to confer monopoly power on the dairy interests. Suppliers of butter and of margarine are in like circumstances as competitors in the marketplace and should have been treated equally. As the New York Court of Appeals previously had said in voiding a similar statute: "Who will have the temerity to say these constitutional principles are not violated by an enactment which absolutely prohibits an important branch of industry for the sole reason that it competes with another, and may reduce the price of an article of food for the human race? . . . Equal rights to all are what are intended to be secured by the establishment of constitutional limit to legislative power, and impartial tribunals to enforce them."[140]

Outside the field of taxation, few cases have found a violation of equal protection in state statutes regulating business. In 1902 an Illinois antitrust statute that exempted agricultural products in the hands of the producer was invalidated.[141] Because small farmers engaged in joint marketing are not in like circumstances with large manufacturers who conspire in restraint of trade, the decision seems wrong, and it has been overruled.[142] In *Smith* v. *Cahoon*[143] the Court invalidated a Florida statute under equal protection that required certain private motor carriers to obtain certification and insurance, but did not require it of others. In *Mayflower Farms* v. *Ten Eyck*,[144] an anticompetitive New York Milk Control Act that set minimum prices for sellers without well-advertised trade names below that of established firms was held to violate equal protection because it in effect barred entry of new firms. In *Hartford Co.* v. *Harrison*,[145] a Georgia statute was held to violate equal protection when it permitted mutual insurance companies to act through salaried resident employees, but denied the same agencies to stock companies.

Morey v. *Doud*[146] was a leading exception to the Court's usual refusal to invalidate economic regulation on the grounds of violating equal protection. In *Morey*, an Illinois act for licensing of currency exchanges that contained a special exemption for American Express Co. was held arbitrary. It was clear that the legislative purpose was "to afford the public *continuing* protection"[147] in its transactions with currency exchanges. Although American Express was a large, financially sound firm at the passage of the statute, the exemption would continue even if its financial conditions changed. The effect of barring rival firms from selling money orders in retail establishments was discriminatory because it created a closed class of one firm for preferential treatment.[148]

The sound reasoning of *Morey* in holding a grant of monopoly to violate the equal protection clause was overruled in *City of New Orleans v. Dukes*.[149] A city ordinance banning pushcart food vendors in the French Quarter exempted those who had previously been operating there for eight years or more. Only two vendors came under this exception, and they had operated in the area for over twenty years. The plaintiff had operated in the area only two years, but she demonstrated that she had invested money and time in developing a trade in reasonable reliance on the right to participate in that market. The Supreme Court upheld the ordinance as rationally related to a legitimate state interest.[150] The decision illustrates the fallacy of the rationality test. The ordinance was rationally related to the objective of preserving "the appearance and custom valued by the Quarter's residents and attractive to tourists."[151] But the plaintiff was in like circumstances with other vendors who had invested in reliance on the existence of that market, and she should have been treated in the same way.

A similar reversal of an antimonopoly holding took place for statutes whose effect was to bar the entry into a state of chain drugstores. In *Liggert Co. v. Baldridge*,[152] the Court had invalidated a Pennsylvania statute requiring all stockholders of drugstores to be registered pharmacists. No detriment to public health could arise from ownership of drugstores by corporate chains, because other state statutes prohibited the sale of impure drugs and required that prescriptions be compounded by registered pharmacists.[153] The problem with the decision was that it rested primarily on substantive due process rather than equal protection. No analysis was made of the efficiencies that would derive from competition of chain and local drugstores as equal participants in free markets. *Liggett* was overruled in 1973 in *North Dakota State Bd. v. Snyder's Drug Stores*,[154] sustaining a state statute requiring that a corporate owner of a pharmacy must have a majority of its stock owned by registered pharmacists. Here again the reasoning centered on substantive due process.[155] The Court missed the point that all owners of drugstores are in like circumstances as competitors in markets and that protection of public health is a separate issue.

The Supreme Court's great deference to state legislatures in refusing to protect equal access to the marketplace is exemplified by the 5-to-4 decision in *Kotch v. Board of River Port Pilot Com'rs*.[156] A Louisiana statute restricted piloting of ocean vessels on the Mississippi into New Orleans to persons appointed by the governor upon recommendation of a state board composed of the pilots themselves. The unlimited discretion of board members enabled them to recommend their relatives and friends exclusively for the required six-month apprenticeship. The plaintiffs, who had at least fifteen years experience elsewhere as pilots, sought relief under the equal protection clause. Justice Black, for the majority, upheld the law and adopted the rational basis test. The object of the law was to secure "the safest and most efficiently operated pilotage system practicable. We cannot say that the method adopted in Louisiana for the selection of pilots is unrelated to this objective."[157] Here again one sees persons in like circumstances denied access to markets by state statute. Justice Rutledge, for the dissenters, stated: "The door is thereby closed to all not having blood relationship to presently licensed pilots. Whether the occupation is considered as having the status of 'public officer' or of highly regulated private employment, it is beyond legislative power to make entrance to it turn upon such a criterion."[158]

Other cases centering on the rejection of substantive due process have failed to give adequate analysis to parallel claims of violation of equal protection. *Williamson* v. *Lee Optical Co.*[159] is a prime example. An Oklahoma statute aimed at reinforcing monopoly power in optometrists and ophthalmologists prohibited others, such as opticians, from fitting lenses to a face or duplicating or replacing lenses into frames without a prescription from the named professionals. The effect was to forbid opticians from doing these mechanical tasks at minimal cost to consumers. In upholding the statute, Justice Douglas, for the Court, failed to discuss whether opticians were similarly situated with the doctors in guaranteeing quality work in duplicating a cracked lens or in placing old lenses in new frames and fitting them to the buyer's face. Instead, he generalized: "The prohibition of the Equal Protection Clause goes no further than the invidious discrimination. We cannot say that point has been reached here."[160]

The filled milk cases represent another instance where discriminatory legislation was approved as conforming to due process standards, side-stepping valid claims of violation of equal protection.[161] The conclusion here is that the famous *Carolene Products*[162] decision was wrong. Strict scrutiny of economic regulation under the equal protection clause to prevent monopolistic exploitation of consumers is just as important as defending the political rights of "discrete and insular minorities."[163] Filled milk is a combination of nonfat milk and vegetable oils that can be manufactured for approximately one-half the price of evaporated milk. It was bought mainly by very low-income people, a discrete social minority. The farm bloc in many states caused their legislatures to pass statutes absolutely prohibiting the sale of filled milk, even though it was healthful food and could clearly be labeled as "not evaporated milk or cream." In the leading case of *Sage Stores Co.* v. *Kansas,*[164] the Supreme Court affirmed a 4-to-3 decision of the Kansas Supreme Court upholding such a prohibitory statute. By emphasizing nutritional inferiority and possible deception of retailers in spite of well-labeled cans, the U.S. Supreme Court used a rational-basis test to summarily dispose of the equal protection issue.[165]

In *Strehlow* v. *Kansas State Board of Agriculture,*[166] the truth finally prevailed. In *Strehlow,* the Kansas court overruled its *Sage Stores* decision, noting that the dissent in 1943 had "hit the nail on the head."[167] The food was found wholesome, nutritious, and healthful. It was clearly labeled and not conducive to deception or fraud. As applied to this product, the statute was held to violate the due process and equal protection clauses. The opinion followed an earlier finding of a U.S. district court that the similar Arkansas statute as applied to filled milk violated the equal protection clause.[168]

On the national level, the Filled Milk Act of 1923 that had been passed by pressure of the dairy interests prohibited the shipment of filled milk in interstate commerce. In *Carolene Products Co.* v. *United States,*[169] the Court upheld the federal statute against a due process challenge as a protective against fraudulent substitution for milk. This was in spite of a finding of equal nutritional value.[170] In 1972 a U.S. district court made an opposite finding, relying on the concept of equal protection as incorporated in the due process clause of the Fifth Amendment.[171] The application of the prohibition to filled milk and not to other products combining nonfat milk and vegetable oils was discriminatory. Without mentioning the leading case of *Bolling* v. *Sharpe,*[172] the district court presumed that the due process clause incorporated equal protection of the laws.

In a significant number of other cases, the Supreme Court has denied equal protection to persons in business firms through summary application of the rational-basis test. Absent argument on whether parties are in like circumstances in relation to a valid statutory purpose, the Court in many cases has failed to consider the true issue. In *Goesaert* v. *Cleary,*[173] it upheld a Michigan statute forbidding women to be licensed as bartenders unless they were wives or daughters of the male owner of the bar. Three dissenting justices argued that the act denied equal protection to female owners of bars since they and their daughters were not permitted to tend their own bars.[174] In *Daniel* v. *Family Security Life Ins. Co.,*[175] the Court upheld a South Carolina statute that forbade insurance companies and their agents from engaging in the undertaking business and forbade undertakers from serving as sales agents for life-insurance companies. The evidence had shown that insurance companies represented by morticians and those not so represented were in like circumstances as competitors in the market. The district court had found the statute to be "arbitrary and discriminative" since its sole objective was to restrain competition.[176]

In *Ferguson* v. *Skrupa*,[177] the Court upheld a Kansas statute that prohibited any person other than lawyers from engaging in the business of debt adjustment. Persons skilled in problems of family finance and budgeting were barred from competing with lawyers. Evidence showed that some states had regulated any abuses of debt adjusting without eliminating competition of those persons who might be most skilled in the field.[178] In *Martin* v. *Walton*,[179] the Court upheld a Kansas Supreme Court rule that required a member of the Kansas bar residing nearby in Missouri to appear with local associate counsel when appearing in Kansas courts. Since all members of the bar must be presumed to know the procedural law of the state, the only purpose of the rule was to reduce competition. The dissenters found the statute "invidious in its application."[180]

Recent decisions have continued the rejection of the plea for equal protection in the marketplace. In *Rice* v. *Norman Williams Co.*,[181] claims under the Sherman Act and the supremacy clause were combined with the issue of equal protection. California liquor wholesalers had induced the state legislature to enact a "designation" statute under which a licensed wholesaler was prohibited from buying any brand of distilled liquor unless he was designated as the authorized wholesaler by the distiller who owned the brand name. The objective was to create monopoly wholesalers for each brand and thus prevent intrabrand competition by preventing a California wholesaler from acquiring branded liquor from an out-of-state wholesaler. Reversing the California Court of Appeal, the Supreme Court held that there was not a per se violation of the Sherman Act because the distiller's designation of an exclusive wholesaler was a vertical, nonprice restraint.[182] As to the equal protection clause, the Court held that the discrimination between designated and nondesignated wholesalers was rationally related to the statute's legitimate purpose. The asserted purpose was to restrain intrabrand competition in order to foster interbrand competition.[183] There was no evidence that this interaction ever had occurred or could occur in the marketing structure of the liquor industry. In fact, interbrand competition was the weaker of the two, because of the contrived product differentiation due to distillers' intensive advertising of brand names.[184] The statutory curtailment of intrabrand rivalry wiped out the most effective element of competition in liquor marketing by depriving wholesalers in like circumstances of equal opportunity in the marketplace.

In theory, the equal protection clause as applied to markets should reinforce the national commerce power in protecting and maintaining a nationwide, free economy. In a few instances, however, the Congress has delegated an aspect of the commerce power to the states. In *Northeast*

Bancorp v. *Board of Governors, FRS*,[185] a federal statute required bank holding companies to obtain approval of the Federal Reserve Board before they acquired any bank and prohibited such acquisition by an out-of-state holding company unless it was authorized by the state in which the bank was located. Connecticut and Massachusetts passed statutes allowing only out-of-state bank holding companies of New England to acquire in-state banks, and only on the basis of reciprocal privileges. Under the commerce, compact, and equal protection clauses, the Supreme Court unanimously upheld the state statutes against challenges of discrimination against bank holding companies outside New England. As to the equal protection challenge, this opinion in part faces the issue of whether New England bank holding companies are in like circumstances with those outside New England. Regional bank holding companies combined "the beneficial effect of increasing the number of banking competitors with the need to preserve a close relationship between those in the community who need credit and those who provide credit."[186]

State Taxation and Equal Protection

Issues of state discrimination in the taxation of interstate commerce are usually litigated under the commerce clause rather than the equal protection clause. The nationwide free market for goods and services is protected by the exclusive power in the national government to regulate commerce between states. Consequently, a state may not impose a franchise tax on foreign corporations for the privilege of coming into the state to execute interstate transactions.[187] On the other hand, the Court held in *Atlantic Refining Co.* v. *Virginia*[188] that there is no constitutional right of a foreign corporation to come into a state to engage in intrastate commerce. In *Atlantic Refining Company* an entrance fee, payable once as a price for admission to engage in intrastate business, was distinguished from an annual tax. Here, a fee that was a fixed percentage of authorized capital was upheld even though domestic corporations paid a lower charter fee.[189]

After a foreign corporation has been admitted to a state to engage in intrastate transactions, however, it is entitled to equal treatment with domestic corporations. Annual sales or operating taxes must be assessed against all corporations equally.[190] *Hanover Ins. Co.* v. *Harding*[191] was a classic case of illegal discrimination. A tax of 2 percent of net receipts was levied on foreign fire and marine insurance companies, but not on domestic ones. In voiding this section of the Illinois statute, the Court ruled that a state may not avoid the requirement of equal treatment by labeling the fee a condition of continuing business in the state.[192]

In 1945 Congress removed all commerce clause limitations on the authority of the states to regulate and tax the insurance business.[193] This congressional action brought equal protection issues to the center of litigation on state discriminatory taxes in the insurance industry. The Court initially upheld discriminatory taxes on a foreign corporation that had entered the state where one condition on entry was that it would consent to pay all future taxes that might be assessed,[194] but later overruled this decision.[195] In *Western & Southern L.I. Co. v. Bd. of Equalization,*[196] California had imposed an extra tax on foreign insurers when their states of incorporation imposed higher taxes on California insurers than California would usually impose on their insurance companies. The Court held that this retaliatory tax did not violate the equal protection clause because it bore a rational relation to a legitimate state purpose. The objective was to deter other states from enacting discriminatory or excessive taxes on California insurance companies.[197] Retaliatory state taxes had been promoted by the insurance industry in order to limit state taxation of that industry. From an economics viewpoint, the objective is positive, since special taxes on one industry are likely to misallocate resources.

Efficiency criteria received unusually strong recognition in a recent case concerning discriminatory annual taxes on foreign insurance companies. In *Metropolitan Life Ins. Co. v. Ward,*[198] the Court invalidated an Alabama statute that taxed foreign life insurance companies at 3 percent of gross premiums, foreign companies selling other types of insurance at 4 percent, and all domestic companies at only 1 percent. The foreign companies could reduce the differential in tax rates partially by investing prescribed percentages of their worldwide assets in specified Alabama assets and securities. On motion for summary judgment, the trial court had found no violation of equal protection because the statute served two purposes in addition to raising revenue: (1) encouraging the formation of new insurance companies in Alabama, and (2) encouraging capital investment by foreign insurance companies in Alabama assets and governmental securities.[199] The companies waived their rights to an evidentiary hearing on whether the statute's classification bore a rational relationship to the two purposes, thus challenging the purposes themselves under the equal protection clause.

In rejecting the first purpose, Justice Powell wrote: "Alabama's aim to promote domestic industry is purely and completely discriminatory, designed only to favor domestic industry within the State, no matter what the cost to foreign corporations seeking to do business there."[200] As to the second purpose, promoting the purchase of assets that the foreign insurance companies do not consider the most efficient investment, Powell noted that this does not lower the discriminatory premiums tax: "The State's investment incentive provision therefore does not cure, but reaffirms, the statute's impermissible classification based solely on residence."[201]

For most types of state classification in assessing taxes, the Supreme Court has denied claims of discrimination under the equal protection clause. In *Allied Stores of Ohio* v. *Bowers*,[202] Ohio law exempted from personal property taxation "merchandise or agricultural products belonging to a nonresident . . . if held in a storage warehouse for storage only."[203] This exemption was challenged by a resident operator of department stores who stored merchandise for sale in Ohio. The Supreme Court upheld the exemption against a charge of discrimination against resident businesses, noting that "it may reasonably have been the purpose and policy of the State Legislature, in adopting the proviso, to encourage the construction or leasing and operation of warehouses in Ohio by nonresidents with the attendant benefits to the states economy."[204] The Court found that the plaintiff was not in like circumstances with nonresidents who were merely storing goods in Ohio. If other states tax-exempted goods held in the state solely for storage, the Ohio exemption would merely be equalizing tax liability between states. If Ohio were unique in this exemption, the exemption might divert warehouse investment to a location that was not the most efficient.[205]

There are only a few cases in which state taxation has been held to violate the equal protection clause. A Virginia tax was invalidated that applied to all profits of firms doing business in the state whether earned in the state or outside, while exempting corporations chartered in Virginia that had no income within the state.[206] In Nebraska, the systematic undervaluation of some property for tax purposes while other property was assessed at full value was held to be illegal discrimination.[207] A Wisconsin tax statute was voided that created a conclusive presumption that all gifts made within six years of death were made in contemplation of death.[208] A Kentucky tax on the privilege of recording mortgages that applied only to those that did not mature within five years was held invalid.[209] A Pennsylvania tax on receipts of taxicab owners that applied to corporate owners but not to individuals and partnerships was held to violate equal protection, but this decision was later overruled.[210] An Iowa statute was invalidated that taxed a nationally chartered bank at a higher rate than competing financial firms.[211] An Illinois statute that taxed receipts of some foreign insurance companies selling casualty insurance but not others was held to be illegal discrimination.[212]

The most noted case holding a state taxing statute invalid occurred during the 1930s. In *Colgate* v. *Harvey*[213] Vermont exempted from income tax interest on money loaned within the state at not more than 5 percent interest. The clear objective was to divert lending from its most efficient use, and the Court held the statute invalid. This decision was overruled in *Madden* v. *Kentucky*,[214] which upheld a state property tax on bank deposits of ten cents per $100 for money in local banks and fifty cents per $100 for deposits in out-of-state banks.

The cases sustaining chainstore taxes during the 1930s are an outstanding example of the Supreme Court's failure to protect equal opportunity in the marketplace.[215] The majority of retailers, owning single stores, were politically organized to secure anticompetitive legislation that increased the tax burdens of their rivals operating chains. Three of the four major decisions affecting chainstores were written by Justice Roberts, and they are arguably inconsistent. The first was a 5-to-4 decision in 1931, *State Board of Tax Com'rs* v. *Jackson*.[216] A graduated tax starting at $3 for one store rose to $25 for each store over twenty. The plaintiff grocer operated 225 stores and paid an annual fee of $5,443 on about $1 million total sales, while two department stores, each with over $8 million sales, paid only the $3 fee.[217] The State Board presented evidence of the efficiencies of chainstores' operation to support the classification that justified oppressive taxes on such efficiencies. The Supreme Court, reversing the trial court's finding that the classification was arbitrary, upheld the tax: "The fact that a statute discriminates in favor of a certain class does not make it arbitrary, if the discrimination is founded upon a reasonable distinction."[218] The evidence that some independent grocers formed buying associations that allowed them to achieve many of the economies of the chains did not convince the majority that all grocers were in like circumstances as competitors in the market.

In *Fox* v. *Standard Oil Co.*,[219] another 5-to-4 decision, the Court upheld a West Virginia chainstore tax as applied to service stations. The graduated tax began at $2 for one store and rose to $250 for each store in excess of seventy-five. Standard Oil Co. had 949 service stations and 54 bulk plants in the state. The trial court had decided that the application of the tax to gasoline stations was so much harsher and heavier than the operation of the tax when applied to other chains that it constituted a denial of equal protection of the laws. The Supreme Court reversed and upheld the tax. Following the decision in the *Jackson* case, Justice Cardozo held that a chain of stations was in a different class from those owned individually, largely because of efficiencies in distribution and advertising.[220] Furthermore, he held that oppressive rates did not amount to arbitrary discrimination or to unlawful confiscation. "Even if the tax should destroy a business, it would not be made invalid or require compensation upon that ground alone."[221] The use of taxation as a regulatory device was a legislative issue. "The tax now assailed may have its roots in an erroneous conception of the ills of the body politic or of the efficacy of such a measure to bring about a cure. We have no thought in anything we have written to declare it expedient or even just, or for that matter to declare the contrary. We deal with the power only."[222]

But two months after *Fox*, the Court invalidated a graduated tax on annual gross retail sales in *Stewart Dry Goods Co.* v. *Lewis*.[223] The tax ranged from 1/20th of one percent on the first $400,000 sales to 1 percent on sales over $1,000,000. Justice Roberts, for the majority, in an opinion that seems inconsistent with *Jackson* and *Standard Oil,* held the statute to be "unjustifiably unequal, whimsical and arbitrary."[224]

In the former cases, the Court had rejected the argument that the number of stores in a chain bore no necessary relation to net profits, but here the Court accepted the argument that gross sales bore no necessary relation to profits. Firms with larger grosses but lower net incomes would suffer glaring inequalities of burden. Furthermore, firms selling the same item would pay different sales taxes on the item because their gross sales were different. Here, the Court recognized that smaller and larger firms were in like circumstances as competitors in the market. Justice Cardozo, with Brandeis and Stone concurring, dissented.[225] He felt that the Court should accept the legislative assumption that efficiency increased with size. The maximum rate here could not be confiscatory, and the precedents supported a conclusion that graduated tax rates were not arbitrary.

In *Great Atlantic & Pacific Tea Co.* v. *Grosjean,*[226] the Court reaffirmed the power of a state to impose a graduated tax on chainstores in a state. By a vote of 4 to 3, it upheld a Louisiana tax whose rate was determined by the total number of stores operated by the chain, including those outside the state. The rate on stores in Louisiana rose from $15 each on chains of two to five stores to $550 each for chains owning more than 500 stores. The district court had found efficiencies determined by aggregate size of the chains.[227] The Court rejected the argument that there was discrimination in favor of chains operating only in Louisiana, even though both sets of stores were in like circumstances as competitors. The tax rate based on total stores operated was held not to be discriminatory, even though the evidence showed that A&P's Louisiana stores had earnings below the average for all its stores.

The more recent cases, like the earlier ones, exhibit no consistent pattern. In *Wheeling Steel Corp.* v. *Glander,*[228] the Court invalidated an Ohio ad valorem tax on intangibles, such as notes and accounts receivables, of nonresident firms. Ohio was taxing intangibles that were never within Ohio but arose from goods shipped from Ohio plants. Wheeling, operating from West Virginia and holding all notes and accounts there, complained that part of these intangibles deriving from Ohio shipments were subject to Ohio property tax. As a reciprocity, Ohio was exempting Ohio firms from tax on those intangibles arising from goods shipped from plants outside Ohio. By implication, Ohio was inviting the states where plants were located to tax the notes and accounts situated anywhere that arose from shipments in their states. There was no indication that other states adopted this scheme.[229] Since Ohio had many plants and fewer home offices of firms, where intangible money claims were held, the tax method would have been discriminatory even if other states had accepted the offered reciprocity.

The more typical modern case upholds unequal treatment of firms that are in like circumstances. In *Lenhausen* v. *Lake Shore Auto Parts Co.*,[230] the Court approved an Illinois constitutional provision exempting individuals from ad valorem taxes on personal property while retaining such taxes on corporations and other associations. The plaintiff, a small corporation with substantial personal property, was subject to the tax while competitive firms owned by individuals were exempt. The Court restated its earlier view that the only classifications that were prohibited by the equal protection clause were those found palpably arbitrary or invidious. "State taxes which have the collateral effect of restricting or even destroying an occupation or a business have been sustained, so long as the regulatory power asserted is properly within the limits of the federal-state regime created by the Constitution."[231] This generalization was based on the decision in *Magnano* v. *Hamilton*,[232] in which a destructive tax on oleomargarine was held consistent with equal protection. The Court there had recognized that butter and margarine were in like circumstances as competitors in the market,[233] and that a tax of 15 cents per pound would destroy the plaintiff's firm, yet it rejected the equal protection claim in a single sentence.

Conclusion

Judicial interpretation of the equal protection clause as applied to the economy will continue to be inconsistent and unpredictable as long as the Supreme Court refuses to adopt sound functional reasoning. The rational-basis test merely requires that method have a rational relation to objective; there is usually no remedy if the statutory objective is in itself discriminatory. This was the basic message of *City of New Orleans* v. *Dukes* and *Kotch* v. *Board of River Port Pilots Com'rs*. Functional analysis should center first on whether there is constitutionally valid statutory objective. If the Court finds this first criterion satisfied, it should go on to inquire whether the classification that has been adopted assigns all persons who are in like circumstance to the same class. Only an analysis that centers on the factual question of like circumstances can discover and invalidate arbitrary and oppressive classifications.

Afterword

AN OBJECTIVE THEORY of documentary interpretation, based on the meaning of language to reasonably educated readers at the time of the writing, together with established common-law rules of documentary construction, was existent in 1787 when the Constitution was framed. Objective theory rejects searching for "intent of framers." While some commentators used the word "intent," it is clear that they did not mean subjective intent as that term is used today, because they knew that a reliable search for subjective intent is an impossibility.[1] The application of the objective theory to constitutional construction is detailed in Justice Joseph Story's long chapter on rules of interpretation in his *Commentaries on the Constitution*.[2] Every law student should be required to read that chapter as he or she begins a course on constitutional law.

The objective theory of constitutional interpretation results in an originalist study of the document as opposed to a theory that holds that Supreme Court justices are noninterpretivists, that they are empowered to reinterpret the Constitution over time to fit their personal value judgments.[3] An originalist study of the Constitution is undertaken on the assumption that the people expect to be governed by the principles incorporated in a document that was submitted to their ancestors for approval and ratified by them. The key implication of the originalist method is that justices of the Supreme Court of the United States are bound to act with great restraint. Each constitutional decision of the Court must be based on an analysis of the original meaning of the clause or clauses applicable to the contested issues. The rejection of stare decisis in Supreme Court constitutional decision making means that earlier decisions on the same clauses may be advisory but they are not binding. In constitutional cases, the Court is never bound by the analytical errors of their predecessors.

The originalist method is reenforced by the fact that the amending power is reserved to the people in Article V. If, for example, American society needs additional civil rights against government, citizens should petition their representatives in Congress to begin the amending process. Those who feel that there should be a national constitutional right to privacy should not expect the judiciary to create this right out of whole cloth, as happened in *Roe* v. *Wade.*[4] The court is bound not to usurp the amending process. Those who adopt the contrary philosophy and urge the judicial power to create new civil rights face the possibility that the Court would also have the power to cancel existing civil rights.

An originalist interpretation results in dividing the analysis of judicial review in three separate categories. Both the philosophical foundations of our political system and the structural characteristics of our Constitution raise strong presumptions in favor of the legislative branch over the judiciary as the site for resolution of social conflict. In chapter 3, it was argued that the structure and function of the judiciary supported judicial review for enforcement of the express constitutional limitations in order to protect individual rights and for review of statutes regulating the judicial function. As to the legislative powers delegated to the Congress, there is neither structural nor functional basis for judicial review. It is remarkable that the obiter dictum of Chief Justice Marshall in *Marbury* v. *Madison,*[5] supporting judicial review of all congressional acts, has been given so much weight by later courts and commentators. While law students are drilled in the idea that the scope of precedent is determined by the facts of the case, not by the *obiter dictum,* few people have applied this principle to *Marbury.*[6] There has been little recognition that *Marbury* was a case of judicial self-defense, departmental review of a statute regulating the judiciary.

A key issue of law and economics of the Constitution is the structural one of separated powers, leading to the question of which department of government shall have the main duty and authority to make economic policy for the nation. The economic fallacies of Congress can be corrected at the next session; the economic fallacies of the Supreme Court remain law until overruled. The view of this study has been that in Article I, Section 8, the Constitution vested in the Congress with finality the power to make economic policy. While the Court was expected to refuse enforcement of national laws on purely local topics such as wills, it was likewise expected to leave the scope of the delegated powers to Congress. There is substantial evidence that in 1789 this was the general understanding of both Federalists and anti-Federalists.[7] A fear of strong national legislative power had led some anti-Federalists to oppose ratification, but they were outvoted. It was only after the Civil War, when laissez-faire and states-rights ideologies overcame the thinking of a majority of the Court, that they assumed the power to review the scope and breadth of the powers delegated to Congress. In the *Dewitt,*[8] *Trademark,*[9] and *Employer's Liability*[10] cases, the Court invalidated economic regulation that was most efficient at the national level. From an economic viewpoint, all three of the statutes invalidated in those cases can be justified as correcting market failures.

Few of the erroneous and now overruled decisions on economic regulation can be attributed to deliberate distortion in order to accomplish political goals. Forgotten original meanings of language and neglected rules of documentary interpretation must account for many errors. Without a rigorous methodology, justices slipped unconsciously into the changed meanings of words by accepting the arguments of business lawyers concerning the then-current meaning of language. Once a constitutional clause had been misinterpreted, later justices, also failing to investigate original meanings, carried these new interpretations into the usual language of the Court. Thus, "interstate commerce," a phrase which distorts the Commerce Clause, is to this day part of the operating vocabulary of the Court. In some cases, the repeated misinterpretations can be attributed to the erroneous application by the Supreme Court of *stare decisis* to constitutional decisions.

The task of constitutional interpretation is highly complex, a fact not always recognized by the commentators. Some clauses under Article I, such as the commerce and taxing powers, vested in Congress plenary power to govern on those topics. All that is required to interpret these clauses is a recognition of their great breadth and of the fact that the constitutional structure implies legislative finality on these topics in absence of any charge of violation of express constitutional limitations. A great body of litigation on the scope of the clauses should have been summarily dismissed by the courts. Other clauses are less clear. Since general language often is ambiguous in the abstract, it must be analyzed in context, and extrinsic evidence of context is important.[11] Textual analyses frequently must be supplemented with rules of documentary interpretation and with search for the social purposes for enacting any given clause.

In contrast to the Congressional powers that derive all their meaning from the time of adoption, some of the constitutional limitations combine original meaning with language that incorporates current value judgments. The term "unreasonable" in "unreasonable search and seizure" is a value term that cannot be confined to eighteenth-century meaning.[12] New technology for search and new types of warrants require current evaluation. The meaning of "due process of law" as required or appropriate procedure contains the element of full and fair hearing. However, the idea of fairness cannot be confined to eighteenth-century meaning because novel modern procedures require modern evaluation.[13] Similarly, cruel and unusual punishment contains value terms and cannot be confined to eighteenth-century examples, because the philosophically general language refers to socially acceptable governmental behavior over time.[14]

In surveying the key constitutional limitations, one must be especially careful to separate those which are procedural and those which are substantive. In Section 1 of the Fourteenth Amendment,[15] for example, the privileges-or-immunities clause and the equal protection clause are substantive. The due process clause is procedural. It was lack of vigilance on this elementary distinction that led to the erroneous judicial creation of substantive due process.

The three clauses of Section 1 were each shown to have specific functions and yet to be complementary to each other. The privileges-or-immunities clause was shown to concern national constitutional limitations and to bar the state governments from engaging in those practices. The due process was concerned with fair procedure in all branches of government. The equal protection clause mandated states to treat persons in like circumstance in the same way. It is immediately clear that these three requirements must not be confused if the rights of citizens are to be protected. In *Bradwell* v. *Illinois*,[16] for example, a woman was denied equal protection of the laws when she passed the bar examination but was denied admission to the bar by state statute. Yet the Supreme Court applied the wrong clause and held that Bradwell was not denied a privilege or immunity of citizenship.

* * *

An objective interpretation of the Constitution and its judicial construction results in the recognition of a few jurists who are true heroes and others who are demiheroes. The true genius of the nineteenth-century Supreme Court was Justice Joseph Story.[17] His mastery of the law merchant as a branch of the law of nations was equal to that of Lord Mansfield. His encyclopedic treatises on many areas of the law merchant were recognized even in England as authoritative. Story's great law-merchant opinion on *Swift* v. *Tyson*[18] has been misunderstood by common lawyers for 148 years in spite of the fact that Justice Field explained in 1893 that *Swift* was not a common-law precedent.[19] One must observe, however, that persons of genius are human beings and occasionally fallible. Those same legal historians who mistakenly degrade Story's opinion in *Swift* also mistakenly praise Story's defective concurring opinion in the *Dartmouth College* case.[20] In *Dartmouth College,* Story failed to write a penetrating explanation of promise as the first essential of contract or of bargained consideration as a second essential. If he had done so, he would not have applied the contract clause but would have realized that the correct issue was one of eminent domain.

Justice Benjamin Curtis's analytical dissent in the *Dred Scott* case[21] was just one example of the high quality of his work. The antebellum rights of citizenship of free African-Americans could not have been more firmly explained. Chief Justice Taney, who wrote the majority opinion, was a lawyer of great ability who was overwhelmed by his own political biases in this case. He has rightfully been "hooted down the page of history."[22]

Justice John Marshall Harlan the elder wrote heroic dissenting opinions on the true meaning of Section 1 of the Fourteenth Amendment. His lone dissent in *Plessy* v. *Ferguson*[23] recognized a key factual truth, that racial segregation statutes were designed to perpetuate inequality for African-

Americans as a lower caste of persons. Historians and sociologists who have studied the effects of "Jim Crow" legislation all confirm his opinion. We had racial apartheid in America. Justice Harlan's dissents on the meaning of due process of law have also been vindicated. The due-process clause of the Fourteenth Amendment was *in pari materia* with the due process clause of the Fifth Amendment. The idea that minimal procedural protections in criminal cases could differ between the state and national systems was inconsistent with basic principles of fairness in the clauses. On the other hand, Justice Harlan succumbed to the erroneous thinking of substantive due process.

Justice Oliver Wendell Holmes, Jr., was clearly the hero of objective constitutional interpretation in the twentieth century. He dissented to the reduction of the commerce power to less than its facial meaning and to the judicial creation of substantive due process. Holmes was one of the few great theorists of common law and constitutional law, yet he too had human frailties. His positivism left him unable to comprehend the true character of the law of nations, and he was therefore unable to see the shining truth of Justice Story's opinion in *Swift* v. *Tyson*. Private international law is not a "brooding omnipresence in the sky."[24] It is the cumulation of very similar positive laws of many nations in both the common-law and civil-law systems. If a novel issue concerning international transactions arises in the federal courts and no federal statutes or precedents apply, the litigants should reasonably expect our courts to adopt the common established principles found in English decisions and continental codes.

Justice Hugo L. Black held the torch for objective interpretation of the Constitution from 1937 to 1971. Some critics mistakenly attacked him as limiting his analyses solely to the constitutional text. It is clear, however, that Black understood and utilized the full methodology that is reviewed in chapter 2 of this volume. Black's dissent in *Adamson* v. *California*[25] asserted that the total incorporation of the Bill of Rights against states was accomplished by Section 1 of the Fourteenth Amendment. This view is confirmed by chapter 10, where it is demonstrated that, from the Charter of Virginia to the framing of the Fourteenth Amendment, the phrase "privileges and immunities" was a synonym for constitutional limitations. Black's uncompromising defense of absolutes in the First Amendment must be understood in light of a definition of "speech" as concerned with the expression of views on controversial issues in the society. Defamation and falsely shouting "fire" in a crowded theater are utterances of words, but they are not "speech" in the constitutional sense. Black was concerned with protecting true speech and not balancing it against some other value judgment designed to restrict expression.

Notes

Introduction

1. 41 U.S. (16 Pet.) 1 (1842). See chapter 7.

2. Erie v. Tompkins, 304 U.S. 64, 78 (1938) (law applicable to common-law torts in diversity cases is governed by section 34 of the Judiciary Act of 1789).

3. United States v. Carolene Products Co., 304 U.S. 144 (1938). See chapter 12.

4. See Bolling v. Sharpe, 347 U.S. 497 (1954); Tussman and tenBroek, The Equal Protection of the Laws, 37 Calif. L. Rev. 341 (1949).

5. 304 U.S. at 152–153 n. 4.

6. 163 U.S. 537 (1896), *overruled*, Gayle v. Browder, 352 U.S. 903 (1956). See chapter 12.

7. See T. Shibutani and K. Kwan, Ethnic Stratification: A Comparative Approach (1965); C. Woodward, The Strange Career of Jim Crow (3d ed. 1974).

8. See R. Posner, Economic Analysis of Law (3d ed. 1986); R. Cooter and T. Ulen, Law and Economics (1988); W. Hirsch, Law and Economics (1979); A. Polinsky, An Introduction to Law and Economics (2d ed. 1989).

9. See F. Knight, The Economic Organization 3–4 (1951); K. Arrow, Social Choice and Individual Values (2d ed. 1963).

10. H. Hochman and G. Peterson, Redistribution through Public Choice (1974).

11. Knight, *supra* note 9, at 10.

12. See Coleman, Economics and the Law: A Critical Review of the Foundations of the Economic Approach to Law, 94 Ethics 649 (1984).

13. In technical economic language, the value of the marginal product of each factor is equal to its price in every use. Since the price of the factor is competitively determined, any disequilibrium is caused by differences in marginal physical productivities. In such a case, it is more efficient to switch some of the input from a firm with lower marginal productivity to one with higher marginal productivity. The operation of competitive bidding for inputs in free markets automatically should result in each firm minimizing the long-run average cost of producing any given output.

14. See Stigler, The Economics of Scale, in the Organization of Industry 71 (1968); Stigler, The Division of Labor is Limited by the Extent of the Market, *id.* at 129.

15. 94 U.S. 113 (1877).

16. See W. Baxter, People or Penguins: The Case for Optimal Pollution (1974).

17. The Daniel Ball, 77 U.S. (10 Wall.) 557 (1871).

18. 196 U.S. 45 (1905).

19. 261 U.S. 525 (1923), *overruled* in West Coast Hotel Co. v. Parrish, 300 U.S. 379 (1937).

Chapter 1

1. See C. McIlwain, Constitutionalism: Ancient and Modern, ch. 1 (1947); Grey, Constitutionalism: An Analytical Framework, in Constitutionalism, Nomos 20, 189 (J. Pennock and J. Chapman eds. 1979).

2. See J. Buchanan and G. Tullock, The Calculus of Consent 13 (1962).

3. E. Hoebel, The Law of Primitive Man 330 (1954).

4. N. Machiavelli, History of Florence 240 (C. W. Colby, ed. 1901). See generally, F. Schevill, History of Florence (1936).

5. See G. Trevelyan, Garibaldi and the Thousand (1909).

6. M. Farrand, Records of the Federal Convention of 1787, I, 19, 166 (1911) [Hereinafter cited as Farrand].

7. Scott v. Sandford, 60 U.S. (19 How.) 393 (1857). See D. Fehrenbacher, The Dred Scott Case: Its Significance in American Law and Politics (1978); C. Warren, The Supreme Court in United States History, II: ch. 26 (1926).

8. 3 Stat. 545–48 (1820).

9. Scott, 60 U.S. at 452.

10. See Strader v. Graham, 51 U.S. (10 How.) 82 (1850).

11. U.S. Const. preamble.

12. McCulloch v. Maryland, 17 U.S. (4 Wheat.) 316, 404 (1819).

13. A. Hayek, Law, Legislation and Liberty, I, Rules and Order 134–36 (1973).

14. 1 Will. and Mary, sess. 2, c. 2 (1689).

15. See R. L. Perry and J. C. Cooper, Sources of our Liberties 245–50 (1959).

16. 31 Car. 2, c. 2 (1679); 56 Geo. III, c. 100 (1816).

17. See W. Duker, A Constitutional History of Habeas Corpus (1980); R. Perry and J. Cooper, *supra* note 15, at 189–203; A. V. Dicey, Introduction to the Study of the Law of the Constitution 209–33 (7th ed. 1908).

18. See R. Posner, Economic Analysis of Law 581–82 (3d ed. 1986).

19. The commerce clause is reviewed in chapter 5.

20. Posner, *supra* note 18, at 582.

21. See H. Scheiber, Federalism and the Constitution: The Original Understanding, in American Law and the Constitutional Order: Historical Perspectives 85–98 (L. Friedman and H. Scheiber eds. 1978).

22. Federalist 39, at 262 (E. Borne, ed. 1947) [cited hereinafter as Federalist]. "This government is acknowledged by all, to be one of enumerated powers." McCulloch v. Maryland, 17 U.S. (4 Wheat.) 316, 404 (1819).

23. Federalist 45, at 319.

24. U.S. Const., art. I, § 8, cl. 18.

25. Federalist 44, at 308. For comments of Hamilton, see Federalist 33, at 211–13.

26. F. McDonald, Novus Ordo Seclorum 267 (1985) citing H. Storing, ed., Complete Anti-Federalist, II: 58, 118, 159–60, 366; III: 36, 202–3; IV: 36; VI: 35 (1981).

27. Express prohibition on states exercising some of these exclusive federal powers, but not all of them, are stated in U.S. Const., art. I, § 10.

28. Home Building and Loan Ass'n v. Blaisdell, 290 U.S. 398, 427 (1934), per Chief Justice Hughes.

29. Farrand I: 21, 250, 318, 337, 438, 447; II: 440, 589; III: 24, 56, 65, 73, 112.

30. U.S. Const., art. VI, cl. 2. See Federalist 33, at 214–15.

31. Hines v. Davidowitz, 312 U.S. 52 (1941); Rice v. Santa Fe Elevator Co., 331 U.S. 218 (1947); Pennsylvania v. Nelson, 350 U.S. 497 (1956).

32. 317 U.S. 341 (1943). See Conant, The Supremacy Clause and State Economic Controls, 10 Hastings Con. L. Q. 255, 269–74 (1983).

33. Federal grants to state and local governments in 1986 totaled $112.6 billion. U.S. Dept. of Commerce, Bureau of the Census, Federal Expenditures by State for Fiscal Year 1986, 2 (1987).

34. See Tullock, Federalism: Problems of Scale, 6 Public Choice 19 (1969).

35. See G. Becker, Human Capital (2d ed. 1975).

36. Federal expenditures for elementary, secondary, and vocational education rose from $2.5 billion in 1969 to $7.8 billion in 1986. U.S. Office of Management and Budget, Historical Tables: Budget of the United States Government, table 3.3 (1987).

37. Tiebout, A Pure Theory of Local Expenditures, 64 J. Pol. Econ. 416 (1956).

38. Rose-Ackerman, Does Federalism Matter? 89 J. Pol. Econ. 152 (1981).

39. See Posner, *supra* note 18, ch. 26.

40. 453 U.S. 609 (1981). See Williams, Severance Taxes and Federalism, 53 U. Colo. L. Rev. 281 (1982).

41. See M. Vile, Constitutionalism and the Separation of Powers (1967); W. B. Gwyn, The Meaning of the Separation of Powers (1965); Sharp, The Classical American Doctrine of "the Separation of Powers," 2 U. Chi. L. Rev. 385 (1935); Wright, The Origins of the Separation of Powers in America, 13 Economica 169 (1933).

42. Federalist 48, quoting T. Jefferson, Notes on the State of Virginia 195; Federalist 50.

43. Myers v. United States, 272 U.S. 52, 293 (1926).

44. "James Wilson, one of the framers of the Constitution and a Justice of this court, in one of his law lectures said that the independence of each department required that its proceedings 'should be free from the remotest influence, direct or indirect, of either of the other two powers.' Andrews, The Works of James Wilson (1896), vol. 1, p. 367. And the importance of such independence was similarly recognized by Mr. Justice Story when he said that in reference to each other neither of the departments 'ought to possess, directly or indirectly, an overruling influence in the administration of their respective powers.' I. Story on the Constitution (4th ed.), Sec. 530. To the same effect, the Federalist (Madison) No. 48." O'Donoghue v. United States, 289 U.S. 516, 530–31 (1933).

45. Humphrey's Ex's v. United States, 295 U.S. 602 (1935), holding that the president may not at his will and in violation of statute remove a member of Federal Trade Commission, since FTC members perform subsidiary legislative functions.

46. U.S. Const. Art. I, §§ 2–5, and amend. XVII; art. II, § 1, and amend. XII. Each house shall be the Judge of the Elections, Returns and Qualifications of its own Members. Article I, Section 5.

47. U.S. Const., art. III, § 1.

48. U.S. Const., art. I, § 6.

49. The legislature may not usurp the executive or judicial powers. Springer v. Philippine Islands, 277 U.S. 189 (1928); Kilbourn v. Thompson, 103 U.S. 168 (1881). The executive may not usurp the legislative or judicial powers.

Youngstown Sheet and Tube Co. v. Sawyer. 343 U.S. 579 (1952); In Re Yamashita, 327 U.S. 1 (1946). The judiciary may not usurp legislative or executive powers. United States v. National City Lines, 334 U.S., 588–89 (1948); National City Bank of New York v. Republic of China, 348 U.S. 356, 358 (1955).

50. J. Locke, The Second Treatise of Government, § 144, at 74 (J. W. Gough ed. 1956).

51. *Id.*, § 160, at 82.

52. See Miller, An Inquiry in the Relevance of the Intentions of the Founding Fathers, 27 Ark. L. Rev. 583, 588 (1973).

53. J. Wilson, Works of James Wilson, I: 294, 296 (R. McCloskey ed. 1967).

54. Federalist 70, at book II, 49.

55. *Id.* at 50.

56. Effective separation of powers in England is said to date from the passage of a statute making judges removable from office only by impeachment by Parliament for misconduct. 12 Will. 3, c. 2 (1701). See Parker, Historic Basis of Administrative Law, 12 Rutgers L. Rev. 449, 450 (1958).

57. O'Donoghue v. United States, 289 U.S. 516, 531–34 (1933); Evans v. Gore, 253 U.S. 245, 248–53 (1920). "The complete independence of the courts of justice is peculiarly essential in a limited constitution." Hamilton in Federalist 78, at 100 (Bourne ed. 1947).

58. For citations and discussions see Corwin, The "Higher Law" Background of American Constitutional Law, 42 Harv. L. Rev. 365, 370 (1929). See L. Mason, Language of Dissent 303 (1959); Berger, Removal of Judicial Functions from Federal Trade Commission to a Trade Court, 59 Mich. L. Rev. 199, 204–6 (1960).

59. "[B]ias from strong and sincere conviction as to public policy may operate as a more serious disqualification than pecuniary interest." Great Britain, Report of the Committee on Ministers' Powers (Cmd. 4060, 1932). "Unlike a judge, who is theoretically neutral about government programs, an administrator often has an affirmative program to carry out; he often has a mission, a purpose, a policy." Professor Davis, in Report of the Special Subcommittee on Legislative Oversight of the House Committee on Interstate and Foreign Commerce, Independent Regulatory Commissions, H. R. 2711, 85th Cong. 2d Sess., 1959, p. 78. See Cooper, The Executive Department of Government and the Rule of Law, 59 Mich. L. Rev. 515, 517–18 (1961).

60. "From a body which had even a partial agency in passing bad laws, we could rarely expect a disposition to temper and moderate them in the application. The same spirit which had operated in making them would be too apt to influence their construction; still less could it be expected that men who had infringed the Constitution in the character of legislators would be disposed to repair the breach in that of Judges." Hamilton in Federalist 81, at 121.

61. Federalist 47, at book I, 330.

62. U.S. Const., art. I, § 1.

63. Cheadle, the Delegation of Legislative Functions, 27 Yale L. J. 842, 897 (1918).

64. Legislation involves the creation or extinction of general classes of rights or immunities for all persons who engage in the action treated by the particular laws. See Dash v. Van Kleeck, 7 Johns (N. Y. Ch.) 477, 502 (1811), per Kent, C. J.; San Diego Land & Town Co. v. Jasper, 189 U.S. 439, 440 (1903), per Holmes, J.; Prentis v. Atlantic Coast Line, 211 U.S. 210, 226 (1908), per Holmes, J.

65. Munn v. Illinois, 94 U.S. 113 (1877).

66. Kendall v. United States, 37 U.S. (12 Pet.) 524, 610 (1838).

67. See E. Levi, An Introduction to Legal Reasoning 31 (1948); Miller, Statutory Language and the Purposive Use of Ambiguity, 42 Va. L. Rev. 23 (1956).

68. "Congress legislated on the subject as far as was reasonably practicable, and from the necessities of the case was compelled to leave to executive officers the duty of bringing about the result pointed out by the statute. To deny the power of Congress to delegate such a duty would, in effect, amount but to declaring that the plenary power vested in Congress to regulate foreign commerce could not be efficaciously exerted." Buttfield v. Stranahan, 192 U.S. 470, 496 (1904). See F. Goodnow, Principles of Administrative Law of the United States 324 (1905); E. Freund, Standards of American Legislation 301 (1917); Rosenberry, Administrative Law and the Constitution, 23 Am. Pol. Sci. Rev. 32, 35 (1929).

69. Hampton & Co. v. United States, 276 U.S. 394, 404–6 (1928), holding delegating power to president to adjust tariffs to equalize costs of production is constitutional.

70. 48 Stat. 195 (1933).

71. Panama Refining Co. v. Ryan, 293 U.S. 388 (1935); Schechter Poultry Co. v. United States, 295 U.S. 495 (1935).

72. 295 U.S. at 529, 537–38.

73. Industrial Union Department v. American Petroleum Institute, 448 U.S. 607 (1980).

74. American Textile Manufacturers Institute V. Donavan, 452 U.S. 490, 543–48 (1981).

75. See H. Friendly, The Federal Administrative Agencies (1962).

76. United States v. Atkins, 556 F. 2d 1028, 1058–71 (Ct. Cl. 1977) (per curiam), cert. denied, 434 U.S. 1009 (1978).

77. Bruff and Gelhorn, Congressional Control of Administrative Regulation, 90 Harv. L. Rev. 1369 (1977); Watson, Congress Steps Out, 63 Calif. L. Rev. 983 (1975).

78. Buckley v. Valeo, 424 U.S. 1, 140n (1976).

79. 462 U.S. 919 (1983). For critical comments, see L. Tribe, Constitutional Choices 66–83 (1985); Elliot, INS v. Chadha: The Administrative Constitution, the Constitution and the Legislative Veto, 1983 Sup. Ct. Rev. 125; Strauss, Was There a Baby in the Bathwater? 1983 Duke L. J. 789; Tribe, The Legislative Veto Decision, 21 Harv. J. Legis. 1 (1984).

80. U.S. Const., art. I, § 7, cl. 2, 3.

81. Id., art. I, §§ 1 and 7, cl. 2.

82. Process Gas Consumers Group v. Consumers Energy Council of America, 463 U.S. 1216 (1983).

83. U.S. Senate v. F.T.C., 463 U.S. 1216 (1983).

84. See A. Howard, The Road from Runnymede, (1968).

85. See Stigler, infra note 115.

86. 22 U.S. (9 Wheat.) 1 (1824).

87. 83 U.S. (16 Wall.) 36 (1873).

88. 8 Co. 114a, 77 Eng. Rep. 646 (C. P. 1610). See McGovney, The British Origin of Judicial Review of Legislation, 93 U. Pa. L. Rev. 1 (1944); Plucknett, Bonham's Case and Judicial Review, 40 Harv. L. Rev. 30 (1926).

89. 14 & 15 Hen. 8, c. 5 (1523); 1 Mary, 2d sess. c. 9 (1553).

90. See Tumey v. Ohio, 273 U.S. 510 (1927).

91. 8 Co. 114a, 118a, 77 Eng. Rep. 646, 652.

92. Wagner, Coke and the Rise of Economic Liberalism, 6 Econ. Hist. Rev. 30 (1935).

93. Hayek, The Use of Knowledge in Society, 35 Am. Econ. Rev. 519 (1945).

94. See F. Knight, Risk, Uncertainty, and Profit, ch. 7 (1921).

95. See Stigler, The Economics of Information, 69 J. Pol. Econ. 213 (1961), reprinted in G. Stigler, The Organization of Industry 171 (1968).

96. See E. MacKaay, Economics of Information and Law, ch. 5 (1982).

97. See Bolger v. Youngs Drug Products Corp., 463 U.S. 60 (1983).

98. This distinction has been noted and thoroughly explained by the commentators. See, e.g., Stone, Restrictions of Speech Because of Its Content, 46 U. Chi. L. Rev. 81 (1978).

99. See G. Anastaplo, The Constitutionalist, ch. 5 (1971).

100. See A. Meiklejohn, Political Freedom 25 (1948).

101. See Meiklejohn, The First Amendment is an Absolute, 1961 Sup. Ct. Rev. 245, 261.

102. See V. Countryman, Advertising Is Speech, in A. Hyman and M. Johnson, eds., Advertising and Free Speech 35, 39 (1977).

103. 316 U.S. 52 (1942).

104. Schneider v. State (Town of Irvington), 308 U.S. 147 (1939).

105. 316 U.S. at 54.

106. Cammarano v. United States, 358 U.S. 498, 514 (1959) (concurring opinion).

107. 341 U.S. 622 (1951).

108. Martin v. City of Struthers, 319 U.S. 141 (1943). The Court also invalidated a license tax as applied to the sales of religious books by Jehovah's Witnesses. Murdock v. Pennsylvania, 319 U.S. 105 (1943).

109. City of Watseka v. Illinois Public Action Council, 107 S. Ct. 919 (1987).

110. 376 U.S. 254 (1964).

111. Id. at 266.

112. Meiklejohn, supra note 101, at 257.

113. 421 U.S. 809 (1975).

114. Id. at 822.

115. On the efforts of firms to secure legislative protection from competition, see Stigler, The Theory of Economic Regulation, 2 Bell J. Econ. & Mgmnt. Sci. 3 (1971); Posner, Theories of Economic Regulation, 5 Bell J. Econ. & Mgmnt. Sci. 335 (1974).

116. 425 U.S. 748 (1976). See Merrill, First Amendment Protection for Commercial Advertising, 44 U. Chi. L. Rev. 205 (1976).

117. "If there is a right to advertise, there is a reciprocal right to receive the advertising, and it may be asserted by these appellees." 425 U.S. 757. See Thornhill v. Alabama, 310 U.S. 88, 102 (1940).

118. Virginia State Board of Pharmacy, 425 U.S. at 760.

119. Id. at 762.

120. Id. at 763.

121. Id. at 765.

122. See In re R. M. J., 455 U.S. 191 (1982); Bates v. State Bar of Arizona, 433 U.S. 350 (1977).

123. 471 U.S. 626 (1985).

124. 471 U.S. at 639–41.

125. Id. at 650–53.

126. 436 U.S. 447 (1978).

127. Id. at 545. On the necessary distinction between speech and conduct, see Cox v. Louisiana, 379 U.S. 559 (1965), and especially the dissent of Justice Black. Id. at 581. Compare L. Tribe, American Constitutional Law 825–32 (2d ed. 1988).

128. 475 U.S. 1 (1986).

129. Consolidated Edison Co. v. Public Service Comm'n of New York, 447 U.S. 530 (1980).

130. *Pacific Gas & Electric* 475 U.S. at 14.

131. See Banzhof v. F.C.C., 405 F. 2d 1082 (D.C. Cir. 1968), cert. denied sub nom. Tobacco Institute, Inc. v. F.C.C., 396 U.S. 842 (1969). On the fairness doctrine, see Red Lion Broadcasting Co. v. F.C.C. 395 U.S. 367 (1969); B. Schmidt, Freedom of the Press v. Public Access 166 (1976).

132. 425 U.S. 765 (1978).

133. *Id.* at 776, citing Thornhill v. Alabama, 310 U.S. 88, 101–2 (1940).

134. 425 U.S. at 784. See Brudney, Business Corporations and Stockholders' Rights under the First Amendment, 91 Yale L. J. 235 (1981).

135. 435 U.S. 802–22.

136. 447 U.S. 557 (1980).

137. *Id.* at 566.

138. *Id.* at 566–68.

139. *Id.* at 568–69.

140. *Id.* at 569–73.

141. *Id.* at 583.

142. 478 U.S. 328 (1986).

143. *Id.* at 341–42.

144. *Id.* at 352–53.

145. *Id.* at 346.

146. *Id.* at 354, n.4 (Brennan, dissenting).

147. *Id.* at 359–63.

Chapter 2

1. See Laycock, Constitutional Theory Matters, 65 Texas L. Rev. 767 (1987).

2. See the critique of the present scope of judicial review in chapter 3.

3. U.S. Const., art. 6, cl. 3.

4. Fletcher v. Peck, 10 U.S. (6 Cranch) 87, 128 (1810); Hylton v. United States, 3 U.S. (3 Dallas) 171, 175 (1796). See Thayer, The Origin and Scope of the American Doctrine of Constitutional Law, 7 Harv. L. Rev. 129 (1893).

5. Statutory rules are much narrower than constitutional principles, and the entire community relies on the first comprehensive interpretation of a statute by the highest court as a controlling precedent. Consequently, the highest court considers itself bound to follow this precedent in later similar cases. The legislature is expected to amend or replace statutes that it feels the highest court has misinterpreted. See E.H. Levi, Introduction to Legal Reasoning 27–33 (1961).

6. Northern Virginia Reg. Pk. Auth. v. United States Civ. Serv. Com., 437 F2d 1346, 1350 (4th Cir. 1971), cert. denied, 403 U.S. 936 (1971).

7. See chapter 1, notes 11 and 12, and accompanying text.

8. Graves v. New York, 306 U.S. 466, 491–492 (1939), overruling Dobbins v. Commissioners of Erie County, 41 U.S. (16 Pet.), 435 (1842); Collector v. Day 78 U.S. (11 Wall.) 113 (1871); New York ex rel. Rogers v. Graves, 299 U.S. 401 (1937); Brush v. Commissioner, 300 U.S. 352 (1937).

9. 247 U.S. 251 (1918), *overruled in* United States v. Darby, 312 U.S. 100 (1941).

10. Scott v. Sandford, 60 U.S. (19 How.) 393 (1857).

11. Congressional Globe, 39th Cong., 1st Sess., 3917 (July 19, 1866).

12. Douglas, Stare Decisis, 49 Colum. L. Rev. 735, 736 (1949). See License Cases, 46 U.S. (5 How.) 504, 612 (1847) (Daniel, J.).

13. Only four amendments have been passed specifically to overrule Supreme Court decisions: the Eleventh to overrule Chisholm v. Georgia, 2 U.S. (2 Dall.) 419 (1793); the Fourteenth, Sec. 1, to overrule Scott v. Sandford, 60 U.S. (19 How.) 393 (1857); the Sixteenth to overrule Pollock v. Farmers' Loan & Trust Co., 157 U.S. 429 (1895), 158 U.S. 601 (1895); the Twenty-sixth to overrule Oregon v. Mitchell, 400 U.S. 112 (1970).

14. Burnet v. Coronado Oil & Gas Co.: 285 U.S. 393, 406–8 (1932) (dissenting opinion), *overruled* in Helvering v. Mountain Producers Corp., 303 U.S. 376 (1938). Other justices have reiterated this view on overruling constitutional error. Justice Reed, for the Court, held racial discrimination in party primary elections to violate the Fifteenth Amendment. In overruling Grovey v. Townsend, 295 U.S. 45 (1935), he commented: "In constitutional questions, where correction depends upon amendment and not upon legislative action, this Court throughout its history has freely exercised its power to reexamine the basis of its constitutional decisions. This has long been accepted practice, and this practice has continued to this day" (Smith v. Allwright, 321 U.S. 649, 655 [1944]).

Justice Black contrasted statutory and constitutional method as follows: "I do not believe that the principle of stare decisis forecloses all reconsiderations of earlier decisions. In the area of constitutional law, for example, where the only alternative to action by this Court is the laborious process of constitutional amendment and where the ultimate responsibility rests with this Court, I believe reconsideration is always proper" (Boys Markets v. Retail Clerks Union, 398 U.S. 235, 259 [1970]).

15. Passenger Cases, 48 U.S. (7 How.) 283, 470 (1849). Two years later, Chief Justice Taney, writing for the Court, adopted the principle of rejecting constitutional stare decisis when he expressly overruled the decision in The Steamboat Thomas Jefferson, 23 U.S. (10 Wheat.) 428 (1825). He explained the rationale of overruling:

> It is the decision in the case of *The Thomas Jefferson* which mainly embarrasses the court in the present inquiry. We are sensible of the great weight to which it is entitled. But at the same time we are convinced that, if we follow it, we follow an erroneous decision into which the court fell, when the great importance of the question as it now presents itself could not be foreseen; and the subject did not therefore receive that deliberate consideration which at this time would have been given to it by the eminent men who presided here when that case was decided. . . . And as we are convinced that the former decision was founded in error, and that the error, if not corrected, must produce serious public as well as private inconvenience and loss, it becomes our duty not to perpetuate it.

Genesee Chief v. Fitzhugh, 53 U.S. (12 How.) 443, 456, 459 (1851).

16. See Blaustein and Field, "Overruling" Opinions in the Supreme Court, 57 Mich. L. Rev. 151 (1958); L. Jayson et al., eds., The Constitution of the United States of America: Analysis and Interpretation 1790–97 (S. Doc. 92–82, 92d Cong., 2d Sess. 1973) and supplement (1983).

17. 304 U.S. 64 (1938).

18. 41 U.S. (16 Pet.) 1 (1842). See chapter 7, which notes that *Swift* was a law-merchant case, a class distinct from the common law, and was the one case that should not have been overruled.

19. Jackson, Decisional Law and Stare Decisis, 30 A.B.A. J. 334 (1944).

20. Many commentators have noted the intention fallacy. For example, Charles Curtis writes: "The intention of the framers of the Constitution, even assuming we could discover what it was, when it is not adequately expressed in the Constitution, that is to say, what they meant when they did not say it, surely that has no binding force upon us. If we look behind or beyond what they set down in the document, prying into what else they wrote and what they said, anything we may find is only advisory. They may sit in at *our* councils. There is no reason why we should eavesdrop on theirs" (Lions under the Throne 2 [1947]). See T. Cooley, A Treatise on the Constitutional Limitations 80–81 (6th ed. 1890); Kelly, Clio and the Court: An Illicit Love Affair, 1965 Sup. Ct. Rev. 119; Wofford, The Blinding Light: The Uses of History in Constitutional Interpretation, 31 U. Chi. L. Rev. 502 (1964); Anderson, The Intention of the Framers, 49 Am. Pol. Sci. Rev. 340 (1955).

21. See R. Berger, Federalism 15–17 (1987); R. Berger, Government by Judiciary 7–9, 363–72, 411–12 (1977); Monaghan, Our Perfect Constitution, 56 N.Y.U. L. Rev. 353, 375–81 (1981). See critique in Murphy, Constitutional Interpretation, 87 Yale L. J. 1752 (1978).

22. James Madison to Thomas Ritchie, Sept. 15, 1821, in Farrand III, 447.

23. United States v. Wong Kim Ark, 169 U.S. 649, 699 (1898).

24. See Powell, The Original Understanding of Original Intent, 98 Harv. L. Rev. 885, 894–96 (1985).

25. J. Powell, Essay upon the Law of Contracts and Agreements 372–73 (1790).

26. Hotchkiss v. National City Bank of New York, 200 F. 287, 293 (S.D.N.Y. 1911).

27. See Powell, *supra* note 24, at 897–902.

28. See Stigler, The Theory of Economic Regulation, 5 Bell J. Econ. & Mgmnt. Sci. 335 (1974).

29. Henry Adams reports the following comment of his time about congressmen: "You can't use tact with a congressman! A congressman is a hog! You must take a stick and hit him on the snout!" (H. Adams, The Education of Henry Adams: An Autobiography 261 [1918]).

30. Schwegmann Bros. v. Calvert Distillers Corp., 341 U.S. 384, 396 (1951).

31. See citations in Powell, *supra* note 24, at 903–13.

32. See G. Wood, The Creation of the American Republic, 524–43 (1969).

33. See Bork, Neutral Principles and Some First Amendment Problems, 47 Ind. L. J. 1, 8 (1971); Linde, Judges, Critics, and the Realist Tradition, 82 Yale L. J. 227, 254 (1972); Ely, The Wages of Crying Wolf, 83 Yale L. J. 920, 949 (1973); Laycock, Taking Constitutions Seriously, 59 Texas L. Rev. 343 (1981); Monaghan, Our Perfect Constitution, 56 N.Y.U. L. Rev. 353 (1981); Wallace, The Jurisprudence of Judicial Restraint, 50 Geo. Wash L. Rev. 1 (1981); White, Law as Language, 60 Texas L. Rev. 415 (1982); Nagel, Interpretation and Importance in Constitutional Law, in Liberal Democracy, Nomos 25, 181 (J. Pennock and J. Chapman, eds. 1983). See generally, L. Hand, How Far Is a Judge Free in Rendering a Decision? in The Spirit of Liberty 103 (2d ed. 1953).

34. H. Black, A Constitutional Faith 1 (1968); R. Epstein, Takings, ch. 3 (1985); M. Merrill, Constitutional Interpretation: The Obligation to Respect the Text, in Perspectives of Law 260 (R. Pound et al., eds. 1964).

35. See M. Farrand, The Framing of the Constitution of the United States, ch. 9 (1913).

36. Wright v. United States, 302 U.S. 583, 588 (1938), quoting Holmes v. Jennison, 39 U.S. (14 Pet.) 540, 570–71 (1840). See Martin v. Hunter's Lessee, 14 U.S. (1 Wheat.) 304, 333–34 (1816).

37. U.S. Const., art. I, § 2 & 3; art. II, § 1.

38. On the theory of two types of clauses, see Corwin, Judicial Review in Action, 74 U. Pa. L. Rev. 639, 659–60 (1926); Monaghan, *supra,* note 33, at 361–67.

39. U.S. Const., art. I, § 8.

40. U.S. Const., art. I, § 9.

41. T. Rutherforth, Institutes of Natural Law, II, ch. 7 (1756); M. Bacon, A New Abridgement of The Laws of England (3rd ed. 1768).

42. J. Story, Commentaries on the Constitution of the United States, I, ch. 5 (1833) [hereinafter cited as Story].

43. Stuart v. Laird 5 U.S. (1 Cranch.) 299, 309 (1803); Martin v. Hunter's Lessee 14 U.S. (1 Wheat.) 304 (1816); Cohens v. Virginia, 19 U.S. (6 Wheat.) 264, 418–21 (1821).

44. Story, I: 390.

45. See chapter 5.

46. See chapter 11 on the distinction between expanded procedural protections to meet the needs of a changing society and the illegitimate creation of substantive due process.

47. Miranda v. Arizona, 384 U.S. 436 (1966).

48. O. Holmes, Theory of Legal Interpretation, in Collected Legal Papers 203, 204, 207 (1920).

49. Story, I: 383.

50. Story, I: 387.

51. Story, I: 404. See Conant, Systems Analysis in the Appellate Decisionmaking Process, 24 Rutgers L. Rev. 293, 317 (1970).

52. H. Maine, Popular Government 253 (1886).

53. W. McKechnie, Magna Carta, ch. 39 (2d ed. 1914). See E. Corwin, Liberty against Government (1948); R. Pound, The Development of Constitutional Guarantees of Liberty (1957); C. Stevens, Source of the Constitution of the United States (1894).

54. See chapter 1, notes 16 and 17.

55. Story, I: 393. See Posner, Economics, Politics and the Reading of Statutes and the Constitution, 49 U. of Chi. L. Rev. 263, 282 (1982).

56. Story, I: 404.

57. The rules of interpretation, which Justice Story explains in detail, are stated here in summary form:

1. Where the power is granted in general terms, the power is to be construed as coextensive with the terms, unless some clear restriction upon it is deducible from the context.

2. A power given in general terms is not to be restricted to particular cases merely because it may be susceptible of abuse, and if abused, may lead to mischievous consequences.

3. On the other hand, a rule of equal importance is not to enlarge the construction of a given power beyond the fair scope of its terms merely because the restriction is inconvenient, impolitic, or even mischievous.

4. No construction of a given power is to be allowed which plainly defeats or impairs its avowed objects.

5. Where a power is remedial in its nature, it should be construed liberally.
6. In the interpretation of a power, all the ordinary and appropriate means to execute it are to be deemed a part of the power itself.
7. In the interpretation of the Constitution, there is no solid objection to implied powers.
8. Exclusive delegation of power to the federal government would only exist in three cases: where the Constitution in express terms granted an exclusive authority to the Union; where it granted in one instance an authority to the Union, and in another prohibited the states from exercising the like authority; and where it granted an authority to the Union in which similar authority in the states would be absolutely and totally *contradictory* and *repugnant*.
9. In order to ascertain how far an affirmative or negative provision excludes others or implies others, we must look to the nature of the provision, the subject matter, the objects, and the scope of the instrument.
10. The natural import of a single clause is not to be narrowed so as to exclude implied powers resulting from its character simply because there is another clause, which enumerates certain powers, which might otherwise be deemed implied powers within its scope.
11. Every word employed in the Constitution is to be expounded in its plain, obvious, and common sense, unless the context furnishes some ground to control qualify, or enlarge it.
12. Define words in reference to the context, and shape the particular meaning so as to make it fit that of the connecting words and agree with the subject matter.
13. Where clearly technical words are used, the technical meaning is to be applied to them, unless it is repelled by the context.
14. It is not a correct rule of interpretation to construe the same word in the same sense wherever it occurs in the same instrument.
15. A constitution of government does not, and cannot, from its nature, depend in any great degree upon more verbal criticism, or upon the import of single words. Story, I: 407–41.

58. U.S. Const., amendment 14, § 1. See chapter 12.

59. See R. Berger, *supra* note 21, ch. 10.

60. See *supra* note 44 and accompanying text.

61. See E. Levi, *supra* note 5, at 58. A significant counterexample is the implied recognition of slavery in the Constitution of 1787.

62. Wright, Professor Bickel, The Scholarly Tradition and the Supreme Court, 84 Harv. L. Rev. 769, 784–85 (1971).

63. See Bickel, The Original Understanding and the Segregation Decision, 69 Harv. L. Rev. 1 (1955).

64. See chapter 12.

65. 163 U.S. 537, 559 (1896), *overruled* in Gayle v. Browder, 352 U.S. 903 (1956).

66. K. Llewellyn, The Common Law Tradition 374 (1960).

67. Wright, *supra* note 62. 785–786. See Wofford, The Blinding Light, 31 U. Chi. L. Rev. 502, 425–427 (1964).

68. Oneida Indian Nation of N.Y. v. State of N.Y., 649 F. Supp. 420, 427 (N. D. N.Y. 1986).

69. See R. Perry and J. Cooper, Sources of Our Liberties (1952); C. Stevens, Sources of the Constitution of the United States, ch. 6 (1894).

70. As Judge Wright noted: "Naturally there will be differences over purposes and underlying political theories of the various constitutional protections. But they will be reasoned differences, subject to argument. . . . Judicial decisions of which we disapprove can best be challenged on their merits, and in a wholly reasonable manner. Arguments over purposes and theories will be healthy, aiding both judges and the political officials who appoint them" (Wright, *supra* note 62, at 786–87).

71. Sturges v. Crowninshield, 17 U.S. (4 Wheat.) 122, 202 (1819).

72. Compare R. Berger, Federalism, ch. 6 (1987).

73. 83 U.S. (16 Wall.) 36 (1873).

74. "We doubt very much whether any action of a state not directed by way of discrimination against the negroes as a class, or on account of their race, will ever be held to come within the purview of this provision." (*Id.* at 81).

75. J. Ely, Democracy and Distrust: A Theory of Judicial Review, chs. 4 and 5 (1980).

76. 313 U.S. 299.

77. *Id.* at 317–18.

78. *Id.* at 315–16.

79. M. Curtis, No State Shall Abridge, chs. 1 and 2 (1986). See Graham, The Early Antislavery Backgrounds of the Fourteenth Amendment, 1950 Wis. L. Rev. 479, 610, reprinted in H. J. Graham, Everyman's Constitution, ch. 4 (1968); R. Kaczorowski, The Politics of Judicial Interpretation (1985); Kelly, Clio and the Court, 1965 Sup. Ct. Rev. 119, 132–34; Yarbrough, The Fourteenth Amendment and Incorporation, 30 U. Miami L. Rev. 231 (1976).

80. 332 U.S. 46, 68–123 (1947). See Fairman, Does the Fourteenth Amendment Incorporate the Bill of Rights? 2 Stan. L. Rev. 5 (1949). Compare Crosskey, Charles Fairman "Legislative History" and the Constitutional Limitations on State Authority, 22 U. Chi. L. Rev. 1 (1954).

81. 17 U.S. (4 Wheat.) 316 (1819).

82. Fairbank v. United States, 181 U.S. 283, 288–89 (1901) (stamp tax on foreign bills of lading held a tax on exports violating art. I, § 9).

83. 71 U.S. (4 Wall.) 2 (1866).

84. 323 U.S. 283 (1944).

85. 323 U.S. 214 (1944). See J. ten Broek, E. Barnhart and F. Matson, Prejudice, War and the Constitution, ch. 6 (1954).

86. E. Vattel, Law of Nations, bk. I, sec. 228 (Chitty ed. 1870). See, e.g., Rex v. Lewis, 168 Eng. Rep. 1308 (1932); People v. Baum, 251 Mich. 187, 231 N.W. 95 (1930).

87. McCulloch v. Maryland, 17 U.S. (4 Wheat.) 316, 429 (1819).

88. See Acker v. C. I. R. 258 F. 2d 568, 577 (6th Cir. 1958).

89. Panhandle Oil Co. v. State of Mississippi ex rel. Knox, 277 U.S. 218, 223 (1928) (dissenting opinion), *overruled,* Alabama v. King & Boozer, 314 U.S. 1 (1941).

90. Baltimore & Ohio R. Co. v. United States, 345 U.S. 146 (1953).

91. Louisville Joint Stock Land Bank v. Radford, 295 U.S. 555 (1935).

92. 310 U.S. 586 (1940).

93. See Exodus, 20: 4–5.

94. 310 U.S. at 591.

95. *Id.* at 599 (footnote omitted).

96. 319 U.S. 624 (1943).

97. *Id.* at 638.

98. *Id.* at 639.

99. *Id.*

100. 25 U.S. (12 Wheat.) 213 (1827).

101. 290 U.S. 398 (1934).

102. 379 U.S. 497 (1965).

103. O. Holmes, Jr., Collected Legal Papers 295–96 (1920).

104. 17 U.S. (4 Wheat.) 316, 436 (1819).

105. 22 U.S. (9 Wheat.) 1, 210–11 (1824).

106. 36 U.S. (11 Pet.) 102, 139 (1837), *overruled,* Edwards v. California, 314 U.S. 160 (1941).

107. 46 U.S. (5 How.) 504 (1847).

108. 78 U.S. (11 Wall.) 113, 124 (1870), *overruled,* Graves v. New York ex rel. O'Keefe, 306 U.S. 466 (1939).

109. 247 U.S. 251 (1918), *overruled,* United States v. Darby, 314 U.S. 100 (1941).

110. *Id.* at 123–24.

111. 317 U.S. 341 (1943).

112. Ray v. Atlantic Richfield Co., 435 U.S. 151 (1978); Jones v. Rath Packing Co., 430 U.S. 519 (1977); Florida Lime & Avocado Growers, Inc. v. Paul, 373 U.S. 132 (1963); Hines v. Davidowitz, 312 U.S. 52 (1941).

113. The revered status of the antitrust laws was explained by Justice Marshall:

Antitrust laws in general, and the Sherman Act in particular, are the Magna Carta of free enterprise. They are as important to the preservation of economic freedom and our free-enterprise system as the Bill of Rights is to the protection of our fundamental personal freedoms. And the freedom guaranteed each and every business, no matter how small, is the freedom to complete—to assert with vigor, imagination, devotion, and ingenuity whatever economic muscle it can muster. Implicit in such freedom is the notion that it cannot be foreclosed with respect to one sector of the economy because certain private citizens or groups believe that such foreclosure might promote greater competition in a more important sector of the economy.

United States v. Topco Associates, Inc., 405 U.S. 596, 610 (1972).

114. 1933 Cal. Stat., ch. 754, *amended by* 1935 Cal. Stat., chs. 471, 743; 1938 Extra Sess., ch. 6; 1939 Cal. Stat., chs. 363, 548, 894; 1941 Cal. Stat., chs. 603, 1150, 1186 (current version at Cal. Agric. Code §§ 59641–662 (West 1968)).

115. "We find nothing in the language of the Sherman Act or in its history which suggests that its purpose was to restrain a state or its officers or agents from activities directed by its legislature" (*Parker,* 317 U.S. at 350–51).

116. "In a dual system of government in which, under the Constitution, the states are sovereign, save only as Congress may constitutionally subtract from their authority, an unexpressed purpose to nullify a state's control over its officers and agents is not lightly to be attributed to Congress" (*Id.* at 351).

117. *Parker,* 317 U.S. at 350.

118. See *supra* note 92.

119. *Parker,* 317 U.S. at 351.

120. On the presumptions against antitrust exemptions, see Group Life & Health Ins. Co. v. Royal Drug Co., 440 U.S. 205, 231 (1979). See also Carnation Co. v. Pacific Westbound Conf., 383 U.S. 213, 217–18 (1966), *modified,* 383 U.S. 932 (1966); California v. Federal Power Comm'n, 369 U.S. 482, 485 (1962).

121. "Sec. 1. Every contract, combination in the form of trust or otherwise, or conspiracy, in restraint of trade or commerce among the several States, or with foreign nations is hereby declared to be illegal" (15 U.S.C. § [1976]).

"Sec. 2. Every person who shall monopolize, or attempt to monopolize, or combine or conspire with any other person or persons, to monopolize any part of the trade or commerce among the several states, or with foreign nations, shall be deemed guilty of a felony" (15 U.S.C. § 2 [1976]).

122. See, e.g., Catalano, Inc. v. Target Sales, Inc., 446 U.S. 643 (1980); United States v. Topco Assocs., Inc., 405 U.S. 596 (1972); United States v. Socony-Vacuum Oil Co., 310 U.S. 150 (1940); United States v. Trenton Potteries Co., 273 U.S. 392 (1927). In light of the unswerving application of the per se illegality rule in price fixing cases both before and after Appalachian Coals, Inc. v. United States, 288 U.S. 344 (1933), that case must be considered a depression aberration and without value as precedent.

123. See *Parker*, 317 U.S. at 367–68.

Chapter 3

1. Muskrat v. United States, 219 U.S. 346 (1911); Massachusetts v. Mellon, 262 U.S. 447 (1923). See L. Levy, Judicial Review and the Supreme Court 1–42 (1967).

2. For an analysis of the literature on justice and efficiency, see R. Posner, The Economics of Justice 13–115 (1983).

3. The literature is reviewed in J. Agresto, The Supreme Court and Constitutional Democracy (1984); McCleskey, Judicial Review in a Democracy, 3 Houston L. Rev. 354 (1966). See Lindgren, Beyond Cases, 1983 Wis. L. Rev. 583, 585–91.

4. See W. McKecknie, Magna Carta, ch. 39 (2d ed. 1914). See *infra* note 53 and accompanying text.

5. On the creation of substantive due process, see chapter 11.

6. D. Lutz, The Origins of American Constitutionalism 92–95, 105–6 (1988); A. Dicey, Introduction to the Study of the Law of the Constitution, ch. 1 (7th ed. 1908); E. Wade and G. Phillips, Constitutional Law, ch. 4 (6th ed. 1960).

7. See C. Haines, The American Doctrine of Judicial Supremacy 27–28 (1932); R. Jackson, The Struggle for Judicial Supremacy, ch. 10 (1941); H. Commager, Majority Rule and Minority Rights (1943).

8. Roosevelt and Frankfurter 384 (M. Freedman, ed., 1967) (emphasis added). Frankfurter's charge of usurpation must be read in light of his earlier attack on those who had asserted that all judicial review was usurpation. Frankfurter, A Note on Advisory Opinions, 37 Harv. L. Rev. 1002, 1003, n. 4 (1924). See W. Hamilton and D. Adair, The Power to Govern, ch. 7 (1938).

9. O. Holmes, The Path of the Law (1897), reprinted in Collected Legal Papers 167, 184 (1920).

10. B. Twiss, Lawyers and the Constitution 168–70, 196–97 (1942); Cohen, Field Theory and Judicial Logic, 59 Yale L. J. 238, 244–45 (1950).

11. See chapter 5.

12. See chapter 11.

13. See L. Levy, ed., American Constitutional Law 130 (1966).

14. 5 U.S. (1 Cranch) 137 (1803).

15.

It is emphatically the province and duty of the judicial department to say what the law is. Those who apply the rule to particular cases must of necessity expound and interpret that rule. If two laws conflict with each other, the courts must decide on the operation of each.

So if a law be in opposition to the Constitution; if both the law and the Constitution apply to a particular case, so that the court must either decide that case conformably to the law, disregarding the Constitution; or conformably to the Constitution, disregarding the law; the court must determine which of these conflicting rules governs the case. This is of the very essence of judicial duty.

Id. at 177–78. See Nelson, The Eighteenth-Century Background of John Marshall's Constitutional Jurisprudence, 76 Mich. L. Rev. 893 (1978).

16. A. Bickel, The Least Dangerous Branch 1–14 (1962); R. McCloskey, The American Supreme Court 40–43 (1960); L. Hand, The Bill of Rights 3–6 (1958); T. Powell, Vagaries and Varieties in Constitutional Interpretation 12–23 (1956); H. Commager, Majority Rule and Minority Rights (1943); Thayer, The Origin and Scope of the American Doctrine of Constitutional Law, 7 Harv. L. Rev. 129 (1893).

17. See P. Bobbit, Constitutional Fate 7 (1982). This assumes, of course, that the appointed elite of the judiciary have limited interpretive functions and are not empowered to impose extra-constitutional moral standards on the elected legislature. Compare M. Perry, The Constitution, the Courts and Human Rights (1982).

18. The power to amend the Constitution is reserved to the people in Article V.

19. See chapter 7.

20. See Crandall v. Nevada, 73 U.S. (6 Wall.) 35, 44 (1868) (structure of national polity includes the right of citizens to travel unimpeded from state to state); C. Black, Structure and Relationship in Constitutional Law (1969).

21. For a detailed analysis of the supremacy clause as mandating national judicial review of state laws, see A. Bickel, The Least Dangerous Branch 8–10 (1962); C. Black, The People and The Court, ch. 5 (1960); W. Crosskey, Politics and the Constitution in the History of the United States, II, 984–90 (1953).

22. U.S. Constitution, article VI.

23. "The Senators and Representatives before mentioned, and the Members of the several State Legislatures, and all executive and judicial Officers, both of the United States and of the several States, shall be bound by Oath or Affirmation, to support this Constitution; but no religious Test shall ever be required as a Qualification to any Office of public Trust under the United States" (U.S. Const., article VI, cl. 3.

24. M. Farrand, The Records of the Federal Convention of 1787, I, 21 (1911) [cited hereinafter as Farrand]. This resolution received unanimous assent. *Id.* 54

25. Farrand, I: 164.

26. *Id.* at 168. The vote was 7 to 3 with one delegation divided.

27. "That the legislative acts of the United States, made by virtue and in pursuance of the articles of union, and all treaties made and ratified under authority of the United States, shall be the supreme law of the respective states, so far as those acts or treaties shall relate to the said states or their citizens, and that the judiciaries of the several states shall be bound thereby in their decisions, any thing in the respective laws of the individual states to the contrary notwithstanding" *Id.* at II: 28–29.

28. *Id.* at III: 286–87.

29. *Id.* at II: 183.

30. *Id.* at II: 381–82.

31. "Section 2. [1] The judicial Power shall extend to all Cases, in Law and

Equity, arising under this Constitution, the Laws of the United States, and Treaties made, or which shall be made, under their authority; . . . [2] In all Cases affecting Ambassadors, other public Ministers and Consuls, and those in which a State shall be a Party, the supreme Court shall have original Jurisdiction. In all other Cases before mentioned, the supreme Court shall have appellate Jurisdiction, both as to Law and Fact, with such Exceptions, and under such Regulations as the Congress shall make" (U.S. Const., art. III).

32. 1 Stat. 85–88 (1789).

33. 14 U.S. (1 Wheat.) 304 (1816). See Cohens v. Virginia, 19 U.S. (6 Wheat.) 264 (1821). See generally, G. White, The Marshall Court and Cultural Change, 1815–35, History of the Supreme Court of the United States, III–IV, 495–524 (1988); C. Warren, The Supreme Court in United States History, I, 442–53, 547–64 (1926). See modern application in Cooper v. Aaron, 358 U.S. 1 (1958) (governor and legislature of Arkansas bound by Supreme Court decision forbidding enforced racial segregation in public schools).

34. Fairfax's Devisee v. Hunter's Lessee, 11 U.S. (7 Cranch) 603 (1812).

35. Crosskey, II, *supra* note 21, at 991–93. See the similar view of Taney in Ableman v. Booth, 62 U.S. (21 How.) 506, 520 (1858).

36. Bickel, *supra* note 16, at 9. A few members of the ratifying conventions spoke of "pursuant" in a narrower sense as a synonym of "consistent with," but none of these suggested that the Supreme Court would review the scope and breadth of the affirmative governing powers delegated to Congress. Furthermore, they did not pretend objective linguistic analysis. These delegates made persuasive speeches deliberately minimizing the scope of national power in order to induce other reluctant delegates to support ratification. See *infra*, notes 83 to 88. Compare R. Berger, Congress v. Supreme Court 228–36 (1969).

37. U.S. Const., art. I, § 8, par. 18.

38. Hylton v. United States, 3 U.S. (3 Dallas) 171 (1796), holding a carriage tax valid against attack under Article I, Sec. 9, Cl. 4.

39. A. Dicey, Introduction to the Study of the Law of the Constitution, chs. 4–7 (7th ed. 1908).

40. *Id.* at 183.

41. *Id.* at 189.

42. *Id.* at 191.

43. *Id.* at chs. 14 and 15.

44. A. Howard, The Road from Runnymede, ch. 1 (1968); A.Sutherland, Constitutionalism in America, ch. 8 (1965); R. Perry and J. Cooper, eds., Sources of Our Liberties (1959); R. Pound, The Development of Constitutional Guarantees of Liberty (1957).

45. Case of the Writs of Assistance, Quincey's Report 51–57 (Mass. 1761).

46. 8 Coke's Reports 107, 77 Eng. Rep. 638 (1610). See Smith, Dr. Bonham's Case and the Modern Significance of Lord Coke's Influence, 41 Wash. L. Rev. 297 (1966).

47. "As to Acts of Parliament. An Act against the Constitution is void; an act against natural equity is void; and if an act of Parliament should be made, in the very words of this petition, it would be void The executive Courts must pass such acts into disuse. 8 Rep. 118 from Viner. Reason or the common law to control an act of Parliament" (J. Adams, The Works of John Adams, II, 522 [C.F. Adams, ed. 1850]).

48. See E. Corwin, Liberty against Government 39 (1948).

49. 5 Journals of the Continental Congress 546, 547 (reprint 1906). Article VII of the first draft reads as follows: "The Inhabitants of each Colony shall

enjoy all the Rights, Liberties, Privileges, Immunities, and Advantages, in Trade, Navigation, and Commerce, in any other Colony, and in going to and from the same from and to any Part of the World, which the Natives of such Colony . . . enjoy."

50. Farrand, II: 582, 587–88; III, 143–44, 161–62 (Rev. ed. 1937).

51. See Dunbar, James Madison and the Ninth Amendment, 42 Va. L. Rev. 627 (1956).

52. See C. Stevens, Sources of the Constitution of the United States, ch. 8 (1894); R. Rutland, The Birth of the Bill of Rights, chs. 1 and 2 (1955).

53. Annals of Congress, I, 454 (1834). See Z. Chafee, How Human Rights Got into the Constitution 19–21 (1952).

54. Annals of Congress, I, 457 (1834).

55. T. Jefferson, Writings of Thomas Jefferson, V, 80–81 (P. Ford, ed. 1895). See Krislov, Jefferson and Judicial Review, 9 J. Pub. L. 374 (1960).

56. C. Warren, Congress, The Constitution and the Supreme Court, 91–93 (1925). Justice James Wilson contrasted British legislative supremacy with the United States Constitution as follows:

In the United States, the legislative authority is subjected to another control, beside that arising from natural and revealed law; it is subjected to the control arising from the constitution. From the constitution, the legislative department, as well as every other part of government, derives it power: by the constitution, the legislative, as well as every department, must be directed; of the constitution, no alteration by the legislature can be made or authorized. In our system of jurisprudence, these positions appear to be incontrovertible. The constitution is the supreme law of the land: to that supreme law every other power must be inferiour and subordinate.

J. Wilson, Works of James Wilson, I, 329 (R. McCloskey, ed. 1967).

57. U.S. Const., amend. V.

58. Field v. Clark, 143 U.S. 649 (1892). See Van Alstyne, A Critical Guide to Marbury v. Madison, 1969 Duke L. J. 1, 20.

59. See J. Choper, Judicial Review and the National Political Process 64 (1980).

60. 5 U.S. (1 Cranch) 137 (1803).

61. *Id.* at 179.

62. See L. Levy, ed., Judicial Review and the Supreme Court 8–10 (1967).

63. See C. Haines, The American Doctrine of Judicial Supremacy 88–121 (2d ed. 1932). Since many of these cases are not found in official reports, the citations will be to Haines.

64. Turner, A Phantom Precedent, 48 Am. L. Rev. 321 (1914). See Haines, *supra* note 63 at 89.

65. Scott, Holmes v. Walton, the New Jersey Precedent, 4 Am. Hist. Rev. 456 (1899). See Haines, *supra* note 63, at 92; Crosskey, II, *supra* note 21, at 948–52.

66. 4 Call. (Va.) 5 (1782).

67. (1784) in Select Cases of the Mayor's Court of New York City 302 (R. Morris, ed. 1935). See J. Goebel, The Law Practice of Alexander Hamilton: Documents and Commentary, I, 415 (1964).

68. Kirby (Conn.) 444–53 (1785).

69. J. Varnum, The Case, Trevett against Weeden (R.I. 1787). See Haines, *supra* note 63, at 105.

70. 1 Martin (N.C.) 42 (1787).

71. See *supra* note 63. See Ware v. Hylton, 3 U.S. (3 Dallas) 198 (1796),

explaining the later supremacy of treaties over state laws under Article VI, Clause 2 of the Constitution.

72. U.S. Const., amend. V.

73. U.S. Const., art. III.

74. Farrand, I: 97.

75. See Corwin, The Supreme Court and Unconstitutional Laws of Congress, 4 Mich. L. Rev. 616, 620 (1906); L. Boudin, Government by Judiciary, I, 114 (1932); R. Berger, *supra* note 36, at 154–65; W. Crosskey, II, *supra* note 21, at 1002–7.

76. 5 U.S. (1 Cranch) 137 (1803). See R. Clinton, Marbury v. Madison and Judicial Review (1989).

77. 1 Stat. 81, Sec. 13 (1789). See United States v. Lawrence, 3 U.S. (3 Dallas) 42 (1795). See generally, A. Beveridge, The Life of John Marshall, III, ch. 3 (1919); G. Haskins and H. Johnson, Foundations of Power, John Marshall, 1801–1815, History of the Supreme Court of the United States, Vol. II, part 1, ch. 6 (1981).

78. See E. Corwin, The Doctrine of Judicial Review 4–10 (1914); W. Crosskey, II, *supra* note 21, at 1035–46; Van Alstyne, A Critical Guide to Marbury v. Madison, 1969 Duke L. J. 1; Bloch and Marcus, John Marshall's Selective Use of History in Marbury v. Madison, 1986 Wis. L. Rev. 301.

79. See Nelson, The Eighteenth-Century Background of John Marshall's Constitutional Jurisprudence, 76 Mich. L. Rev. 893, 936–42 (1978).

80. See L. Boudin, I, *supra* note 75 at 230–33; Van Alstyne, *supra* note 78 at 34.

81. 5 U.S. (1 Cranch) at 165–66.

82. "The interpretation of the laws is the proper and peculiar province of the courts. A constitution is, in fact, and must be regarded by the judges, as a fundamental law. It therefore belongs to them to ascertain its meaning, as well as the meaning of any particular act proceeding from the legislative body. If there should happen to be an irreconcilable variance between the two, that which has the superior obligation and validity ought, of course, to be preferred; or, in other words, the Constitution ought to be preferred to the statute, the intention of the people to the intention of their agents" Federalist 78, book 2 at 101 (Bourne ed. 1947). See Nelson, *supra* note 15, at 937.

83. See J. Smith, The Spirit of American Government 73–85 (1911); Trickett, Judicial Dispensation from Congressional Statutes, 41 Am. L. Rev. 65, 83 (1907).

84. At the convention, Madison said: "Experience in all the States had evinced a powerful tendency in the Legislature to absorb all power into its vortex. This was the real source of danger to the American Constitutions; & suggested the necessity of giving every defensive authority to the other departments that was consistent with republican principles" (Farrand, II: 74). See R. Berger, *supra* note 36 at 8–12.

85. The leading historian of the Constitutional Convention commented: "Hamilton was out of touch with the situation. He was aristocratic rather than democratic, and while his ideas may have been excellent, they were too radical for the convention and found but little support" (M. Farrand, The Framing of the Constitution of the United States 197 [1913]). See J. Sparks, The Life of Gouverneur Morris, III, 260–62 (1832).

86. Federalist 78, *supra* note 82, at 99. Hamilton reiterated: "It proves incontestably that the judiciary is beyond comparison the weakest of the three departments of power" (*Id.*) See Bickel, *supra* note 16.

87. An objective theory of constitutional interpretation precludes taking comments on the Constitution at face value. The legal context and circumstances

under which constitutional language was adopted does not include subsequent comments on the language itself. See O. Holmes, Theory of Legal Interpretation (1899), reprinted in Collected Legal Papers 203, 204, 207 (1920); ten Broek, Admissibility and Use by the United States Superior Court of Extrinsic Aids in Constitutional Construction, 26 Calif. L. Rev. 287 (1938).

88. See, e.g., Hamilton's minimization of the significance of the supremacy clause of Article VI, Cl. 2 in Federalist 33, at 214–15 (Bourne ed. 1947). See generally, Billias, The Federalists (1970).

89. J. Choper, Judicial Review and the National Political Process, ch. 6 (1980).

90. 2 U.S. (2 Dallas) 409 (1792). See Keller v. Potomac Electric Power Co., 261 U.S. 428 (1923).

91. American Insurance Co. v. Canter, 26 U.S. (1 Peters) 511 (1828); Lockerty v. Phillips, 319 U.S. 182 (1943).

92. Northern Pipeline Const. Co. v. Marathon Pipe Line Co., 458 U.S. 50 (1982).

93. R. Jackson, The Supreme Court in the American System of Government 22 (1955); Bickel, *supra* note 16, at 5–6; Crosskey, II, *supra* note 21, at 983; Hand, *supra* note 16, at 10.

94. See Nelson, Changing Conceptions of Judicial Review, 120 U. Pa. L. Rev. 1166 (1972).

95. Farrand, II: 186. Except for omitting the Constitution, the proposed jurisdictional clause was limited to classes of cases and controversies similar to those that were eventually ratified in Article III, Section 2. The language indicates a general understanding of following the English practice of limiting courts to actual adversary litigation.

96. Farrand, II: 430.

97. *Id.* It seems clear that "cases of a judiciary nature" did not refer to the "case-or-controversy" rule, barring advisory opinions. See *supra* note 95.

98. Madison on Jefferson's Draft of a Constitution for Virginia, Papers of Thomas Jefferson, VI, 315 (Boyd ed. 1955). See Miller, Cases of a Judiciary Nature, 8 St. Louis U. Pub. L. Rev. 47 (1989).

99. Annals of Congress, I, 520 (1834). One day earlier, Madison had emphasized the same point: "The legislative powers are vested in Congress, and are to be exercised by them uncontrolled by any other department, except the constitution has qualified it otherwise. The constitution has qualified the legislative power, by authorizing the President to object to any act it may pass, requiring, in this case, two-thirds of both Houses to concur in making a law; but still the absolute legislative power is vested in the Congress with this qualification alone" (*Id.* at 481). See G. Anastaplo, The Constitutionalist 54–65 (1971).

100. Jefferson to Mrs. Adams, Sept. 11, 1804, Writings of Thomas Jefferson, VIII, 311 (Ford ed. 1897). See D. Morgan, Congress and the Constitution 71–82 (1966).

101. Farrand, II: 73 (emphasis added).

102. H. Maine, Popular Government 253 (1886). The Constitution must be interpreted as a unified whole within the English constitutional and common-law legal environment of its adoption. *Ex Parte* Grossman, 267 U.S. 87, 108–9 (1925); United States v. Wong Kim Ark, 169 U.S. 649, 668–72 (1898). See the comments of Justice Henry Baldwin, Origin and Nature of the Constitution and Government of the United States 9 L. Ed. 869, 893–94 (1837).

103. See A. Dicey, Introduction to the Law of the Constitution, ch. 1 (7th ed. 1908); C. McIlwain, The High Court of Parliament and Its Supremacy, ch. 5

(1910). Concerning the presumption that the same legal system would stay in force in the former colonies until changed by affirmative law, see Blankard v. Galdy, 91 Eng. Rep. 356, 357 (1693).

104. W. Blackstone, Commentaries on the Laws of England, I, 49–52 (1st Am. ed. 1771–72). See W. Crosskey, II, *supra* note 21 at 1326 n. 3; Nolan, Sir William Blackstone and the New Republic, 51 N.Y.U. L. Rev. 731 (1976).

105. See W. Crosskey, II, *supra* note 21, at 1325, n. 25; D. Lutz, The Origins of American Constitutionalism 92–95 (1988).

106. See A. Vanderbilt, The Doctrine of the Separation of Powers and its Present-Day Significance (1953); Sharp, The Classical American Doctrine of "The Separation of Powers," 2 U. of Chi. L. Rev. 385 (1935).

107. 5 U.S. (1 Cranch) 137 (1803).

108. See E. Corwin, Court over Constitution 6–7, 69–73 (1938); L. Hand, The Bill of Rights 4 (1958).

109. Rejecting Chief Justice Marshall's statements in Marbury v. Madison, Bickel asserts:

> Far from supporting Marshall, the oath is perhaps the strongest textual argument against him. For it would seem to obligate each of these officers, in the performance of his own function, to support the Constitution. . . . [I]t may be deduced that everyone is to construe the Constitution with finality insofar as it addresses itself to the performance of his own peculiar function. Surely the language lends itself more readily to this interpretation than to Marshall's apparent conclusion, that everyone's oath to support the Constitution is qualified by the judiciary's oath to do the same, and that every official of government is sworn to support the Constitution as the judges, in pursuance of the same oath, have construed it, rather than as his own conscience may dictate.

Bickel, *supra* note 16 at 8. This critique adopts the views of J. Gibson in Eakin v. Raub, 12 S.&R. 330, 353 (Pa. 1825) (dissent).

110. "The President acting in his executive capacity may yield to the opinion of the Court and accept its decisions as practically a part of the Constitution; but under the theory of the separation of powers he is not under strict technical constitutional obligation. He too can interpret the Constitution. . . . The President is no more bound by an unconstitutional law than is the Court. Johnson refused to be bound by the Tenure of Office Act, though it was passed by a two-thirds vote over his veto. No one probably would deny now that in so refusing he was within his constitutional power" (A. McLaughlin, The Courts, the Constitution and Parties 60–61 [1912]).

111. M., K. & T. Ry. Co. v. May, 194 U.S. 267, 270 (1904). See J. Thayer, John Marshall 98 (1904).

112. Messages and Papers of the Presidents, II, 581–82 (J.D. Richardson, ed. 1897).

113. Scott v. Sandford, 60 U.S. (19 How.) 393 (1857).

114. J. Richardson, ed., Messages and Papers of the Presidents, VI, 9 (1897).

115. See W. Crosskey, II, *supra* note 21, at 1013–18; R. Berger, *supra* note 36, at 49–63.

116. 1 Stat. 85–88 (1789). See W.W. Crosskey, II, *supra* note 21 at 1029–35.

117. D. Morgan, *supra* note 100, at 82–89.

118. 17 U.S. (4 Wheat.) 316 (1819).

119. See C. Black, Structure and Relationship in Constitutional Law 14 (1969).

120. W. Smith, Economic Aspects of the Second Bank of the United States, ch. 12 (1953).

121. McCulloch, 17 U.S. at 407.

122. See Federalist 33 at 212–13 (Bourne ed. 1947). Hamilton, in a structural analysis wrote that the clause is "only declaratory of a truth which would have resulted by necessary and unavoidable implication from the very act of constituting a federal government, and vesting it with certain specified powers. . . . The declaration itself, though it may be chargeable with tautology, or redundancy, is at least perfectly harmless" (*Id.*).

123. McCulloch, 17 U.S. at 415.

124. *Id.* at 421.

125. See the similar examples of Hamilton in Federalist 33 at 213–14 (Bourne ed. 1947).

126. U.S. Const., amend. X.

127. On the presumptions in favor of national regulation and against the Tenth Amendment, see Hodel v. Virginia Surface Min. and Reclam. Ass'n, 452 U.S. 264, 266–67 (1981); United States v. Darby, 312 U.S. 100, 123–24 (1941). On the general presumption of constitutionality and the proof that should be needed to rebut it, see Thayer, *supra* note 16.

128. "Marshall's opinion in Marbury v. Madison satisfactorily explained judicial refusal to give effect, in litigation before a court, to a governmental act inconsistent with the Constitution, but not why such a determination of unconstitutionality binds the other branches of the government. This power, which is the essential element of judicial review of constitutionality, is difficult to reconcile with the theory of the judiciary as a coordinate branch of government, which is so clearly the theory of the Constitution of the United States and of all the State constitutions. No attempt at reconciliation has ever satisfactorily met Mr. Justice Gibson's analysis in Eakin v. Raub (12 S. & R. 330, 334 *et seq.* [Pa. 1825])." Strong, Judicial Review: A Tri-Dimensional Concept of Administrative-Constitutional Law, 69 W.Va. L. Rev. 111, 118–19 (1967). See Kutler, John Bannister Gibson, 14 J. Pub. Law 181 (1965); W. Meigs, The Relation of the Judiciary to the Constitution, ch. 10 (1919).

129. West Coast Hotel Co. v. Parrish (300 U.S. 379), in overruling Adkins v. Children's Hospital (261 U.S. 525) made the District of Columbia minimum-wage law of the latter case again valid and enforceable. 39 Opinions of the Atty. Gen. 22 (1937). See O. Field, The Effect of an Unconstitutional Statute (1935).

130. H. Commager, *supra* note 7.

131. See, *e.g.,* J. Frank, Law and the Modern Mind (1930).

132. See C. Black, *supra* note 21; Rostow, The Democratic Character of Judicial Review, 56 Harv. L. Rev. 193 (1952).

133. B. Cardozo, The Nature of the Judicial Process 92–94 (1921).

134. L. Hand, The Spirit of Liberty 164 (2d ed. 1953).

135. See Dennis v. United States, 341 U.S. 494 (1951); Korematsu v. United States, 323 U.S. 214 (1944).

136. Worcester v. Georgia, 31 U.S. (6 Pet.) 515 (1832). See C. Warren, *supra* note 33, ch. 19 (1926).

137. 5 U.S. (1 Cranch) 137 (1803).

138. See C. Wolfe, The Rise of Modern Judicial Review (1986).

139. For an argument for termination of judicial review of legislation, see Haines, Judicial Review of Acts of Congress and the Need for Constitutional Reform, 45 Yale L. J. 816, 852–56 (1936).

140. United States v. Sanchez, 340 U.S. 42 (1950); Wickard v. Filburn, 317 U.S. 111 (1942).

Chapter 4

1. (1913) (Reissued 1935) [cited hereinafter as Beard].

2. See M. Blinkoff, The Influence of Charles A. Beard upon American Historiography, ch. 2 (1936).

3. See R. Brown, Charles Beard and the Constitution (1956); F. McDonald, We the People (1958).

4. Beard at 6.

5. Beard, ch. 2.

6. Beard at 324.

7. Beard, chs. 3–5.

8. Brown, *supra* note 3, ch. 5.

9. *Id.* at 89.

10. McDonald, *supra* note 3, at 349.

11. U.S.Const. art I, § 10.

12. McDonald, *supra* note 3 at 350–55.

13. *Id.* at 355–57.

14. Brown, *supra* note 3, at 95. See D. Adair, The Tenth Federalist Revisited, in Fame and the Founding Fathers 75 (1974).

15. J. Locke, The Second Treatise of Government 18 (J. Gough ed. 1966).

16. J. Madison, Federalist 10, at 64–65 (E. Bourne ed. 1947).

17. M. Farrand, Records of the Federal Convention of 1787, I, 486, 601 (1911).

18. J. Madison, Federalist 10, at 69–70.

19. See, e.g., Singer Sewing Machine Co. v. Brickell, 233 U.S. 304, 316 (1914).

20. W. Blackstone, Commentaries on the Law of England, II, 1 (A. Simpson ed. 1979) [hereinafter cited W. Blackstone, Commentaries]. See J. Reid, Constitutional History of the American Revolution, I, 44–46 (1986); K. Minogue, The Concept of Property and its Contemporary Significance, in Property, Nomos 22, 3 (J. Pennock and J. Chapman eds. 1980); Burns, Blackstone's Theory of the "Absolute" Rights of Property, 54 Cin. L. Rev. 67 (1985).

21. Blackstone labels the two classes as corporeal and incorporeal. He asserts that there were then ten principal sorts of incorporeal property rights. W. Blackstone, Commentaries, II, ch. 3.

22. See Cohen, Dialogue on Private Property, 9 Rutgers L. Rev. 373 (1954).

23. A. Honore, Ownership, in Oxford Essays in Jurisprudence, First Series 107 (A. Guest ed. 1961); L. Becker, The Moral Basis of Property Rights, in Property, Nomos 22, 187 (J. Pennock and J. Chapman eds. 1980).

24. Becker, *supra* note 23, at 190–91. See also L. Becker, Property Rights: Philosophic Foundations, ch. 2 (1977).

25. W. Blackstone, Commentaries, II, at 40.

26. Densmore v. Scofield, 102 U.S. 375, 378 (1880).

27. Roth v. Pritikin, 710 F. 2d 934, 939 (2d Cir. 1983).

28. West River Bridge v. Dix, 47 U.S. (6 How.) 507, 534 (1848); Monongahela Navigation Co. v. United States, 148 U.S. 312, 341 (1893); W. Blackstone, Commentaries II, 37–40.

29. Rea v. Missouri, 84 U.S. 532, 544 (1873). See Stoebuck, A General Theory of Eminent Domain, 47 Wash. L. Rev. 553, 599–606 (1972).

30. United States v. General Motors Corp., 323 U.S. 373, 377–78 (1945).

31. *Id.* at 378.

32. On the problems of defining physical invasion of another's property, see Miller v. Schoene, 276 U.S. 272 (1928). See the analysis of Buchanan, Politics, Property and the Law, 15 J. Law & Econ. 439 (1972).

33. See Sax, Takings and the Police Power, 74 Yale L. J. 36 (1964); Sax, Takings, Private Property and Public Rights, 81 Yale L. J. 149 (1971); Michelman, Property, Utility and Fairness, 80 Harv. L. Rev. 1165 (1967).

34. J. Locke, *supra* note 15, at 14–27. See Telly, The Classical Economic Model and the Nature of Property in the Eighteenth and Nineteenth Centuries, 13 Tulsa L. J. 406, 436–442 (1978).

35. J. Locke, *supra* note 15, at 15.

36. *Id.* at 16. See Rose, Possession as the Origin of Property, 52 U. of Chi. L. Rev. 73 (1985).

37. See R. Posner, Economic Analysis of Law 30 (3d ed. 1986).

38. See F. Knight, Risk, Uncertainty and Profit 332–35 (1921).

39. Lynch v. Household Finance Corp., 405 U.S. 538, 552 (1972). See Baker, Property and its Relation to Constitutionally Protected Liberty, 134 U. Pa. L. Rev. 741 (1986).

40. See Hardin, The Tragedy of the Commons, 162 Science 1243–48 (1968).

41. See D. North and R. Thomas, The Rise of the Western World (1973).

42. See Demsetz, Toward a Theory of Property Rights, 57 Am. Econ. Rev., Papers and Proceedings 347 (1967); Alchian and Demsetz, The Property Rights Paradigm, 33 J. Econ. History 16 (1973).

43. See Posner, *supra* note 37, at 30–33.

44. On transaction costs as an impediment to market remedies for negative externalities, see Coase, The Problem of Social Cost, 3 J. Law & Econ. 1 (1960); Demsetz, The Exchange and Enforcement of Property Rights, 7 J. Law & Econ. 11 (1964).

45. A. Simpson, Introduction to book II of W. Blackstone, Commentaries ix (1979). See Burns, Blackstone's Theory of the "Absolute" Rights of Property, 54 U. Cin. L. Rev. 67 (1985).

46. W. Blackstone, Commentaries, II, 2. See J. Reid, *supra* note 20, chs. 3–5.

47. M. Farrand, Records of the Federal Convention of 1787, I, 533 (G. Morris), 5–41 (R. King) (1911).

48. Vanhorne's Lessee v. Dorrance, 2 U.S. (2 Dall.) 304, 310 (C. C. Pa. 1795).

49. Wilkinson v. Leland, 27 U.S. (2 Pet.) 627, 657 (1829).

50. J. Adams, Works of John Adams, VI, 280 (C. Adams ed. 1851).

51. J. Story, A Discourse Pronounced at the Inauguration of the Author as Dane Professor of Law in Harvard University, August 25, 1829, in Miscellaneous Writings of Joseph Story 501, 519 (W. Story ed. 1852).

52. A. Howard, The Road from Runnymede, ch. 5 (1968); A. Sutherland, Constitutionalism in America (1965).

53. Declaration and Resolves of the First Continental Congress, Resolve 5 (October 14, 1774), in R. Perry and J. Cooper, Sources of Our Liberties 288 (1959).

54. On Private Revenge, Boston Gazette, Sept. 5, 1763, quoted in H. Colburn, The Lamp of Experience 25 (1965).

55. J. Madison, Federalist 10.

56. U.S. Const., art. I, § 10. See chapter 7 on the national monetary power.

57. U.S. Const., art. I, § 10. See chapter 8 on the contract clause.

58. J. Reid, *supra* note 20, 3–15; A. Howard, *supra* note 52, at ch. 10.

59. Howard at 220–231.

60. *Id.*, ch. 16.

61. U.S. Const., amend. 5.

62. See chapter 10 on the due process clause.

63. See A. Howard, *supra* note 52, at 38, 210. See also Grant, The "Higher Law" Background of the Law of Eminent Domain, 6 Wis. L. Rev. 67 (1931). Chapter 28 of the Magna Charta was stated as a protection for chattels and was later extended in British statutes for the public taking of real property. P. Nichols, Law of Eminent Domain I, §1.21 (3d ed. 1985). On the denial of compensation in colonial times for public roads through undeveloped lands that increased their value, see Treanor, The Origins and Original Significance of the Just Compensation Clause of the Fifth Amendment, 94 Yale L. J. 694, 695 (1985).

64. Chicago, B & Q. R. Co. v. Chicago, 166 U.S. 226 (1897).

65. J. Kent, Commentaries on American Law, II 425–31 (10th ed. 1860).

66. J. Story, Commentaries on the Constitution of the United States, II, §1790 (5th ed. 1891). See F. Hayek, The Constitution of Liberty 140–42 (1960).

67. Demorest v. City Bank Farmers Trust Co., 321 U.S. 36, 42–43 (1944).

68. 363 U.S. 603 (1960).

69. Social Security Act, 68 Stat. 1083 as amended, §201, 42 U.S.C. §401 (1983).

70. Social Security Act, §202n, 42 U.S.C. §402(n) (1983).

71. E. Vattel, Law of Nations, Bk. I, § 228 (Chitty ed. 1870). See, e.g., Rex v. Lewis, 1 Mood 372, 168 Eng. Rep. 1308 (Crown 1832); People v. Baum, 251 Mich. 187, 231 N.W. 95 (1930).

72. Nestor v. Folsom, 169 F. Supp. 922 (D.C.D.C. 1959).

73. 363 U.S. at 611.

74. *Id.* at 610.

75. *Id.*

76. It cannot "be deemed irrational for Congress to have concluded that the public purse should not be utilized to contribute to the support of those deported on the grounds specified in the statute" (*Id.* at 612).

77. Lynch v. United States, 292 U.S. 571 (1934); Samuels v. Quartin, 108 F.2d 789, 790 (2d Cir. 1940); Whitely v. United States, 214 F. Supp. 489 (W.D. Wash. 1963); Osgood v. Massachusetts Mut. Life Ins. Co., 93 N.H. 160, 37 A.2d 12, 13 (1944).

78. Lynch v. United States, 292 U.S. 571, 579 (1934). See comments of Justice Black, dissenting in Fleming, 363 U.S. at 622–623.

79. Long Island Water Supply Co. v. Brooklyn, 166 U.S. 685, 690 (1897). See W. Stoebuck, Nontrespassory Takings in Eminent Domain 132–33 (1977).

80. R. Epstein, Takings (1985); E. Paul, Property Rights and Eminent Domain (1987). Compare B. Ackerman, Private Property and the Constitution (1977); L. Tribe, Constitutional Choices 165–87 (1985).

81. See R. Posner, Economic Analysis of Law 48–53 (3d ed. 1986).

82. See R. Sherman, The Economics of Industry 287 (1974).

83. Munch, An Economic Analysis of Eminent Domain, 84 J. Pol. Econ. 473 (1976).

84. T. Cooley, Constitutional Limitations 479 (1968).

85. McCulloch v. Maryland, 17 U.S. (4 Wheat.) 316, 429 (1819).

86. See Martin v. District of Columbia, 205 U.S. 135, 139 (1907); Acker v. C.I.R., 258 F.2d 568, 577 (6th Cir. 1958).

87. Panhandle Oil Co. v. State of Mississippi ex rel. Knox, 277 U.S. 218, 223 (1928) (dissenting opinion), *overruled* Alabama v. King & Boozer, 314 U.S. 1 (1941).

88. Baltimore & Ohio R. Co. v. United States, 345 U.S. 146 (1953).

89. Louisville Joint Stock Land Bank v. Radford, 295 U.S. 555 (1935).

90. Pennsylvania Coal Co. v. Mahon, 260 U.S. 393, 413 (1922).

91. Lockner v. New York, 198 U.S. 45, 53 (1905).

92. Munn v. Illinois, 94 U.S. 113 (1877).

93. See Federal Power Commission v. Hope Natural Gas Co., 320 U.S. 591, 601 (1944).

94. 458 U.S. 419, 435 (1982). On the scope of the *Loretto* rule, see FCC v. Florida Power Corp., 107 S. Ct. 1107 (1987).

95. 407 U.S. 551 (1972). See Hudgens v. NLRB, 424 U.S. 507 (1976).

96. 407 U.S. at 567.

97. 447 U.S. 74 (1980).

98. *Id.* at 83.

99. *Id.* at 84.

100. See Mandelker, Land Use Takings, 8 Hastings Const. L. J. 491 (1981); Cunningham, Inverse Condemnation as a Remedy for "Regulatory Takings," 8 Hastings Const. L. Q. 517 (1981).

101. 80 U.S. (13 Wall.) 166 (1871).

102. *Id.* at 177–78.

103. 260 U.S. 393 (1922). See Rose, *Mahon* Reconstructed, 57 S. Calif. L. Rev. 561 (1984).

104. 260 U.S. at 415. See note 90 *supra* and accompanying text.

105. 123 U.S. 623 (1887).

106. *Id.* at 667.

107. 272 U.S. 365 (1926).

108. Ambler Realty Co. v. Euclid, 297 F. 307, 317 (N. D. Ohio 1924).

109. 272 U.S. at 388–89.

110. *Id.* at 391.

111. Nectow v. City of Cambridge, 277 U.S. 183 (1928).

112. 369 U.S. 590 (1962).

113. See *id.* at 595.

114. Hadechek v. Sebastian, 239 U.S. 394 (1915).

115. 447 U.S. 255 (1980).

116. Agins v. City of Tiburon, 24 Calif. 3d 266, 598 P. 2d 25, 157 Calif. Rptr. 372 (1979).

117. *Id.* at 273, 598 P. 2d at 28, 157 Calif. Rptr. at 375.

118. *Id.* at 277, 598 P. 2d at 31, 157 Calif. Rptr. at 378.

119. *Agins*, 447 U.S. at 262.

120. 438 U.S. 104 (1978).

121. *Id.* at 124.

122. *Id.* at 136.

123. *Id.* at 151 (Rehnquist dissenting).

124. San Diego Gas & Elec. v. City of San Diego, 450 U.S. 621 (1981); Williamson County Regional Planning Com'n v. Hamilton Bank, 473 U.S. 172 (1985); MacDonald, Sommer & Frates v. Yolo County, 477 U.S. 340 (1986).

125. 107 Sup. Ct. 2378 (1987).

126. 24 Calif. 3d 266, 598 P. 2d 25 (1979), *aff'd on other grounds,* 477 U.S. 255 (1980).

127. 107 Sup. Ct. at 2386, citing United States v. Clarke, 445 U.S. 253, 257 (1980).

128. Kimball Laundry Co. v. United States, 338 U.S. 1 (1948); United States v. Petty Motor Co., 327 U.S. 372 (1946).

129. United States v. General Motors Corp., 323 U.S. 373 (1945).

130. *First English Evan. Luth. Ch.*, 107 S. Ct. at 2388.

131. *Id.* at 2389.

132. *Id.* at 2388, citing Armstrong v. United States, 364 U.S. 40, 49 (1960).

133. 276 U.S. 272 (1928).

134. See Buchanan, Politics, Property and the Law, 15 J. Law & Econ. 439 (1972).

135. Reich, The New Property, 73 Yale L. J. 733 (1964); Reich, Individual Rights and Social Welfare, 74 Yale L. J. 1245 (1965). Leading critiques include Van Alstyne, Cracks in "The New Property," 62 Cornell L. Rev. 445 (1977); Williams, Liberty and Property, 12 J. of Legal Studies 3 (1983).

136. 397 U.S. 254 (1970).

137. *Id.* at 261.

138. See *supra* note 135.

139. 397 U.S. at 271.

140. *Id.* at 275.

141. 408 U.S. 564 (1972). See Simon, Liberty and Property in the Supreme Court, 71 Calif. L. Rev. 146 (1983); Monaghan, Of "Liberty" and "Property," 62 Cornell L. Rev. 405 (1977).

142. 408 U.S. at 577.

143. *Id.*

144. 397 U.S. 254 (1970).

145. 408 U.S. 593 (1972).

146. *Id.* at 595.

147. *Id.* at 601.

148. 416 U.S. 134 (1974).

149. *Id.* at 166.

150. 419 U.S. 565 (1975).

151. *Id.* at 574.

152. *Id.* at 576 n. 8.

153. See Michelman, In Pursuit of Constitutional Welfare Rights, 121 U. Pa. L. Rev. 962 (1973); Michelman, Welfare Rights in a Constitutional Democracy, 1979 Wash. U. L. Q. 659; Stone, Equal Protection and the Search for Justice, 22 Ariz. L. Rev. 1 (1980).

154. Bork, The Impossibility of Finding Welfare Rights in the Constitution, 1979 Wash. U. L. Q. 694.

155. 198 U.S. 45 (1905).

156. See H. Hochman and G. Peterson, eds., Redistribution through Public Choice (1974).

Chapter 5

1. U.S Const., art. I, § 8, cl. 3.

2. U.S. Const., art I, § 10, cl. 2: "No State shall, without the Consent of the Congress, lay any Imposts or Duties on Imports or Exports, except what may be absolutely necessary for executing it's inspection Laws: and the net Produce of all Duties and Imposts, laid by any State on Imports or Exports, shall be for the Use of the Treasury of the United States; and all such Laws shall be subject to the Revision and Controul of the Congress."

3. W. Crosskey, Politics and the Constitution in the History of the United States, I, 295–323 (1953).

4. Woodruff v. Parham, 75 U.S. (8 Wall.) 123, (1868).

5. Baldwin v. G.A.F. Seelig, Inc., 294 U.S. 511 (1935). See Sholley, The

Negative Implications of the Commerce Clause, 3 Univ. of Chi. L. Rev. 556 (1936).

6. L. Gipson, The British Empire before the American Revolution, III, 291–94 (rev. ed. 1960).

7. G. Schmoller, The Mercantile System and Its Historical Significance 69 (Reprint 1967). On the economics of colonial dependency under mercantilism, see J. Dorfman, The Economic Mind in American Civilization, I, 135–141 (1946).

8. A. Smith, An Inquiry into the Nature and Causes of the Wealth of Nations (1776).

9. W. Hamilton and D. Adair, The Power to Govern, ch. 5 (1937). See F. McDonald, Novus Ordo Seclorum, ch. 4 (1985).

10. U.S. Cong., Am. State Papers, Class III, Finance, I, 123, 135–37 (1832).

11. Hood & Sons v. DuMond, 336 U.S. 525, 533 (1949), citing U.S. Cong., Documents, Formation of the Union, 12 H. Docs., 69th Cong., 1st Sess., 38 (1927). See W. Rutledge, A Declaration of Legal Faith 25–26 (1947).

12. The report of the Annapolis meeting is reprinted in J. Elliot, Debates in the Several State Conventions on the Adoption of the Federal Constitution, I, 116–19 (1836).

13. Id. at 119–20.

14. M. Farrand, ed., Records of the Federal Convention of 1787, I, 20–23 (1911). [hereinafter cited as Farrand].

15. Farrand, I: 21.

16. Id. at I: 54.

17. Id. at I: 243.

18. Farrand II: 181.

19. Stern, That Commerce which Concerns More States Than One, 47 Harv. L. Rev. 1335, 1344–45 (1934).

20. See G. Caines, An Enquiry into the Law Merchant of the United States (1802).

21. See, e.g., Luke v. Lyde, 2 Burr. 882, 97 Eng. Rep. 61 (K.B. 1759); Pelly v. Company of the Royal Exchange Assurance, 1 Burr. 341, 97 Eng. Rep. 342 (K.B. 1757).

22. A commerce dictionary of the times devoted 23 pages to examples of different types of bills of exchange. M. Postlethwayt, Universal Dictionary of Trade and Commerce (1774). See J. Holden, The History of Negotiable Instruments in English Law, ch. 5 (1955).

23. See W. Crosskey, supra note 3, I, 3–186 (1953); W. Hamilton and D. Adair, supra note 9, 42–53.

24. A. Anderson, Historical and Chronological Deduction of the Origin of Commerce (1787).

25. T. Coxe, A View of the United States of America 7 (1794).

26. Alexander Hamilton, The Federalist, No. XI, 71 (Bourne ed., 1947).

27. 22 U.S. (9 Wheat.) 1, 196 (1824).

28. See A. Hamilton, Federalist VI, 35; VII, 42 (Bourne ed. 1947).

29. The Committee of Stile did not alter the language adopted by the Committee of Detail. Farrand II: 595.

30. W. Crosskey, supra note 3, at 50–55.

31. Gibbons v. Ogden, 22 U.S. (9 Wheat.) 1, 194.

32. Madison, in discussing whether the Constitution was adopted as a compact of the states, noted the different uses of the word "states":

It is indeed true that the term "states" is sometimes used in a vague sense, and sometimes in different senses, according to the subject to which it is applied. Thus it sometimes means the separate sections of territory occupied by the political societies within each; sometimes the particular governments established by those societies; sometimes those societies as organized into those particular governments; and lastly, it means the people composing those political societies, in their highest sovereign capacity. Although it might be wished that the perfection of language admitted less diversity in the signification of the same words, yet little convenience is produced by it, where the true sense can be collected with certainty from the different applications. In the present instance, whatever different construction of the term "states," in the Resolution, may have been entertained, all will at least concur in the last mentioned; because in that sense the Constitution was submitted to the "states"; in that sense the "states" ratified it; and in that sense of the term "states," they are consequently parties to the compact from which the powers of the federal government result.

J. Madison, Report on the Virginia Resolutions, in Debates of the Several State Conventions on the Adoption of the Federal Constitution, IV, 547 (J. Elliot ed. 1836).

33. See sources cited in W. Crosskey, *supra* note 3, at 55–69 and 1267–74. Crosskey cites a number of dictionaries, including S. Johnson, Dictionary of the English Language (1755), noting "state" as a group of persons and not citing any use of the term as a territory. It was common parlance of the times to say "I am of Vermont" or "I belong to Vermont." *Id.* at 57–58. See J. Story, Commentaries on the Constitution of the United States, I, 441 (1833).

34. U.S. Const., art. 1, sec. 3 (emphasis added).

35. See W. Ritz, Rewriting the History of the Judiciary Act of 1789, 83–86 (1990).

36. T. Coxe, *supra* note 25, at 32–33.

37. An Act for Registering and Clearing Vessels, Regulating the Coasting Trade, and for other purposes, 1st Cong. Sess. 1, ch. 11, Sept. 1, 1789, 1 Stat. 55.

38. 28 Fed. Cas. 614 (No. 16,700) (D. Mass. 1808). See G. Haskins and H. Johnson, Foundations of Power, John Marshall, 1801–15, History of the Supreme Court of the United States, II, 305–7 (1981). On the politics of the embargo, see A. Kelly, W. Harbison, and H. Belz, The American Constitution 150–53 (6th ed. 1983).

39. 28 Fed. Cas. at 621.

40. *Id.* at 620–21.

41. 30 Fed. Cas. 239 (no. 17, 846) (C.C. Va. 1820).

42. *Id.* at 243.

43. 8 Fed. Cas. 493 (no. 4,366) (C.C. S.C. 1823). See Donald Morgan, Justice William Johnson: The First Dissenter 192–202 (1954).

44. 8 Fed. Cas. at 495.

45. See A. Beveridge, The Life of John Marshall, IV, 398–405 (1919), describing the original grant of monopoly and its renewals.

46. See H. Fox, Monopolies and Patents 57 (1947). The British constitutional tradition is founded in the Case of Monopolies, 11 Coke 84, 77 Eng. Rep. 1260 (K.B. 1602) and the Statute of Monopolies, 21 Jac. 1, Ch. 3 (1624). On the antimonopoly tradition in America, see chapter 10.

47. A. Beveridge, *supra* note 45, at 403–5; G. Haskins, Marshall and the Commerce Clause of the Constitution, in Chief Justice Marshall 145, 147 (W. Jones ed. 1956).

48. 9 Johns. 507 (N.Y. 1812).

49. An Act for enrolling and licensing ships or vessels to be employed in the coasting trade and fisheries, and for regulating the same, 2d Cong., Sess. 2, ch. 8, Feb. 18, 1793, 1 Stat. 305.

50. 9 Johns. at 514–21.

51. 9 Johns. at 578.

52. North River Steamboat Co. v. Livingston, 3 Cowen 713 (N.Y. 1825), citing Gibbons v. Ogden, 22 U.S. (9 Wheat.) 1 (1824).

53. 22 U.S. (9 Wheat.) 1 (1824). See G. White, The Marshall Court and Cultural Change, 1815–35, History of the Supreme Court of the United States, III–IV, 568–80 (1988); M. Baxter, The Steamboat Monopoly (1972); C. Warren, The Supreme Court in United States History, I, 587–632 (rev. ed. 1926).

54. Ogden v. Gibbons, 4 Johns. ch. 150 (N.Y. 1819).

55. Gibbons v. Ogden, 17 Johns. 488 (N.Y. 1820). See Campbell, Chancellor Kent, Chief Justice Marshall and the Steamboat Cases, 25 Syracuse L. Rev. 497, 513 (1974).

56. 30 Fed. Cas. 239 (no. 17, 846) (C.C. Va. 1820).

57. *Gibbons*, 22 U.S. at 189–90.

58. *Id.* at 190.

59. *Id.* at 194, 196.

60. *Id.* at 194.

61. *Id.* at 194–195.

62. Marshall devotes many pages to a demonstration that the power of Congress over foreign and interstate commerce is exclusive. *Id.* at 197–209.

63. The statute applied to ships or vessels "found trading between district and district, or between different places in the same district." Coasting Act of 1793, sec. 6, 1 Stat. 307.

64. *Gibbons*, 22 U.S. at 200.

65. *Id.* at 221.

66. *Id.* at 222.

67. 8 Fed. Cas. 493 (no. 4, 366) (C.C. S.C. 1823).

68. 22 U.S. at 227.

69. *Id.* at 235.

70. See Abel, Commerce Regulation before *Gibbons v. Ogden,* 25 N.C. L. Rev. 121 (1947).

71. 3 Cowen 713 (N.Y. 1825).

72. North River Steamboat Co. v. Livingston, 1 Hopkins Ch. 149 (N.Y. 1824).

73. 3 Cowen at 714–715.

74. 3 Cowen at 752.

75. 1 Stat. 305 (1793).

76. 25 U.S. (12 Wheat.) 419 (1827). See the application of the original package doctrine in Leisy v. Hardin, 135 U.S. 100 (1890).

77. U.S. Const. art. 1, § 10, cl. 2. See *supra* note 2.

78. 25 U.S. at 446–47. In Woodruff v. Parham, 75 U.S. (8 Wall.) 123 (1869), the original package doctrine was held inapplicable to interstate commerce. It was in effect overruled for foreign commerce in Michelin Tire Co. v. Wages, 423 U.S. 276 (1976), *overruling* Low v. Austin, 80 U.S. (13 Wall.) 29 (1872).

79. 27 U.S. (2 Pet.) 245 (1829).

80. *Id.* at 252.

81. 36 U.S. (11 Pet.) 102 (1837). See C. Swisher, The Tancy Period 1836–64, History of the Supreme Court of the United States, V, 360–65 (1974).

82. 36 U.S. at 139.

83. *Id.* at 138.

84. An Act Respecting Quarantine and Health Laws, ch. 12, Feb. 25, 1799, 1 Stat. 619.

85. 36 U.S. at 156.

86. 92 U.S. 259 (1876).

87. 314 U.S. 160 (1941).

88. 46 U.S. (5 How.) 504 (1847). See C. Swisher, *supra* note 81, at 370–77.

89. 25 U.S. (12 Wheat.) 419 (1827).

90. 46 U.S. at 579. See F. Frankfurter, The Commerce Clause under Marshall, Taney and Waite 51–53 (1937).

91. 48 U.S. (7 How.) 28 (1849). See C. Swisher, *supra* note 81, at 382–91; C. Warren, *supra* note 53, at II, 174–181.

92. 53 U.S. (12 How.) 299 (1851). See C. Swisher, *supra* note 81, at 404–6.

93. Stat. 54 (1789).

94. 22 U.S. 1, 207–8 (1824).

95. 53 U.S. at 319.

96. 77 U.S. (10 Wall.) 557 (1871). See L. Hunter, Steamboats on the Western Rivers, ch. 13 (1949).

97. 24 Stat. 379 (1887).

98. 230 U.S. 352 (1913).

99. Houston, E. & W. Texas Railway v. United States, 234 U.S. 342 (1914).

100. *Id.* at 358–59.

101. Railroad Com'n of Wisconsin v. Chicago, B. & Q. R. R., 257 U.S. 563 (1922).

102. Southern Ry. v. United States, 222 U.S. 20 (1911).

103. Baltimore & Ohio R. R. v. ICC, 221 U.S. 612 (1911).

104. Corwin, Congress' Power to Prohibit Commerce, 18 Cornell L. Q. 477 (1933).

105. Champion v. Ames, 188 U.S. 321 (1903).

106. Hipolite Egg Co. v. United States, 220 U.S. 45 (1911).

107. Hoke v. United States, 227 U.S. 308 (1913).

108. Wilson v. New, 243 U.S. 332 (1917).

109. United States v. Ferger, 250 U.S. 199 (1919).

110. Brooks v. United States, 267 U.S. 432 (1925).

111. Thornton v. United States, 271 U.S. 414 (1926).

112. Stafford v. Wallace, 258 U.S. 495 (1922); Board of Trade v. Olsen, 262 U.S. 1 (1923); Tagg Bros. & Moorhead v. United States, 280 U.S. 420 (1930).

113. See B. Twiss, Lawyers and the Constitution (1942); Tucker, The Congressional Power over Interstate Commerce, 11 A.B.A. Rep. 260 (1888).

114. 75 U.S. (8 Wall.) 168, 183 (1869), *overruled in* United States v. South Eastern Underwriters Ass'n, 332 U.S. 533 (1944).

115. 75 U.S. (8 Wall.) at 183. See contrary view of Justice Holmes in Fidelity & Deposit Co. of Md. v. Tafoya, 270 U.S. 426, 434 (1926).

116. 22 U.S. (9 Wheat.) 1, 195–196 (1824).

117. 76 U.S. (9 Wall.) 41 (1870). On market failure based on consumer ignorance and the costs of search, see E. MacKaay, Economics of Information and Law 107–15, 150–52 (1982).

118. 76 U.S. at 44.

119. 82 U.S. (15 Wall.) 232 (1873).

120. 100 U.S. 82 (1878). Since there have been no constitutional challenges to

the intrastate application of twentieth-century U.S. trademark statutes, the Supreme Court has not had an opportunity to overrule the 1878 decision.

121. See R. Posner, Economic Analysis of Law 37–38 (3d ed. 1986); Conant, Multiple Trademarks and Oligopoly Power, 1 Industrial Org. Rev. 115 (1973).

122. 100 U.S. at 96.

123. 128 U.S. 1 (1888).

124. *Id.* at 20.

125. 26 Stat. 209 (1890), 15 U.S.C.A. §1 (supp. 1986).

126. 156 U.S. 1 (1895). See Twiss, *supra* note 113, ch. 9.

127. 128 U.S. 1 (1888). See 156 U.S. at 14.

128. 156 U.S. at 16.

129. Hopkins v. United States, 171 U.S. 578 (1898); Anderson v. United States, 171 U.S. 604 (1898).

130. 196 U.S. 375 (1905). The Sherman Act was applied to direct restraints on shipping goods between states. Addyston Pipe & Steel Co. v. United States, 175 U.S. 211 (1899).

131. 221 U.S. 1, 68–69 (1911).

132. See R. Posner, *supra* note 121, at 235.

133. 207 U.S. 463 (1908), *overruled in* Southern Pacific Co. v. Gileo, 351 U.S. 493 (1956); Reed v. Pennsylvania R. Co., 351 U.S. 502 (1956). See 34 Stat. 232 (1906).

134. 35 Stat. 65 (1908), 45 U.S.C. 51–60 (1972).

135. Second Employers' Liability Cases, 223 U.S. 1 (1912).

136. 208 U.S. 161 (1908), *overruled in* Lincoln Federal Labor Union v. Northwestern, 335 U.S. 525 (1949). See Erdman Act, §10, 30 Stat. 424 (1898). The *Adair* rule was not followed in 1930 when the Railway Labor Act of 1926 was held constitutional even though local railway clerks were guaranteed the right to choose their own representatives for collective bargaining. Texas & N.O.R.R. v. Brotherhood of Railway Clerks, 281 U.S. 548 (1930).

137. See R. Posner, *supra* note 121, at 137–43; G. Becker, Human Capital (2d ed. 1975).

138. 247 U.S. 251 (1918), *overruled in* United States v. Darby, 312 U.S. 100, 116–17 (1941). See 39 Stat. 675 (1916).

139. 247 U.S. at 272.

140. *Id.* at 279.

141. 259 U.S. 20 (1920). On the broad power of Congress to use taxation as a method of regulation, see McCray v. United States, 195 U.S. 27 (1904).

142. 48 Stat. 195 (1933).

143. 293 U.S. 388 (1935).

144. 295 U.S. 495 (1935).

145. Railroad Retirement Board v. Alton R. Co., 295 U.S. 330 (1935).

146. See L. Lecht, Experience under Railway Labor Legislation 123–31 (1955).

147. 298 U.S. 238 (1936), *overruled in effect* on delegation issue in Sunshine Coal Co. v. Adkins, 310 U.S. 381 (1940), and on commerce issue in United States v. Darby, 312 U.S. 100, 118 (1941).

148. House Doc. 142, 75th Cong., 1st sess. (1937). See R. Jackson, The Struggle for Judicial Supremacy (1941); Leuchtenburg, The Origin of Franklin D. Roosevelt's "Court-Packing" Plan, 1966 Sup. Ct. Rev. 347.

149. 301 U.S. 1 (1937). See Stern, The Commerce Clause and the National Economy, 59 Harv. L. Rev. 645, 883 (1946).

150. 49 Stat. 449 (1935). Section 2(7) of the act: "The term 'affecting com-

merce' means in commerce, or burdening or obstructing commerce or the free flow of commerce, or having led or tending to lead to a labor dispute burdening or obstructing commerce or the free flow of commerce."

151. See R. Posner, *supra* note 121, at 302–5.

152. 301 U.S. at 41–42.

153. Santa Cruz Fruit Packing Co. v. N.L.R.B., 303 U.S. 453 (1938) (NLRA applicable to processors of agricultural products grown in a single state but shipped in interstate commerce); N.L.R.B. v. Fainblatt, 306 U.S. 601 (1939) (NLRA applicable to New Jersey manufacturer whose input materials and products were delivered and picked up by a New York marketer).

154. 312 U.S. 100 (1941). By 1941 the four dissenters in the *Jones & Laughlin* case had left the court.

155. 52 Stat. 1060 (1938).

156. On the economics of minimum wages, see R. Posner, *supra* note 121, at 308–10.

157. 22 U.S. (9 Wheat.) 1, 196. See A. Mason, Harlan Fiske Stone 551–55 (1956).

158. 312 U.S. at 114.

159. 247 U.S. 251 (1918).

160. 312 U.S. at 121.

161. *Id.* at 124. On the Tenth Amendment, see E. Corwin, The Commerce Power versus States Rights 115–72 (1936).

162. Kirschbaum v. Walling, 316 U.S. 517 (1942) (FLSA applicable to local building employees where building tenanted by firms in interstate commerce); Martino v. Michigan Window Cleaning Co., 327 U.S. 173 (1946) (FLSA applicable to watchmen and window cleaners employed by local independent contractor to work in factories producing for commerce); Warren-Bradshaw Drilling Co. v. Hall, 317 U.S. 88 (1942) (FLSA applicable to employees of firm that drilled oil wells in only one state); Mabee v. White Plains Publishing Co., 327 U.S. 178 (1946) (FLSA applicable to employees of newspaper that shipped only forty-five copies to other states).

163. D. Johnson, Farm Commodity Programs 31 (1973). See French, Fruit and Vegetable Marketing Orders, 64 Am. J. Agr. Econ. 916 (1982).

164. 307 U.S. 533 (1939) (regulation of sales by dairy farmers to local dealers who later resold in interstate commerce). See United States v. Wrightwood Dairy Co., 315 U.S. 110 (1942).

165. 317 U.S. 111 (1942).

166. *Id.* at 125. See United States v. Haley Jr., 358 U.S. 644 (1959) (forty acres of wheat, withdrawn from 60 million acres in national market, was not too small for federal regulation).

167. 322 U.S. 533 (1944) *overruling* Paul v. Virginia, 75 U.S. (8 Wall.) 168, 183 (1869). See *supra* notes 114 and 115 and accompanying text.

168. 322 U.S. at 539.

169. *Id.* at 551–52.

170. 334 U.S. 219 (1948).

171. *Id.* at 232.

172. United States v. Women's Sportswear Manufacturers Ass'n, 336 U.S. 460 (1949).

173. *Id.* at 464.

174. 78 Stat. 241, 243 (1964), 42 U.S.C.A. §2000a (1981).

175. 379 U.S. 241 (1964).

176. *Id.* at 258.

177. 379 U.S. 294 (1964).

178. E.E.O.C. v. Wyoming, 460 U.S. 226, 248 (1983).

179. 22 U.S. (9 Wheat.) 1, 196–197 (1824).

180. 460 U.S. at 248–249.

181. Southern Pacific v. Arizona, 325 U.S. 761, 769 (1945).

182. See B. Gavit, The Commerce Clause of the United States Constitution 541–52 (1932); F. Ribble, State and National Power over Commerce 182–229 (1937); Maltz, How Much Regulation is Too Much, 50 Geo. Wash. L. Rev. 47 (1981); Eule, Laying the Dormant Commerce Clause to Rest, 91 Yale L. J. 425 (1982); Sedler, The Negative Commerce Clause as a Restriction on State Regulation and Taxation, 31 Wayne L. Rev. 885 (1985).

183. Helson V. Kentucky, 279 U.S. 245, 248 (1929); Shafer v. Farmers Grain Co., 268 U.S. 189, 199 (1925). See Dowling, Interstate Commerce and State Power, 27 Va. L. Rev. 1 (1940); Dowling, Interstate Commerce and State Power—Revised Version, 47 Colum. L. Rev. 597 (1947). Note the views of Justice Johnson, *supra* notes 43 and 68 and accompanying text.

184. 118 U.S. 557 (1886), *overruling* Peik v. Chicago & Nw. Ry. Co., 94 U.S. 164 (1877). Justice Miller noted:

> It cannot be too strongly insisted upon that the right of continuous transportation from one end of the country to the other is essential in modern times to that freedom of commerce from the restraints which the State might choose to impose upon it, that the commerce clause was intended to secure. This clause, giving to Congress the power to regulate commerce among the States and with foreign nations, as this court has said before, was among the most important of the subjects which prompted the formation of the Constitution. . . . And it would be a very feeble and almost useless provision, but poorly adapted to secure the entire freedom of commerce among the States which was deemed essential to a more perfect union by the framers of the Constitution, if, at every stage of the transportation of goods and chattels through the country, the State within whose limits a part of this transportation must be done could impose regulations concerning the price, compensation, or taxation, or any other restrictive regulation interfering with and seriously embarrassing this commerce.

118 U.S. at 572–73.

185. 325 U.S. 761 (1945).

186. "The decisive question is whether in the circumstances the total effect of the law as a safety measure in reducing accidents and casualties is so slight or problematical as not to outweigh the national interest in keeping interstate commerce free from interferences which seriously impede it and subject it to local regulation which does not have a uniform effect on the interstate train journey which it interrupts" (*Id.* at 775–76).

187. 393 U.S. 129 (1968). See Brotherhood of Locomotive Firemen & Enginemen v. Chicago, R.I.&P. R.R. Co., 382 U.S. 423 (1966).

188. 393 U.S. at 142.

189. See, e.g., J. Nelson, Railroad Transportation and Public Policy 271–80 (1959).

190. 393 U.S. at 132–33.

191. *Id.* at 136.

192. 303 U.S. 177 (1938).

193. *Id.* at 190.

194. *Id.*

195. *Id.* at 191.
196. 359 U.S. 520 (1959).
197. *Id.* at 529.
198. 434 U.S. 429 (1978).
199. *Id.* at 441.
200. *Id.* at 477–48.
201. 450 U.S. 662 (1981).
202. *Id.* at 672–73.
203. *Id.* at 674.
204. McLeod v. J. E. Dilworth Co., 322 U.S. 327, 330 (1944). See Brown, The Open Economy: Mr. Justice Frankfurter and the Position of the Judiciary, 67 Yale L. J. 219 (1957).
205. 294 U.S. 511 (1935).
206. Nebbia v. New York, 291 U.S. 502 (1934); Hegeman Farm Corp. v. Baldwin, 293 U.S. 163 (1934).
207. 294 U.S. at 521.
208. 336 U.S. 525 (1949). See Michel, Hood v. Dumond, A Study of the Supreme Court and the Ideology of Capitalism, 134 U. Pa. L. Rev. 657 (1986).
209. 336 U.S. at 533–34. See *supra* note 12 and accompanying text.
210. 340 U.S. 349 (1951).
211. *Id.* at 354.
212. *Id.* at 356.
213. 397 U.S. 137 (1970). See Farber, State Regulation and the Dormant Commerce Clause, 18 Urban Lawyer 567, 570–72 (1986).
214. 397 U.S. at 142.
215. *Id.* at 145, citing Foster-Fountain Packing Co. v. Haydel, 278 U.S. 1 (1928); Johnson v. Haydel, 278 U.S. 16 (1928); Toomer v. Witsell, 334 U.S. 385 (1948).
216. Great A & P Tea Co. v. Cottrell, 424 U.S. 366, 371 (1976).
217. 424 U.S. 366 (1976).
218. *Id.* at 375.
219. *Id.* at 380.
220. 432 U.S. 333 (1977).
221. *Id.* at 353.
222. 457 U.S. 624 (1982).
223. *Id.* at 642.
224. "The effects of allowing the Illinois Secretary of State to block a nation-wide tender offer are substantial. Shareholders are deprived of the opportunity to sell their shares at a premium. The reallocation of economic resources to their highest-valued use, a process which can improve efficiency and competition, is hindered. The incentive the tender offer mechanism provides incumbent management to perform well so that stock prices remain high is reduced" (*Id.* at 643).
225. 362 U.S. 440 (1960).
226. *Id.* at 448.
227. 437 U.S. 117 (1978).
228. *Id.* at 121.
229. *Id.* at 136.
230. 313 U.S. 109 (1941), *overruling* Di Santo v. Pennsylvania, 273 U.S. 34 (1927).
231. See, e.g., Southern Pacific Co. v. Arizona, 325 U.S. 761, 784 (1945); Hood & Sons v. Du Mond, 336 U.S. 525, 545 (1949). See Sedler, *supra* note 182.

Chapter 6

1. See chapter 5. The Supreme Court raised a false issue of federalism when, after 1870, it erroneously curtailed the scope of the commerce power over private transactions. Hammer v. Dagenhart, 247, U.S. 251 (1918) *overruled in* United States v. Darby, 312 U.S. 100 (1941).

2. See Stigler, The Theory of Economic Regulation, 2 Bell J. Econ. & Mgmnt. Sci. 3 (1971); Peltzman, Toward a More General Theory of Regulation, 19 J. L. & Econ. 211 (1976).

3. 469 U.S. 528 (1985).

4. 426 U.S. 833 (1976).

5. U.S. Const., art. VI, cl. 2. See Edgar v. Mite Corp., 457 U.S. 624, 631 (1982), for a summary of standards for application of the supremacy clause.

6. 456 U.S. 742 (1982). See Hodel v. Virginia Surface Min. & Recl. Ass'n, 452 U.S. 264, 290–93 (1981).

7. 456 U.S. at 769–71.

8. Nagel, Federalism as a Fundamental Value, 1981 Sup. Ct. Rev. 81, 83–89. See C. Black, Structure and Relationship in Constitutional Law (1969).

9. Justice Stone summarized the true meaning of the Tenth Amendment: "The amendment states but a truism that all is retained which has not been surrendered. There is nothing in the history of its adoption to suggest that it was more than declaratory of the relationship between the national and state governments as it had been established by the Constitution before the amendment or that its purpose was other than to allay fears that the new national government might seek to exercise powers not granted, and that the states might not be able to exercise fully their reserved powers" (United States v. Darby, 312 U.S. 100, 124 [1941]).

10. Rapaczynski, From Sovereignty to Process, 1985 Sup. Ct. Rev. 341, 346–59. Compare Kaden, Politics, Money and State Sovereignty, 79 Colum. L. Rev. 847, 849–57 (1979).

11. See Wechsler, The Political Safeguards of Federalism, 54 Colum. L. Rev. 543, 558–60 (1954).

12. Texas v. White, 74 U.S. (7 Wall.) 700, 725 (1869).

13. Federalist 46, at 321 (E. Bourne ed. 1947).

14. 221 U.S. 559 (1911).

15. *Id.* at 565.

16. See Baker v. Carr, 369 U.S. 186 (1962); Reynolds v. Sims, 377 U.S. 533 (1964). See U.S. Const., art. IV, § 4.

17. See chapter 3.

18. See Van Alstyne, The Second Death of Federalism, 83 Mich. L. Rev. 1709, 1729 (1985); Nagel, *supra* note 8, at 97–109.

19. See C. Black, *supra* note 8, at 7.

20. See generally, Wells and Hellerstein, The Governmental-Proprietary Distinction in Constitutional Law, 66 Va. L. Rev. 1073 (1980).

21. 297 U.S. 175 (1936). This holding was reaffirmed in California v. Taylor 353 U.S. 553 (1957) and Parden v. Terminal R. Co., 377 U.S. 184 (1964).

22. 297 U.S. 183.

23. 326 U.S. 572 (1946).

24. 326 U.S. 582.

25. Garcia, 469 U.S. at 542.

26. 326 U.S. 579.

27. 455 U.S. 678 (1982).

28. N.Y. Civ. Serv. Law, sec. 204–14 (McKinney 1983).

29. The Metropolitan Transportation Authority was not the alter ego of the Long Island Railroad Co. Bujosa v. Metropolitan Transportation Auth., 355 N.Y.S. 2d 801 (N.Y. Sup. Ct. App. Div. 1974).

30. 455 U.S. 685. See California v. Taylor, 353 U.S. 553 (1957).

31. 455 U.S. 687. See *National League of Cities*, 426 U.S. 851, discussed *infra*, at note 69.

32. Kramer v. New Castle Area Transit Authority, 677 F. 2d 308 (3d Cir. 1982), *cert. denied* 459 U.S. 1146 (1983); Alewine v. City Council of Augusta, 699 F. 2d 1060 (11th Cir. 1983), *cert. denied* 470 U.S. 1027 (1985); Dove v. Chattanooga Area Regional Trans. Authority, 701 F. 2d 50 (6th Cir. 1983). See Francis v. City of Tallahassee, 424 So. 2d 61 (Fla. App. 1982).

33. 677 F.2d 308 (3d Cir. 1982), *cert. denied* 459 U.S. 1146 (1983).

34. 699 F. 2d 1060 (11th Cir. 1983), *cert. denied* 470 U.S. 1027 (1985).

35. *Id.* at 1067–68.

36. 701 F. 2d. 50 (6th Cir. 1983).

37. *Id.* at 52–53.

38. *Id.* at 53, citing United Transportation Union v. Long Island Railroad, 455 U.S. 678, 687 (1982).

39. Hughes v. Alexandria Scrap Corp., 426 U.S. 794 (1976); Reeves v. Stake, 447 U.S. 429 (1980).

40. 426 U.S. 794 (1976).

41. MD. Code Ann., Art. 66 1/2, §§ 5-201 to 210 (1970), § 11-1002(f)(5) (supp. 1975).

42. A subsidy is a negative tax and is a technique of regulation. See K. Boulding, Economic Analysis 155–58 (1941); E. Malinvaud, Lectures on Microeconomic Theory 209–10 (1972).

43. 426 U.S. at 806, 809. Since *Alexandria Scrap* was not in fact a proprietary case, it should have been treated like other state regulatory cases. Whether the Maryland statute burdened commerce among the several states was the prime contested issue of fact. The case should not have been decided on summary judgment. Alexandria Scrap v. Hughes, 391 F. Supp. 46, 63 (D. Md. 1975). A trial might have established that the greater documentation required of out-of-state processors was necessary to prevent false subsidy claims by firms outside the jurisdiction of Maryland enforcement officers.

44. 426 U.S. 809.

45. *Id.* at 810. The Supreme Court also held the amended statute not to violate the equal protection clause. *Id.* at 810–14.

46. 447 U.S. 429 (1980).

47. See summary, *id.* at 433–34.

48. *Id.* at 434–436.

49. *Id.* at 437, citing L. Tribe, American Constitutional Law 336 (1978).

50. 447 U.S. 439. The Court rejected four other arguments against the State. First, the response to the charge of economic protectionism was that this was merely use of local taxation to assure a healthy building industry. Free markets did not require the state to offer the same services in neighboring states. Second, the state cement program was held not to be a hoarding of resources since cement is not a national resource. It can be produced in any state. Third, the South Dakota program did not give its suppliers of ready-mix concrete an unfair advantage in the out-of-state markets. Barring these suppliers from out-of-state markets would

be the essence of protectionism. Fourth, the Court rejected the argument that since South Dakota had "replaced" the free market, it should be forced to replicate that market by selling to all buyers. The reason South Dakota had built the plant was because of market failure. Because of great fluctuations in demand, the free market failed to supply adequate cement when demand was highest.

51. In 1986 the per capita personal income in Connecticut was $18,089, and in New York $16,050; while in Mississippi it was $9,187, and in West Virginia $10,193. U.S. Dept. of Commerce, Survey of Current Business 24 (August 1986).

52. On the issue of whether minimum-wage laws result mainly in wage raises for lowest-income earners or mainly in unemployment, see J. Hirshleifer, Price Theory and Applications 372–77 (1976).

53. See J. Choper, Judicial Review and the National Political Process 182 (1980).

54. See J. Buchanan, The Demand and Supply of Public Goods (1968); R. Musgrave and P. Musgrave, Public Finance in Theory and Practice, chs. 2 and 3 (4th ed. 1984); M. Olson, The Logic of Collective Action (1965).

55. R. Musgrave and P. Musgrave, *supra* note 54, at 48–51.

56. 392 U.S. 183 (1968).

57. 80 Stat. 831, 832 (1966), 29 U.S.C.A. §§203d, 203(s)(4)(1978).

58. 392 U.S. 195.

59. 297 U.S. 175 (1936), cited at 392 U.S. 197–99.

60. *Id.* at 198–99.

61. *Id.* at 201.

62. *Id.* at 205.

63. 426 U.S. 833 (1976).

64. For citations and review of the commentaries, see Nagel, Federalism as a Fundamental Value, 1981 Supreme Court Rev. 81; Rotunda, The Doctrine of Conditional Preemption and other Limitations on Tenth Amendment Restrictions, 132 U. of Pa. L. Rev. 289, 291–95 (1984).

65. 88 Stat. 55 (1974), 29 U.S.C.A. §§ 203(d), 203(s)(5), 203x(v). For estimations that the increased costs or decreased state and local services resulting from the act would have its major impact on low-income citizens, see Michelman, States' Rights and States' Roles, 86 Yale L. J. 1165, 1178–79 (1977); Tribe, Unraveling National League of Cities, 90 Harv. L. Rev. 1065, 1076 (1977).

66. 426 U.S. 841.

67. "We have repeatedly recognized that there are attributes to sovereignty attaching to every state government which may not be impaired by Congress, not because Congress may lack an affirmative grant of legislative authority to reach the matter, but because the Constitution prohibits it from exercising the authority in that manner" (*Id* at 845).

68. *Id.* at 849.

69. *Id.* at 851.

70. *Id.*

71. *Id.* at 841.

72. 426 U.S. at 843, citing Fry v. United States, 421 U.S. 542, 547 (1975).

73. See the statement of Justice Stone in *supra* note 9.

74. 426 U.S. at 862.

75. *Wirtz,* 392 U.S. 183 (1968).

76. 421 U.S. 542 (1975).

77. *Id.* at 547.

78. Commentators have criticized the standard, "traditional governmental

functions" as unworkable. La Pierre, Political Safeguards of Federalism Redux, 60 Wash. U. L. Q. 779, 956–58 (1982); Wells and Hellerstein, *supra* note 20, at 1086–87; Van Alstyne, *supra* note 18, at 1717.

79. 426 U.S. 854.

80. 452 U.S. 264 (1981). See Rotunda, *supra* note 64, at 300–4.

81. Pub. L. No. 95–87, 91 Stat. 445 (codified as amended at 30 U.S.C.A. §§ 1201–1328 (1986).

82. *Id.* § 504(a), 30 U.S.C.A. § 1254 (a) (1986).

83. Virginia Surface Mining and Reclamation Association, Inc. v. Andrus, 483 F. Supp. 425 (W.D. Va. 1980), *reversed* 452 U.S. 264 (1981); Indiana v. Andrus, 501 F. Supp. 452 (S.D. Ind. 1980), *reversed* 452 U.S. 314 (1981).

84. 452 U.S. at 287–88: "[I]n order to succeed, a claim that congressional commerce power legislation is invalid under the reasoning of *National League of Cities* must satisfy *each* of three requirements. First, there must be a showing that the challenged statute regulates the 'States as States.' Second, the federal regulation must address matters that are indisputably 'attribute[s] of state sovereignty.' And third, it must be apparent that the States' compliance with the federal law would directly impair their ability 'to structure integral operations in areas of traditional functions.' "

85. National League of Cities v. Usery, 426 U.S. 833, 845, citing Coyle v. Oklahoma, 221 U.S. 559 (1911).

86. National League of Cities v. Usery, 426 U.S. 833, 849.

87. 452 U.S. at 290: "[I]t is clear that the Commerce Clause empowers Congress to prohibit all—and not just inconsistent—state regulation of such activity. . . . Although such Congressional enactments obviously curtail or prohibit the States' prerogatives to make legislative choices respecting subjects the States may consider important, the Supremacy Clause permits another result . . . "It is elementary and well settled that there can be no divided authority over interstate commerce, and that the Acts of Congress on that subject are supreme and exclusive.' "

88. 456 U.S. 742 (1982). See Rotunda, *supra* note 64, at 307–18 for a detailed analysis of this case.

89. Pub. L. No. 95–617, 92 Stat. 3117 (1978) (codified as amended in sections of 15, 16, 30, 42 and 43 U.S.C.A.).

90. PURPA, sec. 111, 16 U.S.C.A. § 2621 (1985); *Id.* § 113, 16 U.S.C.A. Section 2623 (1985).

91. PURPA, section 210, 16 U.S.C.A. § 824a-3 (1985).

92. Federal Energy Regulatory Commission, 456 U.S. 752. The district court opinion is unreported.

93. 456 U.S. 764.

94. *Id.* at 766.

95. *Id.* at 775–80.

96. 460 U.S. 226 (1983). See Rotunda, *supra* note 64, at 319–21.

97. This chapter does not treat in detail the cases holding that statutes enforcing the Thirteenth, Fourteenth and Fifteenth amendments override state power. There are no state immunities to those key civil rights. The extension of Title VII of the Civil Rights Act of 1964, 78 Stat. 253 (1964) as amended, 42 U.S.C.A. § 2000e et. seq. (1981), to states and their subdivisions, for example, was upheld in a sex-discrimination case as valid enforcement of section 5 of the Fourteenth Amendment (Fitzpatrick v. Bitzer, 427 U.S. 445 [1976]). The Civil War amendments "were specifically designed as an expansion of federal power and an intrusion on state sovereignty" (City of Rome v. United States, 446 U.S. 151, 179 [1980]).

98. 81 Stat. 602 (1967), 29 U.S.C.A. §§ 621 et. seq. 630 (b) (1985).

99. 88 Stat. 74 (1974), 29 U.S.C.A. §630b (1985).

100. E.E.O.C. v. State of Wyoming, 514 F. Supp. 595, 598–600 (D. Wyom. 1981).

101. E.E.O.C. 460 U.S. 237.

102. *Id.* at 238–39.

103. *Id.* at 239.

104. Cases on age discrimination subsequent to *Wyoming* have centered on whether the statutory age limit was a bona fide occupational qualification. See E.E.O.C. v. County of Allegheny, 705 F. 2d 679 (3d Cir. 1983); E.E.O.C. v. County of Los Angeles, 706 F. 2d 1039 (9th Cir. 1983), *cert. denied* 464 U.S. 1073 (1984); E.E.O.C. v. U. of Texas Health Center, 710 F.2d (1091 (5th Cir. 1983).

105. E.E.O.C. 460 U.S. at 239.

106. *Id.* at 242.

107. *Id.* at 243. The district court, citing Penhurst State School v. Halderman, 451 U.S. 1, 16 (1981), had held that application of the Age Discrimination Act to the states could not be justified as an exercise of Congress's power under Section 5 of the Fourteenth Amendment because Congress did not explicitly state that it had invoked that power in passing the 1972 amendments (E.E.O.C. v. State of Wyoming 514 F. Supp. 596, 598–600 [D. Wyoming 1981]). This statement seems unsound. All statutes are presumptively constitutional. U.S. v. National Dairy Products, 372 U.S. 29, 32 (1963). Even if Congress fails to mention a constitutional basis for a statute, the Court must uphold the statute if there is any constitutional basis for it. Had the Supreme Court found the commerce clause to be an inadequate basis of regulating states in this instance because of the principle of federalism, as expounded in *National League of Cities,* it was fully capable of upholding the statute under the Fourteenth Amendment.

108. See E.E.O.C. 460 U.S. at 229.

109. See Conant, Systems Analysis in the Appellate Decisionmaking Process, 24 Rutgers L. Rev. 293, 317–19 (1970).

110. E.E.O.C. 460 U.S. at 252.

111. *Id.* at 252–54.

112. *Id.* at 255–56.

113. 452 U.S. 264, 287–88 (1981).

114. Garcia, 469 U.S. 528, 538.

115. Gold Cross Ambulance v. Kansas City, 538 F. Supp. 956, 967–69 (W.D.Mo. 1982), *aff'd on other grounds,* 705 F. 2d 1005 (8th Cir. 1983), *cert. denied* 471 U.S. 1003 (1985); Hybud Equipment Corp. v. Akron, 654 F. 2d 1187 (6th Cir. 1981). See Parker v. Brown, 317 U.S. 314 (1943). For a critique of this case, see Conant, The Supremacy Clause and State Economic Controls, 10 Hastings Con. L. Q. 255, 268–72 (1953).

116. United States v. Best, 573 F. 2d 1095, 1102–1103 (9th Cir. 1978).

117. Amersbach v. Cleveland, 598 F.2d 1033, 1037–1038 (6th Cir. 1979) (municipal airport employees); Enrique Molina-Estrada v. Puerto Rico Highway Authority, 680 F. 2d 841, 845–46 (1st Cir. 1982) (irregular highway employees not entitled to overtime pay).

118. Garcia, 469 U.S. 528, 538–39.

119. Oklahoma ex. rel. Derryberry v. FERC, 494 F. Supp. 636, 657 (W.D. Okla. 1980), *aff'd* 661 F.2d 832 (10th Cir. 1981), *cert. denied sub nom.* Texas v. F.E.R.C., 457 U.S. 1105 (1982) (federal regulation of intrastate natural gas prices); Friends of the Earth v. Carey, 552 F. 2d. 25, 38 (2d Cir. 1977), *cert.*

denied 434 U.S. 902 (1977) (Clean Air Act governs state regulation of traffic on public roads); Hughes Air Corp. v. Public Utilities Com'n, 644 F.2d 1334, 1340–41 (9th Cir. 1981) (federal regulation of air transport overrides state regulation).

120. Woods v. Homes and Structures of Pittsburgh, Kansas, 489 F. Supp. 1270, 1296–97 (Kan. 1980) (issuance of local industrial development bonds held subject to federal securities regulation); Puerto Rico Tel. Co. v. F.C.C., 553 F. 2d. 694, 700-01 (1st Cir. 1977) (publicly owned telephone company held subject to FCC regulation); Public Service Co. v. FERC, 587 F. 2d 716, 721 (5th Cir. 1979), *cert. denied sub nom.* Louisiana v. F.E.R.C., 444 U.S. 879 (1979) (state-owned natural gas subject to federal regulation).

121. Williams v. Eastside Mental Health Center, 669 F. 2d. 671, 680–81 (11th Cir. 1982), *cert. denied* 459 U.S. 976 (1982); (not-for-profit mental-health institution is not state agency and does not perform integral state function); Bonnette v. California Health and Welfare Agency, 704 F. 2d. 1465, 1472 (9th Cir. 1983) (chore workers hired by state agency to perform in-home services for the disabled do not perform traditional governmental function).

122. 644 F. 2d, 1334, 1340–41 (9th Cir. 1981).

123. 598 F. 2d 1033, 1037–38 (6th Cir. 1979).

124. 469 U.S. 528 (1985).

125. Fair Labor Standards Amendments of 1974, § 21b, 88 Stat. 68, 29 U.S.C. 207 n.

126. J. Meyer, J. Kain, and M. Wohl, The Urban Transportation Problem 88–98 (1965). Local bus and trolley companies have a morning peak-load demand from about 6:30 to 9:00 AM and an evening peak-load demand from 4:00 to 6:30 PM.

127. U.S. Cong., House Committee on Education and Labor, Fair Labor Standards Amendments of 1973, Hearings on H.R. 4757 and H.R. 2831, 163–67 (93d Cong. 1st sess. 1973).

128. *Id.* at 169–70.

129. 469 U.S. at 531.

130. *Id.* at 534.

131. *Id.*

132. In 1981, the district court granted SAMTA's motion for summary judgment, ruling that "local mass transit systems constitute integral operations in areas of traditional governmental functions" (469 U.S. at 535). The Secretary of Labor and Garcia appealed. While the appeals were pending, the Supreme Court decided United Transportation Union v. Long Island R. Co., 455 U.S. 678 (1982), ruling that a state-owned commuter rail service with a private proprietary history was not a traditional governmental function and hence not immune from requirements of the Railway Labor Act under *National League of Cities.* The Supreme Court in *Garcia* vacated the District Court judgments and remanded them for further consideration in the light of *Long Island.* Garcia v. San Antonio Met. Transit Authority, 457 U.S. 1102 (1982). On remand, the District Court refused to apply the *Long Island* ruling to SAMTA and adhered to its original view of constitutional immunity. San Antonio Met. Transit Authority v. Donavan, 557 F. Supp. 445 (W. D. Texas 1983).

133. In its first footnote, the Court cited the three courts of appeal decisions and a state appellate decision holding local mass transit to be proprietary and not immune from FLSA. 469 U.S. at 530. See *supra* note 32.

134. 469 U.S. at 539–44.

135. *Id.* at 538–39. These cases are discussed, *supra* notes 115 to 123 and accompanying text.

136. Justice Blackmun writes of "state tax immunity recognized in Collector

v. Day," 78 U.S. (11 Wall.) 113 (1870), cited at 469 U.S. 540. That case did not concern state-tax immunity but was the classic case concerning immunity from federal income taxation of state employees and was expressly overruled in Graves v. New York ex rel. O'Keefe. 306 U.S. 466, 486 (1939). The Court puts substantial weight on the *obiter dicta* in Brush v. Commissioner, 300 U.S. 352 (1937), a case concerning whether the salary of the chief engineer of New York City's water supply bureau was subject to federal income taxation. This case was overruled by *Graves*, as was expressly noted in the dissent (306 U.S. at 492) (McReynolds dissenting). In the *obiter dicta* of Flint v. Stone, Tracy Co., 220 U.S. 107, 172 (1911), the Supreme Court had ruled that if a private corporation supplied city water, it would be subject to a federal corporation tax. The Court stated that since a private firm could be granted a public monopoly, the supply of water was not an essential governmental function. This is erroneous since a city or state could employ a private firm to supply a public good. In *Brush, Flint* was distinguished as *dictum* and the supply of water was held governmental (300 U.S. at 373). The alleged inconsistency of these two cases did not exist. Neither concerned taxation of states or their agencies. *Flint* was limited to federal taxation of private corporations. *Brush* concerned federal income taxation of individuals. Blackmun also fails to note that other cases he cites concern taxation of individuals, not state agencies. Thus, Helvering v. Powers, 293 U.S. 214 (1934) held that the compensation of members of boards of a state-run commuter-rail system were not immune from federal income taxation. Herlvering v. Gebhardt (304 U.S. 405 (1938) held that federal income-tax laws applied to salaries of employees of the Port of New York Authority.

137. Justice Blackmun cited Indian Towing Co. v. United States, 350 U.S. 61 (1955), cited at 469 U.S. 545 to assert that the notion of a "uniquely" governmental function is unmanageable. But the main holding of that case was that the distinction in municipal corporation law between governmental and nongovernmental is not applicable in construction of Federal Tort Claims Act. The Court in dictum stated "all Government activity is inescapably 'uniquely governmental' in that it is performed by the government" (350 U.S. at 126). The total refusal in the federal claims context to distinguish types of activity performed by governments is no test of whether one can usefully distinguish proprietary activities of government from those that are uniquely governmental, such as policing a city or state.

138. 469 U.S. 546.

139. *Id.*

140. *Id.* at 548.

141. *Id.* at 550–51, citing J. Choper, *supra* note 53, 175–84; Wechsler, *supra* note 11.

142. *Id.* at 552–53.

143. *Id.* at 554.

144. *Id.* at 558–60. "I note that it does not seem to have occurred to the Court that *it*—an unelected majority of five Justices—today rejects almost 200 years of the understanding of the constitutional status of federalism" (*Id.* at 560).

145. *Id.* at 562.

146. *Id.* at 564–67.

147. *Id.* at 571.

148. *Id.* at 573–75.

149. *Id.* at 575.

150. Field, *Garcia v. San Antonio Metropolitan Transit Authority,* 99 Harv. L. Rev. 84, 89–95 (1985).

151. *Id.* at 96–103.

152. Garcia, 469 U.S. at 572 (Powell, J., dissenting); 469 U.S. at 584–85 (O'Conner, J., dissenting).

153. See, e.g., Howard, Garcia and the Values of Federalism, 19 Ga. L. Rev. 789 (1985).

154. On separated powers, see Immigration and Naturalization Service v. Chadha, 462 U.S. 919 (1983); United States v. Nixon, 418 U.S. 683 (1974).

155. Garcia, 469 U.S. at 568–70 (Powell, J., dissenting). See Brooks, Garcia, the Seventeenth Amendment, and the Role of the Supreme Court in Defending Federalism, 10 Harv. J. L. & Pub. Pol. 189, 192–96 (1987); Van Alstyne, *supra* note 18, at 1727–31; Rapaczynski, *supra* note 10, at 380–95. Compare J. Choper, *supra* note 53, ch. 4.

156. See Brooks, *supra* note 155, at 199–208.

157. Baird, State Empowerment after Garcia, 18 Urban Lawyer 491 (1986). See authorities at 503 n. 62.

158. McCulloch v. Maryland, 17 U.S. (4 Wheat.) 316, 403 (1819).

159. Madison, Federalist 10, at 62 (E. Bourne ed. 1947).

160. See Stigler, *supra* note 2.

161. U.S. Cong., House Committee on Education and Labor, Hearing on the Fair Labor Standards Act 5, 7 (99th Cong., 1st sess. 1985). See U.S. Cong., Senate Committee on Labor and Human Resources, Fair Labor Standards Amendments of 1985, Hearings (99th Cong., 1st sess. 1985). See generally, Overtime Work, 109 Monthly Labor Rev. 36 (Nov. 1986).

162. Fair Labor Standards Amendments of 1985, 99 Stat. 787, 29 U.S.C.A. Section 207(o). See Murphy and Nickles, The Fair Labor Standards Act Amendments of 1985, 37 Labor L. J. 67 (1986).

Chapter 7

1. U.S. Const., art III, § 2.

2. U.S. Const., art. I, § 8, cl. 3.

3. U.S. Const., art VI, cl. 2.

4. 41 U.S. (16 Pet.) 1 (1842).

5. See W. Crosskey, Politics and the Constitution in the History of the United States, II, 856–60 (1953); R. Bridwell and R. Whitten, The Constitution and the Common Law 1–4, 61–70, 90–91 (1977); Heckman, The Relationship of Swift v. Tyson to the Status of Commercial Law in the Nineteenth Century and the Federal System, 17 Am. J. of Legal History 246 (1973); Dickinson, The Law of Nations as Part of the National Law of the United States, 101 U. of Penn. L. Rev. 792, 797–90 (1953).

6. Act of Sept. 24, 1789, ch. 20, § 34, 1 Stat. 92 (1789).

7. An elementary principle of *stare decisis* is that the language used in an opinion must always be read in light of the issues presented, and the *ratio decidendi* is limited to the facts under discussion. Cohens v. Virginia, 19 U.S. (6 Wheat.) 264, 399 (1821); Humphrey's Ex'r. v. United States, 295 U.S. 602, 626–27 (1935). See, generally, Goodhart, Determining the Ratio Decidendi of a Case, 40 Yale L. J. 161 (1930); J. Stone, Legal System and Lawyers' Reasonings 267–74 (1964).

8. 304 U.S. 64 (1938).

9. See W. Crosskey, *supra* note 5, at I, 567–70; R. Bridwell and R. Whitten, *supra* note 5, 52–53. See generally, F. Savigny, Private International Law and the Retrospective Operation of Statutes 194–272 (2d English ed. 1880).

10. Gloucester Insurance Co. v. Younger, 10 Fed. Cas. 495, 500 (no. 5487)

(C.C.D. Mass. 1855); J. Story, Commentaries on the Law of Bills of Exchange 146–52 (2d ed. 1847).

11. Chancellor Kent's commentaries, part V, entitled "Of the Law Concerning Personal Property" begins with a chapter on the history of maritime law followed by a survey of the law merchant. J. Kent, Commentaries on American Law, III, 1019 (10th ed. 1860). This historical relationship is illustrated by the English precedents in commercial law. See, e.g., Luke v. Lyde, 2 Burr. 882, 97 Eng. Rep. 614 (K.B. 1759); Pelly v. Company of the Royal Exchange Assurance, 1 Burr. 341, 97 Eng. Rep. 342 (K.B. 1757).

12. J. Story, Progress of Jurisprudence, in Miscellaneous Writings 198, 214–15 (W. Story ed. 1852).

13. See R. Bridwell and R. Whitten, *supra* note 5, at 61–68. See generally W. Mitchell, Essay on the Early History of Law Merchant, ch. 2 (1904); F. Sanborn, Origins of the Early English Maritime and Commercial Law (1930); L. Trakman, The Law Merchant (1983); Berman and Kaufman, The Law of International Commercial Transactions, 19 Harv. Int'l L. J. 221 (1978).

14. See W. Holdsworth, History of English Law, I, 535–44 (7th ed. 1956); John Macdonell, Introduction to J. Smith, Compendium of Mercantile Law (10th ed. 1890).

15. Vanheath v. Turner, Winch 24, 124 Eng. Rep. 20 (C.P. 1621); Pierson v. Pounteys, Yelverton 135, 80 Eng. Rep. 91 (K.B. 1609).

16. Oaste v. Taylor, Cro. Jac. 306, 79 Eng. Rep. 262 (K.B. 1613).

17. Brandoa v. Barnett, 12 Clark & Finnelly 787, 8 Eng. Rep. 1622 (H.L. 1846); Ereskine v. Murray, 2 Ld. Raym. 1542, 92 Eng. Rep. 500 (K.B. 1728); Mogadara v. Holt, 1 Show K.B. 317, 89 Eng. Rep. 597 (K.B. 1691). If evidence showed a clearly established and settled usage among merchants on the issue in contest, no evidence of particular usages of the litigants would be admitted. Edie v. East India Co., 2 Burr. 1216, 97 Eng. Rep. 797 (K.B. 1761).

18. Goodwin v. Robarts, L.R. 10 Exch. 337, 346 (1875), *affirmed*, H.L., 1 App. Cas. 476 (1876).

19. See C. Fried, Contract as Promise 9–21 (1981); Sharp, Promissory Liability, 7 U. Chi. L. Rev. 1, 250 (1939–40).

20. 20 Fed. Cas. 458 (No. 11, 657) (C.C.D. Mass. 1837).

21.

The true and appropriate office of a usage or custom is, to interpret the otherwise indeterminable intentions of parties, and to ascertain the nature and extent of their contracts, arising not from express stipulations, but from mere implications and presumptions, and acts of a doubtful or equivocal character. It may also be admitted to ascertain the true meaning of a particular word, or of particular words in a given instrument, when the word or words have various senses, some common, some qualified, and some technical, according to the subject-matter, to which they are applied. But I apprehend, that it can never be proper to resort to any usage or custom to control or vary the positive stipulations in a written contract, and a fortiori, not in order to contradict them. An express contract of the parties is always admissible to supersede, or vary, or control, a usage or custom; for the latter may always be waived at the will of the parties. But a written and express contract cannot be controlled, or varied, or contradicted by a usage or custom; for that would not only be to admit parol evidence to control, vary, or contradict written contracts; but it would be to allow mere presumptions and implications, properly arising in the absence of any positive expressions of intention, to control, vary or contradict the most formal and deliberate written declarations of the parties.

Id. at 459.

22. Brandoa v. Barnett, 12 Clark & Finnelly 787, 8 Eng. Rep. 1622, 1629 (H.L. 1846) (Lord Campbell).

23.

It is no doubt true that negotiability can only be attached to a contract by the law merchant or by a statute; and it is also true that, in determining whether a usage has become so well established as to be binding on the Courts of law, the length of time during which the usage has existed is an important circumstance to take into consideration; but it is to be remembered that in these days usage is established much more quickly than it was in days gone by; more depends on the number of the transactions which help to create it than on the time over which the transactions are spread; and it is probably no exaggeration to say that nowadays there are more business transactions in an hour than there were in a week a century ago. Therefore the comparatively recent origin of this class of securities in my view creates no difficulty in the way of holding that they are negotiable by virtue of the law merchant; they are dealt in as negotiable instruments in every minute of a working day, and to the extent of many thousands of pounds. It is also to be remembered that the law merchant is not fixed and stereotyped; it has not yet been arrested in its growth by being moulded into a code; it is . . . capable of being expanded and enlarged so as to meet the wants and requirements of trade in the varying circumstances of commerce, the effect of which is that it approves and adopts from time to time those usages of merchants which are found necessary for the convenience of trade; our common law, of which the law merchant is but a branch, has in the hands of the judges the same facility for adapting itself to the changing needs of the general public; principles do not alter, but old rules of applying them change, and new rules spring into existence.

Edelstein v. Schuler & Co. [1902] 2 K.B. 144, 154–55.

24. T. Scrutton, The Influence of the Roman Law on the Law of England, ch. 15 (1885). Justice Story commented on the origins of modern contract law: "The truth is, that the common law, however reluctant it may be to make the acknowledgment, and however boastful it may be of its own perfection, owes to the civil law, and its elegant and indefatigable commentators . . . almost all its valuable doctrines and expositions of the law of contract. The very action of assumpsit, in its modern refinements, breathes the spirit of its origin. It is altogether Roman and Praetorian." (J. Story, Growth of the Commercial Law, in Miscellaneous Writings 262, 280 [W. Story, ed., 1852]). See W. Buckland, A Manual of Roman Private Law, ch. 12 (1953).

25. 43 Eliza. c. 12 (1601), *reenacted and amended* 13–14 Car. II, c. 23 (1661). See W. Holdsworth, The Development of the Law Merchant and its Courts, in Select Essays in Anglo-American Legal History, I, 289, 329 (1907). In spite of efficient, summary procedure, the court had a short life because it was held in 1658 that the proceedings were not a bar to an action at common law. Came v. Moye, 2 Sid. 121, 82 Eng. Rep. 1290 (K.B. 1658).

26. See W. Holdsworth, *supra* note 14, at 535–44.

27. The first reported case on a negotiable instrument in the common-law courts was Martin v. Boure, Cro. Jac. 6, 79 Eng. Rep. 6 (Ex. Ch. 1603).

28. See T. Scrutton, Elements of Mercantile Law 13 (1891); Burdick, What is the Law Merchant? 2 Colum. L. Rev. 470, 479 (1902).

29. See review of this phenomenon in C. Fifoot, Lord Mansfield, ch. 4 (1936). W. Holdsworth, History of English Law, XII, 524–42 (1938).

30. Carter v. Downish, 1 Show K.B. 127, 89 Eng. Rep. 492, 493 (K.B. 1689); Williams v. Williams, Carthew 269, 90 Eng. Rep. 759, 760 (Ex. Ch. 1693).

31. M. Bigelow, The Law of Bills, Notes, and Cheques 6 (2d ed. 1900).

32. Lickbarrow v. Mason, 2 T.R. 63, 100 Eng. Rep. 35, 40 (K.B. 1787).

33. 2 Burr. 882, 97 Eng. Rep. 614 (K.B. 1759).

34. J. Wilson, Works of James Wilson, I, 279 (R. McCloskey ed. 1967).

35. W. Blackstone, Commentaries on the Laws of England, I, 273 (Reprint 1979). For additional citations, see W. Crosskey, *supra* note 5, I, at 33–35, 78–79, 569.

36. J. Story, *supra* note 12.

37. Walden v. LeRoy, 2 Caines R. 263, 265 (N.Y. Sup. Ct. 1805).

38. Petrie v. Clark, 11 S. & R. 377, 389 (Pa. 1824).

39. Atkinson v. Brooks, 26 Vt. 569 (1854). He summarized the process as follows:

> The more important question growing out of the case is, perhaps, what is the true commercial rule established upon this subject? And it is of vital importance in regard to commercial usages, that they should, as far as practicable, be uniform throughout the world. And such is necessarily the ultimate desideratum, and will inevitably be the final result. It is therefore, always a question of time as to uniformity in such usages. The basis of such uniformity is convenience and justice combined. And until such rules become measurably settled by practice, they have to be treated as matters of fact, to be passed upon by juries; and when the rule acquires the quality of uniformity, and the character of general acceptance, it is then regarded as matter of law. It is thus that most of the commercial law has from time to time grown up.

Id. at 578.

40. Act of Sept. 24, 1789, ch. 20, §34; 1 Stat. 73, 92 (1789).

41. An Act to Regulate Processes in the Courts of the United States, Act of Sept. 29, 1789, ch. 21, §2, 1 Stat. 93 (1789). For modern practice, see Hanna v. Plumer, 380 U.S. 460 (1965); C. Wright, Law of Federal Courts 358 (4th ed. 1983).

42. W. Crosskey *supra* note 5, II, at 868. See also the titles of treatises on both statute and case law such as W. Blackstone, Commentaries on the Laws of England (1765–1769); R. Wooddeson, A Systematical View of the Laws of England (1792); Z. Swift, System of the Laws of the State of Connecticut (1795). The prior drafts of the Judiciary Act are reviewed in Warren, New Light on the History of the Federal Judiciary Act of 1789, 37 Harv. L. Rev. 49 (1923). See critique in W. Ritz, Rewriting the History of the Judiciary Act of 1789, 165–79 (1990).

43. See, e.g., Jackson ex dem. St. John v. Chew, 25 U.S. (12 Wheat.) 153 (1827); Wheaton v. Peters, 33 U.S. (8 Pet.) 591 (1834).

44. 149 U.S. 368, 391 (1893). In his extensive discussion of the meaning of Section 34 of the Judiciary Act of 1789 in trials at common law, Field did not mention *Swift*. One possible inference is that Field correctly understood that Section 34 did not apply to the law merchant.

45. For an example of a context where "laws" had to be a synonym for legislation, see the "necessary and proper" clause of Article I, Section 8. There,

the entire article is concerned with legislation. Similarly the word "Laws" on the title page of a code, such as the Laws of New York, has the restricted context of legislation only.

46. 149 U.S. 398.

47. See chapter 5.

48. See R. Bridwell and R. Whitten, *supra* note 5, at 61–62, 95.

49. U.S. Const., amend. 10.

50. See the concurring opinion of Justice Johnson in Gibbons v. Ogden, 22 U.S. (9 Wheat.) 1, 222, 224–26 (1824); Edgar v. Mite Corp., 457 U.S. 624, 640 (1982).

51. Southern Pacific Co. v. Arizona, 325 U.S. 761 (1945); Lewis v. BT Inv. Managers, Inc., 447 U.S. 27, 35–37 (1980).

52. H. Maine, Popular Government 253 (1886). The Constitution must be interpreted as a unified whole within the English constitutional and common-law legal environment of its adoption. *Ex parte* Grossman, 267 U.S. 87, 108–9 (1925); United States v. Wong Kim Ark, 169 U.S. 649, 668–72 (1898). See the comments of Justice Henry Baldwin, Origin and Nature of the Constitution and Government of the United States, 9 L. Ed. 869, 893–94 (1837).

53. International commerce was a significant part of the life of the nation even before the revolution. As a part of British commerce, its disputes were governed by the law merchant. After ratification of the constitution, and absent congressional regulation, interstate commerce was of the same legal character as international. Buckner v. Finley, 27 U.S. (2 Pet.) 586, 590–91 (1829).

54. Donnell v. Columbian Insurance Co., 7 Fed. Cas. 889, 895 (no. 3, 978) (C.C.D. Mass. 1836); The Seneca, 21 Fed. Cas. 1081, 1082–84 (no. 12, 670) (C.C.E.D. Pa. 1829). See J. Story, Growth of the Commercial Law, in Miscellaneous Writings 262, 268, 281 (1852).

55. United States v. Burr, 25 F. Cas. 187, 188 (no. 14, 694) (C.C.D. Va. 1807). This view was reiterated by Chief Justice Taney in United States v. Reid, 53 U.S. (12 How.) 361, 363 (1851): "The language of this section cannot, upon any fair construction, be extended beyond civil cases at common law as contradistinguished from suits in equity."

56. 1 Stat. 93 (1789).

57. W. Rawle, A View of the Constitution of the United States of America 248 (1825).

58. Pennsylvania v. Wheeling & Belmont Bridge Co., 54 U.S. (13 How.) 518, 563 (1852). See United States v. Coolidge, 25 Fed. Cas. 619, 620 (no. 14, 857) (C.C.D. Mass. 1813). Justice Story on circuit in Maine stated, "The equity jurisdiction of this court is wholly independent of the local laws of any state; and is the same in its nature and extent, as the equity jurisdiction of England, from which ours is derived, and is governed by the same principles." Gordon v. Hobart, 10 Fed. Cas. 795, 797 (no. 5, 609) (C.C.D. Me. 1836). See G. Dunne, Joseph Story and the Rise of the Supreme Court 415–20 (1970); C. Swisher, The Taney Period: 1836–64, History of the Supreme Court of the United States, V, ch. 13 (1974).

59. 41 U.S. (16 Pet.) 1, 19.

60. Heckman, *supra* note 5, at 247–48.

61. Hawkins v. Barney's Lessee, 30 U.S. (5 Pet.) 457, 464 (1831). See Peter S. Du Ponceau, A Dissertation on the Nature and Extent of the Jurisdiction of the Courts of the United States 36–37 (1824; reprint 1972); W. Rawle, *supra* note 57, at 246–47 (1825); W. Rose, A Code of Federal Procedure, I, 67–69 (1907).

62. The conflict-of-laws principles were of international origin and were thus part of the law of nations. See, e.g., Ogden v. Saunders, 25 U.S. (12 Wheat.) 213,

359 (1827) (Johnson, J.). Justice Story's treatise on the conflict of laws contains an early chapter entitled "General Maxims of International Jurisprudence." J. Story, Commentaries on the Conflict of Laws, ch. 2 (1834). Story relied greatly on the writings of the European civilians and especially on Ulricus Huber, *De Conflictu Legum in Diversis Imperiis.* See Note, 3 U.S. (3 Dallas) 370–77 (1797); Lorenzen, Huber's De Conflictu Legum, 13 Ill. L. Rev. 375 (1919); Lorenzen, Story's Commentaries on the Conflict of Laws, 48 Harv. L. Rev. 18 (1934).

63. See Erie v. Tompkins, 304 U.S. 64, 74–76 (1938); R. Bridwell and R. Whitten, *supra* note 5, at 1–3.

64. *Id.* at 3–4, 61–97.

65. Swift v. Tyson, 41 U.S. (16 Pet.) 1, 18 (1842).

66. 25 U.S. (12 Wheat.) 153 (1827). See W. Rose, A Code of Federal Procedure, I, 71 (1907).

67. 11 U.S. (7 Cranch) 115 (1812) (Story, J.).

68. 33 U.S. (8 Pet.) 591 (1834). See G. White, The Marshall Court and Cultural Change, 1815–35, History of the Supreme Court of the United States, III–IV, 384–426 (1988); R. Kent Newmyer, Supreme Court Justice Story 140–43 (1985).

69. 33 U.S. at 658.

70. 41 U.S. (16 Pet.) 1 (1842).

71. 31 U.S. (6 Pet.) 291 (1832).

72. *Id.* at 299–300.

73. 46 U.S. (5 How.) 134 (1847).

74. 40 U.S. (15 Pet.) 449 (1841).

75. 46 U.S. (5 How.) at 139. The basic principle of *Rowan,* protecting the obligation of contract, was followed in Gelpcke v. Dubuque, 68 U.S. (1 Wall.) 175 (1864).

76. Wilson v. Mason, 5 U.S. (1 Cranch) 45, 94–95 (1801).

77. Fletcher, The General Common Law and Section 34 of the Judiciary Act of 1789, 97 Harv. L. Rev. 1513, 1539 (1984).

78. Thurston v. Koch, 1 L. Ed. (4 Dall.) 862, 929 (C.C.D. Pa. 1800). Peters further stated, "I deem myself bound to follow what was the established law and custom of merchants of England, at the time of becoming an independent nation: not because it was the law merely of that country; but because it was, and is, our law" (*Id.* at 930).

79. Marine Insurance Co. v. Tucker, 7 U.S. (3 Cranch) 357, 393 (1806).

80. Fletcher, *supra* note 77, at 1576.

81. See J. Story, Growth of the Commercial Law, in Miscellaneous Writings 262–94 (W. Story ed. 1852).

82. Donnell v. Columbian Insurance Co., 7 Fed. Cas. 889, 893–94 (no. 3,987) (C.C.D. Mass. 1836); Robinson v. Commonwealth Ins. Co., 20 Fed. Cas. 1002, 1004 (no. 11,949) (C.C.D. Mass. 1838); Williams v. Suffolk Ins. Co., 29 Fed. Cas. 1402, 1405 (no. 17,738) (C.C.D. Mass. 1838).

83. Williams, 29 Fed. Cas. at 1405.

84. W. Blackstone, Commentaries on the Laws of England, *supra* note 35; R. Wooddeson, The Elements of Jurisprudence 92 (1783); S. Marshall, A Treatise on the Law of Insurance 18–20 (1st American ed. 1805); J. Sullivan, History of Land Titles in Massachusetts 337–38 (1801); St. G. Tucker, ed., Blackstone's Commentaries 429–30 (1803); Z. Swift, A Digest of the Law of Evidence in Criminal Cases and a Treatise on Bills of Exchange and Promissory Notes 245 (1810); J. Wilson, Works of James Wilson, *infra* note 141 and accompanying text; P. Du Ponceau, Dissertation on the Nature and Extent of the Jurisdiction of

the Courts of the United States 39–41 (1824); W. Rawle, *supra* note 57, 225; T. Sergeant, Constitutional Law 148–50 (2d ed. 1830). One could also cite the extrajudicial writings of Story, such as his 1821 article (see *supra* note 12).

85. 9 Fed. Cas. 62 (no. 4,791) (C.C.D. Ohio 1839).

86. *Id.* at 64.

87. *Id.* at 65.

88. 27 U.S. (2 Pet.) 586 (1829).

89. *Id.* at 592.

90. 28 Fed. Cas. 1062 (no. 16,871) (C.C.D. R.I. 1812), affirmed in part but reversed on other grounds *sub nom.* Clark v. Van Reimsdyk, 13 U.S. (9 Cranch) 153 (1815).

91. See J. Story, Commentaries on the Law of Bills of Exchange, *supra* note 11. The first American conflict-of-laws treatise was published in 1828. S. Livermore, Dissertation on the Questions which Arise from the Contrariety of the Positive Laws of Different States and Nations. The first edition of Joseph Story's *Commentaries on the Conflict of Laws* was 1834.

92. 28 Fed. Cas. at 1065.

93. *Id.*

94. 15 U.S. (2 Wheat.) 66 (1817). See G. White, *supra* note 68, at 795–99, 810–13.

95. Payson v. Coolidge, 19 Fed. Cas. 19 (no. 10,860) (C.C.D. Mass. 1814).

96. 19 Fed. Cas. at 21.

97. 27 U.S. (2 Pet.) 170 (1829).

98. 20 Fed. Cas. 801 (no. 11,835) (C.C.D. Ohio 1841).

99. 41 U.S. (16 Pet.) 1 (1842). The history of this case and citations to the many commentaries thereon is in T. Freyer, Harmony and Dissonance (1981).

100. 20 Fed. Cas. 801 (no. 11,835) (C.C.D. Ohio 1841).

101. Story has been criticized for stating the entire test in terms of valuable consideration when the precedents required proof that the bill of exchange was taken in the ordinary course of business or trade. See K. Llewellyn, The Common Law Tradition 410–16 (1960).

102. Coolidge v. Payson, 15 U.S. (2 Wheat.) 66 (1817); Townsley v. Sumrall, 27 U.S. (2 Pet.) 170 (1829).

103. 41 U.S. (16 Pet.) at 18 (emphasis added). See W. Crosskey, *supra* note 5, II, at 857–58. This jurisprudential approach was borrowed from the then-common British practice, where most recorded opinions were not settled law because they were not decided in the highest appeals court, the House of Lords. Lord Mansfield stated: "[T]he law of England would be a strange science indeed if it were decided upon precedents only. Precedents serve to illustrate principles and give them a fixed certainty. But the law of England, which is exclusive of positive law enacted by statute, depends upon principles and these principles run through all the cases according as the particular circumstances of each have been found to fall within the one or the other of them" (Jones v. Randall, 1 Cowper 37, 39, 98 Eng. Rep. 754, 755 [K.B. 1774]). See Salmond, The Theory of Judicial Precedents, 16 L. Quart. Rev. 376, 379–80 (1900). As to the adoption by early American Courts of this method of writing opinions on the basis of general principles with little citation of precedents, see J. Goebel, The Common Law and the Constitution, in Chief Justice John Marshall 101, 108–15 (W. Jones ed. 1956).

104. 41 U.S. (16 Pet.) at 18–19. See Chief Justice Taney's reaffirmation of his support for Story's opinion in *Swift* by his later express adoption of the *Swift* rationale. Meade v. Beale, 16 Fed. Cas. 1283, 1291 (no. 9371) (C.C.D. Md. 1850).

105. The rules of documentary interpretation and construction, though not usually classified as a part of the law of nations, can be traced to the civil law. H. Jolowicz, The Roman Foundations of Modern Law, ch. 2 (1957). T. Rutherforth, Institutes of Natural Law 404–35 (2d. Amer. ed. 1832) relies primarily on Grotius as authority. The rules are thus international in character and not dependent on the law of any single state.

In Lane v. Vick, 44 U.S. (3 How.) 464 (1845), the Court applied general rules of documentary construction to a will and refused to follow the contrary precedent of the Mississippi Supreme Court. Justice McKinley, in dissent, argued that the Court should have followed *lex loci rei sitae* because the effect of the decision was to determine title to real property. *Id.* at 482.

106. 2 Burr. 882, 97 Eng. Rep. 614 (K.B. 1759).

107. *Id.* at 617.

108. Justice Story was a nationalist on a court of states' righters. He was not the leader or even dominant on the Taney Court. For example, he felt it necessary to dissent in three leading cases during the first term that Taney was chief justice. Charles River Bridge v. Warren Bridge, 36 U.S. (11 Pet.) 420, 583ff (1837); New York v. Miln 36 U.S. (11 Pet.) 102, 1530 (1837); Briscoe v. Bank of Kentucky, 36 U.S. (11 Pet.) 257, 328s (1837). See letter of Joseph Story to James Kent, June 26, 1837, in Life and Letters of Joseph Story, II, 270 (W. Story ed. 1851).

109. See, e.g., Brown v. Van Braam, 3 U.S. (3 Dallas) 334 (1797) (conflict-of-laws rules required that the right to damages be determined under a Rhode Island statute of 1743). See R. Bridwell and R. Whitten, *supra* note 5, at 78–79.

110. 41 U.S. (16 Pet.) 495 (1842).

111.

We have not thought it necessary upon this occasion to go into an examination of the cases cited from the New York and Massachusetts Reports, either upon this last point, or upon the former point. The decisions in those cases are certainly open to some of the grave doubts and difficulties suggested at the bar, as to their true bearing and results. The circumstances however, attending them are distinguishable from those of the case now before us, and they certainly cannot be admitted to govern it. The questions under our considerations are questions of general commercial law, and depend upon the construction of a contract of insurance, which is by no means local in its character, or regulated by any local policy or customs. Whatever respect, therefore, the decisions of State tribunals may have on such a subject, and they certainly are entitled to great respect, they cannot conclude the judgment of this court. On the contrary, we are bound to interpret this instrument according to our own opinion of its true intent and objects, aided by all the lights which can obtained from all external sources whatsoever; and if the result to which we have arrived differs from that of these learned State courts, we may regret it, but it cannot be permitted to alter our judgment.

41 U.S. 511–512.

112. 59 U.S. (18 How.) 517 (1855).

113. *Id.* at 521. Justice Daniel was considered the most extreme states' rights proponent of the Taney Court. He would never have written this nationalist opinion if it were not a clear expression of standing law. See J. Frank, Justice Daniel Dissenting (1964).

114. 28 Fed. Cas. 1062 (no. 16,871) (C.C.D. R.I. 1812). See *supra* notes 85 to 88 and accompanying text.

115. U.S. Const., art. VI, cl. 2.

116. See *supra* note 42 and accompanying text.

117. The fact that an earlier draft of this clause was in terms of "the legislative acts of the United States" is not a contextual fact to limit its scope. The shift to "laws of the United States" was most likely a deliberate choice to broaden the language to include national decisional law to be adopted by the new judiciary. See W. Crosskey, *supra* note 5, II, at 994. Crosskey's contrary conclusion fails to consider the law of nations as separate from the common law for application of the supremacy clause.

118. U.S. Const., art. VI, cl. 2.

119. See sources cited in note, Federal Common Law and Article III: A Jurisdictional Approach to Erie, 74 Yale L. J. 325, 335 (1964).

120. Village of Bensenville v. City of Chicago, 16 Ill. App. 3d 733, 306 N.E. 2d 512 (1973) (state common law of nuisance for noise pollution preempted by the Federal Aviation Act and the Federal Noise Control Act of 1972); In re Hendricksen's Estate, 15 Neb. 463, 56 N.W. 2d 711, 719 (1953) (U.S. Treasury regulations relating to U.S. bonds preempt state law of decedent estates).

121. Standard Oil Co. of New Jersey v. United States, 340 U.S. 54, 59–60 (1950). See J. Story, Commentaries on the Conflict of Laws 24 (1834). The suggestion that federal courts were bound to adopt English maritime law rather than the civil codes of continental Europe on the few issues where they differed is erroneous. In De Lovio v. Boit, 7 Fed. Cas. 418 (No. 3, 776) (C.C.D. Mass. 1815), Justice Story held a policy of marine insurance was a maritime contract cognizable in admiralty. To reach this decision, he had to reject the restricted view that had come to prevail in England at the time the Constitution was adopted. Instead he applied the broader rule of the civil codes. When the precisely same question finally reached the Supreme Court in 1870, Justice Story's opinion was praised as "a monument of his great erudition" and his conclusion on marine insurance was approved as correct. Insurance Company v. Dunham, 78 U.S. (11 Wall.) 1, 35 (1870). See G. White, *supra* note 68, at 428–44.

122. Justice M'Kean of the Pennsylvania Supreme Court, in an action on an international bill of exchange, observed:

> This is an action of very considerable importance, not only as it affects the present parties but as it affects every holder, drawer, or indorser of a bill of exchange. The honor and justice of the state are, indeed, likewise interested, that the decision should be conformably to the generally mercantile law of nations, lest a deviation should be imputed to our ignorance or disrespect, of what is right and proper. It should be remembered too, that the defendant is a stranger, and that the event of this suit can be no further obligatory, elsewhere, than as it corresponds with the universal and established usage of all countries; for, upon the present question, that, and not the local regulations of Pennsylvania, must furnish the rule of determination.

Steinmetz v. Currie, 1 U.S. (1 Dallas) 270 (Pa. 1788).

123. R. Perry and J. Cooper, eds., Sources of Our Liberties, 303, 309, 346, 381 (1959); J. McClellan, Joseph Story and the American Constitution 189–93 (1971).

124. U.S. Const., art. III, § 2.

125. 1 Stat. 76–77 (1789), as modified still in effect in 28 U.S.C. § 1333 (1966).

126. New Jersey Steam Nav. Co. v. Merchants' Bank, 47 U.S. (6 How.) 344, 386 (1848) (contract for the carriage of goods by sea was maritime). This decision, in which Chief Justice Taney concurred, construed the breadth of the national maritime jurisdiction in an opinion comparable to that of Justice Story in De

Lovio v. Boit, 7 Fed. Cas. 418 (no. 3, 776) (C.C.D. Mass. 1815). See *supra* note 121.

127. See Hill, The Law-Making Power of the Federal Courts, 67 Colum. L. Rev. 1024, 1032–33 (1967).

128. Pope & Talbot, Inc. v. Hawn, 346 U.S. 406, 409 (1953); Levinson v. Deupree, 345 U.S. 648, 651 (1953). See Stevens, Erie R.R. v. Tompkins and the Uniform General Maritime Law, 64 Harv. L. Rev. 246 (1950).

129. Sears v. The Scotia, 81 U.S. (14 Wall.) 170, 187–88 (1872); The Maggie Hammond v. Morland, 75 U.S. (9 Wall.) 435, 453–53 (1870). For an earlier explanation by Justice Washington of the importance of civil codes as one source of the law of nations see The Seneca, 21 Fed. Cas. 1081, 1083 (no. 12, 670) (C.C.E.D. Pa. 1829). See G. Gilmore and C. Black, The Law of Admiralty 45 (2d ed. 1975); D. Robertson, Admiralty and Federalism 136 (1970).

130. Moragne v. States Marine Lines, Inc., 398 U.S. 375 (1970), *overruling* The Harrisburg, 119 U.S. 199 (1886).

131. See note: The Legitimacy of Civil Law Reasoning in the Common Law: Justice Harlan's Contribution, 82 Yale L.J. 258 (1972).

132. 244 U.S. 205, 215 (1917) (New York Workmen's Compensation Act held unconstitutional as applied to employees engaged in maritime work). The Court's refusal to apply the saving clause of section 9 of the Judiciary Act of 1789 (1 Stat. 76, 77, §9) governing common-law remedies seems wrong, even though the remedy provided by the compensation act was unknown to the common law. Under the Seventh Amendment, for example, the right to trial by jury in suits at common law includes statutory civil actions for damages unknown to the common law. Curtis v. Loether, 415 U.S. 189 (1974).

133. See a review of the history in Dickinson, *supra* note 5, at 804–16.

134. Pope & Talbot, Inc. v. Hawn, 346 U.S. 406, 409–10 (1953).

135. Byrd v. Byrd, 657 F.2d 615, 617 (4th Cir. 1981) (admiralty rules preempt state doctrines of interspousal immunity in negligence action by wife against husband for maintaining unsafe boat).

136. Wilburn Boat Co. v. Fireman's Fund Insurance Co., 348 U.S. 310 (1955).

137. *Id.* at 314.

138. Garrett v. Moore-McCormick Co., 317 U.S. 239 (1942) (national customary admiralty rules on the burden of proof required to invalidate a release preempt state law).

139. Roberson v. N.V. Stoomvaart Maatschappij, 504 F.2d 994 (5th Cir. 1975) (state statute requiring substitution of plaintiff for the deceased within one year was preempted by national customary admiralty law). For earlier authority, see The Moses Taylor, 71 U.S., (4 Wall.) 411 (1866); The Hine v. Trevor, 71 U.S. (4 Wall.) 555 (1866).

140. Pope & Talbot Inc. v. Hawn, 346, U.S. 406, 410 (1953).

141. J. Wilson, The Works of James Wilson, I, 279 (R. McCloskey ed. 1967). In the footnote to this paragraph, Wilson quotes Justice Wilmot's statement in Pillans v. Van Mierop., 3 Burr. 1663, 1670, 97 Eng. Rep. 1035, 1040 (K.B. 1765): In commercial cases, "all nations ought to have their laws conformable to each other. *Fides sevanda est; simplicitas juris gentium praevaleat.*" (Faith must be kept; the simplicity of the law of nations must prevail.)

142. 15 U.S. (2 Wheat.) 66 (1817).

143. *Id.* at 75.

144. *Id.* at 76.

145. 27 U.S. (2 Pet.) 586 (1829).

146. Townsley v. Sumrall, 27 U.S. (2 Pet.) 170, 179, n.a. (1829).

147. See W. Crosskey, *supra* note 5, II, at 843.

148. 20 Fed. Cas. 801 (no. 11,835) (D. Ohio 1841).

149. *Id.* at 802.

150. 11 Ohio 172 (1842).

151. *Id.* at 191–92.

152. See, e.g., Bank of Mobile v. Hall, 6 Ala. 639, 644 (1844); Bostwick v. Dodge, 1 Douglas 413 (Mich. 1844); Reddick v. Jones, 28 N.C. 107, 110 (1847); Allaire v. Hartshorne, 21 N.J. 665, 667–68 (1847); Blanchard v. Stevens, 57 Mass. 162, 166 (1849).

153. Stalker v. McDonald, 6 Hill 93 (N.Y. 1843). The rejection of *Swift* was unnecessary in this case because the facts showed the transaction was clearly outside the ordinary course of business. See K. Llewellyn, *supra* note 101, 416–17.

154. For an analysis of state-court deviation from the *Swift* rule, see Heckman, Uniform Commercial Law in the Nineteenth Century Federal Courts, 27 Emory L. J. 45, 50–51 (1978).

155. *Id.* See, e.g., Burns Mortgage Co. v. Fried, 292 U.S. 487 (1934); Beutel, Common Law Judicial Technique and the Law of Negotiable Instruments—Two Unfortunate Decisions, 9 Tulane L. Rev. 60, 65–67 (1934).

156. 304 U.S. 64 (1938). See analyses of W. Crosskey, *supra* note 5, II, at 912–37; C. Wright, *supra* note 41, at 352–64. The Congress could have preempted the common law in the fact situation of *Erie* with a statute pursuant to the commerce clause regulating tort liabilities of carriers in commerce among the several states. *Id.* at 363 n. 17. Absent congressional preemption, section 34 of the Judiciary Act of 1789, by incorporating established conflict-of-laws rules, mandated application of the law of the state where the tort occurred.

157. 313 U.S. 487 (1941). See critique in Hart, The Relations between State and Federal Law, 54 Colum. L. Rev. 489, 513–15 (1954); Hill, The Erie Doctrine and the Constitution, 53 Nw. U. L. Rev. 427, 541 (1958).

158. In re King Porter Co., 446 F. 2d 722, 732 (5th Cir. 1971).

159. United Overseas Bank v. Veneers, Inc., 375 F. Supp. 596, 601 (D.C. Md. 1974).

160. Walter v. Marine Office of America, 537 F.2d 89, 94 (5th Cir. 1976).

161. Kuhn v. Fairmont Coal Co., 215 U.S. 349, 370 (1910) (Holmes, J., dissenting); Black & White Taxicab & Transfer Co. v. Brown & Yellow Taxicab & Transfer Co., 276 U.S. 518, 532 (1928) (Holmes, J., dissenting).

162. While Holmes's summary of *Swift* centered on the jurisprudential *obiter dictum* on the meaning of laws and indicates that he did not understand *Swift* as a law-merchant case, his instinct was correct when he wrote: "I should leave Swift v. Tyson undisturbed, as I indicated in Kuhn v. Fairmont Coal Co, but I would not allow it to spread the assumed dominion into new fields" (*Id.* at 535). Writing to Sir Frederick Pollock, Holmes stated that *Swift* v. *Tyson* "was unjustifiable in theory but did no great harm when confined to what Story dealt with" Holmes-Pollack Letters, II, 215 (M. Howe ed. 1941).

163. 304 U.S. 64 (1938).

164. *Id.* at 78. Justice Brandeis correctly asserted that judicial creation of a federal common law had a legal significance that extended beyond misconstruction of section 34 of the Judiciary Act. The issue was constitutional because section 34 merely reiterated for trials at common law the principle of federalism that is the truism of the Tenth Amendment. See Friendly, In Praise of Erie, 39 N.Y.U. L. Rev. 383, 385–91 (1964).

165. See K. Llewellyn, The Common Law Tradition 417 (1960).

166. Brandeis should have overruled City of Chicago v. Robbins, 67 U.S. (2 Blk.) 418 (1862); Baltimore & Ohio R. Co. v. Baugh, 249 U.S. 368 (1893); and the other cases creating a federal common law of torts.

167. Act of June 25, 1948, c. 646, 62 Stat. 944, 28 U.S.C.A. §1652 (1966).

168. Pope & Talbot, Inc. v. Hawn, 346 U.S. 406, 409 (1953).

169. United States v. Guaranty Trust Co., 293 U.S. 340 (1934); Oken-Frankman Livestock, etc. v. Citizens Nat., 605 F.2d 1082, 1085 (8th Cir. 1979).

170. Noting the civil-law origins of the law merchant, Professor Beutel asserted in writing of a predecessor code, "There is overwhelming evidence that the N.I.L. is a codification of law in the truly civilian sense, that it was so intended by the framers and the bar, and that such is the understanding of Anglo-American jurists" (Beutel, *supra* note 155, at 67, n. 20). See also Beutel, The Necessity of a New Technique of Interpreting the N.I.L., 6 Tulane L. Rev. 1 (1931). As to the Uniform Commercial Code as a source for the federal law of sales, see United States v. Wegematic Corporation, 360 F.2d 674, 676 (2d Cir. 1966).

171. U.S. Const., art. III, §2.

172. 72 Stat. 415, 28 U.S.C. §1331 (1958).

Chapter 8

1. J. Hicks, A Theory of Economic History 63–68 (1969); K. Polanyi, The Great Transformation 68–76 (1957).

2. M. Friedman, The Optimum Quantity of Money and Other Essays, ch. 1 (1969).

3. The technical issue for economists is whether in a growing economy there should be statutory growth rates for the money supply in order to limit the discretion of public officials. See M. Miller and C. Upton, Macroeconomics, chs. 11–13 (1974); A. Leijonhufvud, Constitutional Constraints on the Monetary Powers of Government, in Constitutional Economics, ch. 5 (R. McKenzie ed. 1984).

4. J. Dorfman, The Economic Mind in American Civilization, I, 93–111 (1946).

5. *Id.* at 142.

6. D. Dewey, Financial History of the United States 21–24 (12th ed. 1939).

7. C. Bullock, Essays on the Monetary History of the United States 44–45 (1900).

8. *Id.* at 33.

9. *Id.* at 64.

10. *Id.*

11. *Id.* at 66.

12. B. Hammond, Banks and Politics in America from the Revolution to the Civil War 50 (1957).

13. *Id.* at 51.

14. *Id.* at 65.

15. U.S. Const., art. I, § 8, cl. 3, 5.

16. U.S. Const., art. I, § 10.

17. M. Farrand, The Records of the Federal Convention of 1787, II, 182 (1911).

18. *Id.* at 308–9. The motion carried by a vote of 9 states to 2. *Id.* at 310.

19. The most complete analysis of the national power to emit bills of credit and make them legal tender is in Thayer, Legal Tender, 1 Harv. L. Rev. 73 (1887).

20. A. Hepburn, A History of Currency in the United States 90 (rev. ed. 1967).

21. See G. Bancroft, History of the Formation of the Constitution of the United States of America, I, ch. 6 (1882).

22. J. Madison in Federalist 44, at 306 (E. Bourne ed. 1947).

23. J. Story, Commentaries on the Constitution of the United States, II, § 1365 (5th ed. 1891) [hereinafter cited as Story].

24. 29 U.S. (4 Pet.) 410 (1830).

25. 29 U.S. (4 Pet.) at 432.

26. *Id.* at 433.

27. 36 U.S. (11 Pet.) 257 (1837). See C. Swisher, The Taney Period 1836–64, History of the Supreme Court of the United States, V, 105–9 (1974).

28. 36 U.S. (11 Pet.) at 327.

29. *Id.* at 328.

30. *Id.* at 330.

31. *Id.* at 340.

32. *Id.* at 344.

33. Story, II, § 1120.

34. *Id.*

35. U.S. Const., art. I, § 8, cl. 5.

36. For statistical tables on types of money, see A. Hepburn, *supra* note 20, at 129, 160, 178.

37. C. Bullock, *supra* note 7, ch. 6 (1900).

38. W. Gouge, A Short History of Paper Money and Banking in the United States 132–33, 166–68 (1833).

39. Act of July 17, 1861, ch. 5, 12 Stat. 259.

40. Act of July 13, 1866, ch. 184, § 9, 14 Stat. 146.

41. 75 U.S. (8 Wall.) 533 (1864). See D. Currie, The Constitution in the Supreme Court 317–20 (1985).

42. 75 U.S. (8 Wall.) at 544.

43. *Id.* at 549.

44. Merchant's Nat. Bank v. United States, 101 U.S. 1 (1880).

45. See C. Fairman, Reconstruction and Reunion, 1864–88, History of the Supreme Court of the United States, VI, 677–775; C. Warren, The Supreme Court in United States History, II, ch. 31 (2d ed. 1926); Thayer, *supra* note 19.

46. See *supra* notes 17–19 and accompanying text.

47. 75 U.S. (8 Wall.) 603 (1870).

48. *Id.* at 615–16.

49. *Id.* at 625.

50. See Fairman, Mr. Justice Bradley's Appointment to the Supreme Court and the Legal Tender Cases, 54 Harv. L. Rev. 977, 1128 (1941).

51. 79 U.S. (12 Wall.) 457 (1871). On the economics of the greenback period, see M. Friedman and A. Schwartz, A Monetary History of the United States, ch. 2 (1963).

52. 79 U.S. (12 Wall.) at 549.

53. *Id.* at 554.

54. 110 U.S. 421 (1884). See Dam, The Legal Tender Cases, 1981 Sup. Ct. Rev. 367, 410–11.

55. 110 U.S. at 449–50.

56. Bronson v. Rodes, 74 U.S. (7 Wall.) 229 (1869).

57. Joint Resolution of June 5, 1933, 48 Stat. 113, sec. 1.

58. 294 U.S. 330 (1935). See Nortz v. United States, 294 U.S. 317 (1935).

59. 49 Stat. 939, § 2; 31 U.S.C.A. § 773b (1935). See Smyth v. United States,

302 U.S. 329 (1937); Guaranty Trust Co. of N.Y. v. Henwood, 307 U.S. 247 (1939).

60. 294 U.S. 240 (1935).

61. For a history of this period, see B. Hammond, *supra* note 12, ch. 4.

62. M. Farrand, *supra* note 17, II, 615.

63. *Id.* at 616.

64. A. Hamilton, National Bank, American State Papers, Finance, I, 67–76 (Rep. No. 18, 1st Cong., 3d sess. 1790).

65. Debates and Proceedings of the Congress of the United States, II, 1791 (Gales & Seaton eds. 1834).

66. *Id.* at 1947.

67. *Id.* at 1949.

68. *Id.* at 2011.

69. See R. Hammond, *supra* note 12, ch. 5.

70. M. Clarke and D. Hall, Legislative and Documentary History of the Bank of the United States 86–94 (1832).

71. *Id.* at 95–112.

72. See B. Hammond, *supra* note 12, ch. 8.

73. *Id.* at 214.

74. M. Clarke and D. Hall, *supra* note 70, at 274.

75. See B. Hammond, *supra* note 12, ch. 9.

76. M. Clarke and D. Hall, *supra* note 70, at 472–608.

77. *Id.* at 594.

78. *Id.* at 706, 712.

79. *Id.* at 713. See Act of April 10, 1816, ch. 44, § 1, 3 Stat. 266 (expired 1836).

80. W. Smith, Economic Aspects of the Second Bank of the United States 236, 244 (1953). For a detailed history of the bank, see R. Catterall, The Second Bank of the United States (1903).

81. B. Hammond, *supra* note 12, at 263.

82. 17 U.S. (4 Wheat.) 316 (1819). See G. White, The Marshall Court and Cultural Change, 1815–35, History of the Supreme Court of the United States, III–IV, 541–67 (1988).

83. See chapter 3, notes 119–124 and accompanying text.

84. 17 U.S. (4 Wheat.) at 407.

85. *Id.* at 421–422.

86. 22 U.S. (9 Wheat.) 738 (1824). See G. White, *supra* note 82, at 524–35.

87. *Id.* at 860–62.

88. Act of June 3, 1864, ch. 106, § 5, 13 Stat. 100, 12 U.S.C.A. §§ 21–213 (1945).

89. 91 U.S. 29 (1875).

90. "The constitutionality of the Act of 1864 is not questioned. It rests on the same principle as the Act creating the second Bank of the United States. The reasoning of Secretary Hamilton and of this court in McCulloch v. Maryland, . . . therefore, applies. The national banks organized under the Act are instruments assigned to be used to aid the government in the administration of an important branch of the public service. They are means appropriate to that end. Of the degree of the necessity which existed for creating them, Congress is the sole judge" (*Id.* at 33–34).

91. Act of Dec. 23, 1913, c. 6, 38 Stat. 251, 12 U.S.C.A. § 221 et seq. (1945).

92. 244 U.S. 416 (1917).

93. [A]lthough a business be of such a character that it is not inherently considered susceptible of being included by Congress in the powers conferred on national banks, that rule would cease to apply if, by state law, state banking corporations, trust companies, or others which, by reason of their business, are rivals or *quasi*-rivals of national banks, are permitted to carry on such business. This must be, since the state may not by legislation create a condition as to a particular business which would bring about actual or potential competition with the business of national banks, and at the same time deny the power of Congress to meet such created condition by legislation appropriate to avoid the injury which otherwise would be suffered by the national agency" (*Id.* at 425–26).

94. See J. Head, Public Goods and Public Welfare (1974); J. Buchanan, The Demand and Supply of Public Goods (1968).

95. See H. Hochman and G. Peterson, eds., Redistribution through Public Choice (1974).

96. See G. Brennan and J. Buchanan, The Power to Tax 2–12 (1980); G. Brennan, Constitutional Constraints on the Fiscal Powers of Government, in Constitutional Economics, ch. 6 (R. McKenzie, ed. 1984).

97. U.S. Const., art. 1, § 8, cl. 1. The original meaning of the key terms is found in the following: "Monies raised on lands, polls, houses, cattle, &c, are usually called taxes. Monies raised on goods imported or exported are called duties and imposts. Monies raised on manufactures and the retailing of liquors are called excises. But in a more enlarged sense, taxes and imposts comprehend every method of levying money on real or personal estate. Duties is usually restricted to taxes on goods, wares, and merchandize; excise only being confined, to a particular mode of laying duties, and, for the most part, to duties on manufactures" (Gazette of the United States, New York, January 23, 1790, 328, quoted in W. Crosskey, Politics and the Constitution in the History of the United States, II, 1317–18 [1953]).

98. U.S. Const., art. I, § 9, cl. 5. The prohibition of state duties on imports and exports is in art. I, § 10, cl. 2. See chapter 5, notes 2–4 and accompanying text.

99. The uniformity clause was proposed at the Constitutional Convention on August 25 in the following terms: "All duties imposts & excises, prohibitions or restraints laid or made by the Legislature of the U——S——shall be uniform and equal throughout the U——S——" (M. Farrand, *supra* note 17, at II, 418).

100. Head Money Cases, 112 U.S. 580, 594 (1884).

101. Story, I, § 957.

102. 326 U.S. 340 (1945).

103. 462 U.S. 74 (1983).

104. *Id.* at 81.

105. Brushaber v. Union Pac. R. R., 240 U.S. 1, 12 (1916).

106. Garcia v. San Antonio Metro Transit Auth., 469 U.S. 528, 550–51 (1985).

107. 17 U.S. (4 Wheat.) 316 (1819). See T. Powell, Vagaries and Varieties in Constitutional Interpretation, ch. 4 (1956).

108. 17 U.S. (4 Wheat.) at 426.

109. 22 U.S. (9 Wheat.) 738 (1924).

110. *Id.* at 865.

111. *Id.* at 867.

112. Weston v. Charleston, 27 U.S. (2 Pet.) 449 (1829). The immunity of the obligations of the national government from state taxation is codified in 31 U.S.C.A. § 3124(a) (1983).

113. Hibernia Savings & Loan Society v. San Francisco, 200 U.S. 310 (1906).

114. 392 U.S. 339 (1968).

115. 306 U.S. 466 (1939), *overruling* Collector v. Day, 78 U.S. (11 Wall.) 113 (1871) and N.Y. ex rel. Rogers v. Graves, 299 U.S. 401 (1937).

116. Fox Film Corp. v. Doyal, 286 U.S. 123 (1932), *overruling* Long v. Rockwood, 277 U.S. 142 (1928).

117. Panhandle Oil Co. v. Knox, 277 U.S. 218 (1928); Graves v. Texas, 298 U.S. 393 (1936). These cases were both overruled in Alabama v. King & Boozer, 314 U.S. 43, 45 (1941).

118. Trinityfarm Co. v. Grosjean, 291 U.S. 466 (1934).

119. 282 U.S. 509 (1931).

120. 302 U.S. 134 (1937).

121. *Id.* at 152.

122. *Id.* at 160.

123. *Id.* at 149.

124. 314 U.S. 1 (1941), *overruling* Panhandle Oil Co. v. State of Mississippi ex rel. Knox, 277 U.S. 218 (1928), and Graves v. Texas Co., 298 U.S. 393 (1936).

125. 314 U.S. at 10.

126. *Id.* at 8.

127. 347 U.S. 110 (1954).

128. *Id.* at 122.

129. 455 U.S. 720 (1982).

130. *Id.* at 734.

131. *Id.* at 735.

132. 460 U.S. 536 (1983).

133. *Id.* at 547.

134. 355 U.S. 466 (1958).

135. United States v. Railroad Company, 84 U.S. (17 Wall.) 322 (1873).

136. 304 U.S. 405 (1938).

137. 303 U.S. 376 (1938), *overruling* Gillespie v. Oklahoma, 257 U.S. 501 (1922), and Burnet v., Coronado Oil & Gas Co., 285 U.S. 393 (1932).

138. Metcalf & Eddy v. Mitchell, 269 U.S. 514 (1926).

139. Board of Trustees v. United States, 289 U.S. 48 (1933).

140. 157 U.S. 429 (1895), 158 U.S. 601 (1895).

141. 158 U.S. 618.

142. 99 L. Ed. 592 (1988).

143. *Id.* at 602–4.

144. Garcia v. San Antonio Metro. Transit Auth., 469 U.S. 528 (1985).

145. 99 L. Ed. at 611.

146. *Id.* at 610, citing among others, Washington v. United States, 460 U.S. 536, 540 (1983); United States v. New Mexico, 455 U.S. 720, 735 (1982).

147. 326 U.S. 572 (1946).

148. *Id.* at 589–90.

149. See Cushman, Social and Economic Control through Federal Taxation, 18 Minn. L. Rev. 759 (1934).

150. 75 U.S. (8 Wall.) 422 (1869). See text at notes 40–43.

151. 32 Stat. 193 (1902).

152. 195 U.S. 27 (1904). See Cushman, The National Police Power under the Taxing Clause of the Constitution, 4 Minn. L. Rev. 247 (1920).

153. "Undoubtedly, in determining whether a particular act is within a granted power, its scope and effect is to be considered. Applying this rule to the acts assailed, it is self-evident that on their face they levy an excise tax. That being their necessary scope and operation, it follows that the acts are within the grant

of power. The argument to the contrary rests on the proposition that, although the tax be within the power, as enforcing it will destroy or restrict the manufacture of artificially colored oleomargarine, therefore the power to levy the tax did not obtain. This, however, is but to say that the question of power depends, not on the authority conferred by the constitution, but upon what may be the consequence arising from the exercise of the lawful authority" (195 U.S. 59).

154. See chapter 12, notes 25–29 and accompanying text.

155. See W. McKechnie, Magna Carta, chs. 39, 40 (2d ed. 1914).

156. In re Kollack, 165 U.S. 526 (1897) (regulation of packaging of taxed margarine); Felsenheld v. United States, 186 U.S. 126 (1902) (packaging of taxed tobacco); United States v. Doremus, 249 U.S. 86 (1919) (tax of $1 per year in order to force registration of narcotics dealers); Sonzinsky v. United States, 300 U.S. 506 (1937) (tax to force licensing of firearms).

157. 276 U.S. 394 (1928).

158. Id. at 412.

159. Bailey v. Drexel Furniture Co., 259 U.S. 20 (1922).

160. 247 U.S. 251 (1918), overruled in United States v. Darby, 312 U.S. 100, 116–17 (1941).

161. 259 U.S. at 39.

162. Hill v. Wallace, 259 U.S. 44 (1922). In 1923 Congress corrected the purported defects by passing a similar statute applicable only to interstate commerce, and this was held constitutional. Board of Trade v. Olsen, 262 U.S. 1 (1923).

163. United States v. Constantine, 296 U.S. 287 (1935).

164. United States v. Butler, 297 U.S. 1 (1936). See Mulford v. Smith, 307 U.S. 38 (1939), sustaining similar legislation under the commerce power.

165. See chapter 5.

166. Fernandez v. Weiner, 316 U.S. 340, 362 (1945).

167. 301 U.S. 548 (1937).

168. 301 U.S. 619 (1937).

169. 340 U.S. 42 (1950).

170. 340 U.S. 44–45, quoting Magnano Co. v. Hamilton, 292 U.S. 40, 47 (1934): "From the beginning of our government, the courts have sustained taxes although imposed with the collateral intent of effecting ulterior ends which, considered apart, were beyond the constitutional power of the lawmakers to realize by legislation directly addressed to their accomplishments."

171. 345 U.S. 22 (1953), overruled on other grounds in Marchetti v. United States, 390 U.S. 39 (1968).

172. "Penalty provisions in tax statutes added for breach of a regulation concerning activities in themselves subject only to state regulation have caused this court to declare the enactments invalid. Unless there are provisions extraneous to any tax need, courts are without authority to limit the exercise of the taxing power. All the provisions of this excise are adopted to the collection of a valid tax" (345 U.S. 31).

173. U.S. Const., art. I, § 2, cl. 3.

174. U.S. Const., art. I, § 9, cl. 4.

175. See E. Corwin, Court over Constitution 181–85 (1938).

176. M. Farrand, Records of the Federal Convention, I, 589–97 (1927). See recollections of Justice Patterson, who helped draft the clause. Hylton v. United States, 3 U.S. (3 Dall.) 171, 177 (1796).

177. 3 U.S. (3 Dall.) 171 (1796). See D. Currie, supra note 41, at 31–37.

178. Pacific Insurance Co. v. Soule, 74 U.S. (7 Wall.) 433 (1869).

179. Veazie Bank v. Fenno, 75 U.S. (8 Wall.) 533 (1869).

180. Scholey v. Rew, 90 U.S. (23 Wall.) 331 (1875).

181. 102 U.S. 586 (1881).

182. *Id.* at 602.

183. Act of Aug. 27, 1894, 28 Stat. 553.

184. 157 U.S. 429, 158 U.S. 601 (1895), *overruling* Hylton v. United States, 3 U.S. (3 Dall.) 171 (1796). See E. Corwin, Court over Constitution, ch. 4 (1938).

185. 158 U.S. 635.

186. 220 U.S. 107 (1911).

187. Act of Aug. 5, 1909, § 38, 36 Stat. c. 6, 11, 112–17.

188. Scott v. Sandford, 60 U.S. (19 How.) 393 (1857).

189. See C. Hughes, The Supreme Court of the United States, 50, 53 (1928).

190. United States v. E. C. Knight Co., 156 U.S. 1 (1895).

191. 3 U.S. (3 Dall.) 171 (1796).

192. R. Musgrave and P. Musgrave, Public Finance in Theory and Practice 258 (4th ed. 1984).

193. *Id.* at 469–75.

194. U.S. Const., amend. 16.

195. Stanton v. Baltic Mining Co., 240 U.S. 103, 112 (1916).

196. See R. McKean, Public Spending (1968).

197. J. Head, Public Goods and Public Welfare 170–71 (1974).

198. See G. Becker, Human Capital (2d ed. 1975).

199. See J. Lawson, The General Welfare Clause (1934).

200. See W. Crosskey, *supra* note 97, at I, 374.

201. See C. Warren, Congress at Santa Claus or National Donations and the General Welfare Clause of the Constitution (1932); Corwin, The Spending Power of Congress, 36 Harv. L. Rev. 548 (1923).

202. 297 U.S. 1 (1936).

203. *Id.* at 66.

204. 301 U.S. 548 (1937).

205. 301 U.S. 591.

206. 301 U.S. 619 (1937).

207. *Id.* at 640.

208. 339 U.S. 725 (1950).

209. *Id.* at 738.

210. See G. Break, Financing Government in a Federal System (1980).

211. See chapter 1, notes 33–37 and accompanying text.

212. 392 U.S. 309, 333 (1968).

213. 107 Sup. Ct. 2793 (1987).

214. *Id.* at 2796.

Chapter 9

1. U.S. Const., art. I, § 10. See B. Wright, The Contract Clause of the Constitution (1938); B. Schwartz, A Commentary on the Constitution of the United States, Part 2, The Rights of Property 266–306 (1965); Hale, The Supreme Court and the Contract Clause, 57 Harv. L. Rev. 512, 621, 852 (1944); Clarke, The Contract Clause, 39 U. Miami L. Rev. 183 (1985).

2. U.S. Const., art. I, § 8.

3. Pothier defines contract as "[a]n agreement by which two parties reciprocably promise and engage, or one of them singly promises and engages to the other to give some particular thing, or to do or abstain from doing some particular

act" (R. Pothier, A Treatise on the Law of Obligations, or Contracts, I, 3–4 [W. Evans trans. 1826]). See C. Fried, Contract as Promise (1981).

4. See R. Posner, Economic Analysis of Law, ch. 4 (3d ed. 1986); W. Hirsch, Law and Economics, ch. 5 (1979).

5. See A. Corbin, Contracts, IA, 193–209 (1963); Goetz and Scott, Enforcing Promises, 89 Yale L. J. 1261 (1980).

6. See D. North and R. Thomas, The Rise of the Western World 109–15 (1973).

7. See generally, Toward a Theory of the Rent-Seeking Society (J. Buchanan, R. Tollison & G. Tullock eds. 1980).

8. Klein, Crawford and Alchian, Vertical Integration, Appropriable Rents, and the Competitive Contracting Process, 21 J. L. & Econ. 297–98 (1978). This study contains many examples of rent-seeking behavior.

9. Federalist 44, at 307 (E. Bourne ed. 1947).

10. Epstein, Toward A Revitalization of the Contract Clause, 51 U. Chi. L. Rev. 703, 713 (1984).

11. U.S. Const., art. I, § 10. See C. Bullock, Monetary History of the United States, ch. 5 (1900); D. Dewey, Financial History of the United States, ch. 2 (12th ed. 1939).

12. Home Building and Loan Association v. Blaisdell, 290 U.S. 398, 427 (1934). On the same point, see the dissent of Justice Sutherland, *id.* at 454–55. See G. Bancroft, History of the Formation of the Constitution of the United States, I, ch. 6 (1883).

13. See B. Wright, *supra* note 1, at 4.

14. Sturges v. Crowninshield, 17 U.S. (4 Wheat.) 122, 199 (1819).

15. M. Farrand, The Records of the Federal Convention of 1787, II, 440 (1911); J. Elliot, ed., Debates in the Several State Conventions on the Adoption of the Federal Constitution, IV, 183–84, 191 (1836); See Epstein, *supra* note 10, at 705–17.

16. M. Farrand, *supra* note 15, at 440.

17. *Id.* at 597.

18. *Id.* at 619.

19. Sturges v. Crowninshield, 17 U.S. (4 Wheat.) 122, 197 (1819).

20. *Id.* at 198. Justice Story elaborated on the meaning of "impairing":

It is perfectly clear, that any law, which enlarges, abridges, or in any manner changes the intention of the parties, resulting from the stipulations in the contract, necessarily impairs it. The manner or degree in which this change is effected can in no respect influence the conclusion; for whether the law affect the validity, the construction, the duration, the discharge, or the evidence of the contract, it impairs its obligation, though it may not do so to the same extent in all the supposed cases. Any deviation from its terms by postponing or accelerating the period of performance which it prescribes, imposing conditions not expressed in the contract, or dispensing with the performance of those which are a part of the contract, however minute or apparently immaterial in their effect upon it, impairs its obligation.

J. Story, Commentaries on the Constitution of the United States, II, § 1385 (1833).

21. Home Building and Loan Association v. Blaisdell, 290 U.S. 398, 431 (1934).

22. U.S. Const., amend. 5. For the Supreme Court holding that this amendment did not limit state action, see Barron v. Mayor of Baltimore, 32 U.S. (7 Pet.)

243, 250–51 (1833). For a critique of this case, see W. Crosskey, Politics and the Constitution in the History of the United States, II, 1056–82 (1953).

23. Chicago Burlington & Quincy Railroad Company v. City of Chicago, 166 U.S. 226 (1897); Webb's Fabulous Pharmacies v. Beckwith, 449 U.S. 155, 159 (1980).

24. Ogden v. Saunders 25 U.S. (12 Wheat.) 213, 348 (1827).

25. Seibert v. Lewis, 122 U.S. 284 (1887); Edwards v. Kearzey, 96 U.S. 595 (1878).

26. This conclusion rejects the argument that one prime purpose of the contract clause was to prohibit all state regulation of commerce. See W. Crosskey, *supra* note 22, I, ch. 12 (1953); Epstein, *supra* note 10, at 725–30.

27. Ogden v. Saunders, 25 U.S. (12 Wheat.) 213 (1827).

28. Justice Johnson tried in vain to convince the later majorities that this limitation on the *ex post facto* clause was in error and should be overruled. Ogden v. Saunders, 25 U.S. (12 Wheat.) 213, 286 (1827); Satterlee v. Matthewson, 27 U.S. (2 Pet.) 380, 681–87 app. no. 1 (1829) (Johnson, J., concurring, note on the exposition of the phrase *ex post facto* in the Constitution of the United States) (original ed. Philadelphia 1829). Other authorities supporting the civil application include one editor of Blackstone's Commentaries on the Laws of England 132 (Hammond ed. 1890); Field, Ex Post Facto in the Constitution, 20 Mich. L. Rev. 315 (1922); W. Crosskey, Politics and the Constitution in the History of the United States, I, 324–51 (1953).

29. 3 U.S. (3 Dall.) 386 (1798). The "statute" in *Calder* was an appellate judicial decision by a state legislature. Pursuant to the customary constitution of Connecticut, the state legislature passed a "statute" granting parties to a single probate proceeding a new hearing in probate after right of appeal to the ordinary courts to obtain such a hearing was barred by lapse of time. The beneficiary under the original proceedings appealed the decision in the second proceeding to the Supreme Court of the United States on the ground that the Connecticut "statute" was an unconstitutional *ex post facto* law in violation of Article I, Section 10. Justice Chase held that the "statute" was a law but that the prohibition on *ex post facto* laws applied only to criminal statutes. In fact, the Connecticut legislature was openly performing a judicial function under a customary constitution that did not provide for separation of powers. The "statute" was not a law in the sense of a general, prospective rule of conduct, but a judicial decision. All judicial decisions are retrospective, but they are not laws. The appeal should have been dismissed for lack of a federal question. *Calder* should have been overruled long ago. Instead, it stands today for all lower courts as authority that the *ex post facto* protection applies only to criminal statutes. See Galvan v. Press, 347 U.S. 522, 531 (1954).

30. E. Corwin, The Twilight of the Supreme Court 56 (1934). See E. Corwin, American Constitutional History 24–45 (1964).

31. Vanhorne's Lessee v. Dorrance, 2 U.S. (2 Dall.) 304, 310 (C.C.D. Pa. 1795). See Corwin, The "Higher Law" Background of American Constitutional Law, 42 Harv. L. Rev. 149 (1928).

32. Marbury v. Madison, 5 U.S. (1 Cranch) 137, 176 (1803).

33. Fletcher v. Peck, 10 U.S. (6 Cranch) 87, 133 (1810).

34. 10 U.S. (6 Cranch) 87 (1810). The factual background of this case is reviewed in A. Beveridge, Life of John Marshall, III, 546–602 (1919); G. Haskins and H. Johnson, Foundations of Power: John Marshall, 1801–15, History of the Supreme Court of the United States, II, 336–53 (1981); C. Warren, The Supreme Court in United States History, I, 392–99 (rev. ed. 1926); C. Magrath, Yazoo: Law and Politics in the New Republic: The Case of *Fletcher* v. *Peck* (1966).

35. Every member of the state legislature who had voted for the land sale, except one, owned shares of stock in the purchasing companies. A. Beveridge, *supra* note 34, at 561.

36. *Id.* at 563; Magrath, *supra* note 34, at 33.

37. *Fletcher*, 10 U.S. (6 Cranch) at 134, 139. Justice Johnson voiced concern that this was "a mere feigned case." *Id.* at 147. See D. Currie, The Constitution in the Supreme Court 139 n. 27 (1985); E. Corwin, John Marshall and the Constitution 151 (1921). Under modern law, such a case would be dismissed for lack of a case or controversy. See United States v. Johnson, 319 U.S. 302, 305 (1943).

38. Fletcher, 10 U.S. (6 Cranch) at 131.

39. *Id.* at 139.

40. "It is the peculiar function of the legislature, to prescribe general rules for the government of society; the application of those rules to individuals in society would seem to be the duty of other departments" (*Id.* at 136).

41. "[T]here are certain general principles of justice, whose authority is universally acknowledged, that ought not to be entirely disregarded" (*Id.* at 133). Justice Johnson, concurring on the invalidity of the annulling statute, relied entirely on natural law. "I do it on a general principle, on the reason and nature of things: a principle which will impose laws even on the Diety" (*Id.* at 143). See the similar statement of Justice Chase in Calder v. Bull, 3 U.S. (3 Dall.) 386, 388 (1798): "There are certain vital principles in our free republican governments, which will determine and overrule an apparent and flagrant abuse of legislative power."

42. See Ely, Legislative and Administrative Motivation in Constitutional Law, 79 Yale L. J. 1205 (1970).

43. Fletcher, 10 U.S. (6 Cranch) at 137. See Hagan, Fletcher v. Peck, 16 Geo. L. J. 1 (1927); Trickett, Is a Grant a Contract? 54 Am. L. Rev. 718 (1920).

44. Fletcher, 10 U.S. (6 Cranch) at 137.

45. B. Poore, The Federal and State Constitutions, Colonial Charters and Other Organic Laws of the United States, I, 384–86 (1877–78).

46. See P. Nichols, Law of Eminent Domain, I, § 1.21 (rev. 3d ed. 1985).

47. J. Kent, Commentaries on American Law, II, 339 (1827), at 426 in 10th ed. (1860). On the origins of right of compensation in eminent domain beginning with Magna Charta, see chapter 4.

48. Fletcher, 10 U.S. (6 Cranch) at 137.

49. *Id.*

50. *Id.* at 138.

51. 11 U.S. (7 Cranch) 164 (1812). See A. Beveridge, *supra* note 34, IV, 221–23; G. Haskins and H. Johnson, *supra* note 34, 598–600; B. Wright, *supra* note 1, 34–37.

52. State v. Wilson, 2 N.J.L. 282 (1807).

53. *Id.*

54. See Worcester v. Georgia, 31 U.S. (6 Pet.) 515, 559 (1832); G. White, The Marshall Court and Cultural Change, 1815–35, History of the Supreme Court of the United States, III–IV, 730–40 (1988). See, generally, W. Washburn, Red Man's Land/White Man's Law (1971).

55. See Given v. Wright, 117 U.S. 648, 655 (1886) (taxation of land in the same tract allowed).

56. Wilson, 11 U.S. (7 Cranch) at 166–67.

57. Fletcher, 10 U.S. (6 Cranch) 87, 135 (1810).

58. Piqua Branch of State Bank v. Knoop, 57 U.S. (16 How.) 369 (1853).

59. B. Wright, *supra* note 1, at 36.

60. 17 U.S. (4 Wheat.) 518 (1819). The background of the case is discussed in G. White, *supra* note 54, at 612–28; A. Beveridge, *supra* note 34, IV, 220–81; C. Warren, *supra* note 34, I, 475–92; J. Shirley, The Dartmouth College Causes and the Supreme Court of the United States (1895); F. Stites, Private Interest and Public Gain 1819 (1972).

61. Trustees of Dartmouth College v. Woodward, 1 N.H. 111 (1817), *reversed* 17 U.S. (4 Wheat.) 518 (1819).

62. 17 U.S. (4 Wheat.) at 625. Later Marshall asserts: "This is plainly a contract to which the donors, the trustees, and the crown (to whose rights and obligations New Hampshire secedes), were the original parties. It is a contract made on a valuable consideration" (*Id.* at 643–44). As questionable as these assertions were, Marshall did make a correct statement on the limited use of evidence of intent of the framers:

> It is not enough to say that this particular case was not in the mind of the convention when the article was framed, nor of the American people when it was adopted. It is necessary to go farther, and to say that, had this particular case been suggested, the language would have been so varied, as to exclude it, or it would have been made a special exception. The case being within the words of the rule, must be within its operation likewise, unless there be something in the literal construction so obviously absurd, or mischievous, or repugnant to the general spirit of the instrument, as to justify those who expound the constitution in making it an exception.

Id. at 644–45.

63. 10 U.S. (6 Cranch) 87 (1810).

64. Trustees of Dartmouth College, 17 U.S. (4 Wheat.) at 682.

65. J. Shirley, *supra* note 60 at 424–25 (1895); Thompson, Abuses of Corporate Privileges, 26 Am. L. Rev. 169, 175 (1892). See Isaacs, John Marshall on Contracts, 7 Va. L. Rev. 413 (1921).

66. On the general common-law requirement of consideration in contract, see Rann v. Hughes, 7 Term Rep. 350, 101 Eng. Rep. 1014 (H.L. 1778). The attempt of Lord Mansfield, in dicta, to excuse the consideration requirement in written documents was in the context of the law merchant, not the common law. Pillans v. Van Mierop, 3 Burr. 1663, 97 Eng. Rep. 1035 (K.B. 1765). For a later emphasis on the consideration requirement for agreements to receive protection under the contract clause, see Grand Lodge F. & A. Masons v. New Orleans, 166 U.S. 143 (1897).

67. See the attempt of Justice Story to turn these acts into implied contract. Trustees of Dartmouth College, 17 U.S. (4 Wheat.) at 684–85.

68. See J. Shirley, *supra* note 60, at 398; Hagan, The Dartmouth College Case, 19 Geo. L. J. 411, 420 (1931); Denham, An Historical Development of the Contract Theory in the Dartmouth College Case, 7 Mich. L. Rev. 201, 211 (1909).

69. Trustees of Dartmouth College, 1 N.H. at 134.

70. 36 U.S. (11 Pet.) 420 (1837). See S. Kutler, Privilege and Creative Destruction (1971); C. Swisher, History of the Supreme Court of the United States, V, The Taney Period: 1836–64, 71–98 (1974).

71. Charles River Bridge, 36 U.S. (11 Pet.) at 544, *quoting* Proprietors of the Stourbridge Canal v. Wheeley, 2 Barn. & Adol. 793, 109 Eng. Rep. 1336, 1337 (K.B. 1831).

72. See Conant, Antimonopoly Tradition under the Ninth and Fourteenth Amendments, 31 Emory L. J. 785, 792–97 (1982); chapter 10.

73. Charles River Bridge, 36 U.S. (11 Pet.) at 539.

74. See Miller v. New York, 82 U.S. (15 Wall.) 478 (1873); Greenwood v. Freight Company, 105 U.S. 13 (1882).

75. 29 U.S. (4 Pet.) 514 (1830).

76. 97 U.S. 25 (1878).

77. 101 U.S. 814 (1880).

78. *Id.* at 819. This rule was adopted in Butchers Union Co. v. Crescent City Co., 111 U.S. 746 (1884). See chapter 12, page 260.

79. See C. Warren, Bankruptcy in United States History (1935). The First Bankrupt Act of 1800, 2 Stat. 19–36 (1800), was repealed in 1803. The Bankrupt Act of 1841, 5 Stat. 1440 (1841), became effective on February 1, 1842, and was repealed in 1843. The Bankrupt Act of 1867, 15 Stat. 227 (1867), was repealed in 1878.

80. 17 U.S. (4 Wheat.) 122 (1819). See A. Beveridge, *supra* note 34, at IV, 209–18; C. Warren, *supra* note 34, at I, 492–98; Hale, *supra* note 1, at 519–22.

81. Sturges, 17 U.S. (4 Wheat.) at 206–207.

82. U.S. Const., art. I, § 8.

83. 17 U.S. (4 Wheat.) at 194.

84. *Id.* at 203. See Mason v. Haile, 25 U.S. (12 Wheat.) 370 (1827); Penniman's Case, 103 U.S. 714 (1881).

85. Sturges, 17 U.S. (4 Wheat.) at 196–97.

86. *Id.* at 197.

87. *Id.* at 202. "[I]f, in any case, the plain meaning of a provision, not contradicted by any other provision in the same instrument, is to be disregarded because we believe the framers of that instrument could not intend what they say, it must be one in which the absurdity and injustice of applying the provision to the case, would be so monstrous, that all mankind would, without hesitation, unite in rejecting the application" (*Id.* at 202–3).

88. 17 U.S. (4 Wheat.) 209 (1819).

89. *Id.* at 212.

90. 25 U.S. (12 Wheat.) 213 (1827). See A. Beveridge, *supra* note 34, at IV, 480–82; C. Warren, *supra* note 34, at I, 680–93; Hale, *supra* note 1, at 522–33.

91. *Ogden*, 25 U.S. (12 Wheat.) at 266 (Washington, J.)

92. *Id.* at 266–67 (Washington, J.); *id.* at 283–85 (Johnson, J.) *id.* at 297–303 (Thompson, J.); *id.* at 316–21 (Trimble, J.).

93. *Id.* at 254.

94. *Id.* at 264. Justice Washington's views were stated in Golden v. Prince, 3 Wash. C.C. 313, 10 Fed. Cas. 542, 545 (no. 5,509) (C.C.D. Pa. 1814).

95. *Ogden*, 25 U.S. (12 Wheat.) at 283–84. See D. Morgan, Justice William Johnson 220–24 (1954).

96. *Ogden,* 25 U.S. (12 Wheat.) 285–86.

97. *Id.* at 290.

98. *Id.* at 272–73.

99. *Id.* at 286.

100. *Id.* at 347 (Marshall C., dissenting).

101. See Lochner v. New York, 198 U.S. 45 (1905); Isaacs, *supra* note 65, at 426.

102. Ogden, 25 U.S. (12 Wheat.) at 348.

103. See Green v. Biddle, 21 U.S. (8 Wheat.) 1 (1823).

104. Ogden, 25 U.S. (12 Wheat.) at 357.

105. Ogden, 25 U.S. (12 Wheat.) at 286, citing Calder v. Bull, 3 U.S. (3 Dall.) 386 (1798). See *supra* note 28.

106. See International Shoe Company v. Pinkus, 278 U.S. 261, 264–65 (1929).

107. Kalb v. Feurstein, 306 U.S. 433 (1940).

108. 42 U.S. (1 How.) 311 (1843). See C. Swisher, *supra* note 70, at 148–51; C. Warren, *supra* note 34, at 102–5.

109. *Bronson,* 42 U.S. (1 How.) at 319.

110. *Id.* at 319–20.

111. McCracken v. Hayward, 43 U.S. (2 How.) 608 (1844); Lessee of Gantley v. Ewing, 44 U.S. (3 How.) 707 (1845); Howard v. Bugbee, 65 U.S. (24 How.) 461 (1861).

112. Gunn v. Barry, 82 U.S. (15 Wall.) 610 (1872); Edwards v. Kearzy, 96 U.S. 595 (1878).

113. 290 U.S. 398 (1934). See C. Miller, The Supreme Court and the Uses of History, ch. 3 (1969).

114. *Id.* at 426.

115. *Id.* at 435.

116. *Id.* at 465.

117. 292 U.S. at 426 (1934).

118. *Id.* at 434. See W. B. Worthen v. Kavanaugh, 295 U.S. 56 (1935) (contract clause violated when postponed foreclosure provides no payment to lender for loss of possession.)

119. New York Savings Bank v. Hahn, 326 U.S. 230 (1945).

120. 379 U.S. 497 (1965).

121. *Id.* at 506–7.

122. *Id.* at 509.

123. *Id.* at 515.

124. *Id.* at 517.

125. *Id.* at 522.

126. 431 U.S. 1 (1977). See Clarke, *supra* note 1, at 194–98; Epstein, *supra* note 10, at 720–21.

127. United States Trust Company, 431 U.S. at 35.

128. *Id.*

129. 438 U.S. 234 (1978). See Clarke, *supra* note 1, at 198–200.

130. Allied Structural Steel Company, 438 U.S. at 246.

131. *Id.* at 244.

132. *Id.* at 257.

133. 3 U.S. (3 Dall.) 386 (1798). See *supra* note 29.

134. Welch v. Henry, 305 U.S. 134 (1938).

135. Usery v. Turner-Elkhorn Mining Company, 428 U.S. 1 (1976). See R. Epstein, Takings 257–58 (1985).

136. 459 U.S. 400 (1983).

137. *Id.* at 410.

138. *Id.* at 411, citing Hudson Water Company v. McCarter, 209 U.S. 349 (1908) (Holmes, J.).

139. 459 U.S. at 416.

140. 462 U.S. 176 (1983).

141. *Id.* at 190.

142. *Id.* at 191.

Chapter 10

1. U.S. Const., amend. 14, § 1. See R. Cortner, The Supreme Court and the Second Bill of Rights (1981); M. Curtis, No State Shall Abridge (1986).

2. Colgate v. Harvey, 296 U.S. 404 (1935), *overruled in* Madden v. Kentucky, 309 U.S. 83 (1940).

3. U.S. Const., art. I, § 9.

4. 83 U.S. (16 Wall.) 36 (1873).

5. W. Blackstone, Commentaries on the Laws of England, II, 37 (1765), C. Viner, A General Abridgement of Law and Equity, VIII, 508 (2d ed. 1791). The usage is traced to the Magna Charta in Commonwealth v. Alger, 61 Mass. (7 Cush.) 53, 71 (1851).

6. See G. Jacob, Law Dictionary 389 (1811). In the Slaughter-House Cases, 83 U.S. (16 Wall.) 36 (1873), retired Justice Campbell, for appellants, cited similar definitions. See N. Lindley, An Introduction to the Study of Jurisprudence, §§ 30–32, app. note § 31 (1855).

7. F. Thorpe, ed., The Federal and State Constitutions, Colonial Charters and Other Organic Laws, VII, 3788 (1909) [hereinafter cited as Colonial Charters]. The same language was repeated in Virginia's revised charters of 1609 and 1612. *Id.,* VII at 3800, 3805. The earlier letters patent to Sir Humfrey Gylberte and Sir Walter Raleigh granted colonialists the "privileges of free denizens," *id.,* I at 51, 55.

8. *Id.,* III at 1839.

9. *Id.* at 1635.

10. *Id.,* II at 773.

11. *Id.,* III at 1857. The Charter of Massachusetts Bay of 1691 used the terms "liberties and immunities." *Id.* at 1881.

12. *Id.,* II at 533.

13. *Id.,* VI at 3230.

14. *Id.,* III at 1681.

15. *Id.,* V at 2747, 2765.

16. See A. Howard, The Road from Runnymede 103–4 (1968).

17. R. Perry and J. Cooper, Sources of Our Liberties 148 (1959).

18. Letter from Richard Nicolls to the residents of Long Island (1664), quoted in A. Howard, *supra* note 16, at 71.

19. R. Perry and J. Cooper, *supra* note 17, at 212.

20. *Id.* at 256.

21. The Massachusetts Resolves, October 29, 1765, reprinted in E. Morgan, Prologue to Revolution 56 (1959).

22. The resolutions provided in part as follows:

Resolved, That the first Adventurers and Settlers of this his Majesty's Colony and Dominion of *Virginia* brought with them, and transmitted to their Posterity, and all other his Majesty's Subjects since inhabiting in this his Majesty's said Colony, all the Liberties, Privileges, Franchises and Immunities, that have at any Time been held, enjoyed, and posessed, by the people of *Great Britain.*

Resolved, that by two royal Charters, granted by King *James* the First, the Colonists aforesaid are declared entitled to all Liberties, Privileges, and Immunities of Denizens and natural Subjects, to all Intents and Purposes, as if they had been abiding and born within the Realm of *England.*

Resolutions of the House of Burgesses of Virginia against the Stamp Act, reprinted in A. Howard, *supra* note 16, at 430.

23. Resolution II of the Stamp Act Congress provided: "That his Majesty's liege subjects in these colonies, are intitled to all the inherent rights and liberties of his natural born subjects, within the kingdom of Great Britain" (Resolution II

of the Stamp Act Congress, reprinted in A. Sutherland, Constitutionalism in America 135 [1965]). On the constitutional importance of the Stamp Act crisis, see E. Morgan and H. Morgan, The Stamp Act Crisis 295 (1953).

24. The resolutions provided in part as follows:

> Resolved, That this Colony and Dominion of *Virginia* cannot be considered as a conquered country, and, if it was, that the present inhabitants are the descendants, not of the conquered, but of the conquerors. That the same was not settled at the national expense of *England,* but at the private expense of the adventurers, our ancestors, by solemn compact with, and under the auspices and protection of, the *British* Crown, upon which we are, in every respect, as dependent as the people of *Great Britain,* and in the same manner subject to all his Majesty's just, legal, and constitutional prerogatives; that our ancestors, when they left their native land, and settled in *America,* brought with them, even if the same had not been confirmed by Charters, the civil Constitution and form of Government of the country they came from, and were by the laws of nature and Nations entitled to all its privileges, immunities, and advantages, which have descended to us, their posterity, and ought of right to be as fully enjoyed as if we had still continued within the Realm of *England.*

Fairfax County Resolutions, reprinted in A. Howard, *supra* note 16, at 423–33.

25. The October 14 resolutions read in part:

> Resolved, N.C.D.2. That our ancestors, who first settled these colonies, were at the time of their emigration from the mother country, entitled to all the rights, liberties, and immunities of free and natural-born subjects, within the realm of England.
> Resolved, N.C.D.3. That by such emigration they by no means forfeited, surrendered, or lost any of those rights, but that they were, and their descendants now are, entitled to the exercise and enjoyment of all such of them, as their local and other circumstances enable them to exercise and enjoy.

Journals of the Continental Congress, I, 68 (1904).

26. Articles of Confederation, art. IV, reprinted in Journals of the Continental Congress, IX, 908 (1907).

27. For a detailed, comprehensive review of this development, see A. Howard, *supra* note 16, at 1–202.

28. Journals of the Continental Congress, V, 547 (1906). Article VII of the first draft read as follows: "The Inhabitants of each Colony shall enjoy all the Rights, Liberties, Privileges, Immunities, and Advantages, in Trade, Navigation, and Commerce, in any other Colony, and in going to and from the same from and to any Part of the World, which the Natives of such Colony . . . enjoy."

29. The final version of Article IV read: "The better to secure and perpetuate mutual friendship and intercourse among the people of the different states in this union, the free inhabitants of each of these states, paupers, vagbonds, and fugitives from justice excepted, shall be entitled to all privileges and immunities of free citizens in the several states; and the people of each State shall have free ingress and regress to and from any other State, and shall enjoy therein all the privileges of trade and commerce, subject to the same duties, impositions, and restrictions, as the inhabitants thereof respectively" (Journals of the Continental Congress, IX, 908 [1907]).

30. U.S. Const., art. IV, § 2.

31. On June 25, 1778, South Carolina delegates moved to amend Article IV by inserting the word "white" between the words "free" and "inhabitants," so that constitutional protections would be available only to white visitors from other states. This was defeated, eight states against two, and one state had a divided delegation. Journals of the Continental Congress, XI, 652 (1908).

32. Scott v. Sandford, 60 U.S. (19 How.) 393, 403–4, 585 (1857). Justice Curtis, following the rules of documentary interpretation, reported that he had examined the forms of expression commonly used in the State Papers of 1789. *Id.* at 584.

33. U.S. Const., preamble.

34. Madison seems in error in suggesting that free inhabitants who were not technically citizens of their state of domicile would have greater privileges under this clause in a state they visited than at home. He seems to confuse civil rights and rights of citizenship, e.g., voting. Federalist 42, at 291–92 (J. Madison) (E. Bourne ed. 1947).

35. See generally, A. Dicey, Introduction to the Study of the Law of the Constitution, ch. 5 (7th ed. 1908); J. Story, Commentaries on the Constitution of the United States, II, 499 (1833).

36. L. Spooner, The Unconstitutionality of Slavery (1845; reprint 1965), and J. Tiffany, A Treatise on the Unconstitutionality of American Slavery (1849), are cited on the issue in J. ten Broek, The Antislavery Origins of the Fourteenth Amendment 49–50, 86–93 (1951). As part of antislavery constitutional theory, Tiffany and others felt that the decision in Barron v. Baltimore, 32 U.S. (7 Pet.) 243 (1833) was wrong, and that the Bill of Rights, except Amendments I and VII, which expressly referred to Congress and the federal courts, was a constraint on the states. See H. Graham, Everyman's Constitution 174–84 (1968).

37. See *supra* notes 34–35 and accompanying text.

38. 6 F. Cas. 546 (C.C.E.D. Pa. 1823) (no. 3,230) (New Jersey statute forbidding nonresidents from gathering oysters in state's waters did not violate Article IV, § 2).

39. *Id.* at 551. The opinion continues as follows:

What these fundamental principles are, it would perhaps be more tedious than difficult to enumerate. They may, however, be all comprehended under the following general heads: Protection by the government; the enjoyment of life and liberty, with the right to acquire and possess property of every kind, and to pursue and obtain happiness and safety; subject nevertheless to such restraints as the government may justly prescribe for the general good of the whole. The right of a citizen of one state to pass through, or to reside in any other state, for purposes of trade, agriculture, professional pursuits, or otherwise; to claim the benefit of the writ of habeas corpus; to institute and maintain actions of any kind in the courts of the state; to take, hold and dispose of property, either real or personal; and an exemption from higher taxes or impositions than are paid by the other citizens of the state; may be mentioned as some of the particular privileges and immunities of citizens, which are clearly embraced by the general description of privileges deemed to be fundamental: to which may be added, the elective franchise, as regulated and established by the laws or constitution of the state in which it is to be exercised. These, and many others which might be mentioned, are, strictly speaking, privileges and immunities, and the enjoyment of them by the citizens of each state, in every other state, was manifestly calculated (to use the expressions of the preamble of the corresponding provision in the old articles of confederation) "the better to secure and perpetuate mutual friend-ship and intercourse among the people of the different states of the Union."

Id. at 551–52.

40. *See* Hague v. CIO, 307 U.S. 496, 511 (1939); L. Tribe, American Constitu-tional Law 529–31 (2d ed. 1988).

41. The expression "fundamental" law as a synonym for constitutional be-came current during the controversy over the tax known as ship money around 1635. A. Dicey, *supra* note 35, at 141. This usage continued on through the eighteenth century. J. Gough, Fundamental Law in English Constitutional History 207 (rev. ed. 1971). Some colonies used "fundamental" to label their basic laws adopted pursuant to their charters, such as the *Fundamental Orders of Connecti-cut* (1639), the *Fundamentals of Massachusetts* (1646), and *Fundamental Laws of West New Jersey* (1676). Dean Pound noted that early American lawyers equated the idea of fundamental law with the "law of the land" to which all official and governmental action was bound to conform. R. Pound, The Development of Constitutional Guarantees of Liberty 61 (1957). He further stated: "American lawyers were taught to believe in a fundamental law which, after the Revolution, they found declared in written constitution" (*Id.* at 78). *See* Bayard v. Singleton, 1 N.C. (Mart.) 48 (1787).

The other use of "fundamental law," as a reference to natural law, was used in America in the 1770s primarily in political writings to rationalize the Revolu-tion. See C. Mullett, Fundamental Law and the American Revolution 1760–1776 (1933).

42. See chapter 4 on the English origins of property rights.

43. See R. Howell, The Privileges and Immunities of State Citizenship (1918); L. Tribe, American Constitutional Law 528–45 (2d ed. 1988); S. Doc. no. 82, 92nd Cong., 2d sess., 830–38 (1973).

44. 436 U.S. 371 (1978).

45. 75 U.S. (8 Wall.) 168, 180 (1869).

46. 436 U.S. at 388.

47. *Id.* at 383, 386 (citing Ward v. Maryland, 79 U.S. [12 Wall.] 418 [1871], which concerned a discriminatory tax on nonresidents for the privilege of selling goods produced in other states). See also Toomer v. Witsell, 334 U.S. 385 (1948) (discriminatory license fees for nonresident commercial shrimpers).

48. Article IV of the Articles of Confederation provided nonresidents with protection of "privileges and immunities of free citizens" and of "privileges of trade and commerce." In the Constitution the protection for privileges of trade and commerce was moved to Article I, Section 8, Clause 3, and Article I, Section 10, Clause 2.

49. 470 U.S. 274 (1985).

50. *Id.* at 279.

51. The New Hampshire Court asserted that nonresidents would be less likely: (1) to become, and remain familiar with local rules and procedures; (2) to behave ethically; (3) to be available for court proceedings; and (4) to do *pro bono* and other volunteer work in the State. *Id.* at 285.

52. Bradwell v. Illinois, 83 U.S. (16 Wall.) 130 (1873).

53. The words "citizens of the United States" in the Fourteenth Amendment are not words of limitation. They were necessary to help define which class of civil rights were to be protected and were not inserted to limit the persons protected. Green, The Bill of Rights, the Fourteenth Amendment and the Supreme Court, 46 Mich. L. Rev. 869, 904 (1948). See Baldwin, The Citizen of the United

States, 2 Yale L. J. 85 (1893). On the meaning of "citizens" in Article IV, see *supra* note 32 and 33 and accompanying text.

54. 60 U.S. (19 How.) 393 (1857). The Supreme Court's express view that a purpose of Section 1 of the Fourteenth Amendment was to overrule *Dred Scott* is stated in the Slaughter-House Cases, 83 U.S. (16 Wall.) 36, 73 (1873). See M. Curtis, *supra* note 1, at 26–56.

55. Scott, 60 U.S. (19 How.) at 403.

56. *Id.* at 426–27.

57. *Id.* at 406, 422–23.

58. 32 U.S. (7 Pet.) 243 (1833) (takings clause of Fifth Amendment held not applicable to the states; therefore, Baltimore not required to pay just compensation for taking of plaintiff's property). See W. Crosskey, Politics and the Constitution in the History of the United States, II, 1089–95 (1953); H. Flack, The Adoption of the Fourteenth Amendment 233 (1908); Graham, Our "Declaratory" Fourteenth Amendment, reprinted in Everyman's Constitution 295, 316–17 (1968).

59. See Twining v. New Jersey, 211 U.S. 78, 114 (1908) (Harlan, J., dissenting) (the immunity from self-incrimination was a fundamental civil right under English law and was incorporated as such in the U.S. Constitution); Maxwell v. Dow, 176 U.S. 581, 605 (1900) (Harlan, J., dissenting) (trial by a jury of twelve was an implicit right of a citizen at the time of the adoption of the Constitution).

60. 332 U.S. 46, 68–123 (1947) (Black, J., dissenting). The pursuit of the differing and conflicting subjective intents of the framers of the Fourteenth Amendment by Justice Black and Professor Fairman is a prime example of the futile search for intent when the correct methodology requires search for meaning of language. See Fairman, Does the Fourteenth Amendment Incorporate the Bill of Rights? 2 Stan. L. Rev. 5 (1949). Compare M. Curtis, *supra* note 1, at 92–130.

61. See Duncan v. Louisiana, 391 U.S. 145, 148 (1968). In the *Palko* case, which is cited as the standard for selective incorporation, immunity from double jeopardy had been held not implicit in the 1791 concept of ordered liberty. Palko v. Connecticut, 302 U.S. 319, 324 (1937). *Palko* was overruled in Benton v. Maryland, 395 U.S. 784 (1969). The *Palko* Court's view was not consistent with Blackstone: "It is contrary to the genius and spirit of the law of England to suffer any man to be tried twice for the same offense in a criminal way, especially if acquitted upon the first trial" (W. Blackstone, *supra* note 5, IV, at 259). In fact, all of the first eight amendments are explicit requirements of ordered liberty.

62. 176 U.S. 581 (1900). *Maxwell's* general holding regarding incorporation of the right to jury trial was overruled in Duncan v. Louisiana, 391 U.S. 146, 149 n. 14 (1968).

63. 144 U.S. 323 (1892), *questioned in* Furman v. Georgia, 408 U.S. 238, 325 (1972). The dissent of Justice Field in *O'Neill*, explaining the true meaning of privileges and immunities of citizens of the United States, is reviewed in M. Curtis, *supra* note 1, at 189–91.

64. 211 U.S. 78 (1908), *overruled in* Griffin v. California, 380 U.S. 609 (1965).

65. 332 U.S. 46 (1947), *overruled in* Griffin v. California, 380 U.S. 609 (1965).

66. See, e.g., Cantwell v. Connecticut, 310 U.S. 296 (1940); De Jonge v. Oregon, 299 U.S. 353 (1937); Near v. Minnesota, 283 U.S. 697 (1931); Gitlow v. New York, 268 U.S. 652 (1925). See chapter 11, notes 114–127 and accompanying text.

67. See, e.g., Ferguson v. Skrupa, 372 U.S. 726, 730 (1963), *overruling* Adams v. Tanner, 244 U.S. 590 (1917); Williamson v. Lee Optical, 348 U.S. 483, 487–

88 (1955); Day-Brite Lighting v. Missouri, 342 U.S. 421, 423 (1952). See chapter 11, notes 88–113.

68. 83 U.S. (16 Wall.) 36 (1973). See *infra* notes 148–176 and accompanying text for a further discussion of the *Slaughter-House Cases*.

69. J. Ely, Democracy and Distrust 196 n. 59 (1980).

70. 83 U.S. (16 Wall.) at 79. In commenting on the meaning of Amendments XIII through XV in the context of the history of the times at their adoption, Justice Miller asserted: "Fortunately that history is fresh within the memory of us all, and the leading features, as they bear upon the matter before us, free from doubt" (*Id.* at 68).

71. 83 U.S. (16 Wall.) at 118–19 (Bradley, J., dissenting).

72. United States v. Hall, 26 F. Cas. 79 (C.C.S.D. Ala. 1871) (No. 15,282). See M. Curtis, *supra* note 1, at 171–72; R. Kaczorowski, The Politics of Judicial Interpretation, 14–17 (1985).

73. 6 F. Cas. 546 (C.C.E.D. Pa. 1823) (No. 3230).

74. "We think, therefore, that the right of freedom of speech, and the other rights enumerated in the first eight articles of amendment to the constitution of the United States, are the privileges and immunities of citizens of the United States, that they are secured by the constitution, that congress has the power to protect them by appropriate legislation. We are further of opinion that the act on which this indictment is founded applies to cases of this kind, and that it is legislation appropriate to the end in view, namely, the protection of the fundamental rights of citizens of the United States" (Hall, 26 F. Cas. at 82).

75. See M. Goodman, The Ninth Amendment (1981); B. Patterson, The Forgotten Ninth Amendment (1955); Kelley, The Uncertain Renaissance of the Ninth Amendment, 33 U. Chi. L. Rev. 814 & nn.2 & 5 (1966); Caplan, History and Meaning of the Ninth Amendment, 69 Va. L. Rev. 223 (1983).

76. M. Farrand, The Records of the Federal Convention of 1787, II, at 582, 587–88 (rev. ed. 1937); *id.* III, at 143–44, 161–62. See Federalist 84, book II, 152–58 (Hamilton) (E. Bourne ed. 1947).

77. See J. Goebel, History of the Supreme Court of the United States, I, 430–39 (1971); E. Dumbauld, The Bill of Rights and What It Means Today 33–38 (1957); Dunbar, James Madison and the Ninth Amendment, 42 Va. L. Rev. 627, 630 (1956).

78. Debates and Proceedings in the Congress of the United States 452 (J. Gales and W. Seaton eds. 1834). Madison's explanation of reasons for the clause was made on June 8, 1789, as follows:

> It has been objected also against a bill of rights, that, by enumerating particular exceptions to the grant of power, it would disparage those rights which were not placed in that enumeration; and it might follow, by implication, that those rights which were not signaled out, were intended to be assigned into the hands of the General Government, and were consequently insecure. This is one of the most plausible arguments I have ever heard urged against the admission of a bill of rights into this system; but, I conceive, that it may be guarded against, I have attempted it, as gentlemen may see by turning to the last clause of the fourth resolution.

Id. at 456.

79. Livingston v. Moore, 32 U.S. (7 Pet.) 551 (1833). See E. Dumbauld, *supra* note 77, at 207–8.

80. U.S. Const., amend. IX.

81. J. Story, *supra* note 35, at II, § 1905.

82. See chapter 2, notes 43 and 44 and accompanying text.

83. The Ninth Amendment refers only to substantive constitutional law because the due process clause of the Fifth Amendment was designed to incorporate, *inter alia,* all procedural protections of standing English constitutional law. Murray's Lessee v. Hoboken Land & Improvement Co., 59 U.S. (18 How.) 272 (1855). See Van Loan, Natural Rights and the Ninth Amendment, 48 B.U.L. Rev. 1, 13–14 (1968).

84. Kent, Under the Ninth Amendment What Rights Are the "Others Retained by the People?" 28 Fed. B. J. 219 (1970).

85. *Id.* at 234–35.

86. J. Ely, *supra* note 69, at 203.

87. See Reid, In an Inherited Way, 49 S. Calif. L. Rev. 1109, 1120–23 (1976).

88. G. Dietze, In Defense of Property 52–59 (1963). See chapter 4, notes 41 to 63 and accompanying text.

89. U.S. Const., amend. V.

90. Corfield v. Coryell, 6 F. Cas. 546 (C.C.E.D. Pa. 1823) (No. 3,230). See Shelley v. Kraemer, 334 U.S. 1, 10 (1948).

91. W. Holdsworth, History of English Law, XI, 392–94, 507–12 (7th ed. 1938).

92. Cases in which the Ninth Amendment has been pleaded are reviewed in B. Patterson, *supra* note 75, at 19–26; and Kelley, *supra* note 75, at 825–32; Rhoades and Patula, The Ninth Amendment, 50 Den. L. J. 153 (1973).

93. 381 U.S. 479 (1965).

94. Griswold, 381 U.S. at 492.

95. A search through W. Blackstone, *supra* note 5, and W. Holdsworth, History of English Law (1903–1938) reveals no such category.

96. The dynamics of the common law that had led to the development of the private tort remedy for invasion of privacy should have no bearing on public law. See Griswold, The Right to Be Let Alone, 55 Nw.U. L. Rev. 217 (1960); Warren and Brandeis, The Right to Privacy, 4 Harv. L. Rev. 193 (1890). The historical dynamics of the common law are explained in E. Levi, An Introduction to Legal Reasoning 8–27 (1948). Injecting such broad judicial discretion in constitutional law results in bold usurpations of the amending power, like substantive due process. New classes of substantive civil rights and remedies against government should be created by statute or constitutional amendment. See chapter 11.

97. "All merchants shall have safe and secure exit from England, and entry to England, with the right to tarry there and to move about as well by land as by water, for buying and selling by the ancient and right customs, quit from all evil tolls, except (in time of war) such merchants as are of the land at war with us. And if such are found in our land at the beginning of the war, they shall be detained, without injury to their bodies or goods, until information be received by us, or by our chief justiciar, how the merchants of our land found in the land at war with us are treated; and if our men are safe there, the others shall be safe in our land" Magna Charta, ch. 41, translated and reprinted in W. McKechnie, Magna Carta 399 (2d ed. 1914).

98. W. McKechnie, *supra* note 97, at 399–400.

99. See H. Fox, Monopolies and Patents 57 (1947).

100. 9 Edw. 3, Stat. 1, ch. 1 (1335); 25 Edw. 3, Stat. 4, ch. 2 (1350); 2 Rich. 2, Stat. 1, ch. 1 (1378).

101. See, e.g., 12 Hen. 7, ch. 6 (1497).

102. Sandys argued: "All free Subjects are borne inheritable as to ther Lands, soe alsoe to the free exercise of ther industrie in those trads wherto they applie

themselves and wherby they are to live. Merchandise being the chiefe and richest of all other, and of greater extent and importance than all the rest, it is against the naturall right and liberty of the Subjects of England to restrain it into the hands of some fewe" (Sandys, Instructions towchinge the Bill for Free Trade, quoted in W. Cunningham, The Growth of English Industry and Commerce, II, 287 [5th ed. 1912]).

103. H. Fox, *supra* note 99, at 74–75.

104. Moore 576, 72 Eng. Rep. 769 (K.B. 1599). See H. Fox, *supra* note 99, at 311.

105. 11 Coke 84, 77 Eng. Rep. 1260 (K.B. 1602). See J. Gordon, Monopolies by Patents and the Statutable Remedies Available to the Public 193–231 (1897); Davies, Further Light on the Case of Monopolies, 48 L.Q. Rev. 394 (1932).

106. See Wagner, Coke and the Rise of Economic Liberalism 6 Econ. Hist. Rev. 30 (1935). See generally W. Holdsworth, History of English Law, IV, 343–62 (1924).

107. J. Thayer, Cases on Constitutional Law (1895), reprinted in R. Pound, *supra* note 41, at 145–48.

108. 11 Coke 53a, 77 Eng. Rep. 1218 (K.B. 1614).

109. Palmer 1, 81 Eng. Rep. 949 (K.B. 1619).

110. See H. Fox, *supra* note 99, at 330.

111. *Id.* at 336.

112. State Trials, II, 1119, 1130–32 (T. Howell ed. 1816).

113. 21 Jac. 1, ch. 3 (1624). See J. Tanner, Constitutional Documents of the Reign of James I, at 268–72 (1930).

114. See H. Fox, *supra* note 99, at 130.

115. *Id.* at 180.

116. J. Rushworth, Historical Collections of Private Passages of State, II, 103 (1721).

117. See H. Fox, *supra* note 99, at 129.

118. 16 Car. 1, ch. 10 (1640).

119. R. Perry and J. Cooper, *supra* note 17, at 222.

120. H. Levy, Monopolies, Cartels and Trusts in British Industry 62–72 (1927).

121. On the constitutional conventions in England, see A. Dicey, Introduction to the Study of the Law of the Constitution, ch. 14 (7th ed. 1908).

122. Debates and Proceedings in the Congress of the United States 436 (J. Gales and W. Seaton eds. 1834). See Z. Chafee, How Human Rights Got into the Constitution 19–21 (1952). See also chapter 3, notes 53–56 and accompanying text.

123. See *supra* notes 7–15 and accompanying text.

124. The Colonial Laws of Massachusetts 1672, at 33–61 (W. Whitmore ed. 1890).

125. *Id.* at 35.

126. Reinsch, The English Common Law in the Early American Colonies, in Select Essays in Anglo-American Legal History, I, 367, 373 (1907).

127. W. Penn, The Excellent Privilege of Liberty & Property Being the Birth-Right of the Free-Born Subjects of England (1687), *excerpts reprinted in* A. Howard, *supra* note 16, at 413–25.

128. Moore 576, 72 Eng. Rep. 679 (K.B. 1599).

129. 11 Coke 84, 77 Eng. Rep. 1260 (K.B. 1602).

130. A. Howard, *supra* note 16, at 421.

131. Colonial Charters, *supra* note 7, at VII, 3790, 3802.

132. See The Genesis of the United States, I, 207 (A. Brown ed. 1891); E. Channing, History of the United States, I, 193 (1928).

133. See *supra* notes 7–15.

134. R. Perry and J. Cooper, *supra* note 17, at 309–10. See R. Rutland, The Birth of the Bill of Rights 41–77 (1955).

135. Colonial Charters, *supra* note 7, at III, 1686–1691.

136. Colonial Charters, *supra* note 7, at V, 2788. After Tennessee was established as a separate state, it adopted the same prohibition. Colonial Charters, *supra* note 7, at VI, 3423.

137. See J. Story, *supra* note 35, at I, §§ 301, 304; II, §§ 1858–68.

138. Letter from Jefferson to Madison (Dec. 20, 1787), reprinted in T. Jefferson, The Papers of Thomas Jefferson, XII, 438, 440 (J. Boyd ed. 1955) (emphasis added). The need for a clause in the Bill of Rights prohibiting monopolies was repeated in letters to Madison in 1788 and in 1789. *Id.*, XIII at 440, 442; *id.*, XIV at 364, 368.

139. Debates in the Several State Conventions on the Adoption of the Federal Constitution, I, 323 (J. Elliot ed. 1836) [hereinafter cited as Debates].

140. *Id.* at 326; *id.*, III at 210–215.

141. *Id.*, I at 330.

142. *Id.* at 337. Congress completed action on the Bill of Rights on September 25, 1789, and sent the proposal to the states for ratification.

143. See E. Dumbauld, *supra* note 77, at 160–65 for tables showing the sources of the Bill of Rights.

144. See James Madison, Writings, V, 34 (G. Hunt ed. 1906).

145. Debates, *supra* note 139, I at 496. See K. Rowland, The Life of George Mason, II, 387, 389, 1725–92 (1892).

146. See generally, Colonial Charters, *supra* note 7, at III, 1690.

147. J. Senate 122 (1st Cong., 1789); J. H. Rep. 111 (1st Cong., 1789). See E. Dumbauld, *supra* note 77, at 24, 34.

148. 83 U.S. (16 Wall.) 36 (1873). See C. Fairman. Reconstruction and Reunion, 1864–88, History of the Supreme Court of the United States, VI, 1864–88, 1320–63 (1971); Franklin, The Foundation and Meaning of the Slaughterhouse Cases, 18 Tulane L. Rev. 1, 218 (1943).

149. C. Warren, The Supreme Court in United States History, II, 533–61 (1926).

150. See A. Lien, Concurring Opinion 111 n. 8 (1957).

151. Live-Stock Assoc. v. Crescent City Co., 15 F. Cas. 649 (C.C.D. La. 1870) (no. 8,408).

152. An Act to Protect All Person's in the United States in their Civil Rights and Furnish the Means of their Vindication, 14 Stat. 27 (1866).

153. 15 F. Cas. at 652.

154. *Id.* at 653.

155. An Act to Establish the Judicial Courts of the United States, 1 Stat. 333, 335 (1845).

156. Slaughter-House Cases, 83 U.S. (16 Wall.) at 82.

157. *Id.* at 74.

158. See *supra* notes 38–42 and accompanying text. Cf. L. Lusky, By What Right? 191 (1975).

159. State v. Fagan, 22 La. Ann. 545 (La. 1870).

160. L. Lusky, *supra* note 158 at 197, 198.

161. *Id.* at 194.

162. Slaughter-House Cases, 83 U.S. (16 Wall.) at 75. Justice Bradley in dissent,

stated: "It is pertinent to observe that both the clause of the Constitution referred to, and Justice Washington in his comment on it, speak of the privileges and immunities of citizens *in* a state; not of citizens *of* a state" (*Id.* at 117 [Bradley, J., dissenting] [emphasis added]).

163. 83 U.S. (16 Wall.) at 76. See L. Lusky, *supra* note 158, at 195–196.

164. L. Lusky, *supra* note 158 at 196.

165. See, e.g., L. Tribe, American Constitutional Law 550–53 (2d ed. 1988); W. Crosskey, Politics and the Constitution in the History of the United States, II, 1119–30 (1953); Borchard, The Supreme Court and Private Rights, 47 Yale L. J. 1051, 1063 (1938); Royall, The Fourteenth Amendment: The Slaughter-House Cases, 4 S.L. Rev. (n.s.) 558 (1878); Taylor, The Slaughter-House Cases, 3 S.L. Rev. 476 (1874).

166. See *supra* note 2.

167. Referring to the Privileges and Immunities Clause of Article IV, Field stated:

> What the clause in question did for the protection of the citizens of one State against hostile and discriminating legislation of other states, the fourteenth amendment does for the protection of every citizen of the United States against hostile and discriminating legislation against him in favor of others, whether they reside in the same or in different States. If under the fourth article of the Constitution equality of privileges and immunities is secured between citizens of different States, under the fourteenth amendment the same equality is secured between citizens of the United States. . . . Now, what the clause in question does for the protection of citizens of one State against the creation of monopolies in favor of citizens of other States, the fourteenth amendment does for the protection of every citizen of the United States against the creation of any monopoly whatever. The privileges and immunities of citizens of the United States, of every one of them, is secured against abridgement in any form by any State. The fourteenth amendment places them under the guardianship of the National authority.

Slaughter-House Cases, 83 U.S. (16 Wall.) at 100–101 (Field, J., dissenting).

168. 83 U.S. (16 Wall.) at 102 (Field, J., dissenting).

169. 77 Eng. Rep. 1260 (K.B. 1602).

170. 72 Eng. Rep. 769 (K.B. 1599).

171. 21 Jac. 1, ch. 3 (1623).

172. See *supra* note 25.

173. Slaughter-House Cases, 83 U.S. (16 Wall.) at 110 (Field, J., dissenting).

174. Two other legal arguments in the *Slaughter-House* cases received summary disposition by the majority. The Court rejected substantive due process in one sentence. *Id.* at 81. For the recent law on substantive due process, see chapter 11. In light of the later overwhelming rejection of this concept by the Supreme Court with respect to economic regulation, Justice Miller clearly was correct, and dissenting Justice Bradley clearly was wrong. The dissent of Justice Bradley is considered one of the historical foundations of substantive due process. 83 U.S. at 114–15, 122–23 (Bradley, J., dissenting). The Court also rejected an argument based on equal protection, stating that the equal protection clause was primarily for protection of freed slaves and that the plaintiffs had made no case for creating an exception. *Id.* at 81. See chapter 12.

175. See, e.g., Ippolito and Masson, The Social Cost of Government Regulation of Milk, 21 J. L. & Econ. 33 (1978); Smith, The Monopoly Component of

Inflation in Food Prices, 14 U. Mich. J. L. Ref. 149 (1981); Moore, The Beneficiaries of Trucking Regulation, 21 J. L. of Econ. 327, 342 (1978).

176. See, e.g., New Motor Vehicle Board v. Orrin W. Fox Co., 439 U.S. 96 (1978); City of New Orleans v. Dukes, 427 U.S. 297 (1976); Moore, The Purpose of Licensing, 4 J. L. & Econ. 93 (1961); Kitch, Issacson and Kasper, The Regulation of Taxicabs in Chicago, 14 J. L. & Econ. 285 (1971).

Chapter 11

1. Barron v. Baltimore, 32 U.S. (7 Pet.) 243 (1833).

2. Adamson v. California, 332 U.S. 46, 66 (1947) (Frankfurter, J., concurring).

3. See Mathews v. Diaz, 426 U.S. 67, 77 (1976).

4. Conn. Gen. Life Ins. Co. v. Johnson, 303 U.S. 77, 82 (1938); First Nat. Bank of Boston v. Bellotti, 435 U.S. 765, 781 (1978).

5. J. Story, Commentaries on the Constitution of the United States, I, § 453 (1833).

6. *Id.*, § 452.

7. See the comments of Justice Frankfurter, chapter 3, note 8 and accompanying text.

8. See W. McKechnie, Magna Carta, ch. 39 (2d ed. 1914); M. Bigelow, History of Procedure in England from the Norman Conquest 155 (1880); Jurow, Untimely Thoughts, 19 Am. J. Legal Hist. 265 (1975).

9. Corwin, Due Process of Law before the Civil War, 24 Harv. L. Rev. 366, 460 (1911), reprinted in American Constitutional History 46–47 (1964).

10. 1 Stats. 93 (1789).

11. See J. Goebel, History of the Supreme Court of the United States, I, 509 (1971).

12. G. Jacob, A New Law Dictionary (7th ed. 1756), s.v. Process.

13. J. Goebel, *supra* note 11, at 514.

14. See W. Crosskey, Politics and the Constitution in the History of the United States, II, 1103–16 (1953).

15. Dartmouth College v. Woodward, 17 U.S. (4 Wheat.) 518, 581 (1819) (argument of Webster, D.).

16. 59 U.S. (18 How.) 272, 276–77 (1855).

17. Hurtado v. California, 110 U.S. 516, 539 (1884) (dissenting opinion).

18. See International Shoe Co. v. Washington, 326 U.S. 310, 316 (1945).

19. Snyder v. Massachusetts, 291 U.S. 97, 105 (1934).

20. Malinski v. New York, 324 U.S. 401, 414 (1945).

21. 110 U.S. 516 (1884) (grand jury clause of Fifth Amendment not applicable to the states). The dissent of Justice Harlan clearly demonstrated that under the rule of *Murray's Lessee,* due process incorporated Amendments Five through Eight. *Id.* at 542–43.

22. See, e.g., Maxwell v. Dow, 176 U.S. 581 (1900) (Sixth Amendment right to jury trial not applicable to states), *overruled in* Duncan v. Louisiana, 391 U.S. 145 (1968); Twining v. New Jersey, 211 U.S. 78 (1908) (Fifth Amendment privilege against self-incrimination not applicable to the states), *overruled in* Malloy v. Hogan, 378 U.S. 1 (1964); Palko v. Connecticut, 302 U.S. 319 (1937) (Fifth Amendment immunity from double jeopardy not applicable to states), *overruled in* Benton v. Maryland, 395 U.S. 784 (1969).

23. See Duncan v. Louisiana, 319 U.S. 145 (1968).

24. 96 U.S. 97 (1878).

25. *Id.* at 105.

26. *Id.* at 102. Later in the opinion, Miller emphasizes, inconsistently, that there is no eminent domain clause in the Fourteenth Amendment. *Id.* at 105.

27. *Id.* at 104.

28. B. Twiss, Lawyers and the Constitution, ch. 2 (1942); A. Paul, Conservative Crisis and the Rule of Law (1969); B. Siegan, Economic Liberties and the Constitution, ch. 2 (1980).

29. E. Corwin, Liberty against Government, ch. 3 (1948); Corwin, Due Process of Law before the Civil War, 24 Harv. L. Rev. 366, 460 (1911).

30. W. Wiecek, The Sources of Antislavery Constitutionalism in America (1977); Graham, Procedure to Substance, 40 Calif. L. Rev. 483 (1952), reprinted in Everyman's Constitution, ch. 5 (1968).

31. 13 N.Y. 378 (1850).

32. Scott v. Sandford, 60 U.S. (19 How.) 393 (1857). See D. Fehrenbacher, The Dred Scott Case (1978); E. Corwin, The Doctrine of Judicial Review and Other Essays ch. 4 (1914); C. Warren, The Supreme Court in United States History, II, ch. 26 (1926).

33. 60 U.S. (19 How.) at 450. The Illinois constitution of 1848, Art. 13, § 16, contained an absolute prohibition on slavery in the state. This was notice to all owners in slave states not to bring slaves into Illinois because no person could be held in slavery there. This notice met the procedural requirements of due process. See Rodney v. Illinois Central Railroad Co., 19 Ill. 42 (1857). The automatic emancipation rule adopts the standing constitutional law of England when the United States was founded. See chapter 12, *infra,* note 22.

34. 83 U.S. (16 Wall.) 36 (1873). See C. Warren, *supra* note 32, II, at ch. 32 (1926).

35. 83 U.S. (16 Wall.) at 116.

36. *Id.* at 122.

37. See G. Kolko, Railroads and Regulation (1965); P. MacAvoy, The Economic Effects of Regulation (1965).

38. 94 U.S. 113 (1877). On the *Granger* cases, see C. Warren, *supra* note 32, II, at 574–89; C. Swisher, Stephen J. Field 362–95 (1930); Kitch and Bowler, The Facts of Munn v. Illinois, 1978 Sup. Ct. Rev. 313.

39. 94 U.S. at 134. See Siegel, Understanding the Lochner Era, 70 Va. L. Rev. 187 (1984).

40. 116 U.S. 307, 331 (1886).

41. 134 U.S. 418 (1890). See Corwin, The Supreme Court and the Fourteenth Amendment, 7 Mich. L. Rev. 643 (1909).

42. 169 U.S. 466 (1898).

43. 123 U.S. 623 (1887).

44. *Id.* at 661.

45. *Id.*

46. 127 U.S. 678 (1888).

47. *Id.* at 686.

48. *Id.* at 686–87.

49. See chapter 10.

50. 83 U.S. (16 Wall.) 36 (1873).

51. 165 U.S. 578 (1897).

52. 165 U.S. 589.

53. Shattuck, The True Meaning of the Term "Liberty" in Those Clauses in the Federal and State Constitutions which Protect "Life, Liberty, and Property," 4 Harv. L. Rev. 365 (1891). See Warren, The New "Liberty" under the Fourteenth Amendment, 39 Harv. L. Rev. 431, 440 (1926).

54. See B. Siegan, *supra* note 28, ch. 5; R. Hale, Freedom through Law, ch. 12 (1952); Pound, Liberty of Contract, 18 Yale L. J. 454 (1909).

55. 169 U.S. 366 (1898).

56. 169 U.S. 398.

57. 198 U.S. 45 (1905). The majority included Justices Brewer and Peckham, who had dissented in Holden v. Hardy, plus three justices who had found the regulation of hours in *Holden* to be reasonable and therefore constitutional.

58. 198 U.S. 56. See B. Siegan, *supra* note 28, at 113–20.

59. 198 U.S. 75–76.

60. Justice Holmes was essentially a philosopher who turned to law and was immune from the laissez-faire business ideology of the times. See F. Frankfurter, Mr. Justice Holmes and the Supreme Court 55 (1961).

61. 208 U.S. 412 (1908). See Powell, The Judiciality of Minimum Wage Legislation, 37 Harv. L. Rev. 545 (1924). On the economic issues, see R. Posner, Economic Analysis of Law 593 (3d ed. 1986).

62. See Brandeis, Living Law, 10 Ill. L. Rev. 461 (1916); A. Mason, Brandeis 248–52 (1946).

63. 243 U.S. 426 (1917). Justice McKenna, who had joined the majority in *Lochner*, wrote the opinion sustaining the Oregon law. Justice White, who had dissented in *Lochner*, changed sides and dissented in *Bunting*.

64. See statement to this effect by Chief Justice Taft. Adkins v. Children's Hospital, 261 U.S. 525, 528 (1923) (dissenting opinion); Powell. The Logic and Rhetoric of Constitutional Law, 15 J. Phil., Psych & Scientific Method 654 (1918), reprinted in Essays in Constitutional Law 85, 98 (R. McCloskey ed. 1962).

65. 261 U.S. 525 (1923) *overruled in* West Coast Hotel Co. v. Parrish, 300 U.S. 379 (1937). See B. Siegan, *supra* note 28, at 143–50; R. Hale, *supra* note 54, ch. 14.

66. 261 U.S. 568, 570.

67. Murphy v. Sardell, 269 U.S. 530 (1925), Donham v. West-Nelson Co., 273 U.S. 657 (1927).

68. 298 U.S. 587 (1936), *holding overruled in* West Coast Hotel Co. v. Parrish, 300 U.S. 379 (1937).

69. 208 U.S. 161 (1908), *overruled in* Lincoln Union v. Northwestern, 335 U.S. 525 (1949).

70. 208 U.S. 174.

71. *Id.* at 191.

72. 236 U.S. 1 (1915), *overruled in* Phelps Dodge Corp. v. Labor Board, 313 U.S. 177 (1941).

73. 236 U.S. 40.

74. 244 U.S. 590 (1917), *overruled in* Ferguson v. Skrupa, 372 U.S. 726 (1963).

75. 264 U.S. 504 (1924).

76. 270 U.S. 402 (1926).

77. 94 U.S. 113 (1877). See *supra* notes 38 and 39 and accompanying text.

78. See R. Hale, *supra* note 54, ch. 13.

79. Wolff Packing Co. v. Court of Industrial Relations, 262 U.S. 522 (1923) (Kansas compulsory arbitration act as applied to the meat-packing industry); Tyson & Bro. United Theatre Ticket Offices v. Banton, 273 U.S. 418 (1927), *overruled in* Gold v. DiCarlo, 380 U.S. 520 (1965) (per curiam), *affirming* 235 F. Supp. 817, 819 (S.D.N.Y. 1964) (New York statute limiting prices in the resale of theater tickets to fifty cents in excess of box-office price); Ribnik v. McBride, 277 U.S. 350 (1928) *overruled in* Olsen v. Nebraska, 313 U.S. 236 (1941) (New

Jersey law requiring licensing and price regulation of employment agencies; Williams v. Standard Oil Co., 278 U.S. 235 (1929) (Tennessee statute regulating gasoline prices); New State Ice Co. v. Liebmann, 285 U.S. 262 (1932) (Oklahoma statute requiring license to enter ice business).

80. Tyson v. Banton, 273 U.S. at 446.

81. 285 U.S. 262 (1932). See B. Siegan, *supra* note 28, at 132–38; R. Posner, *supra* note 60, at 590–93.

82. 285 U.S. 302.

83. *Id.* at 279.

84. 83 U.S. (16 Wall.) 36 (1873).

85. 285 U.S. at 279.

86. See B. Wright, The Growth of American Constitutional Law 154 (1942; reprint 1967).

87. 96 U.S. 97 (1878).

88. 291 U.S. 502 (1934). See R. Hale, *supra* note 54, at 425–29.

89. 285 U.S. 263 (1932). See *supra* notes 81 to 85 and accompanying text.

90. Nebbia, 291 U.S. 523.

91. *Id.* at 533.

92. *Id.* at 536.

93. See B. Siegan, *supra* note 28, at 138–43.

94. 313 U.S. 236 (1941), *overruling* Ribnik v. McBride, 277 U.S. 350 (1928). See *supra* note 79 and accompanying text.

95. Olsen, 313 U.S. at 246.

96. 320 U.S. 591 (1944). See R. Hale, *supra* note 54, ch. 15 (1952).

97. 169 U.S. 466 (1898). See *supra* note 42 and accompanying text.

98. Federal Power Commission, 320 U.S. at 601.

99. *Id.* at 605.

100. 300 U.S. 379 (1937). See B. H. Siegan, *supra* note 28, at 145 to 148; McCloskey, Economic Due Process and the Supreme Court, 1962 Sup. Ct. Rev. 34.

101. See *supra* note 65 and 66 and accompanying text.

102. See *supra* note 68 and accompanying text.

103. See *supra* note 89 and accompanying text.

104. Smith v. Allwright, 321 U.S. 649, 699 (1944).

105. West Coast Hotel Co., 300 U.S. 391–92.

106. 335 U.S. 525 (1949), *overruling* Adair v. United States, 208 U.S. 161 (1908).

107. 335 U.S. 536–37.

108. 342 U.S. 421 (1952).

109. *Id.* at 423.

110. 348 U.S. 483 (1955).

111. *Id.* at 487. Douglas added: "We emphasize again what Chief Justice Waite said in Munn v. Illinois, . . . 'For protection against abuses by legislatures, the people must resort to the polls, not to the Courts' " (*Id.* at 488).

112. 372 U.S. 726 (1963), *overruling* Adams v. Tanner, 244 U.S. 590 (1917).

113. 372 U.S. at 730, 732. For comment on the demise of economic due process, see McCloskey, *supra* note 100.

114. It was only in 1931 that the Court expressly held that the due process clause of the Fourteenth Amendment incorporated the First Amendment. Stromberg v. California, 283 U.S. 359 (1931).

115. 262 U.S. 390 (1923).

116. 268 U.S. 510 (1925).

117. *Id.* at 534.

118. Wisconsin v. Yoder, 406 U.S. 205 (1972) (forcing members of Amish church to send children to public school after eighth grade impaired the free exercise of religion).

119. 268 U.S. 652 (1925). See Warren, The New Liberty under the Fourteenth Amendment, 39 Harv. L. Rev. 431 (1926); Heberle, From Gitlow to Near, 34 J. Politics 458 (1972).

120. Gitlow, 268 U.S. at 666.

121. *Id.* at 672.

122. See Brandenburg v. Ohio, 395 U.S. 444 (1969) (per curiam); BeVier, The First Amendment and Political Speech, 30 Stan. L. Rev. 299 (1979).

123. 283 U.S. 359 (1931).

124. 283 U.S. 697 (1931).

125. 293 U.S. 245 (1934).

126. DeJonge v. Oregon, 299 U.S. 353 (1937).

127. Hague v. CIO, 307 U.S. 496 (1939); Bridges v. California, 314 U.S. 252 (1941).

128. See R. Posner, The Economics of Justice 231–347 (1983); Karst, The Freedom of Intimate Association, 80 Yale L. J. 624 (1980); Richards, Sexual Autonomy and the Constitutional Right to Privacy, 30 Hast. L. J. 957 (1979).

129. 381 U.S. 479 (1965). For background to this case, see A. Bickel, The Least Dangerous Branch 143–56 (1962). For a critique of this case and of the subsequent development by the Supreme Court of a constitutional right of privacy, see Stoneking, Penumbras and Privacy, 87 W. Va. L. Rev. 859 (1985).

130. See Poe v. Ullman, 367 U.S. 497 (1961), on the disused nature of the statute.

131. 198 U.S. 45 (1905). See *supra* notes 55 and 56 and accompanying text.

132. Griswold, 381 U.S. at 482.

133. 268 U.S. 510 (1925). See *supra* note 116 and accompanying text.

134. 262 U.S. 390 (1923). See *supra* note 115 and accompanying text.

135. Griswold, 381 U.S. at 483.

136. *Id.* at 484.

137.

The Due Process Clause with an "arbitrary and capricious" or "shocking to the conscience" formula was liberally used by this Court to strike down economic legislation in the early decades of this century, threatening, many people thought, the tranquility and stability of the Nation. See, e.g., Lochner v. New York, 198 U.S. 45. That formula, based on subjective considerations of "natural justice," is no less dangerous when used to enforce this Court's views about personal rights than those about economic rights. I had thought that we had laid that formula, as a means for striking down state legislation, to rest once and for all in cases like West Coast Hotel Co. v. Parrish, 300 U.S. 379; Olsen v. Nebraska ex rel. Western Reference & Bond Assn., 313 U.S. 236, and many other opinions.

Id. at 522–23.

138. See, e.g., benShalom v. Secretary of Army, 489 F. Supp. 964 (E. D. Wis. 1980) (sexual preference); Hawaii Psychiatric Soc'y v. Ariyoshi, 481 F. Supp. 1028 (D. Hawaii 1979) (decision to seek psychiatric aid); Murphy v. Pocatello School Dist., 94 Idaho 32, 480 P. 2d 878 (1971) (length of student's hair); Voichahoske v. Grand Island, 194 Neb. 175, 231 N. W. 2d 124 (1975) (right to

marry). For a survey of earlier cases, see Rhoades and Patula, The Ninth Amendment, 50 Den. L. Rev. 153 (1973).

139. Katz v. United States, 389 U.S. 347, 350–51 (1967).

140. 410 U.S. 113 (1973). See A. Cox, The Role of the Supreme Court in American Government 113 (1976); Ely, The Wages of Crying Wolf, 82 Yale L. J. 920 (1973); Epstein, Substantive Due Process by Any Other Name, 1973 Sup. Ct. Rev. 159; Symposium on the Law and Politics of Abortion, 77 Mich. L. Rev. 1579–1827 (1979).

141. Roe, 410 U.S. 152–53.

142. *Id.* at 221–22. Archibald Cox commented on the unsatisfactory opinion: "My criticism of *Roe* v. *Wade* is that the Court failed to establish the legitimacy of the decision by articulating a precept of sufficient abstractness to lift the ruling above the level of political judgment based on the evidence currently available from the medical, physical, and social sciences. . . . The failure to confront the issue in principled terms leaves the opinion to read like a set of hospital rules and regulations, whose validity is good enough this week but will be destroyed with new statistics upon the medical risks of childbirth and abortion or new advances in providing for the separate existence of a foetus" (A. Cox, *supra* note 140, at 113–14).

143. Planned Parenthood v. Danforth, 428 U.S. 52 (1976).

144. City of Akron v. Akron Center for Reproductive Health, 462 U.S. 416 (1983).

145. 431 U.S. 494 (1977). The Court had earlier upheld a city ordinance that limited occupancy of dwellings to persons related either by blood or marriage. Village of Belle Terre v. Boraas, 416 U.S. 1 (1974). In *Moore,* the owner lived with her son and grandson plus a second grandson who was a cousin of the first and whose mother had died. The second grandson was outside the definition of family in the ordinance. Having found this restraint on family living invalid, Justice Powell cited Justice Harlan for limits. "Appropriate limits on substantive due process come not from drawing arbitrary lines but rather from careful 'respect for the teaching of history [and], solid recognition of the basic values that underlie our society' " (431 U.S. 503). The only problem is that in American society there are conflicting values and no consensus. See M. Perry, The Constitution, the Courts and Human Rights 93–97 (1982). Since there were no procedural issues to bring this case under the true meaning of due process, it should have been litigated under the equal protection clause. The issue is whether limiting occupancy to families so narrowly defined that it excludes a grandson treats people who are in like circumstances as different.

146. 431 U.S. 678 (1977). The Court held the decision whether or not to beget a child holds a particularly important place in the history of the right of privacy. *Id.* at 685. Limiting distribution of contraceptives to licensed pharmacists was found to impose a significant burden on users. There was no compelling state interest to grant the monopoly in terms of limiting minors as salespeople or quality control of the product. As to sales to persons under sixteen, there was no evidence that limiting access to contraceptives would reduce teenage sexual activity. In this case, as in *Moore,* there were no issues of procedure and thus no basis to invoke the true meaning of due process. The monopoly of the pharmacists should have been contested under the Sherman Act. Since the monopoly was granted by the state, it might also have been attacked as a violation of the Anglo-American antimonopoly tradition. On the other hand, the prohibition of sale to minors under sixteen years of age, though voided here, was probably not subject to valid constitutional attack under another clause.

147. 478 U.S. 186 (1986).

148. *Id.* at 192. Justice White commented on the scope of the judicial power: "Nor are we inclined to take a more expansive view of our authority to discover new fundamental rights imbedded in the Due Process Clause. The Court is most vulnerable and comes nearest to illegitimacy when it deals with judge-made constitutional law having little or no cognizable roles in the language or design of the Constitution. . . . There should be therefore great resistance to expanding the substantive reach of those Clauses, particularly if it requires redefining the category of rights deemed to be fundamental. Otherwise the Judiciary necessarily takes to itself further authority to govern the country without express constitutional authority" (*Id.* at 194–95).

149. See L. Tribe, American Constitutional Law 1349–62 (2d ed. 1988).

150. On the Ninth Amendment, see Van Alstyne, Slouching toward Bethlehem with the Ninth Amendment, 91 Yale L. J. 207 (1981), reviewing C. Black, Decision according to Law (1981).

151. O. Holmes, Natural Law, in Collected Legal Papers 310–16 (1920). See Corwin, Standpoint in Constitutional Law, 17 B.U.L. Rev. 513, 516 (1937); Dickinson, The Law behind the Law, 29 Colum. L. Rev. 285, 307 (1929); Pound, Common Law and Legislation, 21 Harv. L. Rev. 383, 393 (1908). See generally L. Hand, The Bill of Rights 70 (1958); Rehnquist, The Notion of a Living Constitution, 54 Tex. L. Rev. 693, 698 (1976).

152. J. Ely, Democracy and Distrust 48–54 (1980). For a contrary view, see Sherry, The Founders' Unwritten Constitution, 54 U. Chi. L. Rev. 1127 (1987).

153. See Federalist 78, at 99 (A. Hamilton) (E. Bourne ed. 1947); A. Bickel, The Least Dangerous Branch (1962).

154. On the separation of law and politics, see Nedelsky, Confining Democratic Politics, 96 Harv. L. Rev. 340 (1982). On the preconstitutional rejection of natural law, see Reid, In the Taught Tradition, 14 Suffolk U. L. Rev. 931 (1980).

155. "My surmise is that intellectual Americans between 1765 and 1791 thought a good deal about the rights of man, but that almost all Americans were thinking then and for a long time before about the rights of Englishmen. . . . It is just a question of more or less, of course, but I am impressed with the great importance which the Continental Congress was attaching to the rights of Englishmen almost on the eve of the Revolution" (Z. Chafee, How Human Rights Got into the Constitution 13 [1952]).

156. The historian Clinton Rossiter has argued: "Throughout the colonial period and right down to the last months before the Declaration of Independence, politically conscious Americans looked upon the British Constitution rather than natural law as the bulwark of their cherished liberties. Practical political thinking in eighteenth-century America was dominated by two assumptions: that the British Constitution was the best and happiest of all possible forms of government, and that the colonists, descendants of freeborn Englishmen, enjoyed the blessings of this constitution to the fullest extent consistent with a wilderness environment" (C. Rossiter, Seedtime of the Republic 270 [1953]).

157. The more recent study of Professor Cover presents the same view: "It was, however, in the task of 'constituting' the states and the federal union that eighteenth-century Americans disclosed how deeply ran their constitutional positivism and how sharply they perceived its implications for the judiciary. . . . [T]hose giants who managed the awesome transition from revolutionaries to 'constitutionaries—men like Adams and Jefferson; Dickinson and Wilson; Jay, Madison, Hamilton, and, in a sense, Mason and Henry—were seldom, if ever, guilty of confusing law with natural right. These men, before 1776, used nature

to take the measure of law and to judge their own obligations of obedience, but not as a source for rules of decision" (R. Cover, Justice Accused: Antislavery and the Judicial Process 26–27 [1975]).

158. Calder v. Bull, 3 U.S. (3 Dall.) 386 (1798); Fletcher v. Peck, 10 U.S. (6 Cranch) 87, 143 (1810) (Johnson, J., concurring).

159. 3 U.S. (3 Dall.) 386 (1798).

160. *Id.* at 399.

161. 281 U.S. 586 (1930).

162. *Id.* at 595.

163. 332 U.S. 46 (1947), *overruled* in Griffin v. California, 380 U.S. 609 (1965).

164. 332 U.S. 90–92 (dissenting opinion), citing Federal Power Commission v. Natural Gas Pipeline Co., 315 U.S. 575, 599, 601, n. 4 (1942). See Justice Black's similar statements in his dissent in Griswold v. Connecticut, *supra* note 137.

165. H. Wechsler, Principles, Politics and Fundamental Law 21 (1961). See Nelson, *supra* note 8 at 1262–86.

166. Public Choice and Constitutional Economics (J. Gwartrey and R. Wagner, eds. 1988); Economic Liberties and the Judiciary (J. Dorn and H. Manne eds. 1987); B. Siegan, *supra* note 28, ch. 15.

167. See Siegan, Rehabilitating Lockner, 22 San Diego L. Rev. 453 (1985).

168. Scalia, Economic Affairs as Human Affairs, in Economic Liberties and the Judiciary 31–37 (J. Dorn and H. Manne eds. 1987).

Chapter 12

1. U.S. Const., amend. 14, § 1. See W. Nelson, The Fourteenth Amendment (1988); H. Meyer, The History and Meaning of the Fourteenth Amendment (1977).

2. Chief Justice Marshall noted the rule of construction: "It cannot be presumed that any clause in the Constitution is intended to be without effect; and, therefore, such a construction is inadmissible, unless the words require it" (Marbury v. Madison, 5 U.S. [1 Cranch] 137, 174 [1803]).

3. It also bars unequal application of common-law rules. Jersey Shore, etc. v. Estate of Baum, 84 N.J. 137, 417 A.2d 1003, 1007 (1980).

4. Santa Clara Co. v. Southern Pacific R. Co., 118 U.S. 394, 396 (1886); Wheeling Steel Corp. v. Glander, 337 U.S. 562, 574–76 (1949).

5. Pacific States Box & Basket Co. v. White, 296 U.S. 176, 184 (1935).

6. City of New Orleans v. Dukes, 427 U.S. 297, 303 (1976); Williamson v. Lee Optical Co., 348 U.S. 483, 489 (1955); Smith v. Cahoon, 283 U.S. 553, 567 (1931).

7. L. Tribe, American Constitutional Law 1439–43 (2d ed. 1988).

8. Note, Legislative Purpose, Rationality, and Equal Protection, 82 Yale L. J. 123, 128 (1972). See Gunther, The Supreme Court 1971 Term, Forward, 86 Harv. L. Rev. 1 (1972).

9. See chapter 10, explaining the error in the Slaughter-House Cases, 83 U.S. (16 Wall.) 36 (1873).

10. See Stigler, The Theory of Economic Regulation, 2 Bell J. Econ. & Mgmnt. Sci. 3 (1971); Peltzman, Toward a More General Theory of Regulation, 19 J. Law & Econ. 211 (1976).

11. Slaughter-House Cases, 83 U.S. (16 Wall.) 36, 71 (1973). See J. ten Broek, The Antislavery Origins of the Fourteenth Amendment (1951).

12. See, e.g., Morey v. Doud, 354 U.S. 459 (1957), *overruled in* City of New Orleans v. Dukes, 427 U.S. 297, 306 (1976).

13. On the early meanings of political equality as a self-evident truth, see J. Pole, The Pursuit of Equality in American History, ch. 2 (1978).

14. F. Thorpe, ed., The Federal and State Constitutions, Colonial Charters and Other Organic Laws, VII, 3812–13 (1909) (Virginia); id., V, 3081–82 (Pennsylvania); id., VI, 3739 (Vermont); id., IV, 2453 (New Hampshire); id., III, 1888–1889 (Massachusetts); id., I, 536–37 (Connecticut); id., V, 2599 (New Jersey).

15. R. Cover, Justice Accused, ch. 3 (1975).

16. See J. tenBroek, *supra* note 11, at 175–79 (1951).

17. See Avins, The Equal "Protection" of the Laws, 12 N.Y. L. Forum 385 (1966).

18. Cong. Globe, 39th Cong., 1st sess., 438 (Jan. 26, 1866).

19. See J. tenBroek, *supra* note 11, at 163–64.

20. Cong. Globe, 39th Cong., 1st sess., 2764–65 (May 23, 1866).

21. 60 U.S. (19 How.) 393 (1857).

22. 1 Lofft's Rep. 1, 20 Howell's State Trials 1, 98 Eng. Rep. 499 (1772). See Wiecek, Somerset: Lord Mansfield and the Legitimacy of Slavery in the Anglo-American World, 42 U. Chi. L. Rev. 86 (1974).

23. Plyler v. Doe, 457 U.S. 202, 216 (1982); Royster Guano Co. v. Virginia, 253 U.S. 412, 415 (1920). See Tussman and tenBroek, The Equal Protection of the Laws, 37 Calif. L. Rev. 341, 345 (1949).

24. Home Insurance Co. v. New York, 134 U.S. 594, 606 (1890).

25. W. McKechnie, Magna Carta 395 (2d ed. 1914). Note the judicial citation of Magna Charta for equal protection in Malinski v. New York, 324 U.S. 401, 413–14 (1945) (Frankfurter, J.); Griffin v. Illinois, 351 U.S. 12, 16–17 (1956) (Black, J.). See A. Howard, The Road from Runnymede 311–15 (1968).

26. A. Dicey, Introduction to the Study of the Law of the Constitution 202 (10th ed. 1962). As to colonial Americans' claims to equality of rights with citizens in England, see J. Reid, Constitutional History of the American Revolution 60–64, 82–86 (1986).

27. R. Perry and J. Cooper, Sources of Our Liberties 148 (1959).

28. *Id.* at 375.

29. United States v. Cruikshank, 92 U.S. 542, 555 (1876).

30. Frank and Munro, The Original Understanding of "Equal Protection of the Laws," 1972 Wash. U. L. Q. 421, 432. Compare, Bickel, The Original Understanding of the Segregation Decision, 69 Harv. L. Rev. 1 (1955).

31. Political rights of former slaves were protected in U.S. Const., amend. XIV, § 2, and in amend. XV.

32. Dimond, Strict Construction and Judicial Review of Racial Discrimination under the Equal Protection Clause, 80 Mich. L. Rev. 462, 494–502 (1982).

33. See, e.g., R. Berger, Government by Judiciary, ch. 10 (1977); Fairman, Does the Fourteenth Amendment Incorporate the Bill of Rights? 2 Stan. L. Rev. 5, 44 (1949).

34. Act of April 9, 1866, c. 31, 14 Stat. 27.

35. United States v. Wong Kim Ark, 169 U.S. 649, 699 (1898).

36. See *supra* note 34.

37. Cong. Globe, 39th Cong, 1st sess., 1290–92 (Mar. 9, 1866). See H. Flack, The Adoption of the Fourteenth Amendment 30–31 (1908).

38. Reed v. Reed, 404 U.S. 71, 76 (1971); Lehr v. Robertson, 463 U.S. 248, 265 (1983).

39. Ex parte Virginia, 100 U.S. 339 (1879).

40. Strauder v. West Virginia, 100 U.S. 303 (1880).

41. Ex parte Virginia, 100 U.S. 339 (1879).

42. See Oregon v. Mitchell, 400 U.S. 112, 264n (1970) (Brennan, J.).

43. See G. Becker, The Economics of Discrimination (2d ed. 1971). See R. Posner, The Economics of Justice 351–63 (1983).

44. R. Kluger, Simple Justice 52–53 (1975); G. Myrdal, An American Dilemma, I, ch. 13 (1944), C. Johnson, Patterns of Negro Segregation, ch. 4 (1943).

45. C. Woodward, Origins of the New South (1951); E. Ginzberg and A. S. Eichner, The Troublesome Presence, ch. 8 (1964).

46. M. Weinberg, A Chance to Learn ch. 2 (1977).

47. Id. at 44. The percentage of Negro children enrolled in school rose to 44.8 in 1910; 53.5 in 1920; 60.3 in 1930; and 68.4 in 1940. Id.

48. Claybrook v. Owensboro, 16 F. 297, 302 (D.C.Ky. 1883); Puitt v. Commissioners, 94 N.C. 514, 519 (1886) (ruling under Art. 9, § 2 of N.C. Constitution).

49. M. Weinberg, supra note 46, at 48. In 1920–1921, in the nineteen Black counties of Mississippi where 78.1 per cent of the population was Negro, per capita public school expenditure on white children was $30.22, while the per capita expenditure on Negro children was $3.59. The latter was 11.9 per cent of the former. Id. at 60.

50. On the optimum social investment in education, see G. Becker, Human Capital (2d ed. 1975).

51. Suspect classification has been explained by the Court:

Some classifications are more likely than others to reflect deep-seated prejudice rather than legislative rationality in pursuit of some legislative objective. Legislation predicated on such prejudice is easily recognized as incompatible with the constitutional understanding that each person is to be judged individually and is entitled to equal justice under the law. Classifications treated as suspect tend to be irrelevant to any proper legislative goal. . . . Legislation imposing special disabilities upon groups disfavored by virtue of circumstances beyond their control suggests the kind of "class or caste" treatment that the Fourteenth Amendment was designed to abolish.

Plyler v. Doe, 457 U.S. 202, 216 n. 14 (1982). See J. Baer, Equality under the Constitution, ch. 5 (1983); Linde, Due Process of Lawmaking, 55 Neb. L. Rev. 197, 201–2 (1976).

52. Strauder v. West Virginia, 100 U.S. 303, 307–8 (1880).

53. See R. Fischer, The Segregation Struggle in Louisiana, ch. 1 (1974).

54. C. Woodward, The Strange Career of Jim Crow 16 (rev. ed. 1957); H. Rabinowitz, Race Relations in the Urban South, ch. 8 (1978).

55. G. Johnson, The Ideology of White Supremacy, 1876–1910, in James Sprunt Studies in History and Political Science, XXXI, Essays in Southern History, 124, 136–140 (F. M. Green ed. 1949).

56. 95 U.S. 485 (1878).

57. Id. at 490.

58. 133 U.S. 587 (1890).

59. Id. at 593–95.

60. See chapter 5.

61. 328 U.S. 373 (1946).

62. Id. at 386.

63. 109 U.S. 3 (1883). See R. Carr, Federal Protection of Civil Rights (1947).

64. Act of March 1, 1875, 18 Stat. 336, §§ 1, 2.

65. See Frank and Munro, *supra* note 30, at 452–56.

66. 109 U.S. at 13. See H. Hyman and W. Wiecek, Equal Justice under Law 490–500 (1982).

67. Justice Bradley asserted that "no one will contend that the power to pass it was contained in the Constitution before the adoption of the last three amendments" (109 U.S. 10).

68. Civil Rights Act of 1964, 78 Stat. 214, 42 U.S.C.A. § 2000a–2000a-6 (1981).

69. Heart of Atlanta Motel v. United States, 379 U.S. 241 (1964); Katzenbach v. McClung, 379 U.S. 294 (1964).

70. 163 U.S. 537 (1896), *overruled in* Gayle v. Browder, 352 U.S. 903 (1956). See C. Lofgren, The Plessy Case (1987).

71. The statute provided "that all railway companies carrying passengers in their coaches in this state, shall provide equal but separate accommodations for the white, and colored races, by providing two or more passenger coaches for each passenger train, or dividing the passenger coaches by a partition so as to secure separate accommodations" (Plessy, 163 U.S. 540).

72. F. Johnson, Development of State Legislation Concerning the Free Negro (1919); G. Myrdal, An American Dilemma, I, chs. 28–31 (1944); C. Woodward, The Strange Career of Jim Crow (3d ed. 1974); T. Shibutani and K. Kwan, Ethnic Stratification 315–16 (1965); H. Rabinowitz, *supra* note 54 at 329–39.

73. Black, The Lawfulness of the Segregation Decisions, 69 Yale L. J. 421, 422n.8 (1960).

74. R. Harris, The Quest for Equality 101 (1960).

75. Plessy, 163 U.S. at 544.

76. *Id.* at 551. See Glennon, Justice Henry Billings Brown, 44 U. Colo. L. Rev. 553 (1973).

77. Plessy, 163 U.S. at 559.

78. *Id.*

79. See Watt and Orlikoff, The Coming Vindication of Mr. Justice Harlan, 44 Ill. L. Rev. 13 (1949).

80. Plyler v. Doe, 457 U.S. 202, 213 (1982).

81. See Lofgen, *supra* note 70, ch. 6; Frank and Munro, *supra* note 30, at 452–56.

82. Plessy, 163 U.S. at 553–54.

83. 84 U.S. (17 Wall.) 445 (1873).

84. *Id.* at 452.

85. *Id.* at 452–53.

86. See, e.g., United States v. Buntin, 10 F. 730 (C.C.S.D. Ohio, 1882). See note on public school segregation following this case. *Id.* at 737.

87. G. Myrdal, *supra* note 44; J. Dollard, Caste and Class in a Southern Town (1957); E. Frazier, The Negro Family in the United States (1939).

88. M. Weinberg, *supra* note 46; H. Bullock, A History of Negro Education in the South (1967); L. Harlan, Separate and Unequal (1958); H. Bond, The Education of the Negro in the American Social Order (1934).

89. 59 Mass. (5 Cush.) 198 (1850). See Levy and Jones, Jim Crow Education: Origins of the "Separate But Equal" Doctrine, in L. Levy, Judgments: Essays on American Constitutional History 316–41 (1972).

90. 59 Mass. (5 Cush.) at 200.

91. Mass. Declaration of Rights, art. 1. (1780). See R. L. Perry and J. C. Cooper, *supra* note 27 at 374.

92. 59 Mass. (5 Cush.) at 206–7. The later assertion of Chief Justice Taft that

the Massachusetts constitutional injunction was the same as the equal protection clause of the Fourteenth Amendment was in error. Gong Lum v. Rice, 275 U.S. 78, 86 (1927).

93. 59 Mass. (5 Cush.) at 201. See C. Sumner, Works, III, 51–100 (1900).

94. Mass. St. 1855, ch. 256 sec. 1; Mass. Gen. Stat., ch. 41, sec. 9 (1860).

95. Kelly, The Congressional Controversy over School Segregation, 64 Am. Hist. Rev. 537, 540 (1959).

96. Id.

97. Id. at 542–44.

98. 175 U.S. 528 (1899).

99. 211 U.S. 45 (1908).

100. Kluger, supra note 44 at 88.

101. 275 U.S. 78 (1927).

102. Id. at 86.

103. Missouri ex rel. Gaines v. Canada, 305 U.S. 337 (1938); Sipuel v. Board of Regents, 332 U.S. 631 (1948); Sweatt v. Painter, 339 U.S. 629 (1950); McLaurin v. Oklahoma State Regents, 339 U.S. 637 (1950).

104. 347 U.S. 483 (1954). The four cases were from Kansas, South Carolina, Virginia, and Delaware.

105. The evidence is summarized and quoted in Kluger, supra note 44, chs. 13–18.

106. Brown v. Board of Education, 98 F. Supp. 797 (D. Kan. 1951). See Kluger, supra note 44, at 424.

107. Belton v. Gebhart, 32 Del. Ch. 343, 87 A. 2d 862 (1952).

108. Id. at 865.

109. Brown, 347 U.S. 495.

110. Id. at 494–495.

111. Plessy was overruled without opinion in Gayle v. Browder, 352 U.S. 903 (1956) (per curiam) aff'g, 142 F. Supp. 707 (M.D. Ala. 1956).

112. Compare Wechsler, Toward Neutral Principles of Constitutional Law, 73 Harv. L. Rev. 1 (1959), with Pollack, Racial Discrimination and Judicial Integrity, 108 U. Pa. L. Rev. 1 (1959).

113. Brown, 347 U.S. at 489.

114. A. Bickel, The Least Dangerous Branch 102 (1962). For similar views, see Sandalow, Constitutional Interpretation, 79 Mich. L. Rev. 1033, 1036 (1981); Dimond, supra note 32.

115. 347 U.S. 497 (1954).

116. Id. at 499, citing Korematsu v. United States, 323 U.S. 214 (1944); Hirabashi v. United States, 320 U.S. 81 (1943).

117. 347 U.S. 500.

118. See supra notes 25–29 and accompanying text.

119. See A. Berle and G. Means, The Modern Corporation and Private Property (rev. ed. 1968).

120. N. Butler, Politics and Business, in Why Should We Change Our Form of Government? 77, 82 (1912).

121. 118 U.S. 394 (1886). See C. Magrath, Morrison R. Waite 221–24 (1963); H. Graham, Everyman's Constitution 566–70 (1968).

122. Id. at 396.

123. Orient Insurance Co. v. Daggs, 172 U.S. 557, 561 (1899). This follows the rule that corporations are not citizens under the privileges and immunities clause of U.S. Const., art. IV, § 2. Pembina Mining Co. v. Pennsylvania, 125 U.S. 181, 187 (1888).

124. Metropolitan Life Ins. Co. v. Ward, 470 U.S. 869, 881 (1985); Western & Southern L. I. Co. v. Bd. of Equalization, 451 U.S. 648, 660 (1981); Grosjean v. American Press Co., 297 U.S. 233, 244 (1936).

125. 83 U.S. (16 Wall.) 36 (1873).

126. *Id.* at 81.

127. Butchers Union Co. v. Crescent City Co., 111 U.S. 746, 748 (1884).

128. 111 U.S. 746 (1884).

129. 101 U.S. 814 (1880).

130. 111 U.S. at 754, 760.

131. 111 U.S. 766. Justice Field quoted Adam Smith, Wealth of Nations, bk. 1, ch. 10: "The property which every man has in his own labor, as it is the original foundation of all other property, so it is the most sacred and inviolable. The patrimony of the poor man lies in the strength and dexterity of his own hands, and to hinder his employing this strength and dexterity in what manner he thinks proper, without injury to his neighbor, is a plain violation of this most sacred property. It is a manifest encroachment upon the just liberty both of the workman and of those who might be disposed to employ him. As it hinders the one from working at what he thinks proper, so it hinders the others from employing whom they think proper."

132. 118 U.S. 356 (1886). See Barbier v. Connolly, 113 U.S. 27 (1885); Soon Hing v. Crowley, 113 U.S. 703 (1885).

133. 118 U.S. at 374.

134. 239 U.S. 33 (1915).

135. *Id.* at 41.

136. *Id.*

137. 127 U.S. 678 (1888). See chapter 10, notes 46 to 49.

138. This reasoning has been criticized as an "easy dismissal of the equal protection issue on the grounds that the law applies equally to all to whom it applies. . . . By the same token, a law applying to all red-haired makers of margarine would satisfy the requirements of equality" (Tussman and tenBroek, The Equal Protection of the Laws, 37 Calif. L. Rev. 341, 345 [1949]).

139. 127 U.S. at 681.

140. *Id.* at 694 (Field, J., dissenting), citing People v. Marx, 99 N.Y. 377, 387 (1885).

141. Connolly v. Union Sewer Pipe Co., 184 U.S. 540 (1902).

142. Tigner v. Texas, 310 U.S. 141 (1940).

143. 283 U.S. 553 (1931).

144. 297 U.S. 266 (1936).

145. 301 U.S. 459 (1937).

146. 354 U.S. 457 (1957).

147. *Id.* at 466.

148. *Id.* at 467.

149. 427 U.S. 297 (1976).

150. *Id.* at 303.

151. *Id.* at 304.

152. 278 U.S. 105 (1928).

153. *Id.* at 113–14.

154. 414 U.S. 156 (1973).

155. *Id.* at 164–67.

156. 330 U.S. 552 (1947).

157. *Id.* at 564.

158. *Id.* at 565.

159. 348 U.S. 483 (1955). See chapter 11, notes 124–25.

160. 348 U.S. 489. See Gunther, *supra* note 8, at 45–46.

161. See Miller, The True Story of Carolene Products, 1987 Sup. Ct. Rev. 397; Conant, Systems Analysis in the Appellate Decisionmaking Process, 24 Rutgers L. Rev. 293, 317–22 (1970).

162. United States v. Carolene Products Corp., 304 U.S. 144 (1938).

163. *Id.* at 152, note 4.

164. 323 U.S. 32 (1944) *affirming* State v. Sage Stores Co., 157 Kan. 404, 141 P. 2d 655 (1943). The defendants contended unsuccessfully that the classification was arbitrary and in violation of the equal protection clause in two aspects. First, they argued that it was arbitrary to control only this one combination of milk and oil or fat, other than milk fat, while other combinations of these same ingredients, such as evaporated milk with fish-oil vitamins, chocolate drink, infants' food, and margarines, were not subject to legislative control. Second, they urged that it was arbitrary to prohibit sale of these products when protection against possible deception in the sale of most other products was accomplished by adequate regulation of the selling. 323 U.S. 34–35.

165. "Apparently the objection under the equal protection clause is that the Kansas statute permits the sale of skimmed milk which has less calories and fewer vitamins than petitioners' compound and yet forbids the sale of the compound despite its higher nutritive value. Such an objection is governed by the same standards of legislation as objections under the due process clause. It is a matter of classification and the power of the legislature to classify is as broad as its power to prohibit. A violation of the Fourteenth Amendment in either case would depend upon whether there is any rational basis for the action of the legislature" (323 U.S. 34–35).

166. 232 Kan. 589, 659 P. 2d 785 (1983).

167. *Id.* at 797.

168. Milnot Co. v. Arkansas State Bd. of Health, 388 F. Supp. 901 (E.D. Ark. 1975).

169. 323 U.S. 18 (1944). For contrary views on the due process issue see People v. Carolene Products Co., 345 Ill. 166, 177 N.E. 698 (1931); Carolene Products Co. v. Thomson, 276 Mich. 172, 267 N.W. 608 (1936); Carolene Products Co. v. Banning, 131 Neb. 429, 268 N.W. 313 (1936); Coffee-Rich, Inc. v. Comm'r of Pub. Health, 348 Mass. 414, 204 N.E.2d 281 (1965).

170. 323 U.S. 28–29.

171. Milnot Company v. Richardson, 350 F. Supp. 221 (1972).

172. 347 U.S. 497 (1954).

173. 335 U.S. 464 (1948). In more recent cases, the Court has invalidated most types of sex discrimination. Orr v. Orr, 440 U.S. 268 (1979); Kirchberg v. Feenstra, 450 U.S. 455 (1981).

174. 335 U.S. 467–68.

175. 336 U.S. 220 (1949).

176. Family Security Life Ins. Co. v. Daniel, 79 F. Supp. 62, 70 (E.D.S.C. 1948).

177. 372 U.S. 726 (1963). See chapter 11, notes 126–27.

178. 372 U.S. 727.

179. 368 U.S. 25 (1961).

180. *Id.* at 28 (Douglas, J., dissenting).

181. 458 U.S. 654 (1982). For condemnation of the earlier version of the statute that contained resale price maintenance, see California Retail Liquor Dealers Assn. v. Midcal Aluminum, Inc., 445 U.S. 97, 100–2 (1980).

182. 458 U.S. at 659–70, citing Continental T.V., Inc. v. GTE Sylvania Inc., 433 U.S. 36 (1977).

183. 458 U.S. 665.

184. On the distinction between the information function of selling activities and contrived product differentiation, see E. Chamberlin, The Theory of Monopolistic Competition, ch. 5 (7th ed. 1956); R. Sherman, The Economics of Industry, ch. 16 (1974).

185. 472 U.S. 159 (1985).

186. Id. at 178.

187. Western Union Telegraph Co. v. Kansas, 216 U.S. 1, 21 (1910). This opinion was based on the commerce clause and the due process clause.

188. 302 U.S. 22 (1937).

189. Id. at 31. The fee was $5000 on an authorized capital of $100,000,000.

190. Southern R. Co. v. Greene, 216 U.S. 400 (1909); Air-Way Electric Appliance Corp. v. Day, 266 U.S. 71 (1924).

191. 272 U.S. 494 (1926).

192. Id. at 514.

193. Act of Mar. 9, 1945, c. 20, § 1, 59 Stat. 33, 15 U.S.C.A. § 1011 et seq. (1976). See Prudential Ins. Co. v. Benjamin, 328 U.S. 408 (1946).

194. Lincoln National Life Ins. Co. v. Read, 325 U.S. 673 (1945).

195. Western & Southern L.I. Co. v. Bd. of Equalization, 451 U.S. 648, 667 (1981).

196. 451 U.S. 648 (1981).

197. Id. at 668.

198. 470 U.S. 869 (1985).

199. Id. at 873.

200. Id. at 878.

201. Id. at 883.

202. 358 U.S. 522 (1959).

203. Id. at 522–23.

204. Id. at 528–29. The Court stated the principles for judicial review:

The States have a very wide discretion in the laying of their taxes. When dealing with their proper domestic concerns, and not trenching upon the prerogatives of the National Government or violating the guaranties of the Federal Constitution, the States have the attribute of sovereign powers in devising their fiscal systems to ensure revenue and foster their local interests. Of course, the States, in the exercise of their taxing power, are subject to the requirements of the Equal Protection Clause of the Fourteenth Amendment. But that clause imposes no iron rule of equality, prohibiting the flexibility and variety that are appropriate to reasonable schemes of state taxation. The State may impose different specific taxes upon different trades and professions and may vary the rate of excise upon various products. It is not required to resort to close distinctions or to maintain a precise, scientific uniformity with reference to composition, use or value. . . . To hold otherwise would be to subject the essential taxing power of the State to an intolerable supervision, hostile to the basic principles of our Government and wholly beyond the protection which the general clause of the Fourteenth Amendment was intended to assure.

358 U.S. at 526–27.

205. See E. Hoover, The Location of Economic Activity 27–46 (1948).

206. Royster Guano Co. v. Virginia, 253 U.S. 412 (1920).

207. Sioux City Bridge Co. v. Dakota County, 260 U.S. 441 (1922).
208. Schlesinger v. Wisconsin, 270 U.S. 230 (1926).
209. Louisville Gas Co. v. Coleman, 277 U.S. 32 (1928).
210. Quaker City Cab Co. v. Pennsylvania, 277 U.S. 389 (1928) *overruled in* Lehnhausen v. Lake Shore Auto Parts Co., 410 U.S. 356 (1973).
211. Iowa-Des Moines Nat. Bank v. Bennett, 284 U.S. 239 (1931).
212. Concordia Fire Ins. Co. v. Illinois, 392 U.S. 535 (1934).
213. 296 U.S. 404, 424–26 (1935).
214. 309 U.S. 83, 93 (1940).
215. M. Lee, Anti-Chain-Store Tax Legislation (1939).
216. 283 U.S. 527 (1931).
217. *Id.* at 534.
218. *Id.* at 537.
219. 294 U.S. 87 (1935).
220. *Id.* at 97–99.
221. *Id.* at 99, quoting Magnano v. Hamilton, 292 U.S. 40, 46 (1934).
222. 294 U.S. 101.
223. 294 U.S. 550 (1935).
224. *Id.* at 557.
225. *Id.* at 566–80.
226. 301 U.S. 412 (1937).
227. *Id.* at 419–20.
228. 337 U.S. 562 (1949).
229. *Id.* at 573.
230. 410 U.S. 356 (1973).
231. *Id.* at 360.
232. 292 U.S. 40 (1934).
233. *Id.* at 43.

Afterword

1. See Powell, the Original Understanding of Original Intent, 98 Harv. L. Rev. 885 (1985).
2. J. Story, Commentaries on the Constitution of the United States (1833).
3. Professor Perry summarizes the primary problem of a Supreme Court that decides constitutional cases based on values not found in the constitution:

The tension between noninterpretive review and the principle of electorally accountable policymaking seems especially acute in light of the fact that the decisional norms the Court elaborates and enforces in the exercise of such review are derived not from some authoritative source of value, external to the Court, to which "the people" subscribe, but from the justices' own values. "Thus the recurring embarrassment of the noninterpretivists: majoritarian democracy is, they know, the core of our entire system, and they hear in the charge that there is in their philosophy a fundamental inconsistency therewith something they are not sure they can deny."

M. Perry, the Constitution, the Courts and Human Rights 125 (1982), citing J. Ely, Democracy and Distrust 7 (1980).
4. 410 U.S. 113 (1973).
5. 5 U.S. (1 Cranch) 137 (1803).
6. See Van Alstyne, A Critical Guide to *Marbury* v. *Madison,* 1969 Duke L. J. I.

7. See *supra,* chapter 2, notes 93–114; J. Agresto, the Supreme Court and Constitutional Democracy (1984); D. G. Morgan, Congress and the Constitution chs. 1 and 2 (1966). A key concern of the delegates to the Constitutional Convention who refused to sign the final document was the very broad powers in the national government for which the Constitution did not prescribe express controls. See H. J. Storing, The Complete Anti-Federalist, II, Part 1 (1981), reprinting the recorded objections of the nonsigners.

8. *United States* v. *Dewitt,* 76 U.S. (9 Wall) 41 (1870).

9. Trade-Mark Cases, 100 U.S. 82 (1879).

10. Employer's Liability Cases, 207 U.S. 463 (1908).

11. See Nelson, History and Neutrality in Constitutional Adjudication, 72 Va. L. Rev. 1237, 1246–1256 (1986).

12. U.S. Const., Amend. IV. See *Mapp* v. *Ohio,* 367 U.S. 643 (1961); *Payton* v. *New York,* 445 U.S. 573 (1980).

13. This does not mean that the courts are empowered to designate acts that are not part of the procedures of courts or administrative agencies a subject of due process. The majority opinion in *Rochin* v. *California,* 342 U.S. 165 (1952), is clearly wrong. See H. L. Black, A Constitutional Faith 28–30 (1968); Haigh, Defining Due Process of Law: The Case of Mr. Justice Hugo L. Black, 17 S. Dak. L. Rev. 1 (1971).

14. U.S. Const., Amend. VIII. See *Coker* v. *Georgia,* 433 U.S. 584 (1977); *Robinson* v. *California,* 370 U.S. 660 (1962).

15. U.S. Const., Amend. XIV. See W. Crosskey, Politics and the Constitution in the History of the United States, ch. 31 (1953).

16. 83 U.S. (16 Wall.) 130 (1873).

17. See R. Newmyer, Supreme Court Justice Joseph Story (1985).

18. 41 U.S. (16 Pet.) 1 (1842).

19. *Baltimore & Ohio R. Co.* v. *Baugh,* 149 U.S. 368, 391 (1893) (dissenting opinion).

20. *Trustees of Dartmouth College* v. *Woodward,* 17 U.S. (4 Wheat.) 518 (1819).

21. *Scott* v. *Sandford,* 60 U.S. (19 How.) 393 (1857).

22. Senator Charles Sumner. Congressional Globe, 38th Cong., 2d Sess. 1012 (1865).

23. 163 U.S. 537 (1896).

24. *Southern Pacific Co.* v. *Jensen,* 244 U.S. 205, 221 (1917) (dissenting opinion).

25. 332 U.S. 46 (1947).

Bibliography

Books

Ackerman, Bruce A. *Private Property and the Constitution*. New Haven, Conn.: Yale University Press, 1977.

Adair, Douglass. *Fame and the Founding Fathers*. New York: Norton, 1974.

Adams, Henry. *The Education of Henry Adams: An Autobiography*. Boston: Houghton Mifflin, 1918.

Adams, John. *The Works of John Adams*. Edited by C. F. Adams. Boston, Mass.: Little Brown, 1852.

Agresto, John. *The Supreme Court and Constitutional Democracy*. Ithaca, N.Y.: Cornell University Press, 1984.

American State Papers, Finance, vol. 1, Washington, D.C.: 1st Cong., 3rd Sess., 1790.

Anastaplo, George. *The Constitutionalist: Notes on the First Amendment*. Dallas, Texas: Southern Methodist University Press, 1971.

Anderson, Adam. *Historical and Chronological Deduction of the Origin of Commerce*. London, England: J. Walter, 1787.

Arrow, Kenneth. *Social Choice and Individual Values*. 2d ed. New York: Wiley, 1963.

Association of American Law Schools. *Select Essays in Anglo-American Legal History*. Boston, Mass.: Little, Brown, 1907–1909.

Bacon, Matthew. *A New Abridgement of the Laws of England*. 3d ed. London, England: A. Strahan, 1768.

Baer, Judith A. *Equality Under the Constitution*. Ithaca, N.Y.: Cornell University Press, 1983.

Bailyn, Bernard. *The Ideological Origins of the American Revolution*. Cambridge, Mass.: Harvard University Press, 1967.

Bancroft, George. *History of the Formation of the Constitution of the United States of America*. New York: D. Appleton and Co., 1885.

Baxter, Maurice G. *Daniel Webster and the Supreme Court*. Amherst, Mass.: University of Massachusetts Press, 1966.

———. *The Steamboat Monopoly: Gibbons v. Ogden, 1824*. New York: A. Knopf, 1972.

Baxter, William F. *People or Penguins: The Case for Optimal Pollution*. New York: Columbia University Press, 1974.

Beard, Charles A. *An Economic Interpretation of the Constitution of the United States*. New York: Macmillan, 1913.

Becker, Gary. *The Economics of Discrimination*. 2d ed. Chicago: University of Chicago Press, 1971.

————. *Human Capital: A Theoretical and Empirical Analysis with Special Reference to Education*. 2d ed. New York: National Bureau of Economic Research, 1975.

Becker, Lawrence C. *Property Rights: Philosophic Foundations*. London, England: Routledge and Kegan Paul, 1977.

Berger, Raoul. *Congress v. The Supreme Court*. Cambridge, Mass.: Harvard University Press, 1969.

————. *Federalism: The Founders' Design*. Norman: University of Oklahoma Press, 1987.

————. *Government by Judiciary: The Transformation of the Fourteenth Amendment*. Cambridge, Mass.: Harvard University Press, 1977.

Berle, Adolf A., and Means, Gardiner. *The Modern Corporation and Private Property*. Rev. ed. New York: Harcourt, Brace, 1968.

Beveridge, Albert J. *The Life of John Marshall*. Boston, Mass.: Houghton Mifflin, 1916.

Bickel, Alexander M. *The Last Dangerous Branch*. Indianapolis, Ind., Bobbs-Merrill, 1962.

————. *The Supreme Court and the Idea of Progress*. New York: Harper and Row, 1970.

Bigelow, Melville M. *History of Procedure in England from the Norman Conquest*. London, England: Macmillan, 1880.

————. *The Law of Bills, Notes, and Cheques*. 2d ed. Boston, Mass.: Little Brown, 1890.

Billias, George A. *The Federalists: Realists or Idealogues*. Lexington, Mass.: D.C. Heath, 1970.

Black, Charles L. *The People and the Court*. New York: Macmillan, 1960.

————. *Structure and Relationship in Constitutional Law*. Baton Rouge, Louisiana State University Press, 1969.

Black, Hugo. *A Constitutional Faith*. New York: Alfred A. Knopf, 1968.

Blackstone, William. *Commentaries on the Laws of England*. 1765–1769. Reprint. Chicago: University of Chicago Press, 1979.

Blinkoff, Maurice. *The Influence of Charles A. Beard Upon American Historiography*. University of Buffalo Monographs in History, 12. Buffalo, N.Y.: n.p., 1936.

Bobbit, Philip. *Constitutional Fate: Theory of the Constitution*. New York: Oxford University Press, 1982.

Bond, Horace M. *The Education of the Negro in the American Social Order*. Englewood Cliffs, N.J.: Prentice-Hall, 1934.

Boudin, Louis. *Government by Judiciary*. New York: W. Goodwin, 1932.

Boulding, Kenneth. *Economic Analysis*. New York: Harper and Bros., 1941.

Break, George. *Financing Government in a Federal System*. Washington, D.C.: Brookings Institution, 1980.

Brennan, Geoffrey and Buchanan, James M. *The Power to Tax*. Cambridge, England: Cambridge University Press, 1980.

Bridwell, Randall and Whitten, Ralph U. *The Constitution and the Common Law*. Lexington, Mass.: D. C. Heath, 1977.

Brown, Alexander, ed. *The Genesis of the United States*. Boston, Mass: Houghton Mifflin, 1891.

Brown, Robert E. *Charles Beard and the Constitution*. Princeton: Princeton University Press, 1956.

Buchanan, James M. *Demand and Supply of Public Goods.* Chicago: Rand McNally, 1968.

———; Tollison, Robert D.; and Tullock, Gordon. *Towards a Theory of the Rent-Seeking Society.* College Station, Texas: Texas A&M University Press, 1980.

———, and Tullock, Gordon. *The Calculus of Consent.* Ann Arbor: University of Michigan Press, 1962.

Buckland, William W. *A Manual of Roman Private Law.* Cambridge, England: University Press, 1953.

Bullock, Charles J. *Essays on the Monetary History of the United States.* New York: Macmillan, 1900.

Bullock, Henry A. *A History of Negro Education in the South.* Cambridge, Mass. Harvard University Press, 1967.

Butler, Nicholas M. *Why Should We Change Our Form of Government?* New York: Scribner, 1912.

Cahn, Edmond, ed. *Supreme Court and Supreme Law.* Bloomington: Indiana University Press, 1954.

Caines, George. *An Enquiry into the Law Merchant of the United States; or Lex Mercatoria Americana, on Several Head of Commercial Importance.* New York: Isaac Collins, 1802.

Cardozo, Benjamin N. *The Nature of the Judicial Process.* New Haven, Conn.: Yale University Press, 1921.

Carr, Robert K. *Federal Protection of Civil Rights: Quest for a Sword.* Ithaca, N.Y.: Cornell University Press, 1947.

Catterall, Ralph C. H. *The Second Bank of the United States.* Chicago: Chicago University Press, 1903.

Chafee, Zechariah. *How Human Rights Got into the Constitution.* Boston, Mass.: Boston University Press, 1952.

Chamberlin, Edward H. *The Theory of Monopolistic Competition.* Cambridge, Mass.: Harvard University Press, 7th ed. 1956.

Channing, Edward. *History of the United States.* New York: Macmillan, 1928.

Choper, Jesse H. *Judicial Review and the National Political Process.* Chicago, Ill.: University of Chicago Press, 1980.

Clarke, M. and Hall, D. *Legislative and Documentary History of the Bank of the United States.* Washington, D.C.: Gales and Seaton, 1832.

Clinton, Robert L. *Marbury v. Madison and Judicial Review.* Lawrence: University of Kansas Press, 1989.

Colburn, H. Trevor. *The Lamp of Experience: Whig History and the Intellectual Origins of the American Revolution.* Chapel Hill: University of North Carolina Press, 1965.

Commager, Henry S. *Majority Rule and Minority Rights.* New York: Oxford University Press, 1943.4.

Cooley, Thomas. *Constitutional Limitations.* 6th ed. Boston, Mass.: Little Brown and Co., 1890.

Cooter, Robert, and Ulen, Thomas. *Law and Economics.* Glenview, Ill.: Scott, Foresman, 1988.

Corbin, Arthur. *Contracts.* St. Paul, Minn.: West Publishing Co., 1963.

Cortner, Richard, C. *The Supreme Court and the Second Bill of Rights.* Madison, Wis.: University of Wisconsin Press, 1981.

Corwin, Edward S. *American Constitutional History.* New York: Harper and Row, 1964.

———. *Commerce Power versus State Rights*. Princeton, N.J.: Princeton University Press, 1936.

———. *Court over Constitution*. Princeton, N.J.: Princeton University Press, 1938.

———. *Doctrine of Judicial Review and Other Essays*. Princeton, N.J.: Princeton University Press, 1914.

———. *The "Higher Law" Background of American Constitutional Law*. Ithaca, N.Y.: Cornell University Press, 1955.

———. *John Marshall and the Constitution*. New Haven, Conn.: Yale University Press, 1921.

———. *Liberty against Government*. Baton Rouge, La., Louisiana University Press, 1948.

———. *Twilight of the Supreme Court*. New Haven, Conn.: Yale University Press, 1934.

Cover, Robert M. *Justice Accused: Antislavery and the Judicial Process*. New Haven, Conn.: Yale University Press, 1975.

Cox, Archibald. *The Court and the Constitution*. Boston, Mass.: Houghton Mifflin, 1987.

———. *The Role of the Supreme Court in American Government*. New York: Oxford University Press, 1976.

Coxe, Tench. *A View of the United States of America*. London, England: J. Johnson, 1794.

Crosskey, William W. *Politics and the Constitution in the History of the United States*. Chicago, Ill.: University of Chicago Press, 1953.

Cunningham, William. *The Growth of English Industry and Commerce*. 5th ed. Cambridge, England: University Press, 1912.

Currie, David P. *The Constitution in the Supreme Court, The First Hundred Years, 1789–1888*. Chicago, Ill.: University of Chicago Press, 1985.

Curtis, Charles P. *Lions under the Throne*. Boston, Mass.: Houghton Mifflin, 1947.

Curtis, Michael K. *No State Shall Abridge: The Fourteenth Amendment and the Bill of Rights*. Durham, N.C., Duke University Press, 1986.

Debates and Proceedings in the Congress of the United States. Washington, D.C.: Gales and Seaton, 1834–1856.

Dewey, Davis R. *Financial History of the United States*. New York: Longmans Green, 1939.

Dicey, A. V. *Introduction to the Study of the Law of the Constitution*. London, Macmillan, 1908.

Dietze, Gottfried. *In Defense of Property*. Chicago: H. Regnery, 1963.

Dollard, John. *Caste and Class in a Southern Town*. New Haven, Conn.: Yale University Press, 1937.

Dorfman, Joseph. *The Economic Mind in American Civilization 1606–1865*. New York: Viking Press, 1946.

Dorn, James A., and Manne, Henry G. *Economic Liberties and the Judiciary*. Fairfax, Va.: George Mason University Press, 1987.

Duker, William F. *A Constitutional History of Habeas Corpus*. Westport, Conn.: Greenwood Press, 1980.

Dumbauld, Edward. *The Bill of Rights and What It Means Today*. Norman: Oklahoma University Press, 1957.

Dunham, Allison and Kurland, Philip B., eds. *Mr. Justice*. Chicago, Ill.: University of Chicago Press, 1964.

Dunne, Gerald T. *Joseph Story and the Rise of the Supreme Court*. New York: Simon and Schuster, 1970.

Du Ponceau, Peter S. *A Dissertation on the Nature and Extent of the Jurisdiction of the Courts of the United States* 1824. Reprint. New York: Arno Press, 1972.

Elliot, Jonathan, ed. *Debates in the Several State Conventions on the Adoption of the Federal Constitution*. Philadelphia: Lippincott, 1836–1845.

Ely, John H. *Democracy and Distrust: A Theory of Judicial Review*. Cambridge, Mass.: Harvard University Press, 1980.

Epstein, Richard A. *Takings: Private Property and the Power of Eminent Domain*. Cambridge, Mass.: Harvard University Press, 1985.

Fairman, Charles. *Reconstruction and Reunion 1864–88*, vol. 6 of *History of the Supreme Court of the United States*. New York: Macmillan Co., 1971.

Farrand, Max. *The Framing of the Constitution of the United States*. New Haven, Conn.: Yale University Press, 1913.

———. *The Records of the Federal Convention of 1787*. New Haven, Conn.: Yale University Press, 1911.

Federalist, The. By Alexander Hamilton, James Madison and John Jay. Edited by E. Bourne. New York: Tudor Publishing, 1947.

Fehrenbacher, Don E. *The Dred Scott Case: Its Significance in American Law and Politics*. New York: Oxford University Press, 1978.

Field, Oliver P. *The Effect of an Unconstitutional Statute*. Minneapolis: University of Minnesota Press, 1935.

Fifoot, Cecil H. S. *Lord Mansfield*. Oxford, England: Clarendon Press, 1936.

Fischer, Roger A. *The Segregation Struggle in Louisiana, 1862–77*. Urbana: University of Illinois Press, 1974.

Flack, Harry. *The Adoption of the Fourteenth Amendment*. Baltimore, Md.: Johns Hopkins University Press, 1908.

Fox, Harold G. *Monopolies and Patents*. University of Toronto Studies, Legal Series. Toronto, Canada: n.p., 1947.

Frank, Jerome. *Law and the Modern Mind*. New York: Brentano's, 1930.

Frank, John P. *Justice Daniel Dissenting*. Cambridge, Mass.: Harvard University Press, 1964.

Frankfurter, Felix. *The Commerce Clause under Marshal, Taney and Waite*. Chapel Hill: University of North Carolina Press, 1937.

———. *Mr. Justice Holmes and the Supreme Court*. Cambridge, Mass.: Harvard University Press, 1938.

Frazier, E. Franklin. *The Negro Family in the United States*. Chicago, Ill.: University of Chicago Press, 1939.

Freedman, Max, ed. *Roosevelt and Frankfurter, Their Correspondence 1928–1945*. Boston, Mass.: Little Brown, 1967.

Freund, Ernst. *Standards of American Legislation*. Chicago, Ill.: University of Chicago Press, 1917.

Freyer, Tony. *Harmony and Dissonance: The Swift and Erie Cases in American Federalism*. New York: New York University Press, 1981.

Fried, Charles. *Contract as Promise: A Theory of Contractual Obligation*. Cambridge, Mass.: Harvard University Press, 1981.

Friedman, Lawrence M. and Scheiber, Harry M., eds. *American Law and Constitutional Order: Historical Perspectives*. Cambridge, Mass.: Harvard University Press, 1978.

Friedman, Milton. *The Optimum Quantity of Money and Other Essays*. Chicago, Ill.: Aldine Publishing, 1969.

———, and Schwartz, Anna J. *A Monetary History of the United States 1867–1960.* Princeton, N.J.: Princeton University Press, 1963.

Friendly, Henry J. *The Federal Administrative Agencies: The Need for Better Definition of Standards.* Cambridge, Mass.: Harvard University Press, 1962.

Galitin, Malcolm and Leiter, Robert D., eds. *Economics of Information.* Boston, Mass.: Martinus Nijhoff, 1981.

Gavit, Bernard C. *The Commerce Clause of the United States Constitution.* New York: AMS Press, Reprint 1970, 1932.

Gilmore, Grant and Black, Charles. *The Law of Admiralty.* 2d ed. Mineola, N.Y.: Foundation Press, 1975.

Ginzberg, Eli and Eichner, Alfred S. *The Troublesome Presence: American Democracy and the Negro.* New York: Free Press of Glencoe, 1964.

Gipson, Lawrence H. *The British Empire before the American Revolution,* vol. 3, *The British Isles and the American Colonies: The Northern Plantations 1748–1754.* Rev. ed. New York: Alfred Knopf, 1960.

Goebel, Julius. *Antecedents and Beginnings to 1801,* vol. 1, *History of the Supreme Court of the United States.* New York: Macmillan, 1971.

———. *The Law Practice of Alexander Hamilton.* New York: Columbia University Press, 1964–1981.

Goodman, Mark N. *The Ninth Amendment.* Smithtown, N.Y.: Exposition Press, 1981.

Goodnow, Frank J. *Principles of the Administrative Law of the United States.* New York: G. P. Putnam's, 1905.

Gordon, John W. *Monopolies and Patents and the Statutable Remedies Available to the Public.* London, England: Stevens and Sons, 1897.

Gouge, William M. *A Short History of Paper Money and Banking in the United States.* Philadelphia, Pa.: T. W. Ustick, 1833.

Gough, John W. *Fundamental Law in English Constitutional History.* Rev. ed. Oxford, England: Clarendon Press, 1971.

Graham, Howard J., ed. *Everyman's Constitution.* Madison: State Historical Society of Wisconsin, 1968.

Guest, Anthony G., ed. *Oxford Essays in Jurisprudence.* London, England: Oxford University Press, 1961.

Gunther, Gerald, ed. *John Marshall's Defense of McCulloch v. Maryland.* Stanford, Calif.: Stanford University Press, 1969.

Gwartney, James D., and Wagner, Richard E., eds. *Public Choice and Constitutional Economics.* Greenwich, Conn.: JAI Press, 1988.

Gwyn, William B. *The Meaning of the Separation of Powers.* New Orleans, La.: Tulane University, 1965.

Haar, Charles M., and Kayden, Jerold S. *Zoning and the American Dream.* Chicago, Ill.: APA Planners Press, 1989.

Haines, Charles G. *The American Doctrine of Judicial Supremacy.* New York: Russell and Russell, 1959.

Hale, Robert L. *Freedom through Law.* New York: Columbia University Press, 1952.

Hamilton, Walton H. and Adair, Douglass. *The Power to Govern.* New York: W. W. Norton, 1937.

Hammond, Bray. *Banks and Politics in America from the Revolution to the Civil War.* Princeton, N.J.: Princeton University Press, 1957.

Hand, Learned. *The Bill of Rights.* Cambridge, Mass.: Harvard University Press, 1958.

———. *The Spirit of Liberty.* New York: Alfred A. Knopf, 1953.

Harlan, Louis R. *Separate and Unequal: Public School Campaigns and Racism in the Southern Seaboard States, 1901–1915.* Chapel Hill: University of North Carolina Press, 1958.

Harris, Robert J. *The Quest for Equality.* Baton Rouge, La.: Louisiana University Press, 1960.

Haskins, George L. and Johnson, Herbert A. *Foundation of Power: John Marshall, 1801–15,* vol. 2, *History of the Supreme Court of the United States.* New York: Macmillan, 1981.

Hayek, Friedrich A. *The Constitution of Liberty.* Chicago, Ill.: University of Chicago Press, 1960.

———. *Law, Legislation and Liberty,* vol. 1, *Rules and Order.* Chicago Ill.: University of Chicago Press, 1973.

Head, John G. *Public Goods and Public Welfare.* Durham, N.C.: Duke University Press, 1974.

Hepburn, Alonzo B. *A History of Currency in the United States.* Rev. ed. New York: A. M. Kelley, 1967.

Hicks, John. *A Theory of Economic History.* London, England: Oxford University Press, 1969.

Hirsch, Werner Z. *Law and Economics: An Introductory Analysis.* New York: Academic Press, 1967.

Hirshleifer, Jack. *Price Theory and Applications.* Englewood Cliffs, N.J.: Prentice Hall, 1976.

Hochman, Harold M. and Peterson, George E., eds. *Redistribution through Public Choice.* New York: Columbia University Press, 1974.

Hoebel, E. Adamson. *The Law of Primitive Man.* Cambridge, Mass.: Harvard University Press, 1954.

Holden, James M. *The History of Negotiable Instruments in English Law.* London, England: University of London Athlone Press, 1955.

Holdsworth, William. *History of English Law.* 7th ed. Boston, Mass.: Little Brown, 1956.

Holmes, Oliver W. *Collected Legal Papers.* New York: Harcourt Brace, 1920.

Hoover, Edgar M. *The Location of Economic Activity.* New York: McGraw Hill, 1948.

Horwitz, Morton J. *The Transformation of American Law 1780–1860.* Cambridge, Mass.: Harvard University Press, 1977.

Howard, A. E. Dick. *The Road from Runnymede: Magna Carta and Constitutionalism in America.* Charlottesville: University Press of Virginia, 1968.

Howe, Mark DeWolfe. *Holmes-Pollack Letters.* Cambridge, Mass.: Harvard University Press, 1941.

Howell, Roger. *The Privileges and Immunities of State Citizenship.* Baltimore, Md.: Johns Hopkins University Press, 1918.

Hughes, Charles E. *The Supreme Court of the United States.* New York: Columbia University Press, 1928.

Hunter, Louis C. *Steamboats on the Western Rivers.* Cambridge, Mass.: Harvard University Press, 1949.

Hyman, Allen and Johnson, M. Bruce, eds. *Advertising and Free Speech.* Lexington, Mass.: Lexington Books, 1977.

Hyman, Harold M. and Wiecek, William M. *Equal Justice under Law.* New York: Harper and Row, 1982.

Jackson, Robert H. *The Struggle for Judicial Supremacy.* New York: Alfred A. Knopf, 1941.

————. *The Supreme Court in the American System of Government*. Cambridge, Mass.: Harvard University Press, 1955.

Jacob, Giles. *A New Law-Dictionary*. 7th ed. London: R. Ware, 1756.

James, Joseph B. *The Framing of the Fourteenth Amendment*. Urbana: University of Illinois Press, 1965.

————. *The Ratification of the Fourteenth Amendment*. Macon, Ga.: Mercer University Press, 1984.

Jayson, L. S., et al., eds., *The Constitution of the United States of America: An Analysis and Interpretation*. Washington, D.C.: U.S. Government Printing Office, 1973.

Jefferson, Thomas. *The Papers of Thomas Jefferson*. Edited by J. Boyd. Princeton, N.J.: Princeton University Press, J. Boyd, ed. 1955.

————. *Writings of Thomas Jefferson*. Edited by P. L. Ford, 1895.

Jensen, Merrill. *The Articles of Confederation*. Madison: University of Wisconsin Press, 1940.

Johnson, Charles S. *Patterns of Negro Segregation*. New York: Harper and Bros., 1943.

Johnson, D. Gale. *Farm Commodity Programs: An Opportunity for Change*. Washington, D.C.: American Enterprise Institute, 1973.

Johnson, Franklin. *Development of State Legislation Concerning the Free Negro*. 1919. Reprint. Westport, Conn.: Greenwood Press, 1979.

Johnson, Samuel. *Dictionary of the English Language*. 1755. Reprint. New York: AMS Press Reprint 1967.

Jolowicz, Herbert F. *Roman Foundations of Modern Law*. Oxford, England: Clarendon Press, 1957.

Jones, W. Melville, ed. *Chief Justice John Marshall: A Reappraisal*. Ithaca, N.Y.: Cornell University Press, 1956.

Kaczorowski, Robert J. *The Politics of Judicial Interpretation: The Federal Courts, Department of Justice and Civil Rights 1866–1876*. Dobbs Ferry, N.Y.: Oceana Publications, 1985.

Kelly, Alfred H.; Harbison Winfred A.; and Belz, Herman. *The American Constitution: Its Origins and Development*. 6th ed. New York: Norton, 1983.

Kendrick, Benjamin B. *The Journal of the Joint Committee of Fifteen on Reconstruction*. New York: Columbia University Press, 1914.

Kent, James. *Commentaries on American Law*. 10th ed. Boston, Mass.: Little Brown, 1860.

Kluger, Richard. *Simple Justice*. New York: Alfred A. Knopf, 1976.

Knight, Frank H. *The Economic Organization*. New York: Harper and Row, 1951.

————. *Risk, Uncertainty, and Profit*. Boston, Mass.: Houghton Mifflin, 1921.

Kolko, Gabriel. *Railroads and Regulation 1877–1916*. Princeton, N.J.: Princeton University Press, 1965.

Kutler, Stanley I. *Privilege and Creative Destruction: The Charles River Bridge Case*. Philadelphia, Pa.: Lippincott, 1971.

Lawson, James F. *The General Welfare Clause*. Washington, D.C.: author, 1934.

Lecht, Leonard A. *Experience under Railway Labor Legislation*. New York: Columbia University Press, 1955.

Lee, Maurice W. *Anti–Chain Store Tax Legislation*. University of Chicago Studies in Business. Chicago: University of Chicago Press, 1939.

Levi, Edward H. *An Introduction to Legal Reasoning*. Chicago, Ill.: University of Chicago Press, 1948.

Levy, Hermann. *Monopolies, Cartels and Trusts in British Industry*. 1927. Reprint. New York: A. M. Kelley Reprint, 1968.

Levy, Leonard W., ed. *American Constitutional Law: Historical Essays*. New York: Harper and Row, 1966.

————. *Judgments: Essays on American Constitutional History*. Chicago: Quadrangle Books, 1972.

————. *Judicial Review and the Supreme Court*. New York: Harper and Row, 1967.

Lien, Arnold J. *Concurring Opinion: The Privileges or Immunities Clause of the Fourteenth Amendment*. Washington University Studies. St. Louis, Mo.: 1957.

Lindley, Nathaniel. *An Introduction to the Study of Jurisprudence*. 1855. Reprint. Littleton, Col.: F. B. Rothman, 1985.

Livermore, Samuel. *Dissertation on the Questions which arise from the Contrariety of the Positive Laws of Different States and Nations*. New Orleans, La.: B. Levy, 1828.

Llewellyn, Karl N. *The Common Law Tradition: Deciding Appeals:* Boston, Mass.: Little Brown, 1960.

Locke, John. *The Second Treatise of Government*. Edited by J. W. Gough. Oxford, England: Blackwell, 1956.

Lofgren, Charles A. *The Plessy Case: A Legal-Historical Interpretation*. New York: Oxford University Press, 1987.

Lusky, Louis. *By What Right?*. Charlottesville, Va.: Michie, 1975.

Lutz, Donald. *The Origins of American Constitutionalism*. Baton Rouge: Louisiana State University Press, 1988.

MacAvoy, Paul W. *The Economic Effects of Regulation: The Trunk-Line Railroad Cartels and the Interstate Commerce Commission before 1900*. Cambridge, Mass.: M.I.T. Press, 1965.

Machiavelli, Niccolo. *History of Florence*. Edited by Charles W. Colby. New York: Columbia Press, 1901.

MacKaay, Ejan. *Economics of Information and Law*. Boston, Mass.: Kluwer-Nijhoff, 1982.

Madison, James. *Writings*. Edited by G. Hunt. New York: Putnam, 1900–1910.

Magrath, C. Peter. *Morrison R. Waite: The Triumph of Character*. New York: Macmillan, 1963.

————. *Yazoo: Law and Politics in the New Republic: The Case of Fletcher v. Peck*. Providence, R.I.: Brown University Press, 1966.

Maine, Henry. *Popular Government*. London, England: Murray, 1886.

Malinvaud, Edmond. *Lectures on Microeconomic Theory*. Amsterdam, The Netherlands: North Holland: 1972.

Marshall, Samuel. *A Treatise on the Law of Insurance*. 1st Amer. ed. Boston, Mass.: Manning and Loring, 1805.

Mason, Alpheus T. *Brandeis: A Free Man's Life*. New York: Viking Press, 1946.

————. *Harlan Fiske Stone: Pillar of the Law*. New York: Viking Press, 1956.

Mason, Lowell B. *The Language of Dissent*. Cleveland, Ohio: World Publishing, 1959.

McClellan, James. *Joseph Story and the American Constitution*. Norman: University of Oklahoma Press, 1971.

McCloskey, Robert G. *The American Supreme Court*. Chicago: University of Chicago Press, 1960.

————. *Essays in Constitutional Law*. New York: Alfred A. Knopf, 1962.

McDonald, Forrest. *E Pluribus Unum*. Boston, Mass.: Houghton Mifflin, 1965.

————. *Novus Ordo Seclorum.* Lawrence, Kan., University Press of Kansas, 1985.

————. *We the People, Economic Origins of the Constitution.* Chicago: University of Chicago Press, 1958.

————, and McDonald, Ellen S. *Confederation and Constitution, 1781–1789.* New York: Harper and Row, 1968.

McIlwain, Charles H. *Constitutionalism Ancient and Modern.* Ithaca, N.Y.: Cornell University Press, 1947.

————. *The High Court of Parliament and Its Supremacy.* New Haven, Conn.: Yale University Press, 1910.

McKean, Roland N. *Public Spending.* New York: McGraw-Hill, 1968.

McKechnie, William S. *Magna Carta.* 2d ed. Glasgow, Scotland, J. Maclehose and Sons, 1914.

McKenzie, Richard B., ed. *Constitutional Economics.* Lexington, Mass.: Lexington Books, 1984.

McLaughlin, Andrew C. *The Courts, the Constitution and the Parties.* Chicago: University of Chicago Press, 1912.

Meigs, William M. *The Relation of the Judiciary to the Constitution.* New York: Neale Publishing, 1919.

Meiklejohn, Alexander. *Political Freedom.* New York: Harper and Bros., 1948.

Mendelson, Wallace, ed. *Supreme Court: Law and Discretion.* Indianapolis, Ind.: Bobbs-Merrill, 1967.

Meyer, Hermine H. *The History and Meaning of the Fourteenth Amendment.* New York: Vantage Press, 1977.

Meyer, J. R.; Kain, J. F., and Wohl, M. *The Urban Transportation Problem.* Cambridge, Mass.: Harvard University Press, 1965.

Miller, Charles A. *The Supreme Court and the Uses of History.* Cambridge, Mass.: Harvard University Press, 1969.

Mitchell, William. *Essay on the Early History of the Law Merchant.* 1904. Reprint. New York: Burt Franklin, 1969.

Morgan, Donald G. *Congress and the Constitution.* Cambridge, Mass.: Harvard University Press, 1966.

————. *Justice William Johnson: The First Dissenter.* Columbia: University of South Carolina Press, 1954.

Morgan, Edmund. *Prologue to Revolution: Sources and Documents on the Stamp Act Crisis 1764–1766.* Chapel Hill: University of North Carolina Press, 1959.

————, and Morgan, Helen. *The Stamp Act Crisis: Prologue to Revolution.* Chapel Hill: University of North Carolina Press, 1953.

Mullett, Charles F. *Fundamental Law and the American Revolution 1760–1776.* New York: Columbia University Press, 1933.

Musgrave, Richard A., and Musgrave, Peggy B. *Public Finance in Theory and Practice.* 4th ed. New York: McGraw-Hill, 1984.

Myrdal, Gunnar. *An American Dilemma.* New York: Harper and Bros., 1944.

Nelson, James C. *Railroad Transportation and Public Policy.* Washington, D.C.: Brookings, 1959.

Nelson, William E. *The Fourteenth Amendment: From Political Principle to Judicial Doctrine.* Cambridge, Mass.: Harvard University Press, 1988.

Newmyer, R. Kent. *Supreme Court Justice Joseph Story.* Chapel Hill: University of North Carolina Press, 1985.

Nichols, Philip. *Law of Eminent Domain.* 3d ed. Albany, N.Y.: Mathew Bender, 1985.

North, Douglass C., and Thomas, Robert P. *The Rise of the Western World: A New Economic History.* New York: Cambridge University Press, 1973.

Olson, Mancur. *The Logic of Collective Action.* Cambridge, Mass.: Harvard University Press, 1965.

Patterson, Bennett. *The Forgotten Ninth Amendment.* Indianapolis, Ind.: Bobbs-Merrill, 1955.

Paul, Arnold M. *Conservative Crisis and the Rule of Law.* Ithaca, N.Y.: Cornell University Press.

Paul, Ellen F. *Property Rights and Eminent Domain.* New Brunswick, N.J.: Transaction Books, 1987.

Pennock, J. Rowland, and Chapman, John W., eds. *Constitutionalism,* Nomos 20. New York: New York University Press, 1979.

———, and Chapman, John W., eds. *Liberal Democracy,* Nomos 25. New York: New York University Press, 1983.

———, and Chapman, John W., eds. *Property,* Nomos 22. New York: New York University Press, 1980.

Perry, Michael. *The Constitution, The Courts and Human Rights.* New Haven, Conn.: Yale University Press, 1982.

Perry, Richard L., and Cooper, John C. *Sources of Our Liberties.* Chicago: American Bar Foundation, 1959.

Polanyi, Karl. *The Great Transformation.* Boston, Mass.: Beacon Press, 1957.

Polinsky, A. Mitchell. *An Introduction to Law and Economics.* 2d ed. Boston: Little Brown, 1989.

Pole, Jack R. *The Pursuit of Equality in American History.* Berkeley, Calif.: University of California Press, 1978.

Poore, Benjamin P. *The Federal and State Constitutions, Colonial Charters and Other Organic Charters of the United States.* Washington, D.C.: U.S. Government Printing Office, 1877–1878.

Posner, Richard A. *Economic Analysis of Law.* 3d ed. Boston, Mass.: Little Brown, 1986.

———. *The Economics of Justice.* Cambridge, Mass.: Harvard University Press, 1983.

Postlethwayt, Malachy. *The Unviersal Dictionary of Trade and Commerce.* London, England: W Straham, 1774.

Pothier, Robert J. *A Treatise on the Law of Obligations or Contract.* Translated by W. Evans. Philadelphia, Pa.: R. H. Small, 1826.

Pound, Roscoe. *The Development of Constitutional Guarantees of Liberty.* New Haven, Conn.: Yale University Press, 1957.

———, et al. *Perspectives of Law: Essays for Austin Wakeman Scott.* Boston, Mass.: Little Brown, 1964.

Powell, John. *Essay upon the Law of Contracts and Agreements.* London, England: J. Johnson, 1790.

Powell, Thomas R. *Vagaries and Varieties in Constitutional Interpretation.* New York: Columbia University Press, 1956.

Rabinowitz, Howard N. *Race Relations in the Urban South 1865–1890.* New York: Oxford University Press, 1978.

Rawle, William. *A View of the Constitution of the United States of America.* Philadelphia, Pa.: H. C. Carey and I. Lea, 1825.

Reid, John P. *Constitutional History of the American Revolution.* Madison: University of Wisconsin Press, 1986.

Ribble, Frederick D. G. *State and National Power Over Commerce.* New York: Columbia University Press, 1937.

Richardson, James O. *Compilation of the Messages and Papers of the Presidents 1789–1897.* New York: Bureau of National Literature, 1917.

Ritz, Wilfred J. *Rewriting the History of the Judiciary Act of 1789.* Norman: University of Oklahoma Press, 1990.

Robertson, David W. *Admiralty and Federalism.* Mineola, N.Y.: Foundation Press, 1970.

Rose, Walter M. *A Code of Federal Procedure.* San Francisco, Calif.: Bancroft-Whitney, 1907.

Rossiter, Clinton. *Seedtime of the Republic.* New York: Harcourt Brace, 1953.

Rowland, Kate M. *The Life of George Mason.* New York: G. P. Putnam, 1892.

Rushworth, John. *Historical Collections of Private Passages of State.* London, England: D. Browne, 1721.

Rutherforth, Thomas. *Institutes of Natural Law.* Cambridge, England: J. Bentham, 1756.

Rutland, Robert. *The Birth of the Bill of Rights, 1776–1791.* Chapel Hill: University of North Carolina Press, 1955.

———. *The Ordeal of the Constitution, The Antifederalist Ratification Struggle of 1787–1788.* Norman: University of Oklahoma Press, 1965.

Rutledge, Wiley. *A Declaration of Legal Faith.* Lawrence, Kan., University of Kansas Press, 1947.

Sanborn, Frederick. *Origins of the Early English Maritime and Commercial Law.* New York: Century Co., 1930.

Savigny, Friedrick Carl. *Private International Law and the Retrospective Operation of Statutes.* Edinburgh, Scotland: T. and T. Clark, 1880.

Schevill, Ferdinand. *History of Florence.* New York: Frederick Unger, 1961.

Schmidt, Benno. *Freedom of the Press v. Public Access.* New York: Praeger, 1976.

Schmoller, Gustav. *The Mercantile System and Its Historical Significance.* 1884. Reprint. New York: A. M. Kelley, 1967.

Schwartz, Bernard. *A Commentary on the Constitution of the United States, Part II, The Rights of Property.* New York: Macmillan, 1965.

Scrutton, Thomas E. *The Influence of the Roman Law on the Law of England.* 1885. Reprint. Littleton, Colo.: Rothman, 1985.

———. *Elements of Mercantile Law.* London, England: W. Clowes, 1891.

Select Essays in Anglo-American Legal History. Edited by Association of American Law Schools. Boston: Little Brown, 1907–1909.

Sergeant, Thomas. *Constitutional Law.* 2d ed. Philadelphia, Pa.: P. H. Nicklin and T. Johnson, 1830.

Sherman, Roger. *The Economics of Industry.* Boston, Mass.: Little Brown 1974.

Shibutani, Tamotsu, and Kwan, Kian M. *Ethnic Stratification: A Comparative Approach.* New York: Macmillan, 1965.

Shirley, John M. *The Dartmouth College Causes and the Supreme Court of the United States.* Chicago: G. I. Jones, 1895.

Siegan, Bernard. *Economic Liberties and the Constitution.* Chicago: University of Chicago Press, 1980.

Smith, Adam. *An Inquiry into the Nature and Causes of the Wealth of Nations.* 1776. Reprint. Oxford, England: Clarendon Press, 1869.

Smith, James A. *The Spirit of American Government.* New York: Macmillan, 1911.

Smith, John W. *Compendium of Mercantiie Law.* 10th ed. London, England: Stevens and Sons, 1890.

Smith, Walter B. *Economic Aspects of the Second Bank of the United States.* Cambridge, Mass.: Harvard University Press, 1953.

Sparks, Jared. *The Life of Gouverneur Morris.* Boston, Mass.: Gray and Brown, 1832.

Spooner, Lysander. *The Unconstitutionality of Slavery.* 1845. Reprint. New York: B. Franklin, 1965.

Stevens, C. Ellis. *Sources of the Constitution of the United States.* New York: Macmillan, 1894.

Stigler, George J. *The Organization of Industry.* Homewood, Ill.: Richard D. Irwin, 1968.

Stites, Francis N. *Private Interest and Public Gain: The Dartmouth College Case, 1819.* Amherst: University of Massachusetts Press, 1972.

Stoebuck, William B. *Nontresspassory Takings in Eminent Domain.* Charlottesville, Va.: Michie, 1977.

Stone, Julius. *Legal System and Lawyers' Reasonings.* Stanford, Calif.: Stanford University Press, 1964.

Storing, Herbert J. *The Complete anti-Federalist.* Chicago: University of Chicago Press, 1981.

Story, Joseph. *Miscellaneous Writings of Joseph Story.* Edited by W. W. Story. Boston, Mass.: Little Brown, 1852.

―――. *Commentaries on the Conflict of Laws.* Boston, Mass.: Hilliard, Gray, 1834.

―――. *Commentaries on the Constitution of the United States.* Boston, Mass.: Hilliard, Gray, 1833.

―――. *Commentaries on the Law of Bills of Exchange.* 2d ed. Boston, Mass.: Little Brown, 1847.

Story, William W., ed. *Life and Letters of Joseph Story.* Boston, Mass.: Little Brown, 1851.

Sullivan, James. *History of Land Titles in Massachusetts.* Boston, Mass.: I. Thomas and E. T. Andrews, 1801.

Sumner, Charles. *Charles Sumner: His Complete Works.* Boston, Mass.: Lee and Shepard, 1909.

Sutherland, Arthur E. *Constitutionalism in America.* New York: Blaisdell Pub. Co., 1965.

―――, ed. *Government under Law.* Cambridge, Mass.: Harvard University Press, 1956.

Swift, Zephaniah. *A Digest of the Law of Evidence in Criminal Cases and a Treatise on Bills of Exchange and Promissory Notes.* Hartford, Conn.: Oliver D. Cooke, 1810.

―――. *System of the Laws of the State of Connecticut.* Windham, Conn.: John Byrne, 1795.

Swisher, Carl B. *Stephen J. Field, Craftsman of the Law.* Chicago: University of Chicago Press, 1969.

―――. *The Taney Period 1836–64,* vol. 5, *History of the Supreme Court of the United States.* New York: Macmillan, 1974.

Tanner, Joseph R. *Constitutional Documents of the Reign of James I.* Cambridge, England: University Press, 1930.

ten Broek, Jacobus. *The Antislavery Origins of the Fourteenth Amendment.* Berkeley, Calif.: University of California Press, 1951.

―――, Barnhart, Edward N., and Matson, Floyd W. *Prejudice, War and the Constitution.* Berkeley, Calif.: University of California Press, 1968.

Thayer, James B. *John Marshall.* New York: Houghton, Mifflin, 1904.

Thorpe, Francis ed. *The Federal and State Constitutions, Colonial Charters and Other Organic Laws.* Washington, D.C.: U.S. Government Printing Office, 1909.

Tiffany, Joel. *A Treatise on the Unconstitutionality of American Slavery: Together with the Powers and Duties of the Federal Government in Relation to That Subject.* Cleveland, Ohio, J. Calyer, 1849.

Trakman, Leon E. *The Law Merchant.* Littleton, Colo.: F. B. Rothman, 1983.

Trevelyan, George M. *Garibaldi and the Thousand.* London, England: Longmans Green, 1909.

Tribe, Lawrence H. *American Constitutional Law.* 1978. 2d ed. Mineola, N.Y.: Foundation Press, 1988.

―――. *Constitutional Choices.* Cambridge, Mass.: Harvard University Press, 1985.

Tucker, St. George, ed. *Blackstone's Commentaries.* Philadelphia, Pa.: W. Y. Birch and A. Small, 1803.

Twiss, Benjamin R. *Lawyers and the Constitution: How Laissez Faire Came to the Supreme Court.* Princeton, N.J.: Princeton University Press, 1942.

U.S. Congress. *Debates and Proceedings in the Congress of the United States.* Washington, D.C.: Gales and Seaton, 1834–1856.

U.S. Continental Congress. *Journals of the Continental Congress, 1774–1789.* Washington, D.C.: U.S. Government Printing Office, 1904–1937.

U.S. Office of Management and Budget. *Historical Table: Budget of the United States Government.* Washington, D.C.: U.S. Government Printing Office, 1987.

Vanderbilt, Arthur T. *The Doctrine of Separation of Powers and the Present-Day Significance.* Lincoln, Neb.: University of Nebraska Press, 1953.

Varnum, James M. *The Case of Trevett v. Weeden.* Providence, R.I.: John Carter, 1787.

Vattel, Emer de. *Law of Nations.* Edited by Chitty. Philadelphia, Pa.: T. and J. W. Johnson, 1870.

Vile, M. J. C. *Constitutionalism and the Separation of Powers.* Oxford, England: Clarendon Press, 1967.

Viner, Charles. *A General Abridgement of Law and Equity.* 2d ed. London, England: G. G. J. and J. Robinson, 1791.

Wade, E. C. S., and Phillips, G. Godfrey. *Constitutional Law.* 6th ed. London, England: Longmans, 1960.

Warren, Charles. *Bankruptcy in United States History.* Cambridge, Mass.: Harvard University Press, 1935.

―――. *Congress as Santa Clause; or, National Donations and the General Welfare Clause of Constitution.* Charlottesville, Va.: Michie, 1932.

―――. *Congress, the Constitution and the Supreme Court.* Boston, Mass.: Little Brown, 1925.

―――. *The Supreme Court in United States History.* Boston, Mass.: Little Brown, 1926.

Washburn, Wilcomb E. *Red Man's Land / White Man's Law: A Study of the Past and Present Status of the American Indian.* New York: Scribner, 1971.

Wechsler, Herbert. *Principles, Politics and Fundamental Law.* Cambridge, Mass.: Harvard University Press, 1961.

Weinberg, Meyer. *A Chance to Learn, The History of Race and Education in the United States.* New York: Cambridge University Press, 1977.

White, G. Edward. *The Marshall Court and Cultural Change, 1815–35,* vol. 3–4, *History of the Supreme Court of the United States.* New York: Macmillan, 1988.

Whitmore, William H., ed. *The Colonial Laws of Massachusetts 1672*. Boston, Mass.: Rockwell and Churchill, 1890.

Wiecek, William M. *The Sources of Antislavery Constitutionalism in America 1769–1848*. Ithaca, N.Y.: Cornell University Press, 1977.

Wilson, James. *Works of James Wilson*. Edited by R. G. McCloskey, Cambridge, Mass.: Harvard University Press, 1967.

Wolfe, Christopher. *The Rise of Modern Judicial Review*. New York: Basic Books, 1986.

Wood, Gordon S. *Creation of the American Republic, 1776–1787*. New York: Norton, 1972.

Wooddeson, Richard. *The Elements of Jurisprudence*. 1783. Reprint. Littleton, Colo.: F. B. Rothman, 1979.

———. *A Systematical View of the Laws of England*. London, England: T. Payne, 1792.

Woodward, C. Vann. *Origins of the New South 1877–1913*. Baton Rouge: Louisiana State University Press, 1951.

———. *The Strange Career of Jim Crow*. 3d ed. New York: Oxford University Press, 1974.

Wright, Benjamin F. *The Growth of American Constitutional Law*. Chicago: University of Chicago Press, 1967.

———. *The Contract Clause of the Constitution*. Cambridge, Mass.: Harvard University Press, 1938.

Wright, Charles. *Law of Federal Courts*. 4th ed. St. Paul, Minn., West Publishing, 1983.

Articles

Abel, Albert S. "Commerce Regulation before *Gibbons* v. *Ogden:* Interstate Transportation Facilities." 25 *North Carolina Law Review* 121 (1947).

Alchian, Armen A., and Demsetz, Harold. "The Property Rights Paradigm." 33 *Journal of Economic History* 16 (1973).

Alexander, Gregory. "The Concept of Property in Private Constitutional Law: The Ideology of the Scientific Turn in Legal Analysis." 82 *Columbia Law Review* 1545 (1982).

Anderson, William. "The Intention of the Framers: A Note on Constitutional Interpretation." 49 *American Political Science Review* 340 (1955).

Avins, Alfred. "The Equal 'Protection' of the Laws: The Original Understanding." 12 *New York Law Forum* 385 (1966).

Baird, Zoe. "State Empowerment after *Garcia*." 18 *Urban Lawyer* 491 (1986).

Baker, C. Edwin. "Property and its Relation to Constitutionally Protected Liberty." 134 *University of Pennsylvania Law Review* 741 (1986).

Baldwin, Simeon E. "The Citizen of the United States." 2 *Yale Journal* 85 (1893).

Baldwin, Henry. "Origin and Nature of the Constitution and Government of the United States." 9 *U.S. Supreme Court Reports*, Lawyers' Edition 869 (1837).

Berger, Raoul, "Removal of Judicial Functions from Federal Trade Commission to a Trade Court: A Reply to Mr. Kintner." 59 *Michigan Law Review* 199 (1960).

Berman, Harold, and Kaufman, Colin. "The Law of International Commerce Transactions (Lex Mercatoria)." 19 *Harvard International Law Journal* 221 (1978).

Beutel, Frederick R. "Common Law Judicial Technique and the Law of Negotiable Instruments—Two Unfortunate Decisions." 9 *Tulane Law Review* 60 (1934).

―――. "The Necessity of a New Technique of Interpreting the N.I.L.—The Civil Law Analogy." 6 *Tulane Law Review* 1 (1931).

BeVier, Lillian. "The First Amendment and Political Speech: An Inquiry into the Substance and Limits of Principle." 30 *Stanford Law Review* 299 (1979).

Bickel, Alexander. "The Original Understanding and the Segregation Decision." 69 *Harvard Law Review* 1 (1955).

Black, Charles. "The Lawfulness of the Segregation Decisions." 69 *Yale Law Journal* 421 (1960).

Blaustein, Albert R. and Field, Andrew H. " 'Overruling' Opinions in the Supreme Court." 57 *Michigan Law Review* 151 (1958).

Bloch, Susan L., and Marcus, Maeva. "John Marshall's Selective Use of History in Marbury v. Madison." 1986 *Wisconsin Law Review* 301.

Blume, Lawrence and Rubinfeld, Daniel L. "Compensation for Takings: An Economic Analysis." 72 *California Law Review* 569 (1984).

Borchard, Edwin M. "The Supreme Court and Private Rights." 47 *Yale Law Journal* 1051 (1938).

Bork, Robert. "The Impossibility of Finding Welfare Rights in the Constitution." 1979 *Washington University Law Quarterly* 694.

―――. "Neutral Principles and Some First Amendment Problems." 47 *Indiana Law Journal* 1 (1971).

Brandeis, Louis D. "Living Law." 10 *Illinois Law Review* 461 (1916).

Brooks, Roger G. "*Garcia,* the Seventeenth Amendment, and the Role of the Supreme Court in Defending Federalism." 10 *Harvard Journal of Law and Public Policy* 189 (1987).

Brown, Ernest, "The Open Economy: Mr. Justice Frankfurter and the Position of the Judiciary." 67 *Yale Law Journal* 219 (1957).

Brudney, Victor. "Business Corporations and Stockholders' Rights under the First Amendment." 91 *Yale Law Journal* 235 (1981).

Bruff, Harold, and Gelhorn, Ernest. "Congressional Control of Administrative Regulation: A Study of Legislative Vetoes." 90 *Harvard Law Review* 1369 (1977).

Buchanan, James. "Politics, Property and the Law: An Alternative Interpretation of *Miller et al. v. Schoene.*" 15 *Journal of Law and Economics,* 439 (1972).

Burdick, Francis M. "What is the Law Merchant?." 2 *Columbia Law Review* 470 (1902).

Burns, Robert, "Blackstone's Theory of the 'Absolute' Rights of Property." 54 *University of Cincinnati Law Review* 67 (1985).

Calabressi, Guido, and Melamed, A. Douglas. "Property Rules, Liability Rules, and Inalienability: One View of the Cathedral." 85 *Harvard Law Review* 1089 (1972).

Campbell, Thomas P. "Chancellor Kent, Chief Justice Marshall and the Steamboat Cases." 25 *Syracuse Law Review* 497 (1974).

Caplan, Russel. "History and Meaning of the Ninth Amendment." 69 *Virginia Law Review* 223 (1983).

Cheadle, John B. "The Delegation of Legislative Functions." 27 *Yale Law Journal* 842 (1918).

Clarke, Leo. "The Contract Clause: A Basis for Limited Judicial Review of State Economic Regulation." 39 *University of Miami Law Review* 183 (1985).

Coase, Ronald H. "The Problem of Social Cost." 3 *Journal of Law and Economics* 1 (1960).

Cohen, Felix S. "Field Theory and Judicial Logic." 59 *Yale Law Journal* 238 (1950).

——. "Dialogue on Private Property." 9 *Rutgers Law Review* 373 (1954).

Coleman, Jules. "Economics and the Law: A Critical Review of the Foundations of the Economic Approach to Law." 84 *Ethics* 648 (1984).

Conant, Michael. "Multiple Trademarks and Oligopoly Power: A Legislative Proposal." 1 *Industrial Organization Review* 115 (1973).

——. "The Supremacy Clause and State Economic Controls: The Antitrust Maze." 10 *Hastings Constitutional Law Quarterly* 255 (1983).

——. "Antimonopoly Tradition under the Ninth and Fourteenth Amendments: *Slaughter-House Cases* Re-examined." 31 *Emory Law Journal* 785 (1982).

——. "Systems Analysis in the Appellate Decisionmaking Process." 24 *Rutgers Law Review* 293 (1970).

Cooper, Frank E. "The Executive Department of Government and the Rule of Law." 59 *Michigan Law Review* 515 (1961).

Corwin, Edward S. "Congress' Power to Prohibit Commerce, a Crucial Constitutional Issue." 18 *Cornell Law Quarterly* 477 (1933).

——. "Due Process of Law before the Civil War." 24 *Harvard Law Review* 366 (1911).

——. "The 'Higher Law' Background of American Constitutional Law." 42 *Harvard Law Review* 365 (1929).

——. "Judicial Review in Action." 74 *University of Pennsylvania Law Review* 639 (1926).

——. "The Spending Power of Congress—Apropos the Maternity Act." 36 *Harvard Law Review* 548 (1923).

——. "Standpoint in Constitutional Law." 17 *Boston University Law Review* 513 (1937).

——. "The Supreme Court and the Fourteenth Amendment." 7 *Michigan Law Review* 643 (1909).

——. "The Supreme Court and Unconstitutional Laws of Congress." 4 *Michigan Law Review* 616 (1920).

Crosskey, William W. "Charles Fairman 'Legislative History' and the Constitutional Limitations on State Authority." 22 *University of Chicago Law Review* 1 (1954).

Cunningham, Roger A. "Inverse Condemnation as a Remedy for 'Regulatory Takings'." 8 *Hastings Constitutional Law Quarterly* 517 (1981).

Cushman, Robert E. "The National Police Power under the Taxing Clause of the Constitution." 4 *Minnesota Law Review* 247 (1920).

——. "Social and Economic Control through Federal Taxation." 18 *Minnesota Law Review* 759 (1934).

Dam, Kenneth. "The Legal Tender Cases." 1981 *Supreme Court Review* 367.

Davies, D. Seaborne. "Further Light on the Case of Monopolies." 48 *Law Quarterly Review* 394 (1932).

Demsetz, Harold. "The Exchange and Enforcement of Property Rights." 7 *Journal of Law and Economics* 11 (1964).

——. "Minorities in the Market Place." 43 *North Carolina Law Review* 271 (1965).

——. "Toward a Theory of Property Rights." 57 *American Economic Review, Papers and Proceedings* 347 (1967).

Denham, Clarence P. "An Historical Development of the Contract Theory in the Dartmouth College Case." 7 *Michigan Law Review* 201 (1909).

Dickinson, John. "The Law behind the Law." 29 *Columbia Law Review* 285 (1929).

Dickinson, Edwin, D. "The Law of Nations as Part of the National Law of the United States." 101 *University of Pennsylvania Law Review* 792 (1953).

Dimond, Paul, "Strict Construction and Judicial Review of Racial Discrimination under the Equal Protection Clause: Meeting Raoul Berger on Interpretivist Grounds." 80 *Michigan Law Review* 462 (1982).

Douglas, William O. "Stare Decisis." 49 *Columbia Law Review* 735 (1949).

Dowling, Noel T. "Interstate and State Power." 27 *Virginia Law Review* 1 (1940).

———. "Interstate Commerce and State Power—Revised Version." 47 *Columbia Law Review* 597 (1947).

Dunbar, Leslie. "James Madison and the Ninth Amendment." 42 *Virginia Law Review* 627 (1956).

Elliot, E. Donald. "*INS* v. *Chadha:* The Administrative Constitution, the Constitution and the Legislative Veto." 1983 *Supreme Court Review* 125.

Ely, John H. "Legislative and Administrative Motivation in Constitutional Law." 79 *Yale Law Journal* 1205 (1970).

———. "The Wages of Crying Wolf: A Comment on *Roe* v. *Wade.*" 83 *Yale Law Journal* 920 (1973).

Epstein, Richard A. "Substantive Due Process by Any Other Name: The Abortion Cases." 1973 *Supreme Court Review* 159.

———. "Toward a Revitalization of the Contract Clause." 51 *University of Chicago Law Review* 703 (1984).

Eule, Julian N. "Laying the Dormant Commerce Clause to Rest." 91 *Yale Law Journal* 425 (1982).

Fairman, Charles. "Does the Fourteenth Amendment Incorporate the Bill of Rights?" 2 *Stanford Law Review* 5 (1949).

———. "Mr. Justice Bradley's Appointment to the Supreme Court and the Legal Tender Cases." 54 *Harvard Law Review* 977 (1941).

Farber, Daniel. "State Regulation and the Dormant Commerce Clause." 18 *Urban Lawyer* 567 (1986).

"Federal Common Law and Article III: A Jurisdictional Approach to *Erie.*" 74 *Yale Law Journal* 325 (1964).

Field, Oliver P. "*Ex Post Facto* in the Constitution." 20 *Michigan Law Review* 315 (1922).

Field, Martha A. "*Garcia* v. *San Antonio Metropolitan Authority:* The Demise of a Misguided Doctrine." 99 *Harvard Law Review* 84 (1985).

Fiss, Owen M. "Objectivity and Interpretation." 34 *Stanford Law Review* 739 (1982).

Fletcher, William. "The General Common Law and Section 34 of the Judiciary Act of 1789: The Example of Marine Insurance." 97 *Harvard Law Review* 1513 (1984).

Frank, John P., and Munro, Robert. "The Original Understanding of 'Equal Protection of the Laws.' " 1972 *Washington University Law Quarterly* 421.

Frankfurter, Felix. "A Note on Advisory Opinions." 37 *Harvard Law Review* 1002 (1924).

Franklin, Mitchell. "The Foundation and Meaning of the *Slaughterhouse Cases.*" 18 *Tulane Law Review* 1 (1943).

French, Ben C. "Fruit and Vegetable Marketing Orders: A Critique of the Issues and State of Analysis." 64 *American Journal of Agricultural Economics* 916 (1982).

Friendly, Henry J. "In Praise of *Erie*—And of the New Federal Common Law." 39 *New York University Law Review* 383 (1964).

Glennon, Robert J. "Justice Henry Billings Brown: Values in Tension." 44 *University of Colorado Law Review* 553 (1973).

Goetz, Charles, and Scott, Robert. "Enforcing Promises: An Examination of the Basis of Contract." 89 *Yale Law Journal* 1261 (1980).

Goodhart, Arthur L. "Determining the Ratio Decidendi of a Case." 40 *Yale Law Journal* 161 (1930).

Graham, Howard J. "Procedure to Substance: Extra-Judicial Rise of Due Process, 1830–1860." 40 *California Law Review* 483 (1952).

Grant, J.A.C. "The 'Higher Law' Background of the Law of Eminent Domain." 6 *Wisconsin Law Review* 67 (1931).

Green, John R. "The Bill of Rights, the Fourteenth Amendment and the Supreme Court." 46 *Michigan Law Review* 869 (1948).

Greer, F.A. "Custom in the Common Law." 9 *Law Quarterly Review* 153 (1893).

Griswold, Erwin N. "The Right to Be Let Alone." 55 *Northwestern University Law Review* 217 (1960).

Gunther, Gerald. "The Supreme Court 1971 Term, Forward: A Model for a Newer Equal Protection." 86 *Harvard Law Review* 1 (1972).

Hagan, Horace H. "The Dartmouth College Case." 19 *Georgetown Law Journal* 411 (1931).

———. "Fletcher v. Peck." 16 *Georgetown Law Journal* 1 (1927).

Haines, Charles G. "Judicial Review of Acts of Congress and the Need for Constitutional Reform." 45 *Yale Law Journal* 816 (1936).

Hale, Robert L. "The Supreme Court and the Contract Clause." 57 *Harvard Law Review* 512, 621, 852 (1944).

Hardin, Garrett. "The Tragedy of the Commons." 162 *Science* 1243 (1968).

Hart, Henry M. "The Relations between State and Federal Law." 54 *Columbia Law Review* 489 (1954).

Hayek, Friedrich. "The Use of Knowledge in Society." 35 *American Economic Review* 519 (1945).

Heberle, Klaus H. "From Gitlow to Near: Judicial 'Amendment' by Absent-Minded Incrementalism." 34 *Journal of Politics* 458 (1972).

Heckman, Charles A. "The Relationship of Swift v. Tyson to the Status of Commercial Law in the Nineteenth Century and the Federal System." 17 *American Journal of Legal History* 246 (1973).

———. "Uniform Commercial Law in the Nineteenth Century Federal Courts: The Decline and Abuse of the Swift Doctrine." 27 *Emory Law Journal* 45 (1978).

Hill, Alfred. "The Erie Doctrine and the Constitution." 53 *Northwestern University Law Review* 427 (1958).

———. "The Law-Making Power of the Federal Courts: Constitutional Preemption." 67 *Columbia Law Review* 1024 (1967).

Howard, A.E. Dick. "*Garcia* and the Values of Federalism: On the Need for a Recurrance to Fundamental Principles." 19 *Georgia Law Review* 789 (1985).

Ippolito, Richard, and Masson, Robert. "The Social Cost of Government Regulation of Milk." 21 *Journal of Law and Economics* 33 (1978).

Isaacs, Nathan. "John Marshall On Contracts: A Study in Early American Juristic Theory." 7 *Virginia Law Review* 413 (1921).

Jackson, Robert H. "Decisional Law and Stare Decisis." 30 *American Bar Association Journal* 334 (1944).

Johnson, Gion G. "The Ideology of White Supremacy, 1876–1910," in *James

Sprunt Studies in History and Political Science vol. 31, *Essays in Southern History* 124. Edited by F. M. Green (1949).

Jurow, Keith. "Untimely Thoughts: A Reconsideration of the Origins of Due Process of Law." 19 *American Journal of Legal History* 265 (1975).

Kaden, Lewis B. "Politics, Money and State Sovereignty: The Judicial Role." 79 *Columbia Law Review* 847 (1979).

Karst, Kenneth. "The Freedom of Intimate Association." 80 Yale Law Journal 624 (1980).

Kelley, James F. "The Uncertain Renaissance of the Ninth Amendment." 33 *University of Chicago Law Review* 814 (1966).

Kelly, Alfred. "Clio and the Court: An Illicit Love affair." 1965 *Supreme Court Review* 119.

———. "The Congressional Controversy over School Segregation, 1867–1875." 64 *American History Review* 537 (1959).

Kent, Irvin. "Under the Ninth Amendment What Rights Are the 'Others Retained by the People?' " 28 *Federal Bar Journal* 219 (1970).

Kitch, Edmund, and Bowler, Clara. "The Facts of *Munn* v. *Illinois*." 1978 *Supreme Court Review* 313.

Kitch, Edmund; Isaacson, Marc; and Kasper, Daniel. "The Regulation of Taxicabs in Chicago." 14 *Journal of Law and Economics* 285 (1971).

Klein, Benjamin; Crawford, Robert; and Alchian, Armen. "Vertical Integration, Appropriable Rents, and the Competitive Contracting Process." 21 *Journal of Law and Economics* 297 (1978).

Krislov, Samuel. "Jefferson and Judicial Review: Refereeing Cahn, Commager and Mendelson." 9 *Journal of Public Law* 374 (1960).

Kutler, Stanley I. "John Bannister Gibson: Judicial Restraint and the Positive State." 14 *Journal of Public Law* 181 (1965).

La Pierre, D. Bruce. "Political Safeguards of Federalism Redux: Intergovernmental Immunity and the States as Agents of the Nation." 60 *Washington University Law Quarterly* 779 (1982).

Laycock, Douglas. "Constitutional Theory Matters." 65 *Texas Law Review* 767 (1987).

———. "Taking Constitutions Seriously: A Theory of Judicial Review." 59 *Texas Law Review* 343 (1981).

"Legislative Purpose, Rationality, and Equal Protection." 82 *Yale Law Journal* 123, 128 (1972).

"Legitimacy of Civil Law Reasoning in the Common Law: Justice Harlan's Contribution." 82 *Yale Law Journal* 258 (1972).

Leuchtenburg, William. "The Origin of Franklin D. Roosevelt's 'Court-Packing' Plan." 1966 *Supreme Court Review* 347.

Linde, Hans. "Due Process of Lawmaking." *Nebraska Law Review* 197 (1976).

———. "Judges, Critics, and the Realist Tradition." 82 *Yale Law Journal* 227 (1972).

Lindgren, Janet S. "Beyond Cases: Reconsidering Judicial Review." 1983 *Wisconsin Law Review* 583.

Lorenzen, Earnest G. "Huber's De Conflictu Legum." 13 *Illinois Law Review* 375 (1919).

———. "Story's Commentaries on the Conflict of Laws—One Hundred Years After." 48 *Harvard Law Review* 18 (1934).

Maltz, Earl M. "How Much Regulation is Too Much—An Examination of Commerce Clause Jurisprudence." 50 *George Washington Law Review* 47 (1981).

Mandelker, Daniel R. "Land Use Takings: The Compensation Issue." 8 *Hastings Constitutional Law Journal* 491 (1981).

McCleskey, Clifton. "Judicial Review in a Democracy: A Dissenting Opinion." 3 *Houston Law Review* 354 (1966).

McCloskey, Robert G. "Economic Due Process and the Supreme Court: An Exhumation and Reburial." 1962 *Supreme Court Review* 34.

McGovney, Dudley. "The British Origin of Judicial Review of Legislation."93 *University of Pennsylvania Law Review* 1 (1944).

Meiklejohn, Alexander. "The First Amendment is an Absolute." 1961 *Supreme Court Review* 245.

Merrill, Thomas W. "First Amendment Protection for Commercial Advertising: The New Constitutional Doctrine." 44 *University of Chicago Law Review* 205 (1976).

Michel, Jack. "*Hood v. Dumond:* A Study of the Supreme Court and the Ideology of Capitalism." 134 *University of Pennsylvania Law Review* 657 (1986).

Michelman, Frank I. "In Pursuit of Constitutional Welfare Rights: One View of Rawls' Theory of Justice." 121 *University of Pennsylvania Law Review* 962 (1973).

———. "Welfare Rights in a Constitutional Democracy." 1979 *Washington University Law Quarterly* 659.

———. "Property, Utility and Fairness: Comments on the Ethical Foundation of 'Just Compensation' Law." 80 *Harvard Law Review* 1165 (1967).

———. "States' Rights and States' Roles: Permutations of 'Sovereignty' in National League of Cities v. Usery." 86 *Yale Law Journal* 1165 (1977).

Miller, Arthur S. "An Inquiry in the Relevance of the Intentions of the Founding Fathers, with Special Emphasis on the Doctrine of Separation of Powers." 27 *Arkansas Law Review* 583, 588 (1973).

———. "Statutory Language and the Purposive Use of Ambiguity." 42 *Virginia Law Review* 23 (1956).

Miller, Geoffrey. "The True Story of Carolene Products." 1987 *Supreme Court Review* 397.

Miller, William. "Cases of a Judiciary Nature." 8 *St. Louis University Public Law Review* 47 (1986).

Monaghan, Henry P. " 'Liberty' and 'Property'." 62 *Cornell Law Review* 405 (1977).

———. "Our Perfect Constitution." 56 *New York University Law Review* 353 (1981).

Moore, Thomas G. "The Beneficiaries of Trucking Regulation." 21 *Journal of Law and Economics* 327 (1978).

———. "The Purpose of Licensing." 4 *Journal of Law and Economics* 93 (1961).

Munch, Patricia. "An Economic Analysis of Eminent Domain." 84 *Journal of Political Economy* 473 (1976).

Murphy, Walter. "Constitutional Interpretation: The Art of the Historian, Magician, or Statesman?." 87 *Yale Law Journal* 1752 (1978).

Murphy, Austin, and Nickles, Don. "The Fair Labor Standards Act Amendments of 1985." 37 *Labor Law Journal* 67 (1986).

Nadelmann, Kurt H. "Joseph Story's Contribution to American Conflicts Law: A Comment." 5 *American Journal of Legal History* 230 (1961).

Nagel, Robert F. "Federalism as a Fundamental Value: "National League of Cities in Perspective." 1981 *Supreme Court Review* 81.

Nedelsky, Jennifer. "Conflicting Democratic Politics: Anti-Federalists, Federalists, and the Constitution." 96 *Harvard Law Review* 340 (1982).

Nelson, William E. "Changing Conceptions of Judicial Review: The Evolution of Constitutional Theory in the United States, 1790–1860." 120 *University of Pennsylvania Law Review* 1166 (1972).

———. "The Eighteenth-Century Background of John Marshall's Constitutional Jurisprudence." 76 *Michigan Law Review* 893 (1978).

———. "History and Neutrality in Constitutional Adjudication." 72 *Virginia Law Review* 1236 (1986).

Nolan, Dennis R. "Sir William Blackstone and the New Republic: A Study of Intellectual Impact." 51 *New York University Law Review* 731 (1976).

Parker, Reginald. "Historic Basis of Administrative Law: Separation of Powers and Judicial Supremacy." 12 *Rutgers Law Review* 449 (1958).

Peltzman, Sam. "Toward a More General Theory of Regulation." 19 *Journal of Law and Economics* 211 (1976).

Plucknett, Theodore. "Bonham's Case and Judicial Review." 40 *Harvard Law Review* 30 (1926).

Pollack, Louis H. "Racial Discrimination and Judicial Integrity: A Reply to Professor Wechsler." 108 *University of Pennsylvania Law Review* 1 (1959).

Posner, Richard A. "Economics, Politics and the Reading of Statutes and the Constitution." 49 *University of Chicago Law Review* 263 (1982).

———. "Theories of Economic Regulation." 5 *Bell Journal of Economics and Management Science* 335 (1974).

Pound, Roscoe, "Common Law and Legislation." 21 *Harvard Law Review* 383 (1908).

———. "Liberty of Contract." 18 *Yale Law Journal* 454 (1909).

Powell, Thomas R. "The Judiciality of Minimum Wage Legislation." 37 *Harvard Law Review* 545 (1924).

———. "The Logic and Rhetoric of Constitutional Law." 15 *Journal of Philosophy, Psychology and Scientific Method* 654 (1918).

Powell, H. Jefferson. "The Original Understanding of Original Intent." 98 *Harvard Law Review* 885 (1985).

Rapaczysnki, Andrzej. "From Sovereignty to Process, the Jurisprudence of Federalism after Garcia." 1985 *Supreme Court Review* 341.

Rehnquist, William. "The Notion of a Living Constitution." 54 *Texas Law Review* 693 (1976).

Reich, Charles A. "Individual Rights and Social Welfare: The Emerging Legal Issues." 74 *Yale Law Journal* 1245 (1965).

———. "The New Property." 73 *Yale Law Journal* 733 (1964).

Reid, John P. "In an Inherited Way: English Constitutional Rights, the Stamp Act Debates, and the Coming of the American Revolution." 49 *Southern California Law Review* 1109 (1976).

———. "In the Taught Tradition: The Meaning of Law in Massachusetts-Bay Two Hundred Years Ago." 14 *Suffolk University Law Review* 931 (1980).

Rhoades, Lyman, and Patula, Rodney. "The Ninth Amendment: A Survey of Theory and Practice in the Federal Courts since *Griswold* v. *Connecticut*." 50 *Denver Law Journal* 153 (1973).

Rice, W. G. "The Position of the American Indians in the Law of the United States." 16 *Journal of Comparative Legislation and International Law* (3d. series) 78 (1934).

Richards, David. "Sexual Autonomy and the Constitutional Right to Privacy: A

Case Study in Human Rights and the Unwritten Constitution." 30 *Hastings Law Journal* 957 (1979).

Rose, Carol. "*Mahon* Reconstructed: Why the Takings Issue Is Still a Muddle." 57 *Southern California Law Review* 561 (1984).

——. "Possession as the Origin of Property." 52 *University of Chicago Law Review* 73 (1985).

Rosenberry, Marvin B. "Administrative Law and the Constitution." 23 *American Political Science Review* 32 (1929).

Rose-Ackerman, Susan. "Does Federalism Matter? Political Choice in a Federal Republic." 89 *Journal of Political Economy* 152 (1981).

Rostow, Eugene. "The Democratic Character of Judicial Review." 56 *Harvard Law Review* 193 (1952).

Rotunda, Ronald D. "The Doctrine of Conditional Preemption and other Limitations on Tenth Amendment Restrictions." 132 *University of Pennsylvania Law Review* 289 (1984).

Royall, William L. "The Fourteenth Amendment: The *Slaughter-House Cases*." 4 *Southern Law Review* (n.s.) 558 (1878).

Salmond, John W. "The Theory of Judicial Precedents." 16 *Law Quarterly Review* 376 (1900).

Sandalow, Terrance. "Constitutional Interpretation." 79 *Michigan Law Review* 1033 (1981).

——. "Federalism and Social Change." 43 *Law and Contemporary Problems* 29 (1980).

Sax, Joseph. "Takings and the Police Power." 74 *Yale Law Journal* 36 (1964).

——. "Takings, Private Property and Public Rights." 81 *Yale Law Journal* 149 (1971).

Scalia, Antonin. "Economic Affairs as Human Affairs," in *Economic Liberties and the Judiciary* 31. Edited by J. A. Dorn and H. G. Manne (1987).

Scott, Austin. "Holmes v. Walton, the New Jersey Precedent." 4 *American Historical Review* 456 (1899).

Sedler, Robert. "The Negative Commerce Clause as a Restriction on State Regulation and Taxation: An Analysis in Terms of Constitutional Structure." 31 *Wayne Law Review* 885 (1985).

Sharp, Malcolm P. "The Classical American Doctrine of 'The Separation of Powers.' " 2 *University of Chicago Law Review* 385 (1935).

——. "Promissory Liability." 7 University of Chicago Law Review 1, 250 (1939–40).

Shattuck, Charles E. "The True Meaning of the Term 'Liberty' in Those Clauses in the Federal and State Constitutions which Protect 'Life, Liberty, and Property'." 4 *Harvard Law Review* 365 (1891).

Sherry, Suzanne. "The Founders' Unwritten Constitution." 54 *University of Chicago Law Review* 1127 (1987).

Sholley, John B. "The Negative Implications of the Commerce Clause." 3 *University of Chicago Law Review* 556 (1936).

Siegan, Bernard. "Reabilitating *Lochner*." 22 *San Diego Law Review* 453 (1985).

Siegel, Stephen. "Understanding the Lochner Era: Lessons from the Controversy over Railroad and Utility Rate Regulation." 70 *Virginia Law Review* 187 (1984).

Simon, Peter. "Liberty and Property in the Supreme Court: A Defense of Roth and Perry." 71 *California Law Review* 146 (1983).

Smith, George. "Dr. Bonham's Case and the Modern Significance of Lord Coke's Influence." 41 *Washington Law Review* 297 (1966).

Smith, Neal. "The Monopoly Component of Inflation in Food Prices." 14 *University of Michigan Journal of Law Reform* 149 (1981).

Stern, Robert. "The Commerce Clause and the National Economy, 1933–1946." 59 *Harvard Law Review* 645 (1946).

——. "That Commerce which Concerns More States than One." 47 *Harvard Law Review* 1335 (1934).

Stevens, Theodore, "*Erie R.R.* v. *Tompkins* and the Uniform General Maritime Law." 64 *Harvard Law Review* 246 (1950).

Stigler, George. "The Economics of Information." 69 *Journal of Political Economy* 213 (1961).

——. "The Theory of Economic Regulation." 2 *Bell Journal of Economics and Management Science* 3 (1974).

Stoebuck, William. "A General Theory of Eminent Domain." 47 *Washington Law Review* 553 (1972).

Stone, Julius. "Equal Protection and the Search for Justice." 22 *Arizona Law Review* 1 (1980).

Stone, Geoffrey. "Restrictions of Speech because of its Content: The Peculiar Case of Subject-Matter Restrictions." 46 *University of Chicago Law Review* 81 (1978).

Stoneking, James B. "Penumbras and Privacy: A Study of the Use of Fictions in Constitutional Decision-Making." 87 *West Virginia Law Review* 859 (1985).

Strauss, Peter L. "Was There a Baby in the Bathwater? A Comment on the Supreme Court's Legislative Veto Decision." 1983 *Duke Law Journal* 789.

Strong, Frank. "Judicial Review: A Tri-Dimensional Concept of Administrative-Constitutional Law." 69 *West Virginia Law Review* 111 (1967).

Sunstein, Cass R. "Public Values, Private Interests and the Equal Protection Clause." 1982 *Supreme Court Review* 127.

"Symposium on the Law and Politics of Abortion." 77 *Michigan Law Review* 1579 (1979).

Taylor, M. F. "The *Slaughter-House Cases*." 3 *Southern Law Review* 476 (1874).

Telly, Charles S. "The Classical Economic Model and the Nature of Property in the Eighteenth and Nineteenth Centuries." 13 *Tulsa Law Journal* 406 (1978).

ten Broek, Jacobus. "Admissibility and Use by the United States Superior Court of Extrinsic Aids in Constitutional Construction." 26 *California Law Review* 287 (1938).

Thayer, James B. "Legal Tender." 1 *Harvard Law Review* 73 (1887).

——. "The Origin and Scope of the American Doctrine of Constitutional Law." 7 *Harvard Law Review* 129 (1893).

Thompson, Seymour. "Abuses of Corporate Privileges." 26 *American Law Review* 169 (1892).

Tiebout, Charles M. "A Pure Theory of Local Expenditures." 64 *Journal of Political Economy* 416 (1956).

Treanor, William. "The Origins and Original Significance of the Just Compensation Clause of the Fifth Amendment." 94 *Yale Law Journal* 694 (1985).

Tribe, Lawrence. "The Legislative Veto Decision: A Law by Any Other Name?." 21 *Harvard Journal of Legislation* 1 (1984).

——. "Unraveling National League of Cities: The New Federalism and Affirmative Rights to Essential Government Services." 90 *Harvard Law Review* 1065 (1977).

Trickett, William. "Is a Grant a Contract? A Review of Fletcher v. Peck." 54 *American Law Review* 718 (1920).

———. "Judicial Dispensation from Congressional Statutes." 41 *American Law Review* 65 (1907).

Tucker, John R. "The Congressional Power over Interstate Commerce." 11 *American Bar Association Report* 260 (1888).

Tullock, Gordon. "Federalism: Problems of Scale." 6 *Public Choice* 19 (1969).

Turner, Jesse. "A Phantom Precedent." 48 *American Law Review* 321 (1914).

Tussman, Joseph, and tenBroek, Jacobus. "The Equal Protection of the Laws." 37 *California Law Review* 341 (1949).

U.S. Dept. of Labor. "Monthly Labor Review" (November 1986).

U.S. Dept. of Commerce. "Survey of Current Business" (August 1986).

Van Alstyne, William W. "Cracks in 'The New Property': Adjudicative Due Process in the Administrative State." 62 *Cornell Law Review* 445 (1977).

———. "A Critical Guide to Marbury v. Madison." 1969 *Duke Law Journal* 1.

———. "The Second Death of Federalism." 83 *Michigan Law Review* 1709 (1985).

———. "Slouching toward Bethlehem with the Ninth Amendment." 91 *Yale Law Journal* 207 (1981), reviewing C. Black, *Decision according to Law* (1981).

Wagner, Donald O. "Coke and the Rise of Economic Liberalism." 6 *Economic History Review* 30 (1935).

Wallace, J. Clifford. "A Two Hundred Year Old Constitution in Modern Society." 61 *Texas Law Review* 1575 (1983).

———. "The Jurisprudence of Judicial Restraint: A Return to the Moorings." 50 *George Washington Law Review* 1 (1981).

Warren, Charles. "The New 'Liberty' Under the Fourteenth Amendment." 39 *Harvard Law Review* 431 (1926).

———. "New Light on the History of the Federal Judiciary Act of 1789." 37 *Harvard Law Review* 49 (1923).

Warren, Charles and Brandeis, Louis. "The Right to Privacy." 4 *Harvard Law Review* 193 (1890).

Watson, H. Lee. "Congress Steps Out: A Look at Congressional Control of the Executive." 63 *California Law Review* 983 (1975).

Watt, Richard and Orlikoff, Richard. "The Coming Vindication of Mr. Justice Harlan, 44 *Illinois Law Review* 13 (1949).

Wechsler, Herbert. "The Political Safeguards of Federalism: The Role of the States in the Composition and Selection of the National Government." 54 *Columbia Law Review* 543 (1954).

———. "Toward Neutral Principles of Constitutional Law." 73 *Harvard Law Review* 1 (1959).

Wells, Michael and Hellerstein, Walter. "The Governmental-Proprietary Distinction in Constitutional Law." 66 *Virginia Law Review* 1073 (1980).

White, James B. "Law as Language: Reading Law and Reading Literature." 60 *Texas Law Review* 415 (1982).

Wiecek, William M. "*Somerset:* Lord Mansfield and the Legitimacy of Slavery in the Anglo-American World." 42 *University of Chicago Law Review* 86 (1974).

Williams, Stephen. "Liberty and Property: The Problem of Government Benefits." 12 *Journal of Legal Studies* 3 (1983).

———. "Severance Taxes and Federalism: The Role of the Supreme Court in Preserving a National Common Market for Energy Supplies." 53 *University of Colorado Law Review* 281 (1982).

Wofford, John. "The Blinding Light: The Uses of History in Constitutional Inter-
    pretation." 31 *University of Chicago Law Review* 502 (1964).
Wollan, Laurin. "Crosskey's Once and Future Constitution." 5 *Political Science
    Reviewer* 129 (1975).
Wright, Benjamin. "The Origins of the Separation of Powers in America." 13
    Economica 169 (1933).
Wright, J. Skelly. "Professor Bickel, The Scholarly Tradition, and the Supreme
    Court." 84 *Harvard Law Review* 769 (1971).
Yarbrough, Tinsley. "Justice Black, The Fourteenth Amendment, and Incorpora-
    tion." 30 *University of Miami Law Review* 231 (1976).

Table of Cases

Index